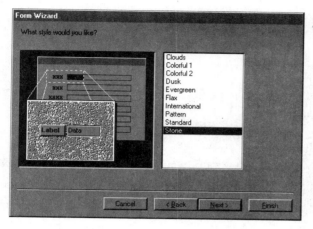

STEP 3: Select a style for your form(s).

STEP 4: Name your form(s) and decide whether you want to make additional design changes or start working with information right away.

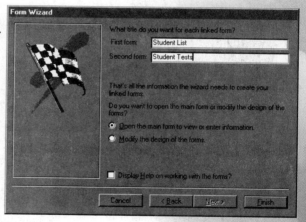

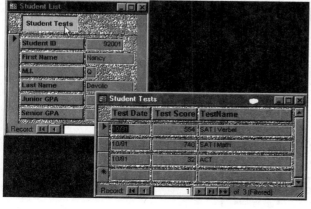

STEP 5: Begin working with your form(s).

Business Professionals, Trainers, and Developers Praise
Running Microsoft Access
by John L. Viescas

I have purchased about 50 pounds of Access books. Yours is the one that gets the most use.

Steve Mongeon
Independent developer and consultant

As a database novice, I found John's book to be a great learning tool. It guides you through all of the Access functions with clearly defined steps and informative examples. *Running Microsoft Access* has more information than you will ever find with the F1 key!

Don Reid
Development manager for a
major computer manufacturer

Each chapter is so well structured that a reader can easily find out how to execute a particular task.

Dan Smith
PC Magazine

Running Microsoft Access by John Viescas has always been at the top of Product Support's list of recommended books for customers looking for a great supplement to the user manuals and online help. It is extremely well written and covers the material that new and experienced users need when they run into database development obstacles. I would love to know how many times customers have not had to reach for their phone to call Product Support because they were wise enough to reach for John's book first.

Steve Alboucq
Microsoft Access Product Support Team Manager

I recommend this book to every class I teach. It's an excellent running start for any Access user or developer. This book covers everything a motivated beginner could possibly need.

Ken Getz
Owner, KNG Consulting

John's clear prose and obvious expertise make this book a standout in a crowded market. It's the first book I recommend to anyone trying to learn Access, and we have used it as Access courseware to the benefit of nearly 200 students. The layout, clarity, problem/solution format, and gradual yet comprehensive progression through the material makes *Running Microsoft Access* an ideal teaching aid. I can't wait to get the next edition.

Jonathan Zuck
V.P., Client/Server Technology
Advanced Paradigms, Inc.

Running Microsoft Access is a must-buy for beginning Access programmers. John really knows his stuff. A lot of Access developers got their start reading *Running Microsoft Access*.

Paul Litwin
Coauthor, *Microsoft Access Developer's Handbook*
Editor, *Smart Access*
President, Litwin Consulting,
a Microsoft Solution Provider
Microsoft Certified Professional

I bought six Access books, but eventually returned them all after using this book. . . . NICE WORK!

Patrick McKnight
Owner, McKnight Consulting

Running Microsoft Access by John Viescas has always been one of the first books I recommend to our users. It covers all of the basics, such as good database design, which helps users start with a solid foundation, as well as advanced topics such as Access SQL.

MariEsther Burnham
Microsoft Access Product Support Team

Just wanted to let you know. . . Excellent book! I have used your book extensively and love it! It is the definitive guide to Microsoft Access! Use it everyday!

Thomas Rizzo
Systems Engineer, United States Air Force Team,
Microsoft Corporation
Microsoft Certified Systems Engineer
Microsoft Certified Solution Developer

I'm about 70 percent through your book and have learned more from it in the past two months than I have fiddling around with Access since it first came out with version 1.0. Thanks again for writing in a style that presents the material in a logical manner that I can follow.

J. J. Johnson
Co-owner, Carrington, Ink!

John L. Viescas

When John Viescas isn't exploring the latest intricacies of Microsoft Access, you're likely to find him "surfing" the internet or zipping around town in his bright green cabriolet—aptly named "Joe" (with apologies to the Pittsburgh Steelers!). Or, if you hang out at any major airport, you might run into him as he flies in to teach a developer seminar on Access or to speak at one of several major conferences. He particularly enjoys the large crowds at the annual Microsoft Tech∗Ed conferences, where he's been invited by Microsoft to speak every year.

Born in Texas, John got started in computing long before many of the current employees at Microsoft were "knee high to a grasshopper." He likes to comment to students that the laptop he carries with him on the road has more than 100 times the memory, has five times the disk space, and is many times faster than the first so-called "mainframe" computer he used to teach himself Autocoder (a computer language spoken by the ancients). John has been working with database systems for most of his career. He began by building large database application systems for El Paso Natural Gas Company in his hometown in the early 1970s. From there, he went to Applied Data Research in Dallas, where he managed the development of database and data dictionary systems for mainframe computers and became involved in the evolution of the SQL database language standard. Before forming his own company a few years ago, he helped market and support NonStop SQL for Tandem Computers in California.

In addition to frequent business travel, John enjoys cashing in his frequent flier miles to go winging somewhere with his wife, Suzanne, just for fun. Between them, John and Suzanne have seven children and (at last count) four grandchildren. When they're not visiting their far-flung family, they like to spend at least part of the Seattle winter in sunnier places like Hawaii. Unless he's on vacation, you can reach John on the Microsoft Network at JohnV@msn.com or on CompuServe at 72110.1451@compuserve.com.

In-Depth Reference

and Inside Tips from

the Software Experts

RUNNING

Microsoft®
ACCESS for
Windows® 95

JOHN L. VIESCAS

PUBLISHED BY
Microsoft Press
A Division of Microsoft Corporation
One Microsoft Way
Redmond, Washington 98052-6399

Library of Congress Cataloging-in-Publication Data
Viescas, John, 1947–
    Running Microsoft Access for Windows 95 / John L. Viescas.
        p.   cm.
    Includes index.
    ISBN 1-55615-886-6
    1. Microsoft Access for Windows.   2. Data base management.
3. Microsoft Windows 95.   I. Title.
QA76.9.D3V554   1995
005.75'65--dc20   94-38997
                                                                   CIP

Printed and bound in the United States of America.

1 2 3 4 5 6 7 8 9 QMQM 0 9 8 7 6 5

Distributed to the book trade in Canada by Macmillan of Canada, a division of Canada Publishing Corporation.

A CIP catalogue record for this book is available from the British Library.

Microsoft Press books are available through booksellers and distributors worldwide. For further information about international editions, contact your local Microsoft Corporation office. Or contact Microsoft Press International directly at fax (206) 936-7329.

Acquisitions Editor: Lucinda Rowley
Project Editor: Ina Chang
Technical Editor: Marc Young

Chapters at a Glance

Table of Contents

For Suzanne.
One day, we'll take a vacation without *my laptop—promise.*

Acknowledgments

The Microsoft Access development team continues to break new ground with exciting new features every time it rolls a new release out the door. Without the team's dedicated efforts, authors like me wouldn't have anything new to write about. Special thanks to David Risher for his excellent leadership and to Jim Sturms for his support on the beta test forums.

This book wouldn't have happened without the outstanding efforts of Ina Chang, my manuscript and project editor, and Marc Young, the excellent technical editor on the book. Thanks to their efforts, I had little to do on subsequent edit passes after I finished the initial manuscript. Marc, especially, did a fine job dealing with not one but *three* major sample databases in this edition. Lots of other folks work behind the scenes at Microsoft Press to ensure the high quality of every book they produce—thanks to all of them. Thanks also to Susan Vinson and Ann Smith of Microsoft Product Support Services, who provided the PSS Q&A troubleshooting tips.

I also owe a debt of gratitude this time around to a couple of fine developers who helped with some key chapters of this book. Thanks to Mike Hernandez of DataTex Consulting Group for his assistance with the chapters on database design and macros. There's a bottle of

Conmemorativo tequila awaiting our attention once this book goes out the door. Thanks also to Steve Saunders for his edit and review of the SQL and VBA (he's a three-letter-acronym kinda guy!) chapters.

Thanks to the Overlake School in Redmond, Washington, for allowing me to use the database my son developed for them as one of the key examples in this book. Although I "tweaked" the example for use in this book, it wouldn't be nearly good enough without the "A+" effort that my son Michael gave the project in the first place.

Special thanks to Ray McCann of RM Productions for graciously allowing me to use a major portion of his scheduling database for many of the advanced examples in the book. He actually uses a much-enhanced version of this database to run his business. I hope he gets a good chuckle out of the group and club names we made up for the sample database!

John Viescas
Redmond, Washington
November 1995

Using the Companion Disc

Bound into the back of this book is a CD-ROM disc. The companion disc contains all of the sample databases discussed in this book as well as additional sample spreadsheet, bitmap, icon, and text files to be used with the various exercises in this book.

To install the companion CD-ROM's files on your hard drive, first insert the disc into your CD-ROM drive. Choose Run from the Start menu, and then type *d:\ setup.exe* in the Run dialog box (where *d* is the drive letter of your CD-ROM drive). After the Setup program executes, follow the on-screen instructions. If you prefer, you can use all of the sample files directly from the CD-ROM disc without installing them on your hard drive. Note, however, that you cannot create any new objects or update any of the sample databases directly on the CD-ROM. If you want to make changes to the data, use the Setup program to copy the samples to your hard drive.

The three main sample databases (Wedding List, College Counseling, and Entertainment Schedule) have startup properties defined to use the three icon files supplied (Wedbell.ico, Ovrlake.ico, and Notes.ico) when you run the applications. These icon files must be in the same directory as the databases; otherwise, you won't see these custom icons when you start the applications.

Every effort has been made to ensure the accuracy of this book and the contents of the companion disc. If you have comments, questions, or ideas regarding this book or the companion disc, please write to Microsoft Press at the following address:

Microsoft Press
Attn: Running Microsoft Access for Windows 95 Editor
One Microsoft Way
Redmond, WA 98052-6399

You can also send feedback to Microsoft Press via electronic mail at mspinput@microsoft.com. Please note that product support is not offered through this e-mail address. For support information on Microsoft Access, you can call Microsoft Access Standard Support at (206) 635-7050 on weekdays between 6 a.m. and 6 p.m. Pacific time.

Introduction

S ince its introduction in 1992, Microsoft Access has sold more than 5 million copies (by Microsoft's count). This certainly gives Access reasonable claim to being the most popular desktop database in the world. As further testament, I've seen overflowing Access sessions at Microsoft's Tech*Ed conferences; I've taught oversold seminars on the product, from introductory to advanced levels; and I've seen everyone from novice end users to developers of advanced database applications making productive use of Access. The high volume of activity on the MSACCESS forum on CompuServe and the Microsoft Access member forum on The Microsoft Network (MSN) are further examples of the high interest in the product.

Access is just one part of Microsoft's overall data management product strategy. Like all good relational databases, it allows you to link related information easily—for example, customer and order data that you enter. But it also complements other database products because it has several powerful connectivity features. As its name implies, Access can work with data from other sources, including many popular PC database programs (such as dBASE, Paradox, and Microsoft FoxPro) and many SQL (structured query language) databases on servers, minicomputers, and mainframes. It also fully supports Microsoft's Object Linking and Embedding (OLE) technology, so an Access application can be either a client or a server to other applications such as Microsoft Word, Microsoft Excel, Microsoft PowerPoint, and Microsoft Schedule+.

Access also provides a very sophisticated application development system for the Microsoft Windows operating system that helps you build applications quickly, whatever the data source. In fact, you can build simple applications by defining forms and reports based on your data and linking them with a few simple Visual Basic for Applications (VBA) statements; there's no need to write complex code in the classical programming sense. Because Access uses VBA, you can use the same set of skills with other products such as Microsoft Visual Basic and Excel.

For small businesses (and for consultants creating applications for small businesses), Access is all that's required to store and manage the data used to run the business. Access coupled with Microsoft SQL Server is an ideal way for many medium-sized companies to build new applications for Windows quickly and inexpensively. For large corporations with a big investment in mainframe relational database applications as well as a proliferation of desktop applications that rely on PC databases, Access provides the tools to easily link host and PC data in a single Windows-based application.

About This Book

If you're developing a database application, this book gives you a thorough understanding of "programming without pain" using Access. It provides a solid foundation for designing databases, forms, and reports and getting them all to work together. You'll learn that you can quickly create complex applications by linking design elements with Access's powerful macro facilities or with VBA. Even if someone else has built most of the application for you, you'll find this book useful for understanding how to use an Access application and for learning how to extend that application to suit your changing needs.

Running Microsoft Access for Windows 95 is divided into six major parts:

- Part 1 provides a thorough overview of Access. Chapter 1 describes how Access fits into the world of personal computer database systems; Chapter 2 describes how you might use Access; and Chapter 3 takes you on a tour of Access, introducing you to the basic concepts and terminology. Chapter 3 also provides summaries of all the new features in version 7 (Access for Windows 95).

- Part 2 teaches you how to design, define, and modify database definitions in Access. Starting with a good design is the key to building easy-to-use applications. Chapter 4 explains a fairly simple technique that you can use to design a good relational database application with little effort. Even old pros will appreciate this technique.

- Part 3 focuses on working with data. Here you'll learn not only how to add, update, delete, or replace data in an Access database but also how to design queries to work with data from multiple tables, calculate values, or update many records using one command. The heart of the book is perhaps Chapter 10, which explains how Access can connect to many other popular databases, spreadsheets, and even text files. Chapter 11 includes a comprehensive look at the SQL database language that Access uses to manage and update its data.

- Part 4 is all about forms. Chapter 12 introduces you to forms—what they look like and how they work. The remaining chapters in Part 4 provide an extensive tutorial on designing, building, and implementing simple and complex forms, including use of the Form Wizard feature.

- Part 5 provides detailed information about reports. Chapter 16 leads you on a guided tour of reports and explains their major features. Chapters 17 and 18 teach you how to design, build, and implement both simple and complex reports in your application.

- Part 6 shows you how to use the programming facilities in Access—macros and VBA—to integrate your database objects and make your application "come alive." First, you'll learn how to create Access macros and how to use them to link forms and reports in an application. Then you'll learn the basics of VBA. The last two chapters show you how to use VBA to create robust applications.

Throughout this book, you'll see examples that explain how to build major portions of three sample Access applications: Wedding List (Wedding.mdb), a simple database to track invitees to a wedding; College Counseling (College.mdb), a more complex database to help high school counselors advise students and track their applications to colleges; and Entertainment Schedule (Entertain.mdb), a sophisticated application for running a business that books entertainment groups into nightclubs. You can find these databases on the companion disc provided with this book. (See page xxv, "Using the Companion Disc," for details.) Please note that the invitee names, student names, and entertainment group and club names in these databases are fictitious. The college name and address information was obtained from publicly available lists. For those college records marked as "verified" in the College Counseling database, the data was kindly provided by the admissions offices of the respective colleges.

This book also includes an appendix that provides instructions for installing Access, shows you how to define and manage data source connections using Open Database Connectivity (ODBC), and explains how to convert version 1.*x* or version 2 databases to version 7.

Conventions Used in This Book

The following conventions are used throughout this book to represent keyboard and mouse operations:

Convention	Meaning
Alt-F	While holding down the Alt key, press the F key.
Alt,F	Press the Alt key, release it, and then press the F key.
Choose	Execute an item on a menu.
Select	Highlight a field in a table or an item in a list or pick an option.
Click	Move the mouse pointer to the named item and press the left mouse button once.
Double-click	Move the mouse pointer to the named item and press the left mouse button twice in rapid succession.
Drag	Move the mouse pointer to the named item, press the left mouse button, and then move the mouse pointer while holding down the left mouse button.
Enter	Type in a value in a particular location on your screen.
Press	Push down on a particular key on your keyboard.

Also note that some code and expression examples in this book are too long to fit on a single printed line. A line that ends with the ➥ symbol means that the code shown on the following line should be entered on the same line.

Part 1

SELECT EDITION

Understanding
Microsoft Access

Microsoft Access Is a Database and More

If you've never worked with database software, here's a good place to get an overview of what databases are all about and how they can help you work more efficiently.

Here you'll discover features of Microsoft Access that make it an excellent relational database management system (RDBMS).

Access goes beyond providing only the traditional features of a database management system. It's also a complete application development system.

Now you have an idea of what a database is and what Access can do for you. But if you're comfortable with your spreadsheet or word processing software, why change? This section explains why.

Chapter 1

Microsoft Access Is a Database and More

If you're a serious user of a personal computer, you've probably been using word processing or spreadsheet applications to help you solve problems. You might have started a number of years ago with character-based products running under MS-DOS but subsequently upgraded to software that runs under the Microsoft Windows operating system. You might also own some database software, either as part of an integrated package such as Microsoft Works or as a separate program.

Database programs have been available for personal computers for a long time. Unfortunately, many of these programs have been either simple data storage managers that aren't suitable for building applications or complex application development systems that are difficult to learn and use. Even many computer-literate people have avoided the more complex database systems unless they have been handed a complete, custom-built database application. Microsoft Access, however, represents a significant turnaround in ease of use, and many people are drawn to it to create both simple databases and sophisticated database applications.

Now that Access is in its third release and has become an even more robust product under Microsoft Windows 95, perhaps it's time to take another look at how you work with your personal computer to get the job done. If you've previously shied away from database software because you felt you needed programming skills or because it would take you too much time to become a proficient user, you'll be pleasantly surprised at how easy it is to work with Access. But how do you decide whether you're ready to move up to a database system such as Access? To help you decide, let's take a look at the advantages of using database application development software.

What Is a Database?

In the simplest sense, a *database* is a collection of records and files that are organized for a particular purpose. On your computer system, you might keep the names and addresses of all your friends or customers. Perhaps you collect all the letters you write and organize them by recipient. You might have another set of files in which you keep all your financial data—accounts payable and accounts receivable or your checkbook entries and balances. The word processor documents that you organize by topic are one type of database. The spreadsheet files that you organize according to their uses are another type of database.

If you're very organized, you can probably manage several hundred spreadsheets by using folders and subfolders. When you do this, you're the database manager. But what do you do when the problems you're trying to solve get too big? How can you easily collect information about all customers and their orders when the data might be stored in several document and spreadsheet files? How can you maintain links between the files when you enter new information? How do you ensure that data is being entered correctly? What if you need to share your information with many people but don't want two people to try updating the same data at the same time? Faced with these challenges, you need a *database management system (DBMS)*.

Relational Databases

Nearly all modern database management systems store and handle information using the *relational* database management model. The term *relational* stems from the fact that each record in the database contains information related to a single subject and only that subject. Also, data about two classes of information (such as customers and orders) can be manipulated as a single entity based on related data values. For example, it would be redundant to store customer name and address information with every order that the customer places. In a relational system, the information about orders contains a field that stores data, such as a customer number, that can be used to connect each order with customer information.

In a relational database management system, sometimes called an *RDBMS,* the system manages all data in tables. Tables store information about a subject (such as customers or students) and have columns that contain the different kinds of information about the subject (for example, customers' or students' addresses) and rows that describe all the attributes of a single instance of the subject (for example, data on a specific customer or student). Even when you *query* the database (fetch information from one or more tables), the result is always something that looks like another table.

You can also *join* information on related values from multiple tables or queries. For example, you can join student information with college application information to find out which students applied to which colleges. You can join employee information with contract information to find out which salesperson should receive a commission.

> ## Some Relational Database Terminology
>
> - *Relation*—Information about a single subject such as customers, orders, students, or colleges. A relation is usually stored as a table in a relational database management system.
>
> - *Attribute*—A specific piece of information about a subject, such as the address for a college or the grade point average for a student. An attribute is normally stored as a data column or field in a table.
>
> - *Relationship*—The way information in one relation is related to information in another relation. For example, customers have a *one-to-many relationship* with orders because one customer can place many orders, but any order belongs to only one customer. Students might have a *many-to-many relationship* with colleges because each high-school senior is interested in multiple colleges, and each college receives applications from many students.
>
> - *Join*—The process of linking tables or queries on tables via their related data values. For example, customers might be joined to orders by matching customer ID.

Database Capabilities

An RDBMS gives you complete control over how you define your data, work with it, and share it with others. The system also provides sophisticated features that make it easy to catalog and manage large amounts of data in many tables. An RDBMS has three main types of capabilities: data definition, data manipulation, and data control. All this functionality is contained in the powerful features of Microsoft Access. Let's take a look at how Access implements these capabilities and compare them to what you can do with spreadsheet or word processing programs.

Microsoft Access as an RDBMS

Microsoft Access is a fully functional RDBMS. It provides all the data definition, data manipulation, and data control features you need to manage large volumes of data.

Main Functions of a Database

- *Data definition*—You can define what data will be stored in your database, the type of data (for example, numbers or characters), and how the data is related. In some cases, you can also define how the data should be formatted and how it should be validated.

- *Data manipulation*—You can work with the data in many ways. You can select which data fields you want, filter the data, and sort it. You can join data with other related information and summarize (total) the data. You can also select a set of information and ask the RDBMS to update it, delete it, copy it to another table, or create a new table containing the data.

- *Data control*—You can define who is allowed to read, update, or insert data. In many cases, you can also define how data can be shared and updated by multiple users.

Data Definition and Storage

While you're working with a document or a spreadsheet, you generally have complete freedom to define the contents of the document or each cell in the spreadsheet. Within a given page in a document, you might include paragraphs of text, a table, a chart, or multiple columns of data displayed with multiple fonts. Within a given column on a spreadsheet, you might have text data at the top to define column headers for printing or display, and you might have various numeric formats within the column, depending on the function of the row. You need this flexibility because your word processing document must be able to convey your message within the context of a printed page, and your spreadsheet must store the data you're analyzing as well as provide for calculation and presentation of the result.

This flexibility is great for solving relatively small, well-defined business problems. But a document becomes unwieldy when it extends beyond a few dozen pages, and a spreadsheet becomes difficult to manage when it contains more than a few hundred rows of information. As the amount of data grows, you might also find that you exceed the data storage limits of your word processing or spreadsheet program or of your computer system. If you design a document or spreadsheet to be used by others, it's difficult (if not impossible) to control how they will use the data or enter new data. For example, on a spreadsheet, even though one cell might need a date and another a currency value to make sense, the user might easily enter character data in error.

Some spreadsheet programs allow you to define a "database" area within a spreadsheet to help you manage the information you need to produce the desired result. However, you are still constrained by the basic storage limitations of the spreadsheet program, and you still don't have much control over what's entered in the rows and columns of the database area. Also, if you need to handle more than number and character data, you might find that your spreadsheet doesn't understand such things as pictures or sounds.

An RDBMS allows you to define the kind of data you have and how the data should be stored. You can also usually define rules that the RDBMS can use to ensure the integrity of your data. In its simplest form, a *validation rule* might ensure that you can't accidentally store alphabetic characters in a field that should contain a number. Other rules might define valid values or ranges of values for your data. In the most sophisticated systems, you can define the relationship between collections of data (usually tables or files) and ask the RDBMS to ensure that your data remains consistent. For example, you can have the system automatically check to ensure that every order entered is for a valid customer.

With Access, you have complete flexibility to define your data (as text, numbers, dates, times, currency, pictures, sounds, documents, spreadsheets), to define how Access stores your data (string length, number precision, date/time precision), and to define what the data looks like when you display or print it. You can define simple or complex validation rules to ensure that only accurate values exist in your database. You can request that Access check for valid relationships between files or tables in your database.

Because Access is a state-of-the-art application for Microsoft Windows, you can use all the facilities of *Dynamic Data Exchange (DDE)* and *Object Linking and Embedding (OLE)* technology. DDE lets you execute functions and send data between Access and any other Windows-based application that supports DDE. You can also make DDE connections to other applications using macros or Microsoft Visual Basic for Applications (VBA). OLE is an advanced Windows capability that, in part, allows you to link objects to or embed objects in your Access database. Objects include pictures, graphs, spreadsheets, and documents from other Windows-based applications that also support OLE. Figure 1-1 shows embedded object data from the sample Northwind Traders database that ships with Access. You can see a product category record that not only has the typical name and descriptive information but also has a picture to visually describe each category. Access for Windows 95 can also act as an OLE Automation *server,* allowing you to open and manipulate Access database objects (such as tables, queries, and forms) from other Windows-based applications.

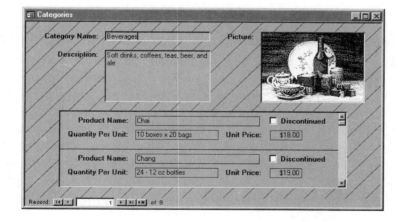

FIGURE 1-1

The Categories form in the Northwind Traders sample database.

Access can also understand and use a wide variety of other data formats, including many other database file structures. You can import and export data from word processing files or spreadsheets. You can directly access and update Paradox, dBASE III, dBASE IV, Btrieve, FoxPro, and other database files. You can also import data from these files into an Access table. In addition, Access can work with most popular databases that support the Open Database Connectivity (ODBC) standard, including Microsoft SQL Server, Oracle, DB2, and Rdb.

Data Manipulation

Working with data in a word processing or spreadsheet program is very different from working with data in an RDBMS. In a word processing document, you can include tabular data and perform a limited set of functions on the data in the document. You can also search for text strings in the original document and, with OLE, include tables, charts, or pictures from other applications. In a spreadsheet, some cells contain functions that determine the desired result, and in other cells you enter the data that provides the source information for the functions. The data in a given spreadsheet serves one particular purpose, and it's cumbersome to use the same data to solve a different problem. You can link to data in another spreadsheet to solve a new problem, or you can use limited search capabilities to copy a selected subset of the data in one spreadsheet to use in problem-solving in another spreadsheet.

An RDBMS provides you with many ways to work with your data. You can, for example, search a single table for information or request a complex search across several related tables or files. You can update a single field or many records with a single command. You can write programs that use RDBMS facilities to read and update your data. Many systems provide data entry and report generation facilities.

Access uses the powerful SQL database language to process data in your tables. Using SQL, you can define the set of information that you need to solve a particular problem, including data from perhaps many tables. But Access simplifies data manipulation tasks. You don't even have to understand SQL to get Access to work for you. Access uses the relationship definitions you provide to automatically link the tables you need. You can concentrate on how to solve information problems without having to worry about building a complex navigation system that links all the data structures in your database. Access also has an extremely simple yet powerful graphical query definition facility that you can use to specify the data you need to solve a problem. Using point and click, drag and drop, and a few keyboard strokes, you can build a complex query in a matter of seconds.

Figure 1-2 shows a complex query under construction in Access. You can find this query in the College Counseling sample database on the disc included with this book. Access displays field lists from selected tables in the upper part of the window, and the lines between field lists indicate the automatic links that Access will use to solve the query. To create the query, you simply select the fields you want from the upper part of the window and drag them to the design grid in the lower part of the window. Choose a few options, type in any criteria, and you're ready to have Access select the information you want.

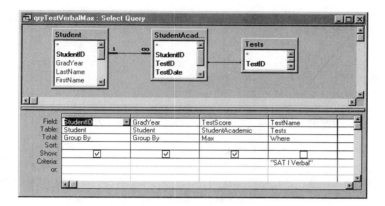

FIGURE 1-2

A query to retrieve student SAT Verbal test scores from the College Counseling database.

Figure 1-3 shows an example of an SQL statement that Access automatically creates from your specifications in the design grid. Figure 1-4 on the next page shows the result of running the query.

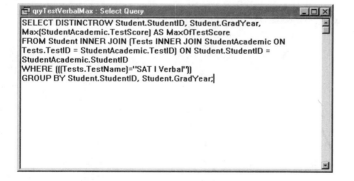

FIGURE 1-3

The SQL statement for a query to retrieve student SAT Verbal test scores.

FIGURE 1-4

The best SAT
Verbal test score
for each student.

Student ID	Graduation Year	MaxOfTestScore
9201	1992	554
9202	1992	727
9203	1992	766
9204	1992	790
9205	1992	757
9206	1992	648
9207	1992	758
9208	1992	787
9210	1992	742
9211	1992	667
9212	1992	712
9301	1993	797
9302	1993	724
9303	1993	683
9304	1993	719
9305	1993	707

qryTestVerbalMax : Select Query

Record: 1 of 44

Data Control

Spreadsheets and word processing documents are great for solving single-user problems, but they are difficult to use when more than one person needs to share the data. Spreadsheets are also useful for providing templates for simple data entry, but they don't do the job well if you need to perform complex data validation. For example, a spreadsheet works well as a template for an invoice for a small business with a single proprietor. But if the business expands and a number of salespeople are entering orders, you need a database. Likewise, a spreadsheet can assist employees with expense reports in a large business, but the data eventually must be captured and placed in a database for corporate accounting.

When you need to share your information with others, true relational database management systems allow you to make your information secure so that only authorized users can read or update your data. An RDBMS that is designed to allow data sharing also provides features to ensure that no two people can change the same data at the same time. The best systems also allow you to group changes (a series of changes is sometimes called a *transaction*) so that either all of the changes or none of the changes appear in your data. For example, while entering new order information for a customer, you probably want to know that all items are recorded or, if you encounter an error, that none of the changes are saved. You probably also want to be sure that no one else can view any part of the order until you have entered all of it.

Access is designed to be used either as a stand-alone RDBMS on a single workstation or in a shared client-server mode across a network. Because you can share your Access data with other users, Access has excellent data security and data integrity features. You can define which users or groups of users can have access to objects (such as tables, forms, and queries) in your database. Access automatically provides locking mechanisms to ensure that no two people can update an object at the same time. Access also understands and honors the locking mechanisms of other database structures (such as Paradox, dBASE, and SQL databases) that you attach to your database.

Microsoft Access as Something More

Being able to define exactly what data you need, how it should be stored, and how you want to access it solves the data management part of the problem. However, you also need a simple way to automate all of the common tasks you want to perform. For example, each time you need to enter a new order, you don't want to have to run a query to search the Customers table, execute a command to open the Orders table, and then create a new record before you can enter the data for the order. And once you've entered the data for the new order, you don't want to have to worry about scanning the table that contains all your products to verify the order's sizes, colors, and prices.

Advanced word processing software lets you define templates and macros to automate document creation, but it's not designed to handle complex transaction processing. In a spreadsheet, you enter formulas that define what automatic calculations you want performed. If you're an advanced spreadsheet user, you might also create macros to help automate entering and validating data. If you're working with a lot of data, you've probably figured out how to use one spreadsheet as a "database" container and use references to selected portions of this data in your calculations.

Although you can build a fairly complex "application" using spreadsheets, you really don't have the debugging and application management tools you need to easily construct a robust data management application. Even something as simple as a wedding guest invitation and gift list is much easier to handle in a database. (See the Wedding List sample database included with this book.) Database systems are specifically designed for application development. They give you the data management and control tools you need and provide facilities to catalog the various parts of your application and manage their interrelationships. You also get a full programming language and debugging tools with a database system.

Developing Application Logic

When you want to build a more complex database application, you need a powerful relational database management system <u>and</u> an *application development system* to help you automate your tasks. Virtually all database systems include application development facilities to allow programmers or users of the system to define the procedures needed to automate the creation and manipulation of data. Unfortunately, many database application development systems require that you know a programming language, such as C or Xbase, to define procedures. Although these languages are very rich and powerful, you must have experience before you can use them properly. To really take advantage of some database systems, you must learn programming, hire a programmer, or buy a ready-made database application (which might not exactly suit your needs) from a software development company.

Fortunately, Microsoft Access makes it easy to design and construct database applications without requiring that you know a programming language. Although you begin in Access by defining the relational tables and the fields in those tables that will contain your data, you will quickly branch out to defining actions on the data via forms, reports, macros, and VBA.

You can use forms and reports to define how you want the data displayed and what additional calculations you want performed—very much like spreadsheets. In this case, the format and calculation instructions (in the forms and reports) are separate from the data (in the tables), so you have complete flexibility to use your data in different ways without affecting the data. You simply define another form or report using the same data. When you want to automate actions in a simple application, Access provides a macro definition facility to make it easy to respond to events (such as clicking a button to open a related report) or to link forms and reports together. When you want to build something a little more complex (like the College Counseling database included with this book), you can quickly learn how to create simple VBA event procedures for your forms and reports. If you want to create more sophisticated applications, such as order entry or scheduling systems (see the Entertainment Schedule sample database), you can employ more advanced techniques using VBA and module objects.

Access provides advanced database application development facilities to process not only data in its own database structures but also information stored in many other popular database formats. Perhaps Access's greatest strength is its ability to handle data from spreadsheets; text files; dBASE files; Paradox, Btrieve, and FoxPro databases; and any SQL database that supports the ODBC standard. This means you can use Access to create a Windows-based application that can process data from a network SQL server or from a mainframe SQL database.

Deciding to Move to Database Software

When you use a word processing document or a spreadsheet to solve a problem, you define both the data and the calculations or functions you need at the same time. For simple problems with a limited set of data, this is an ideal solution. But when you start collecting lots of data, it becomes difficult to manage in many separate document or spreadsheet files. Adding one more transaction (another contract or a new investment in your portfolio) might push you over the limit of manageability. It might even exceed the memory limits of your system or the data storage limits of your software program. Because most spreadsheet programs must be able to load an entire spreadsheet file into memory, running out of memory will probably be the first thing that forces you to consider switching to a database.

If you need to change a formula or the way certain data is formatted, you might find you have to make the same change in many places. When you want to define new calculations on existing data, you might have to copy and modify an existing document or create complex linkages to the files that contain the data. If you make a copy, how do you keep the data in the two copies synchronized?

Before you can use a database such as Microsoft Access to solve problems that require a lot of data or that have complex and changing requirements, you must change the way you think about solving problems with word processing or spreadsheet applications. In Access, you store a single copy of the data in the tables you design. Perhaps one of the hardest concepts to grasp is that you store only your basic data in database tables. For example, in a database you would store the quantity of items ordered and the price of the items, but you would not usually store the extended cost (a calculated value). You use a form or a report to define the quantity-times-price calculation.

You can use the query facility to examine and extract the data in many ways. This allows you to keep only one copy of the basic data yet use it over and over to solve different problems. In a student tracking database, you might create one form to display individual students and the evaluation tests each student has taken. You can use a report defined on the same data to graph the test results for all students during specified time periods. You don't need a separate copy of the data to do this, and you can change either the form or the report independently, without destroying the structure of your database. You can also add new student or test information easily without having to worry about the impact on any of your forms or reports. You can do this because the data (tables) and the routines you define to operate on the data (queries, forms, reports, macros, or modules) are completely independent of each other. Any change you make to the data via one form is immediately reflected by Access in any other form or query that uses the same data.

If you're wondering how you'll make the transition from word processing documents and spreadsheets to Access, you'll be pleased to find features in Access to help you out. You can use the import facilities to copy the data from your existing text or spreadsheet files. You'll find that Access supports most of the same functions you have used in your spreadsheets, so defining calculations in a form or a report will seem very familiar. Within the Help facility, the Answer Wizard can help you find solutions quickly. Help also includes "How Do I" topics that walk you through key tasks you need to learn to begin working with a database and "Tell Me About" and reference topics that enhance your knowledge. In addition, Access provides powerful wizard facilities to give you a jump-start on moving your spreadsheet data to an Access database, including a new Import Spreadsheet Wizard to help you design database tables to store your old spreadsheet data.

Take a long look at the kind of work you're doing today. The sidebar below summarizes some of the key reasons why you might need to move to Access. Is the number of files starting to overwhelm you? Do you find yourself creating copies of old files when you need to answer new questions? Do others need to share the data and update it? Do you find yourself exceeding the limits of your current software or the memory on your system? If the answer to any of these is *yes,* you should be solving your problem with a relational database management system like Microsoft Access.

Reasons to Switch to a Database

Reason 1: You have too many separate files or too much data in individual files. This makes it difficult to manage the data. Also, the data might exceed the limits of the software or the capacity of the system memory.

Reason 2: You have multiple uses for the data—detailing transactions (invoices, for example), summary analysis (such as quarterly sales summaries), and "what if" scenarios. Therefore, you need to be able to look at the data in many different ways, but you find it difficult to create multiple "views" of the data.

Reason 3: You need to share data. For example, numerous people are entering and updating data and analyzing it. Only one person at a time can update a spreadsheet or a word processing document, but many people can simultaneously share and update a database table. Also, databases ensure that people reading the data see only committed updates.

Reason 4: You must control the data because different users access the data, because the data is used to run your business, and because the data is related (such as data for customers and orders). This means you must secure access to data and control data values, and you must ensure data consistency.

In the next chapter, "The Uses of Microsoft Access," you'll read about some uses of the Access application development system in different professional settings. Then, in Chapter 3, "Touring Microsoft Access," you'll open the College Counseling sample database to explore some of the many features and functions of Access.

Chapter 2

The Uses of Microsoft Access

icrosoft Access has all the features of a classic relational database management system (RDBMS)—and more. Access is not only a powerful, flexible, and easy-to-use RDBMS but also a complete database application development facility. You can use Access to create and run under the Microsoft Windows operating system an application tailored to your data management needs. You can limit, select, and total your data using queries. You can create forms for viewing and changing your data. You can also use Access to create simple or complex reports. Both forms and reports "inherit" the properties of the underlying table or query, so in most cases you need to define such things as formats and validation rules only once.

Among the most powerful features of Access are the wizards that you can use to create tables and queries and to customize a wide variety of forms and reports simply by selecting options with your mouse. In its latest version, Access also includes wizards that help you analyze your table design, import spreadsheet or text data, improve database performance, or build and customize one of more than 20 types of applications using built-in templates. Access includes a comprehensive programming language, Microsoft Visual Basic for Applications (VBA), that you can use to create very robust "production" applications that can be shared by many users.

Finally, you get all of these development facilities not only for working with the Access database but also to attach to and work with data stored in many other popular formats. You can build an Access application to work directly with dBASE files; with Paradox, Btrieve, and Microsoft FoxPro databases; and with any SQL database that supports the Open Database Connectivity (ODBC) standard. You can also easily import and export data as text, word processing files, or spreadsheet files.

This chapter describes four scenarios in which Access is used to meet the database and application development needs of the owners of a small business, a PC application developer or consultant, a management information systems (MIS) coordinator in a large corporation, and a home computer user.

In a Small Business

If you're the owner of a small business, you can use the simple yet powerful capabilities of Microsoft Access to manage the data you need to run your business. In addition, you can find dozens of third-party

Access-based applications that will add to your productivity and make running your business much simpler. Because Access's application design facilities are so simple to use, you can be confident in creating your own applications or customizing applications provided by others for your specific needs.

Throughout much of the rest of this book, you'll read about the progressive design and creation of a database application for an entertainment booking agency, RM Productions. This company is an actual small business in western Washington state, owned by a friend who not only handles the booking for many nightclub acts but also is an accomplished musician in his own right.

RM Productions is like many small businesses. The owner, Ray McCann, realized many years ago that a personal computer system could potentially help him run his business more efficiently. At a minimum, he could keep a readily searchable list of all the clubs and groups that hired him as their booking agent, rather than depend on a manual card file. His first personal computer ran on something called CP/M (we won't ask him how long ago that was), and he eventually found a simple little database program that would let him keep track of the clubs and groups and print out contracts.

Even as his business grew, Ray hung on to his old CP/M database program. He even went so far as to install a special emulation card in his PC so that he could still run the program even though he had upgraded to MS-DOS and Windows. As his entertainment booking business grew, Ray needed more sophisticated ways to send out mailings and keep track of clubs and groups that had open future dates. He got pretty creative dumping comma-separated data into an MS-DOS–based word processing program, but he quickly realized that he needed something better.

Ray spent some time in early 1993 taking a look at several new Windows-based database systems. He settled on Microsoft Access. Even though he had virtually no database programming experience, it didn't take Ray long to learn how to import his club and group information into an Access database and create simple queries and mailing labels. Ray contacted me to help him expand his database to run his entire booking business. Figure 2-1 on the next page shows the central contract booking form from that application. In this book, we'll explore many of the key elements of this database. A major portion of Ray's database application is on the sample disc included with this book.

FIGURE 2-1

The Contracts data entry form in the Entertainment Schedule database.

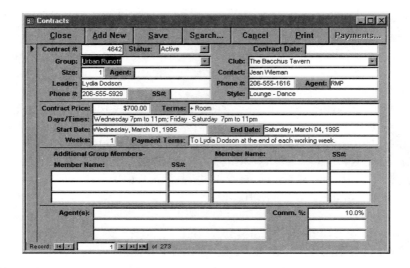

The bottom line? It's true that Ray was already pretty comfortable working with a personal computer. But without Access, he would still be struggling with his outdated database and word processing system. Now he has the database he needs for his growing business. If you're a small business owner who understands that computers should be able to do more than spreadsheets and word processing programs can do, perhaps Access is for you too. You'll find a lot of computer consultants ready and able to put together an Access-based application for you in a short time and at low cost. Even if someone has constructed your database for you, you'll want to know more about Access so that you can take advantage of its native features.

In Contract Work

In today's highly competitive consulting marketplace, the developer who can deliver custom applications quickly and inexpensively will win the lion's share of the business. If you're a PC application developer or consultant, you'll find that the query, form, and report features of Microsoft Access allow you to create applications for your clients in record time. You can also take advantage of VBA, which is built into Access, to satisfy unique requirements and produce truly custom applications. If you've worked with products such as Microsoft Visual Basic for Windows, you'll find the Access application development features very familiar, with the added benefit of a full RDBMS.

If you're a consultant building applications for a vertical market, you'll especially appreciate how Access makes it easy to build your core application and modify the application for each client's needs. You can create optional add-on features that you can price separately. Whether you're building a custom application from scratch or modifying an existing one, your clients will appreciate the fact that you can sit down with them and use Access to prototype the finished application so that they can see exactly what they'll get.

You can scale your application to your clients' needs by taking advantage of the fact that Access can connect to and work with other database management systems. For smaller clients, you'll find the native Access database system more than adequate. For larger clients, you can connect your application to Microsoft SQL Server or other host databases without having to change any of the forms, reports, macros, or modules in your application.

Imagine that your local high school's college counselors use a database to help seniors locate colleges of interest. Suppose the database system was built by you several years ago using an Xbase product. The high school would like to upgrade by converting the system to run under the Microsoft Windows 95 operating system. The school would also like to connect the database system to the current student information that is kept in an SQL Server database. The school wants the new database system to help students locate colleges of interest, to track the application process, and to keep statistics on where students were accepted and where they enrolled.

Sounds like Access might be a perfect solution. You can use the existing Xbase data or convert it easily to Access format. You can also connect the new application to the existing SQL Server student data. Adding search criteria for colleges and tracking student application data is easy. Figure 2-2 on the next page shows a search in progress in the College Counseling sample database included with this book. My son Michael built this database for his high school, the Overlake School in Redmond, Washington, as part of a senior research project. As you might guess, his contract "fee" was a passing grade!

FIGURE 2-2

Searching for information in the College Counseling database.

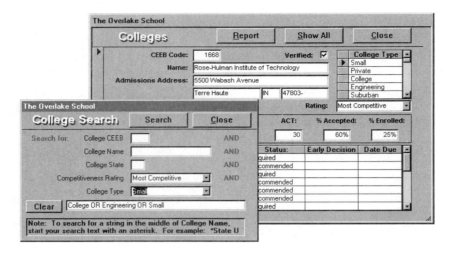

In a Large Corporation

All companies today recognize that one of the ways to remain competitive is to use computer-stored data for more than just day-to-day operations. Creative managers are constantly looking for ways to "turn data into information." As a result, companies no longer have "data processing" units; they have vast MIS departments charged with the care and feeding of the company's valuable computer-stored information.

Nearly all corporations start by building operational data processing systems. These systems collect and process the individual transactional data required to run the business on a day-to-day basis. Examples of transactional data include the following:

- Checks cleared and money withdrawn and deposited in a banking demand deposit system

- Incoming inventory and items sold in a retail system

- Raw materials ordered and received and finished goods shipped in a manufacturing system

- Energy consumed, raw product delivered, and service connection/disconnection data in a utility system

These systems are relatively simple to design and implement in terms of the data input, the processes required on this data, and the data output. They are also easy to justify financially because they can reduce clerical tasks and, at the same time, handle rapidly growing volumes. (Imagine trying to post 10 million checking accounts manually.)

After operational systems are in place and management becomes aware of the vast amounts of data being collected, management often begins to examine the data to better understand how the business interacts with its customers, suppliers, and competitors—to learn how to become more efficient and more competitive. Information processing in most MIS departments usually begins quite innocently as an extension of operational systems. In fact, some information processing almost always gets defined as part of an operational application system design. While interviewing users of a system during the systems analysis phase, the system designer usually hears requests such as, "When the monthly invoices are produced, I'd also like to see a report that tells me which accounts are more than 90 days past due." Printing the invoices is not information processing. Producing the report is.

On the surface, it would seem simple to answer a question about delinquent accounts, given the data about all accounts receivable. However, the operational system might require only 30 days of "current" data to get the job done. The first information request almost always begins to put demands on the data processing systems, and these demands far exceed the data and processing power needed to merely run the business. At some point, the MIS organization decides consciously to reserve additional data storage and processing capability to meet the growing need for information.

This need for information has led companies to build vast networks of departmental systems, which are in turn linked to desktop systems on employees' desks. As more and more data spreads down through the corporation, the data becomes more difficult to manage, locate, and access, as Figure 2-3 on the next page makes clear. Multiple copies of the same data proliferate, and it becomes hard to determine who has the most current and accurate data.

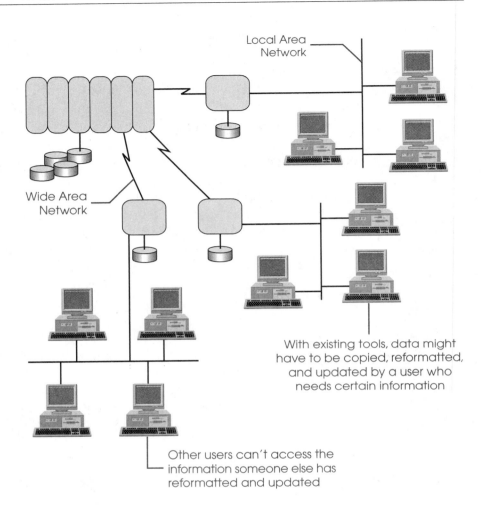

FIGURE 2-3

The typical corporate computing environment, in which data can spread and become difficult to manage, locate, and access.

Local Area Network

Wide Area Network

With existing tools, data might have to be copied, reformatted, and updated by a user who needs certain information

Other users can't access the information someone else has reformatted and updated

Why do so many copies exist? Many copies of data exist because the vast majority of tools aren't designed to work with data in more than one format or to connect to data from multiple sources. Employees must resort to obtaining a copy of the data they want and then converting it to the format understood by their tool of choice.

One major strength of Microsoft Access in a corporate environment is its ability to link to a variety of database formats on the workstation, on database servers, or on host computers. A manager trying to solve a problem no longer has to figure out how to get copies of data from several different sources to plug into a spreadsheet-based graph for analysis. Using Access, the manager can connect directly to the source data, build a query to extract the necessary information, and create a report with an embedded graph—all with one tool. This ability to retrieve data from multiple sources, combined with ease of use, also makes Access a powerful tool for creating information processing systems.

Workgroup Applications

Large corporations find Access especially well suited for creating the workstation portion of client-server applications. Unlike many other Windows-based client application development systems, Access uses its knowledge of the application data and structure to simplify the creation of forms and reports. Applications developed using Access can be made available to users at all levels of the corporation. And with Access it's easy to design truly "user-friendly" applications that fully utilize the investment in employee workstations.

Because Access can link to and share data in many different database formats, it's ideal for creating workgroup applications that maintain data on local departmental servers but need to periodically tap data from applications in other departments or upload data to corporate servers. For smaller workgroup applications, local data can be stored and shared across the workgroup using native Access database files. For larger applications, a true database server such as SQL Server can be used to store the data, with Access as the workstation client. When data must be shared with other workgroups or corporate servers, the Access-based application can use the ODBC standard to execute queries that read or update data that is stored in any of several database formats.

See Also   See Chapter 10, "Importing, Linking, and Exporting Data," for more details about ODBC.

Information Processing Systems

Perhaps a more common use for Access in a corporate environment is as the front-end tool for information processing systems. Many corporations create Executive Information System (EIS) applications using Access so that knowledgeable executives can create their own "drill down" queries, graphs, and reports. MIS departments also find that Access is a great tool for creating the end-user interface for information processing applications.

For example, Microsoft Corporation provides its marketing representatives with an Access database containing information about leading systems and network integrators around the country. When the representatives work with a customer, they can use this tool to quickly search for local companies that might be available to help implement a new system. The representatives can also use the information to provide integrators in their area with information about upcoming products or seminars.

Figure 2-4 shows the main search criteria window of an information database that I helped design and build. The left column shows available search criteria, and the combo boxes provide alphabetic lists of all valid values in the database. It's easy for users of this system to choose criteria to build the search list shown in the boxes on the right. When they have the search list they want, they can click the Go Scout! button to build a list of qualifying companies. From this list, they can "drill down" to detailed descriptive information—a list of company managers, financial data, current clients, and technology specialties. They can also choose a subset of companies from the found list and specify what data they want to print.

FIGURE 2-4

The main search window for the ParaTechnology Systems and Network Integrators database.

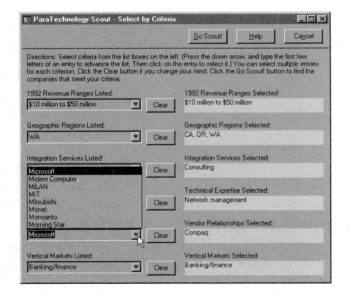

As a Personal RDBMS

Last, but certainly not least, Microsoft Access is a great tool for managing personal information on your home computer. If you're one of the millions of PC users who has a home computer system that can run Microsoft Windows, you can use Access to help you be more productive.

You might want to build a database application to manage your investment portfolio. You can create a directory containing the addresses, birthdays, and anniversaries of all your friends. If you like to cook, a recipe database could be useful. Perhaps you'd like to keep track of your collection of movies or books. I have a friend who uses Access to keep track of his athletic training. The Application Wizard in the latest release of Access shows you how to quickly build and customize an assortment of personal databases.

When one of our daughters got married a couple of years ago, I created a small Access application to keep track of the wedding guest list. You can see the form that I designed for this purpose in Figure 2-5. This was one of the very first Access databases that I created, and it's automated completely with macros. You can find it on the sample disc.

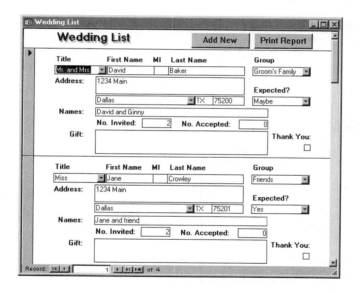

FIGURE 2-5

Keeping track of wedding guests and gifts.

We also used the database to keep track of who had accepted the invitation. It was a snap to produce a summary report by groom's family, bride's family, or friends. After the wedding, we used the form to keep track of the gifts received and thank-you notes written.

Because Access makes it so easy to create forms and reports and link them together with macros or with VBA, you can create small personal applications in a jiffy. Access also supports the OLE standard, so you can get very creative with your applications. Imagine embedding sound snippets from your favorite albums in the database you use to catalog your compact disc collection. The possibilities are endless.

Typical Uses for Microsoft Access

Small Business:

- Accounting
- Order entry
- Customer tracking
- Contact management

Consulting:

- Vertical market applications
- Cross-industry applications

Large Corporation:

- Workgroup applications
- Information processing systems

Personal Use:

- Address book
- Investment management
- Cookbook
- Collections—recordings, books, movies

In the next chapter, you'll learn more about Access's many features as we take a quick tour of the product.

Chapter 3

Touring Microsoft Access

Forms

Use forms to provide a custom way to look at and update your data.

Reports

When you need to analyze and print sets of data from your database, reports are the way to go.

Macros

Macros provide a simple way to automate your forms and reports.

Modules

Modules store the Microsoft Visual Basic for Applications (VBA) procedures that you create and use to build sophisticated database applications.

B

efore you explore the many features of Microsoft Access, it's worth spending a little time looking it over and "kicking the tires." This chapter helps you understand the relationships between the main components in Access and shows you how to move around within the database management system.

Windows Features

Access takes advantage of the many easy-to-use features of the Microsoft Windows operating system. If you've used other Windows-based products, such as Microsoft Excel or Microsoft Word, you'll be right at home with Access's menus, toolbars, and drop-down lists. Even if you're new to Windows, you'll discover that all the techniques you quickly learned in the first chapter of *Introducing Microsoft Windows 95* apply just as easily to Access. When working with data, you'll find familiar cut, copy, and paste capabilities for moving and copying data and objects within Access. In addition, Access supports useful drag and drop capabilities to assist you in designing queries, forms, reports, and macros. For example, you can select a field in a table and then drag the field, dropping it where you want that data to appear in a report.

New General Features in Version 7

- New "Windows 95" look to the Database window

- Long filename support

- Ability to create Windows 95 shortcuts to Access objects

- Ability to set database startup properties such as Application Title, Application Icon, and initial display form

- Ability to create a replica of your database and use the Windows 95 Briefcase to keep the replica objects and data synchronized with the master

- Application Wizard to provide a "jump start" on creating more than 20 common types of applications

- Improved output to Microsoft Excel worksheets (xls), Rich Text Format (rtf) files, and text (txt) files— including the ability to output data in subreports

- Ability to manipulate Access objects from other Windows 95–based applications via OLE Automation

---

Access uses the Multiple Document Interface (MDI) of Windows 95 to allow you to work on multiple objects at one time. This means that you can work with multiple tables, forms, reports, macros, or modules at the same time. If you've used some of the other products included in the Microsoft Office package, you already know how to open multiple Microsoft Word documents; Microsoft Excel spreadsheets, macros, or graphs; and Microsoft PowerPoint slide presentations within a single application window. As an example, Figure 3-1 shows you an Access session with the College Search Summary and Colleges forms open at the same time.

FIGURE 3-1

Two forms open simultaneously within Access.

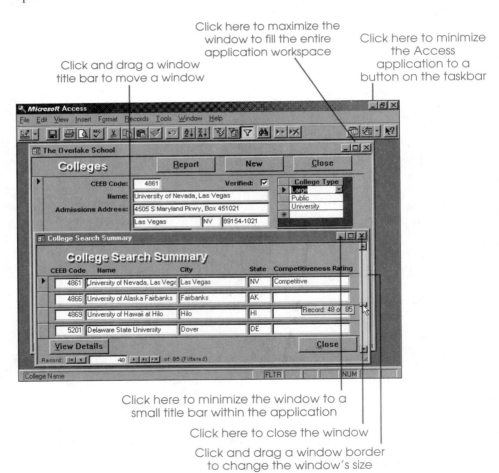

34

Access also fully supports Microsoft's Object Linking and Embedding (OLE) technology. This means that you can embed (in your tables, queries, forms, and reports) objects from other applications, such as pictures, word processing documents, spreadsheets, graphs, sounds, and more. You can use a special type of OLE object, called an *OLE control*, to enhance the way your forms work. You'll learn how to use OLE objects in an Access database later in this book.

The Architecture of Microsoft Access

Microsoft Access calls anything that can have a name an *object*. Within an Access database, the main objects are tables, queries, forms, reports, macros, and modules.

If you have used other database systems on desktop computers, you might have seen the term *database* used to refer to only those files in which you store data. In Access, a database also includes all the major objects related to the stored data, including objects you define to automate the use of your data. Here are the major objects inside an Access database:

Table
: An object you define and use to store data. Each table contains information about a particular subject, such as customers or students. Tables contain *fields* (or *columns*) that store different kinds of data, such as a student name or address, and *records* (or *rows*) that collect all the information about a particular instance of the subject, such as all the information about a student named Jane Smith. You can define a *primary key* (one or more fields that have a unique value for each record) and one or more *indexes* on each table to help retrieve your data more quickly.

Query
: An object that provides a custom view of data from one or more tables. In Access, you can use the graphical query by example (QBE) facility or you can write SQL statements to create your queries. You can define queries to select, update, insert, or delete data. You can also define queries that create new tables from data in one or more existing tables.

(continued)

Form	An object designed primarily for data input or display or for control of application execution. You use forms to completely customize the presentation of data that your application extracts from queries or tables. You can also print forms. You can design a form to run a *macro* or a Visual Basic for Applications (VBA) *procedure* (see below) in response to any of a number of events—for example, to run a procedure when the value of data changes.
Report	An object designed for formatting, calculating, printing, and summarizing selected data. You can view a report on your screen before you print it.
Macro	An object that is a structured definition of one or more actions that you want Access to perform in response to a defined event. For example, you might design a macro that opens a second form in response to the selection of an item on a main form. You might have another macro that validates the contents of a field whenever the value in the field changes. You can include simple conditions in macros to specify when one or more actions in the macro should be performed or skipped. You can use macros to open and execute queries, to open tables, or to print or view reports. You can also run other macros or VBA procedures from within a macro.
Module	An object containing custom procedures that you code using VBA. Modules provide a more discrete flow of actions and allow you to trap errors—something you can't do with macros. Modules can be stand-alone objects containing functions that can be called from anywhere in your application, or they can be directly associated with a form or a report to respond to events on the associated form or report.

Figure 3-2 shows a conceptual overview of how objects in Access are related. Tables store the data that you can extract with queries and display in reports or that you can display and update in forms. Notice that forms and reports can use data directly from tables or from a filtered "view" of the data using queries. Queries can use VBA functions to provide customized calculations on data in your database. Access also has many built-in functions that allow you to summarize and format your data in queries.

Events on forms and reports can "trigger" either macros or VBA procedures. What is an event? An *event* is any change in state of an Access object. For example, on forms you can write macros or VBA procedures to respond to opening the form, closing the form, entering a new row on the form, or changing data either in the current record or in an individual *control* (an object on a form or report that contains data).

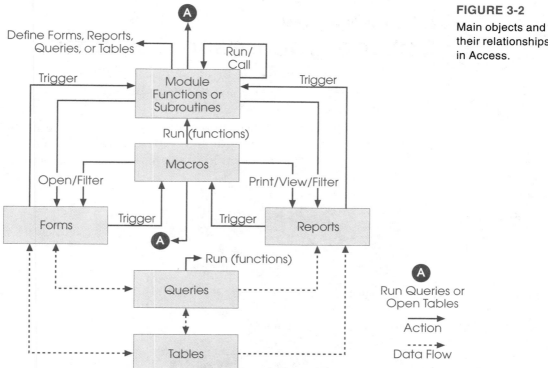

FIGURE 3-2
Main objects and
their relationships
in Access.

You can even design a macro or a VBA procedure that responds to the user pressing individual keys on the keyboard when entering data!

See Also   For a complete list of events on forms and reports, see Chapter 19, "Adding Power with Macros."

Using macros and modules you can change the flow of your application; open, filter, and change data in forms and reports; run queries; and build new tables. Using VBA, you can create, modify, and delete any Access object; manipulate data in your database row by row or column by column; and handle exceptional conditions. Using module code you can even call Windows Application Programming Interface (API) routines to extend your application beyond the built-in capabilities of Access.

See Also   See Chapter 21, "Visual Basic for Applications Fundamentals," and Chapter 22, "Automating Your Application with VBA," for more information about using VBA within Access.

Exploring the College Counseling Database

Now that you know a little bit about the major objects that make up a Microsoft Access database, a good next step is to spend some time exploring the extensive College Counseling database (College.mdb) that comes with this book. First, follow the instructions at the beginning of this book for copying the sample databases to your hard drive. When you start Access, it shows you the opening choices dialog box shown in Figure 3-3.

FIGURE 3-3

The opening choices dialog box in Access.

Select the Open An Existing Database option and click OK to see the Open dialog box shown in Figure 3-4. In the Open dialog box, select the file College.mdb from the folder to which you copied the sample databases, and then click Open. You can also double-click on the filename to open the database. (Note: If you haven't set options in Windows Explorer to show filename extensions for registered applications [choose Options from the View menu in Windows Explorer], you won't see the mdb extension for your database files.) The College Counseling application will start, and you'll see the main switchboard form with buttons for Students, Colleges, Reports, and Exit. Click Exit to close the application and return to the Database window for the College Counseling database, as shown in Figure 3-5 on the next page. (Note: If you hold down the Shift key while you open a database, the application won't start, and you can view just the Database window.)

 TIP   If you have already started Access, you can open the Open dialog box at any time by pressing Alt-F,O or Ctrl-O.

Double-click here to open
the College.mdb database

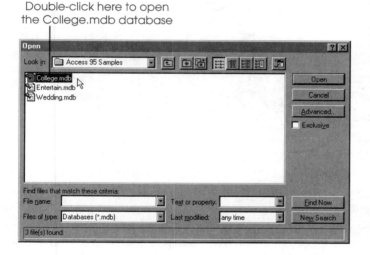

FIGURE 3-4

The Open
dialog box for
databases.

For an existing database, the Database window, shown in Figure 3-5, always remains where you last placed it on your screen. The title bar of the window shows the name of the database that you have open. As you'll learn later in this book, you can set options in the database to change the title bar of the main Access window to show the name of your application instead of "Microsoft Access." Although you can have only one Access database open at a time, you can connect that open database (and its forms, reports, macros, and modules) to tables in other Access databases; to data in Paradox, dBASE, or Btrieve databases; or to data in SQL Server databases on a network.

FIGURE 3-5

The Database
window for the
College Counsel-
ing sample
database.

Tables tab selected

Name of the database

Database window

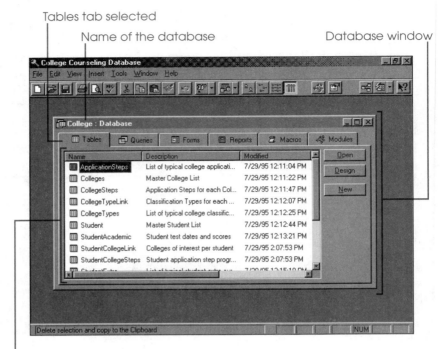

List of tables in the database

Notice in Figure 3-5 that Access makes available most of the buttons on the toolbar after you open a Database window. If you want to see a short tip that describes what a particular toolbar button does, place the mouse pointer over the button, but <u>don't</u> click it. In about a half-second, Access pops up a ToolTip that describes the button's function.

As you explore Access, you'll see that it provides more than a dozen built-in toolbars. Normally, Access shows you the toolbar most appropriate for the work you're currently doing. However, you can control which toolbars are active, and you can customize which buttons appear on which toolbars. You can even define custom toolbars that you display all the time or open and close toolbars from macros or modules. In fact, this sample application includes a custom form toolbar that opens for all the forms in the application. You'll learn how to build a custom form toolbar in Chapter 14, "Customizing Forms."

Across the top of the Database window are tabs that allow you to choose one of the six major object types: tables, queries, forms, reports, macros, and modules.

Tables

When you first open the Database window, Microsoft Access selects the Tables tab and shows you the list of available tables in the database, as shown in Figure 3-5. On the right side of the window are three command buttons. One allows you to create a new table, and the other two allow you to open one of two available views of existing tables:

Open	Lets you view and update the data in the selected table from the table list. Clicking this button opens a Table window in Datasheet view.
Design	Lets you view and modify the selected table's definition. Clicking this button opens a Table window in Design view.
New	Lets you define a new table. When you click this button, Access gives you the option to define a table by entering its data (much like creating a new spreadsheet), to create a new table from scratch, or to start one of the Table Wizards.

When the Database window is active, you can choose any of these command buttons from the keyboard by pressing the first letter of the button name while holding down the Alt key. You can also open a table in Datasheet view by double-clicking on the table name in the Database window with the left mouse button, or you can open the table in Design view by holding down the Ctrl key and double-clicking on the table name using the left mouse button. If you click once with the right mouse button on a table name, Access pops up a *shortcut menu* that lets you perform a number of handy operations on the item you selected, as shown in Figure 3-6 on the next page. Simply choose one of the options on the menu, or left-click anywhere else in the Access window to dismiss the menu.

FIGURE 3-6
A shortcut menu
for a table in the
Database window.

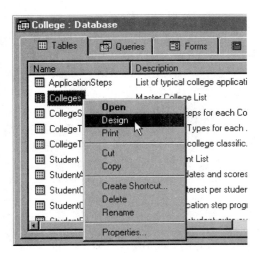

New Table Features in Version 7

- Ability to define a table by entering its data

- Improved Table Wizards

- Performance Analyzer to help make table designs and relationships more efficient

- New "Windows 95" datasheet formatting options

- Ability to define default field-display controls for most fields

- Automatic combo boxes in table datasheets for fields related to other tables (if the Display Control property is set to Combo Box or List Box)

- Ability to set default data type for table design mode

- Datasheet scrollbar "thumb tips" that display the relative record location

- New AutoNumber data type with Random option

Table Window in Design View

When you want to change the *definition* of a table (the structure or design of a table, as opposed to the data in a table), you must open the Table window in Design view. With the College Counseling database open, right-click on the table named Colleges and choose Design from the shortcut menu; this opens the Colleges table in Design view, as shown in Figure 3-7. Notice that the Database window appears behind the active Table window. You can click in any part of the Database window to make it active and bring it to the front. You can also press the F11 key to make the Database window active (or press Alt-F1 on keyboards with 10 or fewer function keys).

Each row defines a field in the table

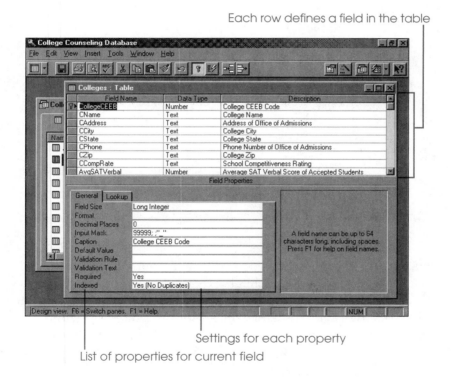

FIGURE 3-7
A Table window in Design view.

Settings for each property

List of properties for current field

Notice that in Design view each row in the top portion of the Table window defines a different field in the table. You can use the mouse to select any field that you want to modify. You can also use the Tab key to move left to right across the screen from column to column. Use

Shift-Tab to move right to left across the screen from column to column. Use the up and down arrow keys to move from row to row in the field list. As you select a different row in the field list in the top portion of the window, you can see the property settings for the selected field in the bottom portion of the Table window. Use the F6 key to move between the top (the field list) and bottom (the field property settings) portions of the Table window in Design view.

Access has many convenient features. Wherever you can choose from a limited list of valid values, Access provides a drop-down list box to assist you in selecting the proper value. For example, when you tab to an area in the Data Type column, a small, gray down arrow button appears at the far right of the column. Click the button or press Alt-down arrow to see the list of available valid data types, as shown in Figure 3-8.

FIGURE 3-8

The Data Type drop-down list box.

Click the down arrow button
to see a list of data types

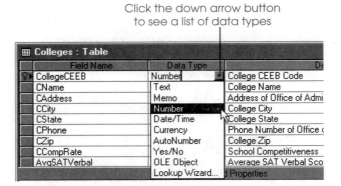

You can open as many as 254 tables (or fewer if you are limited by your computer's memory). You can also minimize any of the windows to an icon by clicking the Minimize button in the upper right corner of the window, or you can maximize the window to fill the Access workspace by clicking the Maximize/Restore button in that same corner. If you don't see a window you want, you can use the list of active windows on the Window menu to bring the window you want to the front. You can choose the Hide command on this menu to make selected windows temporarily disappear, or choose the Show command to make visible any windows that you've previously hidden. Figure 3-9 shows an example of multiple open windows. Choose the Close command from the File menu or click the window's Close button to close any window.

See Also You'll learn about creating table definitions in Chapter 5, "Building Your Database in Microsoft Access."

Choose this command to
reveal a hidden window

Select a window, and then
choose this command to hide it

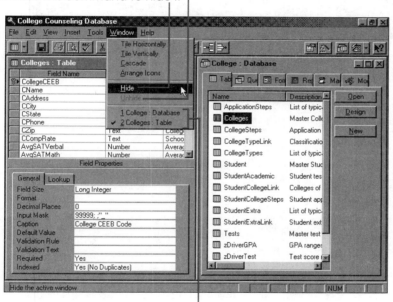

FIGURE 3-9
Working in
multiple windows
in Access.

List of open, unhidden windows
(the Table window has the focus)

Table Window in Datasheet View

To view, change, insert, or delete data in a table, you can use the table's Datasheet view. A datasheet is a simple way to look at your data in rows and columns without any special formatting. You can open a table's Datasheet view by selecting the name of the table you want in the Database window and clicking the Open button. When you open a table in Design view, such as the Colleges table in Figure 3-7, you can also go directly to the Datasheet view of this table (shown in Figure 3-10) by clicking the Table View button on the toolbar. Likewise, when you're in Datasheet view, you can return to Design view by clicking the Table View button. You can also see the list of available views by clicking the small down arrow button to the right of the Table View button and then choosing the view you want by clicking on it.

FIGURE 3-10

A Table window in Datasheet view.

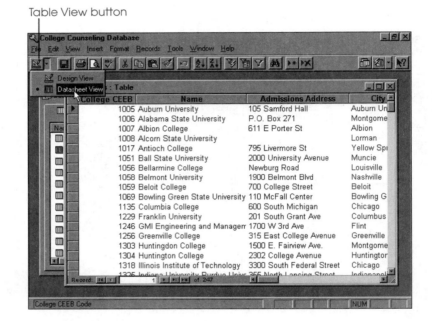

As in the Table window in Design view, in Datasheet view you can move from field to field using the Tab key and move up and down through the records using the arrow keys. You can also use the scroll bars along the bottom and on the right side of the window to move around in the datasheet. To the left of the bottom scroll bar, Access shows you the current record number and the total number of records in the currently selected set of data. You can select the record number with your mouse (or press the F5 key), type a new number, and then press Enter to go to that new record number. As shown in Figure 3-11, you can use the arrows on either side of this record number box to move up or down one record or to move to the first or last record in the table. You can start entering data in a new record by clicking the New Record button on the right.

Click here to move to the first record

Click here to move up one record

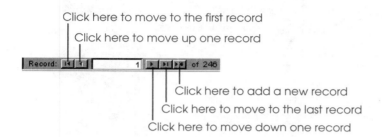

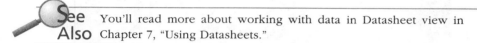

Click here to add a new record

Click here to move to the last record

Click here to move down one record

FIGURE 3-11

Using the record selectors in Datasheet view to move to different records.

See Also You'll read more about working with data in Datasheet view in Chapter 7, "Using Datasheets."

Close the Colleges table now by clicking the window's Close button or by choosing the Close command from the File menu. You should now be back in the Database window for College Counseling.

Queries

You probably noticed that the Datasheet view of the Colleges table gave you all the fields and all the records in the table. But what if you want to see just the college names and addresses? Or maybe you'd like to see information about colleges and all of the students who have applied in one view. To solve these problems, you can create a query. Click on the Queries tab in the Database window to see the list of queries available in the College Counseling database, as shown in Figure 3-12 on the next page. You can see the Large Icon view shown in this figure by clicking the Large Icons button on the toolbar. You can also right-click on the database window (but not on a query name), choose View from the shortcut menu, and then choose Large Icons from the submenu, as shown in Figure 3-12.

FIGURE 3-12
Selecting Large
Icons view from
the shortcut
menu in the
College Coun-
seling database.

Queries tab is selected

Large Icons button

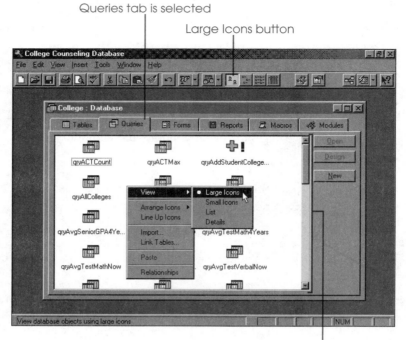

List of queries in the database

New Query Features in Version 7

- Improved Query Wizards

- Performance Analyzer to help make queries more efficient

- New "Windows 95" datasheet formatting options

- Ability to define the field-display control property for most fields

- Automatic combo boxes in query datasheets for fields related to other tables (if the Display Control property is set to Combo Box or List Box)

- Ability to apply sort and filter criteria in Datasheet view

- Datasheet scrollbar "thumb tips" that display the relative record location

On the right side of the Database window are three command buttons:

 Lets you view and possibly update the data gathered by the query selected in the query list. (You might not be able to update all of the data in a query.) Clicking this button opens a Query window in Datasheet view. If the query is an action query, clicking this button runs the query.

Lets you view and modify the definition of the selected query. Clicking this button opens a Query window in Design view.

Lets you define a new query. When you click this button, Access gives you the option to create a new query from scratch or to start one of the Query Wizards.

When the Database window is active, you can choose any of these command buttons from the keyboard by pressing the first letter of the button name while holding down the Alt key. You can also open a query in Datasheet view by double-clicking on the query name in the window using the left mouse button, or you can open the query in Design view by holding down the Ctrl key and double-clicking on the query name using the left mouse button. You can also right-click on a query name and choose an option from the shortcut menu.

Query Window in Design View

When you want to change the definition of a query (the structure or design, as opposed to the data represented in the query), you must open the Design view of the query. Take a look at one of the more complex queries in the College Counseling query list by scrolling to the query named qryStudentCollegeLink. Hold down the Ctrl key and double-click on the query name with the left mouse button to see the query in Design view, as shown in Figure 3-13 on the next page. You can also select the query name with the mouse and then click the Design button on the right side of the Database window, or right-click on the query name and choose Design from the shortcut menu.

FIGURE 3-13

A Query window in Design view showing data from two tables being linked.

Link between tables

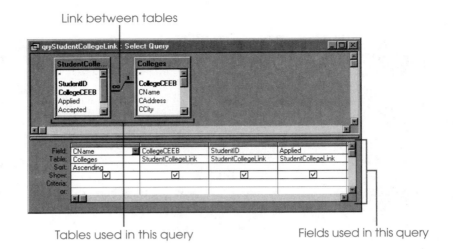

Tables used in this query   Fields used in this query

In the upper part of a Query window in Design view, you can see the field lists of the tables or other queries that this query uses. The line connecting the field lists shows how Access links the tables to solve your query. If you define relationships between tables in your database design, Access draws these lines automatically. (See Chapter 5, "Building Your Database in Microsoft Access," for details.) You can also define relationships when you build the query by dragging a field from one field list and dropping it on another field list.

In the lower part of the Query window, you can see the design grid. The design grid shows fields that Access uses in this query, the tables or queries from which the fields come (when the Table Names command on the View menu has a check mark next to it), any sorting criteria, whether fields show up in the result, and any selection criteria for the fields. You can use the horizontal scroll bar to bring other fields in this query into view. As in the Design view of tables, you can use the F6 key to move between the top and bottom portions of the Query window.

See Also   Chapters 8, 9, and 11 contain details about creating queries.

Query Window in Datasheet View

Click the Query View button on the toolbar to run the query and see
the query results in Datasheet view, as shown in Figure 3-14.

Name	College CEEB Code	Student ID	Applied	Acc
Adams State College	4001	9201	-1	
Adams State College	4001	9308	-1	
Alaska Pacific University	4201	9206	-1	
Albertson College	4060	9530	-1	
Albertson College	4060	9403	-1	
Albertson College	4060	9401	-1	
Alcorn State University	1008	9407	-1	
Alcorn State University	1008	9201	-1	
Alcorn State University	1008	9302	-1	
Arkansas Tech University	6010	9202	-1	
Arkansas Tech University	6010	9307	-1	
Augustana College	6015	9301	-1	
Azusa Pacific University	4596	9404	-1	
Azusa Pacific University	4596	9501	-1	
Ball State University	1051	9408	-1	
Ball State University	1051	9204	-1	
Ball State University	1051	9203	-1	
Baltimore City Community Coll	5131	9508	-1	

FIGURE 3-14
Datasheet view of the qryStudent-CollegeLink query.

The Query window in Datasheet view is similar to a Table window in Datasheet view. Even though the fields in the query datasheet in Figure 3-14 are from two different tables, you can work with the fields as if they were in a single table. If you're designing an Access application for another person, you can use queries to hide much of the complexity of the database and make the application much simpler to use. Depending on how you designed the query, you might also be able to update some of the data in the underlying tables simply by typing in new values as you would in a Table window in Datasheet view.

Close the Query window to see only the Database window.

Forms

Datasheets are useful for looking at and changing data in your database, but they're not particularly attractive or simple to use. If you want to format your data in a special way or automate how your data is used and updated, you need to use a form. Forms provide a number of important capabilities, which are listed on the next page.

■ You can control and enhance the way your data looks on the screen. For example, you can add color and shading or add number formats. You can add controls such as drop-down list boxes and check boxes. You can display OLE objects such as pictures and graphs directly on the form. And you can calculate and display values based on data in a table or a query.

■ You can perform extensive editing of data using macros or VBA procedures.

■ You can link multiple forms or reports by using macros or VBA procedures that are run from buttons on a form. You can also customize the menu bar by using macros associated with your form.

Click on the Forms tab in the Database window to see the list of available forms, shown in Figure 3-15.

New Form Features in Version 7

■ AutoFormat command to design and apply custom form styles

■ Ability to define custom ToolTips for all controls

■ New image control to efficiently display static pictures

■ OLE control properties that are available via the standard Design property sheet

■ New Etched, Shadowed, and Chiseled special effects for controls

■ New Formatting toolbar and Format Painter to make it easier to set the control format

■ Ability to change a control type without having to re-define it

■ Ability to select multiple items in a list box control

■ New PivotTable Wizard

■ Ability for users to Query By Form or Filter By Selection

Forms tab is selected

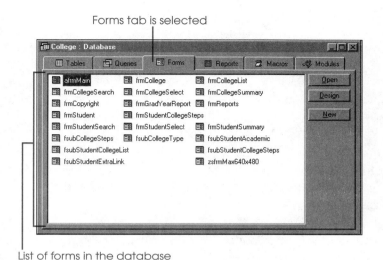

FIGURE 3-15
A Forms list in the
Database window
in Small Icon view.

List of forms in the database

On the right side of the Database window are three command buttons:

Open — Lets you view and update your data through the form selected in the form list. Clicking this button opens a Form window in Form view.

Design — Lets you view and modify the definition of the selected form. Clicking this button opens a Form window in Design view.

New — Lets you define a new form. When you click this button, Access opens a dialog box in which you can choose to build a form from scratch or activate any of the available Form Wizards to help you out.

When the Database window is active, you can choose any of these command buttons from the keyboard by pressing the first letter of the button name while holding down the Alt key. You can also open a form in Form view by double-clicking on the form name in the window using the left mouse button, or you can open the form in Design view by holding down the Ctrl key and double-clicking on the form name using the left mouse button. Finally, you can right-click on a form name and choose a command from the shortcut menu.

Form Window in Design View

When you want to change the definition of a form (the structure or de-sign, as opposed to the data represented in the form), you must open the form in Design view. Take a look at the frmCollege form in the

College Counseling database. It's designed to display all data from the Colleges table, related classification data from the CollegeTypeLink table, and application steps from the CollegeSteps table. Scroll down through the list of forms in the Database window, and then hold down the Ctrl key and double-click on the frmCollege form with the left mouse button to see the form definition, shown in Figure 3-16. You can also select the form name with the mouse and then click the De-sign button on the right side of the Database window. (Don't worry if what you see on your screen doesn't exactly match Figure 3-16. In this figure a few items have been moved around and several options have been selected so that you can see all the main features of the Form win-dow in Design view.)

FIGURE 3-16
The frmCollege form in Design view.

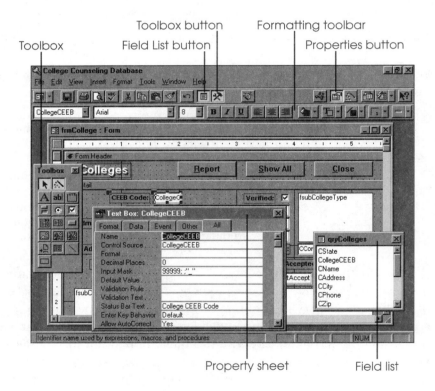

When you first open this form in Design view, you should see the toolbox in the lower left area of the screen. If you don't see it, choose the Toolbox command from the View menu or click the Toolbox button (the crossed hammer and wrench symbol) on the toolbar. This is the action center of form design; you'll use the tools here to add the controls you want, to display data, and to trigger macros or VBA procedures.

See Also You'll learn more about form design in Chapter 12, "Form Basics"; Chapter 13, "Building Forms"; and Chapter 15, "Advanced Form Design."

In the lower right of the window shown in Figure 3-16 you can see a field list labeled *qryColleges*. This query selects all of the fields in the Colleges table and then sorts the rows by State and College Name. You might see the field list near the top of the Form window when you first open the form. If you don't see the field list, choose the Field List command from the View menu or click the Field List button (the mini-datasheet symbol) on the toolbar. You can move the field list by dragging its title bar. When you read about form design in Chapter 13, "Building Forms," you'll see that you can choose a tool from the toolbox and then drag and drop a field from the field list to place a field-display control on the form.

After you place all the controls on a form, you might want to customize some of them. You do this by opening the property sheet, which is in the lower center of Figure 3-16. To see this window, choose the Properties command from the View menu or click the Properties button (a datasheet with a finger-pointing symbol) on the toolbar. The property sheet always shows the property values for the currently selected control in the Form window. Click on a tab at the top of the property sheet to choose all properties or to choose only properties for formats, data, or events. In the example shown in Figure 3-16, the text box called CollegeCEEB, near the top left of the form, has been selected. Looking at the property sheet, you can see that Access displays CollegeCEEB as a numeric field with no decimal places. The designer specified an input mask to assist the user while entering data in this field. If you scroll down the list of other properties for this text box, you can see the wide range of other properties you can set to customize this control. As you learn to build applications using Access, you'll soon discover that you can customize the way your application works by simply setting form and control properties—you don't have to write any code.

If you scroll to the bottom of the property list, or click on the Event tab, you'll see a number of properties that you can set to define macros or VBA procedures that Access will run whenever the associated event occurs on this control. For example, you can use the BeforeUpdate event property to perform additional validation before Access saves any changes typed in this control. You can use the OnClick or

OnDblClick event properties to cause "magic" to happen if the user clicks there. If you need to, you can even look at every individual character the user types there with the OnKey event properties. As you'll discover later, Access provides a rich set of events that you can detect for the form and all controls on the form.

You might have noticed that Access made available some additional boxes and buttons on the Formatting toolbar when you selected the CollegeCEEB control. When you select a text box on a form in Design view, Access shows you drop-down list boxes to make it easy to select a font and font size, and it shows you buttons to let you set the FontWeight, FontItalic, and FontUnderline properties. To the right of these buttons are three buttons that set text alignment: Align Left, Center, and Align Right. You can also set the foreground, background, and border colors; border width; and special effects from buttons on this toolbar.

If all of this looks just a bit too complex, don't worry! Building a simple form is really quite easy. In addition, Access provides Form Wizards that you can use to automatically generate a number of standard form layouts based on the table or query you choose. You'll find it simple to customize a form to your needs once the Form Wizard has done most of the hard work.

See Also   In Chapter 14, "Customizing Forms," you'll learn how to customize a form.

Form Window in Form View

To view, change, insert, or delete data via a form, you can use Form view. Depending on how you've designed the form, not only can you work with your data in an attractive and clear context, but you can also have the form validate the information you enter or you can use it to trigger other forms or reports based on actions you decide to perform. You can open a form in Form view by selecting the form's name in the Database window and then clicking the Open button. Because you have the frmCollege form open in Design view, you can go directly to Form view by clicking the Form View button on the toolbar.

Figure 3-17 shows a fairly complex form that brings together information from five tables into a display that's easy to use and understand. This form includes all the fields from the Colleges table. You can tab or use the arrow keys to move through the fields. You can experiment with the Filter By Form and Filter By Selection buttons on the toolbar to see how easy it is to select only the rows you want to see. For example, you can click in the State field and then click the Filter By Selection button to display rows only for the current state.

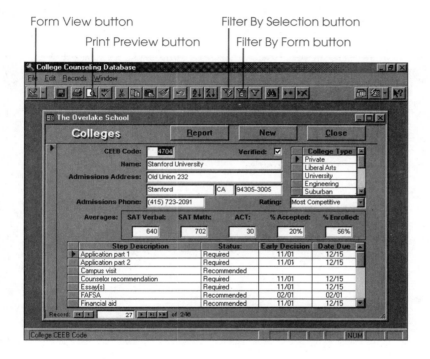

FIGURE 3-17
The frmCollege form in Form view.

There are two other ways to look at a form: in Datasheet view and in Print Preview. You can select Datasheet View from the Form View button drop-down list to see all the fields in the form arranged in a datasheet—similar to a datasheet for a table or a query. You can click the Print Preview button on the toolbar to see what the form will look like on a printed page. You'll read more about Print Preview in the next section. For now, close the frmCollege window so that only the Database window is visible on your screen.

Reports

Although you can print information in a datasheet or a form, neither of these formats provides the flexibility you need to produce complex printed output (such as invoices or summaries) that might include many calculations and subtotals. Formatting in datasheets is limited to sizing the rows and columns, specifying fonts, and setting the colors and gridline effects. You can do a lot of formatting in a form, but because forms are designed primarily for viewing and entering data on your screen, they are not suited for extensive calculations, grouping of data, or multiple totals and subtotals in print.

New Report Features in Version 7

- AutoFormat command to design and apply custom report styles

- New Image control to efficiently display static pictures

- OLE control properties that are available via the standard Design property sheet

- New Etched, Shadowed, and Chiseled special effects for controls

- New Formatting toolbar and Format Painter that make it easier to set the control format

- Ability to change a control type without having to redefine it

- Ability to output subreport data to text and spreadsheet files

- Enhanced Print Preview Zoom capabilities

If your primary need is to print data, you should use a report. Click on the Reports tab to see the list of reports available in the College Counseling database, as shown in Figure 3-18.

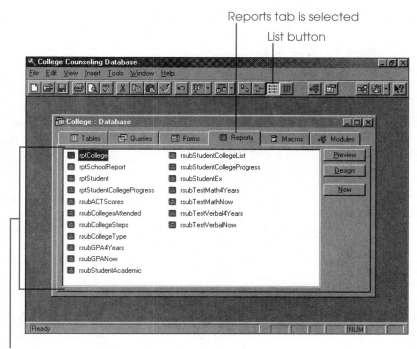

Reports tab is selected

List button

FIGURE 3-18
A list of reports in the Database window in List view.

List of reports in the database

On the right side of the Database window are three command buttons:

Preview   Lets you see how the report you selected will look on a printed page. Clicking this button initiates the Print Preview command.

Design   Lets you view and modify the definition of the selected report. Clicking this button opens a Report window in Design view.

New   Lets you define a new report. When you click this button, Access opens a dialog box in which you can choose to build a report from scratch or activate any of the available Report Wizards to help you out.

When the Database window is active, you can choose any of these command buttons from the keyboard by pressing the first letter of the button name while holding down the Alt key. You can also view the report in Print Preview by double-clicking on the report name in the window using the left mouse button, or you can open the report in

Design view by holding down the Ctrl key and double-clicking on the report name using the left mouse button. Finally, you can right-click on any report name and choose Design from the shortcut menu.

Report Window in Design View

When you want to change the definition of a report, you must open the report in Design view. In the report list for College Counseling, hold down the Ctrl key and double-click on the rptCollege report with the left mouse button to see the design for the report, as shown in Figure 3-19. You can also select the report name with the mouse and then click the Design button on the right side of the Database window. Don't worry if what you see on your screen doesn't exactly match Figure 3-19. A few things were moved around and several options were selected so that you could see all the main features of the Report window in Design view.

FIGURE 3-19
The rptCollege report in Design view.

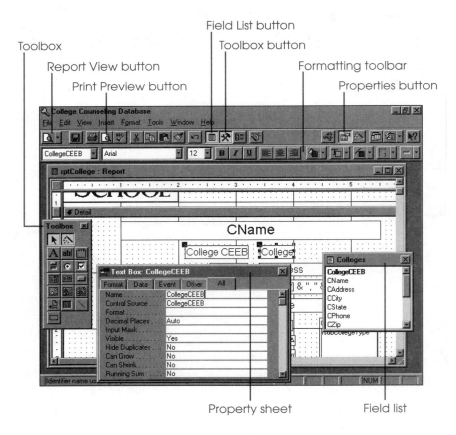

This report is designed to display all the information you saw earlier on the frmCollege form but in a format suitable for printing. You can see that the Design view for reports is similar to the Design view for forms. (For comparison, see Figure 3-16.) Reports provide additional flexibility, allowing you to group items and to total them (either across or down). You can also define header and footer information for the entire report, for each page, and for each subgroup.

When you first open this report in Design view, the toolbox should appear in the lower left area of the screen. If you don't see the toolbox, choose the Toolbox command from the View menu or click the Toolbox button on the toolbar.

In the lower right of Figure 3-19 you can see a window titled Colleges. This is a field list containing all the fields from the Colleges table that provide the data for this report. You might see this list near the top of the report's Design view when you first open it. If you don't see the field list, choose the Field List command from the View menu or click the Field List button on the toolbar. You can move the field list by dragging its title bar.

See Also When you read about report design in Chapter 17, "Constructing a Report," you'll see that you can choose a tool from the toolbox and then drag and drop a field from the field list to place the field-display control on the report.

After you place all the controls on a report, you might want to customize some of them. You do this by opening the property sheet, which you can see in the lower center of Figure 3-19. To see this window, choose the Properties command from the View menu or click the Properties button on the toolbar. The property sheet always shows the property settings for the currently selected control in the Report window. In the example shown in Figure 3-19, the text box called CollegeCEEB is selected. You can see that Access displays the CollegeCEEB field from the Colleges table as the input data for this control. You can also specify complex formulas that calculate additional data for report controls.

You might have noticed that Access made available some additional list boxes and buttons on the Formatting toolbar when you selected the CollegeCEEB control. When you click on a text box in a report in Design view, Access shows you drop-down list boxes that make it easy to select a font and font size, and Access shows you buttons to let you set the FontWeight, FontItalic, and FontUnderline properties. To the right of these buttons are three buttons that set text alignment: Align Left, Center, and Align Right. You can also set the foreground, background, and border colors; border width; and special effects from buttons on this toolbar.

> **NOTE** In version 1 of Access, the text format controls didn't appear until you selected a control. In version 2, they appeared on the Report and Form Design toolbars all the time but were grayed out (disabled) if you hadn't selected a text control. In version 7, these options appear on a separate Formatting toolbar that is normally available when you are in the Design view of a report or the Datasheet view of a form.

Reports can be even more complex than forms, but building a simple report is really quite easy. Access provides Report Wizards that you can use to automatically generate a number of standard report layouts based on the table or query you choose. You'll find it simple to customize a report to suit your needs after the Report Wizard has done most of the hard work.

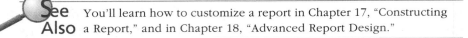 You'll learn how to customize a report in Chapter 17, "Constructing a Report," and in Chapter 18, "Advanced Report Design."

Report Window in Print Preview

Reports do not have a Datasheet view. To see what the finished report looks like, click the Report View button (shown in Figure 3-19) on the toolbar when you're in the Report window in Design view. From the Database window, you can also select the report name and then click the Preview button or right-click on the report name and choose Preview from the shortcut menu. Figure 3-20 shows a Report window in Print Preview.

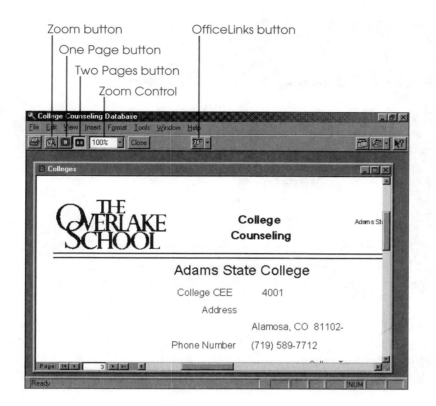

Zoom button
One Page button
Two Pages button
Zoom Control
OfficeLinks button

FIGURE 3-20
The rptCollege report in Print Preview.

Access initially shows you the upper left corner of the report. To see the report centered in full-page view in Print Preview, click the Zoom button on the toolbar. To see two pages side-by-side, click the Two Pages button on the toolbar. This gives you a reduced picture of two pages, as shown in Figure 3-21 on the next page, and an overall idea of how Access arranges major areas of data on the report. Unless you have a large monitor, however, you won't be able to read the data. When you move the mouse pointer over the window in Print Preview, the pointer changes to a magnifying glass icon. To zoom in, place this icon in an area that you want to see more closely, and then press the left mouse button. You can also click the Zoom button on the toolbar again to see a close-up view of the report, and then use the scroll bars to move around in the magnified report. Use the Zoom Control on the

FIGURE 3-21

Two pages of the rptCollege report in Print Preview.

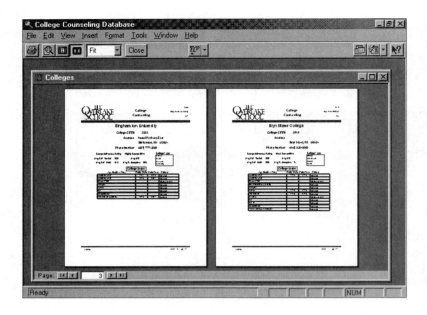

toolbar to magnify or shrink your view. Access also provides an OfficeLinks button on the standard Print Preview toolbar to let you output the report to Microsoft Word or Microsoft Excel.

Close the Report window to return to the Database window.

Macros

You can make working with your data within forms and reports much easier by triggering a macro action. Microsoft Access provides more than 40 actions that you can include in a macro. They perform tasks such as opening tables and forms, running queries, running other macros, selecting options from menus, and sizing open windows. You can even start other applications that support Dynamic Data Exchange (DDE), such as Microsoft Excel, and exchange data from your database with that application. You can group multiple actions in a macro and specify conditions that determine when each set of actions will or will not be executed by Access.

In the Database window, click on the Macros tab to see the list of available macros in the College Counseling database, shown in Figure 3-22.

Macros tab is selected

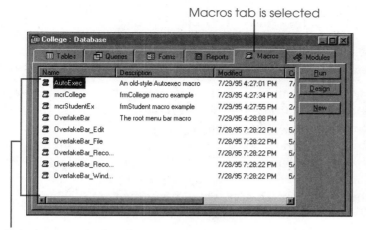

FIGURE 3-22
The macros in the
College Counsel-
ing database.

List of macros in the database

New Macro Features in Version 7

- New SetMenuItem action to gray/ungray, check/uncheck, or hide/unhide custom menu entries

- New Save action to save the definition of any Access object

- New Printout action to print any datasheet, form, report, or module

- Converter tool for forms and reports to convert macros to VBA event procedures

---

On the right side of the Database window are three command buttons:

   Lets you execute the actions in the macro selected in the Database window. A macro object can consist of a single set of commands or multiple named sets (called a *macro group*). If you select a macro group from the Macros list and then click the Run button, Access runs the first macro in the group. You can also choose Macro from the Tools menu to open a dialog box that lets you select a specific macro within a macro group to run.

(continued)

Lets you view and modify the definition of the macro selected in the Database window. Clicking this button opens a Macro window in Design view.

Lets you define a new macro.

When the Database window is active, you can choose any of these command buttons from the keyboard by pressing the first letter of the button name while holding down the Alt key. You can also run a macro by double-clicking on the macro name in the window using the left mouse button, or you can open the Macro window in Design view by holding down the Ctrl key and double-clicking on the macro name using the left mouse button. Finally, you can right-click on a macro name and choose Run or Design from the shortcut menu.

One of the most useful functions of a macro is to test and set data entered on a form. For example, take a look at the SubBeforeUpdate macro in the mcrCollege macro object in the College Counseling database. Scroll down in the Database window until you see this macro object name, select it, and then click the Design button. You'll see a window similar to the one shown in Figure 3-23.

FIGURE 3-23

The mcrCollege macro object in the College Counseling database.

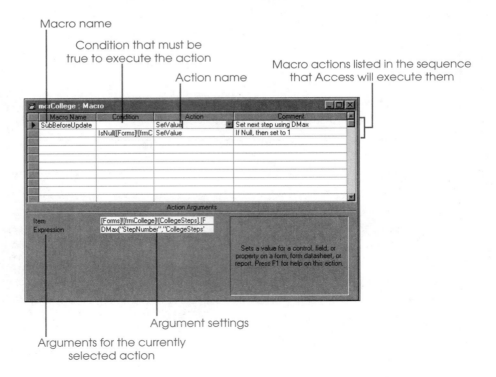

Each college in the database can have a unique set of student application steps. This macro is designed to create the "next" step number for the current college when you decide to enter a new step in the frmCollege form. It does this by calling a function (*DMax*) to find the previous highest step number for the current college and adds one to that number. If the college has no steps yet, the *DMax* function returns a special Null value. The macro tests for this on the second line and sets the value of the step number to 1 if this is the case. Close the Macro window to return to the Database window.

See Also   Chapter 19, "Adding Power with Macros," and Chapter 20, "Automating Your Application with Macros," provide detailed discussions of macros.

Modules

You might find that you keep coding the same complex formula over and over in some of your forms or reports. Although you can easily build a complete Microsoft Access application using only forms, reports, and macros, some actions might be difficult or impossible to define in a macro. You can create a VBA procedure that performs a series of calculations, and then use that procedure in a form or report.

If your application is so complex that it needs to deal with errors (such as two users trying to update the same record at the same time), you must use VBA. Since VBA is a complete programming language with complex logic and the ability to link to other applications and files, you can solve unusual or difficult programming problems by using VBA procedures.

Version 2 of Access introduced the ability to code Basic routines in special modules attached directly to the forms and reports that they support. You can create these procedures from Design view for forms or reports by requesting the code builder in any event property. You can also edit this "code behind forms" by choosing Code from the View menu in Design view for forms and reports. (See Chapter 21, "Visual Basic for Applications Fundamentals," and Chapter 22, "Automating Your Application with VBA," for details.) In fact, once you learn a little bit about VBA, you may find that coding small event procedures for your forms and reports is much more efficient and convenient than try-ing to keep track of many macro modules. You'll also soon learn that you can't fully respond to some sophisticated events, such as KeyPress, in macros because macros can't "see" special additional parameters (such as the value of the key pressed) generated by the event. You can fully handle these events only in VBA.

New Visual Basic Features in Version 7

- Basic in Access is now Visual Basic for Applications, the 32-bit engine that is compatible with all other Microsoft products that use Basic

- Color-coded syntax that allows you to easily distin-guish keywords, variables, comments, and other components in the language as you type them

- Long lines of code that can be continued to new lines

- An Object Browser that lets you see all supported methods and properties for any object

- Improved debugging facilities, including the ability to "watch" variables or expressions

- Ability to define code segments that compile condi-tionally

- Ability to define procedures with optional parameters

Click on the Modules tab in the Database window to display the list of available modules, as shown in Figure 3-24. The College Counseling database has two module objects that contain procedures that can be called from any query, form, report, or other procedure in the database. The modMedian module contains a function to calculate the median value of a column in any table or query. The modUtility module con-tains several functions that you might find useful in your applications.

Modules tab is selected

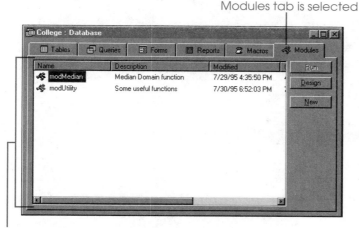

List of modules in the database

FIGURE 3-24
The VBA modules in the College Counseling database.

From the Database window you can either start a new module by clicking the New button or open the design of an existing module by clicking the Design button. You can run a module function from a macro, a form, or a report. You can also use functions in expressions in queries and as validation functions from a table or a form.

Select the modUtility module and click the Design button to open a window containing the VBA code in the module. Use the Proc drop-down list box in the window or choose the Object Browser command from the View menu to look at the procedure names available in the sample. One of the functions in this module, *IsLoaded,* checks all forms open in the current Access session to see whether the form name passed as a parameter is one of the open forms. This function is useful in macros or in other modules to direct the flow of an application based on which forms the user has open. You can see this function in Figure 3-25 on the next page.

See Also   Chapter 21, "Visual Basic for Applications Fundamentals," and Chapter 22, "Automating Your Application with VBA," introduce coding with modules.

FIGURE 3-25

The *IsLoaded*
function.

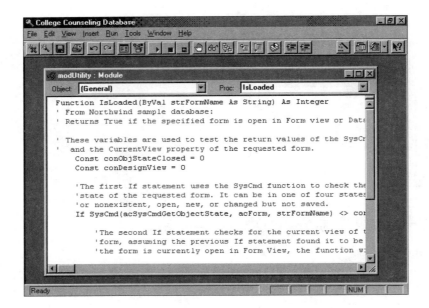

Now that you've had a chance to look at the major objects in the College Counseling sample database, you should be getting comfortable with Access. Perhaps the most important aspect of building an application is designing the database that will support your application. The next chapter describes how you should design your database application and its data structures. Building a solid foundation makes creating the forms and reports for your application easy.

Part 2

Building a Database

Chapter 4

Designing Your Database Application

You could begin building a database in Microsoft Access much as you might begin creating a simple single-sheet problem in a spreadsheet application such as Microsoft Excel—by simply organizing your data into rows and columns and then throwing in calculation formulas where you need them. If you've ever worked extensively with a database or spreadsheet application, you already know that this unplanned approach works in only the most trivial situations. Solving real problems takes some planning; otherwise, you end up rebuilding your application over and over again. One of the beauties of a relational database system such as Access is that it's much easier to make midcourse corrections. However, it's well worth spending time up front designing the tasks you want to perform, the data structures you need to support those tasks, and the flow of tasks within your database application.

You don't have to go deeply into application and database design theory to build a solid foundation for your database project. You'll read about application design fundamentals in the next section, and then you'll apply those fundamentals in the following sections, "An Application Design Strategy" and "Data Analysis." The section titled "Database Design Concepts" teaches you a basic method for designing the tables you'll need for your application and for defining relationships between those tables.

Application Design Fundamentals

Methodologies for good computer application design were first devised in the 1960s by recognized industry consultants such as James Martin, Edward Yourdon, and Larry Constantine. At the dawn of modern computing, building an application or fixing a broken one was so expensive that the experts often advised spending 60 percent or more of the total project time getting the design right before penning a single line of code.

Today's application development technologies make building an application incredibly inexpensive and fast. An experienced user can sit down with Microsoft Access on a PC and build in an afternoon what used to take months to create on an early mainframe system (if it was even possible). It's also easier than ever to go back and fix mistakes or to "redesign on the fly."

Today's technologies also give you the power to build very complex applications. And the pace of computing is several orders of magnitude faster than it was even a decade ago. But even with powerful tools, creating a database application (particularly a moderately complex one) without first spending some time determining what the application should do and how it should operate invites a lot of expensive rework time. If your application design is not well thought out, it will also be very expensive and time-consuming later to track down any problems or to add new functionality.

The following is a brief overview of the typical steps involved in building a database application.

Step 1: Identifying Tasks

Before you start building an application, you'll probably have some idea of what you want it to do. It is well worth your time to make a list of all the major tasks you want to accomplish with the application—including those that you might not need right away but might want to implement in the future. By "major tasks" I mean application functions that will ultimately be represented in a form or a report in your Access database. For example, "Enter customer orders" is a major task that you would accomplish by using a form created for that purpose, while "Calculate extended price" is most likely a subtask of "Enter customer orders" that you would accomplish by using the same form.

Step 2: Charting Task Flow

To make sure your application operates smoothly and logically, you should lay out the major tasks in topic groups and then order those tasks within groups based on the sequence in which the tasks must be performed. For example, you probably want to separate employee-related tasks from sales-related ones. Within sales, a contract must be entered into the system before you can print the contract or examine commission totals.

You might discover that some tasks are related to more than one group or that completing a task in one group is a prerequisite to performing a task in another group. Grouping and charting the flow of tasks helps you discover a "natural" flow that you can ultimately reflect in the way your forms and reports are linked together in your finished application. Later in this chapter, you'll see how I laid out the tasks demonstrated in one of the sample applications included with this book.

Step 3: Identifying Data Elements

After you develop your task list, perhaps the most important design step is to list the data required by each task and the changes that will be made to that data. A given task will require some input data (for example, a price to calculate an extended amount owed on an order); the task might also update the data. The task might delete some data elements (remove invoices paid, for example) or add new ones (insert new order details). Or the task might calculate some data and display it, but it won't save the data anywhere in the database.

Step 4: Organizing the Data

After you determine all the data elements you need for your application, you must organize the data by subject and map the subjects into tables and queries in your database. With a relational database system such as Access, you use a process called *normalization* to help you design the most efficient and flexible way to store the data. (See the section titled "Database Design Concepts" later in this chapter for a simple method of creating a normalized design.)

Step 5: Designing a Prototype and a User Interface

After you build the table structures you need to support your application, you can easily mock up the application flow in forms and tie the forms together using simple macros or Visual Basic for Applications (VBA) event procedures. You can build the actual forms and reports for your application "on screen," switching to Form view or Print Preview periodically to check your progress. If you're building the application to be used by someone else, you can easily demonstrate and get approval for the "look and feel" of your application before you write any complex code that you might need to actually accomplish the tasks. (Parts 4 and 5 of this book show you how to design and construct forms and reports; Part 6 shows you how to use macros and VBA code to link forms and reports to build an application.)

Step 6: Constructing the Application

For very simple applications, you might find that the prototype _is_ the application. Most applications, however, will require that you write code to fully automate all the tasks you identified in your design. You'll probably also need to create certain linking forms that facilitate moving from one task to another. For example, you might need to construct switchboard forms that provide the navigational road map to your application. You might also need to build dialog forms to gather user input to allow users to easily filter the data they want to use in a particular task. You might also want to build custom menus for most, if not all, forms.

Step 7: Testing, Reviewing, and Refining

As you complete various components of your application, you should test each option that you provide. As you'll learn in Part 6 of this book, you can test macros by stepping through the commands you've written, one line at a time. If you automate your application using VBA, you'll have many debugging tools at your disposal to verify application execution and to identify and fix errors.

If at all possible, you should provide completed portions of your application to users so that they can test your code and provide feedback about the flow of the application. Despite your best efforts to identify tasks and lay out a smooth task flow, users will invariably think of new and better ways to approach a particular task after they've seen your application in action. Also, users often discover that some features they asked you to include are not so useful after all. Discovering a required change early in the implementation stage can save you a lot of rework time.

The refinement and revision process continues even after the application is put into use. Most software developers recognize that after they've finished one "release," they often must make design changes and build enhancements. For major revisions, you should start over at Step 1 to assess the overall impact of the desired changes so that you can smoothly integrate them into your earlier work.

Typical Application Development Steps

- Identifying tasks
- Charting task flow
- Identifying data elements
- Organizing the data
- Designing a prototype and a user interface
- Constructing the application
- Testing, reviewing, and refining

An Application Design Strategy

The two major schools of thought on designing databases are *process-driven design* (also known as *top-down design*), which focuses on the functions or tasks you need to perform, and *data-driven design* (also known as *bottom-up design*), which concentrates on identifying and organizing all the bits of data you need. The method used here incorporates ideas from both philosophies.

This method begins with you identifying and grouping tasks to decide whether you need only one database or more than one database. (This is a top-down approach.) As explained previously, databases should be organized around a group of related tasks or functions. For each task, you choose the individual pieces of data you need. Next, you gather all the data fields for all related tasks and begin organizing them into subjects. (This is a bottom-up approach.) Each subject forms the foundation for the individual tables in your database. Finally, you apply the rules you will learn in the "Database Design Concepts" section of this chapter to create your tables.

> **NOTE** The examples in the rest of this chapter are based on the College Counseling sample database application. Later in the book, you'll learn how to build various pieces of the application as you explore the architecture and features of Microsoft Access. The College Counseling application is somewhat more complex than the Northwind Traders application that is included with Access. The College Counseling application also employs some techniques not found in the product documentation.

Analyzing the Tasks

Let's assume that you've been assigned to act as an Access database consultant to the college counselors at the Overlake School, a private liberal-arts primary and secondary school in Redmond, Washington. The counselors' job is to help students identify and apply to colleges and universities that are appropriate to their interests and qualifications. The counselors must also produce an annual report that summarizes the characteristics of the senior class so that they can respond to inquiries from the colleges to which students apply.

The counselors are keeping track of all the information on paper, and they are finding it difficult to keep up with the number of students they work with. They need a more efficient way to keep track of the students as well as the colleges and universities. The counselors need to do the following:

- Record students' college and university preferences

- Enter personal student data

- Track students' test scores and extracurricular activities

- Record basic college and university data

- Track the application steps and the deadline for each step at each college

- Perform college searches based on such criteria as college type, location, and competitiveness

- Track the students' application status

- Create a profile report for each student

- Produce a graduating class analysis report

Figure 4-1 on the next page shows a blank application design worksheet that you would fill out for each task.

Consider the first task—recording students' college and university preferences. For this task, you need to interview each student, perhaps perform a search of colleges and universities based on the student's criteria, and then log the student's preferences. The list of related tasks probably includes entering personal student data, recording basic college and university data, entering the application steps and the deadline for each step at each institution, entering the student's extracurricular activities, and entering the scores for the various tests the student must take. You would fill out one worksheet for each related task, and then you would begin to determine what data you need.

APPLICATION DESIGN WORKSHEET #1 - TASKS			
Task Name:			
Brief Description:			
Related Tasks:			
Data Name	**Usage**	**Description**	**Subject**

Data or Information?

You need to know the difference between data and information before you proceed any further. This bit of knowledge makes it easier to determine what you need to store in your database.

The difference between data and information is that data is the static values you store in the tables of the database, while information is data that is retrieved and organized in a way that is meaningful to the person viewing it. You *store* data and you *retrieve* information. The distinction is important because of the way that you construct a database application. You first determine the tasks that are necessary (what *information* you need to be able to retrieve), and then you determine what must be stored in the database to support those tasks (what *data* you need in order to construct and supply the information).

Whenever you refer to or work with the structure of your database or the items stored in the tables, queries, macros, or code, you're dealing with data. Likewise, whenever you refer to or work with query dynasets, filters, forms, or reports, you're dealing with information. The process of designing a database and its application becomes clearer once you understand this distinction. Unfortunately, this is another set of terms that people in the computer industry have used interchangeably. But armed with this new knowledge, you're ready to go on to the next step.

Selecting the Data

After you identify all the tasks, you must list the data items you need in order to perform each task. On the task worksheet, you enter a name for each data item, a usage code, and a brief description. In the Usage column, you enter one or more usage codes—I, O, U, D, and C—which stand for input, output, update, delete, and calculate. A data item is an *input* if you need to read it from the database (but not update it) to perform a task. For example, a customer name and address are the inputs needed to create an order; a student name is the input needed to record student college preferences. Likewise, data is an *output* if it is new data that you enter as you perform a task or that a task calculates and stores from the input data. For example, the quantities of items you enter for an order are outputs; the student address and phone number you provide for a new student record are outputs as well.

You *update* data in a task if you read data from the database, change it, and write it back. A task such as recording a student's change of address would input the old address, update it, and write the new one back to the database. As you might guess, a task *deletes* data when it removes the data from the database. In the College Counseling database, you might have a task to remove data about interest in a college if the student decides not to apply after all. Finally, *calculated* data creates new values from input data to be displayed or printed but not written back to the database.

In the Subject column, you enter the name of the Access object to which you think each data item belongs. For example, an address might belong to a Students table. A completed application design worksheet for the Record Student College and University Preferences task might look like the one shown in Figure 4-2.

FIGURE 4-2

A completed worksheet for the Record Student College and University Preferences task.

APPLICATION DESIGN WORKSHEET #1 - TASKS			
Task Name:	Record Student College and University Preferences		
Brief Description:	Interview the student. Execute the Search on College Criteria task to find candidate schools. Enter student intent to apply in the database.		
Related Tasks:	Enter personal student data. Record basic college/university data. Perform college searches based on such criteria as college type, location, and competitiveness. Track the application steps and deadlines for each step at each college. Track the student's application status.		

Data Name	Usage	Description	Subject
StudentID	I, O	Student identifier	Students
StudentName	I	Name of the student	Students
GradYear	I, U	Student graduation year	Students
CollegeID	I, O	College identifier	Colleges
CollegeName	I	College name	Colleges
CollegeAddress	I	Address of the college	Colleges
CollegeCity	I	City where college is located	Colleges
CollegeState	I	College state	Colleges
CollegeZip	I	College zip code	Colleges
CollegePhone	I	College admissions phone	Colleges
ApplicationStep1	I	Application step for the college	Colleges
ApplicationStep1	O	Application step for this student	Students
ApplicationStep2	I	Application step for the college	Colleges
ApplicationStep2	O	Application step for this student	Students
...			
ApplicationStep$n$	I	Application step for the college	Colleges
ApplicationStep$n$	O	Application step for the student	Students

Organizing Tasks

You should use task worksheets as a guide in laying out an initial structure for your application. Part of the planning you do on the worksheets is to consider usage—whether a piece of data might be needed as input, for updating, or as output of a given task. Wherever you have something that is required as input, you should have a *precedent* task that creates that data item as output.

For example, for the worksheet shown in Figure 4-2, you must gather college and university data and student data before you can record student preferences. Similarly, you need to create the admissions requirements data in some other task before you can use that data (or update it) in this task. Therefore, you should have a task for gathering the college and university data, a task for gathering basic student data, and a task for recording admissions requirements for each institution. It's useful to lay out all of your defined tasks in a relationship diagram. The relationships among the tasks in the College Counseling application are shown in Figure 4-3. Note that optional precedent tasks are shown with dashed lines. (In other words, a student might know his or her college preferences without performing a criteria search.)

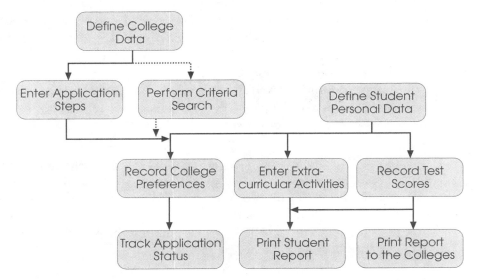

FIGURE 4-3

The relationships among tasks in the College Counseling application.

Data Analysis

Now you're ready to begin a more thorough analysis of your data and to organize the individual items into data subjects. These subjects become candidates for tables in your database design.

Choosing the Database Subjects

If you've been careful in identifying the subject for each data item you need, the next step is very easy. You create another worksheet, similar to the worksheet shown in Figure 4-4, to help you collect all the data items that belong to each subject. In the top part of the worksheet, you list the related subjects that appear in any given task and indicate the kind of relationship—one-to-many or one-to-one. For example, a student might have many college preferences, and a college might have many students who want to apply. A completed worksheet for the Students subject is shown in Figure 4-5.

It's important to understand these relationships because they have a significant impact on the database structure and on how you use certain types of objects in Access. You'll learn more about these relationships later in this chapter.

As you copy each data item to the subject worksheet, you designate the data type (text, number, currency, memo, and so on) and the data length in the Data Type column. You can enter a short descriptive phrase for each data item in the Description column. When you create your table from the worksheet, the description is the default information that Access will display on the status bar at the bottom of the screen whenever the field is selected on a datasheet or in a form or a report.

Finally, in the Validation Rule column, you might make a note of any validation rules that should always apply to the data field. Later, you can define these rules in Access, and Access will check each time you create new data to ensure that you haven't violated any of the rules. Validating data can be especially important when you create a database application for other people to use.

APPLICATION DESIGN WORKSHEET #2 - SUBJECTS			
Subject Name:			
Brief Description:			
Related Subjects: Name Relationship			
Data Name	**Data Type**	**Description**	**Validation Rule**

FIGURE 4-4

An application design worksheet for identifying related subjects.

FIGURE 4-5

A completed
worksheet for the
Students subject.

APPLICATION DESIGN WORKSHEET #2 - SUBJECTS			
Subject Name:	Student		
Brief Description:	Basic student data		
Related Subjects:	Name	Relationship	
	Colleges	Many	
	Application steps	Many	
	Test scores	Many	
	Extracurricular	Many	

Data Name	Data Type	Description	Validation Rule
StudentID	Number(Long)	Student identifier	Number(Long)
GradYear	Number (Integer)	Graduation year	>1968
LastName	Text (15)	Student last name	Required
MiddleInit	Text (1)	Student Middle initial	
FirstName	Text (15)	Student first name	Required
SocSec	Text (13)	Social Security number	nnn-nn-nnnn
Address	Text (50)	Student address	
City	Text (50)	Student city	
State	Text (15)	Student state	
Zip	Text (9)	Student zip code	nnnnn-nnnn
Phone Number	Text (14)	Student home phone	(nnn) nnn-nnnn
JuniorGPA	Number (Single)	Junior grade point average	>0 And < 4.01
SeniorGPA	Number (Single)	Senior grade point average	>0 And < 4.01
Photo	OLE Object	Student picture	
Comments	Memo	Advisor comments	

Mapping Subjects to Your Database

After you fill out all of the subject worksheets, each worksheet becomes a candidate to be a table in your database design. For each table you must confirm that all the data you need is included. You should also be sure that you don't include any unnecessary data.

For example, if any students need more than one line for an address, you should add a second data field. If you expect to have more than one contact person at a college or university, you should create a separate Contacts table that contains records for each name and phone number. In the next section, you'll learn how to use four simple rules to create a flexible and logical set of tables from your subject worksheets.

Database Design Concepts

When using a relational database system such as Microsoft Access, you should begin by designing each database around a specific set of tasks or functions. For example, you might design one database for student admissions that contains personal data about each student, the classes in which the student is enrolled, the student's current grade point average, and the student's academic classification. You might have another database that handles human resources for your school. It would contain all relevant data about the administrative and teaching staffs, such as names, job titles, employment histories, departmental assignments, insurance information, and the like.

At this point you face your biggest design challenge: How do you organize data within each task-oriented database so that you take advantage of the relational capabilities of Access and avoid inefficiency and waste? If you followed the steps outlined earlier in this chapter for analyzing application tasks and identifying database subjects, you're well on your way to creating a logical, flexible, and usable database design. But what if you just "dive in" and start laying out your tables without first analyzing tasks and subjects? The rest of this chapter shows you how to apply some rules to transform a makeshift database design into one that is robust and efficient.

Waste Is the Problem

A table stores the data you need for the tasks you want to perform. A table is made up of columns, or fields, each of which contains a specific kind of data (such as a student name or a test score), and rows, or records, that collect all the data about a particular person, place, or thing. You can see this organization in the College Counseling database's Students table, as shown in Figure 4-6 on the next page.

FIGURE 4-6

The College
Counseling
database's
Students table in
Datasheet view.

Student ID	Graduation	Last Name	M.I.	First Name	Address	City
92001	1992	Davolio	Q	Nancy	507 - 20th Ave. E.	Seattle
92002	1992	Fuller	R	Andrew	908 W. Capital Way	Tacoma
92003	1992	Leverling	S	Sarah	722 Moss Bay Blvd.	Kirkland
92004	1992	Peacock	T	Carol	4110 Old Redmond Rd	Redmond
92005	1992	Viescas	L	Suzanne	15127 NE 24th, #383	Redmond
92006	1992	Thompson	G	Will	122 Spring River Drive	Duvall
92007	1992	Hallmark		Gary	Route 2, Box 203B	Woodinville
92008	1992	Callahan	U	Sally	4726 - 11th Ave. N.E.	Seattle
92010	1992	Buchanan	V	Steven	13920 S.E. 40th Street	Bellevue
92011	1992	Smith	W	Jeffrey	30301 - 166th Ave. N.E	Kent
92012	1992	Patterson	K	Ann	16 Maple Lane	Auburn
93001	1993	Davolio	M	Michael	507 - 20th Ave. E.	Seattle
93002	1993	Fuller	N	Ann	908 W. Capital Way	Tacoma
93003	1993	Leverling	O	James	722 Moss Bay Blvd.	Kirkland
93004	1993	Peacock	P	Kenneth	4110 Old Redmond Rd	Redmond
93005	1993	Viescas	L	John	15127 NE 24th, #383	Redmond

Record: 1 of 45

For the purposes of this design exercise, let's say you want to build a new database (named College Counseling) for college counselors at the Overlake School without the benefit of first analyzing the tasks and subjects you'll need. You might be tempted to put all the data about the task you want to do—keeping track of student college preferences—in a single Student-Colleges table whose fields are represented in Figure 4-7.

Basically, three things are wrong with this technique:

■ Every time a student adds another preference, you have to duplicate the Student Name and Student Address fields in another record for the new preference. Repeatedly storing the same name and address in your database wastes a lot of space—and you can easily make mistakes if you have to enter basic information about a student more than once.

■ You have no way of predicting how many application steps are required by any given college. If you keep track of each step in a separate record, you have to guess the largest number of steps and leave space for Step 1, Step 2, Step 3, and so on, all the way to the maximum number. Again you're wasting valuable space in your database. If you guess wrong, you'll have to change your design just to accommodate a college that requires more application steps. And later, if you want to find out which students had to perform what steps for what colleges, you'll have to search each Application Step field in every record.

■ You have to waste space in the database storing data that can easily be calculated when it's time to print a report. For example, you'll certainly want to summarize a student's test scores to obtain an average overall score, but you do not need to keep the result in a Student Average Overall Test Score field.

Student–Colleges

Student Name	Student Graduation Year	Student Address	Student City	Student State	Student Zip	Student Phone

Student Test Score 1	Student Test Date 1	Student Test Score 2	Student Test Date 2	...	Student Test Score n	Student Test Date n	Student Average Overall Test Score

College Name	College Admissions Address	College State	College Zip	College Phone

Application Step 1 Description	Application Step 1 Required	Application Step 1 Early Due Date	Application Step 1 Final Due Date	Application Step 1 Completed

Application Step 2 Description	Application Step 2 Required	Application Step 2 Early Due Date	Application Step 2 Final Due Date	Application Step 2 Completed

Application Step n Description	Application Step n Required	Application Step n Early Due Date	Application Step n Final Due Date	Application Step n Completed

FIGURE 4-7
The design for the College Counseling database using a single Student-Colleges table.

Normalization Is the Solution

You can minimize the kinds of problems noted above (although it might not always be desirable to eliminate all duplicate values), by using a process called *normalization* to organize data fields into a group of tables. The mathematical theory behind normalization is rigorous and complex, but the tests you can apply to determine whether you have a design that makes sense and is easy to use are quite simple—and can be stated as rules.

Rule 1: Field Uniqueness

Since wasted space is one of the biggest problems with an un-normalized table design, it makes sense to remove redundant fields from a table. So the first rule is about field uniqueness.

Rule 1: Each field in a table should represent a unique type of information.

This means that you should get rid of the repeating Test Score and Application Step fields in the Student-Colleges table. You can do this by creating separate tables for the repeating data and including a link between the new tables and the original one. One possible result is shown in Figure 4-8.

Student–Colleges

Student–Tests

Student–College–Steps

FIGURE 4-8

A design for the College Counseling database that eliminates redundant fields.

These tables are much simpler because you can process one record per test or application step. Also, you don't have to reserve room in your records to hold a large number of test scores or steps. And if you want to find out which students had a high score on a specific test, you need only look in one place in each Student-Tests record.

However, the duplicate data problem is now somewhat worse because you are repeating the Student Name field in each record. You can solve this problem by assigning a unique ID number to each student and moving the college preferences data to another table. The result is represented in Figure 4-9.

Students

Student ID	Student Name	Student Graduation Year	Student Address	Student City	Student State	Student Zip	Student Phone

Student–Colleges

Student ID	Preference Number	Student Average Overall Test Score	College Name

College Admissions Address	College State	College Zip	College Phone

Student–Tests

Student ID	Test Description	Test Score	Test Date

Student–College–Steps

Student ID	College Name	Step Number	Step Description	Step Required	Early Due Date	Final Due Date	Completed

FIGURE 4-9

A design for the College Counseling database that includes separate tables for students and for college preferences.

Although it appears that you've created duplicate data with the Student ID field in each table, you've actually significantly reduced the total amount of data stored. The student name and address data is stored only once in the Students table for each student and not for each preference a student has. You've duplicated only a small piece of data, the Student ID field, which allows you to *relate* the preference data to the appropriate Student data. Relational databases are equipped to support this design technique by giving you powerful tools to bring related information back together easily. (You'll take a first look at some of these tools in Chapter 8, "Adding Power with Select Queries.")

But you still have the college name stored for each student preference. To address this situation, you need to understand a few additional rules about relational tables.

Rule 2: Primary Keys

In a good relational database design, each record in any table must be uniquely identified. That is, some field (or combination of fields) in the table must yield a unique value for each record in the table. This unique identifier is called the *primary key*.

Rule 2: Each table must have a unique identifier, or primary key, that is made up of one or more fields in the table.

In the Students table, the student ID is probably unique, so the Student ID field could well be the primary key for that table, as shown in Figure 4-10.

Students

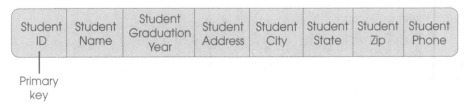

FIGURE 4-10
The primary key for the Students table.

In the Student-Colleges table, the student ID isn't unique if one or more students have multiple college preferences. Likewise, the preference number is not unique—every student has a preference number 1. However, the combination of student ID and preference number is unique and can serve as the primary key for this table, as shown in Figure 4-11.

Student–Colleges

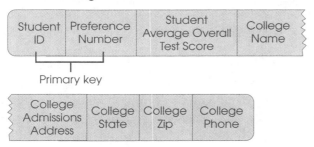

Primary key

FIGURE 4-11

The primary key for the Student-Colleges table.

Whenever you build a table, Access always recommends that you define a primary key for that table. You can let Access build an artificial primary key, in which case it adds an AutoNumber field to each record; Access increments that field by 1 each time you add a new record.

Rule 3: Functional Dependence

After you define a primary key for each table, you can check to see whether you included all the data relevant to the subject of the table. Additionally, you should check to see whether each field is *functionally dependent* on the primary key.

Rule 3: For each unique primary key value, the values in the data columns must be relevant to, and must completely describe, the subject of the table.

This rule works in two ways. First, you shouldn't have any data in a table that is not relevant to the subject (as defined by the primary key) of the table. For example, you don't need Student Average Overall Test Score in the Student-Colleges table. Second, the data in the table should completely describe the subject. For example, if some of your students have both a home address and a mailing address, one address field in the Students table will not be sufficient.

Rule 4: Field Independence

The last rule checks to see whether you'll have any problems when you make changes to the data in your tables.

Rule 4: You must be able to make a change to the data in any field (other than a field in the primary key) without affecting the data in any other field.

Take a look again at the Student-Colleges table in Figure 4-11. After you eliminate the Student Average Overall Test Score field, the first field outside the primary key is College Name. If you need to correct the spelling of a college name, you can do so without affecting any other fields in that record. If you misspelled the same college name for many students, however, you might have to change many records. Also, if you entered the wrong college (the preference is actually for Antioch College, not Columbia College), you can't change the college name without also fixing that record's admissions address and phone data. The College Name, College Admissions Address, and College Phone fields are not independent of one another. In fact, College Admissions Address, College City, College State, and College Phone are functionally dependent on College Name. (See Rule 3 on the previous page.) College Name describes another subject that is different from the subject of preferences. This situation calls for another table in your design: a separate Colleges table, as shown in Figure 4-12.

Now, if you've misspelled a college name, you can simply change the college name in the Colleges table. Note that instead of using the College Name field (which might be 40 or 50 characters long) as the primary key for the Colleges table, you can create a shorter College ID field (perhaps a five-digit number) to minimize the size of the relational data you need in the Student-Colleges table and Student-College-Steps table.

Note also that the Student Average Overall Test Score field has been removed from the database design. Since the database contains all of the test score data, it's easy to calculate the current average overall test score. If you include this field in your database, it fails the independence test—if the student takes another test, the value in the field might have to be recalculated.

An alternative (but less rigorous) way to check for field independence is to see whether you have the same data repeated in your records. In the previous design, whenever a student had more than one college preference, you had to enter the college's name, address, state, zip, and phone number in multiple preference records. With a separate Colleges table, if you need to correct a spelling or change an address, you have to make the change only in one field of one record in the Colleges table. If you entered the wrong college, you have to change only the College ID in the Student-Colleges table to fix the problem.

Students

Student ID	Student Name	Student Graduation Year	Student Address	Student City	Student State	Student Zip	Student Phone

Colleges

College ID	College Name	College Admissions Address	College State	College Zip	College Phone

Student–Colleges

Student ID	Preference Number	College ID	Applied	Accepted	Attended

Student–Tests

Student ID	Test Description	Test Score	Test Date

Student–College–Steps

Student ID	College ID	Step Number	Step Description	Step Required	Early Due Date	Final Due Date	Completed

FIGURE 4-12

A Colleges table that is separate from the Student-Colleges table is added to the College Counseling database.

The actual College Counseling sample database includes nine tables, which are all shown in the Relationships window in Figure 4-13 on the next page. Notice that additional fields were created in each table to fully describe the subject of each table and that other tables were added to support some of the other tasks identified earlier in this section. For example, fields were added to the Colleges table to record the average SAT and ACT test scores of the previous year's incoming freshmen. New tables were added to provide a means to designate college types, such as liberal arts, technical, vocational, and so forth.

FIGURE 4-13

The College
Counseling
sample
database's tables
shown in the
Relationships
window.

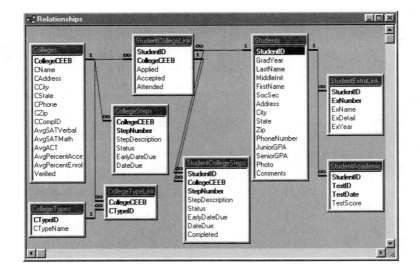

The Four Rules of Good Table Design

Rule 1: Each field in a table should represent a unique type of information.

Rule 2: Each table must have a unique identifier, or primary key, that is made up of one or more fields in the table.

Rule 3: For each unique primary key value, the values in the data columns must be relevant to, and must completely describe, the subject of the table.

Rule 4: You must be able to make a change to the data in any field (other than a field in the primary key) without affecting the data in any other field.

Efficient Relationships Are the Result

When you apply good design techniques, you end up with a database that efficiently links your data. You probably noticed that when you normalize your data as recommended, you tend to get many separate tables as a result. Before relational databases were invented, you had to either compromise your design or manually keep track of the relationships between files or tables. For example, you had to put college data in your StudentCollegeLinks table or write your program to first open and read a record from the StudentCollegeLinks table and then search for the matching record in the Colleges table. Relational databases solve these problems. With a good design you don't have to worry about how to bring the data together when you need it.

Foreign Keys

You might have noticed as you followed along in the College Counseling example above that each time you created a new table, you left behind a field that could link the old and new tables, such as the Student ID and College ID fields in the Student-Colleges table. These "linking" fields are called *foreign keys*.

In a well-designed database, foreign keys result in efficiency. You keep track of related foreign keys as you lay out your database design. When you define your tables in Access, you link primary keys to foreign keys to tell Access how to join the data when you need to retrieve information from more than one table. To improve performance, you also instruct Access to build indexes on your foreign keys.

See Also   For details about defining indexes, see the section titled "Adding Indexes" in Chapter 5.

One-to-Many and One-to-One Relationships

In most cases, the relationship between any two tables is one-to-many. That is, for any one record in the first table, there are many related records in the second table, but for any record in the second table, there is exactly one matching record in the first table. You saw many instances of this pattern of relationship in the College Counseling database design. For example, each student might have several tests stored as records in the Student-Tests table, but a single Student-Tests record applies to only one student.

Occasionally, you might want to further break down a table because you use some of the data in the table infrequently or because some of the data in the table is highly sensitive and should not be available to everyone. For example, you might want to keep track of certain faculty data for promotion purposes, but you don't need access to that data all the time. Or you might have data such as annual salary that should be accessible only to authorized people. In either case, you can create a separate table that also has a primary key of FacultyID. The relationship between the original Faculty table and the FacultyInfo or FacultyPaygrade tables is one-to-one. That is, for each record in the first table, there is exactly one record in the second table.

Creating Table Links

The last step in designing your database is to create the links between your tables. For each subject, look at the subjects for which you wrote *Many* under "Relationship" on the worksheet. Be sure that the corresponding relationship for the other table is *One*. If you see *Many* in both places, you must create a separate *intersection table* to handle the relationship. (Access won't let you define a many-to-many relationship directly between two tables.) In the example of the Record Student College and University Preferences task, a student can prefer "many" colleges and a college can be preferred by "many" students. The StudentCollegeLinks table in the College Counseling database is an intersection table that clears up this many-to-many relationship between Students and Colleges. StudentCollegeLinks works as an intersection table because it has a one-to-many relationship with both Students and Colleges.

After you straighten out the many-to-many relationships, you need to create the links between tables. To complete the links, place a copy of the primary key from the "one" tables into the "many" tables. For example, by looking at the worksheet for Students shown in Figure 4-5, you can surmise that the primary key for the Students table, StudentID, also needs to be included in the StudentCollegeLinks table.

Now that you understand the fundamentals of good database design, you're ready to do something a little more fun with Access—building a database. The next chapter, "Building Your Database in Microsoft Access," shows you how to create a new database and tables; Chapter 6, "Modifying Your Database Design," shows you how to make changes later if you discover that you need to modify your design.

Chapter 5

Building Your Database in Microsoft Access

After you design the tables for your database, defining them in Microsoft Access is incredibly easy. This chapter shows you how it's done. You'll learn how to:

- Create a new database application using the Database Wizard
- Create a new empty database for your own custom application
- Create a simple table by entering data directly in the table
- Get a jump-start on defining custom tables by using the Table Wizard
- Define your own tables "from scratch"
- Select the best data type for your fields
- Set validation rules for your fields and tables
- Tell Access what relationships to maintain between your tables
- Optimize data retrieval by adding indexes
- Print a table definition

Creating a New Database

When you first start Microsoft Access, you see the opening choices dialog box shown in Figure 5-1 on the next page. In this dialog box you specify whether you want to create a brand-new empty database, to use the Database Wizard to create a new database application using any of the more than 20 database application templates, or to open an existing database (mdb) file. If you've previously opened other databases, such as the Northwind Traders sample database that is included with Access, you'll also see a "most recently used" list of up to four database selections in the Open An Existing Database section of the dialog box.

FIGURE 5-1

The Access
opening choices
dialog box.

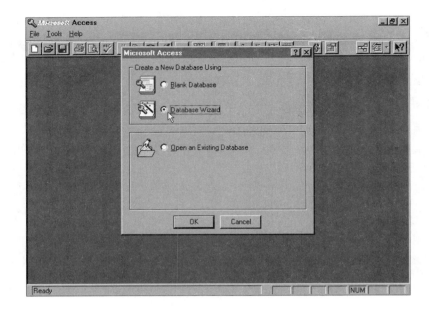

Using the Database Wizard

Just for fun, let's explore the Database Wizard first. If you're a beginner, you can use the Database Wizard to build and customize any of the
more than 20 database application templates included with Access
without needing to know anything about designing database software.
You might find that the application the wizard builds meets most of
your needs right off the bat. As you learn more about Access, you can
customize the basic application design and add new features.

Even if you're an experienced developer, you might find that the
application templates save you lots of time in setting up the basic
tables, queries, forms, and reports for your application. If the application you need to build is covered by one of the templates, the wizard
can take care of many of the simpler design tasks.

When you start Access, you can select the Database Wizard option
in the opening choices dialog box. If you have already started Access,
you can choose New Database from the File menu to open the dialog
box shown in Figure 5-2. You work with all of the templates in the Database Wizard in the same way. This example will show you the steps
that are needed to build a Household Inventory database.

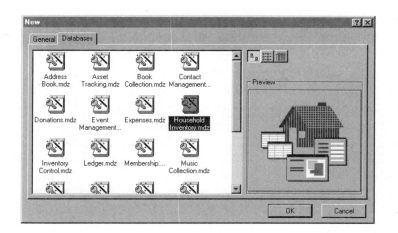

FIGURE 5-2
Some of the
Database Wizard
templates.

Scan the list of available templates. When you click on a template icon, Access shows a preview graphic to give you a further hint about the purpose of the template. You start the Database Wizard by selecting a template and clicking OK or by double-clicking on a template icon. Access opens the File New Database dialog box and suggests a name for your new database file. You can modify the name and then click Create to allocate space for your new database and launch the wizard.

The wizard takes a few moments to initialize and to create a new blank file for your new database application. The wizard first displays a screen with a few more details about the capabilities of the application you are about to build. If this isn't what you want, click Cancel to stop the wizard and delete the database file. You can also click Finish to ask the wizard to quickly build the application by selecting all the default options. Click Next to proceed to a window that provides options for customizing the tables in your application, as shown in Figure 5-3.

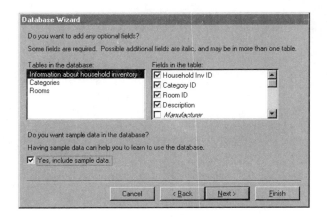

FIGURE 5-3
Selecting optional
fields in the
Database Wizard.

In this window, you can see the names of the tables the wizard plans to build. As you select each table name in the list on the left, the wizard shows you the fields it will include in that table in the list on the right. For many of the tables, you can ask the wizard to include or exclude certain optional fields (which appear in *italics*). In the Household Inventory application, for example, you might not be interested in keeping track of the name of the manufacturer for each inventory item. If this is your first experience using the Database Wizard, it's a good idea to select the Yes, Include Sample Data check box in this window. The wizard will build the database with a small amount of sample data so you can see how the application works without having to enter any of your own data. Click Next when you finish selecting optional fields for your application.

In the next window, shown in Figure 5-4, you select one of several styles for the forms in your database. As you recall from Chapter 3, "Touring Microsoft Access," forms are objects in your database that are used to display data on your screen. Some of the styles, such as Clouds and Dusk, are quite whimsical. The Standard style has a very business-like gray-on-gray look.

FIGURE 5-4

Selecting a style for forms in the Database Wizard.

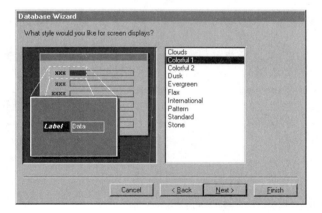

After you select a form style you like, click Next to proceed to the window shown in Figure 5-5, in which you select a report style. You might want to select Bold, Casual, or Compact for personal applications. Corporate, Formal, and Soft Gray are good choices for business applications. Select an appropriate report style, and then click Next.

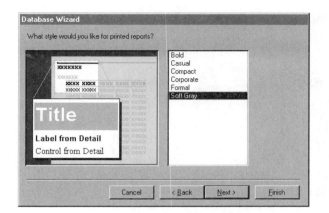

FIGURE 5-5
Selecting a report style in the Database Wizard.

In the next window, shown in Figure 5-6, you specify a title that will appear on the Access title bar when you run the application. You can also ask the wizard to include a specific picture file in all of your reports. This picture file can be a bitmap, a Windows metafile, or an icon file. Click Next after you supply a title for your application.

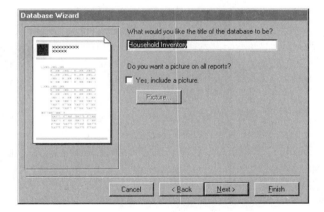

FIGURE 5-6
Naming your database in the Database Wizard.

In the final window, you can choose to start the application immediately after the wizard finishes building it. You can also choose to open a special set of help topics to guide you through using a database application. (See the section titled "More About Microsoft Access Help" later in this chapter for details about special help features in Access.) Select the Yes, Start The Database option and click Finish to create and then start your application. Figure 5-7 on the next page shows the opening "switchboard" form for the Household Inventory database application.

FIGURE 5-7
The switchboard
form for the
Household
Inventory
database
application.

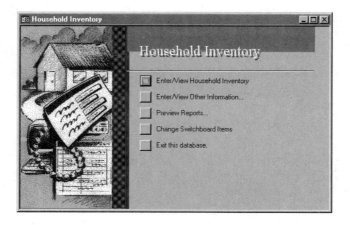

Creating a New Empty Database

To begin creating a new empty database, select Blank Database in the
opening choices dialog box shown in Figure 5-1. You can also choose
the New Database command from the File menu and then double-click
on the Blank Database icon in the New dialog box, shown in Figure 5-2.
This opens the File New Database dialog box, shown in Figure 5-8.
Select the drive and folder you want from the Save In drop-down list.
In this example, the My Documents folder of the current drive is selected. Finally, go to the File Name text box and type the name of your
new database. Access appends an mdb extension to the filename for
you. Access uses a file with an mdb extension to store all your database
objects, including tables, queries, forms, reports, macros, and modules.
For this example, create a new sample database called Kathy's Wedding List to experiment with one way to create a database and tables.
Click the Create button to create your database.

FIGURE 5-8
The File New
Database
dialog box.

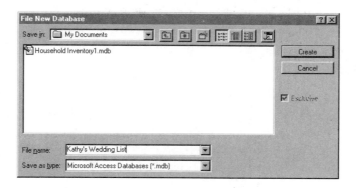

TIP You can create a new database either by choosing the New Database command from the File menu or by clicking the New Database button on the toolbar. The New Database button is the first button at the left end of the toolbar.

Access takes a few moments to create the system files in which to store all the information about the tables, queries, forms, reports, macros, and modules that you might create. When Access completes this process, it displays the Database window for your new database in the center of your Access workspace, as shown in Figure 5-9.

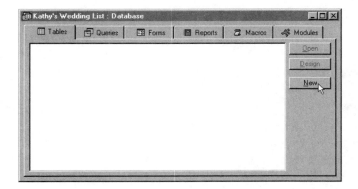

FIGURE 5-9

The Database window for a new database.

When you open any database, Access selects the Tables tab and shows you the available tables in the Database window. Because this is a new database and no tables exist yet, the Database window is empty.

 TIP You can see a short description of any toolbar button by placing your mouse pointer over the button (without clicking the button) and waiting a second. Access displays a small label, called a *ToolTip,* below the button, which contains the name of the button. If you can't see ToolTips, choose the Toolbars command from the View menu while you have a database open and be sure the Show ToolTips check box is selected in the Toolbars dialog box.

Using Microsoft Access Help

Microsoft Access provides several ways to obtain help. Anywhere within Access, you can find a Help button at the far right end of the toolbar. Click this button to turn your mouse pointer into an arrow with a question mark attached, and then click any button, property, or design area to receive context-sensitive help about the area you clicked. You can also place the cursor on a particular area or keyword about which you need more information, and then press F1 to open a related help topic.

You can also explore Access Help by using the Help menu commands shown in Figure 5-10. Choose Microsoft Access Help Topics to see a list of all the major categories of help information presented as a list of book icons. Click on a book and then click Open to see a list of subtopics. When you see a topic you want to explore, double-click on it to display the information on your screen.

FIGURE 5-10

Choosing Microsoft Access Help Topics from the Help menu.

Within the Help Topics dialog box, you can also find tabs that let you explore an alphabetic index of topic titles, or you can enter the Find facility to look for keywords within the text of any help topic. When you click on the Find tab for the first time, Access starts the Find Setup Wizard to build a database of words to make searching faster. You can ask the wizard to index only keywords or all words in the very large Access Help files. After the wizard builds the find list database, you can quickly search for all topics that contain any keyword you specify.

One of the most fascinating capabilities of the new Help system in Access is the Answer Wizard. You can go to this wizard directly from the Help menu, or you can choose Microsoft Access Help Topics and then click on the Answer Wizard tab. Figure 5-11 shows the Answer Wizard tab of the Help Topics dialog box. In the text box, enter a question or a phrase that describes your problem. This works best if you type a phrase that would follow "How do I." In the example shown in

Figure 5-11, I asked the wizard how to "create a new table." The wizard works by first throwing out "noise" words like *a* or *the* and then listing all topics that contain any combination of the remaining keywords in your query. It first lists the topics that contain all of the keywords, and below that it lists the topics that contain only one of the keywords. As you can see in the figure, it listed the Create A Table topic at the top.

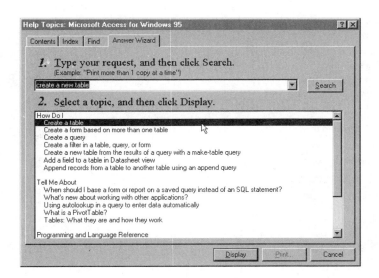

FIGURE 5-11
Asking the Answer Wizard a question, and then selecting a topic.

As you can also see in the figure, the Answer Wizard organizes help topics into three major categories:

- How Do I—These topics give you step-by-step instructions about a specific task. How Do I topics replace the Cue Cards you might have used in previous versions of Access.

- Tell Me About—These topics provide detailed descriptive information. In some cases, the Help facility opens an example image with "hotspots" that you can click on to learn more about particular features.

- Programming and Language Reference—This portion of Access Help provides in-depth coverage of programming techniques related to the topic. For example, after asking how to "create a new table," you'll see entries for various statements, methods, and properties related to tables that you can use in Microsoft Visual Basic for Applications (VBA).

If you select the Create A Table topic under How Do I, you'll see the window shown in Figure 5-12. You can learn more about one of the ways to create a new table by clicking its corresponding arrow button. Each button leads you through the steps you need to perform to create a table. These How Do I windows are designed to stay on top of your work so you can perform the steps with the instructions right there on your screen.

FIGURE 5-12

Step-by-step help topics in the How Do I section.

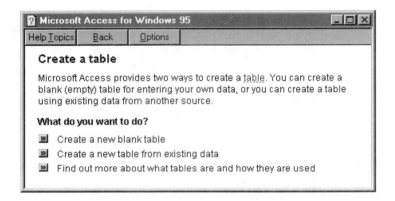

In the next section, you'll see how to create your first new table by entering data in a datasheet.

Creating Your First Simple Table

If you've been following along to this point, you should still have your new empty Kathy's Wedding List database open with an empty Database window, as shown earlier in Figure 5-9. You can also follow these steps in any open database. Make sure the Tables tab in the Database window is selected, and then click the New button to open the New Table dialog box shown in Figure 5-13.

FIGURE 5-13

The New Table dialog box.

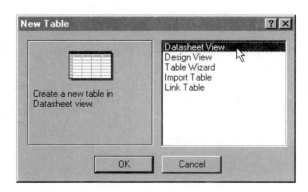

Select Datasheet View in the list and click OK to get started. You can also double-click on Datasheet View in the list. What you see next is an empty datasheet that's quite similar to a spreadsheet. You can enter just about any type of data you want—text, dates, numbers, currency. But unlike a spreadsheet, in a datasheet you can't enter any calculated expressions. As you'll see later in the chapters on queries, you can easily display a calculated result using data from one or more tables by entering an expression in a query.

Since we're starting a list of wedding invitees, we'll need columns containing information such as title, first name, middle initial, last name, street address, city, state, zip code, number of guests invited, number of guests confirmed, gift received, and a gift acknowledged indicator. Be sure to enter the same type of data in a particular column for every row. For example, enter the city name in the same column for every row.

You can see some of the data entered for the wedding invitee list in Figure 5-14. When you start to type in a field in a row, Access displays a pencil icon on the row selector on the far left to indicate that it can see you're changing data. Use the Tab key to move from column to column. When you move to another row, Access saves what you typed. If you make a mistake in a particular row or column, you can click on the data you want to change and type over it or delete it.

Row selector   Field names

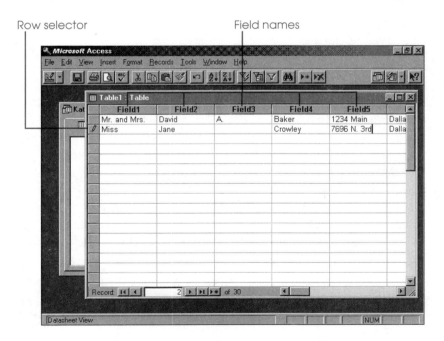

FIGURE 5-14
Creating a table by entering data.

If you created a column of data that you don't want, click any-where in the column and choose Delete Column from the Edit menu. If you want to insert a new blank column between two columns that already contain data, click anywhere in the column to the right of where you want to insert a new column, and then choose Column from the Insert menu. To move a column to a different location, click on the field name at the top of the column to highlight the entire column, and then click again and drag the column to a new location. You can also click on an unselected column and drag your mouse pointer through several adjacent columns to highlight them all. You can then move the columns as a group.

You probably noticed that Access named your columns Field1, Field2, and so forth—not very informative. You can enter a name for each column by double-clicking on the column's field name. You can also click anywhere in the column and then choose Rename Column from the Format menu. In Figure 5-15, two of the columns have been renamed.

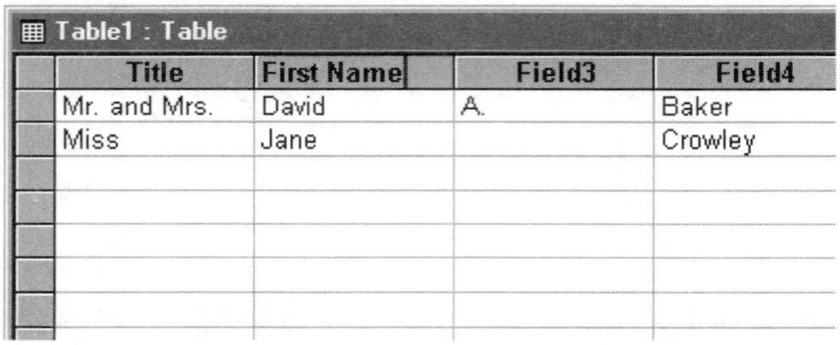

FIGURE 5-15

Renaming a column in Datasheet view.

Title	First Name	Field3	Field4
Mr. and Mrs.	David	A.	Baker
Miss	Jane		Crowley

After you enter several rows of data, it's a good idea to save your table. You can do this by clicking the Save button on the toolbar or by choosing Save Layout from the File menu. Access displays a Save As dialog box, as shown in Figure 5-16. Type an appropriate name for your table and click OK. Access will display a message box warning you that you have no primary key defined and offering to build one for you. If you accept the offer, Access adds a field called ID and assigns it a special data type called AutoNumber (see the section titled "Field Data Types" later in this chapter for details) that automatically gener-ates a unique number for each new row you add. If one or more of the data columns you entered would make a good primary key, click No in the message box. But in this case, click Yes to build a field called ID that's the primary key. In Chapter 6, "Modifying Your Database Design," you'll learn how to use the Design view of the table to define your own primary key(s) or to change the definition of an existing primary key.

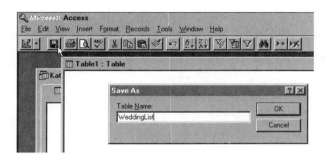

FIGURE 5-16
Saving your new table.

Using the Table Wizard

If you look in the Wedding List sample database (Wedding.mdb) included with this book, you'll find it very simple, with one main table and a few supporting tables for data such as titles, cities, and zip codes. Most databases are usually quite a bit more complex. For example, both the College Counseling and the Entertainment Schedule sample databases contain more than a dozen tables. If you had to create every table "by hand," it could turn out to be quite a tedious process. Fortunately, Microsoft Access comes with a Table Wizard to help you build many common tables. For this exercise, create a new blank database and give it the name Students and Colleges, as shown in Figure 5-17.

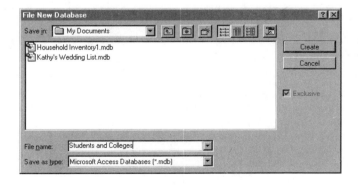

FIGURE 5-17
Creating a blank database named Students and Colleges.

To build a table using the Table Wizard, go to the Database window, click on the Tables tab, and then click the New button. In the New Table dialog box (see Figure 5-13), select Table Wizard from the list and click OK. You'll see the opening window of the wizard, shown in Figure 5-18.

FIGURE 5-18

The opening window of the Table Wizard.

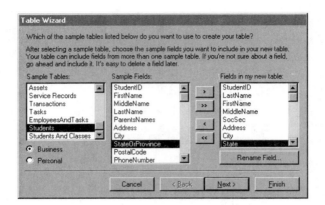

Toward the lower left of the window are two option buttons—Business (to select business-oriented tables) and Personal (to select personal tables). You can find an entry for a Students sample table in the Business category. Scroll down the Sample Tables list until you see Students. When you select it, the wizard displays all the fields in the Students sample table in the Sample Fields list. (You will change the table you create now in Chapter 6, "Modifying Your Database Design," so that it is more like the final Students table in the College Counseling database.)

To select a field, click on it in the Sample Fields list and click the single right arrow (>) button to move it to the Fields In My New Table list. (You can also select a field by double-clicking on it.) You define the sequence of fields in your table based on the sequence in which you select them from the Sample Fields list. If you add a field that you decide you don't want, select it in the Fields In My New Table list box and click the single left arrow (<) button to remove it. If you want to start over, you can remove all fields by clicking the double left arrow (<<) button.

Many of the fields in the Students sample table are fields you'll need in the Students table for the Students and Colleges database. You can pick StudentID, LastName, FirstName, and MiddleName directly from the Students sample table. Scroll up the Sample Tables list and select the Employees sample table. Select the SocialSecurityNumber field from that table, click the Rename Field button, and name it SocSec (the name you'll find in the original Students table in the College Counseling database). Go back to the Students sample table and select Address, City, StateOrProvince (which you should rename State), PostalCode (which you should rename Zip), PhoneNumber, and Notes (which you should rename Comments). As you can see, it's easy to mix and match fields from various sample tables and then rename them to get exactly what you want.

Click the Next button to see the window shown in Figure 5-19. In this window, you can specify a new name for your table. You can also ask the wizard to set a primary key for you, or you can define your own. In most cases, the wizard chooses the most logical field or fields to be the primary key. If the wizard can't find an appropriate field to be the primary key, it creates a new Primary Key field that uses a special data type called AutoNumber. As you'll learn later in this chapter, the AutoNumber data type ensures that each new row in your table will have a unique value. For this example, let the wizard set the primary key for you. Because your table includes the primary key from the Students sample table, a single field called StudentID, the wizard will choose StudentID to be the primary key for your new table.

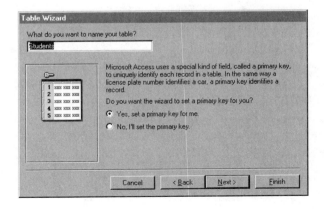

FIGURE 5-19

Specifying a table name and selecting a primary key option in the Table Wizard.

Click the Next button to move to the next window. If you have
other tables already defined in your database, the Table Wizard shows
you a list of those tables and tells you whether it thinks your new table
is related to any of the existing tables. If the wizard finds a primary key
in another table with the same name and data type as a field in your
new table (or vice-versa), it will assume that the tables are related. If
you think the wizard has made a mistake, you can tell it to not create a
relationship (a link) between your new table and the existing table.
You'll learn how to define your own relationships between tables later
in this chapter.

Since this is the first and only table in this database, you won't see
the Relationships window in the Table Wizard. Instead, the wizard
shows you a final window in which you can choose to see the resulting
table in Table Design view, open it as a datasheet, or call the AutoForm
Wizard to create a simple form to let you begin entering data. (See
Figure 5-20.)

FIGURE 5-20

Selecting final
options in the
Table Wizard.

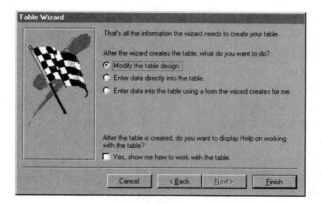

In this case, select the Modify The Table Design option and click
Finish to let the wizard build your table. The table will open in Design
view, as shown in Figure 5-21. In the next chapter, you'll learn how to
modify this table in Design view to exactly match the Students table in
the College Counseling database. For now, close the Table window so
you can go on to building other tables that you need.

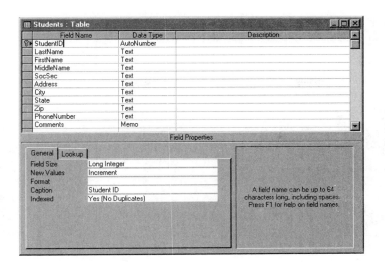

FIGURE 5-21
The Students
table built by the
Table Wizard.

Creating a Table in Design View

Although you could continue to use the Table Wizard to build some of
the other tables in the Students and Colleges database, none of the
wizard's example tables closely matches the other Students and Colleges tables. You could use the Customers or the Suppliers sample
table to get fields for the Colleges table (the next table in the Students
and Colleges database), but you'd spend as much time picking and renaming fields as you would building the table from scratch. So now is a
good time to explore Design view and learn how to build tables that
the Table Wizard can't handle. You'll also see many additional features
that you can use to customize the way your tables (and any queries,
forms, or reports built on these tables) work.

If you want to design a new table in a database, the Database window (shown in Figure 5-9) must be active. Click on the Tables tab (the
leftmost tab), and then click the New button. Access shows you the
New Table dialog box you saw earlier in Figure 5-13. Select Design View
and click OK. Access displays a blank Table window in Design view, as
shown in Figure 5-22 on the next page.

FIGURE 5-22

A blank Table
window in
Design view.

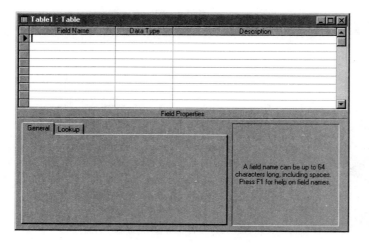

TIP   You can also open a blank Table window in Design view by selecting the New Table option from the
New Object toolbar button's drop-down list.

In the upper part of the Table window in Design view are columns in which you can enter the field names, the data type for each
field, and a description of each field. After you select a data type for a
field, Access allows you to set field properties in the lower left area of
the Table window. In the lower right area of the Table window is a box
in which Access displays information about fields or properties. The
contents of this box change as you move your cursor from one location
to another within the Table window.

Defining Fields

Now you're ready to begin defining the fields for the Colleges table. Be
sure the cursor is in the first row of the Field Name column, and then
type the name of the first field, *CollegeCEEB*. Press the Tab key once to
move to the Data Type column. A button with a down arrow appears
on the right side of the box in the Data Type column. Here and elsewhere in Microsoft Access, this type of button signifies the presence of a
drop-down list. Click the down arrow or press Alt-down arrow to open
the list of data type options, shown in Figure 5-23. In the Data Type
column, you can either type a valid value or select from the list of values

in the drop-down list box. The data type values are explained later in this chapter in the section titled "Field Data Types." For now, select Number to be CollegeCEEB's data type.

> **NOTE** Although you can use spaces anywhere within names in Access, you should try to create field names and table names <u>without</u> embedded spaces. Most SQL databases to which Access can attach do not support spaces within names. If you ever want to move your application into a true client-server environment and store your data in an SQL database such as Microsoft SQL Server or Oracle, you'll have to change every name in your database tables that has an embedded blank space. As you'll learn later in this book, table field names propagate into the queries, forms, and reports that you design using these tables. So any name you decide to change later in a table must also be changed in all your queries, forms, and reports.

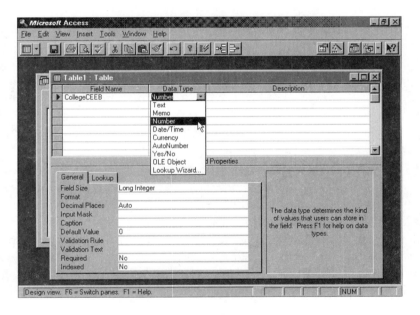

FIGURE 5-23

The drop-down list of data type options.

After you select a data type, Access displays some property boxes in the Field Properties area in the lower part of the window. These boxes allow you to set properties and thereby customize a field. The boxes Access shows you depend on the data type you selected; they appear with some default properties in place, as shown in Figure 5-23.

119

The various property settings for each property box are explained later in this chapter in the section titled "Field Properties."

In the Description column for each field, you can enter a descriptive phrase. Access displays this description in the status bar (at the bottom of the Access window) whenever you select this field in a query in Datasheet view or in a form in Form view or Datasheet view. As you can imagine, paying careful attention to what you type in the Description field can later pay big dividends as a kind of "mini help" on the status bar for the users of your database. Also, since this data propagates automatically, you probably <u>don't</u> want to type something nonsensical or silly. Typing *I don't have a clue what this field does* is probably not a good idea—it will show up on the status bar.

Field Data Types

Access supports eight types of data, each with a specific purpose. These data types are described in Figure 5-24. Access also gives you a ninth option, Lookup Wizard, to help you define the characteristics of foreign key fields that link to other tables. You'll learn how to use the Lookup Wizard in the next chapter.

For each field in your table, select the data type that is best suited to how you will use that field's data. For character data, you should normally select the Text data type. You can control the maximum length of a Text field by using a field property, as explained below. Use the Memo data type only for long strings of text that might exceed 255 characters or that might contain formatting characters such as tabs or carriage returns.

When you select the Number data type, you should think carefully about what you enter as the Field Size property, because this property choice will affect precision as well as length. (For example, integer numbers do not have decimals.) The Date/Time data type is useful for calendar or clock data and has the added benefit of allowing calculations in minutes, seconds, hours, days, months, or years. For example, you can find out the difference in days between two Date/Time values.

Data Type	Usage	Size
Text	Alphanumeric data	Up to 255 bytes
Memo	Alphanumeric data—sentences and paragraphs	Up to 64,000 bytes
Number	Numeric data	1, 2, 4, or 8 bytes (16 bytes for ReplicationID)
Date/Time	Dates and times	8 bytes
Currency	Monetary data, stored with 4 decimal places of precision	8 bytes
AutoNumber	Unique value generated by Access for each new record	4 bytes (16 bytes for ReplicationID)
Yes/No	Boolean data	1 bit
OLE Object	Pictures, graphs, or other OLE objects from another Windows-based application	Up to about 1 gigabyte

FIGURE 5-24

Access data types.

Always use the Currency data type for storing money values. You can also use the Currency data type for any numeric field that must have a precise fractional number of up to four decimal places. Currency has the precision of integers, but with a fixed number of decimal places. The AutoNumber data type is specifically designed for automatic generation of primary key values. Depending on the Field Size and New Values properties you choose for an AutoNumber field, you can have Access create a sequential or random long integer. You can include only one field using the AutoNumber data type in any table.

Use the Yes/No data type to hold Boolean (true or false) values. This data type is particularly useful for flagging accounts paid or not paid or tests passed or not passed. Finally, the OLE Object data type allows you to store complex data, such as pictures, graphs, or sounds, that can be maintained by a dynamic link to another Microsoft Windows 95–based application. For example, Access can store and allow you to edit a Microsoft Word document, a Microsoft Excel spreadsheet, a Microsoft PowerPoint presentation slide, a sound file (wav), a video file (avi), or pictures created using the Paintbrush or Draw application.

Field Properties

You can customize each field by setting specific properties. These properties vary according to the data type you choose. Here are all of the possible properties for a field in a table:

Properties on the General tab:

Field Size
You can specify the length of Text and Number data types. Text can be from 0 through 255 characters long, with a default length of 50 characters. For Number, the field sizes are as follows:

Byte	A single-byte integer containing values from 0 through 255
Integer	A 2-byte integer containing values from $-32,768$ through $+32,767$
Long Integer	A 4-byte integer containing values from $-2,147,483,648$ through $+2,147,483,647$
Single	A 4-byte floating-point number containing values from -3.4×10^{38} through $+3.4 \times 10^{38}$
Double	An 8-byte floating-point number containing values from -1.797×10^{308} through $+1.797 \times 10^{308}$
ReplicationID	A 16-byte Globally Unique Identifier (GUID)

Format
You can control how your data is displayed or printed. The format options vary by data type.

For Text and Memo data types, you can specify a custom format that controls how Access displays the data. For details on custom formats, see the section titled "Setting Control Properties" in Chapter 14 or the "Format Property—Text and Memo Data Types" topic in Access Help.

For Number, Currency, and AutoNumber, the standard format options are as follows:

General Number	The default (no commas or currency symbols; decimal places shown depend on the precision of the data)
Currency	Currency symbols and two decimal places
Fixed	At least one digit and two decimal places

Standard	Two decimal places and separator commas
Percent	Percentage
Scientific	Scientific notation (as in 1.05×10^3)

For the Date/Time data type, the format options follow the patterns of the examples below:

General Date	The default
	04/15/95 05:30:10 PM (US)
	15/04/95 17:30:10 (UK)
Long Date	Saturday, April 15, 1995 (US)
	15 April 1995 (UK)
Medium Date	15-Apr-95
Short Date	4/15/95
Long Time	5:30:10 PM
Medium Time	5:30 PM
Short Time	17:30

For the Yes/No data type, the options are as follows:

Yes/No	The default
True/False	
On/Off	

Decimal Places	For Number and Currency data types, you can specify the number of decimal places that Access displays. The default specification is Auto, which causes Access to display two decimal places for the Currency, Fixed, Standard, and Percent formats and the number of decimal places necessary to show the current precision of the numeric value for General Number format. You can also request a fixed display of decimal places ranging from 0 through 15.
Input Mask	For Text, Number, Date/Time, and Currency data types, you can specify an editing mask that the user sees while entering data in the field. For example, you can have Access provide the delimiters in a date field: (__/__/__). Or you can have Access format a U.S. phone number: (###) 000-0000. See the section titled "Defining Input Masks" later in this chapter for details.
Caption	You can enter a more fully descriptive field name that Access displays in form labels and in report headings. (Note: If you create field names with no embedded spaces, you can use the Caption property to specify a name that includes spaces for Access to use in labels and headers associated with this field in queries, forms, and reports.)

(continued)

Default Value	You can specify a default value for all data types except AutoNumber and OLE Object. For numbers, the default value is 0. Access provides a Null default value for Text and Memo data types.
Validation Rule	You can supply an expression that must be true whenever you enter or change data in this field. For example, *<100* specifies that a number must be less than 100. You can also check for one of a series of values. For example, you can have Access check for a list of valid cities by specifying *"Chicago" Or "New York" Or "San Francisco"*. In addition, you can specify a complex expression that includes any of the built-in functions in Access. (See the section titled "Defining Simple Field Validation Rules" later in this chapter for details.)
Validation Text	You can have Access display text whenever the data entered does not pass your validation rule.
Required	If you don't allow a Null value in this field, set this property to Yes.
Allow Zero Length	For Text and Memo fields, you can set the field equal to a zero length string (" "). (See the sidebar titled "Nulls and Zero-Length Strings" on page 126 for more information.)
Indexed	You can ask that an index be built to speed access to data values for Text, Number, Date/Time, Currency, and AutoNumber data types. You can also require that the values in the indexed field always be unique for the entire table. (See the section titled "Adding Indexes" later in this chapter for details.)

Properties on the Lookup tab (see the next chapter for details):

Display Control	Specifies the default control type for displaying this field in datasheets, forms, and reports. For most fields, select Text Box. If the field is a foreign key (see Chapter 4, "Designing Your Database Application") pointing to another table, you can select List Box or Combo Box to display meaningful values from the related table. You can also select List Box or Combo Box if this field must always contain one of a specific list of values.

Row Source Type	When you select List Box or Combo Box for Display Control, set this property to indicate whether the list of valid values comes from a Table/Query, a Value List that you enter, or a Field List of names of fields from another table.
Row Source	If Row Source Type is Table/Query or Field List, specify the table or query providing the values for the list. If Row Source Type is Value List, enter the values separated by semicolons.
Bound Column	Specify which column in a multiple-column list provides the value that sets this field. If the Row Source is a single column, enter *1*.
Column Count	Enter the number of columns of information provided by the Row Source.
Column Heads	If Yes, the list displays the Caption for each column from the Row Source.
Column Widths	Enter the display width of the columns, separated by semicolons. If you do not want to display a column, enter a width of 0. For example, if this field is a code value, you might not want to display the code that you need to set the value, but you should display the description of the codes being supplied by another table or list. If Display Control is Combo Box, Access shows the value from the first nonzero-width column when the list is closed.
List Rows	When Display Control is Combo Box, specifies the number of rows to display in the combo box's list.
List Width	When Display Control is Combo Box, specifies the width of the combo box's list. The default value of Auto opens a list as wide as the combo box. If the width of the combo box is not wide enough to display all the values in the list, enter a specific value here to make sure the opened list displays all columns.
Limit To List	For combo boxes, if the field can contain only values supplied by the list, enter Yes. If you can enter values not contained in the list, enter No. Note: If you don't display the bound column value as the first column, the combo box behaves as though you specified Yes for Limit To List.

Nulls and Zero-Length Strings

Relational databases support a special value in fields, called a *Null,* that indicates an unknown value. Nulls have special properties. A Null value cannot be equal to any other value, not even to another Null. This means you cannot join (link) two tables on Null values. Also, the test "A = B," when A or B, or both, contains a Null, cannot yield a true result. Finally, Null values do not participate in aggregate calculations involving such functions as *Sum* or *Avg.* You can test a value to determine whether it is a Null by comparing it to the special keyword NULL or by using the *IsNull* built-in function.

In contrast, you can set text or memo fields to a *zero-length string* to indicate that the value of a field is known but the field is empty. You can join tables on zero-length strings, and two zero-length strings will compare to be equal. However, for text and memo fields, you must set the Allow Zero Length property to Yes to allow users to enter zero-length strings. Otherwise, Access converts any zero-length or all-blank string to a Null before storing the value. If you also set the Required property of the text field to Yes, Access stores a zero-length string if the user enters either " " or blanks in the field.

Why is it important to differentiate Nulls from zero-length strings? Here's an example: Suppose you have a database that stores the results of a survey about automobile preferences. For questionnaires on which there is no response to a color-preference question, it is appropriate to store a Null. You don't want to match responses based on an "unknown" response, and you don't want to include the row in calculating totals or averages. On the other hand, some people might have responded "I don't care" for a color preference. In this case, you have a known "nothing" answer, and a zero-length string is appropriate. You can match all "I don't care" responses and include the responses in totals and averages.

Another example might be fax numbers in a customer database. If you store a Null, it means you don't know whether the customer has a fax number. If you store a zero-length string, you know the customer has no fax number. Access gives you the flexibility to deal with both types of "empty" values.

Completing the Fields in the Colleges Table

You now know enough about field data types and properties to finish designing the Colleges table in this example. (You can also follow this example using the Colleges table from the College Counseling sample database.) Use the information listed in Figure 5-25 to design the table shown in Figure 5-26 on the next page.

Field Name	Data Type	Description	Field Size
CollegeCEEB	Number	CollegeCEEB Code	Long Integer
CName	Text	College Name	50
CAddress	Text	Address of Office of Admissions	50
CCity	Text	College City	50
CState	Text	College State	2
CPhone	Text	Phone Number of Office of Admissions	15
CZip	Text	College Zip	10
CCompRate	Text	School Competitiveness Rating	25
AvgSATVerbal	Number	Average SAT Verbal Score of Accepted Students	Integer
AvgSATMath	Number	Average SAT Math Score of Accepted Students	Integer
AvgACT	Number	Average Composite ACT Score of Accepted Students	Integer
AvgPercent-Accept	Number	Average Percentage of Applicants Who Are Accepted	Integer
AvgPercent-Enrolled	Number	Average Percentage of Accepted Students Who Enroll	Integer
Verified	Yes/No	Data has been verified with the school	-

FIGURE 5-25
The field definitions for the Colleges table.

FIGURE 5-26

The fields in the
Colleges table
and a validation
rule on the
AvgSATVerbal
field.

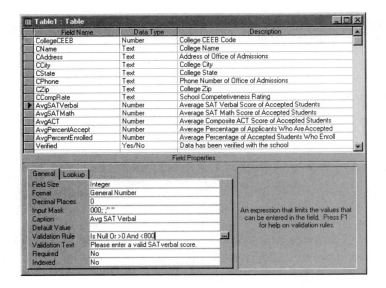

Defining Simple Field Validation Rules

To define a simple check on the values that you allow in a field, enter an expression in the Validation Rule property box for the field. Access won't allow you to enter a field value that violates this rule. Access performs this validation for data entered in a Table window in Datasheet view, in an updatable query, or in a form. You can specify a more restrictive validation rule in a form, but you cannot override the rule in the table by specifying a different rule in a form.

In general, a field validation expression consists of an operator and a comparison value. If you do not include an operator, Access assumes you want an "equals" (=) comparison. You can specify multiple comparisons separated by the Boolean operators OR and AND. For example, in Figure 5-26 you can see a validation rule for the AvgSATVerbal field: *Is Null Or >0 And <800.* If the average SAT verbal score is unknown, you can leave it Null. If you enter a value, it must be greater than 0 and less than 800 (the valid range of Scholastic Aptitude Test scores).

You should always enclose text string values in quotes. If one of your values is a text string containing blanks or special characters, you must enclose the entire string in quotes. For example, to limit the valid entries for a City field to the two largest cities in the state of California, enter *"Los Angeles" Or "San Diego"*. If you are comparing date values, you must enclose date constants in pound sign (#) characters, as in *#01/15/95#*.

You can use the comparison symbols to compare the value in the field to a value or values in your validation rule. For example, you might want to check that a numeric value is always less than 1000. To do this, enter *<1000*. You can use one or more pairs of comparisons to check that the value falls within certain ranges. For example, if you want to verify that a number is in the range of 50 through 100, enter either *>=50 And <=100* or *Between 50 And 100*.

Another way to test for a match in a list of values is to use the IN comparison operator. For example, to test for states surrounding the U.S. capital, enter *In ("Virginia", "Maryland")*.

Operator	Meaning
<	Less than
<=	Less than or equal to
>	Greater than
>=	Greater than or equal to
=	Equal to
<>	Not equal to
IN	Test for "equal to" any member in a list; comparison value must be a list enclosed in parentheses
BETWEEN	Test for a range of values; comparison value must be two values (a low and a high value) separated by the AND operator
LIKE	Test a text or memo field to match a pattern string

FIGURE 5-27
Some comparison symbols that can be used in validation rules.

If you need to validate a text or memo field against a matching pattern (for example, a zip code or a phone number), you can use the LIKE comparison operator. You provide a text string as a comparison value that defines which characters are valid in which positions. Access understands a number of *wildcard characters,* which you can use to define positions that can contain any single character, zero or more characters, or any single number. These characters are shown in Figure 5-28 on the next page.

FIGURE 5-28
LIKE wildcard
characters.

Wildcard Character	Meaning
?	Any single character
*	Zero or more characters; used to define leading, trailing, or embedded strings that don't have to match any of the pattern characters
#	Any single number

You can also specify that any particular position in the text or memo field can contain only characters from a list that you provide. To define a list of valid characters, enclose the list in brackets ([ ]). You can specify a range of characters within a list by entering the low value character, a hyphen, and the high value character, as in *[A-Z]* or *[3-7]*. If you want to test a position for any characters <u>except</u> those in a list, start the list with an exclamation point (!). Some examples of validation rules using LIKE are shown in Figure 5-29.

FIGURE 5-29
Some validation
rules that use the
LIKE comparison
operator.

Validation Rule	Tests For
LIKE "#####" or LIKE "#####-####"	A U.S. zip code
LIKE "[A-Z]#[A-Z]#[A-Z]#"	A Canadian postal code
LIKE "Smith*"	A string that begins with *Smith*
LIKE "*smith##*"	A string that contains *smith* followed by two numbers anywhere in the text
LIKE "??00####"	An eight-character string that contains any first two characters followed by exactly two zeros and then any four numbers
LIKE "[!0-9BMQ]*####"	A string that contains any character other than a number or the letter *B*, *M,* or *Q* in the first position and ends with exactly four numbers

Defining Input Masks

To assist you in entering formatted data, Access allows you to define an *input mask* for any type of field except AutoNumber, Memo, OLE Object, and Yes/No data types. You can use an input mask to do something as simple as forcing all letters entered to be uppercase or as complex as adding parentheses and dashes to phone numbers. You create an input mask by using the special mask definition characters shown in Figure 5-30. You can also embed strings of characters that you want displayed for formatting or stored in the data field.

Mask Character	Meaning
0	A number must be entered in this position. Plus (+) and minus (-) signs are not allowed.
9	A number or a space can be entered in this position. Plus and minus signs are not allowed. If the user skips this position by moving the cursor past the position without entering anything, Access stores nothing.
#	A number, a space, or a plus or minus sign can be entered in this position. If the user skips this position by moving the cursor past the position without entering anything, Access stores a space.
L	A letter must be entered in this position.
?	A letter can be entered in this position. If the user skips this position by moving the cursor past the position without entering anything, Access stores nothing.
A	A letter or a number must be entered in this position.
a	A letter or a number can be entered in this position. If the user skips this position by moving the cursor past the position without entering anything, Access stores nothing.
&	A character or a space must be entered in this position.
C	Any character or a space can be entered in this position. If the user skips this position by moving the cursor past the position without entering anything, Access stores nothing.

FIGURE 5-30

Input mask definition characters used to create an input mask.

(continued)

FIGURE 5-30 *continued*

Mask Character	Meaning
.	Decimal placeholder (depends on the setting in the Regional Settings section of Windows Control Panel).
,	Thousand separator (depends on the setting in the Regional Settings section of Windows Control Panel).
: ; - /	Date and time separators (depends on the settings in the Regional Settings section of Windows Control Panel).
<	Converts to lowercase all characters that follow.
>	Converts to uppercase all characters that follow.
!	Causes the mask to fill from right to left when you define optional characters on the left end of the mask. You can place this character anywhere in the mask.
\	Causes the character immediately following to be displayed as a literal character rather than as a mask character.
"literal"	You can also enclose any literal string in double quotation marks rather than using the \ character repeatedly.

An input mask consists of three parts, separated by semicolons. The first part defines the mask string using mask definition characters and embedded fixed data. The optional second part indicates whether you want the formatting characters stored in the field in the database. Set this second part to 0 to store the characters or to 1 to store only the data entered. The optional third part defines the single character that Access uses as a placeholder to indicate positions where data can be entered. The default placeholder character is an underscore (_).

Perhaps the best way to learn to use input masks is to take advantage of the Input Mask Wizard. In the Colleges table of the Students and Colleges database, for example, the CPhone field could benefit from the use of an input mask. Click on the CPhone field in the upper part of the Table window in Design view, and then click in the Input Mask property box in the lower part of the window. You should see a small button with three dots on it (called a Build button) to the right of the property box, as shown in Figure 5-31.

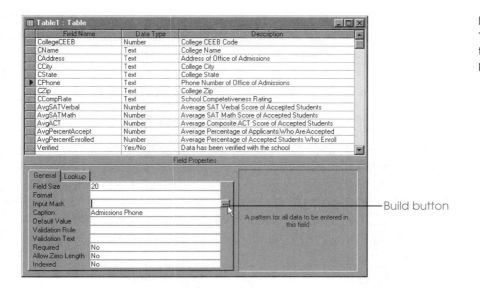

FIGURE 5-31
The Build button for the Input Mask property.

Click the Build button to start the Input Mask Wizard. In the first window, the wizard gives you a number of choices for "standard" input masks that it can generate for you. In this case, click the first one in the list—Phone Number. Your screen should look like the one shown in Figure 5-32. Note that you can type something in the Try It box below the input mask selection box to try out the mask.

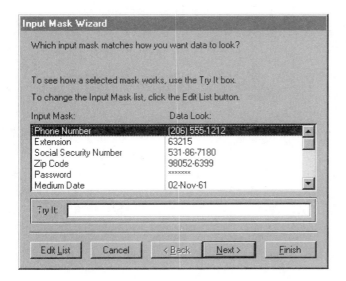

FIGURE 5-32
Selecting an input mask in the Input Mask Wizard.

133

Click the Next button to go to the next window. In this window, shown in Figure 5-33, you can see the mask name, the proposed mask string, a selection box in which you select the placeholder character, and another Try It box. The default underscore character (_) works well as a placeholder character for phone numbers.

FIGURE 5-33

Selecting the
placeholder
character in the
Input Mask
Wizard.

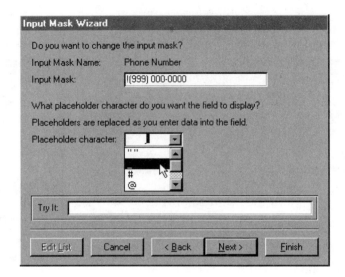

Click Next to go to the next window, where you can choose whether you want the data stored without the formatting characters (the default) or stored with the parentheses, spaces, and dash separator. In Figure 5-34, the data is going to be saved with the formatting characters. Click Next to go to the final window, and then click the Finish button in that window to store the mask in the property setting. Figure 5-35 shows the mask entered in the CPhone field. You'll find this same mask handy for any text field that is meant to contain a U.S. phone number (such as the PhoneNumber field in the Students table).

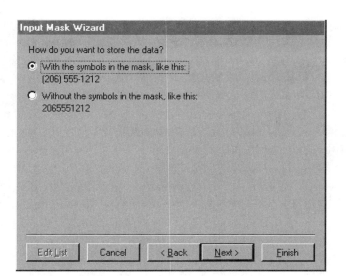

FIGURE 5-34
Opting to store
formatting
characters.

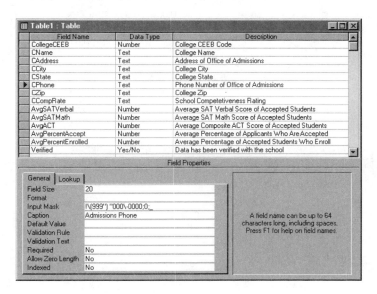

FIGURE 5-35
The CPhone field
input mask.

Defining a Primary Key

Every table in a relational database should have a primary key. If you used the procedure outlined in Chapter 4, "Designing Your Database Application," you should know what fields must make up the primary key for each of your tables.

Telling Microsoft Access how to define the primary key is quite simple. Select the first field for the primary key by clicking the row selector to the left of that field's name in the Table window in Design view. If you need to select multiple fields for your primary key, hold down the Ctrl key and click the row selector of each additional field you need.

After you select all the fields you want for the primary key, click the Primary Key button on the toolbar, or choose the Primary Key command from the Edit menu. Access displays a key symbol to the left of the selected field(s) to acknowledge your definition of the primary key. (To eliminate all primary key designations, see the section titled "Adding Indexes" later in this chapter.) When you've finished creating the Colleges table for the Students and Colleges database, the primary key should be the CollegeCEEB field (a field for the unique code assigned by the U.S. College Entrance Examination Board—the folks who administer the Scholastic Aptitude Tests), as shown in Figure 5-36.

FIGURE 5-36
The Colleges table with a primary key defined.

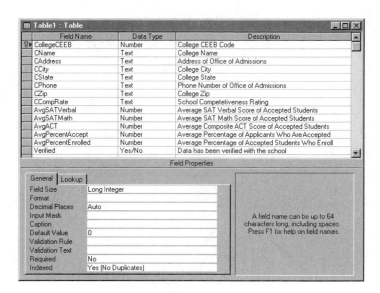

The last step you need to perform for a new table is to save it. From the File menu, choose the Save command or the Save As/Export command. Access opens the Save As dialog box, as shown in Figure 5-37. Type the name of your table, *Colleges,* and click OK to save the table.

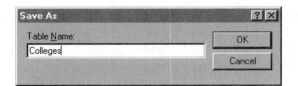

FIGURE 5-37
Saving your table.

Defining a Table Validation Rule

The last detail to define is any validation rule that you want Microsoft Access to check for each row you save in the table. Although field validation rules get checked as you enter each new value, Access checks a table validation rule only when you save or add a row. To define a table validation rule, be sure that the table is in Design view, and then click the Properties button on the toolbar or choose the Properties command from the View menu to open the Table Properties window, shown in Figure 5-38.

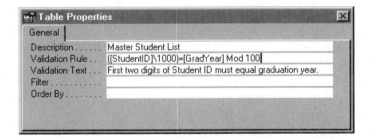

FIGURE 5-38
Defining a table validation rule.

In the Table Properties window, you can enter a description of the table on the first line. On the second line, you can enter any valid comparison expression. The Overlake School in Redmond, Washington (the high school for which my son Michael built the College Counseling database), has a "business rule" that dictates that the first two digits of the StudentID should also be the student's graduation year. Note that here you can compare the contents of one field with the contents of another. In this case, the validation rule makes sure that the first two digits of the StudentID match the last two digits of the GradYear field. To refer to a field name, enclose the name in brackets ([ ]), as shown in Figure 5-38. You'll use this technique whenever you refer to the name of an object anywhere in an expression.

On the third line in the Table Properties window, enter the text that you want Access to display whenever the table validation rule is violated. Additional table properties you can define include Filter and Order By. Filter lets you predefine criteria to limit the data displayed in the Datasheet view of this table. (You'll learn more about filters in Chapter 7, "Using Datasheets.") You can use Order By to define one or more fields that define the default display sequence of rows in this table when in Datasheet view. If you don't define an Order By property, Access displays the rows in primary key sequence.

Defining Relationships

After you have defined two or more related tables, you should tell Microsoft Access how the tables are related. If you do this, Access will be able to link all your tables when you need to use them later in queries, forms, or reports. In the Students and Colleges database, any given student might be interested in many colleges, and any given college might have multiple students apply. As you learned in Chapter 4, "Designing Your Database Application," this is called a *many-to-many relationship*. To create this type of relationship in Access, you need a linking table to connect students to colleges. Within the linking table, you should also include any fields that are related to any specific relationship between a college and a student. In this case, the linking table tracks whether a student applied to a particular college, was accepted at that college, and finally attended the college.

You can easily create the linking table you need in Table Design view, as shown in Figure 5-39. StudentID links to the primary key in the Students table, and CollegeCEEB links to the primary key in the Colleges table. The additional Number/Integer fields will hold the status codes the application will use to keep track of students applying to colleges. When you finish creating the linking table, save it with the name StudentCollegeLink.

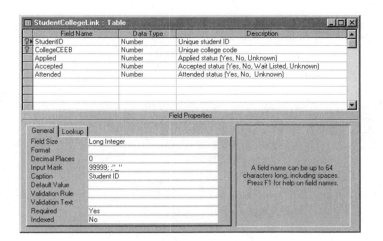

FIGURE 5-39
The table that
links the Students
and Colleges
tables.

To define relationships, you need to return to the Database window by closing any Table windows that are open and by clicking in the
Database window to make it active. Then choose the Relationships
command from the Tools menu. If this is the first time you have defined
relationships in this database, Access opens a blank Relationships window and opens the Show Table dialog box, shown in Figure 5-40.

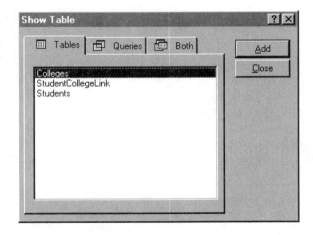

FIGURE 5-40
The Show Table
dialog box.

In the Show Table dialog box, select each table and click the Add button in turn. Click Close to dismiss the Show Table dialog box. Your Relationships window should now look like the one shown in Figure 5-41.

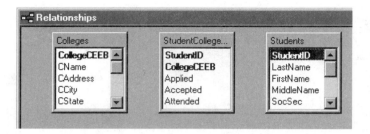

Defining Your First Relationship

If you remember the design work you did in Chapter 4, "Designing Your Database Application," you know that a college can have several interested students, and any student can apply to multiple colleges. This means that colleges have a many-to-many relationship with students. You can see that for the CollegeCEEB primary key in the Colleges table, there is a matching CollegeCEEB foreign key in the StudentCollegeLink table. To create the relationship you need, click in the CollegeCEEB field in the Colleges table and drag and drop it onto CollegeCEEB in the StudentCollegeLink table, as shown in Figure 5-42.

FIGURE 5-42
Dragging the linking field from the "one" table (Colleges) to the "many" table (StudentCollege-Link).

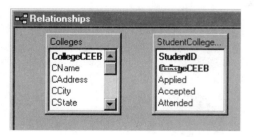

When you release the mouse button, Access opens the Relationships dialog box, shown in Figure 5-43.

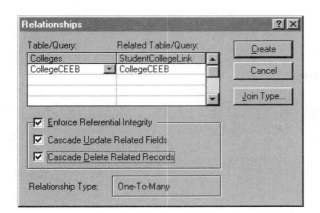

FIGURE 5-43
The Relationships
dialog box.

You'll notice that Access has filled in the field names for you. If you need to define a multiple-field relationship between two tables, you can use the additional blank lines to define those fields. Because you probably don't want any links lying around for nonexistent colleges, click the Enforce Referential Integrity check box. When you do this, Access ensures that you can't add a link for an invalid CollegeCEEB. Also, Access won't let you delete any Colleges records that have links outstanding.

Note that after you click the Enforce Referential Integrity check box, Access makes two additional options available: Cascade Update Related Fields and Cascade Delete Related Records. If you select Cascade Update Related Fields, Access updates all the foreign key values in "child" tables (the "many" table in a one-to-many relationship) if you change a primary key value in a "parent" table (the "one" table in a one-to-many relationship). If you select Cascade Delete Related Records, Access deletes child rows (the related rows in the "many" table of a one-to-many relationship) when you delete a parent row (the related row in the "one" table of a one-to-many relationship). If you decide to remove a college from the database, it's probably a good idea to remove the college's links to the Students table. If you select Cascade Delete Related Records, Access will automatically remove the links for you. Also, from time to time a CollegeCEEB code might change. Select Cascade Update Related Fields to request that Access automatically update any links any time you need to change a college code.

You probably noticed that the Show Table dialog box, shown earlier in Figure 5-40, gives you the option to include queries as well as tables. Sometimes you might want to define relationships between tables and queries or between queries so that Access knows how to join them properly. You can also define what's known as an *outer join* by clicking the Join Type button in the Relationships dialog box and selecting an option in the Join Properties dialog box. With an outer join, you can find out, for example, which colleges have no students that expressed an interest.

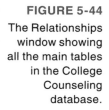

See Also For details on outer joins, see the section titled "Outer Joins" in Chapter 8.

After you click the Create button to finish your relationship definition, Access draws a line between the two tables to indicate the relationship. Notice that when you ask Access to enforce referential integrity, Access displays a *1* at the end of the relationship line, next to the "one" table, and an infinity symbol (∞) next to the "many" table. If you want to delete the relationship, click on the line and press the Del key. If you want to edit or change the relationship, double-click on the line to open the Relationships dialog box again.

You also need to define a similar relationship between the StudentID field in the Students table and the matching field in the StudentCollegeLink table. Figure 5-44 shows the Relationships window for all the main tables in the College Counseling database.

FIGURE 5-44

The Relationships window showing all the main tables in the College Counseling database.

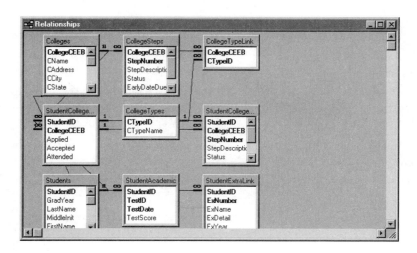

Note that once you define a relationship, you can delete the table or query field lists from the Relationships window without affecting the relationships. To do this, click on the table or query list header and press the Del key. This can be particularly advantageous in large databases that have dozens of tables. You can also display only those tables that you're working with at the moment. To see the relationships defined for any particular table or query, include it in the Relationships window by using the Show Table dialog box, and then click the Show Direct Relationships button on the toolbar or choose Show Direct from the Relationships menu. To redisplay all relationships, click the Show All Relationships button on the toolbar or choose Show All from the Relationships menu.

When you close the Relationships window, Access asks whether you want to save your layout changes. Click Yes to save the latest graphical relationship drawing. That's all there is to it. Later, when you use multiple tables in a query in Chapter 8, "Adding Power with Select Queries," you'll see that Access builds the relationships among tables based on the relationships you've defined.

Adding Indexes

The more data you include in your tables, the more you need indexes to help Microsoft Access search your data efficiently. An *index* is simply an internal table that contains two columns: the value in the field or fields being indexed and the location of each record in your table that contains that value. Let's assume that you often search your Students table by city. Without an index, when you ask Access to find all the students in the city of Bellevue, Access has to search every record in your table. This search is fast if your table includes only a few students but very slow if the table contains hundreds of student records collected over many years. If you create an index on the City field, Access can use the index to directly find the records for the students in the city you specify.

Single Field Indexes

Most of the indexes you'll need to define will probably contain the values from only a single field. Access uses this type of index to help narrow down the number of records it has to search whenever you provide search criteria on the field—for example, *City = Redmond* or *GradYear = 1995*. If you have defined indexes on multiple fields and provided search criteria for more than one of the fields, Access uses the indexes together (using a technology called Rushmore from Microsoft FoxPro) to find the rows you want quickly. For example, if you have created indexes on City and GradYear and you ask for *City = Seattle* and *GradYear = 1994*, Access uses the rows in the City index that equal *Seattle* and matches those with the rows in the GradYear index that equal *1994*. The result is a small set of pointers to the records that match both criteria.

Creating an index on a single field in a table is easy. Open the table in Design view, and select the field for which you want an index. Click the Indexed property box in the lower part of the Table window, and then click the down arrow to drop down the list of choices, as shown in Figure 5-45.

FIGURE 5-45

Using the Indexed property box to set an index on a single field.

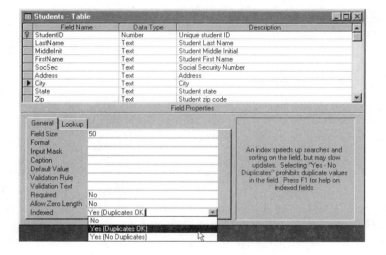

The default indexed property setting for all fields except the primary key is No. If you want to set an index for a field, there are two Yes choices. In most cases, a given field will have multiple records with the same value—perhaps multiple colleges in the state of Texas or multiple students who graduated in 1995. You should select Yes (Duplicates OK) to create an index on this type of field. Note that you can use Access to enforce unique values in any field by creating an index that doesn't allow duplicates: Yes (No Duplicates). Access performs this check automatically for the primary key index.

Multiple Field Indexes

If you often provide multiple criteria in searches against large tables, you might want to consider creating a few multiple field indexes to help Access narrow the search quickly without having to match values from two separate indexes. For example, suppose you often perform a search for students who have a particular last name and first name. If you create an index that includes both of these fields, Access can satisfy your query rapidly.

To create a multiple field index, you must open the Table window in Design view and open the Indexes window (shown in Figure 5-46) by clicking the Indexes button on the toolbar or by choosing the Indexes command from the View menu. You can see the primary key index and the index that you defined on City in the previous section. Each of these indexes comprises exactly one field.

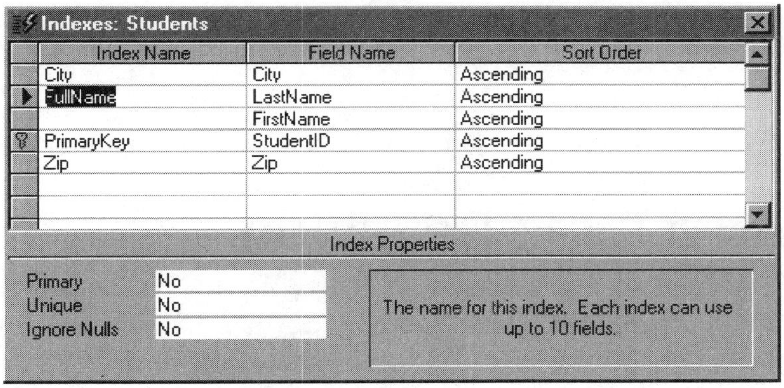

FIGURE 5-46
The indexes for the Students table shown in the Indexes window.

To create a multiple field index, move the cursor down to an empty row in the Indexes window and type a unique name. In this example, you want a multiple field index using LastName and FirstName fields, so *FullName* might be a reasonable index name. Select the LastName field in the field name column of this row. To add other fields, simply skip down to the next row and select another field without typing a new index name. When you're done, your Indexes window should look like the one shown in Figure 5-46.

> **NOTE** You can remove an existing index by simply highlighting the row (by clicking the row selector) that defines the index and then pressing the Del key. Any indexes you define, change, or delete are saved when you save the table definition.

Access will use a multiple field index in a search even if you don't provide search values for all the fields. Access can use a multiple field index as long as you provide search criteria for consecutive fields starting with the first field. Therefore, in the multiple field index shown in Figure 5-46, you can search for last name or for last name and first name. There's one additional limitation on multiple field indexes: Only the last search criterion can be an inequality, such as >, >=, <, or <=. In other words, Access can use the index shown in Figure 5-46 when you specify searches such as this:

LastName = Smith
LastName > Franklin
LastName = Buchanan And FirstName = Steven
LastName = Hallmark And FirstName >= Elizabeth

But Access cannot use the index shown in Figure 5-46 if you ask for

LastName > Davolio And FirstName > John

because only the last field in the search (FirstName) can be an inequality. Access also cannot use this index if you ask for

FirstName = John

because the first field (LastName) is missing from the search criterion.

Printing a Table Definition

After you create several tables, you might want to print out their definitions to provide a permanent paper record. You can do this by choosing Analyze from the Tools menu and then choosing Documentor from the submenu. Microsoft Access displays several options in the Database Documentor dialog box, as shown in Figure 5-47.

FIGURE 5-47
The Database Documentor dialog box.

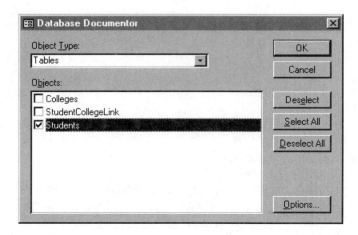

You can select not only the type of object you want to document but also which objects. Click the Options button to select what you want reported. For example, you can ask for the properties, relationships, and permissions for a table; the names, data types, sizes, and properties for fields; and the names, fields, and properties for indexes. Click OK in the Database Documentor dialog box to produce the definition report and view it in Print Preview. You can print the resulting report or save the data in a special Object Definition table by choosing Save As Table from the File menu.

Database Limitations

As you design your database, you should keep in mind the following limitations:

- A table can have up to 255 fields.

- A table can have up to 32 indexes.

- A multiple field index can have up to 10 columns. The sum of the lengths of the columns cannot exceed 255 bytes.

- A row in a table, excluding memo fields and OLE objects, can be no longer than approximately 2 kilobytes.

- A memo field can store up to 1 gigabyte, but you can't display a memo larger than 32 kilobytes in a form or a datasheet.

- An OLE object can be up to 1 gigabyte in size.

- There is no limit on the number of records in a table, but an Access database cannot be larger than 1 gigabyte. If you have several large tables, you might need to define each one in a separate Access database and then attach them to the database that contains the forms, reports, macros, and modules for your applications. See Chapter 10, "Importing, Attaching, and Exporting Data," for details.

Now that you've started to get comfortable with creating databases and tables, you can read the next chapter to learn how to make modifications to tables in an existing database.

Chapter 6

Modifying Your Database Design

149

No matter how carefully you design your database, you can be sure that you'll need to change it at some later date. Here are some of the reasons you might need to change your database:

- You no longer need some of the tables.

- You want to be able to perform some new tasks that require not only creating new tables but also inserting some linking fields in existing tables.

- You find that you use some fields in a table much more frequently than others, so it would be easier if those fields appeared first in the table design.

- You no longer need some of the fields.

- You want to add some new fields that are similar to fields that already exist.

- You discover that some of the data you defined would be better stored as a different data type. For example, a field that you originally designed to be all numbers (such as a U.S. zip code) must now contain some letters (as in a Canadian postal code).

- You have a number field that needs to hold larger values or needs a different number of decimal places than you originally planned.

- You can improve your database design by splitting an existing table into two or more tables using the Table Analyzer Wizard.

- You discover that the field you defined as a primary key isn't always unique, so you need to change your primary key definition.

- You find that some of your queries take too long to run and might execute faster if you add an index to your table.

This chapter takes a look at how you can make these changes easily and relatively painlessly with Microsoft Access. If you want to follow along with the examples in this chapter, you should first create the Students and Colleges database as described in Chapter 5, "Building Your Database in Microsoft Access."

NOTE You might have noticed that the Students table you defined for the Students and Colleges database in Chapter 5 is different from the Students table in the College Counseling database on the companion disc that comes with this book. In this chapter, you'll modify the Students table you built in Chapter 5 so that it is more like the one on the sample disc. You'll also learn how to use the Table Analyzer Wizard to further refine the Colleges table in the College Counseling database.

Before You Get Started

Microsoft Access makes it easy for you to change the design of your database, even when you already have data in your tables. You should, however, understand the potential impact of any changes you plan and take steps to ensure that you can recover if you make a mistake. Here are some things to consider before you make changes:

- Access does not automatically propagate changes that you make in tables to any queries, forms, reports, macros, or modules. You must make changes to dependent objects yourself.

TIP   You can determine which other objects use the tables or fields you plan to change by using the Database Documentor. (Choose Analyze from the Tools menu, and then choose Documentor from the submenu.)

- You cannot change the data type of a field that is part of a relationship definition between tables. You must first delete the relationship definition, change the field's data type, and then rebuild the relationship definition.

- You cannot change the definition of any table that you have open in a query, a form, or a report. You must first close any other objects that refer to the table you want to change before you open that table in Design view. If you give other network users access to your database, you won't be able to change the table definition if someone else has the table (or a query or form based on the table) open.

 TIP Access always prompts you for confirmation before committing any changes that permanently alter or delete data in your database and gives you a chance to cancel the operation.

Making a Backup Copy

The safest way to make changes to your database design is to make a backup copy of the database before you begin. If you plan to make extensive changes to several tables in your database, you should make a copy of the mdb file, which contains your database, using a utility such as Windows Explorer in Microsoft Windows 95.

If you want to change a single table, you can easily make a backup copy of that table right in your database. Use the following procedure to copy any table structure (the contents of the Table window in Design view), table data (the contents of the Table window in Datasheet view), or the structure and the data together:

1. Open the database containing the table you want to copy. If the database is already open, click on the Tables tab in the Database window.

2. Select the table you want to copy by clicking on it in the Database window. The table name will be highlighted.

3. Choose the Copy command from the Edit menu (as shown in Figure 6-1 on the next page), or click the Copy button on the toolbar. This copies the entire table (structure and data) to the Clipboard.

FIGURE 6-1
Using the Copy
command to copy
a table from the
Tables list.

4. Choose the Paste command from the Edit menu, or click the
Paste button on the toolbar. Access opens the Paste Table As
dialog box, shown in Figure 6-2. Type in a new name for your
table. (When naming a backup copy, you can add *Backup* and
the date to the original table name, as shown in Figure 6-2.) The
default option is to copy both the structure and the data. You
also have the option of copying only the table's structure or of
appending the data to another table.

FIGURE 6-2
The Paste Table
As dialog box.

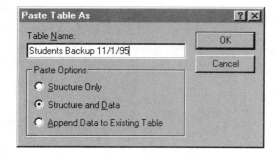

Deleting Tables

You probably won't need to delete an entire table very often. However,
if you set up your application to collect historical information—for example, to collect student test scores in tables by year—you'll eventually
want to delete old information that you no longer need. You also might
want to delete a table if you've made extensive changes that are incorrect and it would be easier to delete your work and restore the table
from a backup.

154

To delete a table, select it in the Database window and press the Del key or choose the Delete command from the Edit menu. Access opens the dialog box shown in Figure 6-3, which asks you to confirm or cancel the delete operation. Even if you mistakenly confirm the deletion, you can immediately select the Undo command from the Edit menu to get your table back.

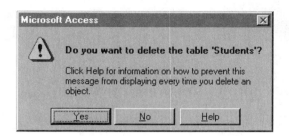

FIGURE 6-3
This dialog box gives you the option of canceling the deletion of a table.

TIP   You can use the Cut command on the Edit menu or the Cut button on the toolbar to delete a table. Both of these methods place a copy of the table on the Clipboard. After you close the database in which you've been working, you can open another database and paste the table that's on the Clipboard.

If you have defined relationships between the table you want to delete and other tables, Access opens another dialog box that alerts you and asks if you want to also delete the relationships. If you click Yes, Access deletes all relationships between any other table and the table you want to delete and then deletes the table. Even at this point, if you find you made a mistake you can choose Undo from the Edit menu to restore both the table and all its relationships.

Renaming Tables

If you keep transaction data (such as receipts, deposits, or checks written), you might want to save that data at the end of each month in a table with a unique name. One way to save your data is to rename the existing table (perhaps by adding a date to the name). You can then create a new table (perhaps by making a copy of the backup table's structure) to start collecting information for the next month.

To rename a table, select it in the Database window and choose the Rename command from the Edit menu. Microsoft Access places the name in edit mode in the Database window so you can type in a new name, as shown in Figure 6-4. Type in the new name and press Enter to save it.

FIGURE 6-4

Renaming a table in the Database window.

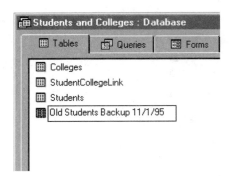

TIP You can also place the name of an object in edit mode by selecting it in the Database window, waiting a second, and then clicking on the name again. This works just like it would in Windows Explorer.

If you enter the name of a table that already exists, Access asks whether you want to replace the existing table, as shown in Figure 6-5. If you click Yes, Access deletes the old table before performing the renaming operation. Even if you replace an existing table, you can undo the renaming operation by immediately choosing the Undo command from the Edit menu.

FIGURE 6-5

This dialog box asks if you want to replace an existing table with the same name.

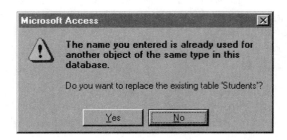

>
> **TIP**   You can use the techniques you just learned for copying, renaming, and deleting tables to copy, rename, and delete queries, forms, reports, macros, or modules.

Changing Field Names

Perhaps you misspelled a field name when you first created one of your tables. Or perhaps you decide that one of the field names isn't descriptive enough. You won't want the hassle of giving the field a new name every time it appears in a query, a form, or a report. Fortunately, Microsoft Access makes it easy to change a field name in a table—even if you already have data in the table.

> **NOTE** The next several examples in this chapter show you how to change the Students table that you created in the previous chapter to match the Students table in the College Counseling database.

Assume that you created the first draft of the Students table using a wizard. Now you need to make a few changes so that it will hold all the data fields that you need for your application. You bypassed your chance in the wizard to rename any sample fields when you originally selected them, but now you decide to rename one of the fields before beginning work on the rest of your application.

Renaming a field is easy. For example, you chose the field "MiddleName" in the wizard, but you decide that you need only the student's middle initial in this database. It makes sense to change the field name to reflect the actual data you intend to store in the field. (Later in this chapter, you'll see how to shorten the length of the field.) Open the Students table in the Students and Colleges database in Design view, and then move the cursor to the MiddleName field. Highlight the characters "Name" at the end of the field name, using the mouse, and then type *Init*. You can also click in the field name, use the arrow keys to position the cursor just before the letter *N,* press the Del key to remove the characters you don't want, and type in the new ones. While you're at it, press F6 to jump down to the Field Properties area of the window and change the field caption. Your result should look something like Figure 6-6 on the next page.

FIGURE 6-6

Changing a field name and a field caption in Design view.

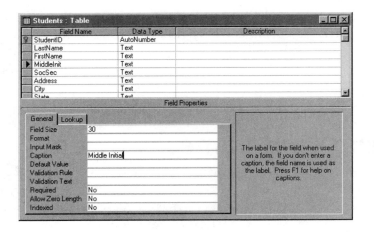

  CAUTION   If you have defined any queries, forms, reports, modules, or macros that use a field whose name you have changed, you must also change the field name in those other objects. You can determine which other objects use this field by running the Database Documentor (by choosing Analyze from the Tools menu and then choosing Documentor from the submenu) for your forms, reports, and queries. If you save the reports that the Database Documentor generates, you can use the search capabilities of most text editors to find references to the name you changed.

Inserting Fields

Perhaps one of the most common changes you'll make to your database is to insert a new field into a table. In the preceding exercise, you changed the field name MiddleName in the Students table to MiddleInit. If you compare this table to the Students table in the College Counseling sample database, you can see that a few more fields are needed. Now you're ready to insert fields to store the student graduation year, a grade-point average, and a student photograph.

First, you must select the row or move your cursor to the row that defines the field <u>after</u> the point where you want to insert the new field. In this case, if you want to insert a new field to contain the graduation year between the StudentID and LastName fields, place the cursor anywhere in the row that defines the LastName field or select the entire row (by using the arrow keys or by clicking the row selector). Next, choose the Field command from the Insert menu (as shown in Figure 6-7), or click the Insert Row button on the toolbar.

Insert Row button

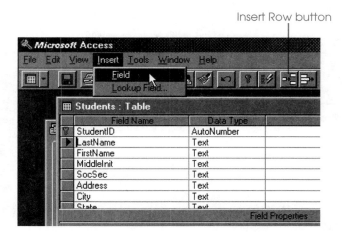

FIGURE 6-7
The Insert Field command inserts a new row above a selected row or above the row in which the cursor is located.

Microsoft Access adds a new blank row that you can use to define your new field. Type in the definition for the GradYear field. Choose the Number data type and set the Field Size property to Integer. Move down to the Comments field and insert two new rows above it: a SeniorGPA field that has the Number data type with a Single field size and a Photo field that has an OLE Object data type. You can also type in field descriptions if you want (note that the wizard didn't supply them). When you finish, your Table window in Design view should look something like the one shown in Figure 6-8 on the next page. Don't worry about setting other properties just yet.

FIGURE 6-8
The Students
table with
additional fields
inserted.

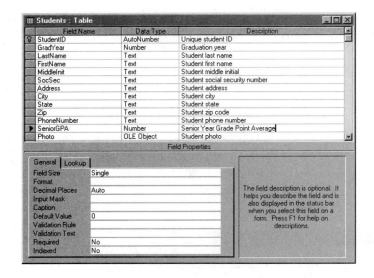

TIP   You can move the cursor between the upper part
and the lower part of any Table or Query window in
Design view by pressing the F6 key.

Copying Fields

As you create table definitions, you might find that several field definitions in your table are similar. Rather than enter each field definition
separately, you can enter one field definition, copy it, and then paste it
as many times as necessary.

You might have noticed that we haven't yet defined the
JuniorGPA field for the Students table. You could insert a blank row
and then type in the data. But the JuniorGPA field is nearly identical
to the SeniorGPA field, so you can save time by copying the definition
of the SeniorGPA field.

Select the entire row containing the SeniorGPA field definition by
clicking the row selector at the far left end of the row. Choose the Copy

command from the Edit menu, as shown in Figure 6-9, or click the Copy button on the toolbar. Move the cursor to the row that should follow your new inserted row. (In this case, you're already in the SeniorGPA field, which should follow your new field.) Insert a new blank row by choosing Field from the Insert menu or by clicking the Insert Row button on the toolbar. Select the new row by clicking the row selector. Choose the Paste command from the Edit menu, or click the Paste button on the toolbar, to insert the copied row, as shown in Figure 6-10 on the next page. You can use the Paste command repeatedly to insert a copied row more than once. Remember to change both the name and the description of the copied field in each location before you save the modified table definition. In this case, it's a simple matter to change the name of the copied row from SeniorGPA to JuniorGPA. Note that this procedure also has the benefit of copying forward any formatting, default value, or validation rule information.

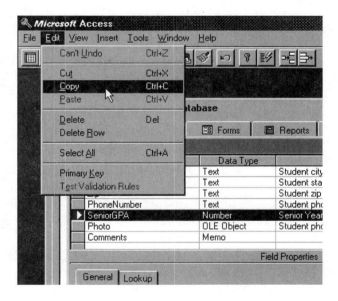

FIGURE 6-9
The SeniorGPA field is selected and copied.

FIGURE 6-10

The copied
SeniorGPA field
can be pasted
into a new
blank row.

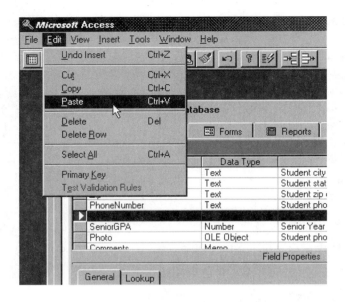

NOTE If you choose the Paste command when a row containing data is selected, the copied row will replace the selected row. Should you make this replacement in error, you can choose the Undo command from the Edit menu to restore the original row.

Deleting Fields

Removing unwanted fields is easy. With the Table window open in Design view, select the field definition that you want to delete by clicking the row selector. You can extend the selection to multiple contiguous fields by holding down the Shift key while you extend the selection using the up and down arrow keys. You can also select multiple contiguous rows by clicking the row selector of the first row and, without releasing the mouse button, dragging up or down to select all the rows you want. After you select the appropriate fields, choose Delete or Delete Row from the Edit menu or press Del to delete the selected fields.

If a table contains one or more rows of data (in Datasheet view), Access displays a warning message when you delete field definitions in Design view, as shown in Figure 6-11. Click Yes to proceed with the deletion of the fields and the data in those fields. Click No if you think you made a mistake.

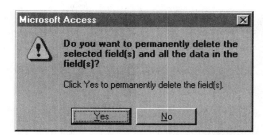

FIGURE 6-11
This dialog box asks you to confirm a field deletion.

Moving Fields

You might want to move a row in a table definition for a number of reasons. Perhaps you made an error as you entered or changed the information in a table. Or perhaps you discover that you're using some fields you defined at the end of a table quite frequently in forms or reports, in which case it would be easier to find and work with those fields if they were nearer the beginning of your table definition.

You can use the mouse to move one or more rows. Simply follow these steps:

1. To select a row you want to move, click its row selector.

2. If you want to move multiple contiguous rows, click the row selector for the first row in the group and scroll until you can see the last row in the group. Hold down the Shift key and click the row selector for the last row in the group. The first and last rows and all rows in between will be selected. Release the Shift key.

3. Click and drag the row selector(s) for the highlighted row(s) to a new location. A small shaded box attaches to the bottom of the mouse pointer while you're dragging, and a highlighted line will appear, indicating the position to which the row(s) will move when you release the mouse button.

In the design for the Students table in the College Counseling database, the MiddleInit field appears between the LastName and FirstName fields. Select the MiddleInit field by clicking its row selector. Click the row selector again and drag up until the line between the LastName field and the FirstName field is highlighted, as shown in Figure 6-12 on the next page.

FIGURE 6-12

The MiddleInit field is being dragged to its new position between the LastName and FirstName fields.

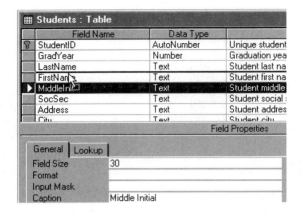

In Figure 6-13, the fields are positioned correctly.

FIGURE 6-13

The MiddleInit field is now correctly placed.

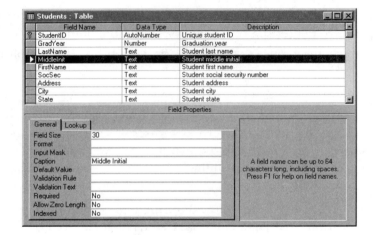

TIP When it comes to moving fields, you might find it easier to use a combination of mouse and keyboard methods. Use the mouse to select the row or rows you want to move. Then activate Move mode by pressing Ctrl-F8, and use the arrow keys to position the row(s). As you experiment with Access, you'll discover more than one way to perform many tasks, and you can choose the techniques that work the best for you.

Changing Data Attributes

As you learned in the previous chapter, Microsoft Access provides a number of different data types. These data types help Access work more efficiently with your data and also provide a base level of data validation; for example, you can enter only numbers in a Number or Currency field.

When you initially design your database, you should match the data type and length of each field to its intended use. You might discover, however, that a field you thought would contain only numbers (such as a U.S. zip code) must now contain some letters (perhaps because you've started doing business in Canada). You might find that one or more number fields need to hold larger values or a different number of decimal places. Access allows you to change the data type and length of many fields, even after you've entered data in them.

Changing Data Types

Changing the data type of a field in a table is simple. Open the table in Design view, click in the data type column of the field definition you want to change, click the down arrow button at the right to see the available choices, and select a new data type. You cannot convert an OLE Object or a ReplicationID to another data type. With a few limitations, Access can successfully convert every other data type to any other data type. Figure 6-14 shows you the possible conversions and potential limitations.

Convert From	Convert To	Limitations
Text	Memo	Access deletes indexes that include the text field
	Number	Text must contain only numbers and valid separators
	Date/Time	Text must contain a recognizable date and/or time, such as 11-Nov-95 5:15 PM
	Currency	Text must contain only numbers and valid separators

FIGURE 6-14
The limitations on converting from one data type to another.

(continued)

FIGURE 6-14 *continued*

Convert From	Convert To	Limitations
	AutoNumber	Not possible if table contains data
	Yes/No	Text must contain only one of the following values: Yes, True, On, No, False, or Off
Memo	Text	Access truncates text longer than 255 characters
	Number	Memo must contain only numbers and valid separators
	Date/Time	Memo must contain a recognizable date and/or time, such as 11-Nov-95 5:15 PM
	Currency	Memo must contain only numbers and valid separators
	AutoNumber	Not possible if table contains data
	Yes/No	Memo must contain only one of the following values: Yes, True, On, No, False, or Off
Number, except ReplicationID	Text	No limitations
	Memo	No limitations
	Date/Time	Number must be between −657,434 and 2,958,465.99998843
	Currency	No limitations
	AutoNumber	Not possible if table contains data
	Yes/No	Zero or Null = No; any other value = Yes
	Number (different precision)	Number must not be larger or smaller than can be contained in the new precision
Date/Time	Text	No limitations
	Memo	No limitations

(continued)

FIGURE 6-14 *continued*

Convert From	Convert To	Limitations
	Number	No limitations
	Currency	No limitations, but value might be rounded
	AutoNumber	Not possible if table contains data
	Yes/No	12:00:00 AM or Null = No; any other value = Yes
Currency	Text	No limitations
	Memo	No limitations
	Number	Number must not be larger or smaller than can be contained in the data type
	Date/Time	Number must be between −$657,434 and $2,958,465.99
	AutoNumber	Not possible if table contains data
	Yes/No	Zero or Null = No; any other value = Yes
AutoNumber, except ReplicationID	Text	No limitations
	Memo	No limitations
	Number	No limitations
	Date/Time	Value must be less than 2,958,466
	Currency	No limitations
	Yes/No	All values evaluate to Yes
Yes/No	Text	Yes = "Yes"; No = "No"
	Memo	Yes = "Yes"; No = "No"
	Number	No = 0; Yes = −1
	Date/Time	No = 12:00:00 AM; Yes = 12/29/1899
	Currency	No = 0; Yes = −$1
	AutoNumber	Not possible

Changing Data Length

For text and number fields, you can define the maximum length of the data that can be stored in the field. Although a text field can be up to 255 characters long, you can restrict the length to as little as 1 character. If you don't specify a length for text, Access normally assigns a default length of 50 characters. Access won't let you enter text field data longer than the defined length. If you need more space in a text field, you can increase the length at any time; but if you try to redefine the length of a text field so that it's shorter, you might get a warning message stating that Access will truncate a number of the data fields when you try to save your change.

 TIP   You can change the default data type for a new field and the default length of new text and number fields by choosing Options from the Tools menu and then clicking on the Tables/Queries tab of the Options dialog box.

Sizes for numeric data types can vary from a single byte (which can contain a value from 0 through 255) to 2 or 4 bytes (for larger integers), 8 bytes (necessary to hold very large floating-point or currency numbers), or 16 bytes (to hold a unique ReplicationID). Except for ReplicationID, you can change the size of a numeric data type at any time, but you might generate errors if you make the size smaller. Access also rounds and truncates numbers when converting from floating-point data types (Single or Double) to Integer or Currency values.

Conversion Errors

When you try to save a changed table definition, Access always warns you if any changes to the data type or length will cause conversion errors. For example, if you change the Field Size property of a Number field from Integer to Byte, Access warns you if any of the records contain a number larger than 255. You'll see a dialog box similar to the one shown in Figure 6-15 warning you about fields that Access will set to a Null value if you proceed with your changes. Click the Yes button to proceed with the changes. You'll have to examine your data to correct any conversion errors.

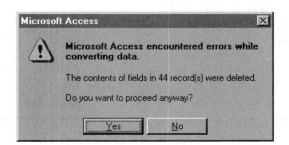

FIGURE 6-15
This dialog box informs you of conversion errors.

If you click the No button, Access opens the dialog box shown in Figure 6-16. If you deleted any fields or indexes, added any fields, or renamed any fields, Access will save those changes. Otherwise, the database will be unchanged. You can correct any data type or length changes you made, and then try to save the table definition again.

FIGURE 6-16
This dialog box appears when you decide not to save a changed table definition because of conversion errors.

Reversing Changes

If you make several changes and then decide you don't want any of them, you can close the Table window without saving it. When you do this, Access opens the dialog box shown in Figure 6-17 on the next page. Simply click the No button to abort all of your changes. Click the Cancel button to return to the Table window without saving or aborting your changes.

FIGURE 6-17

This dialog box
gives you the
option of aborting
unsaved changes
to a table.

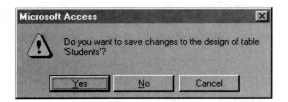

TIP You can always reverse the last change you
made by choosing the Undo command from the Edit
menu.

Using the Table Analyzer Wizard

Even if you follow all the recommendations in Chapter 4, "Designing
Your Database Application," and build a normalized database, you
might not arrive at the best design. In fact, you often cannot fully
evaluate a database design until you have begun to use the database
and store data. Microsoft Access for Windows 95 contains a new Table
Analyzer Wizard that can examine data in your tables (or data you import from another source) and recommend additional enhancements to
your database design.

You'll recall from Chapter 4 that one of the key elements of good
database design is the elimination of redundant data. The Table Analyzer Wizard is particularly good at scanning data in your existing
tables, identifying repeating data in one or more columns, and recom-
mending alterations to your design that break out the redundant data
into separate "lookup" tables. You can find an example of such redundant data in the College Counseling database. The initial design of the
Colleges table included a text field to describe the competitiveness
rating (reflecting the relative difficulty of gaining admission) for each
college in the database. The database uses six different values: Non-
competitive, Less Competitive, Competitive, Very Competitive, Highly

Competitive, or Most Competitive. (These are the descriptive phrases that the colleges themselves use.) Storing the competitiveness rating as a text string in each College row requires up to 18 characters of information. If you move these rating descriptions to another table, you can use a linking field that requires only 1 character per college.

You can see how the Table Analyzer Wizard works by using it on the Colleges4TableAnalyzer table in the College Counseling database. First, hold down the Shift key as you open the College Counseling database—this keeps Access from loading the application. (You'll learn more about startup properties in Chapter 23, "The Finishing Touches.") If you open the database in the normal way, you can return to the Database window by clicking the Exit button on the main switchboard form.

In the Database window, choose Analyze from the Tools menu and then choose Table from the submenu. Access starts the Table Analyzer Wizard and displays the first window, as shown in Figure 6-18.

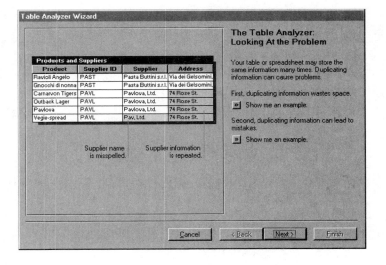

FIGURE 6-18

The opening window of the Table Analyzer Wizard.

This first window is one of two introductory windows that explain what the wizard can do. You can click the "Show me" buttons to get a better understanding of the kinds of problems the wizard solves and to see how the wizard works. Click Next twice to get to the first "action" window in the wizard, shown in Figure 6-19.

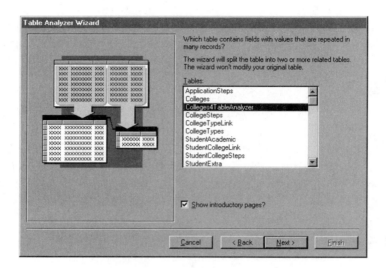

In this window, you select the table you want to analyze. For this exercise, select the Colleges4TableAnalyzer table. Note that you have an option in this window to continue to show the two introductory windows each time you start the wizard. If you think you understand how the wizard works, you can deselect the check box to skip the introductory windows the next time you start the wizard. Click Next to go on to the next step.

In the next window, the wizard asks if you want to decide how to rearrange the fields in the target table or if you want the wizard to decide for you. If you know which field contains redundant data, you can make the decision yourself. Because the wizard handles all the "grunt work" of splitting out lookup data, you might choose the latter option in the future to further normalize tables in your application. For now, select the "let the wizard decide" option to see how it does. Click Next to start the analysis of your table. Figure 6-20 shows the results of the wizard's analysis.

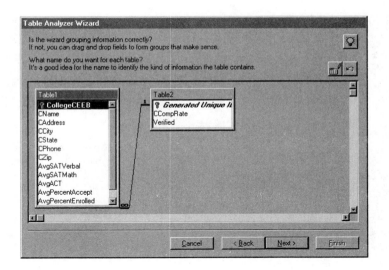

FIGURE 6-20

The initial recommendation of the Table Analyzer Wizard.

In this case, the wizard splits out the CCompRate and Verified fields into a separate lookup table. It does this because it sees that every row with a Competitiveness Rating also has its Verified flag set. (I used the Verified field to indicate colleges that responded to a questionnaire that I mailed out.) You can move the Verified field back to the main table by dragging and dropping it from Table2 to Table1.

If you like the way the wizard split your table, the next step is to give each of the new tables a new name. To rename a table, first click on the table name, and then click the Rename Table button in the upper part of the window. You can also double-click on the table's title bar; the wizard opens a dialog box in which you can enter a new name. Figure 6-21 on the next page shows a new name, CollegeFixed, assigned to Table1; Table2 is selected and ready to be assigned a new name. Type in *CompRating* as the name of Table2. After you name your tables, click Next to go on to the next step.

The next window asks you to verify the primary key fields for these tables. You can select new fields for the primary key of each table or add fields to the primary key. Click Next to accept the settings and go on to an analysis of duplicate values in the lookup tables.

FIGURE 6-21
Renaming the
new tables.

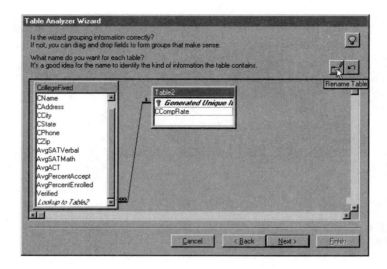

The Table Analyzer Wizard looks at values in any new lookup tables to try to eliminate any possible duplicates created by typing errors. Figure 6-22 shows the result of this analysis on the sample table. Because the wizard sees the word *Competitive* in multiple rows, it suggests that some of these values might, in fact, be the same. You can use this window to tell the wizard any correct values for actual mistyped duplicates. The wizard will store only unique values in the final code table. Click Next when you are done to go on to the next window.

FIGURE 6-22
Looking at
potentially
duplicate lookup
values.

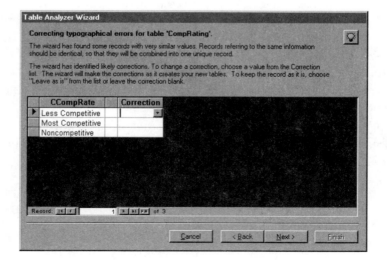

Finally, the wizard offers to create a new query that has the same name as the original table. (See Figure 6-23.) If you've already been using the old table in queries, forms, and reports, creating a new query that integrates the new tables into the original data structure means you won't have to change any other objects in your database. In most cases, the new query will look and operate just like the original table. Old queries, forms, and reports based on the original table will now use the new query and won't know the difference.

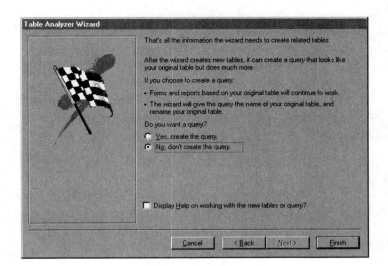

FIGURE 6-23

The final window of the Table Analyzer Wizard.

Click Finish to build your new tables. The wizard also creates relationships among the new tables to make sure you can easily re-create the original data structure in queries. Figure 6-24 on the next page shows the new CollegeFixed table and its related CompRating lookup table built by the wizard. As you'll see in the next section, the final design for the Colleges table uses a special feature of table design to automatically pull in this lookup data whenever you use the Colleges table.

FIGURE 6-24

The tables
produced by the
Table Analyzer
Wizard.

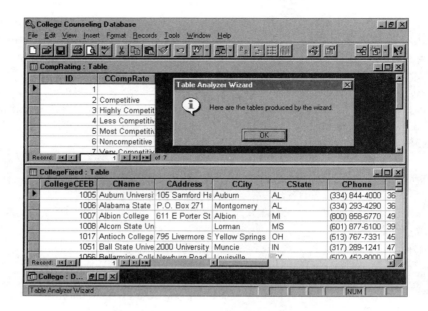

Taking Advantage
of Lookup Properties

In the previous section, you learned how to use the Table Analyzer
Wizard to break out redundant data into more efficient lookup tables.
The end result stores a space-efficient code in the original table. However, when you look at the main data, you probably want to see the
original meaning of the code, not the code number. You can take advantage of Lookup properties on code fields to make this happen automatically.

To see how this works, open the Colleges table in the College
Counseling database in Design view. Click on the Data Type column
for the CCompID field, click the down arrow, and then select Lookup
Wizard from the drop-down list, as shown in Figure 6-25.

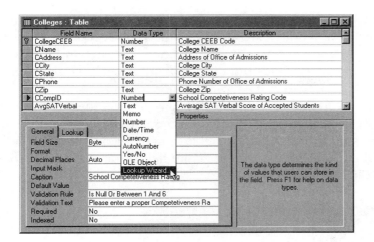

FIGURE 6-25
Starting the
Lookup Wizard
for the competi-
tiveness code
field.

The purpose of the Lookup Wizard is to help you set the Lookup properties of any code field in a table so that you see meaningful values from the lookup table whenever you use the main table—either in Datasheet view, in a query, or in a form or a report. Once you get the hang of it, you can set the lookup values yourself. It's helpful to use the wizard the first few times to become familiar with how this works.

In the first window, shown in Figure 6-26, the wizard asks if you want to type in a list of values or if you want to look up the values in another table or query. In this example, you know that the competitiveness descriptions are in another table, so select that option. Click Next to go on to the next step.

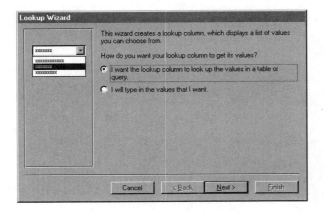

FIGURE 6-26
The first window
of the Lookup
Wizard.

In the next window, select the table named zCompeteList—this is where the lookup values are stored in the College Counseling database. Choose Next to go on. The next window, shown in Figure 6-27, asks you to select the fields from the lookup table that you want to include for the code field in the current table. You must always select the code value. In addition, you can select one or more descriptive fields that will be displayed when you view the code field in the original table. In this case, you need both fields from the zCompeteList table, so click the double right arrow to move the fields from the left list to the right list. Click Next to go on.

FIGURE 6-27
Selecting fields from the lookup table.

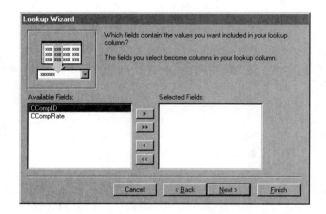

After you select the fields, the wizard shows you how it might display them. (See Figure 6-28.) You can alter the width of the display column by clicking on the right edge of the column heading and dragging it. Since you don't really need to see the code values, the wizard automatically hides them. Click Next to go on.

FIGURE 6-28
Adjusting the width of the display columns.

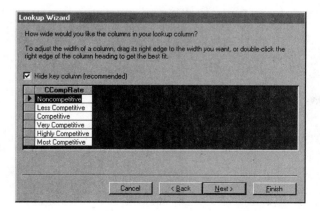

In the final window, the wizard asks you to name the code field in the original table. Unless you have a particular reason to rename the original field, it's probably a good idea to use the same name so that any queries you have defined on this table continue to work.

Figure 6-29 shows the Lookup properties set by the wizard after you click Finish in the final window. The wizard chooses a special type of display control called a combo box to let you see the original code value for the field or to let you select a new one from a drop-down list. The wizard also creates a query to pull in the descriptive values from the lookup table automatically. When you study combo box controls later in Chapter 13, "Building Forms," you'll see how you can also use Lookup properties to display lists from related tables in a form.

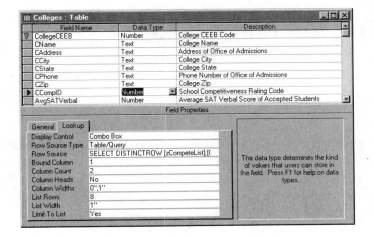

FIGURE 6-29
The resulting Lookup properties.

Save the table design and switch to Datasheet view to see the result, as shown in Figure 6-30 on the next page. You might need to scroll to the right in the datasheet to see the new School Competitiveness Rating column. Instead of a code number, you can now see the matching descriptive value from the lookup table. You can open the drop-down list and select a new value to set the code in the table.

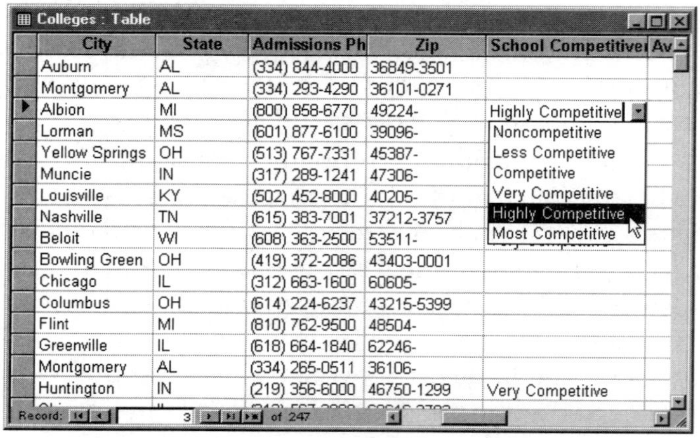

FIGURE 6-30

The lookup
column in
Datasheet view.

City	State	Admissions Ph	Zip	School Competitive	Av
Auburn	AL	(334) 844-4000	36849-3501		
Montgomery	AL	(334) 293-4290	36101-0271		
Albion	MI	(800) 858-6770	49224-	Highly Competitive	
Lorman	MS	(601) 877-6100	39096-	Noncompetitive	
Yellow Springs	OH	(513) 767-7331	45387-	Less Competitive	
Muncie	IN	(317) 289-1241	47306-	Competitive	
Louisville	KY	(502) 452-8000	40205-	Very Competitive	
Nashville	TN	(615) 383-7001	37212-3757	Highly Competitive	
Beloit	WI	(608) 363-2500	53511-	Most Competitive	
Bowling Green	OH	(419) 372-2086	43403-0001		
Chicago	IL	(312) 663-1600	60605-		
Columbus	OH	(614) 224-6237	43215-5399		
Flint	MI	(810) 762-9500	48504-		
Greenville	IL	(618) 664-1840	62246-		
Montgomery	AL	(334) 265-0511	36106-		
Huntington	IN	(219) 356-6000	46750-1299	Very Competitive	

Record: 3 of 247

Changing the Primary Key

Chapter 4, "Designing Your Database Application," discussed the need to have one or more fields that provide a unique value to every row in your table. This field with unique values is identified as the *primary key*. If a table doesn't have a primary key, you can't define a relationship between it and other tables, and Microsoft Access has to guess how to link tables for you. Even if you define a primary key in your initial design, you might discover later that it doesn't actually contain unique values. In that case, you might have to define a new field or fields to be the primary key.

Using the Students and Colleges database as an example, suppose you discover after designing the Students table that StudentID is unique only within the graduation year. To solve this problem, you must remove the StudentID field as the only field in the primary key and redefine the key to include the GradYear field. First, you must remove the primary key definition on StudentID—but don't remove the field. To remove the existing primary key, open the table in Design view and then open the Indexes window by choosing Indexes from the View menu or by clicking the Indexes button on the toolbar. Click on the primary key row, as shown in Figure 6-31, and then press the Del key to remove the index. Access won't let you delete the index if the table has relationships defined with other tables. First, use the Relationships window to remove the table's relationships, and then use the Indexes window to remove the index.

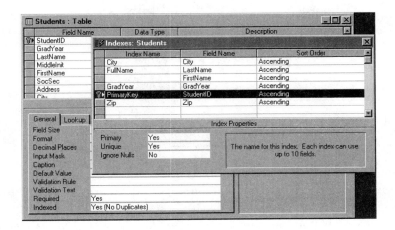

FIGURE 6-31

Click on the primary key row and then press the Del key to remove the primary key designation in the Indexes window.

Next, highlight both the StudentID and GradYear fields in the Table window and click the Primary Key button on the toolbar to make both fields the primary key. When you save the table, Access creates a new index that includes both fields as the primary key.

Compacting Your Database

As you delete old database objects and add new ones, the space within your mdb file can become fragmented. The result is that, over time, your database file can grow larger than it needs to be to store all your definitions and data.

To remove unused space, you should compact your database periodically. No database can be open when you run the compact utility. Also, no other users should be accessing the database you intend to compact. To execute the compact utility, choose Database Utilities from the Tools menu in the Access window after all databases have been closed, and then choose the Compact Database command from the submenu. Access opens the dialog box shown in Figure 6-32 on the next page.

FIGURE 6-32

The dialog box
for specifying
a database
to compact.

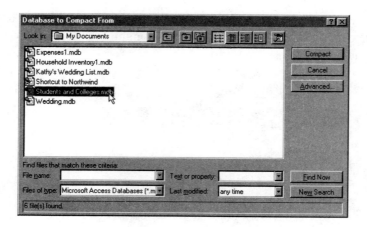

Select the database you want to compact, and then click Compact. Access asks you for a name for the compacted database. You can enter the same name as the database you are compacting, or you can use a different name. If you use the same name, Access warns you that the original database of the same name will be deleted. If you decide to proceed, Access compacts your database into a temporary file. When compaction is successfully completed, Access deletes your old database and automatically gives its name to the new compacted copy.

You now have all the information you need to modify and maintain your database table definitions. In the next chapter, you'll explore working with the data in your tables.

PART 3

SELECT EDITION

Working with Data

Chapter 7

Using Datasheets

The simplest way to look at your data is to open a table in Datasheet view. When you build your application, you'll probably work with your data mostly through forms that you design. Studying datasheets is useful, however, because it improves your understanding of basic concepts such as viewing, updating, inserting, and deleting data. Microsoft Access performs these functions in the same way regardless of whether you're using a datasheet or a specially designed form to work with your data. On some forms, you might decide to embed a Datasheet view to make it easy to look at several rows and columns of data at once. Even after you've built an application to work with your data, you'll find that Datasheet view is often useful for verifying data at the basic table level.

Throughout this chapter, you'll look at examples of operations using the Colleges table in the College Counseling sample database included with this book. Take a moment now to make a copy of the Colleges table. Open the College Counseling database, and then click Exit on the main switchboard form to return to the Database window. The copying procedure is described in Chapter 6, "Modifying Your Database Design." Name your copy *CollegesBackup*.

Viewing Data

To look at data in one of your tables in Datasheet view, do the following:

1. Open your database. By default, Microsoft Access displays the list of tables in the database within the Database window. If you opened the College Counseling database without holding down the Shift key, click Exit on the main switchboard form to return to the Database window.

2. Double-click on the name of the table you want. If you prefer to use the keyboard, press the up or down arrow key to move to the table name you want, and then press Enter or Alt-O.

Figure 7-1 shows the Datasheet view of the Colleges table and identifies some key elements. (Note the change in the toolbar buttons when you view a table in Datasheet view.) Open this table now. If you like, you can make the datasheet fill the workspace by clicking the

Maximize button in the upper right corner of the window. Or you can press Alt-- (hyphen) to open the Control menu and then press *X* to choose the Maximize command.

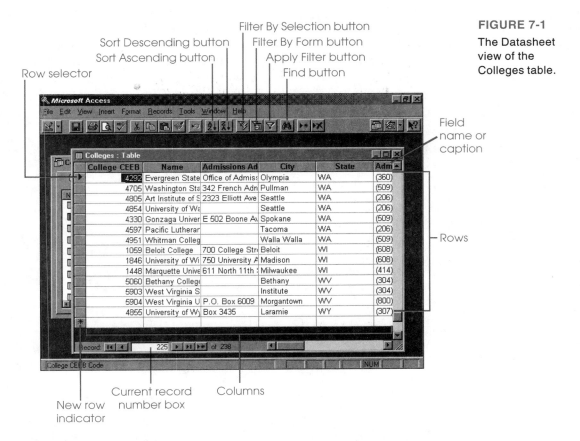

FIGURE 7-1

The Datasheet view of the Colleges table.

Moving Around

Changing the display to show different records or fields is simple. You can use the horizontal scroll bar, shown in Figure 7-2, to scroll through a table's fields, or you can use the vertical scroll bar to scroll through a table's records.

FIGURE 7-2

Use the horizontal scroll bar to change the display of fields.

In the lower left corner of the table in Datasheet view, you can see a record number box, as shown in Figure 7-3. The record number box shows the *relative record number* of the current record (meaning the number of the record in relation to the current recordset). Note that you might not see the current record in the window if you've scrolled the display. The number to the right of the record number box shows the total number of records available in the current recordset. If you've applied a filter against the table (see the section titled "Searching for and Filtering Data" later in this chapter), the number might be less than the total number of records in the table.

FIGURE 7-3

The record number box.

You can use the record number box to quickly move to the record you want. As you'll read about a bit later, you'll usually select some data in a record in order to change it. You can also choose the Go To command from the Edit menu to move to the first, last, next, or previous record, or to a new record. You can also make any record current by clicking anywhere in its row; the number in the record number box will change to indicate the new row you've selected.

Keyboard Shortcuts

You might find it easier to use the keyboard rather than the mouse to move around in a datasheet, especially if you're typing in new data. Figure 7-4 lists the keyboard shortcuts for scrolling in a datasheet. Figure 7-5 lists the keyboard shortcuts for selecting data in a datasheet.

Keys	Scrolling Action
PgUp	Up one page
PgDn	Down one page
Ctrl-PgUp	Left one page
Ctrl-PgDn	Right one page

FIGURE 7-4

The keyboard shortcuts for scrolling in a datasheet.

Keys	Selecting Action
Tab	Next field
Shift-Tab	Previous field
Home	First field, current record
End	Last field, current record
Up arrow	Current field, previous record
Down arrow	Current field, next record
Ctrl-up arrow	Current field, first record
Ctrl-down arrow	Current field, last record
Ctrl-Home	First field, first record
Ctrl-End	Last field, last record
F5	Record number box

FIGURE 7-5
The keyboard shortcuts for selecting data in a datasheet.

Modifying the Datasheet Format

You can make a number of changes to the appearance of a datasheet. You can change the height of rows or the width of columns, rearrange or hide columns, set the display or printing font, and decide whether you want to see gridlines. You can make most of these changes from the Format menu, as shown in Figure 7-6.

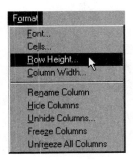

FIGURE 7-6
The Format menu of a Table window in Datasheet view.

Changing Row Height and Column Width

Microsoft Access initially displays all the columns and rows using a default width and height. The standard width is probably wider than it needs to be for columns that contain a small amount of data, but it's not wide enough for columns with a large amount of data. For example, the State column in the Colleges table is wider than it needs to be to display the state abbreviations in the field. The Name and Admissions Address columns, however, are not wide enough to display the data contained in them.

One way to adjust the column width is to select any value in the column that you want to change and then choose the Column Width command from the Format menu. In the Column Width dialog box, shown in Figure 7-7, you can type in a new width value (in number of characters). The "standard" width is approximately 1 inch when printed. (It can vary depending on the current font selection.) If you click the Best Fit button, Access sets the column width to accommodate the longest currently displayed data value in this column. In other words, Access adjusts the column width to show the widest data in the current display window. It does not search all available data. (You probably wouldn't want it to do this, anyway, on a table with thousands of rows!)

FIGURE 7-7

The Column Width dialog box.

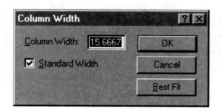

You can also modify the column widths directly on the datasheet by placing the mouse pointer on the line between two column names at the top of the Table window. (See Figure 7-8.) When you do this, the mouse pointer becomes a vertical bar with arrows pointing to the left and right. By dragging the column boundary, you can adjust the size of the column.

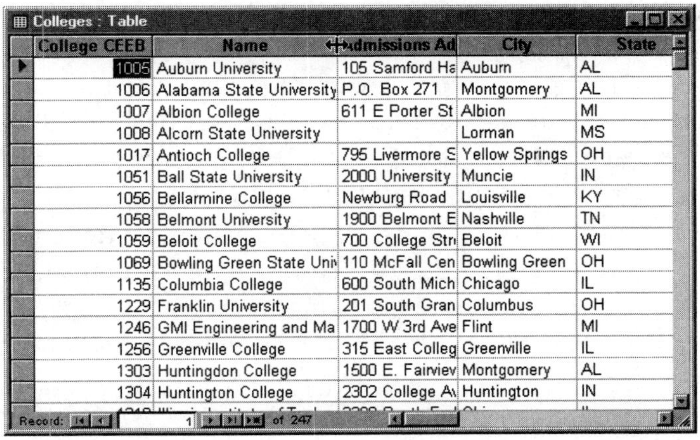

FIGURE 7-8
Using the mouse
to adjust the
column width.

If you plan to print your datasheet, you might want to increase the height of the rows to create some space between records on the report. Choose the Row Height command from the Format menu to open the Row Height dialog box, shown in Figure 7-9. The row height is measured in points—units of approximately $1/72$ inch ($1/28$ centimeter). To allow space between rows, Access calculates a standard height that is approximately 30 percent taller than the current font's point size. You can enter a new height in the Row Height text box. If you specify a number that is shorter than the font size, your rows will overlap when you print the datasheet. You can also change the row height by dragging the row boundary between two row selectors, in the same way that you changed the column width using the mouse. (See Figure 7-8.)

FIGURE 7-9
The Row Height
dialog box.

Arranging Columns

The default order of fields from left to right in Datasheet view is the order in which the fields were defined in the table. You can easily change the column order for viewing or printing. Select the column you want by clicking the field selector (the field name bar at the top of the column). Access highlights the entire column. You can select multiple columns by dragging across several columns in either direction before you release the mouse button. You can also click a field selector and extend the selection by holding down the Shift key while pressing the left or right arrow key to expand the highlighted area.

To move the selected columns, drag the columns' field selectors to the new location. (See Figure 7-10.) To move the columns using the keyboard, press Ctrl-F8 to turn on Move mode. Access displays *MOV* in one of the areas on the status bar. Shift the columns to the left or right using the arrow keys. Press Esc to turn off Move mode.

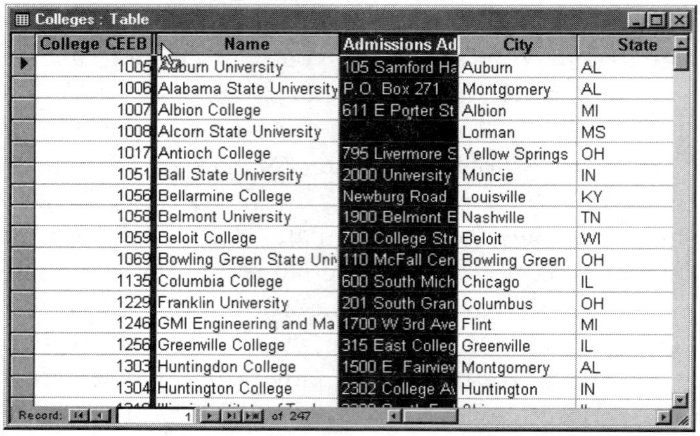

Colleges : Table

College CEEB	Name	Admissions Ad	City	State
1005	Auburn University	105 Samford Ha	Auburn	AL
1006	Alabama State University	P.O. Box 271	Montgomery	AL
1007	Albion College	611 E Porter St	Albion	MI
1008	Alcorn State University		Lorman	MS
1017	Antioch College	795 Livermore S	Yellow Springs	OH
1051	Ball State University	2000 University	Muncie	IN
1056	Bellarmine College	Newburg Road	Louisville	KY
1058	Belmont University	1900 Belmont E	Nashville	TN
1059	Beloit College	700 College Str	Beloit	WI
1069	Bowling Green State Uni	110 McFall Cen	Bowling Green	OH
1135	Columbia College	600 South Mich	Chicago	IL
1229	Franklin University	201 South Gran	Columbus	OH
1246	GMI Engineering and Ma	1700 W 3rd Ave	Flint	MI
1256	Greenville College	315 East Colleg	Greenville	IL
1303	Huntingdon College	1500 E. Fairview	Montgomery	AL
1304	Huntington College	2302 College Av	Huntington	IN

Record: 1 of 247

FIGURE 7-10
You can move a column by first selecting it and then dragging the field selector.

Hiding and Showing Columns

By default, Access displays all of the table's columns in Datasheet view, although you might have to scroll to see some of them. If you're not interested in looking at or printing all these fields, you can hide some of them. One way to hide a column is to drag the right column boundary to the left (from within the field selector) until the column disappears. You can also select one or more columns and choose the Hide Columns command from the Format menu.

To reveal hidden columns or to hide additional ones, choose the Unhide Columns command from the Format menu to open the Unhide Columns dialog box, as shown in Figure 7-11. Select the check box next to a column name to unhide the column. The checked columns are already showing. Click Close to close the dialog box.

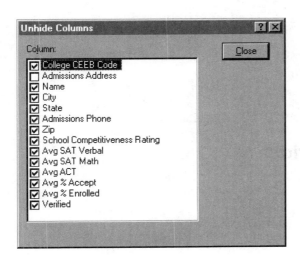

FIGURE 7-11

The Unhide Columns dialog box.

Freezing Columns

Sometimes you might want to keep one column on the screen while scrolling left or right through the other columns. For example, you might want to keep the Name column on the screen as you scroll to the right to see the Admissions Phone column. You can freeze one or more contiguous columns by selecting them and then choosing the Freeze Columns command from the Format menu. (If you want to freeze multiple, noncontiguous columns, you need to select and then freeze each column in turn.) Access moves the selected columns to the far left and freezes them there. These fields do not scroll off the left of the window when you scroll right. To release frozen columns, choose the Unfreeze All Columns command from the Format menu. Figure 7-12 on the next page shows the Name column frozen to the left with the rest of the display scrolled right to show the state, phone number, zip code, and competitiveness rating columns.

FIGURE 7-12

A datasheet with
a frozen column
(Name).

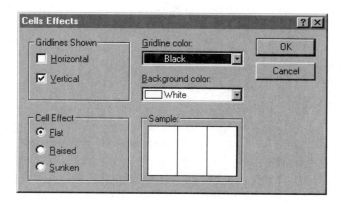

Name	State	Admissions Ph	Zip	School Con
Auburn University	AL	(334) 844-4000	36849-3501	
Alabama State University	AL	(334) 293-4290	36101-0271	
Albion College	MI	(800) 858-6770	49224-	Highly Comp
Alcorn State University	MS	(601) 877-6100	39096-	
Antioch College	OH	(513) 767-7331	45387-	
Ball State University	IN	(317) 289-1241	47306-	
Bellarmine College	KY	(502) 452-8000	40205-	
Belmont University	TN	(615) 383-7001	37212-3757	
Beloit College	WI	(608) 363-2500	53511-	Very Compet
Bowling Green State Uni	OH	(419) 372-2086	43403-0001	
Columbia College	IL	(312) 663-1600	60605-	
Franklin University	OH	(614) 224-6237	43215-5399	
GMI Engineering and Ma	MI	(810) 762-9500	48504-	
Greenville College	IL	(618) 664-1840	62246-	
Huntingdon College	AL	(334) 265-0511	36106-	
Huntington College	IN	(219) 356-6000	46750-1299	Very Compet

Record: |◄| |◄| 1 |►| |►►| |►*| of 247

Removing Gridlines

Datasheet view normally displays gridlines between the columns and
rows. Access also includes these gridlines if you print the datasheet.
You can customize the look of the cells in your datasheet by choosing
Cells from the Format menu. In the Cells Effects dialog box, shown in
Figure 7-13, you can select options to display horizontal or vertical
gridlines and select the color of the gridlines and the background color
of the cells. You can also select a special sunken or raised effect.

FIGURE 7-13

Setting the look of
datasheet cells in
the Cells Effects
dialog box.

Figure 7-14 shows the datasheet from Figure 7-12 without the
gridlines. Notice that a line is present to indicate that the Name column
is frozen. Access includes this line if you print a report with frozen columns, even if you have turned off vertical gridlines.

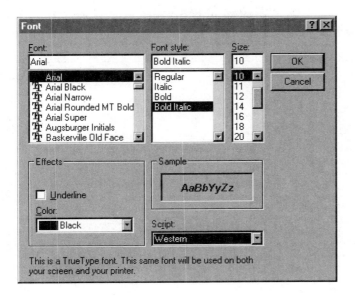

FIGURE 7-14
A datasheet
without gridlines.
The line to the
right of the Name
column indicates
that this column
is frozen.

TIP To print a datasheet without the frozen column line, choose the Unfreeze All Columns command from the Format menu before printing the datasheet.

Selecting Fonts

The last thing you can do to customize the look of a datasheet is to select a different font. Choose the Font command from the Format menu to see the dialog box shown in Figure 7-15.

FIGURE 7-15
The Font
dialog box.

195

In the Font list box at the upper left of the dialog box, you can see all the fonts that are installed in your Windows 95 operating system. You can scroll down the list box and select the font name you want. The icon to the left of the font name indicates whether the font is a printer font (printer icon) or a TrueType font (TT icon) that you can use for both screen display and printing. If there is no icon to the left of the font name, the font is a screen font.

If you select a printer font, Access uses the closest matching screen or TrueType font to display the datasheet on your screen. If you select a screen font, Access uses the closest matching printer or TrueType font when you print. In either case, your printed result might look different from the image on your screen.

When you select a font, Access shows you a sample of the font in the Sample box. Depending on the font you select, you might also see a wide range of font styles (such as italic or bold) and font sizes. Select the Underline check box if you want all the characters underlined. You can also select a specific color for the font characters on your screen. Click OK to set the new font for the entire datasheet. Click Cancel to dismiss the dialog box without changing the font.

You can also reset the default font for all datasheets. To do this, choose the Options command from the Tools menu. On the Datasheet tab of the Options dialog box (see Figure 7-16), you can set the font name, size, and weight (light, normal, or bold) and select italics and underline. You'll also find options here to set colors, horizontal and vertical gridlines, default column width, and special effects, and an option to display the animations that accompany certain actions in Access.

CAUTION If you share your databases over a network, the changes you make in the Options dialog box might affect every user in your workgroup. If you don't have to enter a user ID when you start Access and you think you might be sharing your Access installation with other users, check with your system administrator before making any changes in the Options dialog box.

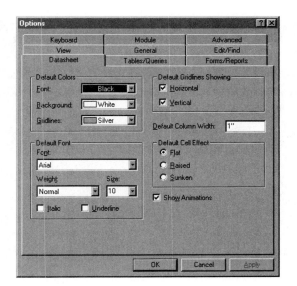

FIGURE 7-16
Setting new
default options for
all datasheets.

Saving Datasheet Formatting

After you have the datasheet formatted the way you want it, you don't have to lose your work when you close the table. Choose the Save Layout command from the File menu to save the format. Access also asks whether you want to save formatting changes when you try to close a table.

Changing Data

Not only can you view and format data in a datasheet, you can also insert new records, change data, and delete records.

Record Indicators

You might have noticed as you moved around in the datasheet that occasionally icons appeared on the row selector at the far left of each row. (See Figure 7-1.) These *record indicators* and their meanings are listed below.

 Indicates that this is the current row.

 Indicates that you are making or have made a change to one or more entries in this row. Microsoft Access saves the changes when you move to another row. Before moving to a new row, you can press Esc once to undo the change to the current value or press Esc twice to undo all changes in the row. If you're updating a database that is shared on a network with other users, Access locks this record when you save the change so that no one else can update it until you're finished. (See the last indicator below.)

⊞   Indicates the blank row at the end of the table that you can use to create a new record.

⊘   Indicates that another user might be changing this record. You'll see this icon only when you're accessing a database that is shared by other users on a network. You should wait until this indicator disappears before attempting to make changes to the record.

Adding a New Record

As you build your application, you might find it useful to place some data in your tables so you can test the forms and reports that you design. You might also find it convenient sometimes to add data directly to your tables by using Datasheet view rather than by opening a form. If your table is empty, Access shows a single blank row when you open Datasheet view. If you have data in your table, Access shows a blank row beneath the last record. You can jump to the blank row to begin adding a new record either by choosing the Go To command from the Edit menu and then choosing New from the submenu, by clicking the New Record button on the toolbar, or by pressing Ctrl-+. Access places the cursor in the first column when you start a new record. As soon as you begin typing, Access changes the record indicator to a pencil icon to show that updates are in progress. You can press Tab to move to the next column.

If the data you enter in a column violates a field validation rule, Access notifies you as soon as you attempt to leave the column. You must provide a correct value before you can move to another column. Press Esc, choose Undo Typing from the Edit menu, or click the Undo button on the toolbar to remove your changes in the current field.

Press Shift-Enter at any place in the record or press Tab in the last column in the record to commit your new record to the database. You can also choose the Save Record command from the Records menu. If the changes in your record violate the validation rule for the table, Access warns you when you try to save the record. You must correct the problem before you can save your changes. If you want to cancel adding the record, press Esc twice or click the Undo button on the toolbar until it turns gray. If you want to use the Edit menu to undo the current record, you must first choose Undo Typing from the Edit menu if you are in a field that contains changes; Access then changes the available Edit menu item to Undo Current Field/Record so that you can undo all changes.

Access provides several keyboard shortcuts to assist you as you enter new data, as shown in Figure 7-17.

Keys	Data Action
Ctrl-; (semicolon)	Enters the current date
Ctrl-: (colon)	Enters the current time
Ctrl-Alt-Spacebar	Enters the default value for the field
Ctrl-' (single quotation mark) or Ctrl-" (double quotation mark)	Enters the value from the same field in the previous record
Ctrl-Enter	Inserts a carriage return in a memo or text field
Ctrl-+ (plus sign)	Adds a new record
Ctrl-- (minus sign)	Deletes the current record

FIGURE 7-17

The keyboard shortcuts for entering data in a datasheet.

Selecting and Changing Data

When you have data in your table, you can easily change the data by editing it in Datasheet view. You must select data before you can change it, and you can do this in several ways:

- Click in the cell containing the data you want to change, just to the left of the first character you want to change, and then drag the highlight to include all the characters you want to change.

- Double-click on any word in a cell to select the entire word.

- Click at the left edge of a cell in the grid (that is, where the mouse pointer turns into a large white cross). Access selects the entire contents of the cell.

Any data you type replaces the old, selected data. In Figure 7-18, the address value for Alabama State University in the Colleges table is selected. In Figure 7-19, that value is changed before the record is saved. Access also selects the entire entry if you tab to the cell in the datasheet grid. If you want to change only part of the data (for example, to correct the spelling of a street name), you can shift to single-character mode by pressing F2 or by clicking the location at which you want to start your change. Use the Backspace key to erase characters to the left of the cursor and use the Del key to remove characters to the right of the cursor. Hold down the Shift key and press the right or left arrow key to select multiple characters to replace. You can press F2 again to select the entire cell. A useful keyboard shortcut for changing data is to press Ctrl-Alt-Spacebar to restore the data to the default value you specified in the table definition.

FIGURE 7-18
The old data is selected.

	1005	Auburn University	105 Samford Hall	Auburn
	1006	Alabama State University	P.O. Box 271	Montgomery
	1007	Albion College	611 E Porter St	Albion
	1008	Alcorn State University		Lorman

FIGURE 7-19
The new data is typed in, replacing the old.

	1005	Auburn University	105 Samford Hall	Auburn
	1006	Alabama State University	Greely Hall	Montgomery
	1007	Albion College	611 E Porter St	Albion
	1008	Alcorn State University		Lorman

You can set two options to control how the arrow keys and the Enter key work as you move from cell to cell. Choose the Options command from the View menu, and click on the Keyboard tab of the Options dialog box, as shown in Figure 7-20. To control what happens in a cell by using the right or left arrow key, in the Arrow Key Behavior section select Next Field (selection moves to the next field in the record) or Next Character (cursor moves over one character). I prefer the Next Character option because it allows me to always use the arrow keys to move one character at a time while reserving the Tab key for moving a field at a time.

In the Move After Enter section, you can select Next Field so that pressing the Enter key completes the update of the current field in the record and tabs to the next field. If you select Next Record, pressing Enter moves you to the next row on the datasheet. If you select Don't Move, pressing Enter selects the current cell.

You can select the Cursor Stops At First/Last Field check box to prevent the arrow keys from causing you to leave the current record. If you leave this option unchecked, you'll move to the first field in the next row when you press the right arrow key while you're at the last character in the row, and you'll move to the last field in the previous row when you press the left arrow key while you're at the first character in the row.

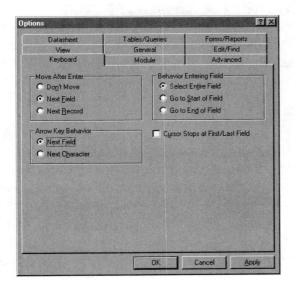

FIGURE 7-20
The Keyboard tab of the Options dialog box.

Replacing Data

What if you need to make the same change in more than one record? Access provides a way to do this quickly and easily. Select any cell in the column whose values you want to change (select the cell in the first row if you want to start at the beginning of the table), and then choose the Replace command from the Edit menu or press Ctrl-H to see the dialog box shown in Figure 7-21 on the next page. For example, to fix the misspelled *Seatle* in the City field in the Colleges table, select the City field in the first row, choose the Replace command, type *Seatle* in the Find What text box, and then type *Seattle* in the Replace With text box, as shown in Figure 7-21. Click the Find Next button to search for the next occurrence of the text in the Find What text box. Click the

Replace button to change data selectively, or click the Replace All button to change all the entries that match the Find What text. Notice that you have the option to search all fields or only the current field, to exactly match the case for text searches (because searches in Access are normally case-insensitive), and to select an entry only if the Find What text matches the entire entry in the field.

FIGURE 7-21
The Replace
dialog box.

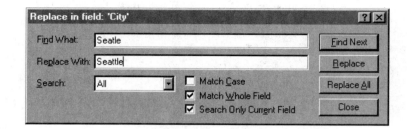

Copying and Pasting Data

You can copy or cut any selected data to the Windows Clipboard and paste this data into another field or record. To copy data, tab to the cell or click at the left edge of the cell in the datasheet grid to select the data within it. Choose the Copy command from the Edit menu or press Ctrl-C. You can also choose the Cut command from the Edit menu or press Ctrl-X to delete (cut) the data you have selected. To paste the data in another location, select the data you want to replace in that location and choose the Paste command from the Edit menu or press Ctrl-V. If the new location is blank, move the cursor to the new location before choosing the Paste command.

To select an entire record to be copied or cut, click the row selector at the far left of the row. If you happen to click the wrong row selector, you can use the up and down arrow keys to move the selection highlight. You can drag through the row selectors or press Shift-up arrow or Shift-down arrow to extend the selection to multiple rows. Choose the Copy command from the Edit menu or press Ctrl-C to copy the contents of multiple rows to the Clipboard. You can open another table and paste the copied rows into the table, or you can use the Paste Append command on the Edit menu to paste the rows at the end of the same table. You can paste copies of records into the same table only if the table has no primary key or if the primary key has the AutoNumber data type. When the primary key is AutoNumber, Access automatically generates new primary key values for you.

Be aware that cutting rows from a table is the same as deleting them. (See the next section.) However, the Cut command is handy for moving data that you don't want in an active table to a backup table. You can have the other table open in Datasheet view at the same time. Simply switch to that window and paste the cut rows using the Paste Append command.

Whenever you paste rows in a table, Access asks you to confirm the paste operation. (See Figure 7-22.) Click Yes to proceed, or click No if you decide to abort the operation.

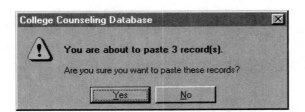

FIGURE 7-22

The dialog box that asks if you want to proceed with a paste operation.

NOTE You can't change the physical sequence of rows in a relational database by cutting rows from one location and pasting them in another location. Access always pastes new rows at the end of the current display. If you close the datasheet after pasting in new rows and then open it again, Access displays the rows in sequence by the primary key you defined. If you want to see rows in some other sequence, see the section titled "Sorting and Searching for Data" later in this chapter.

Deleting Rows

To delete one or more rows, select the rows using the row selectors and then press the Del key. For details on selecting multiple rows, see the previous discussion on copying and pasting data. You can also use Ctrl-- (minus sign) to delete only the current row. When you delete rows, Access gives you a chance to change your mind if you made a mistake. (See Figure 7-23 on the next page.) Click Yes in the dialog box to delete the rows, or click No to abort the deletion.

FIGURE 7-23
The dialog box
that appears
when you delete
a row.

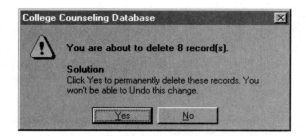

  CAUTION After you click Yes in the confirmation dialog box, you cannot restore the deleted rows. You have to reenter them or copy them from a backup.

Sorting and Searching for Data

When you open a table in Datasheet view, Microsoft Access shows you all the rows sorted in sequence by the primary key you defined for the table. If you didn't define a primary key, you'll see the rows in the sequence in which you entered them in the table. If you want to see the rows in a different sequence or search for specific data, Access provides you with tools to do that.

Sorting Data

Access provides several ways to sort data in Datasheet view. As you might have noticed, two handy toolbar buttons allow you to quickly sort the rows in the table in ascending or descending order, based on the values in a single column. To see how this works, open the Colleges table, click anywhere in the State column, and click the Sort Ascending button on the toolbar. Access sorts the display to show you the rows ordered alphabetically by State, as shown in Figure 7-24.

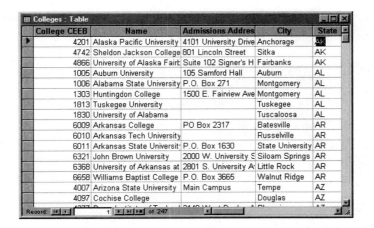

FIGURE 7-24

Sorting colleges
by State.

You can click the Sort Descending button to sort the rows in descending order. It might be useful, for example, to sort student rows by descending grade point average (the JuniorGPA or SeniorGPA fields). You'll see the best students at the top of the list.

If you want to sort more than one field, you must use the filtering and sorting feature. Let's assume you want to sort by State, then by City within State, and then by Name. Here's what you should do:

1. Choose Filter from the Records menu, and then choose Advanced Filter/Sort from the submenu. You'll see the Advanced Filter/Sort window, shown in Figure 7-25 on the next page, with a list of fields in the Colleges table shown in the top part of the window.

2. Access normally places the cursor in the cell in the first row of the first column of the Field row in the lower part of the window. If you don't see the cursor there, click in that cell.

3. Open the field list by clicking the down arrow or by pressing Alt-down arrow on the keyboard. Select the CState field in the list. You can also place the CState field in this first column by finding CState in the list of fields in the Colleges field list in the top part of the window and dragging and dropping it onto the Field row in the first column of the design grid.

4. Click in the Sort row, immediately below the CState field, and select Ascending from the drop-down list.

205

5. Add the CCity and CName fields to the next two columns, and select Ascending in the Sort row for both.

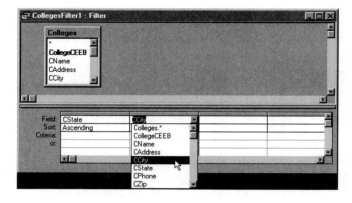

6. Click the Apply Filter toolbar button or choose Apply Filter/Sort from the Filter menu to see the result shown in Figure 7-26.

Searching for and Filtering Data

If you want to look for data anywhere in your table, Access provides several powerful searching and filtering capabilities.

Using Find

To perform a simple search on a single field, first select that field. Open the Find dialog box shown in Figure 7-27 by choosing the Find command from the Edit menu, by pressing Ctrl-F, or by clicking the Find button on the toolbar.

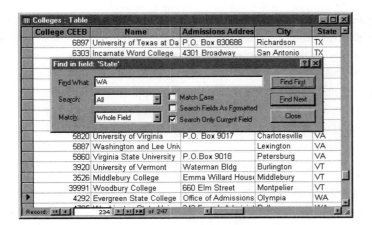

FIGURE 7-27

Using the Find dialog box to search for data.

In the Find What text box, type the data that you want Access to find. You can include wildcard characters to perform a generic search similar to that of the LIKE comparison operator you learned about in the section titled "Defining Simple Field Validation Rules" in Chapter 5. Use an asterisk (*) to indicate a string of unknown characters of any length, and use a question mark (?) to indicate exactly one unknown character (or a space). For example, "*AB??DE*" matches "Aberdeen" and "Tab idea" but not "Lab department." If you're searching a date field for dates in January, you can specify *-Jan-* (provided that you click the Search Fields As Formatted check box and provided that the field uses the Medium Date format).

By default, Access searches the field that your cursor was in before you opened the Find dialog box. To search the entire table, deselect the Search Only Current Field check box. By default, Access searches all records from the top of the recordset unless you change the Search parameter to search down or up from the current record position. Select the Match Case check box if you want to find text that exactly matches the uppercase and lowercase letters you typed. By default, Access is case-insensitive unless you select this check box.

Select the Search Fields As Formatted check box if you need to search the data as it is displayed rather than as it is stored by Access. Although searching this way is slower, you probably should select this check box if you are searching a Date/Time field. You might also want to select this check box when searching a Yes/No field for Yes because any value except 0 is a valid indicator of Yes.

Click the Find First button to start the search from the beginning of the table. Click Find Next to start searching from the current record. After you establish search criteria, you can press Shift-F4 to execute the search from the current record without having to open the Find dialog box again.

Using Filter By Selection

If you want to see all the rows in your table that match any part of a value you can see in a row in the datasheet grid, you can use Filter By Selection. For example, to see all colleges that have the word *University* in their name, find a college that has *University* in its name and highlight that word. Click the Filter By Selection button on the toolbar or choose Filter from the Records menu and then choose Filter By Selection from the submenu. When the search is completed you should see only universities listed.

Alternatively, you can select a complete value in a field to see only rows that match that value. Figure 7-28 shows the value *WA* selected in the State column and the result after clicking the Filter By Selection button. If several contiguous columns contain the filtering data you need, click on the first column, hold down the Shift key and click on the last column to select all of the data, and then click the Filter By Selection button to see only rows that match the data in all the columns you selected.

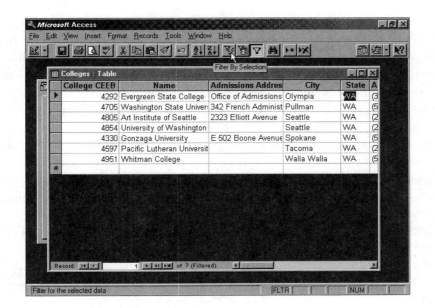

You can also add a filter to a filter. For example, if you want to see all universities in the state of Texas, find a row containing the word *University* in the college name, select the word, and then click the Filter By Selection button. In the filtered list, find the value *TX* in the State column, highlight it, and click Filter By Selection again.

> **NOTE** If you select a word at the beginning of a field and use it to Filter By Selection, you will see only rows whose value is the first word in the column. Likewise, selecting a word at the end of a field finds only rows whose column value ends in a matching value. Selecting a word in the middle of a field searches for that word anywhere in the same column.

Using Filter By Form

Filter By Selection is great for searching for rows that match *all* of several criteria (Name Like "*University*" *and* State equals "TX"), but what if you want to see rows that meet <u>any</u> of several criteria (State equals "WA" *or* State equals "CA" *or* State equals "OR")? You can use Filter By Form to easily build the criteria for this type of search.

209

When you click the Filter By Form button on the Table Datasheet toolbar, Access shows you a Query By Form example that looks like your datasheet but contains no data. (See Figure 7-29.) If you have no filtering criteria previously defined, Access shows you the Look For tab and one Or tab at the bottom of the window. Move to each column where you want to define criteria and either select a value from the drop-down list or enter criteria much the same way that you did to create validation rules in Chapter 5, "Building Your Database in Microsoft Access." For example, you can enter *Like "*University*"* in the Name field to search for the word *University* anywhere in the name. You can use criteria such as *> 5* in a numeric field to find only rows containing values greater than 5. You can enter multiple criteria on one line, but all of the criteria you enter on a single line must be true for a particular row to be selected.

FIGURE 7-29

Using Filter By Form to search for one of several states.

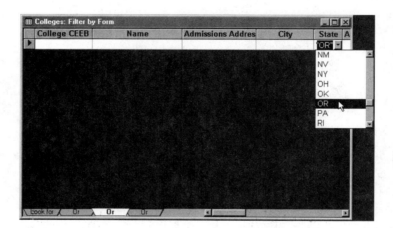

If you want to see rows that contain any of several values in a particular column (for example, rows from several states), enter the first value in the appropriate column, and then click on the Or tab at the bottom of the window to enter additional criteria. In this example, *"WA"* was entered in the State column on the Look For tab and *"CA"* on the first Or tab, and you can see *"OR"* being selected for the third Or tab in Figure 7-29. (As you define additional criteria, Access makes additional Or tabs available at the bottom of the window.) Figure 7-30 shows the result of applying this criteria by clicking the Apply Filter button on the toolbar.

College CEEB	Name	Admissions Addres	City	State
4345	Humboldt State Universit		Arcata	CA
4596	Azusa Pacific University	901 E. Alosta Ave.	Azusa	CA
4833	University of California, B		Berkeley	CA
4341	Harvey Mudd College		Claremont	CA
4852	University of Southern Ca	University Park	Los Angeles	CA
4630	Pepperdine University	24255 Pacific Coast	Malibu	CA
4034	California Institute of Tech	1201 E. California Bl	Pasadena	CA
4671	California State University	6000 J St.	Sacramento	CA
4704	Stanford University	Old Union 232	Stanford	CA
4952	Whittier College	13406 E. Phila, PO E	Whittier	CA
4586	Oregon State University		Corvallis	OR
4846	University of Oregon	PO Box 3175	Eugene	OR
4601	Pacific University	2043 College Way	Forest Grove	OR
4384	Lewis & Clark College	615 SW Palatine Hill	Portland	OR
4654	Reed College	3203 SE Woodstock	Portland	OR
4292	Evergreen State College	Office of Admissions	Olympia	WA

Record: 1 of 22 (Filtered)

FIGURE 7-30

The colleges in the states of "WA," "CA," and "OR."

TIP Access always remembers the last filtering or sorting criteria you defined for a datasheet. The next time you open the datasheet, click the Apply Filter toolbar button to apply the last filter you created. If you want to save a particular filter/sort definition, choose Filter from the Records menu, and then choose Advanced Filter/Sort from the submenu. Choose Save As Query from the File menu and give your criteria a name. The next time you open the table, return to Advanced Filter/Sort, and then choose Load From Query from the File menu to find the criteria you previously saved.

You can actually define very complex filtering criteria using expressions and the Or tabs in the Filter By Form window. If you look at the Advanced Filter/Sort window, you can see that Access builds all your criteria in something that looks similar to the design grid of a Query window in Design view, which you'll study in the next chapter. In fact, filters and sorts use the query capabilities of Access to accomplish the result you want, so in Datasheet view you can use all the same filtering capabilities you'll find for queries.

See Also Chapter 8, "Adding Power with Select Queries," provides details about building complex filtering criteria.

Printing a Datasheet

You can use Datasheet view to print information from your table. If you have applied filter/sort criteria, you can limit which records Microsoft Access prints and you can define the print sequence. You can also control which fields are printed. (You cannot perform any calculations; you must create a query, a form, or a report to do that.) As you discovered earlier in this chapter, you can format the fields you want to print, including setting the font and adjusting the spacing between columns and between rows. If you use the Caption property when defining fields in Design view, you can also customize the column headings.

To produce the datasheet layout shown in Figure 7-31 for the Colleges table, you can hide all but the columns shown, increase the row height to add space between the printed rows, and size the columns so that you can see all the information. You should also eliminate the vertical gridlines—you turn them off by choosing Cells from the Format menu, and then deselecting the Vertical check box in the Cells Effects dialog box.

FIGURE 7-31
A datasheet that's ready to print.

Print Preview

After you format a datasheet the way you want, you can switch to Print Preview to verify that the data fits on a printed page. Choose the Print Preview command from the File menu, or click the Print Preview button on the toolbar, to see the display shown in Figure 7-32. Notice that the mouse pointer changes to a small magnifying glass. You can move the mouse pointer to any part of the report and click to zoom in and see the data up close. You can also click the Zoom button on the toolbar (the magnifying glass icon) to magnify the report and display the upper left corner of the current page. You can set a custom zoom percentage by using the Zoom Control drop-down box. While zoomed in, you can use the arrow keys to move around the displayed page in small increments. Press the PgUp or PgDn key to move around in larger increments. You can press Ctrl-down arrow to move to the bottom of the page, Ctrl-up arrow to move to the top, Ctrl-right arrow to move to the right margin, and Ctrl-left arrow to move to the left margin. Ctrl-Home puts you back in the upper left corner, and Ctrl-End moves the display to the lower right corner. Click the Zoom button again or press the left mouse button to zoom out.

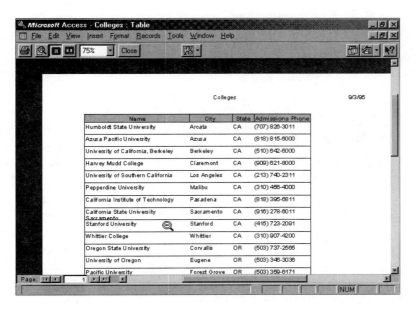

FIGURE 7-32

The datasheet in Print Preview.

   If your printed output has multiple pages, you can use the PgUp and PgDn keys while you are zoomed out to move between pages. Click the Close button to exit Print Preview without printing. Click the Print button to send your formatted datasheet to a printer. Choose Page

Setup from the File menu to specify printer setup options, as explained in the next section. You can use the drop-down list next to the Office Links button to start the Microsoft Word Mail Merge Wizard or to export the report to Word or to Microsoft Excel (if you have these applications installed).

Page Setup

For every table, you can set default page setup attributes that you want Access to use whenever you print the datasheet. With the datasheet open, choose Page Setup from the File menu to see the dialog box shown in Figure 7-33.

FIGURE 7-33

The Page Setup
dialog box.

In this dialog box, click on the Margins tab to specify the top, bottom, left, and right margins. Click on the Page tab to select the paper size and a specific type of printer. In general, it's best to leave the Default Printer option selected. This provides maximum flexibility if you move the database application to another machine. Note also that you can ask Access to print the datasheet in Landscape orientation (sideways across the length of the paper). This is very handy if you want to print more fields than will normally fit across the narrower width of the printer paper.

Printing

To send the datasheet to the printer, click the Print button on the toolbar. You can also print a datasheet directly from the Database window by selecting the table you want and choosing the Print command from the File menu. When you choose the Print command, Access displays a Print dialog box similar to the one shown in Figure 7-34. (This dialog box varies depending on your printer.) If you click the Print button on one of the toolbars, Access sends the report directly to the printer without prompting you.

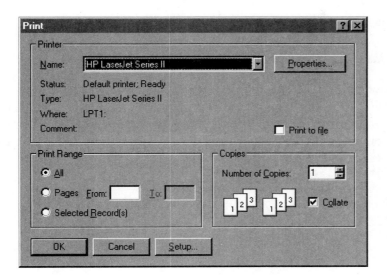

FIGURE 7-34

The Print dialog box.

In all Print dialog boxes, you can choose to print multiple copies. You can also choose to print all pages or a range of pages. If you select the Collate check box, Access prints the first through last pages in sequence and repeats for each set of pages. If you deselect the Collate check box, Access prints the number of copies you requested for the first page, then the number of copies you requested for the second page, and so on. On some printers, printing uncollated is faster because each page is sent to the printer memory only once, and the printer can quickly produce multiple copies once the page is loaded. Printing collated can be slower because each page copy must be sent to the printer individually. You can also tell Access to send your output to a file that you can copy to your printer later.

When you send the output to a printer, Access displays a printing progress report in a dialog box, as shown in Figure 7-35. While Access is sending pages to the print spool, you can switch to other applications to perform other tasks. Once the pages have been spooled, you can go on to other tasks in Access while Windows 95 sends the report to your printer.

FIGURE 7-35

The Printing dialog box, which shows the printing status.

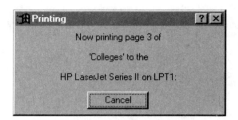

Now that you've worked with data directly out of single tables by using datasheets, it's time to deal with data from multiple tables and to update many rows in a table in one operation. To handle these operations, you need the power of queries, as explained in the next two chapters.

Chapter 8

Adding Power with Select Queries

n the previous chapter, you learned about working with the data in your tables in Datasheet view. Although you can do a lot with datasheets—including browsing, sorting, filtering, updating, and printing your data—you'll find that you often need to perform calculations on your data or retrieve related data from multiple tables. To select a set of data to work with, you use queries.

When you define and run a *select query* (which selects information from the tables and queries in your database, as opposed to an *action query,* which inserts, updates, or deletes data), Microsoft Access creates a *recordset* of the selected data. In most cases, you can work with a recordset in the same way that you work with a table: You can browse through it, select information from it, print it, and even update the data in it. But unlike a real table, a recordset doesn't actually exist in your database. Access creates a recordset from the data in your tables and queries at the time you run the query.

As you learn to design forms and reports later in this book, you'll find that queries are the best way to focus on the specific data you need for the task at hand. You'll also find that queries are useful for providing choices for combo and list boxes, which make entering data in your database much easier.

> **NOTE** The examples in this chapter are based on the tables and data from the Entertainment Schedule sample database (Entertain.mdb) on the companion disc included with this book.

To open a new Query window in Design view, click on the Queries tab in the Database window, and then click the New button to the right of the Query list. A dialog box opens that lets you either start a new query from scratch in Design view or select a Query Wizard. (You'll learn about Query Wizards later in this chapter.) To open an existing query in Design view, click on the Queries tab in the Database window (which, in this case, displays the Query list of the complete Entertainment Schedule database, as shown in Figure 8-1), select the query you want, and click the Design button.

Figure 8-2 shows an existing query whose window has been opened in Design view. The upper part of the Query window contains field lists and the lower part contains the design grid.

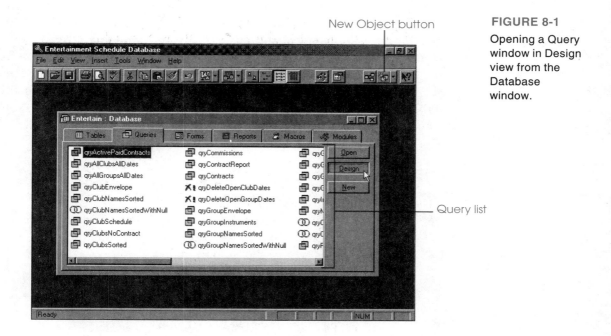

FIGURE 8-1

Opening a Query window in Design view from the Database window.

Query list

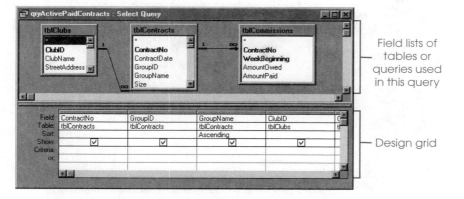

FIGURE 8-2

An existing query opened in Design view.

Field lists of tables or queries used in this query

Design grid

Selecting Data from a Single Table

One advantage of using queries is that they allow you to find data easily in multiple related tables. Queries are also useful for sifting through the data in a single table. All the techniques you use for working with a single table apply equally to more complex multiple-table queries, so this chapter begins by using queries to select data from a single table.

The easiest way to start building a query on a table is to open the Database window, select the table you want, and select New Query from the New Object toolbar button's drop-down list. Do this now with the tblGroups table in the Entertainment Schedule database, and then select Design View in the resulting dialog box. If you can't see the Table row in the lower part of the Query window, choose the Table Names command from the View menu to open the window shown in Figure 8-3.

> **NOTE** The New Object button "remembers" the last new object type that you created. If you've created only new tables up to this point, you have to use the button's drop-down list to select New Query. Once you start a new query in this manner, the New Object button defaults to New Query until you use it to create a different type of new object.

FIGURE 8-3

The Query window in Design view for a new query on tblGroups.

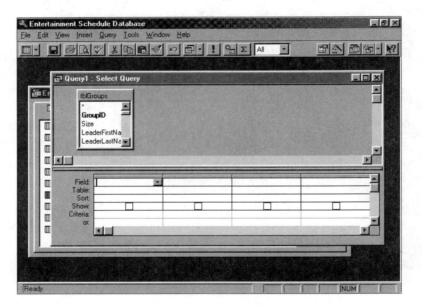

The Query window in Design view has two main parts. In the upper part are field lists with the fields for the tables or queries you chose for this query. The lower part of the window is the design grid, in which you do all the design work. Each column in the grid represents one field that you'll work with in this query. As you'll see later, a field can be a simple field from one of the tables, a calculated field based on several fields in the tables, or a total field using one of the functions provided by Microsoft Access.

You use the first row of the design grid to select fields—the fields you want in the resulting recordset, the fields you want to sort, and the fields you want to test for values. As you'll learn later, you can also generate custom field names (for display in the resulting recordset), and you can use complex expressions or calculations to generate a calculated field.

Because you chose the Table Names command from the View menu, Access displays the table name (which is the source of the selected field) in the second row of the design grid. In the Sort row, you can specify whether Access should sort the selected or calculated field in ascending or in descending order.

 TIP   It's a good idea to select the Show Table Names option on the Tables/Queries tab of the Options dialog box (choose the Options command from the Tools menu) whenever your query is based on more than one table. Because you might have the same field name in more than one of the tables, showing table names in the design grid helps to ensure that you refer to the field you want.

In the Show row, you can use the check boxes to indicate the fields that will be included in the recordset. By default, Access includes all the fields you selected in the design grid. Sometimes you'll want to include a field in the query to allow you to select the records you want (such as the contracts for a certain date range), but you won't need that field in the recordset. You can add that field to the design grid so that you can define criteria, but you should deselect the Show check box beneath the field to exclude it from the recordset.

Finally, you can use the Criteria row and the rows labeled *Or* to enter the criteria you want to use as filters. Once you understand how it's done, you'll find it easy to specify exactly the fields and records that you want.

Specifying Fields

The first step in building a query is to select the fields you want in the recordset. You can select the fields in several ways. Using the keyboard, you can tab to an available column in the design grid and press Alt-down arrow to open the list of available fields. (If you need to move the cursor to the design grid, press the F6 key.) Use the up and down arrow keys to move the highlight to the field you want, and then press Enter to select the field.

Another way to select a field is to drag it from one of the field lists in the upper part of the window to one of the columns in the design grid. In Figure 8-4, the Size field is being dragged to the design grid. When you drag a field, the mouse pointer turns into a small rectangle.

FIGURE 8-4

Dragging a field to a column in the design grid.

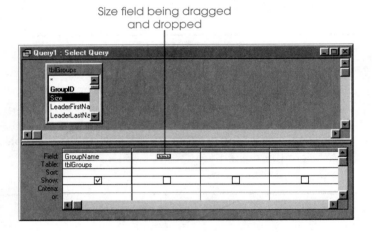

At the top of each field list in the upper part of the Query window (and also next to the first entry in the Field drop-down list in the design grid) is an asterisk (*) symbol. This symbol is shorthand for "all fields in the table or the query." When you want to include all the fields in a table or a query, you don't have to define each one individually in the design grid (unless you also want to define some sorting or selection criteria for specific fields). You can simply add the asterisk to the design grid to include all the fields from a list. Note that you can add individual fields to the grid in addition to the asterisk in order to define criteria for those fields, but you should deselect the Show check box for the individual fields so that they don't appear twice in the recordset.

TIP Another easy way to select all the fields in a table is to double-click on the title bar of the field list in the upper part of the Query window. This highlights all the fields. Simply click in any of the highlighted fields and drag them to the field row in the design grid. While you're dragging, the mouse pointer changes to a multiple rectangle icon, indicating that you're dragging multiple fields. When you release the mouse button, you'll see that Access has copied all the fields to the design grid for you.

For this exercise, select GroupName, Size, City, and State from the tblGroups table in the Entertainment Schedule database. If you switch the Query window to Datasheet view at this point, you'll see only the fields you selected from the records in the underlying table.

Setting Field Properties

In general, fields that are output by a query inherit the properties defined for the field in the table. You can define a different Description property (the information that is displayed on the status bar when you select that field in a Query window in Datasheet view), Format property (how the data is displayed), Decimal Places property (for numeric data), Input Mask property, and Caption property (the column heading). When you learn to define calculated fields later in this chapter, you'll see that it's a good idea to define the properties for these fields. If the field in the query is a foreign key link to another table, you can also set the Lookup properties as described in Chapter 6, "Modifying Your Database Design."

To set the properties of a field, click on any row of the field's column in the design grid and then click the Properties button on the toolbar or choose Properties from the View menu to display the Field Properties dialog box. Even though the fields in your query inherit their properties from the underlying table, you won't see those properties here. For example, the Format property for Size in tblGroups is

Standard, and Decimal Places is 0, although neither value appears in the Field Properties dialog box. You can use these property settings to customize how the fields look when viewed for this query. Try entering new property settings for the Size field, as shown in Figure 8-5. If you make these changes and switch to Datasheet view, you'll see a result similar to that shown in Figure 8-6. Notice that the Size column heading is now *Player Count*, that two digits are displayed, and that the text on the status bar matches the new description.

FIGURE 8-5

Setting properties
for the Size field.

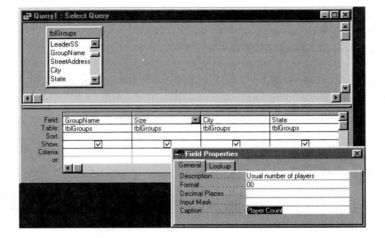

TIP You'll notice that in Datasheet view any new query you build using the tblGroups table will have no vertical gridlines and will use a serif font. These attributes are inherited from the datasheet settings that you saw in the previous chapter. While you are in a query's Datasheet view, you can set the display format exactly as you would for a table in Datasheet view by using the commands on the Format menu. (See the previous chapter for details.) When you save the query, Access saves the custom format settings.

FIGURE 8-6

The Size field displayed with new properties.

Entering Selection Criteria

The next step is to further refine the values in the fields you want. The example shown in Figure 8-7 selects groups in the state of Washington.

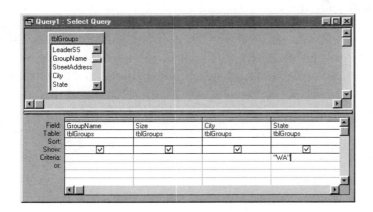

FIGURE 8-7

A design grid that specifies *"WA"* as a selection criterion.

Entering selection criteria in a query is similar to entering a validation rule for a field, which you learned about in Chapter 5, "Building Your Database in Microsoft Access." To look for a single value, simply type it in the Criteria row for the field you want to test. If the field you're testing is a text field and the value you're looking for has any blank spaces in it, you must enclose the value in quotation marks. Note that Access adds quotes for you around single text values. (In Figure 8-7, *WA* was typed, but the field shows *"WA"* after Enter was pressed.)

If you want to test for any of several values, enter the values in the Criteria row, separated by the word *Or*. For example, specifying *WA Or OR* searches for records for Washington or Oregon. You can also test for any of several values by entering each value in a separate Criteria or Or row for the field you want to test. For example, you can enter *OR* in the Criteria row, *WA* in the next row (the first Or row), and so on—but you have to be careful if you're also specifying criteria in other fields, as explained below.

In the next section, you'll see that you can also include a comparison operator in the Criteria row to look for values less than (<), greater than or equal to (>=), or not equal to (<>) the value that you specify.

AND vs. OR

When you enter criteria for several fields, all of the tests in a single Criteria row or Or row must be true for a record to be included in the recordset. That is, Access performs a logical AND operation between multiple criteria in the same row. So if you enter *WA* in the Criteria row for State and *<3* in the Criteria row for Size, the record must be for the state of Washington <u>and</u> must have a group size of less than 3 in order to be selected. If you enter *WA Or OR* in the Criteria row for State and *>=2 And <=5* in the Criteria row for Size, the record must be for the state of Washington or Oregon, <u>and</u> the group size must be between 2 and 5 inclusive.

Figure 8-8 shows the result of applying a logical AND operator between any two tests. As you can see, both tests must be true for the result of the AND to be true and for the record to be selected.

FIGURE 8-8

The result of applying the logical AND operator between two tests.

AND	True	False
True	True (Selected)	False (Rejected)
False	False (Rejected)	False (Rejected)

When you specify multiple criteria for a field separated by a logical OR operator, only one of the criteria must be true for the record to be selected. You can specify several OR criteria for a field, either by entering them all in a single Criteria row separated by the logical OR operator, as shown earlier, or by entering each of the criteria in a separate Or row. When you use multiple Or rows, all the criteria <u>in only one of the Or rows</u> must be true for a record to be selected. Figure 8-9 shows the result of applying a logical OR operation between any two tests. As you can see, only one of the tests must be true for the result of the OR to be true and for the record to be selected.

<u>OR</u>	**True**	**False**
True	True (Selected)	True (Selected)
False	True (Selected)	False (Rejected)

FIGURE 8-9

The result of applying the logical OR operator between two tests.

Let's look at a specific example. In Figure 8-10, you specify *WA* in the first Criteria row of the State field and *<3* in that same Criteria row for the Size field. In the next row (the first Or row), you specify *OR* in the State field. When you run this query, you get all the records for the state of Washington that also have a group size of less than 3. You also get any records for the state of Oregon regardless of the group size.

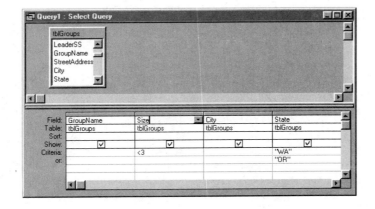

FIGURE 8-10

A design grid that specifies multiple AND and OR selection criteria.

227

In Figure 8-11, you can see the recordset (in Datasheet view) that results from running this query.

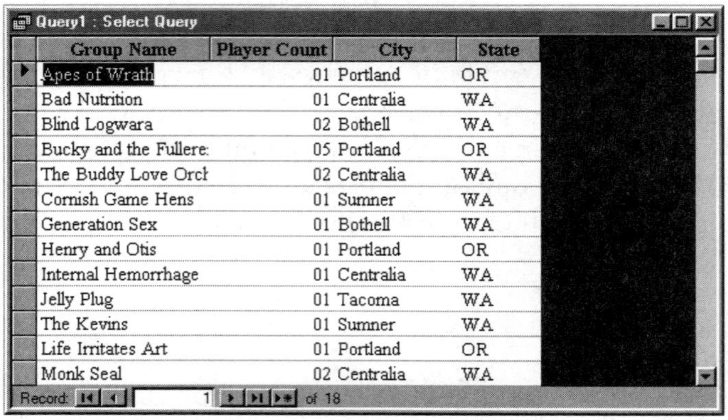

Group Name	Player Count	City	State
Apes of Wrath	01	Portland	OR
Bad Nutrition	01	Centralia	WA
Blind Logwara	02	Bothell	WA
Bucky and the Fullere:	05	Portland	OR
The Buddy Love Orcl	02	Centralia	WA
Cornish Game Hens	01	Sumner	WA
Generation Sex	01	Bothell	WA
Henry and Otis	01	Portland	OR
Internal Hemorrhage	01	Centralia	WA
Jelly Plug	01	Tacoma	WA
The Kevins	01	Sumner	WA
Life Irritates Art	01	Portland	OR
Monk Seal	02	Centralia	WA

FIGURE 8-11 The recordset of the query shown in Figure 8-10.

BETWEEN, IN, and LIKE

In addition to comparison operators, Access provides three special predicate clauses that are useful for specifying the data you want in the recordset:

BETWEEN	Useful for specifying a range of values. The clause *Between 10 And 20* is the same as specifying *>=10 And <=20*.
IN	Useful for specifying a list of values, any one of which can match the field being searched. The clause *In ("WA", "CA", "ID")* is the same as *"WA" Or "CA" Or "ID"*.
LIKE	Useful for searching for patterns in text fields. You can include special characters and ranges of values in the Like comparison string to define the character pattern you want. Use a question mark (?) to indicate any single character in that position. Use an asterisk (*) to indicate zero or more characters in that position. The pound-sign character (#) specifies a single numeric digit in that position. Include a range in brackets ([ ]) to test for a particular range of characters in a position, and use an exclamation point (!) to indicate exceptions. The range [0-9] tests for numbers, [a-z] tests for letters, and [!0-9] tests for any characters except *0* through *9*. For example, the clause *Like "?[a-k]d[0-9]*"* tests for any single character in the first position, any character from *a* through *k* in the second position, the letter *d* in the third position, any character from *0* through *9* in the fourth position, and any number of characters after that.

Suppose you want to find all entertainment groups in the city of Tacoma or in the town of Sumner that have between two and four members and whose name begins with the letter *B*. Figure 8-12 shows how you would enter these criteria. (Note that the test for GroupName checks for names that begin with *B* or the word *The* followed by a name beginning with the letter *B*.) Figure 8-13 shows the recordset of this query.

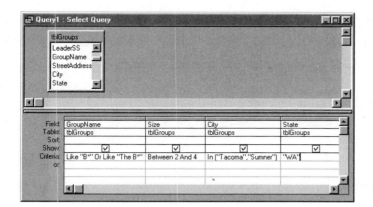

FIGURE 8-12
A design grid that uses BETWEEN, IN, and LIKE.

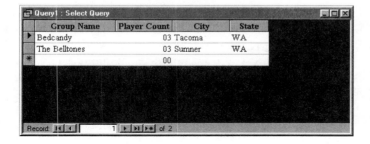

FIGURE 8-13
The recordset of the query shown in Figure 8-12.

For additional examples that use the BETWEEN, IN, and LIKE comparison operators, see the section titled "Defining Simple Field Validation Rules" in Chapter 5 and the "Predicate" sections in Chapter 11.

Working with Dates and Times in Criteria

Access stores dates and times as double-precision floating-point numbers. The value to the left of the decimal point represents the day, and the fractional part of the number stores the time as a fraction of a day. Fortunately, you don't have to worry about converting internal numbers to specify a test for a particular date value because Access handles date and time entries in several formats.

You must always surround date and time values with pound signs (#) to tell Access that you're entering a date or a time. To test for a specific date, use the date notation that is most comfortable for you. For example, *#April 15, 1995#, #4/15/95#,* and *#15-Apr-1995#* are all the same date when you choose English (United States) from the drop-down list on the Regional Settings tab of the Regional Settings Properties dialog box. (You can display the Regional Settings Properties dialog box by double-clicking on the Regional Settings icon in Control Panel.) Also, *#5:30 PM#* and *#17:30#* both specify 5:30 in the evening.

Access has several useful functions to assist you in testing date and time values. These are explained below with examples that use the BeginningDate field in the tblContracts table:

Day(date)	Returns a value from 1 through 31 for the day of the month. For example, if you want to select records with BeginningDate values after the 10th of any month, enter *Day([BeginningDate])* as a calculated field (see the next section), and enter *>10* as the criterion for that field.
Month(date)	Returns a value from 1 through 12 for the month of the year. For example, if you want to find all records that have a BeginningDate value of June, enter *Month([BeginningDate])* as a calculated field (see the next section), and enter *6* as the criterion for that field.
Year(date)	Returns a value from 100 through 9999 for the year. If you want to find a BeginningDate value in 1996, enter *Year([BeginningDate])* as a calculated field (see the next section), and enter *1996* as the criterion for that field.
Weekday(date)	As a default, returns from 1 (Sunday) through 7 (Saturday) for the day of the week. To find business day dates, enter *Weekday([BeginningDate])* as a calculated field (see the next section), and enter *Between 2 And 6* as the criterion for that field.
Hour(date)	Returns the hour (0 through 23). To find a scheduled start time before noon, enter *Hour([BeginningDate])* as a calculated field (see the next section), and enter *<12* as the criterion for that field.
DatePart (interval, date)	Returns a portion of the date or time, depending on the interval code you supply. Useful interval codes are *"q"* for quarter of the year (1 through 4) and *"ww"* for week of the year (1 through 53). For example, to select dates in the second

quarter, enter *DatePart("q", [BeginningDate])* as a calculated field (see the next section), and enter *2* as the criterion for that field.

Date   Returns the current system date. To select dates more than 30 days ago, enter *<Date() - 30* as the criterion for that field.

Calculating Values

You can specify a calculation on any of the fields in your table and make that calculation a new field in the recordset. You can use any of the many built-in functions that Access provides. (See the examples above.) You can also create a field in a query by using arithmetic operators on fields in the underlying table to calculate a value. In a contract record, for example, you might have a NumberOfWeeks field and a ContractPrice (per week) field, but not the extended price (weeks times price). You can include that value in your recordset by typing the calculation in the field of an empty column in the design grid using the NumberOfWeeks field, the multiplication operator (*), and the ContractPrice field.

You can also create a new text (string) field by concatenating fields containing either text or string constants. You create a string constant by enclosing the text in double or single quotation marks. Use the ampersand character (&) between text fields or strings to indicate that you want to concatenate them. For example, you might want to create an output field that concatenates the LastName field, a comma, a blank space, and then the FirstName field.

The operators you can use in expressions include the following:

+	Adds two numeric expressions.
-	Subtracts two numeric expressions.
*	Multiplies two numeric expressions.
/	Divides the first numeric expression by the second numeric expression.
\	Rounds both numeric expressions to integers and divides the first integer by the second integer. The result is rounded to an integer.
^	Raises the first numeric expression to the power indicated by the second numeric expression.
MOD	Rounds both numeric expressions to integers, divides the first integer by the second integer, and returns the remainder.
&	Creates an extended text string by concatenating the first text string to the second text string. If either expression is a number, Access converts it to a text string before concatenating.

231

Try creating a query on the tblGroups table in the Entertainment Schedule database that shows a field containing the group name, followed by a single field containing the street address, a comma and a blank space, the city, another comma and a blank space, the state followed by two blank spaces, and the zip code. Your expression should look like this:

[StreetAddress] & ", " & [City] & ", " & [State] & " " & [ZipCode]

The Query window in Design view for this example is shown in Figure 8-14. Notice that I clicked in the Field row of the column I wanted and then pressed Shift-F2 to open the Zoom window, where it is easier to enter the expression.

FIGURE 8-14

Editing an expression in the Zoom window.

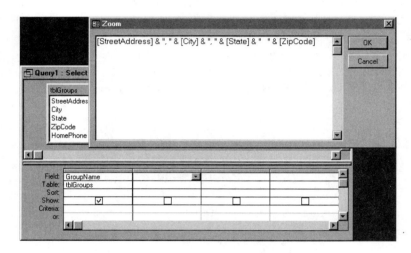

When you look at the query result in Datasheet view, you should see something like that shown in Figure 8-15.

FIGURE 8-15

A query result with concatenated text fields.

232

Try typing in the Expr1 field in Datasheet view. Because this display is a result of a calculation (concatenation of strings), Access won't let you update the data in this column.

Using the Expression Builder

For more complex expressions, Access provides a utility called the Expression Builder. Let's say you want to calculate the total commission owed for a contract in the Entertainment Schedule database. You have to work with several fields to do this: ContractPrice, NumberOfWeeks, and Commission1%. To use the Expression Builder, start a new query on the tblContracts table. Click in an empty field in the design grid, and then click the Build button on the toolbar. Access opens the Expression Builder window shown in Figure 8-16.

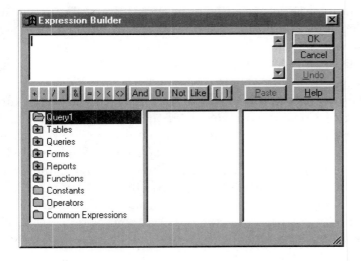

FIGURE 8-16
The Expression
Builder window.

In the upper part of the window is a blank text box in which you can build an expression. You can type the expression yourself, but it's much easier to use the various expression operator buttons just below the text box to help you out. In the lower part of the window are three list boxes you can use to find field names and function names that you need to build your expression.

The basic expression you need looks like this:

[ContractPrice] * [NumberOfWeeks] * [Commission1%]

ContractPrice is a Currency field, and NumberOfWeeks is an integer. Whenever you ask Access to evaluate an arithmetic expression, it returns a result that has a data type sufficiently complex to contain the result. As you might expect, multiplying an integer (a simple data type) with a currency field (a more complex data type) returns a currency field. So far, so good. But what do you suppose happens when you multiply the currency field by the Commission1% field, a floating-point number? Access doesn't know in advance that Commission1% contains only a simple percentage and that a Currency result would do very nicely. Access has to assume that the floating-point field could contain a very large or a very small number, so the data type of the calculation result is a floating-point number.

Floating-point numbers are indeed handy for holding very large or very small numbers, but they don't handle precise decimal fractions very well. This is because floating-point numbers only approximate the fractional portion of a number by adding up negative powers of two. If your fraction isn't exactly a sum of negative powers of two ($\frac{1}{2}$, $\frac{1}{4}$, $\frac{1}{8}$, $\frac{1}{16}$, and so on), the floating-point number might be close but not exact. If you're dealing with money, you not only want fractions of a cent calculated and stored accurately, but you also probably want the result rounded to an even penny.

Access has some built-in data conversion functions to help you deal with these issues. Access does not have a built-in rounding function, but both the Convert to Integer (*CInt*) and Convert to Long (*CLng*) functions perform "banker's" integer rounding—any number greater than .50 rounds up, any number less than .50 rounds down, and when the number is exactly one-half (note that floating-point numbers can accurately store .50 because it's a simple negative power of two), the functions look at the first integer digit and round odd numbers up and even numbers down. So 1.51 becomes 2, 1.49 rounds down to 1, 1.50 rounds up to 2 (because the integer *1* is odd), and 2.50 rounds down to 2 (because the integer *2* is even).

Note, however, that these functions perform <u>integer</u> rounding. If you want to keep rounded pennies, you must first multiply by 100 and then round. This part of the expression is as follows:

CLng([ContractPrice] * [NumberOfWeeks] * [Commission1%] * 100)

This expression gives you the commission owed in rounded pennies as a long integer data type. It's a simple matter to divide this result by 100 and use the Convert to Currency (*CCur*) function to get the exact format you want. This technique works nicely for currency values of up to $21.4 million (because a long value can hold slightly more than 2.1 trillion pennies). Using this technique is particularly important, for example, if you're calculating percentage discount values for an invoice. If you don't do this, your calculations will produce fractions of a cent, which might display correctly but won't add precisely at the bottom of the invoice. As you might guess, you can use the Expression Builder to help you correctly construct this expression.

Because you need a couple of built-in functions, double-click on the Functions folder in the far left list box to expand the list to show categories of functions. As shown in Figure 8-17, the Expression Builder allows you to select any of the built-in functions or any of the user-defined functions in the Entertainment Schedule database. Click on Built-In Functions, and then select Conversion in the second list box. Select *CCur* in the third list box, and then click Paste to move a "skeleton" of the function to the text box in the upper part of the window. You should see *CCur (<<expr>>)* in the list box. Click on *<<expr>>* to highlight it so you can replace it with the next part of your expression. Choose the *CLng* function in the third list box, and then click the Paste button to move the function into your expression. Your result should now look like this:

CCur (CLng (*<<expr>>*))

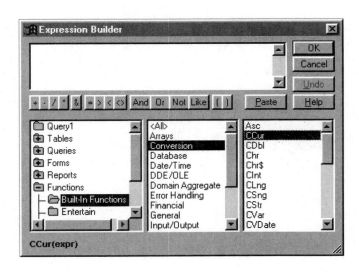

FIGURE 8-17
Selecting from the Built-In Functions list in the Expression Builder window.

TIP   A quick way to select a field in the Expression Builder window is to double-click on the field's name.

Click on *<<expr>>* again to begin entering the field calculation. Because you need fields from the tblContracts table, double-click on the Tables folder in the far left list box. The Tables folder expands to show all the table names. Scroll down in the Expression Builder window until you can see the tblContracts table. Click on the tblContracts table to see the list of fields in the table in the middle list box.

To get the total commission for the contract, you need to start with ContractPrice. Click on that field, and then click the Paste button to move the field to the expression area. You'll notice that Access pastes *[tblContracts]![ContractPrice]* into the expression area, not just *ContractPrice*. There are two good reasons for this. First, you should enclose all names of objects in Access in brackets ([ ]). If you designed the name without any blank spaces, you can leave out the brackets, but it's always best to include them. Second, the Expression Builder doesn't know whether you might include other tables in this query and whether some of those tables might also have field names that are identical to the ones you're selecting now. The way to avoid conflicts is to <u>fully qualify</u> the field names by preceding them with the table name. When using names that you have created, separate the parts of the name with an exclamation point (!). As you'll learn later in Chapter 20, "Automating Your Application with Macros," sometimes you'll need to use a period (.) to separate parts of names.

Next, you need to multiply the price times the commission percentage. Click the small asterisk button (*) to insert a multiplication symbol, and then click on *<<expr>>*. Select the Commission1% field from the tblContracts table and then click the Paste button. Insert another multiplication symbol, click on *<<expr>>,* and then insert the NumberOfWeeks field. You need to calculate pennies first, so insert another multiplication symbol, click on *<<expr>>,* and then type the value *100* directly into the text box. Finally, you need to divide the result from the *CLng* function by 100 to return to dollars and cents. Move the cursor to a point between the two closing right parentheses and insert a division symbol (/). Click on *<<expr>>,* and then type in the value *100* again. Your result should look like that shown in Figure 8-18.

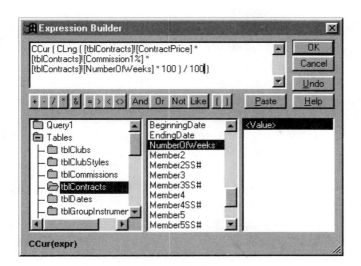

FIGURE 8-18
The completed
commission
expression.

Click OK to paste your result into the design grid. You might also want to include in your query the ContractNo field and all the fields used in the calculation. When you open your query in Datasheet view, it should look something like the one shown in Figure 8-19. (As you might guess from looking at the figure, I set some field properties to change the date format and some of the column headings.)

Contract No.	Begin Date	Weeks	Contract Price	Ray's %	Expr1	Expr2	Expr3
4761	15-Oct-95	2	$450.00	9.0%	$900.00	$81.00	81
4762	10-Sep-95	2	$450.00	10.0%	$900.00	$90.00	90
4763	30-Oct-95	3	$1,350.00	11.0%	$4,050.00	$445.50	445.5
4764	31-Oct-95	2	$1,500.00	10.0%	$3,000.00	$300.00	300
4765	27-Sep-95	1	$450.00	9.0%	$450.00	$40.50	40.5
4767	18-Oct-95	1	$450.00	11.0%	$450.00	$49.50	49.5
4770	05-Mar-96	4	$1,500.00	10.0%	$6,000.00	$600.00	600
4771	06-Oct-95	1	$475.00	7.5%	$475.00	$35.62	35.625
4775	01-Nov-95	2	$450.00	11.0%	$900.00	$99.00	99
4778	04-Aug-95	1	$300.00	10.0%	$300.00	$30.00	30
4779	11-Aug-95	1	$300.00	11.0%	$300.00	$33.00	33
4780	18-Aug-95	1	$400.00	5.0%	$400.00	$20.00	20
4784	10-Nov-95	1	$300.00	10.0%	$300.00	$30.00	30

Record: 73 of 248

FIGURE 8-19
A query with
calculated fields.

Note that in the result in Figure 8-19 I included the total contract amount (Expr1), the correctly calculated commission amount (Expr2), and the commission amount without rounding. If you scroll down (contract number 4771 in the sample database is a good example), you should see some contracts that calculate to a fraction of a cent.

Specifying Field Names

You learned earlier that you can change the caption (column heading) for a field in a query by using the field's property sheet. You might have noticed that when you create an expression in the field row of the design grid, Access adds a prefix such as *Expr1* followed by a colon. Every field in a query must have a name. By default, the name of a field in a query is the name of the field from the source table. Likewise, the default caption for the field is either the field's original caption property or the field name.

You can change or assign field names that will appear in the recordset of a query. This feature is particularly useful when you've calculated a value in the query that you'll use in a form, a report, or another query. In the queries shown in Figures 8-15 and 8-19, you calculated a value and Access assigned a temporary field name. You can replace this name with something more meaningful. For example, in the first query you might want to use something like *FullName:* and *FullAddress:*. In the second query, *ContractAmt:* and *RMPCommission:* might be appropriate. Figure 8-20 shows the second query with the field names changed.

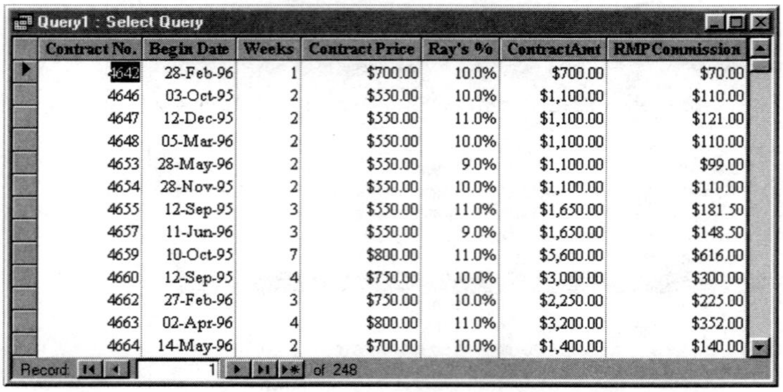

FIGURE 8-20

The result of changing the Expr1 and Expr2 column headings shown in Figure 8-19.

Contract No.	Begin Date	Weeks	Contract Price	Ray's %	ContractAmt	RMP Commission
4642	28-Feb-96	1	$700.00	10.0%	$700.00	$70.00
4646	03-Oct-95	2	$550.00	10.0%	$1,100.00	$110.00
4647	12-Dec-95	2	$550.00	11.0%	$1,100.00	$121.00
4648	05-Mar-96	2	$550.00	10.0%	$1,100.00	$110.00
4653	28-May-96	2	$550.00	9.0%	$1,100.00	$99.00
4654	28-Nov-95	2	$550.00	10.0%	$1,100.00	$110.00
4655	12-Sep-95	3	$550.00	11.0%	$1,650.00	$181.50
4657	11-Jun-96	3	$550.00	9.0%	$1,650.00	$148.50
4659	10-Oct-95	7	$800.00	11.0%	$5,600.00	$616.00
4660	12-Sep-95	4	$750.00	10.0%	$3,000.00	$300.00
4662	27-Feb-96	3	$750.00	10.0%	$2,250.00	$225.00
4663	02-Apr-96	4	$800.00	11.0%	$3,200.00	$352.00
4664	14-May-96	2	$700.00	10.0%	$1,400.00	$140.00

Sorting Data

Normally, Access displays the rows in your recordset in the order in which they're retrieved from the database. You can add sorting information to determine the sequence of the data in a query exactly as you did for tables in the previous chapter. Click in the Sort row for the field you want to sort, and select Ascending or Descending from the drop-down list. In the example shown in Figure 8-21, the query results are to be sorted in descending order based on the calculated RMPCommission field. The recordset will list the contracts paying the most commission first. The resulting Datasheet view is shown in Figure 8-22. (You can find this query saved as *qryXmplCalc* in the Entertainment Schedule database.)

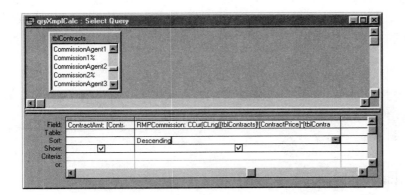

FIGURE 8-21

A query with sorting criteria added.

FIGURE 8-22

The recordset of the query shown in Figure 8-21 in Datasheet view.

You can also sort on multiple fields. Access honors your sorting criteria from left to right in the design grid. If, for example, you want to sort by BeginningDate and then by RMPCommission, you should include the BeginningDate field to the left of the RMPCommission field. If the additional field you want to sort is already in the design grid but in the wrong location, you can click the column selector box above the field to select the entire column. You can then click the selector box again and drag the field to its new location.

239

Total Queries

Sometimes you aren't interested in each and every row in your table. You'd rather see totals of different groups of data. For example, you might want the total contract amount for all clubs in a particular state. Or you might want to know the average of all sales for each month in the last year. To get these answers, you need a *total query*. To calculate totals within any query, click the Totals button on the toolbar in Design view to open the Total row in the design grid, as shown in Figure 8-23.

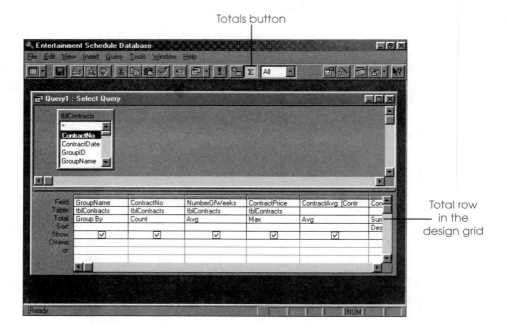

Totals Within Groups

When you first click the Totals button on the toolbar, Access displays *Group By* in the Total row for any fields you already have in the design grid. At this point the records in each field are grouped but not totaled. If you were to run the query now, you'd get one row in the recordset for each set of unique values—but no totals. You can create totals by replacing Group By with some *total functions* in the Total row.

Access provides nine total functions for your use. You can choose the one you want by typing its name in the Total row in the design grid or by selecting it from the drop-down list. The available functions are as follows:

Sum	Calculates the sum of all the values for this field in each group. You can specify this function only with number or currency fields.
Avg	Calculates the arithmetic average of all the values for this field in each group. You can specify this function only with number or currency fields. Access does not include any Null values in the calculation.
Min	Returns the lowest value found in this field within each group. For numbers, returns the smallest value. For text, returns the lowest value in collating sequence ("dictionary" order), without regard to case. Access ignores Null values.
Max	Returns the highest value found in this field within each group. For numbers, returns the largest value. For text, returns the highest value in collating sequence ("dictionary" order), without regard to case. Access ignores Null values.
Count	Returns the count of the rows in which the specified field is not a Null value. You can also enter the special expression COUNT(*) in the Field row to count all rows in each group, regardless of the existence of Null values.
StDev	Calculates the statistical standard deviation of all the values for this field in each group. You can specify this function only with number or currency fields. If the group does not contain at least two rows, Access returns a Null value.
Var	Calculates the statistical variance of all the values for this field in each group. You can specify this function only with number or currency fields. If the group does not contain at least two rows, Access returns a Null value.
First	Returns the first value in this field.
Last	Returns the last value in this field.

You can experiment with total functions by building a query similar to the one shown in Figure 8-23. Start a new query on the tblContracts table, and include the GroupName, ContractNo, NumberOfWeeks, and ContractPrice fields in the design grid. Include the expression *[ContractPrice] * [NumberOfWeeks]* twice in the design grid and name one field *ContractAvg:* and the other *ContractTotal:*. Click the Totals button on the toolbar to show the Total row. For ContractNo, select Count (to count the number of contracts for each group), select Avg for NumberOfWeeks, Max for ContractPrice, Avg for your first calculated field, and Sum for your second calculated field. Figure 8-24 shows the results when you run the query. (Again, I set some field properties to correctly format AvgOfNumberOfWeeks.)

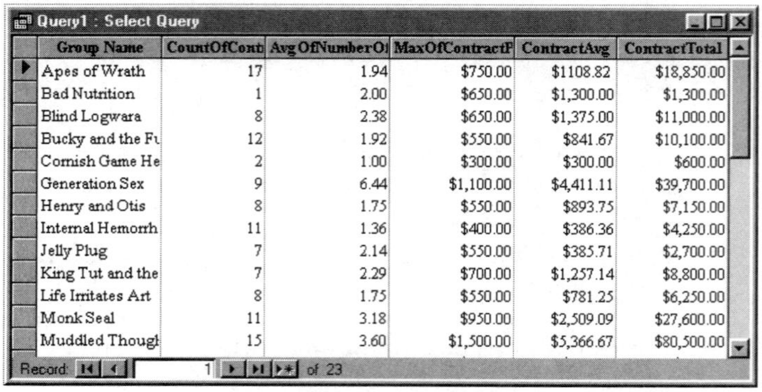

FIGURE 8-24

The recordset of the query shown in Figure 8-23.

Group Name	CountOfCont	AvgOfNumberO	MaxOfContractF	ContractAvg	ContractTotal
Apes of Wrath	17	1.94	$750.00	$1108.82	$18,850.00
Bad Nutrition	1	2.00	$650.00	$1,300.00	$1,300.00
Blind Logwara	8	2.38	$650.00	$1,375.00	$11,000.00
Bucky and the Fu	12	1.92	$550.00	$841.67	$10,100.00
Cornish Game He	2	1.00	$300.00	$300.00	$600.00
Generation Sex	9	6.44	$1,100.00	$4,411.11	$39,700.00
Henry and Otis	8	1.75	$550.00	$893.75	$7,150.00
Internal Hemorrh	11	1.36	$400.00	$386.36	$4,250.00
Jelly Plug	7	2.14	$550.00	$385.71	$2,700.00
King Tut and the	7	2.29	$700.00	$1,257.14	$8,800.00
Life Irritates Art	8	1.75	$550.00	$781.25	$6,250.00
Monk Seal	11	3.18	$950.00	$2,509.09	$27,600.00
Muddled Though	15	3.60	$1,500.00	$5,366.67	$80,500.00

Record: ◄◄ ◄ 1 ► ►► ►* of 23

In the drop-down list for the Total row in the design grid, you'll also find an Expression setting. Select this when you want to create an expression in the Field row that uses one or more of the total functions listed above. For example, you might want to calculate a value that reflects the range of commission percentages in the group, as in the following:

Max([Commission1%]) - Min([Commission1%])

Selecting Records to Form Groups

You might not want to include some records in the groups that form your total query. To filter out certain records from groups, you can add to the design grid the field or fields you want to use as filters. To create the filter, select the Where setting in the Total row, deselect that field's Show check box, and enter criteria that tell Access which records to exclude. In the tblContracts table, Ray McCann (owner of the RM Productions booking agency) is probably most interested in contracts for which he is the commissioning agent. Or he might be interested only in contracts that have been paid. To filter out this data, add the CommissionAgent1 field to the query, set its Total row to Where, and enter *"RMP"* in the Criteria row. Also add the Status field and check for the value *"Pd"*. This example is shown in Figure 8-25.

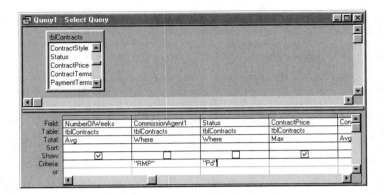

FIGURE 8-25
Using the Commission-Agent1 and Status fields to select the rows that will be included in groups.

Now, when you run the query, you get totals only for paid contracts for which Ray is the commissioning agent. The result is shown in Figure 8-26.

FIGURE 8-26
The recordset of the query shown in Figure 8-25.

Selecting Specific Groups

You can also filter out groups of totals after the query has calculated the groups. To do this, enter criteria for any field that has a Group By setting, one of the total functions, or an Expression using the total functions in its Total row. For example, you might want to find out which groups have more than $10,000 in total sales. To find that out, you would use the settings shown in Figure 8-25 and enter a Criteria setting of *>10000* for the ContractTotal field, as shown in Figure 8-27 on the next page.

FIGURE 8-27

Entering a
Criteria setting
for the Contract-
Total field.

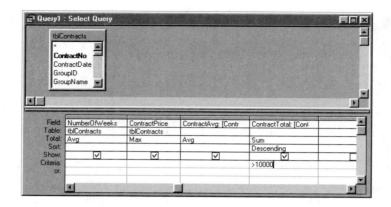

Using Query Parameters

So far you've been entering selection criteria directly in the design grid of the Query window in Design view. However, you don't have to decide at the time you design the query exactly what value you want Access to search for. Instead, you can include a parameter in the query, and Access will prompt you for the criteria before the query runs.

To set a parameter, you enter a name or a phrase enclosed in brackets ([ ]) instead of entering a value in the Criteria row. What you enclose in brackets becomes the name by which Access knows your parameter. Access displays this name in a dialog box when you run the query, so it's a good idea to enter a phrase that accurately describes what you want. You can enter several parameters in a single query, so each parameter name must be unique and informative.

You can adapt the query in Figure 8-25 so that Access will prompt for a particular month of interest each time the query runs. First, create a new calculated field to display a year and month by entering *SchedStart:* and the expression *Format([BeginningDate], "yyyy mmm")* in the Field row of an empty column. (The expression uses the built-in *Format* function to display BeginningDate values as a four-digit year followed by a three-character month.) Enter a parameter in the Criteria row for this field, as shown in Figure 8-28.

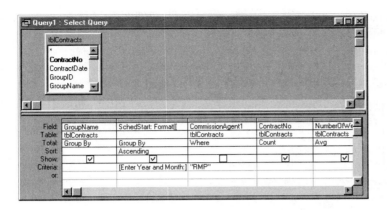

FIGURE 8-28

Setting a query
parameter for the
SchedStart field.

For each parameter in a query, you should tell Access what data type to expect. Access uses this information to validate the value entered. For example, if you define a parameter as a number, Access won't accept alphabetic characters in the parameter value. By default, Access assigns the text data type to query parameters, which is fine for our example. If you need to change a parameter's data type, choose the Parameters command from the Query menu; Access displays the Query Parameters dialog box, as shown in Figure 8-29.

FIGURE 8-29

The Query
Parameters
dialog box.

In the Parameter column, enter each parameter name whose data type you want to specify, exactly as you entered it in the design grid but without the brackets. In the Data Type column, select the appropriate data type from the drop-down list. Click the OK button when you finish defining all your parameters.

When you run the query, Access prompts you for an appropriate value for each parameter, one at a time, with a dialog box like the one shown in Figure 8-30. Because Access displays the "name" of the parameter that you provided in the design grid, you can see why naming the parameter with a phrase can help you enter the correct value later. In this case, *1995 Dec* is typed in the Enter Parameter Value dialog box, and the recordset is shown in Figure 8-31. (You can find this query saved as *qryXmplTotalParameter* in the Entertainment Schedule database.)

FIGURE 8-30

The Enter
Parameter Value
dialog box.

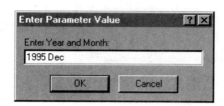

FIGURE 8-31

The recordset of
the query shown
in Figure 8-28,
when *1995 Dec* is
typed in the Enter
Parameter Value
dialog box.

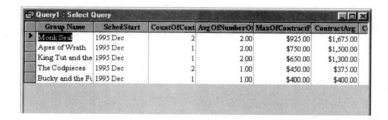

Crosstab Queries

Access supports a special type of total query called a *crosstab query* that allows you to see calculated values in a spreadsheetlike format. For example, you can use this type of query to see total sales by month for each entertainment group in the tblContracts table.

To build a crosstab query, first select the table you want in the Database window, and then select New Query from the New Object toolbar button's drop-down list. Select Design View in the New Query dialog box, and then choose the Crosstab command from the Query menu. Access adds a Crosstab row to the design grid, as shown in Figure 8-32. Each field in a crosstab query can have one of four crosstab settings: Row Heading, Column Heading, Value (calculated in the crosstab grid), or Not Shown. For a crosstab query to work, you must specify at least one field as a row heading, one field as a column heading, and one field as a value in your query. Each column heading must have Group By as the setting in the Total row. Any column that is a row heading can have a Group By setting, one of the total functions (*Count,*

Min, Max, and so on), or an expression that includes a total function. You must select one of the available total functions or enter an expression that uses a total function for the field that contains the Value setting in the design grid.

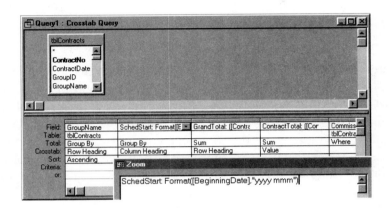

FIGURE 8-32
A crosstab query in Design view.

As in other types of total queries, you can include other fields to filter out values from the result. For these fields you should select the Where setting in the Total row and the Not Shown setting in the Crosstab row and then enter your criteria. You can also enter criteria for any column headings, and you can sort any of the fields. As you'll see a bit later, Access sorts the column heading name values in ascending order by default.

To build the crosstab query referred to above—one that shows contract sales by month for each group and a grand total for each group—start by selecting the tblContracts table in the Database window. Select New Query from the New Object toolbar button's drop-down list. Select Design View in the New Query dialog box, and then choose the Crosstab command from the Query menu. Drag the GroupName field from the field list to the first field in the design grid. Fill in the column as shown in Figure 8-32 (with the Group By, Row Heading, and Ascending settings).

To generate output in the form of monthly sales columns, you can create an expression that uses one of the built-in Access functions. You can use the same expression you saw earlier in the totals parameter query example:

SchedStart: Format([BeginningDate], "yyyy mmm")

This is your column heading. Fill out the second column of the design grid as shown in Figure 8-32 (with the Group By and Column Heading settings).

To calculate a grand total for each group, you need another Row Heading column that sums up the subtotals of ContractPrice times NumberOfWeeks. The expression is as follows:

GrandTotal: [ContractPrice] * [NumberOfWeeks]

Enter *Sum* in the Total row and *Row Heading* in the Crosstab row. To calculate the total for each month, you need to multiply the same two fields and call the result *ContractTotal*. Enter *Sum* in the Total row and *Value* in the Crosstab row. You can also add Where tests to total either paid contracts only or contracts issued by RM Productions (CommissionAgent1 = "RMP"). Figure 8-33 shows the recordset of the query shown in Figure 8-32.

FIGURE 8-33
The recordset of
the query shown
in Figure 8-32.

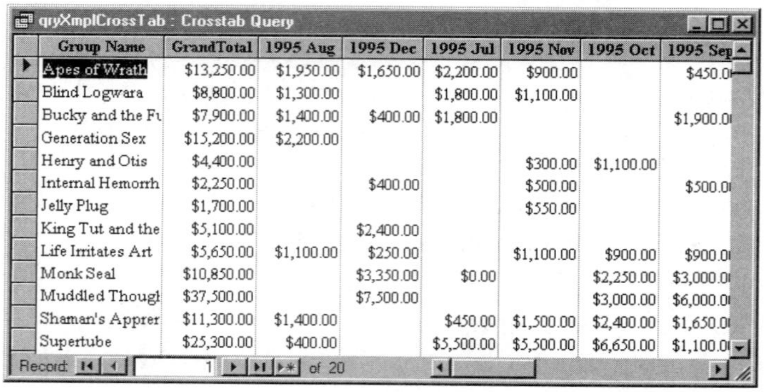

Group Name	GrandTotal	1995 Aug	1995 Dec	1995 Jul	1995 Nov	1995 Oct	1995 Sep
Apes of Wrath	$13,250.00	$1,950.00	$1,650.00	$2,200.00	$900.00		$450.00
Blind Logwara	$8,800.00	$1,300.00		$1,800.00	$1,100.00		
Bucky and the Fu	$7,900.00	$1,400.00	$400.00	$1,800.00			$1,900.00
Generation Sex	$15,200.00	$2,200.00					
Henry and Otis	$4,400.00				$300.00	$1,100.00	
Internal Hemorrh	$2,250.00		$400.00		$500.00		$500.00
Jelly Plug	$1,700.00				$550.00		
King Tut and the	$5,100.00		$2,400.00				
Life Irritates Art	$5,650.00	$1,100.00	$250.00		$1,100.00	$900.00	$900.00
Monk Seal	$10,850.00		$3,350.00	$0.00		$2,250.00	$3,000.00
Muddled Though	$37,500.00		$7,500.00			$3,000.00	$6,000.00
Shaman's Apprer	$11,300.00	$1,400.00		$450.00	$1,500.00	$2,400.00	$1,650.00
Supertube	$25,300.00	$400.00		$5,500.00	$5,500.00	$6,650.00	$1,100.00

Record: 1 of 20

Notice that although you didn't specify a sort sequence on the dates, the years appear left to right in ascending collating order. However, if you run the query as is, you'll get the month names in alphabetic order, not in the desired numeric order.

Access provides a solution for this: You can specifically define the order of columns for any crosstab query by using the query's property sheet. Click in the upper part of the Query window in Design view, and then click the Properties button on the toolbar to see the property sheet, as shown in Figure 8-34.

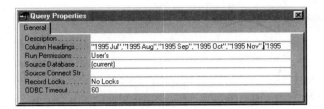

FIGURE 8-34

Entries in the property sheet that fix the order of column headings for the query in Figure 8-32.

To control the order of columns displayed, enter the headings exactly as they are formatted and in the order you want in the Column Headings row. Be careful to include all the column headings that match the result of the query. If you omit (or misspell) a column heading, Access won't show that column. When you run the query again with formatted column headings, you see the recordset shown in Figure 8-35.

FIGURE 8-35

A crosstab query recordset with custom headings, as defined in Figures 8-33 and 8-34.

Group Name	GrandTotal	1995 Jul	1995 Aug	1995 Sep	1995 Oct	1995 Nov	1995 Dec
Apes of Wrath	$13,250.00	$2,200.00	$1,950.00	$450.00		$900.00	$1,650.00
Blind Logwara	$8,800.00	$1,800.00	$1,300.00			$1,100.00	
Bucky and the Fu	$7,900.00	$1,800.00	$1,400.00	$1,900.00			$400.00
Generation Sex	$15,200.00		$2,200.00				
Henry and Otis	$4,400.00				$1,100.00	$300.00	
Internal Hemorrh	$2,250.00			$500.00		$500.00	$400.00
Jelly Plug	$1,700.00					$550.00	
King Tut and the	$5,100.00						$2,400.00
Life Irritates Art	$5,650.00		$1,100.00	$900.00	$900.00	$1,100.00	$250.00
Monk Seal	$10,850.00	$0.00		$3,000.00	$2,250.00		$3,350.00
Muddled Though	$37,500.00			$6,000.00	$3,000.00		$7,500.00
Shaman's Apprer	$11,300.00	$450.00	$1,400.00	$1,650.00	$2,400.00	$1,500.00	
Supertube	$25,300.00	$5,500.00	$400.00	$1,100.00	$6,650.00	$5,500.00	

Record: 1 of 20

You can find this query saved as *qryXmplCrossTab* in the Entertainment Schedule database.

Searching Multiple Tables

At this point, you've been through all the variations on a single theme—queries on a single table. It's easy to build on this knowledge to retrieve related information from many tables and to place that information in a single view. You'll find this ability to select data from multiple tables very useful in designing forms and reports.

Try the following example, in which you combine information about an entertainment contract and about the club where the entertainment is to be performed. Start by bringing the Entertainment Schedule Database window to the front. Click on the Queries tab, and then click the New button. Select Design View in the New Query dialog box to open a new Query window in Design view. Access immediately opens the Show Table dialog box. In this dialog box, you select tables and queries with which to design a new query. Select the tblClubs and tblContracts tables and then close the dialog box.

If you defined the relationships between your tables correctly, the upper part of the Query window in Design view should look like that shown in Figure 8-36. Access links multiple tables in a query based on the relationship information you provided when you designed each table. Access shows the links between tables as a line drawn from the primary key in one table to its matching field in the other table. If you didn't define relationships between tables, Access makes a best guess by linking the primary key field(s) in one table to those that have the same name and matching data type in other tables.

FIGURE 8-36

A query that selects information from the tblClubs and tblContracts tables.

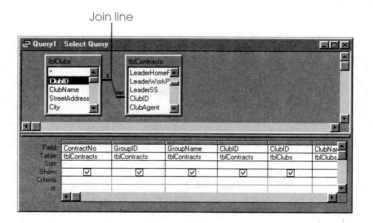

In this example, you want to add to the query the ContractNo, GroupID, GroupName, and ClubID fields from the tblContracts table and the ClubID, ClubName, and StreetAddress fields from the tblClubs table. When you run the query, you see the recordset shown in Figure 8-37. The fields from the tblContracts table appear first, left to right. You can scroll to the right to see the fields you added from the tblClubs table.

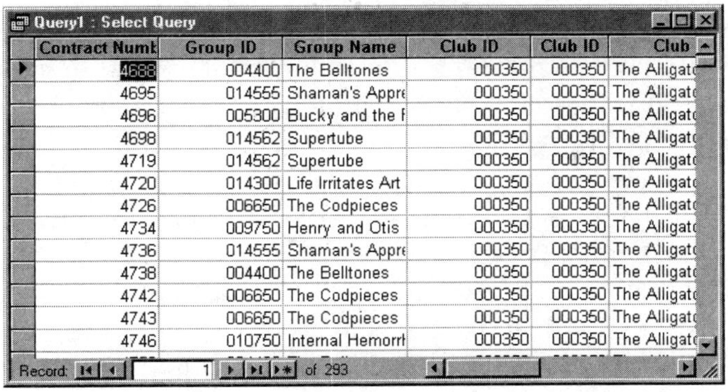

Query1 : Select Query

Contract Numb	Group ID	Group Name	Club ID	Club ID	Club
4688	004400	The Belltones	000350	000350	The Alligat
4695	014555	Shaman's Appre	000350	000350	The Alligat
4696	005300	Bucky and the I	000350	000350	The Alligat
4698	014562	Supertube	000350	000350	The Alligat
4719	014562	Supertube	000350	000350	The Alligat
4720	014300	Life Irritates Art	000350	000350	The Alligat
4726	006650	The Codpieces	000350	000350	The Alligat
4734	009750	Henry and Otis	000350	000350	The Alligat
4736	014555	Shaman's Appre	000350	000350	The Alligat
4738	004400	The Belltones	000350	000350	The Alligat
4742	006650	The Codpieces	000350	000350	The Alligat
4743	006650	The Codpieces	000350	000350	The Alligat
4746	010750	Internal Hemorrh	000350	000350	The Alligat

Record: 1 of 293

FIGURE 8-37
The recordset of the query shown in Figure 8-36.

As mentioned earlier, you can do many of the things with Query windows in Datasheet view that you can do with Table windows in Datasheet view. To see club information alongside group information, you can select the columns containing club data and move them next to the Group Name column. You can also select the columns containing group information, and then choose the Freeze Columns command from the Format menu. This action will lock those fields on the left side of the datasheet. You can then scroll to the right to bring the club columns into view.

One interesting aspect of queries on multiple tables is that in many cases you can update the tables from any of the columns. (See the section titled "Limitations on Using Select Queries to Update Data" later in this chapter for a discussion of when joined queries are not updatable.) For example, you can change either the group name in the tblContracts table or the club name in the tblClubs table by changing the data in this query's datasheet. (Caution: Because the club name comes from a table on the "one" side of a one-to-many relationship [one club has many contracts, but each contract is for only one club], if you change the club name in any row in this query, you change the club name for all contracts for the same club.)

Likewise, you can change the ClubID from the tblContracts table (the one on the left in this example), and Access will automatically update the new related club information. Try changing ClubID in the first row from 350 to 5000. When you leave the field, you should see the Club Name entry change from The Alligator Club to CandyBox. Note that in this case you're changing only the linking ClubID field in tblContracts, not the name of the club in tblClubs.

Outer Joins

Most queries that you create to request information from multiple tables will show results based on matching data in one or more tables. For example, the Query window in Datasheet view shown in Figure 8-37 contains the names of clubs that have contracts in the tblContracts table—and it does not contain the names of clubs that don't have contracts. This type of query is called an *equi-join query*. What if you want to display clubs that do not have any contracts in the database? You can get the information you need by creating an *outer join*.

To create an outer join, you must modify the join properties. Look at the Design view of the query you created in Figure 8-36. Double-click on the join line between the two tables in the upper part of the Query window in Design view to see the Join Properties dialog box, shown in Figure 8-38.

FIGURE 8-38

The Join Properties dialog box with the second option selected.

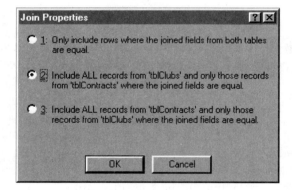

The default setting in the Join Properties dialog box is the first option—when the joined fields from both tables match. You can see that you have two additional options for this query: to see all clubs and any contracts that match or to see all contracts and any clubs that match. If you entered your data correctly, you shouldn't have contracts for nonexistent clubs. If you asked Access to enforce referential integrity (discussed in Chapter 5, "Building Your Database in Microsoft Access") when you defined the relationship between the tblClubs table and the tblContracts table, Access won't let you create any contracts for nonexistent clubs.

Select the second option in the dialog box and then click OK. You should now see an arrow on the join line pointing from the tblClubs field list to the tblContracts field list, indicating that you have asked for an outer join with all records from tblClubs regardless of match, as shown in Figure 8-39. For clubs that have no contracts, Access returns the special Null value in the columns for tblContracts. You can see only the clubs that aren't generating any business by including the Is Null test for any of the columns from tblContracts. When you run this query on the data in the Entertainment Schedule database, you should find exactly one club (the No One Wants to Work Here club, naturally) that has no contracts, as shown in Figure 8-40. The finished query is saved as *qryXmplClubsWithNoContracts* in the Entertainment Schedule database.

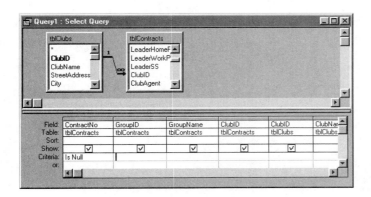

FIGURE 8-39

You can double-click on the join line between two tables in a query to open the Join Properties dialog box.

FIGURE 8-40

The recordset that shows clubs that have no contracts.

Building a Query on a Query

You might have noticed in the Show Table dialog box in the query's Design view that you can select not only tables but also other queries to be the input source for a new query. In fact, another way to build queries using multiple tables is to use another query as input. To solve certain types of problems, you must first build one query to define a subset of data from your tables and then use that query as input to another query to get the final answer.

For example, suppose you want to find out which clubs or groups have no bookings in a certain time period. You might guess that an outer join using the tblContracts table will do the trick. That would work fine if the tblContracts table contained contracts only for the time period in question. Remember, to find clubs that aren't booked, you have to look for a special Null value in the columns from tblContracts. To limit the data in tblContracts to a specific time period—let's say December 1995—you have to be able to test real values. In other words, a column from tblContracts can't be both Null and have a date value at the same time.

To solve this problem, you must first create a query that contains only the contracts for the month you want. As you'll see in a bit, you can then use that query with an outer join in another query to find out which clubs weren't booked in December 1995. Figure 8-41 shows the query you need. This example includes both the ClubID and the GroupID fields, so you can use it to search for either clubs or groups that weren't booked in the target month. A simple Between criterion in the BeginningDate field ensures that this query will return the correct rows. This query is saved as *qryXmplBookDec1995* in the Entertainment Schedule database.

FIGURE 8-41

A query that lists contract data for a particular month.

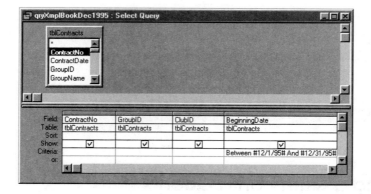

After you save the first query, select it in the Database window and select New Query from the New Object toolbar button's drop-down list to start a new query using the first one as input. In your new query, add tblClubs to the design grid by choosing Show Table from the Query menu and then selecting tblClubs in the Show Table dialog box. Access should automatically link tblClubs to the query on matching ClubID fields. Double-click on the join line to open the Join Properties dialog box, and choose option 3 to see all rows from tblClubs and any matching rows from the query. The join line's arrow should point from tblClubs to the query, as shown in Figure 8-42.

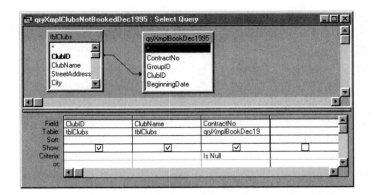

An outer join query searching for clubs not booked in December 1995.

As you did in the previous outer join example, include some fields from the tblClubs table and at least one field from the query that contains contracts only from December 1995. In the field from the query, add the special Is Null criterion. When you run this query (the results of which are shown in Figure 8-43), you should find 17 clubs without bookings in December 1995—including the No One Wants to Work Here club that you found earlier. This query is saved as *qryXmplClubs-NotBookedDec1995* in the Entertainment Schedule database.

Club ID	Club Name	Contract Numb
007000	Geppetto's Rockshop	
007050	Jumpin' Jacks Tavern	
012000	Lucifer's Lighthouse	
014400	Mudskipper's	
014950	The Olympic Bar	
018600	The Putt Putt Club	
018900	The Rickshaw Shack	
022050	The Salt and Pepper Lounge	
023800	Mom's Kitchen Café	
024252	The Ski Haus	
024259	The Wine Seller	
024269	West Coast Comedy Club	
024548	No One Wants to Work Here	

Record: 17 of 17

FIGURE 8-43

The clubs without bookings in December 1995.

Using Multiple Tables in Total Queries

As you might suspect, you can also use multiple tables in a total query or in a crosstab query. Earlier in this chapter, you built a crosstab query to show monthly contract amounts for each group. (See Figure 8-32.) You could do this using a single table as input because the application copies the relevant group name from the tblGroups table each time you create a new contract. You'll see later in Chapter 23, "The Finishing Touches," that some special Visual Basic for Applications (VBA) code can do this in the form you use to create and edit contracts. However, if you want to see totals by club name, you need to include tblClubs in this query so that you can use the related ClubName field to form the groups for the crosstab totals.

Figure 8-44 shows the crosstab query with the tblClubs table added. Instead of using GroupName from the tblContracts table for the row heading, you can now use the ClubName field from the tblClubs table. The settings for the field remain the same (Group By, Row Heading, and Ascending). Figure 8-45 shows the recordset of the query, with club names instead of group names. This example is saved as *qryXmplCrossTabClubs* in the Entertainment Schedule database.

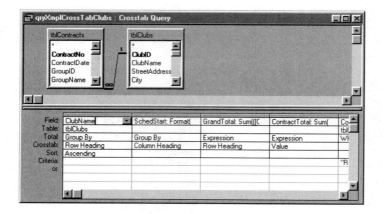

FIGURE 8-44
A crosstab query that uses multiple tables.

FIGURE 8-45
The recordset of the crosstab query shown in Figure 8-44.

Using a Query Wizard

Throughout this chapter, you've seen the tantalizing Query Wizard entries in the New Query dialog box. You can use Query Wizards to help you build certain types of "tricky" queries such as crosstab queries and queries to find duplicate or unmatched rows. For example, you could have used a Query Wizard to build the query shown in Figure 8-39 to locate clubs that have no outstanding contracts. Let's use a Query Wizard to build a query to perform the same search on groups.

To try this, click on the Queries tab in the Database window, and then click the New button. This time, select Find Unmatched Query Wizard in the New Query dialog box, as shown in Figure 8-46.

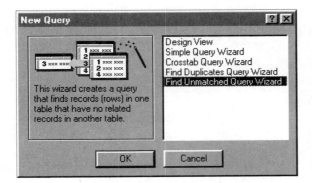

FIGURE 8-46

Selecting a
Query Wizard.

The wizard opens a window with a list of tables from which you can select the inital records, as shown in Figure 8-47 on the next page. If you want to search in an existing query, select the Queries option. If you want to look at all queries and tables, select the Both option. In this case, you're looking for groups that have no outstanding contracts, so select the tblGroups table and then click the Next button.

In the next window, select the table that contains the related information you expect to be unmatched. You're looking for groups that have no outstanding contracts, so select the tblContracts table and then click the Next button to go to the next window, shown in Figure 8-48 on the next page.

FIGURE 8-47

The first window
of the Find
Unmatched
Query Wizard.

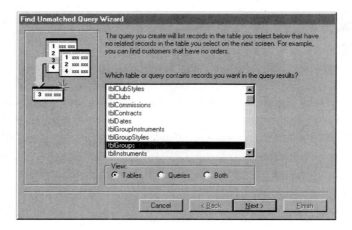

FIGURE 8-48

Defining the
unmatched link.

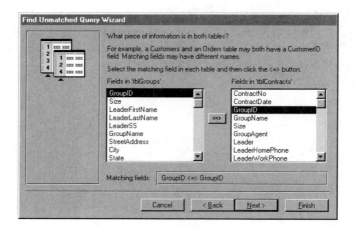

Next, the wizard needs to know the linking fields between the two tables. If you properly defined the table relationships, the wizard should select the related fields correctly. If you didn't do it properly, select the linking field in the first table (GroupID in tblGroups) in the left list box, select the linking field for the second table (GroupID in tblContracts) in the right list box, and then click the <=> button in the center to define the link. Click Next to go to the next window, shown in Figure 8-49.

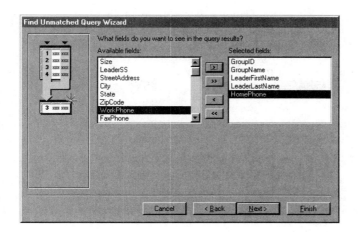

FIGURE 8-49
The window in which you select the fields to be displayed in a query.

Finally, select the fields you want to display and then specify whether you want to open the Query window in Datasheet view or in Design view. Figure 8-50 shows the finished query to find groups that have no contracts.

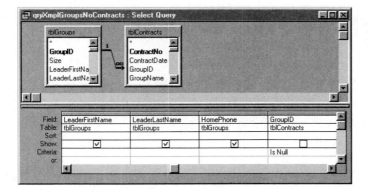

FIGURE 8-50
A query to find groups that have no contracts.

Limitations on Using Select Queries to Update Data

The recordset that Microsoft Access creates when you run a query looks and acts pretty much like a real table containing data. In fact, in most cases you can insert rows, delete rows, and update the information in a recordset, and Access will make the necessary changes to the underlying table or tables for you.

In some cases, however, Access won't be able to figure out what needs to be changed. Consider, for example, any calculated field. If you try to increase the amount in a Total field whose value is a result of multiplying data in the Quantity field by data in the Price field, Access can't know whether you mean to update the Quantity field or the Price field. You can, however, change either the Price field or the Quantity field and then immediately see the change reflected in the calculated Total field.

In addition, Access won't accept any change that might potentially affect many rows in the underlying table. For that reason, you can't change any of the data in a total query or in a crosstab query. Access can't update data in a field that has a Sum or Avg setting when the result might be based on the values in many records.

When working with a recordset that is the result of a join, Access lets you update all fields from the "many" side of a join but only the nonkey fields on the "one" side. For example, one club can have many contracts. In a recordset that results from a join between the tblClubs and tblContracts tables, you can update any fields that come from the tblContracts table, but you can't update any fields that form the primary key of the tblClubs table (in this case, the ClubID field). Access does let you change other fields in the tblClubs table, such as ClubName or the address fields.

This ability to update fields on the "one" side of a query can produce unwanted results if you aren't careful. For example, you could intend to assign a contract to a different club. If you change the club name, you'll change that name for all contracts related to the current club ID. What you should do instead is change the club ID in the tblContracts table, not the club name in the tblClubs table. You'll learn techniques later in Chapter 15, "Advanced Form Design," to prevent inadvertent updating of fields in queries.

Customizing Query Properties

Microsoft Access provides a number of properties associated with queries that you can use to control how a query runs. It's worth spending a moment to examine these properties before going on to the next chapter. Figure 8-51 shows the property sheet for select queries.

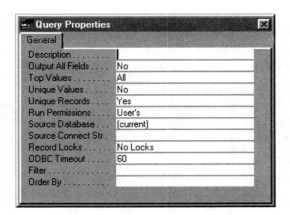

FIGURE 8-51
The property
sheet for select
queries.

You'll normally select only specific fields that you want returned in the recordset when you run a select query. However, if you're designing the query to be used in a form and you want all fields from all tables in the query available to the form, set the Output All Fields property to Yes. It's a good idea to keep the default setting of No and change this option only for specific queries.

TIP To open the property sheet for queries, click in the upper part of a Query window in Design view outside of the field lists, and then click the Properties button.

When a query is very complex, Access might need several seconds (or perhaps minutes) to find all the rows and begin to display information. If you're interested in only the "first" or "top" rows returned by a query, you can use the Top Values property to tell Access that you want to see information as soon as it finds the first n rows or the first $x\%$ of rows. If you enter an integer value, Access displays the result when it finds the number of rows specified. If you enter a decimal value of less than *1*, Access displays the result when approximately that percentage of rows has been found. Note, however, that if you include sorting criteria in your query, Access might have to first retrieve all the rows and then sort them before it can find the first n rows. In this case, specifying a Top Values property does not speed up the query.

When you run a query, Access can often find duplicate rows in the recordset. The default in Access is to return unique records. This means that the identifier for each row (the primary key of the table in a single-table query or the concatenated primary keys of a multiple-table query) is unique. If you don't ask for unique values, Access returns only rows that are different from each other. If you want to see all possible data (including duplicate rows), set both the Unique Values property and the Unique Records property to No. You cannot update fields in a query that has its Unique Records property set to No.

If you have designed your database to be shared by multiple users across a network, you might want to secure the tables and grant access to other users only through queries. The owner of the tables always has full access to the tables. You can deny access to the tables to everyone and still let authorized users see certain data in the tables. You accomplish this by setting the Run Permissions property to User's. If you want to allow users of this query to "inherit" the owner's permission to access tables when they use this query, set Run Permissions to Owner's.

Use the Record Locks property to control the level of editing integrity when this query is designed to access data that is shared across a network. The default is to not lock any records when the user opens the query. Access applies a lock only when it needs to write a row back to the source table. Select the Edited Record setting to lock a row as soon as the user begins entering changes in that row. The most restrictive setting, All Records, locks every record retrieved by the query as long as the user has the query open. Use this setting only when the query must perform multiple updates to a table and other users should not access any data in the table until the query is finished.

Three of the remaining properties—Source Database, Source Connect Str, and ODBC Timeout—apply to attached tables. See Chapter 10, "Importing, Linking, and Exporting Data," for details.

Now that you understand the fundamentals of building select queries with Access, you're ready to move on to updating sets of data with action queries in the next chapter.

SELECT EDITION

Chapter 9

Modifying Data
with Action Queries

Deleting Groups of Rows

An earlier section showed you how to copy old data to an archive table. This section shows you how to use a delete query to remove the data from your active table after you copy the data to an archive table.

Deleting Inactive Data

Here's another interesting example of how to use action queries.

n Chapter 7, "Using Datasheets," you learned how to insert, update, and delete single rows of data within a datasheet. In Chapter 8, "Adding Power with Select Queries," you discovered that you can use queries to select the data you want—even from multiple tables. Now you can take the concept of queries one step further and use *action queries* to quickly change, insert, create, or delete sets of data in your database.

> **NOTE** The examples in this chapter are based on the tables and data from the Entertainment Schedule sample database that comes with this book.

Updating Groups of Rows

It's easy enough to use a table or a query in Datasheet view to find a single record in your database and change one value. But what if you want to make the same change to many records? Changing one record at a time could be very tedious.

As a normal part of business, Ray McCann (the owner of RM Productions) often creates a contract record for entertainment booking dates that are still being negotiated. When he creates a new record for a contract that hasn't been confirmed, he marks it as pending (by using a *P* as the contract status code). Over time, he accumulates anywhere from a few to perhaps dozens of such contracts in his database. He likes to keep a record of these pending contracts—at least for local clubs—but he doesn't need them to be displayed when he's looking at other active contracts.

The Status field in the tblContracts table allows the value *D* to indicate a deleted contract record. As you'll see later, the query that supplies the data for the main contract edit form has a filter to weed out all "D" records. Ray could go through his contracts periodically and set all the old pending contracts to deleted status by hand. But why not let Microsoft Access do the work for him with a single query?

Testing with a Select Query

Before you create and run a query to update many records in your database, it's a good idea to first create a select query using criteria that select the records you want to update. You'll see in the next section that it's easy to convert this select query to an update query or another type of action query after you're sure that Access will process the right records.

To filter out pending contracts for local clubs, you need the club city, state, and zip code information, which is not in the tblContracts table. You can join the tblClubs table with tblContracts to get this information. You could filter on zip code ranges, but in this case searching for clubs in the state of Washington is sufficient. You also need to filter on the contract beginning date to be sure you don't throw away any current contracts. The query shown in Figure 9-1 looks for pending contracts with a proposed start date (the BeginningDate field) that is earlier than January 1, 1996. You can also use the *Date* built-in function to look for contracts dated prior to today's date.

FIGURE 9-1

A select query to find old pending contracts.

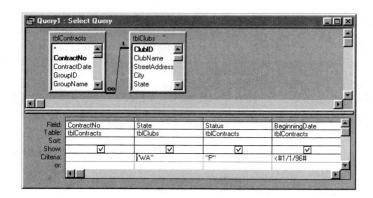

When you run the query, you'll see four contract records that you want to change, as shown in Figure 9-2.

FIGURE 9-2

The recordset of the select query shown in Figure 9-1.

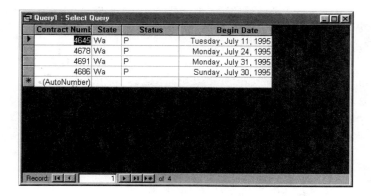

Converting a
Select Query to an Update Query

Now you're ready to change the query so that it will update the table. When you first create a query, Access creates a select query by default. You can find commands for the four types of action queries—make table, update, append, and delete—on the Query menu when the query is in Design view. You can also select one of these options from the Query Type toolbar button's drop-down list, as shown in Figure 9-3. Select Update to convert the select query to an update query.

FIGURE 9-3

The Query Type toolbar button's drop-down list.

When you convert a select query to an update query, Access changes the title bar of the Query window in Design view and adds an Update To row to the design grid, as shown in Figure 9-4. You use this new row to specify how you want your data changed. In this case, you want to change all "P" status contracts in Washington state that originated before January 1, 1996, to "D".

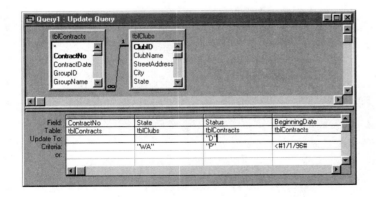

FIGURE 9-4

An update query with its Update To setting.

267

TIP You can enter any valid expression in the Update To row. You can include in the expression one or more of the fields from the source tables in the query. For example, if a particular group wants to raise its contract price for all pending contracts by 10 percent, you can include the ContractPrice field on the design grid and enter

    CCur(CLng(tblContracts.[ContractPrice] * 1.1))

in the Update To row. Note that the above formula uses the *CCur* and *CLng* built-in functions discussed in the previous chapter to round the result to the nearest dollar.

Running an Update Query

If you want to be completely safe, you should make a backup copy of your table before you run an update query. To do that, go to the Database window, select the table you're about to update, and choose the Copy command from the Edit menu. Then choose the Paste command from the Edit menu, and give the copy of your table a different name when Access prompts you with a dialog box. Now you're ready to run the update query.

To run the query, choose the Run command from the Query menu or click the Run button on the toolbar. Access first scans your table to determine how many rows will change based on your selection criteria, and then it displays a confirmation dialog box like the one shown in Figure 9-5.

FIGURE 9-5

The dialog box that reports the number of rows that will be changed by an update query.

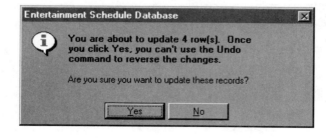

You already know that there are four old pending contract records, so you know that your update query is OK. To perform the update, click the Yes button in the dialog box. (If the number of rows indicated in the dialog box is not what you expected or if you're not sure that Access will update the right records or fields, click the No button to stop the query without updating.) After the update query runs, you can look at the table or create a new select query to confirm that Access made the changes you wanted. Figure 9-6 shows the result—old pending contracts are now marked as deleted.

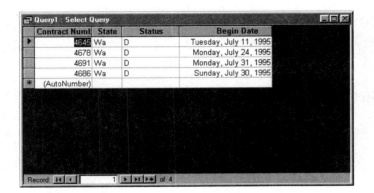

FIGURE 9-6
The updated data in the tblContracts table.

If you think you might want to perform this update again, you can save the query and give it a name. This sample query is saved in the Entertainment Schedule database as *qryXmplUpdateOldPending*. In the Database window, Access distinguishes action queries from select queries by displaying a special icon, followed by an exclamation point, before action query names. For example, Access displays a pencil and an exclamation point next to the new update query that you just created.

To run an action query again, select it in the Database window and click the Open button. When you run an action query from the Database window, Access displays a confirmation dialog box, similar to the one shown in Figure 9-7 on the next page. Click the Yes button to complete the action query. If you want to disable this extra confirmation step, choose the Options command from the Tools menu and, on the Edit/Find tab of the Options dialog box, deselect the Confirm Action Queries check box.

FIGURE 9-7

The dialog box
that asks you
to confirm an
action query.

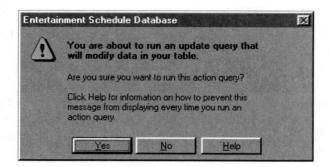

Updating Multiple Fields

When you create an update query, you aren't limited to changing a single field at a time. You can ask Access to update any or all of the fields in the record by including them in the design grid and then specifying an update formula. You can also update one field by using a formula that is based on a different field in the record.

Before Access updates a record in the underlying table or query, it makes a copy of the original record. Access applies the formulas you specify to the values in the original record and places the result in the updated copy. It then updates your database by writing the updated copy to your table. Because updates are made first to the copy, you can, for example, swap the values in a field named *A* and a field named *B* by specifying an Update To setting of [B] for the A field and an Update To setting of [A] for the B field. If Access were making changes directly to the original field, you'd need a third field to swap values to because the first assignment of B to A would destroy the original value of A.

Creating a New Table

Sometimes you might want to save as a new table the data that you extract with a select query. If you find that you keep executing the same query over and over against data that isn't changing, it can be faster to access the data from a table rather than from the query, particularly if the query must join several tables. Saving a query as a table is also useful for gathering summary information that you intend to keep long after you delete the detailed data on which the query is based.

Creating a Make Table Query

Assume that at the end of each year you want to create and save a table that summarizes the sales for the year by group or by club. You might recall from the exercises in building total queries in the previous chapter that the tblContracts table contains the data you need to calculate such information as number of contracts, average number of weeks per contract, and total contract amount for each group.

As with most action queries, it's a good idea to start with a select query to verify that you're working with the right data. In this case, start with the qryXmplTotalParameter query you saw in the previous chapter and make a few modifications to get it ready to store the result in a new table. Remove the SchedStart field (and the parameter) and replace it with a field named *EntertainMonth: Format([BeginningDate], "yyyy mm")*. This gives you a month number (which is easier to sort in ascending order) instead of a month abbreviation. Add a criterion on this field to pick out all of the 1996 contracts: *Between "1996 01" and "1996 12"*. It's probably a good idea to add the GroupID field and then sort the result by EntertainMonth and GroupID. Your result should look something like that shown Figure 9-8.

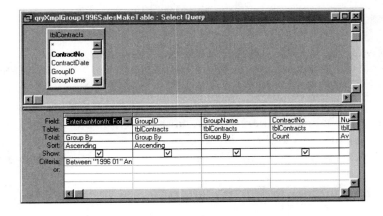

FIGURE 9-8
A select query to calculate contract data by group for 1996.

You can run this query to verify that you'll get the rows you want. Switch to Datasheet view to check out the result, as shown in Figure 9-9 on the next page.

FIGURE 9-9

The recordset
of the select
query shown
in Figure 9-8.

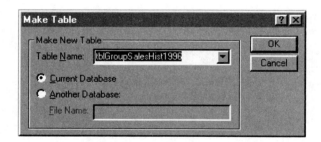

To convert this select query to a make table query, choose the
Make Table command from the Query menu. Access displays the Make
Table dialog box shown in Figure 9-10. Type in an appropriate name
for the summary table you are creating, and click OK to close the dialog box.

FIGURE 9-10

The Make Table
dialog box.

You can change the name of the table you want to create at any
time. Choose the Properties command from the View menu whenever
the query is in Design view and change the Destination Table property.

Running a Make Table Query

After you set up a make table query, you can run it by choosing Run
from the Query menu or by clicking the Run button on the toolbar.
Access creates the records that will be inserted in the new table and
displays a confirmation dialog box, as shown in Figure 9-11, that informs you of how many rows you'll be creating in the new table.

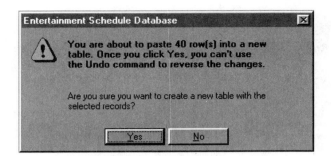

FIGURE 9-11
The dialog box
that asks you
to confirm the
results of a make
table query.

Click the Yes button to create your new table and insert the rows. Switch to the Database window and click on the Tables tab to bring up the table list, which should include the name of your new table. Open the table in Datasheet view to verify the information, as shown in Figure 9-12.

EntertainMonth	GroupID	GroupName	CountOfContract	AvgOfNumber	Max
1996 01	5200	Blind Logwara	1	1	
1996 01	10750	Internal Hemorrh	1	1	
1996 01	11050	Jelly Plug	1	5	
1996 01	14562	Supertube	1	1	
1996 02	6650	The Codpieces	1	1	
1996 02	9750	Henry and Otis	1	2	
1996 02	14300	Life Irritates Art	1	1	
1996 02	14524	Monk Seal	1	3	
1996 03	5200	Blind Logwara	1	2	
1996 03	14555	Shaman's Appre	1	2	
1996 04	14555	Shaman's Appre	1	2	
1996 05	14555	Shaman's Appre	1	2	
1996 05	14615	Urban Runoff	1	2	
1996 06	14555	Shaman's Appre	1	2	
1996 07	5300	Bucky and the F	1	2	
1996 07	6650	The Codpieces	1	2	

tblGroupSalesHist1996 : Table

Record: 1 of 40

FIGURE 9-12
The result of the
qryXmplTotal-
Parameter make
table query.

You might want to switch to Design view, as shown in Figure 9-13 on the next page, to correct field names or to define formatting information. As you can see, Access copies only basic field attributes when creating a new table. At a minimum, you should create a primary key that contains the EntertainMonth and GroupID fields. You might also want to change the CountOfContractNo and AvgOfNumberOfWeeks field names to something more meaningful.

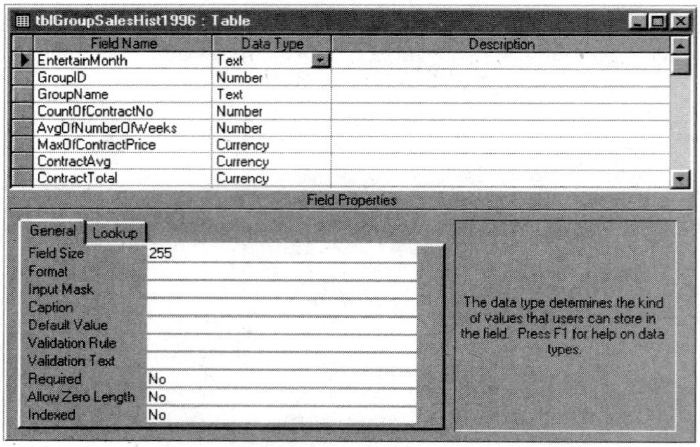

FIGURE 9-13

The Design
view of the
table created
by the qryXmpl-
TotalParameter
make table
query.

Inserting Data from Another Table

Using an append query, you can copy a selected set of information and insert it into another table. You can also use an append query to bring data from another source into your database—for example, a list of names and addresses purchased from a mailing list company—and then edit the data and insert it into an existing table. (In the next chapter, you'll learn how to import data from external sources.)

An append query, like a make table query, provides a way to collect calculated totals and save them in a predefined target. One major advantage to using an append query is that you can fully define the fields and field properties that you want in the final result table. A disadvantage is that it's easier to run into errors either because you're trying to reinsert data that's already there (based on the primary key you defined) or because the data you're adding doesn't match the data type you defined in the table. See the section titled "Troubleshooting Action Queries" later in this chapter for a specific discussion of potential errors.

Creating an Append Query

In the previous example you saw how to take one of the total queries you learned about in the previous chapter and turn it into a make table query. In truth, if you plan to collect such data over several months or years, you should probably design a table to hold the results and use append queries to periodically insert new sales data.

The Entertainment Schedule database includes two tables that were created for this purpose: tblClubSalesHistory and tblGroupSales-History. Both tables have an EntertainMonth field to record the year and month as formatted text, a NumberOfContracts field to record the number of contracts for each club or group for each month, a Contract-AvgWeek field to store the average number of weeks per contract, a HighestContractPrice field for the largest weekly contract price, a ContractAvg field for the average of all contracts, and a ContractTotal field for the sum of the contract amounts for this club or group and month. As you might expect, the tblClubSalesHistory table has ClubID and ClubName fields, and the tblGroupSalesHistory table has GroupID and GroupName fields.

You can use the qryXmplGroup1996SalesMakeTable query as a starting point. (This query is the same as the make table query that you just studied.) In this example, the append query is for the tblClub-SalesHistory table, so you need to include the tblClubs table to get the ClubName field. You should also rename each of the calculated fields to match the names of the fields in the target tblClubSalesHistory table. You can see this query under construction in Figure 9-14. You can find the completed queries saved as *qryXmplAppendClubSales* and *qryXmplAppendGroupSales* in the Entertainment Schedule database.

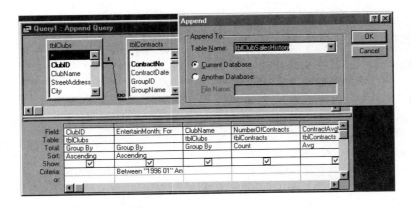

FIGURE 9-14

A query to calculate and append monthly totals for clubs.

Running an Append Query

As with other action queries, you can run an append query as a select query first to be sure that you'll be copying the right rows. You can either start out by building a select query, running it, and then converting it to an append query, or you can build the append query directly and examine the data to be added by the query by switching to Datasheet view from Design view. Although you can find and delete rows that you append in error, you can save time if you make a backup of the target table first.

After you confirm that the query will append the right rows, you can either run it directly from Design view or save it and run it from the Database window. When you run the qryXmplAppendClubSales query, Access should tell you that 40 rows will be appended, as shown in Figure 9-15. If you want to append the rows to the tblClubSalesHistory table, click Yes in the confirmation dialog box. Note that once you click Yes, the only way to undo these changes is to go to the target table and either select and delete the rows manually or build a delete query to do it.

FIGURE 9-15
The dialog box
that asks you
to confirm the
appending of
rows.

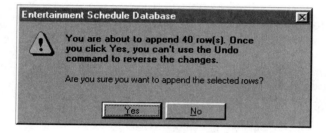

Entertainment Schedule Database

You are about to append 40 row(s). Once you click Yes, you can't use the Undo command to reverse the changes.

Are you sure you want to append the selected rows?

Yes   No

TIP   You probably won't want to create or modify a sales summary append query each time you want to update your summary table with data for different months and years. You can substitute parameters in the Between criteria to prompt you for the date ranges to calculate the next time you run the query.

Example: Using an Append Query to Archive Data

As you've just seen, you can easily convert a total query to an append query to save calculated totals that you think you'll use many times. It's much faster to use calculated data from a stored table than to recalculate the data in a total query.

Another excellent use of append queries is to extract old data from active tables to copy to archive tables. Over time, you might accumulate thousands of rows in your main transaction tables—the contracts, enrollments, or orders you collect in the process of running your business. You probably don't need data that's more than a year old for your day-to-day business. You can improve the performance of the most active parts of your application by periodically moving "old" data to archive tables that you access only infrequently.

To do this, you must first set up some archive tables in which to store the old records. If you need related records in other tables in order to fully understand the data (in this case, the original club and group data for archived contracts), you need to set up archive tables for those records as well. As you'll see in the last section of this chapter, RM Productions uses action queries to purge from the active system any clubs or groups that haven't had any recent activity. If you archive old contracts, you should also archive the related club and group information in case this information ever gets deleted from the active part of the system.

Let's start by building an append query to select certain old contracts from the active tblContracts table. Start a new query on tblContracts, and select all the fields from that table. To make this query easy to use, include a parameter to prompt for the oldest date you want to copy to the archive. You can see this query under construction in Figure 9-16 on the next page. Note that the Criteria row looks for any BeginningDate value that is less than the last date value entered <u>plus one</u>. Remember that date/time values have both a date and a time component. If you look for records containing a value less than or equal to a target last date, you might not get any of the rows for the last date if the date/time field you are checking has a time as well as a date. The date/time value for 8 A.M. on December 31, 1995, is <u>greater</u> <u>than</u> the value for just the date 12/31/95. Adding one to the required date value and looking for any date/time less than that will yield all dates and times on that day.

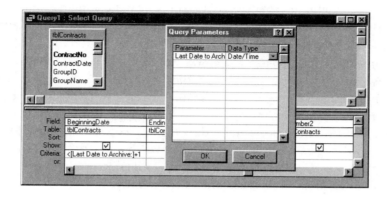

As you did earlier, convert this query to an append query by choosing Append from the Query menu or by selecting Append from the Query Type toolbar button's drop-down list. In the Append dialog box, enter *tblContractHistory* as the target table, as shown in Figure 9-17.

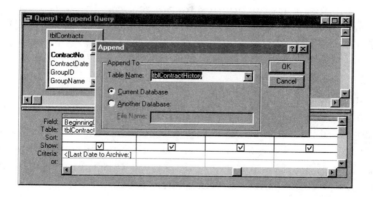

Let's assume that it is now late 1996 and you no longer need any of the contracts from 1995. Save the query (you can find this example saved as *qryXmplArchiveOldContracts* in the Enterainment Schedule database) and run it. When the Enter Parameter Value dialog box appears, type in the last day of 1995, as shown in Figure 9-18.

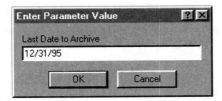

FIGURE 9-18
Entering an
archive cutoff
date.

It's very important to take the time to define the data type of the parameter you included in the query. If you tell Access that this parameter is a date/time value, you cannot type in any invalid value. If you're running the sample query in the database, try typing in letters to see what happens. Access won't run the query until you type in a valid date. If you enter a date of December 31, 1995, Access will ask you to confirm that the query should append 78 rows to the archive table, as shown in Figure 9-19. Click Yes in the confirmation dialog box to copy the old 1995 contracts to the tblContractHistory table. (You'll learn how to delete them later.) There's also a tblClubHistory table in the database that contains club information for rows previously archived and a tblGroupHistory table for old group information. You should check the new rows you just copied to see if you also need to copy any missing club or group rows from the active tables.

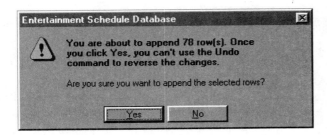

FIGURE 9-19
The dialog box
that asks you
to confirm the
appending of
rows.

You'll recall from the previous chapter how to build a query to find unmatched data between two tables. That's the starting point for the next query you need. You suspect that there might be some rows now in tblContractHistory that don't have matching rows in either tblClubHistory or tblGroupHistory. You could use the Find Unmatched Query Wizard to get a jump-start, but let's build this one "from scratch."

Start a new query on tblContractHistory. Add tblClubHistory to the query—Access will kindly link the two tables on the club ID. Double-click on the join line between the two tables and ask for all the rows in tblContractHistory and any matching rows in tblClubHistory. You should see an arrow pointing from tblContractHistory to tblClubHistory. Add tblClubs to the query—again, Access should link tblClubs to tblContractHistory for you on the club ID. Drag the asterisk field (*) from tblClubs to the design grid. Drag and drop the ClubID field from tblClubHistory to the design grid, deselect its Show check box, and add a criterion of Is Null. Convert your query into an append query with a destination table set to tblClubHistory. The result should look like that shown in Figure 9-20.

FIGURE 9-20

A query to select unmatched clubs to add to the archive table.

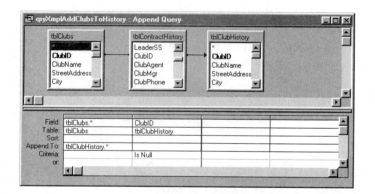

If you switch to Datasheet view, you should see four rows, as shown in Figure 9-21. What's happening? The answer is that the first link (an outer join, remember?) you created between tblContract-History and tblClubHistory asks for all rows in tblContractHistory regardless of whether you have matching rows in tblClubHistory. When you add the criterion to return only Null values from tblClubHistory, you get only rows in tblContractHistory that don't have a matching club yet in tblClubHistory. When you link this result to the main tblClubs table, you can find the data for the four unmatched clubs that you need to insert.

When you run this query, you insert the club data you need into tblClubHistory. Note that if you run this query again, it won't find any unmatched rows, so there will be nothing to append. This query is saved as *qryXmplAddClubsToHistory* in the Entertainment Schedule database. There's also a companion qryXmplAddGroupsToHistory query.

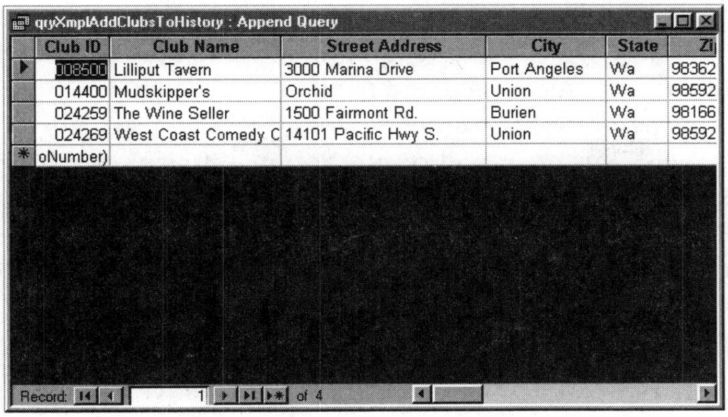

FIGURE 9-21
The four club
rows needed
to match the
archived
contracts.

Troubleshooting Action Queries

Microsoft Access analyzes your action query request and the data you are about to change before it commits changes to your database. When it identifies errors, Access always gives you an opportunity to cancel the operation.

Common Action Query Errors and Problems

Access identifies (traps) four types of errors during the execution of an action query:

- *Duplicate primary keys.* This types of error occurs if you attempt to append a record to a table or update a record in a table when the result is a duplicate primary key or a duplicate of a unique index key value. Access will not update or append any rows that would create duplicate values in primary keys or unique indexes. For example, if the primary key of a contract archive table is ContractID, Access won't append a record that contains a ContractID already in the table. Before attempting to append such rows, you might have to change the primary key values in the source table to avoid the conflict.

- *Data conversion errors.* This type of error occurs when you attempt to append data to an existing table and the data type of the receiving field does not match that of the sending field (and the data in the sending field cannot be converted into the appropriate data type). For example, if you attempt to append a text field to an integer field and the text field contains either alphabetic characters or a number string that is too large for the integer field, this error will occur. You might also encounter a conversion error in an update query if you use a formula that attempts a calculation on a field that contains characters. (For information on data conversions and potential limitations, see Figure 6-14 in Chapter 6, "Modifying Your Database Design.")

- *Locked records*. This type of error can occur when you run a delete query or an update query on a table that you share with other users on a network. Access cannot update records that are in the process of being updated by others. You might want to wait and try again later when no one else is using the affected records to be sure that your update or deletion occurs.

- *Validation rule violations*. If any of the rows being inserted or any row being updated violates either a field validation rule or the table validation rule, Access notifies you of an error and does not insert or update any of the rows that fail the validation test.

Another problem that occurs, although it isn't an error as such, is that Access might truncate data that is being appended to text or memo fields if the data does not fit. Access does not warn you when this happens. You must be sure (especially with append queries) that the receiving text and memo fields have been defined as large enough to store the incoming data.

An Error Example

Earlier in this chapter, you learned how to create an append query to copy old contracts to an archive table. What do you suppose would happen if you copied rows through June 30, 1995; forgot to delete them from the main table; and then later asked to copy rows through December 31, 1995? If you try this starting with an empty archive table in the Entertainment Schedule database, you'll get an error dialog box similar to the one shown in Figure 9-22.

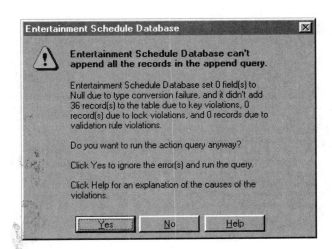

FIGURE 9-22
The dialog box
that alerts you
to action query
errors.

The dialog box declares that 36 records won't be inserted because of duplicate primary key values. Access didn't find any data conversion errors. Note that if some fields have conversion problems, Access might still append the row but leave the field set to Null. Because this table isn't shared on a network, there aren't any locking errors. When you see this dialog box, you can click the Yes button to proceed with the changes that Access can make without errors. You might find it difficult, however, to track down all the records that will not be updated successfully. Click the No button to abort the append query.

Deleting Groups of Rows

You're not likely to keep all the data in your database forever. You'll probably summarize some of your detailed information as time goes by and then delete the data you no longer need. You can remove sets of records from your database using a delete query.

Testing with a Select Query and Parameters

Once you have calculated and saved all the sales data and moved old contracts to the archive table, you should remove the contracts from the active table. This is clearly the kind of query that you will use again and again. You can design the query to automatically calculate which records to delete based on the current system date. (If you do this, you should probably change the qryXmplArchiveOldContracts query to work the same way.) The query can also be designed with a parameter so that a user can specify which data to delete when you run the query. Either design makes it unnecessary to change the query at each use.

As with an update query, it's a good idea to test which rows will be affected by a delete query by first building a select query to isolate these records. Start a new query on tblContracts and include the asterisk (*) field. Add the BeginningDate field to the design grid, deselect the Show check box, and add either a parameter criterion or something like *<Date( ) - 366* (to see all contracts that are more than a year old). If you convert this select query to a delete query, your result should look like that shown in Figure 9-23.

FIGURE 9-23
A delete query to remove archived contracts.

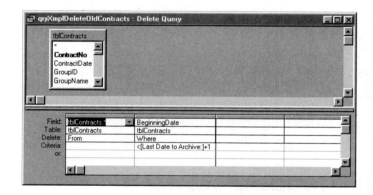

When you switch to Datasheet view for this query, Access prompts you for a date parameter, as shown in Figure 9-24. In the Enter Parameter Value dialog box, enter *12/31/95* to see all the old contracts from 1995. The result is shown in Figure 9-25.

FIGURE 9-24
Entering the delete query date parameter.

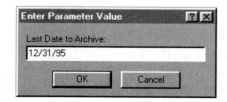

TIP Access recognizes several different formats for date parameters. For example, for the last day in 1995, you can enter any of the following:

12/31/95

December 31, 1995

31-Dec-1995

FIGURE 9-25
Verifying the rows to delete.

Contract Number	Contract Date	Group ID	Group Name	Size	Group
4642	6/24/95	000500	Apes of Wrath	1	RMP
4643	6/29/95	005300	Bucky and the Fu	5	RMP
4644	6/29/95	004400	The Belltones	3	RMP
4645	7/1/95	005200	Blind Logwara	2	MKP
4648	7/10/95	005200	Blind Logwara	2	MKP
4650	7/10/95	014250	King Tut and the	3	RMP
4651	7/10/95	014555	Shaman's Apprer	1	RMP
4652	7/11/95	006650	The Codpieces	3	RMP
4655	7/11/95	004400	The Belltones	3	RMP
4657	7/11/95	009750	Henry and Otis	1	RMP
4661	7/11/95	004400	The Belltones	3	RMP
4664	7/11/95	005300	Bucky and the Fu	5	RMP
4667	7/11/95	014615	Urban Runoff	4	RMP
4669	7/11/95	014524	Monk Seal	2	RMP
4670	7/11/95	014524	Monk Seal	2	RMP

Record: 1 of 78

The append query you saw earlier that moved these rows to an archive table copied 78 rows, which matches what you see here. After you verify that this is what you want, go back to Design view and run the query to actually delete the rows.

NOTE If you have experimented with various action queries to change the data in the Entertainment Schedule database, you might want to reinstall the database from the sample disc before trying other examples in this book.

Using a Delete Query

Because you won't be able to retrieve any deleted rows, it's a good idea to first make a backup copy of your table, especially if this is the first time that you've run this delete query. Use the procedure described previously in the section titled "Running an Update Query" to make a copy of your table.

You can create a delete query from a select query by choosing the Delete command from the Query menu when your query is in Design view. You don't have to make any further changes to select the rows to delete. Simply choose Run from the Query menu or click the Run button on the toolbar to delete the rows you specified. Because you included a parameter in this query, you'll need to respond to the Enter Parameter Value dialog box (shown in Figure 9-24) again. Access selects the rows to be deleted and displays the confirmation dialog box shown in Figure 9-26.

FIGURE 9-26

The dialog box that asks you to confirm the deletion of rows.

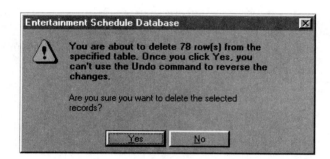

Click the Yes button to proceed with the deletion. Click the No button if you're unsure about the rows that Access will delete.

Deleting Inactive Data

You now know how to copy old contracts to an archive table, how to make sure matching club and group data is also copied to an archive table, and how to delete the old contracts from the main table. Eventually, you should probably also look at the rows in the active tblClubs and tblGroups tables to purge any rows that aren't active. If you have at least six months' worth of active data, you can create some queries to help you identify clubs or groups that haven't done any business in the last half-year. If you have more than six months' worth of contract data but want to limit your search to only the last six months, you must first create and save a query to filter out this data (similar to the example you saw in the previous chapter in the section titled "Building a Query on a Query"). Start a new query on tblContracts and add criteria, as shown in Figure 9-27. Save the query (or you can use the qryXmplContractsInLast6Months query in the Entertainment Schedule database).

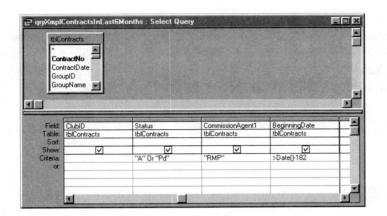

FIGURE 9-27

A query to find active contracts in the last six months.

Start a new query on the first one and add the tblClubs table. Change the link to an outer join that retrieves all the rows from tblClubs. Add the asterisk (*) field from tblClubs. Include any field from the query, deselect its Show check box, and add a criterion of Is Null. In this particular application, there might be a number of recently added clubs that are new prospects but don't yet have a contract. Since ClubID is an AutoNumber field, all the latest clubs have the highest ClubID values in the table. You know that many of these clubs won't find a match on contracts in the last six months, but you don't want to delete them. To solve this, include a test on ClubID from tblClubs using a parameter. Set the query to exclude from consideration any clubs whose primary key is greater than the value entered. Convert your query to a delete query, and the result should look like that shown in Figure 9-28.

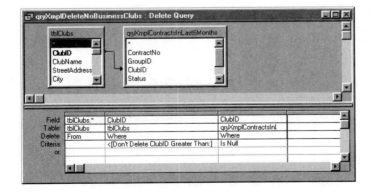

FIGURE 9-28

A query to delete clubs that had no contracts in the last six months.

You can find this query saved as *qryXmplDeleteNoBusinessClubs* in the Entertainment Schedule database. As you might expect, there's also a companion qryXmplDeleteNoBusinessGroups query. If you run the qryXmplDeleteNoBusinessClubs query and respond with *99999*, you should find two clubs to delete.

See Also   For more examples of action queries, see Chapter 11, "Advanced Query Design—SQL."

At this point, you should have a reasonable understanding of how action queries can work for you. In the next chapter, you'll learn how to import data from and export data to outside sources—text files, spreadsheets, other Access databases, or other database management systems.

Chapter 10

Importing, Linking, and Exporting Data

Although you can use Microsoft Access as a self-contained database and application system, one of the primary strengths of the product is that it allows you to work with many kinds of data in other databases, in spreadsheets, or in text files. In addition to using data in your local Access database, you can *import* (copy in) or *link* (connect to) data that's in text files, spreadsheets, other Access databases, dBASE, Paradox, Microsoft FoxPro, Btrieve, and any other SQL database that supports the Open Database Connectivity (ODBC) software standard. You can also *export* (copy out) data from Access tables to the databases, spreadsheets, or text files of other applications.

A Word About Open Database Connectivity

If you look under the hood of Microsoft Access, you'll find that it uses a database language called *SQL (Structured Query Language)* to read, insert, update, and delete data. SQL grew out of a relational database research project conducted by IBM in the 1970s. It has been adopted as the official standard for relational databases by organizations such as the American National Standards Institute (ANSI) and the International Standards Organization (ISO). You can see the SQL statements that Access uses by choosing the SQL command from the View menu or by selecting SQL View from the Query View toolbar button's drop-down list when you're viewing a Query window in Design view.

See Also Chapter 11, "Advanced Query Design—SQL," provides more details on how Access uses SQL.

In an ideal world, any product that "speaks" SQL should be able to "talk" to any other product that understands SQL. You should be able to build an application that can work with the data in several relational database management systems using the same database language. Although standards exist for SQL, most software companies have implemented variations on or extensions to the language to handle specific features of their products. Also, several products evolved before standards were well established, so the companies producing those products invented their own SQL syntax, which differs from the adopted standard. An SQL statement intended to be executed by Microsoft SQL Server might require modification before it can be executed by other databases that support SQL, such as DB2 or Oracle.

To solve this problem, several years ago a group of influential hardware and software companies—more than 30 of them, including Microsoft Corporation—formed the SQL Access Group. The group's goal was to define a common base SQL implementation that its members' products could all use to "talk" to one another. The companies jointly developed the *Common Language Interface (CLI)* for all the major variants of SQL, and they committed themselves to building in CLI support for their products. About a dozen of these companies jointly demonstrated this capability in early 1992.

In the meantime, Microsoft formalized the CLI for workstations and announced that Microsoft products—especially those designed for the Microsoft Windows operating system—would use this interface to access SQL databases. Microsoft calls this formalized interface the *Open Database Connectivity (ODBC) standard.* In the spring of 1992, Microsoft announced that more than a dozen database and application software vendors had committed to providing ODBC support in their products by the end of 1992. With Access, Microsoft provides the basic ODBC driver manager and the driver to translate ODBC SQL to Microsoft SQL Server SQL. Microsoft has also worked with several database vendors to develop drivers for other databases. The ODBC architecture is represented in Figure 10-1.

Access was one of Microsoft's first ODBC-compliant products. You have an option to install ODBC when you install Access on your computer. Once you've added the drivers for the other SQL databases that you want to access, you can use Access to build an application using data from any of these databases.

FIGURE 10-1

The Microsoft ODBC architecture.

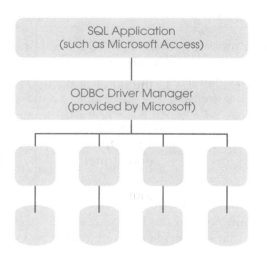

SQL Application
(such as Microsoft Access)

ODBC Driver Manager
(provided by Microsoft)

ODBC Drivers for Specific Relational Databases (provided by database vendor or third party)

SQL Databases, Local or Remote

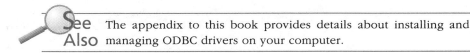

See Also The appendix to this book provides details about installing and managing ODBC drivers on your computer.

Importing vs. Linking Database Files

You have the choice of importing or linking data from other databases, but how do you decide which type of access is best? Here are some guidelines.

You should consider <u>importing</u> another database file when any one of the following is true:

- The file you need is relatively small and is not changed frequently by users of the other database application.

- You don't need to share the data you create with users of the other database application.

- You're replacing the old database application, and you no longer need the data in the old format.

- You need the best performance while working with the data in the other database (because Microsoft Access performs best with a local copy of the data in its native format).

On the other hand, you should consider <u>linking</u> another database file when any one of the following is true:

- The file is larger than the maximum capacity of a local Access database (1 gigabyte).

- The file is changed frequently by users of the other database application.

- You must share the file with users of the other database application on a network.

- You'll be distributing your application to several individual users, and you might offer updates to the application interface you develop. Separating the "application" (queries, forms, reports, macros, and modules) from the "data" (tables) can make it easier to update the application without having to disturb the users' accumulated data.

Importing Data and Databases

You can copy data from a number of different file formats to create a Microsoft Access table. In addition to copying data from a number of popular database file formats, Access can also create a table from data in a spreadsheet or a text file. When you copy data from another database, Access uses information stored by the source database system to convert or name objects in the target Access table. You can import data not only from other Access databases but also from dBASE, Paradox, Microsoft FoxPro, Btrieve, and—using ODBC—any SQL database that supports the ODBC standard.

Importing dBASE Files

To import a dBASE file, do the following:

1. Open the Access database that will receive the dBASE file. If that database is already open, switch to the Database window.

2. Choose the Get External Data command from the File menu, and then choose Import from the submenu. Access opens the Import dialog box, as shown in Figure 10-2.

FIGURE 10-2

The Import dialog box, in which you select a filename and a file type.

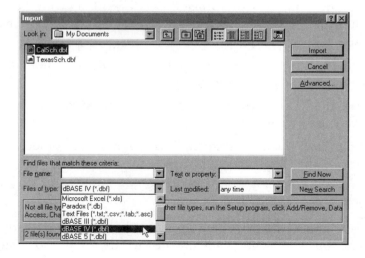

294

3. Select dBASE III, dBASE IV, or dBASE 5, as appropriate, in the Files Of Type drop-down list. Select the source file folder from the Look In drop-down list, and then select or type in the filename in the File Name text box. If you're having difficulty finding the file you want, you can enter part of the filename in the File Name text box and click the Find Now button. If you want to perform a more extensive search, click the Advanced button to open the Advanced Find dialog box.

4. Click the Import button to import the dBASE file you selected. Access displays a message box that informs you of the result of the import procedure, as shown in Figure 10-3.

FIGURE 10-3

The message box that indicates the result of an import procedure.

If the import procedure is successful, the new table will have the name of the dbf file. If Access finds a duplicate filename, it will generate a new name by adding a unique integer to the end of the name. For example, if you import a file named NEWCOLLEGE.DBF and you already have tables named Newcollege and Newcollege1, Access creates a table named NEW-COLLEGE2.

5. Click the OK button to dismiss the message box that confirms the import procedure. Access returns to the Import dialog box, where you can select another file to import or you can click the Cancel button to dismiss the Import dialog box.

You'll find a file named CalSch.dbf on the sample disc included with this book. Follow the procedure described above to import this dBASE 5 file into the College Counseling sample database. When you open the new table that Access creates from this dBASE format data, you'll see additional sample college data, as shown in Figure 10-4 on the next page.

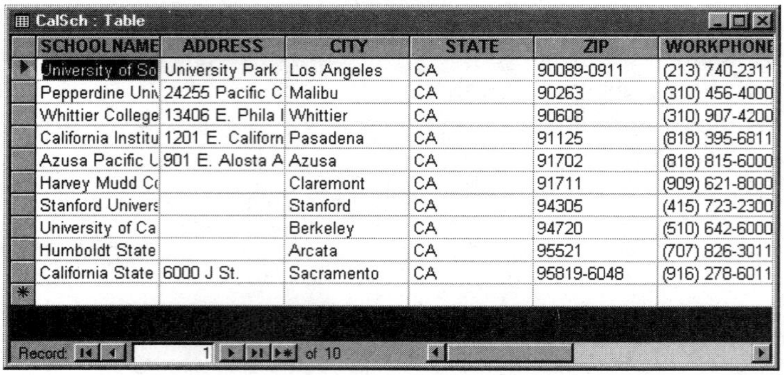

FIGURE 10-4

An imported
dBASE file.

FIGURE 10-4

An imported
dBASE file.

SCHOOLNAME	ADDRESS	CITY	STATE	ZIP	WORKPHONE
University of So	University Park	Los Angeles	CA	90089-0911	(213) 740-2311
Pepperdine Univ	24255 Pacific C	Malibu	CA	90263	(310) 456-4000
Whittier College	13406 E. Phila I	Whittier	CA	90608	(310) 907-4200
California Institu	1201 E. Californ	Pasadena	CA	91125	(818) 395-6811
Azusa Pacific U	901 E. Alosta A	Azusa	CA	91702	(818) 815-6000
Harvey Mudd Co		Claremont	CA	91711	(909) 621-8000
Stanford Univers		Stanford	CA	94305	(415) 723-2300
University of Ca		Berkeley	CA	94720	(510) 642-6000
Humboldt State		Arcata	CA	95521	(707) 826-3011
California State	6000 J St.	Sacramento	CA	95819-6048	(916) 278-6011

Record: 1 of 10

When you look at a table imported from dBASE in Design view, you'll find that Access has converted the data types, as shown in Figure 10-5.

FIGURE 10-5

The dBASE-to-
Access data type
conversions.

dBASE Data Type	Converted to Access Data Type
Character	Text
Numeric	Number, FieldSize property set to Double
Float	Number, FieldSize property set to Double
Logical	Yes/No
Date	Date/Time
Memo	Memo

Importing Paradox Files

The procedure for importing Paradox files is similar to the procedure for importing dBASE files. To import a Paradox file, do the following:

1. Open the Access database that will receive the Paradox file. If that database is already open, switch to the Database window.

2. Choose the Get External Data command from the File menu, and then choose Import from the submenu. Access opens the Import dialog box, as shown earlier in Figure 10-2.

3. Select Paradox in the Files Of Type drop-down list, and then select the folder and the name of the Paradox file you want to import.

4. Click the Import button to import the Paradox file you selected.

5. If the Paradox file is encrypted, Access opens a dialog box that asks for the password. Type in the correct password and click OK to proceed, or click Cancel to start over.

   When you proceed, Access responds with a message box, similar to the one shown earlier in Figure 10-3, that indicates the result of the import procedure. If the import procedure is successful, the new table will have the name of the db file. If Access finds a duplicate filename, it will generate a new name by adding a unique integer to the end of the name. For example, if you import a file named NEWCOLLEGE.DB and you already have tables named Newcollege and Newcollege1, Access creates a table named NEWCOLLEGE2.

6. Click OK to dismiss the message box that confirms the import procedure. Access returns to the Import dialog box. You can select another file to import, or you can click Cancel to dismiss the Import dialog box.

When you look at a table imported from Paradox in Design view, you'll find that Access has converted the data types, as shown in Figure 10-6.

Paradox Data Type	Converted to Access Data Type
Alphanumeric	Text
Number	Number, FieldSize property set to Double
Short Number	Number, FieldSize property set to Integer
Currency	Number, FieldSize property set to Double
Date	Date/Time
Memo	Memo
OLE	OLE Object (but Access won't be able to activate the object)
Graphic, Binary, Formatted Memo	Not supported

FIGURE 10-6
The Paradox-to-Access data type conversions.

Importing FoxPro Files

The procedure for importing FoxPro files is similar to the procedures for importing dBASE files and Paradox files. To import a FoxPro file, do the following:

1. Open the Access database that will receive the FoxPro file. If that database is already open, switch to the Database window.

2. Choose the Get External Data command from the File menu, and then choose Import from the submenu. Access opens the Import dialog box, as shown earlier in Figure 10-2.

3. Select FoxPro or FoxPro 3.0, as appropriate, in the Files Of Type drop-down list, and then select the folder and the name of the FoxPro file you want to import.

4. Click the Import button to import the FoxPro file you selected.

5. If the FoxPro file is encrypted, Access opens a dialog box that asks for the password. Type in the correct password and click OK to proceed, or click Cancel to start over.

   When you click OK, Access displays a message box, similar to the one shown earlier in Figure 10-3, that indicates the result of the import procedure. If the import procedure is successful, the new table will have the name of the FoxPro file. If Access finds a duplicate table name, it will generate a new name by adding a unique integer to the end of the name. For example, if you import a file named NEWCOLLEGE.DBF and you already have tables named Newcollege and Newcollege1, Access creates a table named NEWCOLLEGE2.

6. Click OK to dismiss the message box that confirms the import procedure. Access returns to the Import dialog box. You can select a new file and click the Import button, or you can click the Cancel button to dismiss the Import dialog box.

When you look at a table imported from FoxPro in Design view, you'll find that Access has converted the data types, as shown in Figure 10-7.

FoxPro Data Type	Converted to Access Data Type
Character	Text
Numeric	Number, FieldSize property set to Integer
Float	Number, FieldSize property set to Double
Date	Date/Time
Logical	Yes/No
Memo	Memo
General	OLE Object

FIGURE 10-7
The FoxPro-to-Access data type conversions.

Importing Btrieve Tables

NOTE To import Btrieve tables, you must have the Btrieve for Windows dynamic link library (DLL) installed. This DLL is not provided with Access; it is provided with Btrieve for Windows 95 and some other Windows-based products that use Btrieve. As this book goes to press, the 32-bit driver for Windows 95 is not yet available but is scheduled to be available shortly after the release of Access for Windows 95. Contact Btrieve, Inc., for further details.

To import a table from a Btrieve file, do the following:

1. Open the Access database that will receive the Btrieve table. If that database is already open, switch to the Database window.

2. Choose the Get External Data command from the File menu, and then choose Import from the Submenu. Access opens the Import dialog box, as shown earlier in Figure 10-2.

3. Select Btrieve in the Files Of Type list, and then select the folder and the name of the Btrieve dictionary file containing the description of the table you want to import. Click OK to open the Import Tables dialog box, which displays the list of tables in the dictionary file, as shown in Figure 10-8 on the next page.

FIGURE 10-8

The Import
Tables dialog
box.

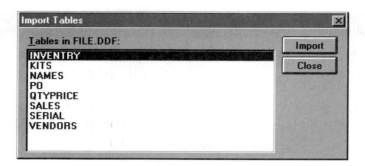

4. In the Import Tables dialog box, select the table you want to import. Click the Import button to import the Btrieve table you selected.

5. If the Btrieve table is password protected, Access opens a dialog box that asks for the password. Type in the correct password and click OK to proceed, or click Cancel to start over.

   When you proceed, Access responds with a message box, similar to the one shown earlier in Figure 10-3, that indicates the result of the import procedure. If the import procedure is successful, the new table will have the name of the Btrieve table. If Access finds a duplicate name, it will generate a new name by adding a unique integer to the end of the name. For example, if you import a table named NewCust and you already have tables named NewCust and NewCust1, Access creates a table named NewCust2.

6. Click OK to dismiss the message box that confirms the import procedure. Access returns to the Import Tables dialog box. You can select another table to import, or you can click Close to dismiss the dialog box.

When you look at the Table window in Design view for a table imported from a Btrieve file, you'll find that Access has converted the data types, as shown in Figure 10-9.

FIGURE 10-9

The Btrieve-to-
Access data type
conversions.

Btrieve Data Type	Converted to Access Data Type
String, lstring, zstring	Text
Integer, 1-byte	Number, FieldSize property set to Byte
Integer, 2-byte	Number, FieldSize property set to Integer

(continued)

FIGURE 10-9 *continued*

Btrieve Data Type	Converted to Access Data Type
Integer, 4-byte	Number, FieldSize property set to Long Integer
Float or bfloat, 4-byte	Number, FieldSize property set to Single
Float or bfloat, 8-byte	Number, FieldSize property set to Double
Decimal or numeric	Number, FieldSize property set to Double
Money	Currency
Logical	Yes/No
Date or Time	Date/Time
Note	Memo
Lvar	OLE Object

Importing SQL Tables

To import a table from another database system that supports ODBC SQL, you must first have the ODBC driver for that database installed on your computer. (For details, see the *Building Applications with Microsoft Access for Windows 95* manual that comes with Access; also see the appendix to this book.) Your computer must also be linked to the network that connects to the SQL server you want, and you must have an account on that server. Check with your system administrator for information about correctly connecting to the SQL server from which you want to import data.

To import data from an SQL table, do the following:

1. Open the Access database that will receive the SQL data. If that database is already open, switch to the Database window.

2. Choose the Get External Data command from the File menu, and then choose Import from the submenu. Access opens the Import dialog box, as shown earlier in Figure 10-2.

3. Select ODBC Databases in the Files Of Type drop-down list. Access opens the SQL Data Sources dialog box, shown in Figure 10-10 on the next page, from which you can select the data source that maps to the SQL server containing the table you want to import. Select a data source and click OK. Access displays the SQL Server Login dialog box for the SQL data source that you selected, as shown in Figure 10-11 on the next page.

FIGURE 10-10
The SQL
Data Sources
dialog box.

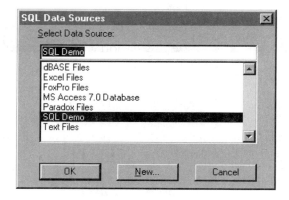

NOTE Although the SQL Data Sources dialog box lists dBASE, FoxPro, Paradox, and other Access databases, you can't import these files into an Access database using ODBC. Instead, Access uses built-in drivers to access these file types directly.

FIGURE 10-11
The SQL
Server Login
dialog box
for an SQL
data source.

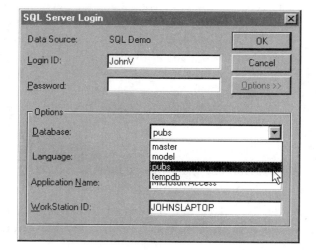

4. Enter your user ID and your password, and click OK. If you are authorized to connect to more than one database on the server and you want to connect to a database other than your default database, enter your user ID and password, and then click the Options button to open the lower part of the dialog box. When you click in the Database text box, Access logs on to the server and returns a list of available database names. Select the one you want and click OK. If you don't specify a database name

and if multiple databases exist on the server, you'll be prompted to select the database you want. When Access connects to the server, you'll see the Import Objects dialog box, which lists the available tables on that server, as shown in Figure 10-12.

FIGURE 10-12
A table list for an SQL data source.

5. From the list of tables, select the ones you want to import. If you select a table name in error, you can click on it again to deselect it, or you can click the Deselect All button to start over. Click the OK button to import the SQL tables you selected.

6. If the import procedure is successful, the new table will have the name of the SQL table. If Access finds a duplicate name, it will generate a new name by adding a unique integer to the end of the name. For example, if you import a table named newcollege and you already have tables named Newcollege and Newcollege1, Access creates a table named newcollege2.

    NOTE You've no doubt noticed by now that the different databases use different style conventions (newcollege, Newcollege, NEWCOLLEGE) for table names.

In general, Access converts SQL data types to Access data types, as shown in Figure 10-13.

SQL Data Type	Converted to Access Data Type
CHAR[ACTER]	Text, or Memo if greater than 255 characters in length
VARCHAR	Text, or Memo if greater than 255 characters in length
TEXT	Memo

FIGURE 10-13
The SQL-to-Access data type conversions.

(continued)

FIGURE 10-13 *continued*

SQL Data Type	Converted to Access Data Type
TINYINT	Numeric, FieldSize property set to Byte
SMALLINT	Numeric, FieldSize property set to Integer
INT	Numeric, FieldSize property set to Long Integer
REAL	Numeric, FieldSize property set to Double
FLOAT	Numeric, FieldSize property set to Double
DOUBLE	Numeric, FieldSize property set to Double
DATE	Date/Time
TIME	Date/Time
TIMESTAMP	Binary
IMAGE	OLE Object

Importing Access Objects

When the database from which you want to import data is another Access database, you can import any of the six major types of Access objects: tables, queries, forms, reports, macros, or modules. To achieve the same result you can also open the source database, select the object you want, choose the Copy command from the Edit menu, open the target database, and then choose the Paste command from the Edit menu. Using the Import command, however, allows you to copy several objects without having to switch back and forth between the two databases.

To import an object from another Access database, take the following steps:

1. Open the Access database that will receive the object. If that database is already open, switch to the Database window.

2. Choose the Get External Data command from the File menu, and then choose Import from the submenu. Access opens the Import dialog box, as shown earlier in Figure 10-2.

3. Select Microsoft Access in the Files Of Type drop-down list, and then select the folder and the name of the mdb file containing the object that you want to import.

4. Click the Import button. Access opens the Import Objects dialog box, shown in Figure 10-14, which is a representation of the source database's Database window. First click on the tab for

the object type, and then select the specific object you want to import. If you select an object in error, you can click on the name again to deselect it. If you want to import all objects of a particular type, click the Select All button. You can import multiple objects of different types by clicking on each object tab in turn and clicking Select All.

NOTE An import procedure might fail if you try to import more than 100 Access objects at one time. Microsoft suggests that you import no more than 50 to 100 objects at one time, depending on the memory available on your computer.

You can also click the Options button (which has been clicked in Figure 10-14) to select additional options. If you import any tables from the source database, you can also select the option to import the table relationships (if any) defined for those tables in the source database. If the object is a table, you can select the option to import the table structure (the table definition) only or to import the structure <u>and</u> the stored data. You can also select special options to import all custom toolbars from the source database (see Chapter 14, "Customizing Forms") or all import/export specifications (see later in this chapter for details). You can also choose to import the results of a query rather than import the query definition. Click OK to copy the objects you selected to the current database.

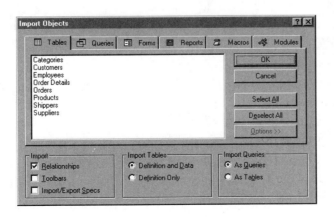

FIGURE 10-14
The Import Objects dialog box.

5. If the import procedure is successful, the new object will have the name of the object you selected. If Access finds a duplicate name, it will generate a new name by adding a unique integer

to the end of the name. For example, if you import a table named Newcollege and you already have tables named Newcollege and Newcollege1, Access creates Newcollege2. Because objects can refer to other objects by name within an Access database, you should carefully check preestablished name references to the new object if the object has to be renamed.

NOTE If the source Access database is secured, you must have at least read permission for the database, read data permission for the tables, and read definition permission for all other objects in order to import objects. Once you import the objects into your database, you will own the copies of those objects in the target database.

Importing Spreadsheet Data

Microsoft Access allows you to import data from spreadsheet files created by Lotus 1-2-3, Lotus 1-2-3 for Windows, and Microsoft Excel versions 2 and later. You can specify a portion of a spreadsheet or the entire spreadsheet file to import into a new table. If the first row of cells contains names suitable for field names in the resulting Access table, as shown in the spreadsheet in Figure 10-15, you can ask Access to use these names for your fields.

FIGURE 10-15

The data in the first row of this Excel spreadsheet can be used as field names when you import the spreadsheet into a new Access table.

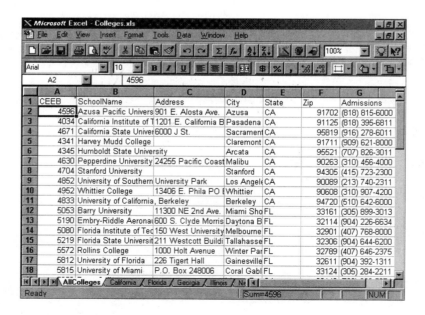

Preparing a Spreadsheet

Access determines the data type for the fields in a new table based on the values it finds in the first 25 rows of data being imported. When you import a spreadsheet into a new table, Access stores alphanumeric data as the Text data type with an entry length of 255 characters, numeric data as the Number type with the FieldSize property set to Double, numeric data with currency formatting as the Currency type, and any date or time data as the Date/Time type. If Access finds a mixture of data in any column in the first 25 rows, it imports that column as Text.

 TIP   If you want to append all or part of a spreadsheet to a target table, you should import or link the entire spreadsheet as a new table and then use an append query to edit the data and move it to the table you want to update.

If the first 25 rows are not representative of all the data in your spreadsheet, you might want to insert a single "dummy" row at the beginning of your spreadsheet with data values that are representative of the data type you want to use for each column. You can easily delete that row after you import the spreadsheet. For example, if you scroll down in the spreadsheet shown in Figure 10-15, you'll find several entries beyond the 25th row that have the zip code in Zip+4 text format, two of which are shown in Figure 10-16. Because Access sees only the numbers in the first 25 rows, it will use a Number data type for the Zip column. As you'll see a bit later, if you attempt to import this spreadsheet without fixing this problem, Access will generate an error for each row that contains data in the other format.

	A	B	C	D	E	F
30	1832	University of Chica	5801 S. Ellis Avenue	Chicago	IL	60637
31	1836	University of Illinois	601 East John Street	Champaign	IL	61820
32	1905	Wheaton College	501 East College Ave	Wheaton	IL	60187-5593
33	1318	Illinois Institute of	3300 South Federal S	Chicago	IL	60616-3793

FIGURE 10-16
Entries beyond the 25th row in the Zip column containing data that can't be stored in numeric format.

Importing a Spreadsheet

To import a spreadsheet into an Access database, do the following:

1. Open the Access database that will receive the spreadsheet. If that database is already open, switch to the Database window.

2. Choose the Get External Data command from the File menu, and then choose Import from the submenu. Access opens the Import dialog box, as shown earlier in Figure 10-2.

3. Select the type of spreadsheet you want to import (Excel or Lotus 1-2-3) in the Files Of Type drop-down list. Select the folder and the name of the spreadsheet file that you want to import. If you want to follow along with this example, select the Colleges.xls file on the sample disc.

4. Click the Import button. If your spreadsheet is from Excel version 5.0 or later, it can contain multiple worksheets. If the spreadsheet contains multiple worksheets or any named ranges, Access shows you the first window of the Import Spreadsheet Wizard, as shown in Figure 10-17. If you want to import a range that isn't yet defined, exit the wizard, open your spreadsheet to define a name for the range you want, save it, and then restart the import process in Access. Select the worksheet or the named range that you want to import, and click Next to continue.

FIGURE 10-17
The first window of the Import Spreadsheet Wizard.

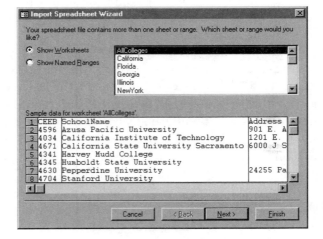

5. After you select a worksheet or a named range, or if your spreadsheet file contains only a single worksheet, the wizard displays the window shown in Figure 10-18. Select the First Row Contains Column Headings check box if you've placed names at the tops of the columns in your spreadsheet. Click Next to go to the next step.

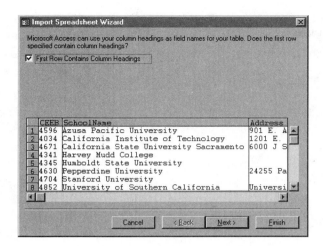

FIGURE 10-18
Selecting column headings from the first row of your spreadsheet.

6. In the next window, you can scroll left and right to the various fields and tell the wizard which fields should be indexed in the final table. Your indexing choices are identical to the ones you'll find for the Indexed property of a table in Design view. In this case, for the CEEB field, select Yes (No Duplicates) from the Indexed drop-down list box, as shown in Figure 10-19, and for the Zip field select Yes (Duplicates OK).

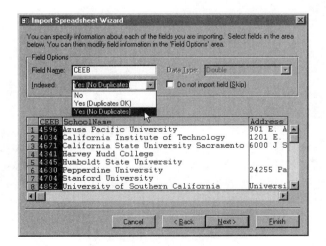

FIGURE 10-19
Identifying fields to index in the new imported table.

As you move from field to field, the Data Type combo box displays the data type that the wizard picks for each field (based on the data it finds in the first 25 rows). If what you see here is incorrect, you should exit the wizard and edit your spreadsheet to correct the data in the column. You can also choose to eliminate certain columns that you don't want to appear in the final table. For example, it's quite common to have intervening blank columns to control spacing in a spreadsheet that you print. You can eliminate such blank columns by scrolling to them and selecting the Do Not Import Field (Skip) check box. Click Next to go to the next step.

7. In the next window, shown in Figure 10-20, you can designate a field as the primary key of the new table. If you want, you can ask the wizard to build an ID field for you that will use the AutoNumber data type. If multiple fields form a unique value for the primary key, you can tell the wizard to not create a primary key. Later, you can open the resulting table in Design view to set the primary key. Click Next to go to the final window.

FIGURE 10-20

Identifying the primary key for the new imported table.

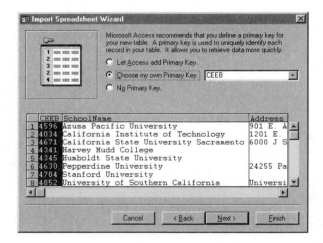

8. In the final window, you can type in the name of your new table and select an option to start the Table Analyzer Wizard to analyze your new table. (See Chapter 5, "Building Your Database in Microsoft Access," for details.) If you enter the name of an existing table, Access asks if you want to replace the old table. Remember, if you want to <u>append</u> the rows in your spreadsheet to an existing table, you must first import or link the spreadsheet (see the section titled "Linking Text and

Spreadsheet Files" later in this chapter) and then create an append query on that data to update your existing table. See Chapter 9, "Modifying Data with Action Queries," for details on append queries.

9. Click Finish in the last window to import your data. Access opens a message box, similar to the one shown earlier in Figure 10-3, that indicates the result of the import procedure. If the procedure is successful, the new table will have the name of the spreadsheet you selected. Click OK to dismiss the message box that confirms the import procedure.

Fixing Errors

Earlier in this chapter, in the section titled "Preparing a Spreadsheet," you learned that Access determines data types for the fields in a new table based on the values it finds in the first 25 rows being imported from a spreadsheet. Figures 10-15 and 10-16, shown earlier, show a spreadsheet whose first 25 rows would generate a wrong data type for the Zip column in a new Access table. The Number data type that Access would generate for that field, based on the first 25 entries, would not work for all the remaining entries, some of which have hyphens in them. In addition, one of the rows doesn't have a value in the CEEB column. If you attempt to use this column as the primary key when you import the spreadsheet, you'll get an additional error.

If you were to import that spreadsheet, Access would first display an error message similar to the one shown in Figure 10-21. This indicates that the wizard found a problem with the column that you designated as the primary key. If you have duplicate values, the wizard will also inform you. When the wizard encounters any problems with the primary key column, it imports your data but does not define a primary key. This gives you a chance to correct the data in the table and then define the primary key yourself.

FIGURE 10-21

Access displays this error message when it encounters a problem with your primary key values.

In addition, if the wizard has any problems with data conversion, it displays a message box similar to the one shown in Figure 10-22.

FIGURE 10-22

Access
displays this
message box
if it encountered
data conversion
errors while
importing a
spreadsheet.

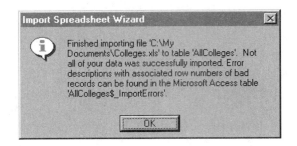

When the wizard has problems with data conversion, it creates an import errors table in your database (with the name of the spreadsheet in the title) that contains a record for each error. Figure 10-23 shows the import errors table that Access creates when you import the spreadsheet shown in Figure 10-15. Notice that the table lists not only the type of error but also the field and row in the spreadsheet in which the error occurred. In this case, it lists the six rows in the source spreadsheet that contain data in Zip+4 text format. The row number listed is the relative row number in the source spreadsheet, not the record number in the resulting table.

FIGURE 10-23

The import
errors table that
results from
importing the
spreadsheet
shown in
Figure 10-15.

Error	Field	Row
Type Conversion Failure	Zip	32
Type Conversion Failure	Zip	33
Type Conversion Failure	Zip	54
Type Conversion Failure	Zip	59
Type Conversion Failure	Zip	61
Type Conversion Failure	Zip	62

AllColleges$_ImportErrors : Table

Record: 1 of 6

If you look at the table that results from importing the spreadsheet shown in Figure 10-15 (see Figure 10-24), you can see that one row has no entry in the CEEB column. You can also find six rows that have no entry in the Zip column. If you switch to Design view, you can see that the Import Spreadsheet Wizard selected the Number data type for the Zip field. If you want to be able to store the values that include hyphens, the Zip field must be a text field.

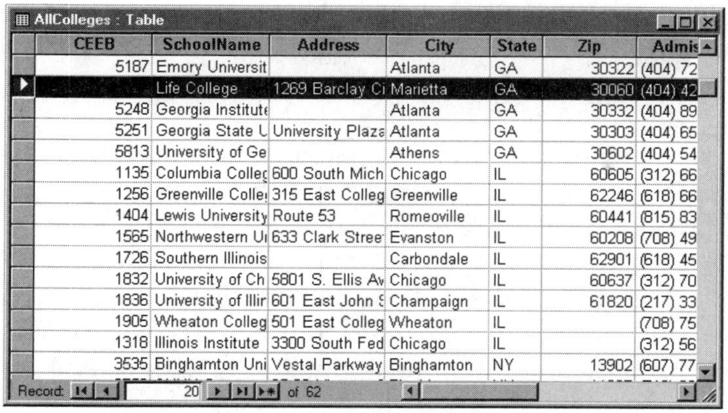

AllColleges : Table

CEEB	SchoolName	Address	City	State	Zip	Admis
5187	Emory Universit		Atlanta	GA	30322	(404) 72
	Life College	1269 Barclay Ci	Marietta	GA	30060	(404) 42
5248	Georgia Institut		Atlanta	GA	30332	(404) 89
5251	Georgia State U	University Plaza	Atlanta	GA	30303	(404) 65
5813	University of Ge		Athens	GA	30602	(404) 54
1135	Columbia Colleg	600 South Mich	Chicago	IL	60605	(312) 66
1256	Greenville Colle	315 East Colleg	Greenville	IL	62246	(618) 66
1404	Lewis University	Route 53	Romeoville	IL	60441	(815) 83
1565	Northwestern U	633 Clark Stree	Evanston	IL	60208	(708) 49
1726	Southern Illinois		Carbondale	IL	62901	(618) 45
1832	University of Ch	5801 S. Ellis Av	Chicago	IL	60637	(312) 70
1836	University of Illir	601 East John S	Champaign	IL	61820	(217) 33
1905	Wheaton Colleg	501 East Colleg	Wheaton	IL		(708) 75
1318	Illinois Institute	3300 South Fed	Chicago	IL		(312) 56
3535	Binghamton Uni	Vestal Parkway	Binghamton	NY	13902	(607) 77

Record: 20 of 62

FIGURE 10-24
After importing the spreadsheet shown in Figure 10-15, one of the rows has no primary key and several rows are missing a Zip entry.

You can correct some of the errors in the Table window in Design view. For example, you can change the data type of the Zip field to Text, save the table, and then enter the six missing zip codes. For the row that has no CEEB entry, you can either delete the row or supply a unique value. You can then set CEEB as the primary key in Design view.

Importing Text Files

You can import data from a text file into Microsoft Access even though the data in a text file, unlike the data in a spreadsheet, isn't arranged in columns and rows in an orderly way. You can enable Access to understand the data in a text file either by creating a *delimited text file,* in which special characters delimit the fields in each record, or by creating a *fixed-width text file,* in which each field occupies the same location in each record.

Preparing a Text File

You might be able to import some text files into Access without changing them, particularly if a text file was created by another program using standard field delimiters. In many cases, you'll have to modify the contents of the file, define the file for Access, or do both before you can import it.

Setting Up Delimited Data

Access needs some way to distinguish where a field starts and ends in each incoming text string. Access supports three standard separator characters: a comma, a tab, and a space. When you use a comma as the separator (a very common technique), the comma (or the carriage return at the end of the record) indicates the end of each field, and the next field begins with the first nonblank character. The commas are not part of the data. To include a comma within a text string as data, you must enclose all text strings within single or double quotation marks. If any of your text strings contain double quotation marks, you must enclose the strings within single quotation marks, and vice versa. Access accepts only single or double quotation marks (but not both) as the text delimiter, so all embedded quotes in a file that you want to import into Access must be of the same type. In other words, you can't include a single quotation mark in one field and a double quotation mark in another field within the same file. Figure 10-25 shows a sample comma-separated and double-quote–delimited text file.

FIGURE 10-25

A comma-separated and double-quote–delimited text file.

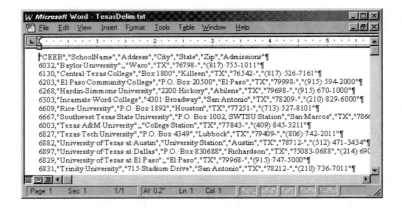

Another common way to separate data is to use the tab character between fields. In fact, when you save a spreadsheet file as text in most spreadsheet programs, the program stores the columns with tab characters between them. Figure 10-26 shows one of the worksheets from the Colleges spreadsheet from Microsoft Excel saved as text in Microsoft Word. Notice that Excel added double quotation marks around text strings that include commas but did not add quotation marks in any other case.

By default, Access assumes that fields in a delimited text file are separated by commas and that text strings are within double quotation marks. As you'll see a bit later, if you want to import a file that is delimited differently, you can specify different delimiters and separators in the Text Import Wizard. The important thing to remember is that your data should have a consistent data type in all the rows for each column—just as it does in spreadsheet files. If your text file is delimited, the delimiters must be consistent throughout the file.

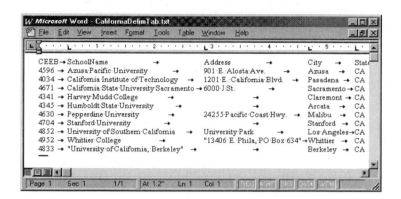

FIGURE 10-26
A tab-separated text file.

Setting Up Fixed-Width Data

Access can also import text files when the fields appear in fixed locations in each record in the file. You might encounter this type of file if you download a print output file from a host computer. Figure 10-27 shows a sample fixed-width text file. Notice that each field begins in exactly the same location in all the records. (Note: To see this sort of fixed spacing on your screen, you must display the file using a monospaced font such as Courier New.) To prepare this type of file for importing, you must first remove any heading or summary lines from the file. The file must contain only records, with the data you want to import in fixed locations.

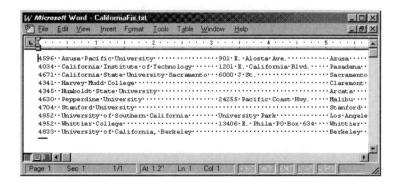

FIGURE 10-27
A fixed-width text file.

Importing a Text File

Before you can import a text file, you'll probably need to prepare the data or define the file for Access, or both, as discussed earlier in the section titled "Preparing a Text File." After you do that, you can import the text file into an Access database by doing the following:

1. Open the Access database that will receive the text data. If that database is already open, switch to the Database window.

2. Choose the Get External Data command from the File menu, and then choose Import from the submenu. Access opens the Import dialog box, as shown earlier in Figure 10-2.

3. Select Text Files in the Files Of Type drop-down list, and then select the folder and the name of the file you want to import. Access starts the Text Import Wizard and displays the first window of the wizard, as shown in Figure 10-28.

FIGURE 10-28
The first window of the Text Import Wizard.

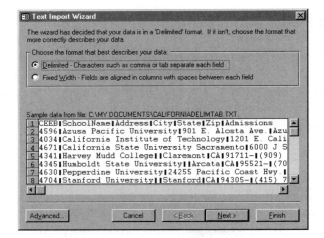

4. In this window, the wizard makes its best guess about whether the data is delimited or fixed-width. It displays the first several rows of data, which you can examine to confirm the wizard's choice. If the wizard has made the wrong choice, your data is probably formatted incorrectly. You should exit the wizard and fix the source file as suggested in the preceding section. If the wizard has made the correct choice, click Next to go to the next step.

5. If your file is delimited, the Text Import Wizard displays the window shown in Figure 10-29. Here you can verify the character that delimits the fields in your text file and the qualifier character that surrounds text strings. Remember that when you save a delimited text file from a spreadsheet program, the field delimiter is a tab character, and you'll find quotation marks around only strings that contain commas. If the wizard doesn't find a text field with quotation marks in the first line, it might assume that no text is surrounded by quotes. You might need to change the Text Qualifier from *{none}* to *"* if this is the case.

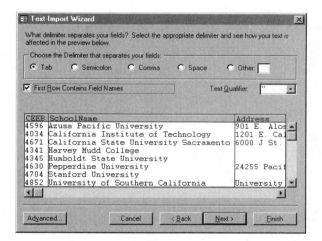

FIGURE 10-29

The window in which you select the field delimiter, the text qualifier, and field names.

If your file is in fixed-width format, the wizard displays the window shown in Figure 10-30 on the next page. Instead of showing delimiting characters, the wizard offers a graphic representation of where it thinks each field begins. You can click on and drag any line to move it. You can also create an additional field by clicking at the position on the display where fields should be separated. If the wizard creates too many fields, you can double-click on any extra delimiting lines to remove them. In the example shown in Figure 10-30 (using the CaliforniaDelimTab.txt file on the sample disc), the wizard assumes that the area code is separate from the rest of the phone number. You can double-click on the extra line following the area code to remove it and place all the characters that make up the phone number in a single field.

After you finish in this window, click Next to go to the next step.

FIGURE 10-30

The Text Import Wizard window for fixed-width text files.

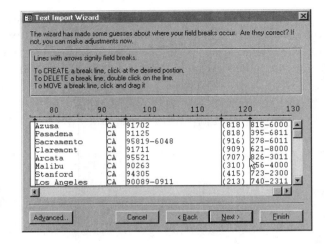

6. In the next window, shown in Figure 10-31, you specify whether you want to import the text into a new table or append the data to an existing table. (Unlike spreadsheet files that you have to import or link before you can append any of the data to an existing table, you can append data directly from a text file.)

FIGURE 10-31

Storing the data in a new table or appending the data to an existing table.

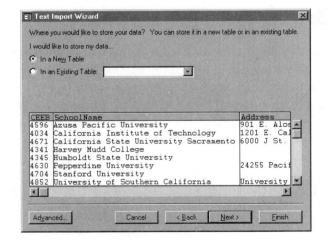

If you decide to create a new table, the wizard displays the window shown in Figure 10-32, in which you can specify or confirm field names (you can change field names even if the first row in the text file contains names), select field data types, and set indexed properties. Click Next to go to the next window, where you can select a primary key, much as you did for spreadsheet files in Figure 10-20.

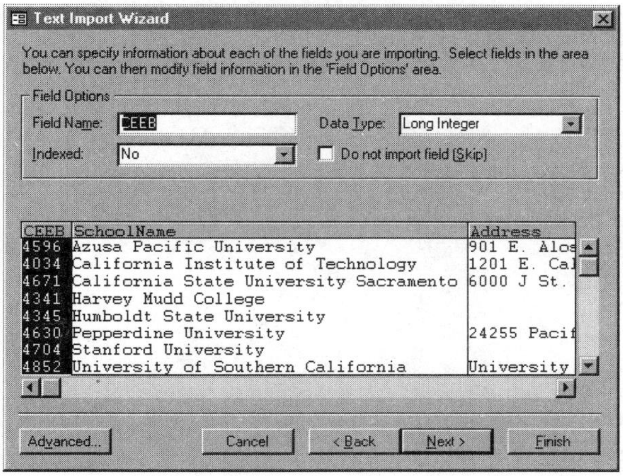

FIGURE 10-32

Setting field names, data types, and indexed properties for a new table.

If you decide to append the data to an existing file, either the columns must exactly match the columns in the target table (left to right) or the file must be a delimited file that has column names in the first row that match column names in the target table.

7. In the final window of the wizard, you confirm the name of the new table or the target table and click Finish to import your data. Access displays a confirmation message box to show you the result of the import procedure. If the wizard encounters an error that prevents any data from being imported, it will reopen the final wizard window. You can click the Back buttons to return to previous settings to correct them.

Defining an Import Specification

If you are likely to import the same fixed-width file often or you want to be able to use a macro or Visual Basic for Applications (VBA) to automate importing a text file, you can use the Text Import Wizard to save an import specification for use by your automation procedures. To do so, use the wizard to examine your file, and verify that the wizard identifies the correct fields. Click the Advanced button to see an Import Specification window like the one shown in Figure 10-33.

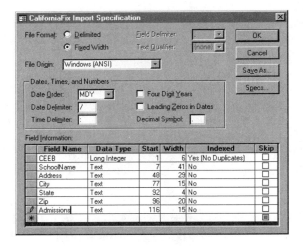

FIGURE 10-33
An Import Specification window.

For fixed-width specifications, you can define the field names, data types, start column, width, and indexed properties. You can also specify in the File Origin combo box whether the text file was created using a program running under MS-DOS or under Microsoft Windows. For fixed-width files, you don't need to make a Field Delimiter selection or a Text Qualifier selection; you use these options only to define a specification for delimited files. You can also specify the way Access recognizes date and time values and numeric fractions. Click the Save As button to save your specification and give it a name. You can also click the Specs button to edit other previously saved specifications.

Fixing Errors

You might encounter errors while importing text files that are similar to those described earlier in the section titled "Importing Spreadsheet Data." When you append a text file to an existing table, some rows might be rejected because of duplicate primary keys. Unless the primary key for your table is an AutoNumber field, the rows you append from the text file must contain the primary key fields and the values in those fields must be unique. For delimited text files, Access determines the data type based on the fields in the first 25 records being imported. If a number appears in a field in the first 25 records but subsequent records contain text data, you must enclose that field in quotation marks in at least one of the first 25 rows so that Access will use the Text data type for that field. If a number first appears without decimal places, Access will use the Number data type with the FieldSize property set to Long Integer. This setting will generate errors later if the numbers in other records contain decimal places.

Access displays a message box similar to the one shown earlier in Figure 10-22 if it encounters any errors. As with errors that are generated when you import a spreadsheet, Access creates an import errors table. The table contains a record for each error. The import errors table lists not only the type of error but also the column and row in the text file in which the error occurred.

You can correct some errors in the Table window in Design view. For example, you can change the data type of fields if the content of the fields can be converted to the new data type. (See Figure 6-14 in Chapter 6 for data conversion limitations.) With other errors you must either add missing data in Datasheet view or delete the imported records and reimport the table after correcting the values in the text file that originally caused the errors.

Modifying Imported Tables

When you import data from an external source, Microsoft Access often has to use default data types or lengths that will accommodate the incoming data but that might not be correct for your needs. For example, Access assigns a maximum length of 255 characters to text data imported from a spreadsheet or a text file. Even when the source of the data is another database, Access might choose numeric data types that can accept the data but that might not be correct. For example, numeric data in dBASE might be of the Integer type, but Access stores all numeric data from dBASE with a FieldSize setting of Double.

Unless you're importing data from an SQL or Paradox database that has a primary key defined, Access does not define a primary key in the new table. Also, if you did not include field names from a text or spreadsheet file, you'll probably want to enter meaningful names in the resulting table.

See Also   You can correctly specify most data types, change field names, and add a primary key in the Table window in Design view. For details about modifying your table design, see Chapter 6, "Modifying Your Database Design."

Linking Files

You can link tables from other Microsoft Access databases—whether the other databases are local or on a network—and work with the data as if these tables were defined in your current Access database. If you want to work with data stored in another database format supported by Access (FoxPro, dBASE, Paradox, Btrieve, or any SQL database that supports ODBC), you can link the data instead of importing it. In most cases, you can read data, insert new records, delete records, or change data just as if the linked file were an Access table. You can also link text and spreadsheet format data so that you can process it with queries, forms, and reports in your Access database. You can update and insert new rows in spreadsheets, but you can't delete rows. You can only read the data in linked text files. This ability to link data is especially important when you need to access data on a host computer or share data from your application with many other users.

Security Considerations

If you attempt to link a file or a table from another database system that is protected, Access asks you for a password. If the security information you supply is correct and Access successfully links the secured data, Access optionally stores the security information with the linked table entry so that you do not have to enter this information each time you or your application opens the table. Although there is no way to directly access this information in your database from Access, a knowledgeable person might be able to retrieve it by scanning the file with a dump utility. Therefore, if you have linked sensitive information to your Access database and have supplied security information, you should consider encrypting your database. Consult Chapter 14, "Securing and Delivering Your Application," in the *Building Applications with Microsoft Access for Windows 95* manual that comes with Access for information about securing and encrypting your Access database.

If you are linking to Microsoft SQL Server tables and are using Microsoft Windows NT domain security, you can set options in SQL Server to accept the Windows NT domain user ID if the user logs on correctly to the network. Therefore, you won't need to store security information with the link. If your server contains particularly sensitive information, you might want to disable this option to guard against unauthorized access from logged on but unattended network workstations.

Performance Considerations

Access always performs best when working with its own files on your local machine. If you link tables or files from other databases, you might notice slower performance. In particular, you can expect slower performance if you connect over a network to a table or a file in another database, even if the remote table is an Access table.

When sharing data over a network, you should consider how you and other people can use the data in a way that maximizes performance. For example, you should use queries with shared data whenever possible to limit the amount of data you need at any one time. When inserting new data in a shared table, you should use an Access form that is set only for data entry so that you don't have to access the entire table to add new data, as explained in Part 4 of this book, "Using Forms."

You should set options so that records are not locked if you are simply browsing through data. If you need to update data and you want to ensure that no one else can change a record that you have begun to update, you should set the RecordLocks property to Edited Record. When other users are updating the data you are using, you'll occasionally notice that you cannot update a record. You can set options to limit the number of times Access will retry an update to a locked record on your behalf and how long it will wait between retries.

You can also control how often Access reviews updates made by other users to shared data. If this refresh interval is set very low, Access will waste time performing this task repeatedly.

You can view and set options for multiple users sharing data by choosing Options from the View menu and clicking on the Advanced tab of the Options dialog box, as shown in Figure 10-34. The original settings for these options are often appropriate when you share data over a network, so it's a good idea to consult your system administrator before making changes.

FIGURE 10-34

The Options dialog box with the Advanced tab selected.

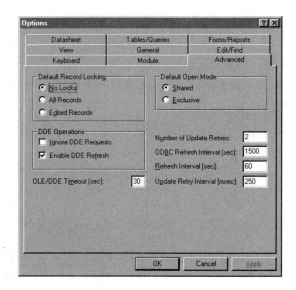

Linking Access Tables

To link a table from another Access database to your database, do the following:

1. Open the Access database to which you want to link the table. If that database is already open, switch to the Database window.

2. Choose the Get External Data command from the File menu, and then choose Link Tables from the submenu. Access opens the Link dialog box, which is similar to the Import dialog box shown earlier in Figure 10-2, and which lists the types of databases you can link.

3. Select Microsoft Access in the Files Of Type drop-down list and then select the folder and the name of the mdb file that contains the table you want to link. If you are connecting over a network, select the logical drive that is assigned to the network server containing the database you want. If you want Access to connect to the network server each time you open the table, type the full network location in the File Name text box instead of selecting a logical drive. For example, on a Microsoft NT network you might enter a network location such as this one:

   \\DBSVR\ACCESS\SHARED\NORTHWIND.MDB

   After you select the Access database file you want, click the Link button to see the tables in that database.

4. Access opens the Link Tables dialog box, shown in Figure 10-35, which lists the tables available in the database you selected. Select one or more tables, and click the OK button to link the tables to the current database. If the link procedure is successful, the new table will have the name of the table you selected. Access marks the icon for linked tables in the Database window with an arrow, as shown in Figure 10-36 on the next page. If Access finds a duplicate name, it generates a new name by adding a unique integer to the end of the name. For example, if you link a table named NEWCOLLEGE and you already have tables named Newcollege and Newcollege1, Access creates a table named NEWCOLLEGE2.

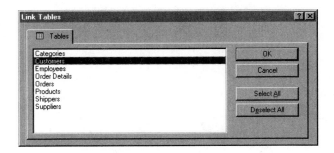

FIGURE 10-35
The Link Tables dialog box.

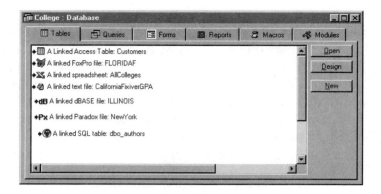

FIGURE 10-36

The Database window showing Access, FoxPro, spreadsheet, text, dBASE, Paradox, and SQL linked tables. Icons marked with an arrow represent linked tables.

Because objects such as forms, reports, macros, and modules might refer to the linked table by its original name, you should carefully check name references if Access has to rename a linked table.

Linking dBASE, FoxPro, and Paradox Files and Btrieve Tables

NOTE To link Btrieve tables, you must have the Btrieve for Windows dynamic link library (DLL) installed. This DLL is not provided with Access; it is provided with Btrieve for Windows 95 and some other Windows-based products that use Btrieve. As this book goes to press, the 32-bit driver for Windows 95 is not yet available but is scheduled to be available shortly after the release of Access for Windows 95. Contact Btrieve, Inc., for further details.

Linking tables from a foreign database is almost as easy as linking an Access table. To link a table from dBASE, FoxPro, Paradox, or Btrieve, do the following:

1. Open the Access database to which you want to link the table. If that database is already open, switch to the Database window.

2. Choose the Get External Data command from the File menu, and then choose Link Tables from the submenu. Access opens the Link dialog box, which lists the types of databases you can link.

3. Select dBASE III, dBASE IV, dBASE 5, Microsoft FoxPro, Paradox, or Btrieve, as appropriate, in the Files Of Type drop-down list, and then select the folder and the name of the database file

that you want to link. If you're linking a table from a Btrieve database, select the dictionary file (a ddf file). If you're connecting over a network, select the logical drive that is assigned to the network server that contains the database you want. If you want Access to automatically connect to the network server each time you open the linked file, type the full network location in the File Name text box instead of selecting a logical drive. For example, on a Microsoft NT network you might enter a network location such as this one:

\\DBSVR\DBASE\SHARED\NEWCOLLEGE.DBF

4. Click the Link button to link the selected dBASE, FoxPro, Paradox, or Btrieve file.

5. If you selected a dBASE file or a FoxPro file, Access opens the Select Index Files dialog box shown in Figure 10-37. In this dialog box you identify any index files that are associated with the file you want to link. You must inform Access of all related indexes if you want the indexes updated properly whenever you make a change to the dBASE or FoxPro file using Access. You must not move or delete these index files or the information (inf) file that Access builds when you link the table; if you do, you will not be able to open the dBASE or FoxPro file from Access. You must also be sure that any dBASE or FoxPro application always maintains these indexes. Access can't open a linked dBASE or FoxPro table if its indexes are not current. Also, if you don't identify the indexes for a FoxPro file, you won't be able to update the data from Access.

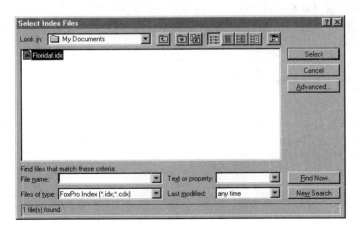

FIGURE 10-37

The Select Index Files dialog box, in which you associate index files with dBASE or FoxPro files that you link to your Access database.

327

Select the index files you need to associate with the dBASE or FoxPro file you're linking. Click the Select button once for each index file you want to add to the information file. Click Close after you select all the appropriate indexes.

6. If you're linking a Btrieve table, Access opens a Tables list box after you select a dictionary file in the Select File dialog box. The Tables list box shows the tables available in the dictionary you selected. Select the table you want, and click the Link button to connect the table you selected to the current database.

7. If the file you selected requires a password to access it (because it's an encrypted Paradox file or a password-protected Btrieve table), Access prompts you for the correct password and then displays a message box that indicates the result of the link procedure. If the link procedure is successful, the new table will have the name of the file you selected. If Access finds a duplicate name, it will generate a new name by adding a unique integer to the end of the name. For example, if you link a table named NEWCOLLEGE and you already have tables named Newcollege and Newcollege1, Access creates a new table named NEWCOLLEGE2.

8. Click the OK button to dismiss the message box that confirms the link action. Access returns you to the Link dialog box (or, with Btrieve, to the Tables list box). You can select another file to link, or you can click the Close button to dismiss the dialog box.

Linking Text and Spreadsheet Files

Linking a text file or an Excel spreadsheet file is almost identical to importing these types of files, as discussed earlier in this chapter. As noted earlier, you can only read linked text files, but you can update and add new rows (but not delete rows) in Excel spreadsheet files.

To link a spreadsheet file or a text file, do the following:

1. Open the Access database to which you want to link the file. If that database is already open, switch to the Database window.

2. Choose the Get External Data command from the File menu, and then choose Link Tables from the submenu. Access opens the Link dialog box, which lists the types of files you can link.

3. Select Microsoft Excel or Text Files, as appropriate, in the Files Of Type drop-down list, and then select the folder and the name of the file that you want to link. If you're connecting over a network, select the logical drive that is assigned to the network server that contains the database you want. If you want Access to automatically connect to the network server each time you open the linked file, type the full network location in the File Name edit box instead of choosing a logical drive. For example, on a Microsoft NT network you might enter a network location such as this one:

    \\FILESVR\EXCEL\SHARED\COLLEGES.XLS

4. Click the Link button to start the Link Spreadsheet Wizard or the Link Text Wizard.

5. Follow the steps in the wizard, which are identical to the steps for importing a text or spreadsheet file, as shown earlier in this chapter.

Linking SQL Tables

To link a table from another database system that supports ODBC SQL, you must have the ODBC driver for that database installed on your computer. (For details, see the *Building Applications with Microsoft Access for Windows 95* manual that comes with Access; also see the appendix to this book.) Your computer must also be linked to the network that connects to the SQL server you want, and you must have an account on that server. Check with your system administrator for information about correctly connecting to the SQL server from which you want to link a table.

To link an SQL table, do the following:

1. Open the Access database to which you want to link the SQL table. If that database is already open, switch to the Database window.

2. Choose the Get External Data command from the File menu, and then choose Link Tables from the submenu. Access opens the Link dialog box, which lists the types of files you can link.

3. Select ODBC Databases in the Files Of Type drop-down list. Access opens the SQL Data Sources dialog box, shown earlier in Figure 10-10, in which you can select the data source that maps to the SQL server containing the table you want to link. Select a data source and click OK. Access displays the SQL Server Login dialog box for the SQL data source that you selected, as shown earlier in Figure 10-11.

4. Enter your user ID and your password, and click OK. If you are authorized to connect to more than one database on the server and you want to connect to a database other than your default database, enter your user ID and password, and then click the Options button to open the lower part of the dialog box. When you click the Database text box, Access logs on to the server and returns a list of available database names. Select the one you want and click OK. If you don't specify a database name and if multiple databases exist on the server, Access will prompt you to select the database you want. When Access connects to the server, you'll see the Link Objects dialog box, similar to the Import Objects dialog box shown earlier in Figure 10-12, which lists the available tables on that server.

5. From the list of tables, select the ones you want to link. If you select a table name in error, you can click it again to deselect it, or you can click the Deselect All button to start over. Click the OK button to link to the SQL tables you selected.

6. If the link procedure is successful, the new table will have the name of the SQL table. If Access finds a duplicate name, it will generate a new name by adding a unique integer to the end of the name. For example, if you link to a table named newcollege and you already have tables named Newcollege and Newcollege1, Access creates a table named newcollege2.

Modifying Linked Tables

You can make some changes to the definitions of linked tables to customize them for use in your Access environment. When you attempt to open the Table window in Design view, Access opens a dialog box to warn you that you cannot modify certain properties of a linked table. You can still click OK to open the linked table in Design view.

You can open a linked table in Design view to change the Format, Decimal Places, Caption, Description, and Input Mask property settings for any field. You can set these properties to customize the way you look at and update data in Access forms and reports. You can also give any linked table a new name for use within your Access database (although the table's original name remains unchanged in the source database) to help you better identify the table or to enable you to use the table with the queries, forms, and reports that you've already designed.

Changing a table's design in Access has no effect on the original table in its source database. Notice, however, that if the design of the table in the source database changes, you must relink the table to Access. You must also unlink and relink any table if your user ID or your password changes.

Unlinking Linked Tables

It is easy to unlink tables that are linked to your Access database. In the Database window, simply select the table you want to unlink and then press the Del key or choose Delete from the Edit menu. Access displays the confirmation message box shown in Figure 10-38. Click the Yes button to unlink the table. Unlinking the table does not delete the table; it simply removes the link from your table list in the Database window.

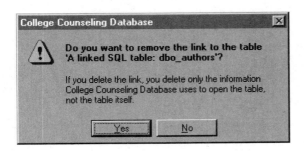

FIGURE 10-38
The confirmation message box that appears when you unlink a table.

Using the Linked Table Manager

If some or all of your linked tables move to a different location, you can easily update the location information by using the Linked Table Manager. This handy utility is provided in the Add-ins facility on the Tools menu. To use the Linked Table Manager, open the database that contains linked tables that need to be relinked, choose Add-ins from the Tools menu, and then choose Linked Table Manager from the submenu. The utility opens a dialog box that displays all the linked tables in your database, as shown in Figure 10-39. Simply select the ones that you think need to be verified and updated, and then click OK. If any of the linked tables have moved to a different location, the Linked Table Manager prompts you with a dialog box so that you can identify the new file location. You can also select the Always Prompt For New Location check box to verify the file location for all linked tables.

FIGURE 10-39
The Linked
Table Manager
dialog box.

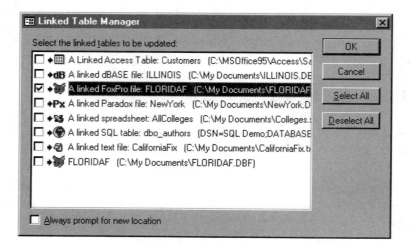

Exporting Data

You can export (copy) any object in a Microsoft Access database to any other Access database. You can also export data from Access tables to spreadsheet files, other databases, text files, Microsoft Word mail merge documents, and SQL tables.

Exporting to Another Access Database

Exporting objects from one Access database to another works much like importing Access objects. To export any object from one Access database to another Access database, do the following:

1. Open the Access database from which you want to export an object. If that database is already open, switch to the Database window.

2. Select the object you want to export in the Database window, and then choose the Save As/Export command from the File menu. Access opens the Save As dialog box shown in Figure 10-40. Note that if you select a macro object, you also have the option to save the macro as a Visual Basic module in the current database. Select the To An External File Or Database option and then click OK.

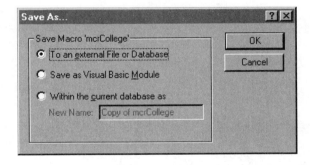

FIGURE 10-40
The Save As
dialog box.

3. Access opens a Save In dialog box, similar to the one shown in Figure 10-41 on the next page, in which you can select the folder and the name of the mdb file to which you want to export the object. After you select these, click Export.

FIGURE 10-41

The Save In
dialog box.

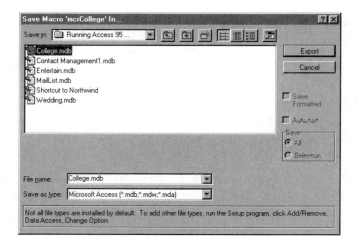

4. Next, Access opens the Export dialog box, shown in Figure 10-42, in which you can specify a name for the object in the target database. You can keep the name that Access suggests, or you can change it to make it more appropriate to the target database. Note that if you're exporting a table, you can choose to export both the table definition and the data or the definition only. Click OK to export the object.

FIGURE 10-42

The Export
dialog box for
naming an
Access object
to export.

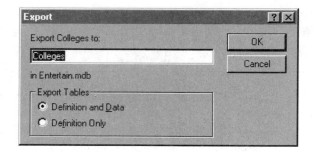

5. If the export name you type in already exists in the target database, Access warns you and asks whether you want to replace the existing object. Click Yes to proceed, or click No to stop the export procedure. If the export procedure is successful, you'll find a new object in the target database. Because objects can refer to other objects by name within an Access database, you should carefully check name references in the target database.

Exporting to a Spreadsheet or to a dBASE, Paradox, or FoxPro File

Use the following procedure to export data from a table, a select query, or a crosstab query to a spreadsheet (Microsoft Excel or Lotus 1-2-3) or to a foreign database (dBASE, Paradox, or FoxPro) file:

1. Open the Access database from which you want to export an object. If that database is already open, switch to the Database window.

2. Select the object you want to export in the Database window, and then choose the Save As/Export command from the File menu. Access opens the Save As dialog box, as shown in Figure 10-40. Select the To An External File Or Database option and then click OK.

3. Access opens the Save In dialog box, shown in Figure 10-41, from which you can select the file type, folder, and name of the file to which you want to export the selected object. After you select these, click Export.

4. If the export procedure is successful, you'll find a new file that you can use with your spreadsheet or with another database program.

TIP   Access truncates long field names when exporting data to dBASE, Paradox, or FoxPro files. If this results in a duplicate field name, Access will not export your data.

To correct this problem, make a temporary copy of your table, edit the field names in the temporary table to avoid duplicates, and try the export procedure again using the temporary table. You should avoid changing the field names in your permanent table because you might cause errors in queries, forms, and reports that use the table.

Quick Export to Microsoft Excel

Access also provides a quick facility to export the data in any table, select query, or crosstab query to an Excel spreadsheet. In the Database window, select the table or query whose data you want to export. Choose Office Links from the Tools menu and then choose Analyze It With MS Excel from the submenu, or select Analyze It With MS Excel from the Office Links toolbar button's drop-down list. Access copies the table to an Excel spreadsheet file and opens the file in Excel. If the filename already exists, Access asks whether you want to replace the file. If you click No, Access asks you to provide a different filename. Figure 10-43 shows the Colleges table in the College Counseling database after it has been exported to Excel.

FIGURE 10-43

An Access table that has been exported to Excel.

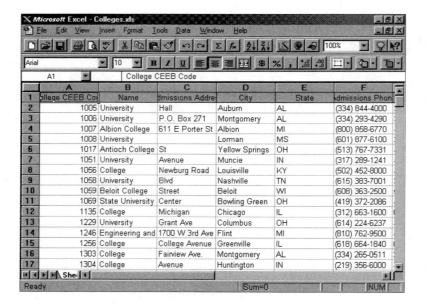

Exporting to a Text File

You can export data from an Access table, a select query, or a crosstab query to a text file in one of two formats: delimited or fixed-width. You might find this procedure particularly useful for copying data from an Access table to a non–Windows-based word processor or text editor or for uploading the data to a host computer.

To export the data from an Access table, a select query, or a crosstab query to a text file, do the following:

1. Open the Access database from which you want to export the data in a table. If that database is already open, switch to the Database window.

2. Choose the Save As/Export command from the File menu. Access opens the Save As dialog box, as shown earlier in Figure 10-40. Select the To An External File Or Database option and then click OK.

3. Access opens the Save In dialog box, in which you can select the text file type, the folder, and the name of the file to which you want to export the data. After you select these, click Export. (See Figure 10-41, shown earlier.)

4. Access starts the Text Export Wizard, in which you can select a delimited or fixed-width output format.

5. If you're exporting to a delimited text file, you can set the delimiter to separate the exported fields and the qualifier character to surround text strings. You can also ask Access to create an optional first record containing your field names. If you're exporting to a fixed-width format, you can adjust the column widths, as shown in Figure 10-44. You can also click the Advanced button to edit or select an import/export specification. In the final window of the wizard, you verify the export file name and click Finish to export your data. If the export procedure is successful, you'll find a new file in the text format you selected.

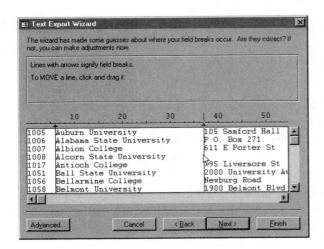

FIGURE 10-44

Setting fixed column widths for a text file export procedure.

Exporting to a Mail Merge Document in Microsoft Word

Perhaps one of the most useful features of Access is that it enables you to embed data from an Access table or query directly in a Word document. To embed data from an Access database in a Word document, do the following:

1. Open your database, and select the table or query whose data you want to embed in a Word document.

2. Choose Office Links from the Tools menu and then choose Merge It from the submenu, or select Merge It from the Office Links toolbar button's drop-down list. This starts the Microsoft Word Mail Merge Wizard, shown in Figure 10-45.

FIGURE 10-45
The Microsoft Word Mail Merge Wizard in Access.

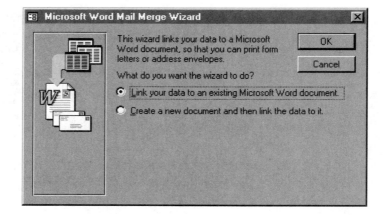

3. Select the option to link to an existing Word document or the option to create a new document. If you want to embed the data in an existing document, the wizard will ask for the document location. When you finish, click OK.

4. The wizard starts Word and activates a mail merge link to your table or query, as shown in Figure 10-46. To solicit actual data for the College Counseling sample database, I created a mail-merge document that I sent out to college admissions directors around the country. You can find this document, Solicit.doc, on the sample disc. The qryMailing query in the sample MailList database provides the data for this document. You can use the various features of the Mail Merge toolbar in Word to build your document with fields embedded from Access.

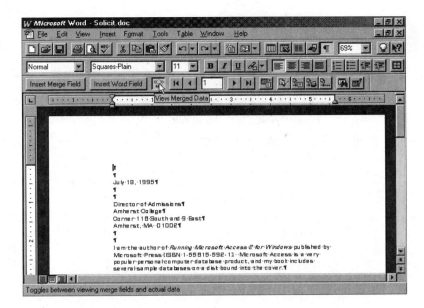

FIGURE 10-46
Creating a mail
merge document
in Word.

Exporting to an SQL Table

You can export data from an Access table or query to define a new
table in any SQL database that supports the ODBC standard. To export
data in an Access table or query to another database system that supports ODBC SQL, you must have the ODBC driver for that database installed on your computer. (For details, see the *Building Applications
with Microsoft Access for Windows 95* manual that comes with Access;
also see the appendix to this book.) Your computer must also be linked
to the network that connects to the SQL server you want, and you must
have an account on that server. Check with your system administrator
for information about correctly connecting to the SQL server to which
you want to export data.

To export data to an SQL table, do the following:

1. Open the Access database from which you want to export your
   data. If that database is already open, switch to the Database
   window.

2. Choose the Save As/Export command from the File menu. Access opens the Save As dialog box, as shown earlier in Figure
   10-40. Select the To An External File Or Database option, and
   then click OK.

3. Access opens the Save In dialog box, as shown earlier in Figure 10-41. Select ODBC Databases in the Save As Type drop-down list, and click Export.

4. Next, Access asks for a name for the new table on the server. Type in the name you want, and click OK.

5. Access opens a dialog box in which you can select the ODBC name of the SQL server that will receive your data. This dialog box is similar to the one shown earlier in Figure 10-10. Select the server alias name, and click OK.

6. Access displays the SQL Server Login dialog box for the SQL data source that you selected. This dialog box is similar to the one shown earlier in Figure 10-11. Enter your user ID and password, and click OK. If you are authorized to create tables in more than one database on the server and you want to connect to a database other than your default database, enter your user ID and password, and then click the Options button to open the lower part of the dialog box. When you click in the Database text box, Access logs on to the server and returns a list of available database names. Select the one you want and click OK. If you don't specify a database name and if multiple databases exist on the server, Access will prompt you to select the database you want. Click OK to store your Access data in a new SQL table on the server. The name of the table on the server will be your user ID, followed by an underscore, followed by the Access table or query name. If the name in Access contains blank spaces, the blank spaces will be replaced by underscores.

Now you have all the information you need to import, link, and export data using Access. The next chapter, "Advanced Query Design—SQL," discusses in detail the Access dialect of SQL. The discussion is intended for intermediate and advanced users. If you're not interested in advanced query design, you can skip to Chapter 12, "Form Basics."

Chapter 11

Advanced Query Design—SQL

U nderlying every query in Microsoft Access is the SQL database command language. Although you can design most queries using the simple Access design grid, Access stores every query you design as an SQL command. For some advanced types of queries that use the results of a second query as a comparison condition, you need to know SQL in order to define the second query (called a *subquery*). Also, you cannot use the design grid to construct all the types of queries available in the product; you must use SQL for some of them.

This chapter explores and explains the various syntax elements in the Access variant of SQL that you can use to build select, total, crosstab, make table, update, append, and delete queries. You'll find brief examples that explain how to use each element. At the end of this chapter are several complex examples that are implemented in the Entertainment Schedule database. This sample database also uses some of the more complex features of SQL in Access to accomplish tasks described in Part 6 of this book. As you become more familiar with SQL, you can learn a lot about the language and how it's implemented in Access by using the design grid to design a query and then switching to SQL view to see how Access interprets the query in SQL statements.

NOTE This chapter is appropriate for intermediate and advanced users who are interested in using the Access dialect of SQL. If you are a beginning user, or if you prefer not to know the details about SQL, you can skip to the next chapter.

A Brief History of SQL

In the early 1970s, IBM created a language called Structured English Query Language (SEQUEL) for a research project on relational database management systems. This language evolved into SEQUEL/2 and finally into Structured Query Language (SQL). Other companies became interested in the concept of relational databases and the emerging SQL interface. Relational Software, Inc., (now the Oracle Corporation) created a relational database product called Oracle in 1979. IBM released its first relational database product, called SQL Data System (SQL/DS), in 1981.

In 1982, the American National Standards Institute (ANSI), realizing the potential significance of the relational model, began work on a Relational Database Language (RDL) standard. By 1984, acceptance in the marketplace of such products as Oracle, SQL/DS, and IBM's DB2 caused the ANSI committee to focus on SQL as the basis for the new

RDL standard. The first version of this standard, SQL-86, was adopted by both ANSI and the International Standards Organization (ISO) in October 1986. An update to SQL-86 covering integrity enhancements was adopted in 1989. The current standard, often referred to as "SQL2" or "SQL-92," reflects extensive work by the international standards bodies to both enhance the language and correct many missing, confusing, or ambiguous features in the original 1986 standard.

The standard as it currently exists is both a common subset of the major implementations and a superset of almost all implementations. That is, the core of the standard contains features found in virtually every commercial implementation of the language, yet the entire standard includes enhanced features that many vendors have yet to implement.

As mentioned in the previous chapter, the SQL Access Group consortium of database vendors has published what could be regarded as the "commercial standard" for SQL—a variant of the language that can be "spoken" by (or mapped to) every major relational database product. An extended version of this "Common Language Interface" (CLI) is part of the draft SQL3 standard under consideration in 1995. Microsoft has implemented support for the CLI in the Open Database Connectivity (ODBC) application programming interface (API) for Windows. This allows vendors of applications for Microsoft Windows to connect to each other via the SQL Access Group standard. Microsoft Access connects to many databases via the ODBC standard and also "speaks" a major subset of the SQL Access Group's standard SQL.

SQL Syntax Conventions

The following table lists the SQL syntax conventions you'll encounter in this chapter:

SQL Convention	Meaning
UPPERCASE	Uppercase letters indicate keywords and reserved words that you must enter exactly as shown. Note that Microsoft Access understands keywords entered in either uppercase or lowercase.
Italic	Italicized words represent variables that you supply.

(continued)

343

continued

SQL Convention	Meaning
Angle brackets < >	Angle brackets enclose syntactic elements that you must supply. The words inside the angle brackets describe the element but do not show the actual syntax of the element.
Brackets [ ]	Brackets enclose optional items. If more than one item is listed, the items are separated by a pipe (I) character. Choose one or none of the elements. Do not enter the brackets or the pipe. Note that Access in many cases requires you to enclose names in brackets. In this chapter, when brackets are required as part of the syntax of variables that you must supply, the brackets are italicized, as in *[MyTable].[MyField]*.
Braces { }	Braces enclose one or more options. If more than one option is listed, the options are separated by a pipe (I) character. Choose one option from the list. Do not enter the braces or the pipe.
Ellipses ...	Ellipses indicate that you can repeat an item one or more times. When a comma is shown with an ellipsis, enter the comma between items.

You must enter all other characters, such as parentheses and colons, exactly as they appear in the syntax line.

TIP When you build a query in SQL view, you can insert a carriage return between elements to improve readability. In fact, Access inserts carriage returns between major clauses when you save and close your query. The only time you might not include carriage returns in an SQL statement is when you're defining an SQL statement on a string literal in Visual Basic for Applications (VBA). VBA requires that a literal be defined as a single line in a procedure. (A *literal* is a value that is expressed as itself rather than as a variable's value or as the result of an expression.)

NOTE This chapter does not document all of the syntax variants accepted by Access, but it does cover all the features of the SELECT statement and of action queries. Wherever possible, ANSI standard syntax is shown to provide portability across other databases that also support some form of SQL. You might discover that Access modifies the ANSI standard syntax to a syntax that it prefers after you define and save a query.

SQL SELECT Syntax in Microsoft Access

The SELECT statement forms the core of the SQL database language. You use the SELECT statement to select or retrieve rows and columns from database tables. The SELECT statement syntax contains five major clauses, generally constructed as follows:

```
SELECT <field list>
   FROM <table list>
   [WHERE <row selection specification>]
   [GROUP BY <grouping specification>]
   [HAVING <group selection specification>]
   [ORDER BY <sorting specification>];
```

Microsoft Access implements four significant extensions to the language: TRANSFORM, to allow you to build crosstab queries; IN, to allow you to specify a remote database connection or to specify column names in a crosstab query; DISTINCTROW, to limit the rows returned from the *<table list>* to rows that have different values in the columns in the *<field list>*; and WITH OWNERACCESS OPTION, to let you design queries that can be run by users who are authorized to use the query but who have no access rights to the tables referenced in the query.

The following sections in this chapter are a reference guide to the Access implementation of SQL for select, total, and crosstab queries. The language elements are presented in alphabetic order.

Expression

Specifies a value in a predicate or in the select list of a SELECT statement or subquery.

345

Syntax:

```
[+|-] {function | (expression) | literal | column-name}
[{+|-|*|/|\|^|MOD|&} {function | (expression) |
literal | column-name}]...
```

Notes:

function—You can specify one of the SQL total functions: AVG, COUNT, MAX, MIN, STDEV, STDEVP, SUM, VAR, or VARP. You can also use any of the functions built into Access or the functions you define using VBA.

(expression)—You can construct an expression from multiple expressions separated by operators. (See the examples later in this section.)

literal—You can specify a numeric or an alphanumeric constant. You must enclose an alphanumeric constant in single or double quotation marks. To include an apostrophe in an alphanumeric constant, enter the apostrophe character twice in the literal string. If the expression is numeric, you must use a numeric constant. Enclose a date/time literal within pound (#) signs. A date/time literal must follow the ANSI standard mim/dd/yy (U.S.) format.

column-name—You can specify the name of a column in a table or a query. You can use a column name only from a table or query that you've specified in the FROM clause of the statement. If the expression is arithmetic, you must use a column that contains numeric data. If the same *column-name* appears in more than one of the tables or queries included in the query, you must fully qualify the name with the query name, table name, or correlation name, as in *[TableA].[Column1]*.

+|-|*|/|\|^|MOD—You can combine multiple numeric expressions with arithmetic operators that specify a calculation. If you use arithmetic operators, all expressions within an expression must be able to be evaluated as numeric data types.

&—You can concatenate alphanumeric constants by using the special & operator.

Examples:

To specify the average of a column named COST, enter the following:

```
AVG(COST)
```

To specify one-half the value of a column named PRICE, enter the following:

```
(PRICE * .5)
```

To specify a literal for 3:00 P.M. on March 1, 1995, enter the following:

```
#3/1/95 3:00PM#
```

To specify a character string that contains the name *Acme Mail Order Company,* enter the following:

```
"Acme Mail Order Company"
```

To specify a character string that contains a possessive noun (requiring an embedded apostrophe), enter the following:

```
'Andy''s Hardware Store'
```

To specify a character string that is the concatenation of the fields containing a person's first and last name, enter the following:

```
[FirstName] & " " & [LastName]
```

See Also   Predicates, SELECT Statement, Subquery, and UPDATE Statement.

FROM Clause

Defines the tables or queries that provide the source data for your query.

Syntax:

```
FROM {{table-name [[AS] correlation-name] |
select-query-name [[AS] correlation-name]} |
<joined table>},...
[IN <source specification>]
```

where *<joined table>* is

```
({table-name [[AS] correlation-name] |
 select-query-name [[AS] correlation-name] |
 <joined table>}

{INNER | LEFT | RIGHT} JOIN
 {table-name [[AS] correlation-name] |
 select-query-name [[AS] correlation-name] |
 <joined table>}

ON <join-specification>)
```

Notes:

You can optionally supply a correlation name for each table name or query name. You can use this correlation name as an alias for the full table name when qualifying column names in the select list, in the

<join-specification>, or in the WHERE clause and subclauses. If you're joining a table or a query to itself, you must use correlation names to clarify which copy of the table or query you're referring to in the select list, join criteria, or selection criteria. If a table name or a query name is also an SQL reserved word (for example, "Order"), you must enclose the name in brackets.

If you include multiple tables in the FROM clause with no JOIN specification but do include a predicate that matches fields from the multiple tables in the WHERE clause, Access in most cases optimizes how it solves the query by treating the query as a JOIN. For example,

```
SELECT *
  FROM TableA, TableB
  WHERE TableA.ID = TableB.ID
```

is treated by Access as if you had specified

```
SELECT *
  FROM TableA
   INNER JOIN TableB
   ON TableA.ID = TableB.ID
```

When you list more than one table or query without join criteria, the source is the *Cartesian product* of all the tables. For example, *FROM TableA, TableB* asks Access to search all the rows of TableA matched with all the rows of TableB. Unless you specify other restricting criteria, the number of logical rows that Access processes could equal the number of rows in TableA <u>times</u> the number of rows in TableB. Access then returns the rows in which the selection criteria specified in the WHERE and HAVING clauses evaluate to True.

Example:

To select information about customers and their purchases of more than $100, enter the following:

```
SELECT Cust.CustomerID, Cust.CompanyName, Ord.OrderDate,
       Cat.CatalogItemID, Cat.Description,
       OrderItem.Quantity, OrderItem.QuotedPrice
  FROM (Catalog AS Cat
    INNER JOIN ((Customer AS Cust
     INNER JOIN [Order] AS Ord
     ON Cust.CustomerID = Ord.CustomerID)
       INNER JOIN OrderItem
       ON Ord.OrderID = OrderItem.OrderID)
    ON Cat.CatalogItemID = OrderItem.CatalogItemID)
  WHERE (OrderItem.Quantity * OrderItem.Price) > 100;
```

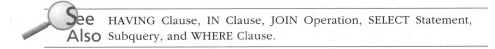

See Also HAVING Clause, IN Clause, JOIN Operation, SELECT Statement, Subquery, and WHERE Clause.

GROUP BY Clause

In a SELECT statement, specifies the columns used to form groups from the rows selected. Each group contains identical values in the specified column(s). In Access, you use the GROUP BY clause to define a total query. You must also include a GROUP BY clause in a crosstab query. (See the TRANSFORM statement for details.)

Syntax:

```
GROUP BY column-name,...
```

Notes:

A column name in the GROUP BY clause can refer to any column from any table in the FROM clause, even if the column is not named in the select list. If the GROUP BY clause is preceded by a WHERE clause, Access creates the groups from the rows selected after it applies the WHERE clause. When you include a GROUP BY clause in a SELECT statement, the select list must be made up of either SQL total functions or column names specified in the GROUP BY clause.

Examples:

To find the largest order from any customer within each zip code, enter the following:

```
SELECT DISTINCTROW Customer.PostalCode,
      MAX(Order.SubTotalCost) AS MaxOfSubTotalCost
  FROM Customer
    INNER JOIN [Order]
    ON Customer.CustomerID = Order.CustomerID
  GROUP BY Customer.PostalCode;
```

To find the average and maximum prices for items in the catalog by category, enter the following:

```
SELECT DISTINCTROW Type.TypeDescription,
      AVG(Catalog.Price) AS AvgOfPrice,
      MAX(Catalog.Price) AS MaxOfPrice
  FROM Type
    INNER JOIN Catalog
    ON Type.ItemTypeCode = Catalog.ItemTypeCode
  GROUP BY Type.TypeDescription;
```

See Also   Total functions—AVG, COUNT, MAX, MIN, STDEV, STDEVP, SUM, VAR, VARP; HAVING Clause; Search-Condition; SELECT Statement; and WHERE Clause.

HAVING Clause

Specifies groups of rows that appear in the logical table (an Access recordset) defined by a SELECT statement. The search condition applies to columns specified in a GROUP BY clause, to columns created by total functions, or to expressions containing total functions. If a group doesn't pass the search condition, it is not included in the logical table.

Syntax:

```
HAVING search-condition
```

Notes:

If you do not include a GROUP BY clause, the select list must be formed using one or more of the SQL total functions.

The difference between the HAVING clause and the WHERE clause is that the WHERE search condition applies to single rows before they are grouped, while the HAVING search condition applies to groups of rows.

If you include a GROUP BY clause preceding the HAVING clause, the search condition applies to each of the groups formed by equal values in the specified columns. If you do not include a GROUP BY clause, the search condition applies to the entire logical table defined by the SELECT statement.

Examples:

To find the largest purchase from each group (categorized by state) whose largest purchase is less than the average of purchases by all customers, enter the following:

```
SELECT DISTINCTROW Customer.State,
       Max(Order.SubTotalCost) AS MaxOfSubTotalCost
  FROM Customer
    INNER JOIN [Order]
    ON Customer.CustomerID = Order.CustomerID
  GROUP BY Customer.State
  HAVING MAX(Order.SubTotalCost) <
    (SELECT AVG(SubTotalCost)
      FROM [Order]);
```

To find the average and maximum order amounts for customers in the state of Washington for every month in which the maximum order amount is less than $4,000, enter the following:

```
SELECT DISTINCTROW Month([OrderDate]) AS Month,
       AVG(Order.SubTotalCost) AS AvgOfSubTotalCost,
       MAX(Order.SubTotalCost) AS MaxOfSubTotalCost
   FROM Customer
     INNER JOIN [Order]
     ON Customer.CustomerID = Order.CustomerID
   WHERE Customer.State = "WA"
   GROUP BY Month([OrderDate])
   HAVING Max(Order.SubTotalCost) < 4000;
```

 See Also   Total functions—AVG, COUNT, MAX, MIN, STDEV, STDEVP, SUM, VAR, VARP; GROUP BY Clause; Search-Condition; SELECT Statement; and WHERE Clause.

IN Clause

Specifies the source for the tables in a query. The source can be another Access database; a dBASE, Microsoft FoxPro, or Paradox file; a Btrieve database; or any database for which you have an ODBC driver. This is an Access extension to standard SQL.

Syntax:

```
IN <"source database name"> <[source connect string]>
```

Enter *"source database name"* and *[source connect string]*. (Be sure to include the quotation marks and the brackets.) If your database source is Access, enter only *"source database name"*. Enter these parameters according to the type of database to which you are connecting, as follows:

Database Name	Source Database Name	Source Connect String
Access	*"drive:\path\filename"*	(none)
dBASE III	*"drive:\path"*	[dBASE III;]
dBASE IV	*"drive:\path"*	[dBASE IV;]
Paradox 3.*x*	*"drive:\path"*	[Paradox 3.x;]

(continued)

351

continued

Database Name	Source Database Name	Source Connect String
Paradox 4.*x*	"*drive:\path*"	[Paradox 4.x;]
Btrieve	"*drive:\path\filename*.DDF"	[Btrieve;]
FoxPro 2.0	"*drive:\path*"	[FoxPro 2.0;]
FoxPro 2.5	"*drive:\path*"	[FoxPro 2.5;]
ODBC	(none)	[ODBC; DATABASE=*defaultdatabase;* UID=*user;* PWD=*password;* DSN=*datasourcename*]

Notes:

The IN clause applies to all tables referenced in the FROM clause and any subqueries in your query. You can refer to only one external database within a query. If you need to refer to more than one external file or database, attach those files as tables in Access and use the logical attached table names instead.

For ODBC, if you omit DSN= or DATABASE=, Access prompts you with a dialog box showing available data sources so that you can select the one you want. If you omit UID= or PWD= and the server requires a UserID and password, Access prompts you with a Login dialog box for each table accessed.

For dBASE, Paradox, FoxPro, and Btrieve databases, you can provide an empty string ("") for *source database name* and provide the path or dictionary filename using the DATABASE= parameter in *source connect string* instead.

Examples:

To retrieve the Company Name field in the Northwind Traders sample database without having to attach the Customers table, enter the following:

```
SELECT DISTINCTROW Customers.[CompanyName]
   FROM Customers
      IN "C:\MSOFFICE\ACCESS\SAMPLES\NORTHWIND.MDB";
```

To retrieve data from the CUST and ORDERS sample files distributed with dBASE IV, enter the following:

```
SELECT DISTINCTROW CUST.CUST_ID, CUST.CUSTOMER,
       ORDERS.DATE_TRANS, ORDERS.PART_ID,
       ORDERS.PART_QTY
  FROM CUST
    INNER JOIN ORDERS
    ON CUST.CUST_ID = ORDERS.CUST_ID
  IN "" [dBASE IV;DATABASE=C:\DBASE\SAMPLES;];
```

See Also   SELECT Statement.

JOIN Operation

Much of the power of SQL derives from its ability to combine (join) information from several tables or queries and present the result as a single logical recordset. In many cases, Access lets you update the recordset of a joined query as if it were a single base table.

Use a JOIN operation in a FROM clause to specify how you want two tables linked to form a logical recordset from which you can select the information you need. You can ask Access to join only matching rows in both tables (called an *inner join*) or to return all rows from one of the two tables even when a matching row does not exist in the second table (called an *outer join*). You can nest multiple join operations to join, for example, a third table with the result of joining two other tables.

Syntax:

```
({table-name [[AS] correlation-name] |
  select-query-name [[AS] correlation-name] |
  <joined table>}
{INNER | LEFT | RIGHT} JOIN
  {table-name [[AS] correlation-name] |
   select-query-name [[AS] correlation-name] |
   <joined table>}
ON <join-specification>)
```

where *<joined table>* is the result of another join operation, and where *<join-specification>* is a search condition made up of comparison predicates that compare fields in the first table with fields in the second table.

Notes:

You can optionally supply a correlation name for each table or query name. You can use this correlation name as an alias for the full table name when qualifying column names in the select list or in the WHERE clause and subclauses. If you're joining a table or a query to itself, you must use correlation names to clarify which copy of the table or the query you're referring to in the select list, join criteria, or selection criteria. If a table name or query name is also an SQL reserved word (for example, "Order"), you must enclose the name in brackets.

Use INNER JOIN to return all the rows that match the join specification in both tables. Use LEFT JOIN to return all the rows from the first table joined on the join specification with any matching rows from the second table. When no row matches in the second table, Access returns Null values for the columns from that table. Conversely, RIGHT JOIN returns all the rows from the second table joined with any matching rows from the first table.

When you use only *equals* comparison predicates in the join specification, the result is called an *equi-join*. Access can graphically display equi-joins in the design grid but cannot display nonequi-joins. If you want to define a join on a nonequals comparison (<, >, <>, <=, or >=), you must define the query using the SQL view. When you join a table to itself using an equals comparison predicate, the result is called a *self-join*.

Examples:

To select information about components and the supplier that provides each component, sorted by ComponentID, enter the following:

```
SELECT DISTINCTROW Component.*, Supplier.SupplierName,
       Supplier.SupplierAddress1,
       Supplier.SupplierAddress2,
       Supplier.SupplierCity,
       Supplier.SupplierState,
       Supplier.SupplierPostal,
       Supplier.SupplierPhone,
       Supplier.SupplierFax
  FROM Supplier
    INNER JOIN Component
    ON Supplier.SupplierID = Component.SupplierID
  ORDER BY Component.ComponentID;
```

To find out which suppliers do not provide component number 25, enter the following:

```
SELECT DISTINCTROW Component.ComponentID,
       Supplier.SupplierID,
       Supplier.SupplierName,
```

```
        Supplier.SupplierCity,
        Supplier.SupplierState
FROM Supplier
  INNER JOIN Component
  ON Supplier.SupplierID <> Component.SupplierID
WHERE Component.ComponentID = 25;
```

To find out which customers do not currently have an order outstanding, enter the following:

```
SELECT DISTINCTROW Customer.CompanyName, Customer.City,
        Customer.State
FROM Customer
  LEFT JOIN [Order]
  ON Customer.CustomerID = [Order].CustomerID
WHERE [Order].CustomerID Is Null;
```

To see a list of products and the amounts currently on order, sorted by product type, enter the following:

```
SELECT DISTINCTROW Type.TypeDescription,
        Catalog.Description, OrderItem.OrderID,
        OrderItem.Quantity
FROM Type
  INNER JOIN (Catalog
    INNER JOIN OrderItem
    ON Catalog.CatalogItemID = OrderItem.CatalogItemID)
  ON Type.ItemTypeCode = Catalog.ItemTypeCode
ORDER BY Type.TypeDescription;
```

See Also   FROM Clause, HAVING Clause, Predicate: Comparison, Search-Condition, SELECT Statement, and WHERE Clause.

ORDER BY Clause

Specifies the sequence of rows to be returned by a SELECT statement or an INSERT statement.

Syntax:

```
ORDER BY {column-name | column-number [ASC | DESC]},...
```

Notes:

You use column names or relative output column numbers to specify the columns on whose values the rows returned are ordered. (If you use relative output column numbers, the first output column is 1.) You can specify multiple columns in the ORDER BY clause. The list is ordered primarily by the first column. If rows exist for which the values of that column are equal, they are ordered by the next column in the ORDER BY list. You can specify ascending (ASC) or descending (DESC) order for each column. If you do not specify ASC or DESC, ASC is assumed. Using an ORDER BY clause in a SELECT statement is the only means of defining the sequence of the returned rows.

Examples:

To select customers who first did business in 1988 or earlier and list them in ascending order by zip code, enter the following:

```
SELECT DISTINCTROW Customer.CompanyName, Customer.City,
       Customer.PostalCode
  FROM Customer
  WHERE 1988 >=
    (SELECT MIN(Year(OrderDate))
      FROM [Order]
      WHERE
        Order.CustomerID = Customer.CustomerID)
  ORDER BY Customer.PostalCode;
```

To find all suppliers and all customers in the state of Washington and list them in descending order by zip code, enter the following:

```
SELECT DISTINCTROW Customer.CompanyName, Customer.City,
       Customer.PostalCode
  FROM Customer
  WHERE Customer.State = "WA"
UNION
  SELECT DISTINCTROW Supplier.SupplierName,
         Supplier.SupplierCity,
         Supplier.SupplierPostal
    FROM Supplier
    WHERE Supplier.SupplierState = "WA"
    ORDER BY 3;
```

NOTE If you decide to use column names in the ORDER BY clause of a UNION query, Access derives the column names from the names returned by the first query. In this example, you would change the ORDER BY clause to read: ORDER BY PostalCode.

See
Also   INSERT Statement, SELECT Statement, and UNION Query Operator.

PARAMETERS Declaration

Precedes an SQL statement to define the data types of any parameters you include in the query. You can use parameters to prompt the user for data values or to match data values in controls on an open form.

Syntax:

    PARAMETERS {[parameter-name] data-type},... ;

Notes:

If your query prompts the user for values, each parameter name should describe the value that the user needs to enter. For example, [Print invoices from orders on date:] is much more descriptive than [Enter date:]. If you want to refer to a control on an open form, use the format

[Forms]![*Myform*]![*Mycontrol*]

To refer to a control on a subform, use the format

[Forms]![*Myform*]![*Mysubformcontrol*].[Form]![*ControlOnSubform*]

Valid data type entries are as follows:

SQL Parameter Data Type	Equivalent Access Data Type
Bit	Yes/No
Binary	Binary
Byte	Byte
Currency	Currency
DateTime	Date/Time
FLOAT	Double
IEEEDouble	Double
IEEESingle	Single
INT[EGER]	Long integer
Long	Long integer
LongBinary	OLE object
LongText	Memo
REAL	Single
Short	Integer
SMALLINT	Integer
Text	Text
Value	Value
VARCHAR	Memo

Example:

To create a parameter query that summarizes the sales and the cost of goods for all items sold in a given month, enter the following:

```
PARAMETERS [Year to summarize:] Short,
            [Month to summarize:] Short;
SELECT DISTINCTROW OrderItem.CatalogItemID,
       SUM(OrderItem.Quantity) AS Quantity,
       SUM(OrderItem.[Quantity] *
         [QuotedPrice]) AS TotalSales,
       SUM(OrderItem.[Quantity] * [OurCost]) AS TotalCost
  FROM [Order]
    INNER JOIN (Catalog
      INNER JOIN OrderItem
      ON Catalog.CatalogItemID = OrderItem.CatalogItemID)
    ON Order.OrderID = OrderItem.OrderID
  WHERE Year([OrderDate]) = [Year to summarize:]
    AND Month([OrderDate]) = [Month to summarize:]
  GROUP BY OrderItem.CatalogItemID;
```

See Also   SELECT Statement.

Predicate: BETWEEN

Compares a value with a range of values.

Syntax:

expression [NOT] BETWEEN *expression* AND *expression*

Notes:

The data types of all expressions must be compatible. Comparison of alphanumeric literals (strings) in Access is case-insensitive.

Let *a*, *b*, and *c* be expressions. Then, in terms of other predicates, *a* BETWEEN *b* AND *c* is equivalent to the following:

a >= *b* AND *a* <= *c*

a NOT BETWEEN *b* AND *c* is equivalent to the following:

a < *b* OR *a* > *c*

The result is undefined if any of the expressions is Null.

Example:

To determine whether the average of Quantity multiplied by QuotedPrice is greater than or equal to $500 and less than or equal to $10,000, enter the following:

```
AVG(Quantity * QuotedPrice) BETWEEN 500 AND 10000
```

See Also   Expressions, SELECT Statement, Subquery, and WHERE Clause.

Predicate: Comparison

Compares the values of two expressions or the value of an expression and a single value returned by a subquery.

Syntax:

```
expression {= | <> | > | < | >= | <=}
{expression | subquery}
```

Notes:

Comparison of strings in Access is case-insensitive. The data type of the first expression must be compatible with the data type of the second expression or with the value returned by the subquery. If the subquery returns no rows or more than one row, an error is returned except when the select list of the subquery is COUNT(*), in which case the return of multiple rows yields one value. If either the first expression, the second expression, or the subquery evaluates to Null, the result of the comparison is undefined.

Examples:

To determine whether the order date was in 1992, enter the following:

```
Year(OrderDate) = 1992
```

To determine whether the order ID is not equal to 50, enter the following:

```
OrderID <> 50
```

To determine whether an order was placed in the first half of the year, enter the following:

```
Month(OrderDate) < 7
```

To determine whether the maximum value for the total order amount in the group is less than the average total order amount found in the Order table, enter the code on the following page.

```
MAX(SubTotalCost - (SubTotalCost * Discount)) <
  (SELECT AVG(SubTotalCost - (SubTotalCost * Discount))
    FROM [Order])
```

See Also   Expressions, SELECT Statement, Subquery, and WHERE Clause.

Predicate: EXISTS

Tests the existence of at least one row that satisfies the selection criteria in a subquery.

Syntax:

```
EXISTS (subquery)
```

Notes:

The result cannot be undefined. If the subquery returns at least one row, the result is True; otherwise, the result is False. The subquery need not return values for this predicate; therefore, you can list any columns in the select list that exist in the underlying tables or queries or use an asterisk (*) to denote all columns.

Example:

To find all suppliers that supply at least one component, enter the following:

```
SELECT DISTINCTROW Supplier.SupplierName
  FROM Supplier
  WHERE Exists
    (SELECT *
      FROM Component
      WHERE Component.SupplierID = Supplier.SupplierID);
```

NOTE In this example, the inner subquery makes a reference to the Supplier table in the SELECT statement by referring to a column in the outer table (Supplier.SupplierID). This forces the subquery to be evaluated for every row in the SELECT statement, which might not be the most efficient way to achieve the desired result.

See Also   Expression, SELECT Statement, Subquery, and WHERE Clause.

Predicate: IN

Determines whether a value is equal to any of the values or is unequal to all values in a set returned from a subquery or provided in a list of values.

Syntax:

```
expression [NOT] IN {(subquery) | ({literal},...) |
expression}
```

Notes:

Comparison of strings in Access is case-insensitive. The data types of all expressions, literals, and the column returned by the subquery must be compatible. If the expression is Null or any value returned by the subquery is Null, the result is undefined. In terms of other predicates, *expression* IN *expression* is equivalent to the following:

```
expression = expression
```

expression IN (*subquery*) is equivalent to the following:

```
expression = ANY (subquery)
```

expression IN (*a*, *b*, *c*,...), where *a*, *b*, and *c* are literals, is equivalent to the following:

```
(expression = a) OR (expression = b) OR
(expression = c) ...
```

expression NOT IN ... is equivalent to the following:

```
NOT (expression IN ...)
```

Examples:

To determine whether State is on the West Coast, enter the following:

```
State IN ("CA", "OR", "WA")
```

To determine whether CustomerID is the same as any SupplierID in Washington state, enter the following:

```
CustomerID IN
  (SELECT SupplierID
    FROM Supplier
    WHERE SupplierState = "WA")
```

See Also   Expressions, Predicate: Quantified, SELECT Statement, Subquery, and WHERE Clause.

Predicate: LIKE

Searches for strings that match a pattern.

Syntax:

```
column-name [NOT] LIKE match-string
```

Notes:

String comparisons in Access are case-insensitive. If the column specified by *column-name* contains a Null, the result is undefined. Comparison of two empty strings or an empty string with the special asterisk (*) character evaluates to True.

You provide a text string as a *match-string value* that defines what characters can exist in which positions for the comparison to be true. Access understands a number of *wildcard characters* that you can use to define positions that can contain any single character, zero or more characters, or any single number, as follows:

Wildcard Character	Meaning
?	Any single character
*	Zero or more characters (used to define leading, trailing, or embedded strings that don't have to match any of the pattern characters)
#	Any single number

You can also specify that any particular position in the text or memo field can contain only characters from a list that you provide. To define a list of comparison characters for a particular position, enclose the list in brackets ([ ]). You can specify a range of characters within a list by entering the low-value character, a hyphen, and the high-value character, as in [A-Z] or [3-7]. If you want to test a position for any characters <u>except</u> those in a list, start the list with an exclamation point (!). If you want to test for one of the special characters *, ?, #, and [, you must enclose the character in brackets.

Examples:

To determine whether CustomerName is at least four characters long and begins with *Smi,* enter the following:

```
CustomerName LIKE "Smi?*"
```

To test whether PostalCode is a valid Canadian postal code, enter the following:

```
PostalCode LIKE "[A-Z]#[A-Z] #[A-Z]#"
```

See Also Expressions, SELECT Statement, Subquery, and WHERE Clause.

Predicate: NULL

Determines whether the expression evaluates to Null. This predicate evaluates only to True or False and will not evaluate to undefined.

Syntax:

```
expression IS [NOT] NULL
```

Example:

To determine whether the customer phone number column has never been filled, enter the following:

```
PhoneNumber IS NULL
```

See Also Expressions, SELECT Statement, Subquery, and WHERE Clause.

Predicate: Quantified

Compares the value of an expression to some, any, or all values of a single column returned by a subquery.

Syntax:

```
expression {= | <> | > | < | >= | <=}
[SOME | ANY | ALL] (subquery)
```

Notes:

String comparisons in Access are case-insensitive. The data type of the expression must be compatible with the data type of the value returned by the subquery.

When ALL is used, the predicate is true if the comparison is true for all the values returned by the subquery. If the expression or any of the values returned by the subquery is Null, the result is undefined. When SOME or ANY is used, the predicate is true if the comparison is true for any of the values returned by the subquery. If the expression is a Null value, the result is undefined. If the subquery returns no values, the predicate is false.

Examples:

To find the components whose cost is greater than all the components whose type code is 008, enter the following:

```
SELECT DISTINCTROW Component.Description,
      Component.OurCost
  FROM Component
  WHERE (Component.OurCost) > ALL
    (SELECT OurCost
      FROM Component
      WHERE ItemTypeCode = "008");
```

To find the components whose cost is greater than any component whose type code is 008, enter the following:

```
SELECT DISTINCTROW Component.Description,
      Component.OurCost
  FROM Component
  WHERE (Component.OurCost) > SOME
    (SELECT OurCost
      FROM Component
      WHERE ItemTypeCode = "008");
```

 See Also Expressions, SELECT Statement, Subquery, and WHERE Clause.

Search-Condition

Describes a simple or compound predicate that is true, false, or undefined for a given row or group. Use a search condition in the WHERE clause of a SELECT statement, a subquery, a DELETE statement, or an UPDATE statement. You can also use it within the HAVING clause in a SELECT statement. The search condition defines the rows that should appear in the resulting logical table or the rows that should be acted upon by the change operation. If the search condition is true when applied to a row, that row is included in the result.

Syntax:

```
[NOT] {predicate | (search-condition)}
[{AND | OR | XOR | EQV | IMP}
[NOT] {predicate | (search-condition)}]...
```

Notes:

Access effectively applies any subquery in the search condition to each row of the table that is the result of the previous clauses. Access then evaluates the result of the subquery with regard to each candidate row.

If you include a comparison predicate in the form of *expression comparison-operator subquery*, an error is returned if the subquery returns no rows.

The order of evaluation of the Boolean operators is NOT, AND, OR, XOR (exclusive OR), EQV (equivalence), and IMP (implication). You can include additional parentheses to influence the order in which the Boolean expressions are processed.

TIP   You can express AND and OR Boolean operations directly using the design grid. If you need to use XOR, EQV, or IMP, you must create an expression in the Field row, deselect the Show check box, and set the Criteria row to <> False.

When you use the Boolean operator NOT, the following holds: NOT (True) is False, NOT (False) is True, and NOT (undefined) is undefined. The result is undefined whenever a predicate references a Null value. If a search condition evaluates to False or undefined when applied to a row, the row is not selected. Access returns True, False, or undefined values as a result of applying Boolean operators (AND, OR, XOR, EQV, IMP) against two predicates or search conditions according to the tables shown in Figure 11-1 on the next page.

Example:

To find all products whose cost is greater than $100 and whose number of days to build is equal to 2 or whose number in stock is less than 5, but not both, enter the following:

```
SELECT DISTINCTROW Catalog.CatalogItemID,
       Catalog.Description, Catalog.OurCost,
       Catalog.DaysToBuild, Catalog.NumberInStock
  FROM Catalog
  WHERE Catalog.OurCost > 100
    AND (Catalog.DaysToBuild = 2
    XOR Catalog.NumberInStock < 5);
```

See
Also
DELETE Statement, Expressions, HAVING Clause, Predicates, SE-
LECT Statement, Subquery, UPDATE Statement, and WHERE
Clause.

FIGURE 11-1

Truth tables for
SQL Boolean
operators.

AND	True	False	undefined (Null)
True	True	False	Null
False	False	False	False
undefined (Null)	Null	False	Null

OR	True	False	undefined (Null)
True	True	True	True
False	True	False	Null
undefined (Null)	True	Null	Null

XOR	True	False	undefined (Null)
True	False	True	Null
False	True	False	Null
undefined (Null)	Null	Null	Null

EQV	True	False	undefined (Null)
True	True	False	Null
False	False	True	Null
undefined (Null)	Null	Null	Null

IMP	True	False	undefined (Null)
True	True	False	Null
False	True	True	True
undefined (Null)	True	Null	Null

SELECT Statement

Performs the select, project, and join relational operations to create a logical table (recordset) from other tables or queries. The items in the select list identify the columns or calculated values to project from the source tables to the new recordset. You identify the tables to be joined in the FROM clause, and you identify the rows to be selected in the WHERE clause. Use GROUP BY to specify how to form groups for a total query, and use HAVING to specify which resulting groups should be included in the result.

Syntax:

```
SELECT [ALL | DISTINCT | DISTINCTROW | TOP number
       [PERCENT]] select-list
  FROM {{table-name [[AS] correlation-name] |
   select-query-name [[AS] correlation-name]} |
   <joined table>},...
  IN <"source database name"> <[source connect string]>
  [WHERE search-condition]
  [GROUP BY column-name,...]
  [HAVING search-condition]
  [UNION [ALL] select-statement]
  [ORDER BY {column-name [ASC | DESC]},...] |
 [WITH OWNERACCESS OPTION];
```

where *select-list* is

```
{* | {expression [AS output-column-name] | table-name.* |
 query-name.* | correlation-name.*},...}
```

and where *<joined table>* is

```
({table-name [[AS] correlation-name] |
 select-query-name [[AS] correlation-name] |
 <joined table>}
{INNER | LEFT | RIGHT} JOIN
  {table-name [[AS] correlation-name] |
  select-query-name [[AS] correlation-name] |
  <joined table>}
ON <join-specification>)
```

Notes:

You can optionally supply a correlation name for each table or query name. You can use this correlation name as an alias for the full table name when qualifying column names in the select list or in the WHERE clause and subclauses. If you're joining a table or a query to itself, you must use correlation names to clarify which copy of the table or query you're referring to in the select list, join criteria, or selection criteria. If a table name or query name is also an SQL reserved word (for example, "Order"), you must enclose the name in brackets.

When you list more than one table or query without join criteria, the source is the Cartesian product of all the tables. For example, *FROM TableA, TableB* asks Access to search all the rows of TableA matched with all the rows of TableB. Unless you specify other restricting criteria, the number of logical rows that Access processes could equal the number of rows in TableA <u>times</u> the number of rows in TableB. Access then returns the rows in which the selection criteria specified in the WHERE and HAVING clauses are true.

You can further define which rows Access includes in the output recordset by specifying ALL, DISTINCT, DISTINCTROW, TOP *n*, or TOP *n* PERCENT. ALL includes all rows that match the search criteria from the source tables, including potential duplicate rows. DISTINCT requests that Access return only rows that are different from any other row. You cannot update any columns in a query that uses ALL or DISTINCT.

DISTINCTROW (the default) requests that Access return only rows in which the concatenation of the primary keys from all tables supplying output columns is unique. Depending on the columns you select, you might see rows in the result that contain duplicate values, but each row in the result is derived from a distinct combination of rows in the underlying tables. Specify TOP *n* or TOP *n* PERCENT to request that the recordset contain only the first *n* or first *n* percent of rows. The parameter *n* must be an integer and must be less than or equal to 100 if you include the PERCENT keyword. Note that if you do not include an ORDER BY clause (see the next page), the sequence of rows returned is undefined.

When you include a GROUP BY clause, the select list must be made up of one or more of the SQL total functions or one or more of the column names specified in the GROUP BY clause. A column name in a GROUP BY clause can refer to any column from any table in the FROM clause, even if the column is not named in the select list. If you want to refer to a calculated expression in the GROUP BY clause, you must assign an output column name to the expression in the select list and then refer to that name in the GROUP BY clause. If the GROUP BY clause is preceded by a WHERE clause, Access forms the groups from the rows selected after it applies the WHERE clause.

If you use a HAVING clause but do not include a GROUP BY clause, the select list must be formed using SQL total functions. If you include a GROUP BY clause preceding the HAVING clause, the HAVING search condition applies to each of the groups formed by equal values in the specified columns. If you do not include a GROUP BY clause, the HAVING search condition applies to the entire logical table defined by the SELECT statement.

You use column names or relative output column numbers to specify the columns on whose values the rows returned are ordered. (If you use relative output column numbers, the first output column is 1.) You can specify multiple columns in the ORDER BY clause. The list is ordered primarily by the first column. If rows exist for which the values of that column are equal, they are ordered by the next column on the ORDER BY list. You can specify ascending (ASC) or descending (DESC) order for each column. If you do not specify ASC or DESC, ASC is assumed. Using an ORDER BY clause in a SELECT statement is the only means of defining the sequence of the returned rows.

Normally, the person running the query not only must have rights to the query but also must have the appropriate rights to the tables used in the query. (These rights include reading data to select rows and updating, inserting, and deleting data using the query.) If your application has multiple users, you might want to secure the tables so that no user has direct access to any of the tables and that all users can still run queries defined by you. Assuming you're the owner of both the queries and the tables, you can deny access to the tables but allow access to the queries. To make sure that the queries run properly, you must add the WITH OWNERACCESS OPTION clause to allow users the same access rights as the table owner when accessing the data via the query. See Chapter 14, "Securing and Delivering Your Application," in the *Building Applications with Microsoft Access for Windows 95* manual that comes with Access for more details on securing your applications.

Examples:

To select information about customers and their purchases of more than $100, enter the following:

```
SELECT Cust.CustomerID, Cust.CompanyName, Ord.OrderDate,
       Cat.CatalogItemID, Cat.Description,
       OrderItem.Quantity, OrderItem.QuotedPrice
   FROM (Catalog AS Cat
     INNER JOIN ((Customer AS Cust
       INNER JOIN [Order] AS Ord
       ON Cust.CustomerID = Ord.CustomerID)
         INNER JOIN OrderItem
         ON Ord.OrderID = OrderItem.OrderID)
     ON Cat.CatalogItemID = OrderItem.CatalogItemID)
   WHERE (OrderItem.Quantity * OrderItem.Price) > 100;
```

To find the largest order from any customer within each zip code, enter the following:

```
SELECT DISTINCTROW Customer.PostalCode,
       Max(Order.SubTotalCost) AS MaxOfSubTotalCost
   FROM Customer
     INNER JOIN [Order]
     ON Customer.CustomerID = [Order].CustomerID
   GROUP BY Customer.PostalCode;
```

To find the average and maximum prices for items in the catalog by category, enter the following:

```
SELECT DISTINCTROW Type.TypeDescription,
       AVG(Catalog.Price) AS AvgOfPrice,
       MAX(Catalog.Price) AS MaxOfPrice
   FROM Type
     INNER JOIN Catalog
     ON Type.ItemTypeCode = Catalog.ItemTypeCode
   GROUP BY Type.TypeDescription;
```

To find the largest purchase from each group (categorized by state) whose largest purchase is less than the average of purchases by all customers, enter the following:

```
SELECT DISTINCTROW Customer.State,
       Max([Order].SubTotalCost) AS MaxOfSubTotalCost
   FROM Customer
     INNER JOIN [Order]
     ON Customer.CustomerID = [Order].CustomerID
   GROUP BY Customer.State
```

```
HAVING Max([Order].SubTotalCost) <
  (SELECT AVG(SubTotalCost)
    FROM [Order]);
```

To find the average and maximum order amounts for customers in the state of Washington for every month in which the maximum order amount is less than $4,000, enter the following:

```
SELECT DISTINCTROW Month([OrderDate]) AS Month,
        AVG([Order].SubTotalCost) AS AvgOfSubTotalCost,
        MAX([Order].SubTotalCost) AS MaxOfSubTotalCost
  FROM Customer
    INNER JOIN [Order]
    ON Customer.CustomerID = [Order].CustomerID
  WHERE Customer.State = "WA"
  GROUP BY Month([OrderDate])
  HAVING Max(Order.SubTotalCost) < 4000);
```

To find the number of different prices for items currently in stock, you need two queries. For the query DistinctPrice, enter the following:

```
SELECT DISTINCT Price
  FROM Catalog
  WHERE NumberInStock > 0;
```

For the query CountDistinctPrice, enter the following:

```
SELECT COUNT(*)
  FROM DistinctPrice;
```

To select information about components and the supplier that provides each component, sorted by ComponentID, enter the following:

```
SELECT DISTINCTROW Component.*, Supplier.SupplierName,
        Supplier.SupplierAddress1,
        Supplier.SupplierAddress2,
        Supplier.SupplierCity,
        Supplier.SupplierState,
        Supplier.SupplierPostal,
        Supplier.SupplierPhone,
        Supplier.SupplierFax
  FROM Supplier
    INNER JOIN Component
    ON Supplier.SupplierID = Component.SupplierID
  ORDER BY Component.ComponentID;
```

To find out which suppliers do not provide component number 25, enter the following:

```
SELECT DISTINCTROW Component.ComponentID,
        Supplier.SupplierID, Supplier.SupplierName,
        Supplier.SupplierCity, Supplier.SupplierState
   FROM Supplier
     INNER JOIN Component
     ON Supplier.SupplierID <> Component.SupplierID
   WHERE Component.ComponentID = 25;
```

To find out which customers do not currently have an order outstanding, enter the following:

```
SELECT DISTINCTROW Customer.CompanyName, Customer.City,
        Customer.State
   FROM Customer
     LEFT JOIN [Order]
     ON Customer.CustomerID = Order.CustomerID
   WHERE (((Order.CustomerID) IS NULL));
```

To see a listing of products and the amount currently on order, sorted by product type, enter the following:

```
SELECT DISTINCTROW Type.TypeDescription,
        Catalog.Description,
        OrderItem.OrderID, OrderItem.Quantity
   FROM Type
     INNER JOIN (Catalog
       INNER JOIN OrderItem
       ON Catalog.CatalogItemID = OrderItem.CatalogItemID)
     ON Type.ItemTypeCode = Catalog.ItemTypeCode
   ORDER BY 1;
```

To select customers who first did business in 1988 or earlier and list them in ascending order by zip code, enter the following:

```
SELECT DISTINCTROW Customer.CompanyName, Customer.City,
        PostalCode
   FROM Customer
   WHERE (((1988) >=
     (SELECT MIN(Year(OrderDate))
       FROM [Order]
         WHERE Order.CustomerID = Customer.CustomerID)))
     ORDER BY Customer.PostalCode;
```

To find all suppliers and all customers in the state of Washington and list them in descending order by zip code, enter the following:

```
SELECT DISTINCTROW Customer.CompanyName, Customer.City,
        PostalCode
   FROM Customer
     WHERE Customer.State = "WA"
UNION
```

```
SELECT DISTINCTROW Supplier.SupplierName,
       Supplier.SupplierCity, Supplier.SupplierPostal
   FROM Supplier
   WHERE Supplier.SupplierState = "WA"
   ORDER BY PostalCode;
```

To find all suppliers that supply at least one component, enter the following:

```
SELECT DISTINCTROW Supplier.SupplierName
   FROM Supplier
   WHERE Exists
     (SELECT *
       FROM Component
       WHERE Component.SupplierID = Supplier.SupplierID);
```

To find the components whose cost is greater than ALL the components whose type code is 008, enter the following:

```
SELECT DISTINCTROW Component.Description,
       Component.OurCost
   FROM Component
   WHERE (Component.OurCost) > ALL
     (SELECT OurCost
       FROM Component
       WHERE ItemTypeCode = "008");
```

To find all products whose cost is greater than $100 and whose number of days to build is equal to 2 or whose number in stock is less than 5, but not both, enter the following:

```
SELECT DISTINCTROW Catalog.CatalogItemID,
       Catalog.Description, Catalog.OurCost,
       Catalog.DaysToBuild, Catalog.NumberInStock
   FROM Catalog
   WHERE (Catalog.OurCost) > 100
     AND ((Catalog.DaysToBuild) = 2
     XOR (Catalog.NumberInStock) < 5);
```

To select from the Customer table and insert into a temporary table names of customers in the state of Oregon, enter the following:

```
INSERT INTO TempCust
   SELECT *
     FROM Customer
     WHERE State = "OR";
```

See Also INSERT Statement, Search-Condition, and UNION Query Operator.

Subquery

Selects from a single column any number of values or no values at all for comparison in a predicate.

Syntax:

```
(SELECT [ALL | DISTINCT] select-list
  FROM {{table-name [[AS] correlation-name] |
   select-query-name [[AS] correlation-name]} |
   <joined table>},...
  [WHERE search-condition]
  [GROUP BY column-name,...]
  [HAVING search-condition])
```

where *select-list* is

```
{* | {expression | table-name.* |
query-name.* | correlation-name.*}}
```

and where *<joined table>* is

```
({table-name [[AS] correlation-name] |
 select-query-name [[AS] correlation-name] |
 <joined table>}
{INNER | LEFT | RIGHT} JOIN
 {table-name [[AS] correlation-name] |
  select-query-name [[AS] correlation-name] |
  <joined table>}
ON <join-specification>)
```

Notes:

You can use the special asterisk (*) character in the select list of a subquery only when the subquery is used in an EXISTS predicate or when the FROM clause within the subquery refers to a single table or query that contains only one column.

You can optionally supply a correlation name for each table or query name. You can use this correlation name as an alias for the full table name when qualifying column names in the select list or in the WHERE clause and subclauses. If you're joining a table or a query to itself, you must use correlation names to clarify which copy of the table or query you're referring to in the select list, join criteria, or selection criteria. If a table name or query name is also an SQL reserved word (for example, "Order"), you must enclose the name in brackets.

When you list more than one table or query without join criteria, the source is the Cartesian product of all the tables. For example, *FROM*

TableA, TableB asks Access to search all the rows of TableA matched with all the rows of TableB. Unless you specify other restricting criteria, the number of logical rows that Access processes could equal the number of rows in TableA <u>times</u> the number of rows in TableB. Access then returns the rows in which the selection criteria specified in the WHERE and HAVING clauses are true.

In the search condition of the WHERE clause of a subquery, you can refer via an outer reference to the columns of any table or query that is defined in the outer queries. You must qualify the column name if the table or query reference is ambiguous.

A column name in the GROUP BY clause can refer to any column from any table in the FROM clause, even if the column is not named in the select list. If the GROUP BY clause is preceded by a WHERE clause, Access creates the groups from the rows selected after the application of the WHERE clause.

When you include a GROUP BY or HAVING clause in a SELECT statement, the select list must be made up of either SQL total functions or column names specified in the GROUP BY clause. If a GROUP BY clause precedes a HAVING clause, the HAVING clause's search condition applies to each of the groups formed by equal values in the specified columns. If you do not include a GROUP BY clause, the HAVING clause's search condition applies to the entire logical table defined by the SELECT statement.

Examples:

To find all suppliers that supply at least one component, enter the following:

```
SELECT DISTINCTROW Supplier.SupplierName
  FROM Supplier
  WHERE Exists
    (SELECT *
      FROM Component
      WHERE Component.SupplierID = Supplier.SupplierID);
```

NOTE In this example, the inner subquery makes a reference to the Supplier table in the SELECT statement by referring to a column in the outer table (Supplier.SupplierID). This forces the subquery to be evaluated for every row in the SELECT statement, which might not be the most efficient way to achieve the desired result.

To find the largest purchase from each group (categorized by state) whose largest purchase is less than the average of purchases by all customers, enter the following:

```
SELECT DISTINCTROW Customer.State,
      Max([Order].SubTotalCost) AS MaxOfSubTotalCost
  FROM Customer
    INNER JOIN [Order]
    ON Customer.CustomerID = [Order].CustomerID
  GROUP BY Customer.State
  HAVING MAX([Order].SubTotalCost) <
    (SELECT AVG(SubTotalCost)
      FROM [Order]);
```

To select customers who first did business in 1988 or earlier and list them in ascending order by zip code, enter the following:

```
SELECT DISTINCTROW Customer.CompanyName, Customer.City,
      Customer.PostalCode
  FROM Customer
  WHERE 1988 >=
    (SELECT MIN(Year(OrderDate))
      FROM [Order]
      WHERE [Order].CustomerID = Customer.CustomerID)
  ORDER BY Customer.PostalCode;
```

To find the inventory item name and supplier name for any item that has an inventory cost of less than $500, enter the following:

```
SELECT DISTINCTROW Component.Description,
      Supplier.SupplierName
  FROM Supplier
    INNER JOIN Component
    ON Supplier.SupplierID = Component.SupplierID
  WHERE EXISTS
    (SELECT *
      FROM Component C2
      WHERE Component.ComponentID = C2.ComponentID
        AND C2.NumberInStock > 0
        AND (C2.NumberInStock * C2.OurCost) < 500);
```

NOTE In this example, the inner subquery makes an outer reference to the Component table in the SELECT statement. Access is then forced to evaluate the subquery for every row in the SELECT statement, which might not be the most efficient way to achieve the desired result.

To find the components whose cost is greater than any component whose type code is 008, enter the following:

```
SELECT DISTINCTROW Component.Description,
        Component.OurCost
  FROM Component
  WHERE (Component.OurCost) > SOME
    (SELECT OurCost
      FROM Component
      WHERE ItemTypeCode = "008");
```

See Also   Expressions, Predicates, and SELECT Statement.

Total Function: AVG

In a logical table defined by a SELECT statement or a subquery, creates a column value that is the numeric average of the values in the expression or column name specified. You can use the GROUP BY clause to create an average for each group of rows selected from the underlying tables or queries.

Syntax:

```
AVG(expression)
```

Notes:

You cannot use another total function reference within the expression. If you use an SQL total function in the select list of a SELECT statement, any other columns in the select list must be derived using a total function, or the column name must appear in a GROUP BY clause. An expression must contain a reference to at least one column name, and the expression or column name must be a numeric data type.

Null values are not included in the calculation of the result. The data type of the result is generally the same as that of the expression or column name. If the expression or column name is an integer, the resulting average is truncated. For example, AVG(n)—where n is an integer and the values of n in the selected rows are equal to 0, 1, and 1—returns the value 0.

Examples:

To find the average and maximum prices for items in the catalog by category, enter the code on the following page.

```
SELECT DISTINCTROW Type.TypeDescription,
       AVG(Catalog.Price)  AS AvgOfPrice,
       MAX(Catalog.Price) AS MaxOfPrice
  FROM Type
    INNER JOIN Catalog
    ON Type.ItemTypeCode = Catalog.ItemTypeCode
  GROUP BY Type.TypeDescription;
```

To find the average inventory cost of items currently in stock, enter the following:

```
SELECT DISTINCTROW Avg([OurCost] *
                       [NumberInStock]) AS AvgInventoryCost
  FROM Component
  WHERE Component.NumberInStock > 0;
```

See Also   Expressions, GROUP BY Clause, HAVING Clause, SELECT Statement, Subquery, and TRANSFORM Statement.

Total Function: COUNT

In a logical table defined by a SELECT statement or a subquery, creates a column value that is equal to the number of rows in the result table. You can use the GROUP BY clause to create a count for each group of rows selected from the underlying tables or queries.

Syntax:

```
COUNT({* | expression})
```

Notes:

You cannot use another total function reference within the expression. If you use an SQL total function in the select list of a SELECT statement, any other columns in the select list must be derived using a total function, or the column name must appear in a GROUP BY clause. An expression must contain a reference to at least one column name.

Null values are not included in the calculation of the result. The data type of the result is a long integer.

Access does not support the ANSI standard COUNT(DISTINCT *expression*).

Examples:

To find the number of customers who first did business in 1988 or earlier and group them by zip code, enter the following:

```
SELECT COUNT(*)
  FROM Customer
  WHERE 1988 >=
    (SELECT MIN(Year(OrderDate))
      FROM [Order]
      WHERE [Order].CustomerID = Customer.CustomerID)))
      GROUP BY Customer.PostalCode;
```

To find the number of different prices for items currently in stock, you need two queries. For the query DistinctPrice, enter the following:

```
SELECT DISTINCT Price
  FROM Catalog
  WHERE NumberInStock > 0;
```

For the query CountDistinctPrice, enter the following:

```
SELECT COUNT(*) FROM DistinctPrice;
```

See Also Expressions, GROUP BY Clause, HAVING Clause, SELECT Statement, Subquery, and TRANSFORM Statement.

Total Function: MAX

In a logical table defined by a SELECT statement or a subquery, creates a column value that is the maximum value in the expression or column name specified. You can use the GROUP BY clause to create a maximum value for each group of rows selected from the underlying tables or queries.

Syntax:

MAX(*expression*)

Notes:

You cannot use another total function reference within the expression. If you use an SQL total function in the select list of a SELECT statement, any other columns in the select list must be derived using a total function, or the column name must appear in a GROUP BY clause. An expression must contain a reference to at least one column name.

Null values are not included in the calculation of the result. The data type of the result is the same as that of the expression or the column name.

Examples:

To find the largest order from any customer within each zip code, enter the following:

```
SELECT DISTINCTROW Customer.PostalCode,
       MAX(Order.SubTotalCost) AS MaxOfSubTotalCost
  FROM Customer
    INNER JOIN [Order]
    ON Customer.CustomerID = Order.CustomerID
  GROUP BY Customer.PostalCode;
```

To find the item currently in stock with the maximum inventory cost, enter the following:

```
SELECT ComponentID, Description, OurCost, NumberInStock
  FROM Component
  WHERE ([OurCost] * [NumberInStock]) =
   (SELECT MAX([OurCost] * [NumberInStock])
     FROM Component);
```

See Also   Expressions, GROUP BY Clause, HAVING Clause, SELECT Statement, Subquery, and TRANSFORM Statement.

Total Function: MIN

In a logical table defined by a SELECT statement or a subquery, creates a column value that is the minimum value in the expression or column name specified. You can use the GROUP BY clause to create a minimum value for each group of rows selected from the underlying tables or queries.

Syntax:

```
MIN(expression)
```

Notes:

You cannot use another total function reference within the expression. If you use an SQL total function in the select list of a SELECT statement, any other columns in the select list must be derived using a total function, or the column name must appear in a GROUP BY clause. An expression must contain a reference to at least one column name.

Null values are not included in the calculation of the result. The data type of the result is the same as that of the expression or the column name.

Examples:

To find the smallest order from any customer within each zip code, enter the following:

```
SELECT DISTINCTROW Customer.PostalCode,
      MIN(Order.SubTotalCost) AS MinOfSubTotalCost
  FROM Customer
    INNER JOIN [Order]
    ON Customer.CustomerID = Order.CustomerID
  GROUP BY Customer.PostalCode;
```

To find the item currently in stock with the smallest inventory cost, enter the following:

```
SELECT ComponentID, Description, OurCost, NumberInStock
  FROM Component
  WHERE ([OurCost] * [NumberInStock]) =
    (SELECT MIN([OurCost] * [NumberInStock])
      FROM Component
      WHERE NumberInStock <> 0);
```

 **See Also** Expressions, GROUP BY Clause, HAVING Clause, SELECT Statement, Subquery, and TRANSFORM Statement.

Total Functions: STDEV, STDEVP

In a logical table defined by a SELECT statement or a subquery, creates a column value that is the standard deviation (square root of the variance) of the values in the expression or column name specified. You can use the GROUP BY clause to create a standard deviation for each group of rows selected from the underlying tables or queries. STDEVP produces an estimate of the standard deviation for the entire population based on the sample provided in each group.

Syntax:

```
{STDEV | STDEVP} (expression)
```

Notes:

You cannot use another total function reference within the expression. If you use an SQL total function in the select list of a SELECT statement, any other columns in the select list must be derived using a total function, or the column name must appear in a GROUP BY clause. An expression must contain a reference to at least one column name, and the expression or column name must be a numeric data type.

Null values are not included in the calculation of the result. The data type of the result is a double number. If there are not at least two members in a group, STDEV returns a Null value. STDEVP returns an estimate if there is at least one non-Null value in the group.

Example:

To find the standard deviation and the population standard deviation of the cost of components, grouped by type of component, enter the following:

```
SELECT DISTINCTROW Type.TypeDescription,
       Count(Description) AS CountOfDescription,
       StDev(Component.OurCost) AS StDevOfOurCost,
       StDevP(Component.OurCost) AS StDevPOfOurCost
   FROM Type
     INNER JOIN Component
     ON Type.ItemTypeCode = Component.ItemTypeCode
   GROUP BY Type.TypeDescription;
```

 See Also Expressions, GROUP BY Clause, HAVING Clause, SELECT Statement, Subquery, and TRANSFORM Statement.

Total Function: SUM

In a logical table defined by a SELECT statement or a subquery, creates a column value that is the numeric sum of the values in the expression or column name specified. You can use the GROUP BY clause to create a sum for each group of rows selected from the underlying tables or queries.

Syntax:

SUM(*expression*)

Notes:

You cannot use another function reference within the expression. Also, a column name must not refer to a column in a query derived from a function. If you use an SQL total function in the select list of a SELECT statement, any other columns in the select list must be derived using a total function, or the column name must appear in a GROUP BY clause. An expression must contain a reference to at least one column name, and the expression or column name must be a numeric data type.

Null values are not included in the calculation of the result. The data type of the result is generally the same as that of the expression or the column name.

Examples:

To create a parameter query that summarizes the sales and cost of goods for all items sold in a given month, enter the following:

```
PARAMETERS [Year to summarize:] Short,
          [Month to summarize:] Short;
SELECT DISTINCTROW OrderItem.CatalogItemID,
      SUM(OrderItem.Quantity) AS Quantity,
      SUM(OrderItem.[Quantity] *
        [QuotedPrice]) AS TotalSales,
      SUM(OrderItem.[Quantity] *
        [OurCost]) AS TotalCost
  FROM [Order]
    INNER JOIN (Catalog
    INNER JOIN OrderItem
    ON Catalog.CatalogItemID = OrderItem.CatalogItemID)
  ON [Order].OrderID = OrderItem.OrderID
  WHERE Year([OrderDate]) = [Year to summarize:]
    AND Month([OrderDate]) = [Month to summarize:]
  GROUP BY OrderItem.CatalogItemID;
```

To find the total inventory cost of items currently in stock, enter the following:

```
SELECT DISTINCTROW SUM([OurCost] *
      [NumberInStock]) AS SumInventoryCost
  FROM Component
  WHERE Component.NumberInStock > 0;
```

 **See Also**   Expressions, GROUP BY Clause, HAVING Clause, SELECT Statement, Subquery, and TRANSFORM Statement.

Total Functions: VAR, VARP

In a logical table defined by a SELECT statement or a subquery, creates a column value that is the variance (average of the square of the difference from the mean) of the values in the expression or column name specified. You can use the GROUP BY clause to create a variance for each group of rows selected from the underlying tables or queries. VARP produces an estimate of the variance for the entire population based on the sample provided in each group.

Syntax:

```
{VAR | VARP} (expression)
```

Notes:

You cannot use another total function reference within the expression. If you use an SQL total function in the select list of a SELECT statement, any other columns in the select list must be derived using a total function, or the column name must appear in a GROUP BY clause. An expression must contain a reference to at least one column name, and the expression or column name must be a numeric data type.

Null values are not included in the calculation of the result. The data type of the result is a double number. If there are not at least two members in a group, VAR returns a Null value. VARP returns an estimate if there is at least one non-Null value in the group.

Example:

To find the variance and the population variance of the cost of components, grouped by type of component, enter the following:

```
SELECT DISTINCTROW Type.TypeDescription,
       Count(Description) AS CountOfDescription,
       Var(Component.OurCost) AS VarOfOurCost,
       VarP(Component.OurCost) AS VarPOfOurCost
   FROM Type
     INNER JOIN Component
     ON Type.ItemTypeCode = Component.ItemTypeCode
   GROUP BY Type.TypeDescription;
```

 **See Also**   Expressions, GROUP BY Clause, HAVING Clause, SELECT Statement, Subquery, and TRANSFORM Statement.

TRANSFORM Statement

Produces a crosstab query that lets you summarize a single value using the values found in a specified column or expression as the column headers and using other columns or expressions to define the grouping criteria to form rows. The result looks similar to a spreadsheet and is most useful as input to a graph object.

Syntax:

```
TRANSFORM total-function-expression
  <select-statement>
PIVOT expression
[IN (<column-value-list>)]
```

where *total-function-expression* is an expression created using one of the total functions, *<select-statement>* contains a GROUP BY clause, and *<column-value-list>* is a list of required values expected to be returned by the PIVOT expression, enclosed in quotes and separated by commas. (You can use the IN clause to force the output sequence of the columns.)

Notes:

total-function-expression is the value that you want to appear in the "cells" of the crosstab datasheet. PIVOT *expression* defines the column or expression that provides the column heading values in the crosstab result. For example, you might use this value to provide a list of months with total rows defined by product categories in the *select-statement* GROUP BY clause. You can use more than one column or expression in the select statement to define the grouping criteria for rows.

Example:

To produce a total sales amount for each month in the year 1993, categorized by catalog item, enter the following:

```
TRANSFORM Sum(MonthlySales.TotalInvoiceAmount) AS
          SumOfTotalInvoiceAmount
SELECT Catalog.Description
  FROM Catalog
    INNER JOIN MonthlySales
    ON Catalog.CatalogItemID = MonthlySales.CatalogItemID
  GROUP BY Catalog.Description
  ORDER BY Catalog.Description,
    Format(DateSerial([Year],[Month],1),"mmm yy")
  PIVOT Format(DateSerial([Year],[Month],1),"mmm yy")
  IN ("Jan 93","Feb 93","Mar 93","Apr 93","May 93",
      "Jun 93","Jul 93","Aug 93","Sep 93","Oct 93",
      "Nov 93","Dec 93");
```

NOTE This example shows a special use of the IN predicate to define not only which months should be selected but also the sequence in which Access displays the months in the resulting recordset.

See Also   GROUP BY Clause, HAVING Clause, SELECT Statement, and Total Functions.

UNION Query Operator

Produces a result table that contains the rows returned by both the first select statement and the second select statement. You must use SQL view to define a UNION query.

Syntax:

```
select-statement
UNION [ALL]
   select-statement
[ORDER BY {column-name | column-number [ASC | DESC]},...]
```

Notes:

If you specify ALL, Access returns all rows in both logical tables. If you do not specify ALL, Access eliminates duplicate rows. The tables returned by each select statement must contain an equal number of columns, and each column must have identical attributes.

You must not use the ORDER BY clause in the select statements that are joined by query operators; however, you can include a single ORDER BY clause at the end of a statement that uses one or more query operators. This action will apply the specified order to the result of the entire statement. Access derives the column names of the output from the column names returned by the first select statement. If you want to use column names in the ORDER BY clause, be sure to use names from the first query. You can also use the output column numbers to define ORDER BY criteria.

You can combine multiple select statements using UNION to obtain complex results. You can also use parentheses to influence the sequence in which Access applies the operators, as shown here:

```
SELECT...UNION (SELECT...UNION SELECT...)
```

Example:

To find the names of all suppliers, current customers, and potential customers from a new mailing list (NewCust) in the state of Washington, to eliminate duplicates, and to sort the names by zip code, enter the following:

```
SELECT DISTINCTROW Customer.CompanyName, Customer.City,
      PostalCode
  FROM Customer
    WHERE Customer.State = "WA"
UNION
  (SELECT DISTINCTROW Supplier.SupplierName,
         Supplier.SupplierCity, Supplier.SupplierPostal
  FROM Supplier
    WHERE Supplier.SupplierState = "WA"
UNION
  SELECT DISTINCTROW NewCust.Company, NewCust.City,
         NewCust.Zip
    FROM NewCust
    WHERE NewCust.Region = "WA")
    ORDER BY PostalCode;
```

 See Also   ORDER BY Clause and SELECT Statement.

WHERE Clause

Specifies a search condition in an SQL statement or an SQL clause. The DELETE, SELECT, and UPDATE statements and the subquery containing the WHERE clause operate only on those rows that satisfy the condition.

Syntax:

```
WHERE search-condition
```

Notes:

Access applies the search condition to each row of the logical table assembled as a result of executing the previous clauses, and it rejects those rows for which the search condition does not evaluate to True. If you use a subquery within a predicate in the search condition (often called an *inner query*), Access must first execute the subquery before it evaluates the predicate.

In a subquery, if you refer to a table or a query that you also use in an outer FROM clause (often called a *correlated subquery*), Access must execute the subquery for each row being evaluated in the outer table. If you do not use a reference to an outer table in a subquery, Access must execute the subquery only once. A correlated subquery can also be expressed as a join, which generally executes more efficiently. If you include a predicate in the search condition in the form

expression comparison-operator subquery

an error is returned if the subquery returns no rows.

The order of evaluation of the Boolean operators used in the search condition is NOT, AND, OR, XOR (exclusive OR), EQV (equivalence), and then IMP (implication). You can include additional parentheses to influence the order in which Access processes Boolean expressions.

Example:

To find all products whose cost is greater than $100 and whose number of days to build is equal to 2 or whose number in stock is less than 5, but not both, enter the following:

```
SELECT DISTINCTROW Catalog.CatalogItemID,
       Catalog.Description, Catalog.OurCost,
       Catalog.DaysToBuild, Catalog.NumberInStock
  FROM Catalog
  WHERE (Catalog.OurCost) > 100
    AND ((Catalog.DaysToBuild) = 2
    XOR (Catalog.NumberInStock) < 5);
```

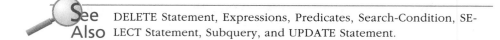 **See Also**   DELETE Statement, Expressions, Predicates, Search-Condition, SELECT Statement, Subquery, and UPDATE Statement.

SQL Action Queries

Use SQL action queries to delete, insert, or update data or to create a new table from existing data. Action queries are particularly powerful because they allow you to operate on sets of data, not single rows. For example, an UPDATE statement or a DELETE statement affects all rows in the underlying tables that meet the selection criteria you specify.

DELETE Statement

Deletes one or more rows from a table or a query. The WHERE clause is optional. If you do not specify a WHERE clause, all rows are deleted from the table or the query that you specify in the FROM clause. If you specify a WHERE clause, the search condition is applied to each row in the table or the query, and only those rows that evaluate to True are deleted.

Syntax:

```
DELETE [select-list]
  FROM {{table-name [[AS] correlation-name] |
  select-query-name [[AS] correlation-name]} |
  <joined table>},...
  [IN <source specification>]
  [WHERE search-condition];
```

where *select-list* is

```
[* | table-name.* | column-list]
```

and where *<joined table>* is

```
({table-name [[AS] correlation-name] |
 select-query-name [[AS] correlation-name] |
 <joined table>}
{INNER | LEFT | RIGHT} JOIN
  {table-name [[AS] correlation-name] |
  select-query-name [[AS] correlation-name] |
  <joined table>}
ON <join-specification>)
```

Notes:

If you specify a query name in a DELETE statement, the query must not be constructed using the UNION query operator. The query also must not contain an SQL total function, the DISTINCT keyword, the GROUP BY or HAVING clause, or a subquery that references the same base table as the DELETE statement.

If you join two or more tables in the FROM clause, you can delete rows only from the "many" side of the relationship if the tables are related one-to-many or on one of the "one" sides if the tables are related one-to-one. When you include more than one table in the FROM clause, you must also specify from which table the rows are to be deleted by using *table-name.** in the select list. When you specify only one table in the FROM clause, you do not need to provide a select list.

You can optionally supply a correlation name for each table or query name. You can use this correlation name as an alias for the full table name when qualifying column names in the WHERE clause and in subclauses. You must use a correlation name when referring to a column name that occurs in more than one table in the FROM clause.

If you use a subquery in the search condition, you must not reference the target table or the query or any underlying table of the query in the subquery.

Examples:

To delete all rows in the MonthlySales table, enter the following:

```
DELETE FROM MonthlySales;
```

To delete all rows in the Component table that are "Hard drives," enter the following:

```
DELETE DISTINCTROW Component.*
  FROM Component
    INNER JOIN Type
    ON Component.ItemTypeCode = Type.ItemTypeCode
WHERE Type.TypeDescription = "Hard drives";
```

See Also   IN Clause, INSERT Statement, Predicates, Search-Condition, and Subquery.

INSERT Statement (Append Query)

Inserts one or more new rows into the specified table or query. When you use the VALUES clause, only a single row is inserted. If you use a select statement, the number of rows inserted equals the number of rows returned by the select statement.

Syntax:

```
INSERT INTO table-name [({column-name},...)]
[IN <source specification>]
{VALUES({literal},...) |
select-statement}
```

Notes:

If you do not include a column name list, you must supply values for all columns defined in the table in the order in which they were declared in the table definition. If you include a column name list, you must supply values for all columns in the list, and the values must be compatible with the receiving column attributes. You must include in the list all columns in the underlying table whose Required attribute is Yes and that do not have a default value.

If you include an IN clause in both the INSERT INTO and the FROM clause of the select statement, both must refer to the same source database.

If you supply values by using a select statement, the statement's FROM clause cannot have the target table of the insert as its table name or as an underlying table. The target table also cannot be used in any subquery.

Because Access allows you to define column-value constraints, a table validation rule, and referential integrity checks, any values that you insert must pass these validations before Access allows you to run the query.

Examples:

To insert a new row in the Customer table, enter the following:

```
INSERT INTO Customer (CompanyName, CustomerName,
        Address1, Address2, City, State, PostalCode,
        Country, PhoneNumber, FaxNumber, CreditLimit,
        AmountOwed)
VALUES ("Books Unlimited", "12345 Camino Real", " "
        "San Jose", "CA", "95000", "USA",
        "(408) 881-2051", "(408) 881-2055", 9000, 0);
```

To calculate the sales totals for a given month and insert them into a summary working table, enter the following:

```
PARAMETERS [Year to summarize:] Short,
        [Month to summarize:] Short;
INSERT INTO zSumSalesWork (CatalogItemID, Quantity,
        TotalSales, TotalCost)
SELECT DISTINCTROW OrderItem.CatalogItemID,
        SUM(OrderItem.Quantity) AS SumOfQuantity,
        SUM([Quantity] * [QuotedPrice]) AS
            TotalInvoiceAmount,
        SUM([Quantity] * [OurCost]) AS TotalCost
```

```
FROM [Order]
  INNER JOIN (Catalog
    INNER JOIN OrderItem
    ON Catalog.CatalogItemID =
      OrderItem.CatalogItemID)
  ON [Order].OrderID = OrderItem.OrderID
WHERE Year([OrderDate]) = [Year to summarize:]
  AND Month([OrderDate]) = [Month to summarize:]
GROUP BY OrderItem.CatalogItemID;
```

Although Access accepts the ANSI-standard VALUES clause, you will discover that Access converts a statement such as

```
INSERT INTO MyTable (ColumnA, ColumnB)
VALUES (123, "Jane Doe");
```

to

```
INSERT INTO MyTable (ColumnA, ColumnB)
SELECT 123 As Expr1, "Jane Doe" as Expr2;
```

See Also   DELETE Statement, IN Clause, SELECT Statement, and Subquery.

SELECT...INTO Statement (Make Table Query)

Creates a new table from values selected from one or more other tables. Make table queries are most useful for providing backup snapshots or for creating tables with rolled-up totals at the end of an accounting period.

Syntax:

```
SELECT [ALL | DISTINCT | DISTINCTROW | TOP number
       [PERCENT]]
  select-list
INTO new-table-name
  [IN <source specification>]
  FROM {{table-name [[AS] correlation-name] |
   select-query-name [[AS] correlation-name]} |
   <joined table>},...
  [IN <source specification>]
  [WHERE search-condition]
  [GROUP BY column-name,...]
  [HAVING search-condition]
```

```
[UNION [ALL] select-statement]
[[ORDER BY {column-name [ASC | DESC]},...] |
IN <"source database name"> <[source connect string]>
[WITH OWNERACCESS OPTION];
```

where *select-list* is

```
{* | {expression [AS output-column-name] | table-name.* |
query-name.* | correlation-name.*},...}
```

and where *<joined table>* is

```
({table-name [[AS] correlation-name] |
 select-query-name [[AS] correlation-name] |
 <joined table>}
{INNER | LEFT | RIGHT} JOIN
 {table-name [[AS] correlation-name] |
 select-query-name [[AS] correlation-name] |
 <joined table>}
ON <join-specification>)
```

Notes:

A SELECT...INTO query creates a new table with the name specified in *new-table-name*. If the table already exists, Access displays a dialog box that asks you to confirm the deletion of the table before it creates a new one in its place. The columns in the new table inherit the data type attributes of the columns produced by the select list.

You can optionally supply a correlation name for each table or query name. You can use this correlation name as an alias for the full table name when qualifying column names in the select list or in the WHERE clause and subclauses. If you're joining a table or a query to itself, you must use correlation names to clarify which copy of the table or query you're referring to in the select list, join criteria, or selection criteria. If a table name or a query name is also an SQL reserved word (for example, "Order"), you must enclose the name in brackets.

When you list more than one table or query without join criteria, the source is the Cartesian product of all the tables. For example, *FROM TableA, TableB* asks Access to search all the rows of TableA matched with all the rows of TableB. Unless you specify other restricting criteria, the number of logical rows that Access processes could equal the number of rows in TableA <u>times</u> the number of rows in TableB. Access then returns the rows in which the selection criteria specified in the WHERE and HAVING clauses are true.

You can further define which rows Access includes in the output recordset by specifying ALL, DISTINCT, DISTINCTROW, TOP *n*, or TOP *n* PERCENT. ALL includes all rows that match the search criteria from the source tables, including potential duplicate rows. DISTINCT requests that Access return only rows that are different from any other row. You cannot update any columns in a query that uses ALL or DISTINCT.

DISTINCTROW (the default) requests that Access return only rows in which the concatenation of the primary keys from all tables supplying output columns is unique. Depending on the columns you select, you might see rows in the result that contain duplicate values, but each row in the result is derived from a distinct combination of rows in the underlying tables. Specify TOP *n* or TOP *n* PERCENT to request that the recordset contain only the first *n* or first *n* percent of rows. The parameter *n* must be an integer and must be less than or equal to 100 if you include the PERCENT keyword. Note that if you do not include an ORDER BY clause (see the facing page), the sequence of rows returned is undefined.

If you include an IN clause for both the INTO and the FROM clauses, both must refer to the same source database.

When you include a GROUP BY clause, the select list must be made up of either SQL total functions or column names specified in the GROUP BY clause. A column name in a GROUP BY clause can refer to any column from any table in the FROM clause, even if the column is not named in the select list. If you want to refer to a calculated expression in the GROUP BY clause, you must assign an *output-column-name* to the expression in *select-list* and then refer to that name in the GROUP BY clause. If the GROUP BY clause is preceded by a WHERE clause, Access forms the groups from the rows selected after it applies the WHERE clause.

If you use a HAVING clause but do not include a GROUP BY clause, the select list must be formed using SQL total functions. If you include a GROUP BY clause preceding the HAVING clause, the HAVING search condition applies to each of the groups formed by equal values in the specified columns. If you do not include a GROUP BY clause, the HAVING search condition applies to the entire logical table defined by the SELECT statement.

You use column names or relative output column numbers to specify the columns on whose values the rows returned are ordered. (If you use relative output column numbers, the first output column is 1.) You can specify multiple columns in the ORDER BY clause. The list is ordered primarily by the first column. If rows exist for which the values of that column are equal, they are ordered by the next column on the ORDER BY list. You can specify ascending (ASC) or descending (DESC) order for each column. If you do not specify ASC or DESC, ASC is assumed. Using an ORDER BY clause in a SELECT statement is the only means of defining the sequence of the returned rows.

Normally, the person running the query not only must have rights to the query but also must have the appropriate rights to the tables used in the query. (These rights include reading data to select rows, updating, inserting, and deleting data using the query.) If your application has multiple users, you might want to secure the tables so that no user has direct access to any of the tables and all users can still run queries defined by you. Assuming you are the owner of both the queries and the tables, you can deny access to the tables but allow access to the queries. To make sure that the queries run properly, you must add the WITH OWNERACCESS OPTION clause to allow the users to have the same access rights as the table owner when accessing the data via the query. (See Chapter 14, "Securing and Delivering Your Application," in the *Building Applications with Microsoft Access for Windows 95* manual that comes with Access for more details on securing your applications.)

Example:

To create a new table that summarizes all sales for the year 1993 by product from the MonthlySales totals table, enter the following:

```
SELECT DISTINCTROW MonthlySales.CatalogItemID,
        Catalog.Description, MonthlySales.Year,
        CLng(Sum([QuantitySold])) AS Quantity,
        Sum(MonthlySales.TotalInvoiceAmount) AS
            TotalSales,
        Sum(MonthlySales.TotalCost) AS TotalCost
    INTO Sales1993
      FROM Catalog
        INNER JOIN MonthlySales
        ON Catalog.CatalogItemID = MonthlySales.CatalogItemID
      WHERE MonthlySales.Year = 1993
      GROUP BY MonthlySales.CatalogItemID,
            Catalog.Description, MonthlySales.Year;
```

See Also   IN Clause, JOIN Operation, Search-Condition, and SELECT Statement.

UPDATE Statement

In the specified table or query, updates the selected columns (either to the value of the given expression or to Null) in all rows that satisfy the search condition. If you do not enter a WHERE clause, all rows in the specified table or query are affected.

Syntax:

```
UPDATE {{table-name [[AS] correlation-name] |
 select-query-name [[AS] correlation-name]} |
 <joined table>},...
[IN <source specification>]
SET {column-name = {expression | NULL}},...
[WHERE search-condition]
```

where *<joined table>* is

```
({table-name [[AS] correlation-name] |
 select-query-name [[AS] correlation-name] |
 <joined table>}
{INNER | LEFT | RIGHT} JOIN
  {table-name [[AS] correlation-name] |
  select-query-name [[AS] correlation-name] |
  <joined table>}
ON <join-specification>)
```

Notes:

If you provide more than one table name, you can update columns only in the table on the "many" side of a one-to-many relationship. If the tables are related one-to-one, you can update columns in either table. Access must be able to determine the relationship between queries in order to update columns in a query. In general, if a table is joined by its primary key to a query, you can update columns in the query (because the primary key indicates that the table is on the "one" side of the join). You cannot update a table joined to a query. If you want to update a table with the results of a query, you must insert the query results into a temporary table that can be defined with a one-to-many or one-to-one relationship with the target table and then use the temporary table to update the target.

If you specify a search condition, you can reference only columns found in the target table or query. If you use a subquery in the search condition, you must not reference the target table or the query or any underlying table of the query in the subquery.

In the SET clause, you cannot specify a column name more than once. Values assigned to columns must be compatible with the column attributes. If you assign the Null value, the column cannot have been defined Required=Yes.

Access lets you define column-value constraints, a table validation rule, or referential integrity checks, so any values that you update must pass these validations or Access will not let you run the query.

Examples:

To raise the price of all video boards by 10 percent, enter the following:

```
UPDATE DISTINCTROW Type
  INNER JOIN Catalog
  ON Type.ItemTypeCode = Catalog.ItemTypeCode
  SET Catalog.Price = [Price] * 1.1
  WHERE Type.TypeDescription = "Video Boards";
```

To discount the price of all items in the catalog by 5 percent, enter the following:

```
UPDATE Catalog
  SET Catalog.Price = [Price] * .95;
```

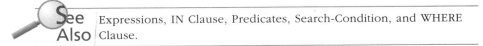

See Also   Expressions, IN Clause, Predicates, Search-Condition, and WHERE Clause.

Complex Query Examples

Although the preceding sections provide many examples, it's useful for you to examine how complex queries are constructed for the Entertainment Schedule sample application. The first example in this section shows you how to create a query that returns the date of every Monday between January 1, 1995, and January 1, 2001. The second example uses the first query to generate a week-by-week booking list for all clubs and groups. It then shows you how to revise an SQL SELECT statement produced by the Access design grid to handle a special JOIN criteria expression. The third example expands the week-by-week booking list to show weeks in which there are no bookings for clubs and groups.

Example 1:
Returning the Date of Every Monday

To produce reports that show weekly bookings for clubs and groups, the Entertainment Schedule sample database uses several scheduling queries. Because you want the reports to show bookings for clubs and groups by week, beginning on each Monday, you need some way to return the date of Monday for every week in which there is a booking. You can accomplish this by creating a query that returns the date of every Monday, and then basing the scheduling queries on a combination of this query and the tables in which the booking information is stored.

To create the Monday dates query, called qryMondays, you start with a table, tblDates, that stores all dates between January 1, 1990, and January 2, 2001. Each date record has a corresponding DayOfWeek field that stores an integer value indicating the day of the week that the date falls on—*1* for Monday, *2* for Tuesday, and so on. Add the tblDates table to the upper part of the Query window in Design view, and then drag the SchedDate and DayOfWeek fields to the design grid. To create a query that returns Monday dates since January 1, 1995, set the criterion for the SchedDate field to ">=#1/1/95#", and then set the criterion for the DayOfWeek field to 1.

Your query should look like the one shown in Figure 11-2.

FIGURE 11-2

A query that returns a list of Monday dates.

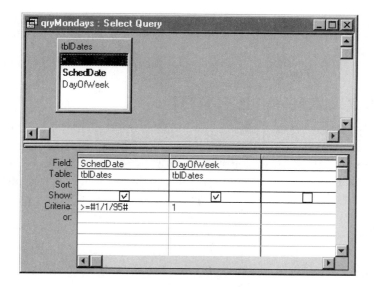

To see the underlying SQL code for the query, select SQL View from the Query View toolbar button's drop-down list. In SQL view, the query should look like this:

```
SELECT DISTINCTROW tblDates.SchedDate, tblDates.DayOfWeek
  FROM tblDates
  WHERE (((tblDates.SchedDate)>=#1/1/95#)
    AND ((tblDates.DayOfWeek)=1));
```

Example 2:
Generating a Week-by-Week Booking List

To see all the weekly bookings for clubs and groups, you need to create a query that combines information about each group's bookings with information about clubs. You can get information about each booking from a group's contract, which is stored in the master contracts table. Information about clubs is stored in the master clubs table. Creating a query that uses these two tables alone won't give you a week-by-week list of bookings, however. That's where the Monday dates query you created in the previous example comes in.

To create the master clubs and groups schedule query, called qrySchedClubsAndGroups, you'll combine information from the master contracts table (tblContracts), the master clubs table (tblClubs), and the Monday dates query (qryMondays). You can start by adding the two tables and the query to the upper part of the Query window in Design view. Because a relationship has already been defined for the contracts and clubs tables, a one-to-many join is already established between the ClubID fields of the two tables. You can then relate the Monday dates query to the contracts table by establishing an equi-join between the SchedDate field in qryMondays and the BeginningDate field in tblContracts. Then drag the following fields to the design grid:

Field	Table/Query
SchedDate	qryMondays
ContractNo	tblContracts
GroupID	tblContracts
GroupName	tblContracts
ClubID	tblContracts

(continued)

399

continued

Field	Table/Query
Status	tblContracts
BeginningDate	tblContracts
EndingDate	tblContracts
ClubName	tblClubs

Because you don't want to include bookings for contracts that have been cancelled, set the criterion for the Status field to <>"D".

Your query should look like the one shown in Figure 11-3.

FIGURE 11-3

A query that returns weekly bookings for clubs and groups.

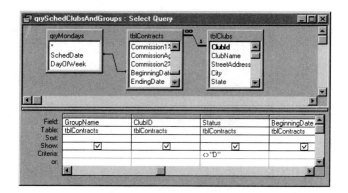

So far, creating the master clubs and groups schedule query is like creating any other simple query. However, if you run the query you'll see that it doesn't yet produce the results you want: It returns only the bookings whose beginning date is a Monday, but most bookings begin on a Friday, a Saturday, or another day of the week. To return a Monday schedule date for a booking that begins on another day, revise the query to include bookings whose beginning date is within seven days of each Monday date. In addition, you need to include bookings whose ending date occurs in the week following the Monday schedule date. When a contract spans multiple weeks, you'll see that this technique generates one output row for each week of the contract.

You can accomplish this by adding criteria to the BeginningDate and EndingDate fields in the master clubs and groups schedule query. Translating what you want into SQL expressions gives you the following criteria:

Field	Criteria
BeginningDate	qryMondays.SchedDate > tblContracts.BeginningDate -7
EndingDate	qryMondays.SchedDate <= tblContracts.EndingDate

Because greater than (>) and less than or equal to (<=) operators can't be represented in the design grid, you need to specify the criteria in a custom join expression in the query's underlying SQL code. Open the query in SQL view and replace the SELECT statement's FROM clause with the following:

```
FROM qryMondays
  INNER JOIN (tblContracts
    INNER JOIN tblClubs
    ON tblClubs.ClubId = tblContracts.ClubID)
    ON (qryMondays.SchedDate >
      tblContracts.BeginningDate -7)
      AND (qryMondays.SchedDate <=
        tblContracts.EndingDate)
```

In SQL view, the completed query should look like this:

```
SELECT DISTINCTROW qryMondays.SchedDate,
        tblContracts.ContractNo, tblContracts.GroupID,
        tblContracts.GroupName, tblContracts.ClubID,
        tblContracts.Status,
        tblContracts.BeginningDate,
        tblContracts.EndingDate, tblClubs.ClubName
  FROM qryMondays
    INNER JOIN (tblContracts
      INNER JOIN tblClubs
      ON tblClubs.ClubId = tblContracts.ClubID)
      ON (qryMondays.SchedDate >
        tblContracts.BeginningDate -7)
        AND (qryMondays.SchedDate <=
          tblContracts.EndingDate)
  WHERE tblContracts.Status <> "D";
```

Example 3: Showing Weeks in Which There Are No Bookings

Now that you've created a master clubs and groups schedule query, you can use it as the basis for other queries. For example, you can create a master schedules query that shows all weeks—those with bookings as well as those without.

To build the master schedules query, called qrySchedules, create a new query and add the qrySchedClubsAndGroups and qryMondays queries to the upper part of the Query window in Design view. Drag the SchedDate field from the qryMondays field list and drop it on the SchedDate field in the qrySchedClubsAndGroups field list. Double-click on the resulting join line, and then select option 2 in the Join Properties dialog box. Then drag the following fields to the design grid:

Field	Table/Query
SchedDate	qryMondays
ContractNo	qrySchedClubsAndGroups
Status	qrySchedClubsAndGroups
GroupID	qrySchedClubsAndGroups
GroupName	qrySchedClubsAndGroups
ClubID	qrySchedClubsAndGroups
ClubName	qrySchedClubsAndGroups
BeginningDate	qrySchedClubsAndGroups
EndingDate	qrySchedClubsAndGroups

Sort the SchedDate field in ascending order. Your query should look like the one shown in Figure 11-4.

FIGURE 11-4

A master schedules query.

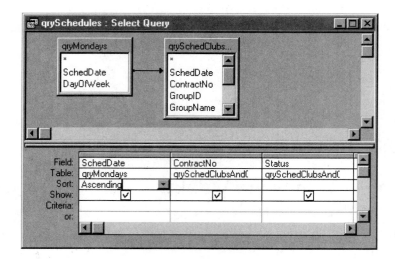

In SQL view, the query should look like this:

```
SELECT DISTINCTROW qryMondays.SchedDate,
       qrySchedClubsAndGroups.ContractNo,
       qrySchedClubsAndGroups.Status,
       qrySchedClubsAndGroups.GroupID,
       qrySchedClubsAndGroups.GroupName,
       qrySchedClubsAndGroups.ClubID,
       qrySchedClubsAndGroups.ClubName,
       qrySchedClubsAndGroups.BeginningDate,
       qrySchedClubsAndGroups.EndingDate
  FROM qryMondays LEFT JOIN qrySchedClubsAndGroups
    ON qryMondays.SchedDate =
       qrySchedClubsAndGroups.SchedDate
  ORDER BY qryMondays.SchedDate;
```

At this point, you should have a good working understanding of how to build complex queries using the SQL syntax understood by Access. In Parts 4 and 5 of this book, you'll learn how to build forms and reports that use queries. In Part 6, you'll learn how to use macros and VBA to tie it all together.

Part 4

SELECT EDITION

Using Forms

Chapter 12

Form Basics

f you've worked through the book to this point, you should understand all the mechanics of designing and building databases (and
connecting to external ones), entering and viewing data in tables, and
building queries. You need to understand tables and queries before
you jump into forms because most of the forms you design will have an
underlying table or recordset.

This chapter focuses on the external aspects of forms—why forms
are useful, what they look like, and how to use them. You'll look at
examples of forms from the College Counseling sample database. In
the next two chapters, you'll learn how to design and build your own
forms by creating portions of the database application for the College
Counseling and Entertainment Schedule databases.

Uses of Forms

Forms are the primary interface between users and your Microsoft Access application. You can design forms for many different purposes.

- *Displaying and editing data.* This is the most common use of
  forms. Forms provide a way to customize the presentation of
  data in your database. You can also use forms to change, add,
  or delete data in your database. You can set options in a form
  to make all or part of your data read-only, to fill in related information from other tables automatically, to calculate the values
  to be displayed, or to show or hide data based on either the
  values of other data in the record or the options selected by the
  user of the form.

- *Controlling application flow.* You can design forms that work
  with macros or with Microsoft Visual Basic for Applications
  (VBA) procedures to automate the display of certain data or the
  sequence of certain actions. You can create special controls on
  your form, called *command buttons,* that run a macro or a VBA
  procedure when you click them. With macros and VBA procedures, you can open other forms, run queries, restrict the data
  that is displayed, execute a menu command, set values in
  records and forms, display menus, print reports, and perform a
  host of other actions. You can also design a form so that macros
  or VBA procedures run when specific events occur—for example, when someone opens the form, tabs to a specific control, clicks an option on the form, or changes data in the form.
  See Part 6 of this book for details on using macros and VBA
  with forms to automate your application.

- *Accepting input.* You can design forms that are used only for entering new data in your database or for providing data values to help automate your application.

- *Displaying messages.* Forms can provide information about how to use your application or about upcoming actions. Access also provides a MsgBox macro action and a *MsgBox* VBA function that you can use to display information, warnings, or errors. (See Chapter 19, "Adding Power with Macros," for details.)

- *Printing information.* Although you should design reports to print most information, you can also print the information in a form. Because you can specify one set of options when Access displays a form and another set of options when Access prints a form, a form can serve a dual role. For example, you might design a form with two sets of display headers and footers, one set for entering an order and another set for printing a customer invoice from the order.

A Tour of Forms

The College Counseling sample database is full of interesting examples of forms. The rest of this chapter takes you on a tour of some of the major features of those forms. In the next chapter, you'll learn how to design and build forms for this database.

Begin by opening the College Counseling database and clicking on the Forms tab in the Database window to see the list of available forms. If you started the application, click Exit on the main switchboard form to return to the Database window.

Headers, Detail Sections, and Footers

You'll normally place the information that you want to display from the underlying table or query in the detail section in the center of the Form window. You can add a header at the top of the window or a footer at the bottom of the window to display information or controls that don't need to change with each different record.

An interesting form in the College Counseling database that includes both a header and a footer is frmCollegeSummary. The application uses this form to display the summary results of a college search whenever the search finds more than 20 matching colleges. You can also open this form directly from the Database window—it will show you all the colleges. Find the frmCollegeSummary form in the forms list in the Database window, select the form, and then click the Open button to see a window similar to the one shown in Figure 12-1.

FIGURE 12-1

The frmCollege-
Summary form,
which has a
header, a detail
section, and
a footer.

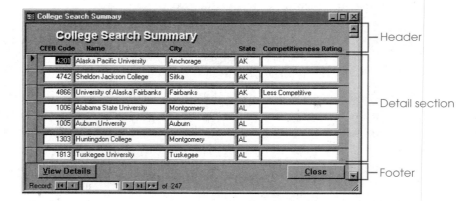

The area at the top of the window containing the title *College Search Summary* is the header for the form. The header also includes the column names. The area at the bottom of the window is the footer for the form. You can click the View Details button to see all details for the currently selected college (the row with the arrow on the row selector), or you can click Close to close the form. At the bottom left corner of the form is the record number box that you saw in tables and queries in Datasheet view. Click the arrow button immediately to the right of the record number, and the row selector arrow will move to the next college record in the detail section of the form; notice that the header and footer don't change when you do this. If you move down several records, you can see the records scroll up in the detail section of the form.

If you click the View Details button in the footer, this form closes and the frmCollege form opens, showing details of the college record that was current when you clicked the button. The way the form is designed, the View Details button opens the frmCollege form using a filter to show you the currently selected college. If you decide that you don't want to see details, you can click the Close button to dismiss the form.

Multiple-Page Forms

When you have a lot of information from each record to display in a form, you can design a *multiple-page form*. Open the frmStudent form in the College Counseling database to see an example. When you open the form, you'll see the first page of the student data for the first student.

You can use the record number box and the buttons in the lower left corner of the form to move through the records, viewing the first page of information for each student. Figure 12-2 shows the first page of the 16th student record. (For those of you who want to drop me a line, that's my real business address in the form! I didn't actually attend the Overlake School, however, and I invented some nice grade point averages for myself.) To see the second page of information for any student, use the scroll bar along the right side of the form or press the PgDn key. Figure 12-3 shows the second page of the 16th student record. (Notice that this form has a header, but no footer.) As you view different pages of a multiple-page form, the header at the top of the form (with the form title and some command buttons) doesn't change.

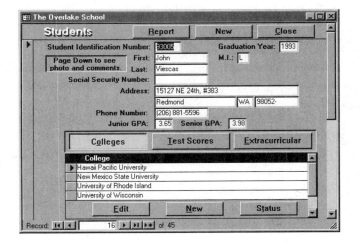

FIGURE 12-2
The first page
of a record in
the multiple-page
frmStudent form.

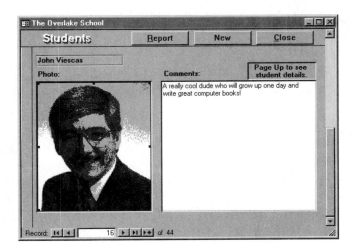

FIGURE 12-3
The second page
of a record in the
frmStudent form.

Continuous Forms

You can create another type of form that is useful for browsing through a list of records when each record has only a few data fields. This type of form is called a *continuous form*. Rather than showing you only a single record at a time, a continuous form displays formatted records back to back, in the manner of a datasheet.

The frmCollegeSummary form shown earlier in Figure 12-1 is a continuous form. The frmStudentSummary form, shown in Figure 12-4, is also a continuous form. You can use the vertical scroll bar to move through the record display, or you can click the record number box and the buttons in the lower left corner of the form to move from record to record. As you might guess, the application uses this form to display the results of a student search that returns more than 20 rows.

FIGURE 12-4
The frmStudent-
Summary form is
a continuous form.

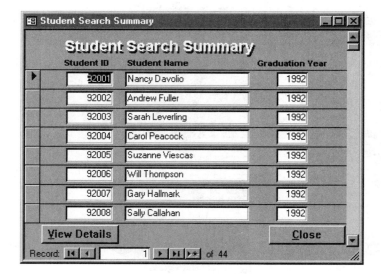

Subforms

Subforms are a good way to show related data from the "many" side of a one-to-many relationship. For example, the frmStudent form shown earlier in Figure 12-2 shows one student and the many colleges to which the student has applied. Another good example of a subform is the frmCollege form, shown in Figure 12-5. Although both of these forms look much like a single display panel, each has a subform (which looks more like a datasheet than a form) embedded in the main form. The main part of the frmCollege form displays information from the Colleges table, while the subform in the lower part of the window shows the application steps and related deadline dates for the displayed college. The form in Figure 12-5 actually has two subforms. The second one, in the upper right corner, displays the various classification categories associated with the current college.

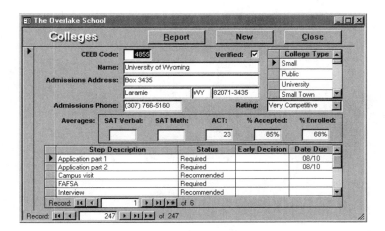

FIGURE 12-5

The frmCollege form with embedded subforms that list the college type and the application step information.

This form looks pretty complicated, but it really isn't difficult to build. Because the College Counseling database is well designed, it doesn't take much effort to build the queries that extract information from three different tables. Most of the work of creating the form goes into selecting and placing the controls that display the data. To link a subform to a main form, you have to set only two properties that tell Access which linking fields to use. In Chapter 15, "Advanced Form Design," you'll build and link a subform to a form.

Pop-up Forms

Sometimes it's useful to provide information in a window that stays on top regardless of where you move the focus. You've probably noticed that the default mode for windows in Microsoft Windows 95 is to bring the active window to the front and move other windows behind the active one. One exception is the Help windows. In particular, the "How Do I" windows are designed to float on top so you can follow the step-by-step instructions when you move the focus to the window in which you're doing the work. This sort of floating window is called a *pop-up window.*

You can create forms in Access that open in pop-up windows. If you open any form in the College Counseling application and then choose About College Counseling from the Help menu, this opens the frmAbout form shown in Figure 12-6, which is designed to be a pop-up. You'll learn more about how to create custom menus for forms in Chapter 23, "The Finishing Touches." For now, switch to the Database window and open the frmAbout form to see how it behaves. Notice that if you click on the Database window behind it, the frmAbout form stays on top. Click the OK button on the form to close it.

FIGURE 12-6
The frmAbout pop-up form "floats" on top of the Database window that has the focus.

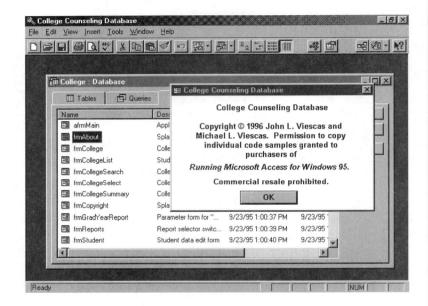

Modal Forms

As you add functionality to your application, you'll find situations in which you need to find some data or convey some important information before Access can proceed. Access provides a special type of form called a *modal form* that requires a response before you can continue working in the application. The frmCollegeSearch dialog box in the College Counseling database, shown in Figure 12-7, is a modal form. This dialog box normally opens when you click the Colleges button on the switchboard form and then click the Search button on the resulting Colleges form, but you can also open the form on which the dialog box is based directly from the Database window. You'll notice that as long as this dialog box is open, you can't select any other window or menu that you can see on the screen. To proceed, you must either enter some search criteria and click the Search button or click the Close button to dismiss the form.

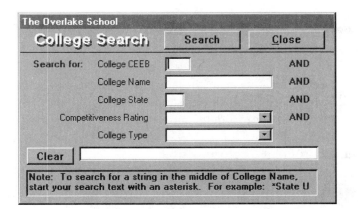

FIGURE 12-7
The frmCollege-
Search dialog box
is a modal form.

Special Controls

The information in a form is contained in *controls*. The most common control you'll use on a form is a simple text box. A text box can display data from an underlying table or query, or it can display data calculated in the form itself. You've probably noticed that many controls allow you to choose from among several values or to see additional content. You can also use controls to trigger a macro. These controls are discussed in the next four sections.

Option Buttons, Check Boxes, Toggle Buttons, and Option Groups

Whenever the data you're displaying can have only two or three valid values, you can use option buttons, check boxes, or toggle buttons to see or set the value you want in the field. For example, when there are two values, as in the case of a simple Yes/No field, you can use a check box to graphically display the value in the field. A check box that's selected means the value is "Yes," and a check box that's deselected means the value is "No." The Verified control on the frmCollege form (see Figure 12-5) is a good example of a use of a check box.

To provide a graphical choice among more than two values, you can place any of these controls in a group. Only one of the controls in a group can have a "Yes" value. For example, the frmStudent form shown earlier in Figure 12-2 actually has the ability to display several categories of information about students—the colleges in which the student is interested, the various test scores for the student, and any of the student's extracurricular activities. Displaying all this information at once would make the form very complex and unwieldy. Instead, the form has three toggle buttons in an option group (shown in detail in Figure 12-8) that let you choose which category you want to see. You can click only one button at a time. When you click a button, the form displays the related information in the subform just below these controls. As you'll read about in more detail later, Access uses the relative numeric value of the control to determine the value in the underlying field. A VBA procedure tests the value when you click a new button and makes the appropriate subform visible.

FIGURE 12-8

An option group on the frmStudent form.

List Boxes and Combo Boxes

When you want to display a list of data values that stays open all the time, a list box is a good choice. When you view objects in the Database window in detail list mode, you're looking at the tables, queries, forms, reports, macros, or modules in a list box. A list box can show a list of values you entered when you designed the control, a list of values from an SQL statement, the value of a field in a table or in a query, or a list of field names from a table or a query. In the example shown in Figure 12-9 (the frmCollegeSelect form), the list includes the set of names from the CName field of the Colleges table.

FIGURE 12-9

A list box can show a list of values or a list of field names.

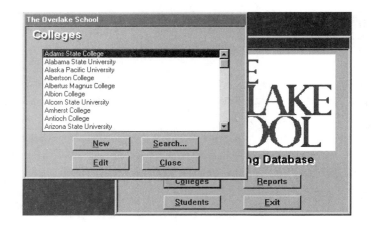

When you select a value from the list, you set the value of the control. If the control represents a field in the underlying table or query, you update that field. A list box like this one can use data from more than one field. You can, for example, display the more meaningful name of the CName field in the list but set the control to the value of the related CollegeCEEB when the name is selected. In the College Counseling database, this sample list box lets you select multiple entries by holding down the Shift key to select a range or by holding down the Ctrl key to select several noncontiguous entries. When you click the Edit button, a VBA procedure evaluates your choices and opens the frmCollege form to display the selected colleges.

Combo boxes are similar to list boxes. The major difference is that a combo box has a text box <u>and</u> a drop-down list. One advantage of a combo box is that it requires space for only one of the values in the underlying list. The Rating field in the frmCollege form is set using a combo box, as shown in Figure 12-10. The combo box uses two fields from the underlying query—CCompRate (the text describing the rating) and CCompID (which you can't see). When you select a rating description, the combo box sets the CCompID field in the underlying record—a very useful feature.

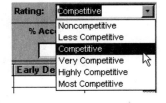

FIGURE 12-10
An open combo box.

OLE Objects

You saw the student picture in the frmStudent form earlier. This picture is stored in a field in the Students table using Microsoft's Object Linking and Embedding (OLE) technology. The logo in the top part of the main switchboard form is a picture that Access has stored as part of the form. The control you use to display a picture or any other OLE object is called an *object frame*. A bound object frame control is used to display an OLE object that is stored in a field in a table. An unbound object frame control is used to display an object that is not stored in a table.

When you include an object frame control on a form and bind the object frame control to an OLE object in the database, you can edit that object by selecting it and choosing the command at the bottom of the Edit menu that starts the object's application, as shown in Figure 12-11. If the object is a picture, a graph, or a spreadsheet, you can see the object in the object frame control, and you can activate its application by double-clicking on the object. If the object is a sound, you can hear it by double-clicking on the object frame control.

FIGURE 12-11

You can select a picture and then edit it by choosing the Bitmap Image Object command from the Edit menu and then choosing Edit from the submenu.

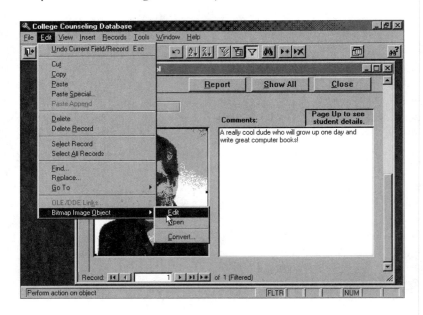

Figure 12-11 shows one of the Photo fields from the Students table that is bound in an object frame control on the frmStudent form. When you double-click on the picture or select the picture and choose Bitmap Image Object from the Edit menu and then choose Edit from the submenu, Access starts the Paint application in which the picture was created. Paint in Windows 95 is an OLE application that can "activate in place," as shown in Figure 12-12. You can still see the Access form, menus, and toolbars, but Paint has added its own toolbars and commands. You can update the picture using any of the Paint tools. You can paste in a different picture by copying a picture to the Clipboard and choosing the Paste command from Paint's Edit menu. After you make your changes, you simply click in another area on the Access form to deactivate Paint and store the result of your edits in the object frame control. If you save the record, Access saves the changed data in your OLE object.

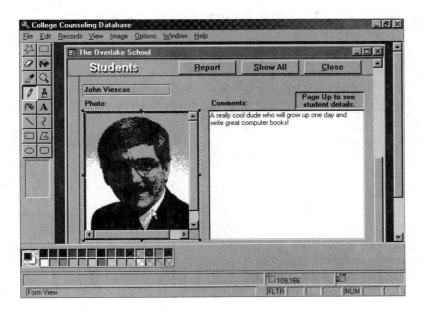

FIGURE 12-12
The OLE object from Figure 12-11 being edited "in place" with its host OLE application.

Command Buttons

Another useful control is the command button, which you can use to link many forms to create a complete database application. In the College Counseling database, for example, most of the sample forms are linked to the main switchboard form (afrmMain), shown in Figure 12-13 on the next page, in which the user can click command buttons to launch various functions in the application. The advantage of command buttons is really quite simple—they offer an easy way to trigger a macro or a VBA procedure. The procedure might do nothing more than open another form, print a report, or run an action query to update many records in your database. As you'll see by the time you get to the end of this book, you can easily build a fairly complex application using forms, reports, macros, and some simple VBA routines.

FIGURE 12-13
The command
buttons on the
afrmMain
switchboard
form.

Moving Around on Forms and Working with Data

The rest of this chapter shows you how to move around on and work with data in the various types of forms discussed earlier in the chapter.

Viewing Data

If you've read Chapter 7, "Using Datasheets," and you have followed along in this chapter with the form examples, you should have a pretty good idea of how to move around on forms and view data in forms. Moving around on a form is similar to moving around in a datasheet, but there are a few subtle differences between forms and datasheets (usually having to do with how a form was designed) that determine how a form works with data. You can use the frmCollege form in the College Counseling database to explore how forms work.

First, open the College Counseling database. If you started the application, click Exit on the main switchboard form to return to the Database window. Next, click on the Forms tab in the Database window. Select the frmCollege form from the list, and click the Open button to see the form shown in Figure 12-14.

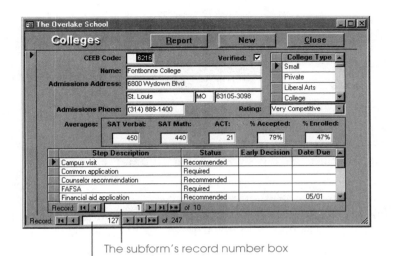

FIGURE 12-14
The frmCollege form in the College Counseling database.

The subform's record number box
The main form's record number box

Moving Around

The way you move around on a form depends in part on the form design. For example, the frmCollege form contains two subforms. To move back and forth between the form and either subform, use the Ctrl-Tab and Ctrl-Shift-Tab key combinations.

The fsubCollegeSteps subform in the lower part of the Form window is a datasheet, and you move around in it as you would move around in any datasheet. The window for this subform is wide enough to display all the fields in the datasheet, but if some columns are not displayed, you can use the horizontal scroll bar at the bottom of the subform to move the display left or right. On this subform you can use the vertical scroll bar on the right side to move the display up or down. The subform can be toggled between two different views—Datasheet view (its current state) and Form view. If you want to see the Form view of the fsubCollegeSteps subform, click in any of the fields on the subform datasheet (to ensure that the focus is on the subform), and then open the View menu. You'll notice that the Subform Datasheet command is checked. This command is a toggle. If you choose the Subform Datasheet command, the fsubCollegeSteps subform will change to look like the one shown in Figure 12-15. Choose the Subform Datasheet command (which is no longer checked) from the View menu again to restore the datasheet display.

FIGURE 12-15

The fsubCollege-
Steps subform in
Form view.

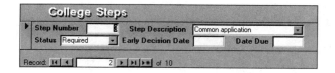

In the frmCollege form, you view different records by using one of two record number boxes. To see the next college, use the main form's record number box; to see different college application steps for a particular college, use the subform's record number box.

Using the mouse, you can also choose the Go To command from the Edit menu to move to the first, last, next, or previous record in the main form or in the subform. You can select any field in the form by clicking anywhere in that field. To use the Go To command you must first move to the form or the subform, depending on which set of records you want to view.

Keyboard Shortcuts

If you're typing in new data, you might find it easier to use the keyboard rather than the mouse to move around on the form. Some of the keyboard shortcuts are listed in Figure 12-16 (for moving around in fields and records) and in Figure 12-17 (for actions in a list box or in a combo box).

FIGURE 12-16

The keyboard shortcuts for moving around in fields and records.

Key(s)	Movement in Fields and Records
Tab	Moves to the next field.
Shift-Tab	Moves to the previous field.
Home	Moves to the first field of the current record.
End	Moves to the last field of the current record.
Up arrow	Moves to the current field of the previous record.
Down arrow	Moves to the current field of the next record.
Ctrl-Up arrow	Moves to the current field of the first record.
Ctrl-Down arrow	Moves to the current field of the last record.
Ctrl-Home	Moves to the first field of the first record.
Ctrl-End	Moves to the last field of the last record.

(continued)

FIGURE 12-16 *continued*

Key(s)	Movement in Fields and Records
Ctrl-Tab	On a subform, moves to the next field in the main form. If the subform is the last field in tab sequence in the main form, moves to the first field in the next main record. If not on a subform, moves to the next field.
Ctrl-Shift-Tab	On a subform, moves to the previous field in the main form. If the subform is the first field in tab sequence in the main form, moves to the last field in the previous main record. If not on a subform, moves to the previous field.
Ctrl-Shift-Home	Moves to the first field in the main form.
F5	Moves to the record number box.

Key(s)	Action in a List Box or a Combo Box
F4 or Alt-Down arrow	Opens a combo box or a drop-down list box.
Down arrow	Moves down one line.
Up arrow	Moves up one line.
PgDn	Moves down to next group of lines.
PgUp	Moves up to next group of lines.
Tab	Exits the box.

FIGURE 12-17
The keyboard shortcuts for actions in a list box or a combo box.

Adding Records and Changing Data

You'll probably design most forms so that you can insert new records, change field values, or delete records in Form view or in Datasheet view. The following sections explain procedures for adding new records and changing data.

Adding a New Record

The procedure for entering a new record varies depending on the design of the form. With a form that's been designed for data entry only, you open the form and type data in the (usually empty) data fields. Sometimes forms of this type open with default values in the fields or with data entered by a macro. Another type of form displays data and also allows you to add new records. You can open the frmStudent form and then choose the Data Entry command from the Records menu or click the New Record button on the toolbar to shift the form into data-entry mode, as shown in Figure 12-18. Notice that the form also provides its own New button that changes the form to data-entry mode when you click it.

After you finish entering new records, you can click the Show All button on the form to return to normal data display.

FIGURE 12-18

The frmStudent form in data-entry mode.

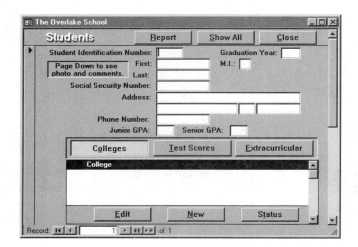

There's also a "blank" row at the end of the normal data display that you can use to enter new rows. You can jump to the blank row to begin adding a new record by choosing the Go To command from the Edit menu and then choosing New from the submenu, or by pressing Ctrl-+. Access places the cursor in the first field when you start a new record. As soon as you begin typing, Access changes the indicator on the row selector (if your form shows the row selector) to a pencil icon to indicate that updates are in progress. Press Tab to move to the next field.

If you violate a field's validation rule, Access notifies you as soon as you attempt to leave the field. You must provide a correct value before you can move to another field. Press Shift-Enter at any point in the record or press Tab in the last field in the record to save your new record in the database. If the data you enter violates a table validation rule, Access displays an error message and does not save the record. You'll recall from Chapter 5, "Building Your Database in Microsoft Access," that the Students table has a validation rule that requires that the first two digits of the student ID match the last two digits of the student's graduation year. If you want to cancel a new record, press Esc twice.

If you're adding a new record to a form such as Students, you'll encounter a special situation. You'll notice when you tab to the picture object frame control that you can't type anything in it. This is because the field in the underlying table is an OLE object. To enter data in this type of field in a new record, you must create the object in an application that supports OLE before you can store the data in Access. To do this, select the Photo control and choose the Object command from the Insert menu. Access displays the Insert Object dialog box shown in Figure 12-19. Select the object type you want (in this case, Bitmap Image), and click OK. Access starts the application that's defined in the Windows 95 registry as the default edit application for this type of data (for bitmaps, usually the Paint application).

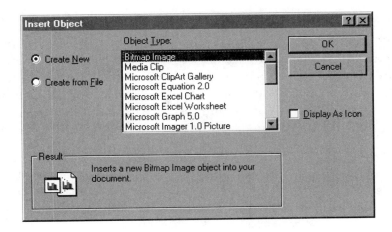

FIGURE 12-19
The Insert Object dialog box.

If you already have an appropriate file available to copy into the OLE object in Access, select the Create From File option button in the dialog box. Access changes the option list to let you enter the path-name and filename, as shown in Figure 12-20 on the next page. You can click the Browse button to open the Browse dialog box, which lets you search for the file you want. After you select a file, select the Link check box to create an active link between the copy of the object in Access and the actual file. Whenever you change the file, the copy in Access will also change. Select the Display As Icon check box to display the Paint application icon instead of the picture in Access.

FIGURE 12-20

Inserting an
object from
a file.

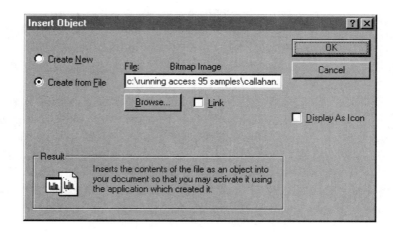

Try adding a new record by using the frmStudent form. Open the form, choose the Go To command from the Edit menu, and choose New from the submenu. You should see a screen similar to the one shown earlier in Figure 12-18. You can start adding information for a new student who will graduate in 1996. Scroll down to the student picture field and follow the procedure discussed above to create a new picture. You can find several appropriately sized bitmap pictures of people on the sample disc.

> **NOTE** As soon as you begin to enter new data in a table that has an AutoNumber field as its primary key, Access assigns a new number to that field. If you decide to cancel the new record, Access won't reuse this AutoNumber value. Access does this to ensure that multiple users sharing a database don't get the same value for a new table row.

To begin adding some extracurricular activities for your new student, click the Extracurricular button on the form to reveal the appropriate subform. Select an activity, as shown in Figure 12-21. Enter a year and a description. When you tab out of the last field or press Shift-Enter, Access adds the new activity for you. Access also inserts the linking information required between the record in the main form and the new record in the subform. Here, Access adds the student ID you entered to the new record in the StudentExtraLink table.

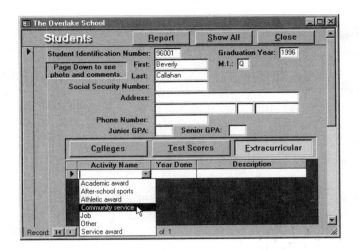

FIGURE 12-21

Adding a new record in the frmStudent form.

Changing and Deleting Data

If your form permits updates, you can easily change or delete existing data in the underlying table or query. If the form is designed to be used in Datasheet view, you can use the same techniques you learned in Chapter 7, "Using Datasheets," to work with your data.

In Form view, your data might appear in one of several formats. If the form is designed to be a single form, you can see the data from only one record at a time. If the form is designed as a continuous form, you might be able to see data from more than one record at a time.

As with datasheets, you must select a field in the form in order to change the data in the field. To select a field, either tab to the field or click in the field with the mouse. After you select a field, you can change the data in it using the same techniques you used for working with data in a datasheet. You can type over individual characters, re-place a sequence of characters, or copy and paste data from one field to another.

You might find that you can't tab to or select some fields in a form. When you design a form, you can set the properties of the controls on the form so that a user can't select the control. These properties pre-vent users from changing fields that you don't want updated, such as calculated values or fields from the "one" side of a query. You can also set the tab order to control the sequence of field selection when you use Tab or Shift-Tab to move around on the form. (See Chapter 14, "Customizing Forms," for details.)

Deleting a record in a single form or in a continuous form is different from deleting a record in a datasheet. First, you must select the record as you would select a record in a datasheet. If the form is designed with row selectors, simply click the row selector to select the record. If the form does not have row selectors, choose the Select Record command from the Edit menu. To delete a selected record, press the Del key or choose the Delete command from the Edit menu. You can also choose the Delete Record command from the Edit menu to delete the current record without first having to select it.

Searching for and Sorting Data

When you use forms to display and edit your data, you can search for data or sort it in a new order in much the same way that you search for and sort data in datasheets. (See Chapter 7, "Using Datasheets.") The following sections show you how to use some of the form filter features to search for data in a form or use the Quick Sort commands to reorder your data.

Performing a Simple Search

You can use Microsoft Access's Find capability in a form just as you would in a datasheet. First, select the field, and then choose the Find command from the Edit menu or click the Find button on the toolbar to open the Find dialog box that you saw in Figure 7-27 in Chapter 7. You can enter search criteria exactly as you would for a datasheet. Note that in a form you can also perform a search on any control that you can select, including controls that display calculated values.

Performing a Quick Sort on a Form Field

As you can with a datasheet, you can select just about any control that contains data from the underlying recordset and click the Sort Ascending or Sort Descending button on the toolbar to reorder the records you see, based on the selected field. You can't quick-sort fields in a subform. If you want to try to quick-sort, open the frmCollege form, click in the Zip field in the form, and then click the Sort Descending button on the toolbar. The college with the highest zip code (the largest number) is displayed first.

Adding a Filter to a Form

One of Access's most powerful features is its ability to further restrict or sort the information displayed in the form without your having to create a new query. This restriction is accomplished with a filter that you define while you're using the form. When you apply the filter, you see only the data that matches the criteria you entered.

As with datasheets, you can define a filter using Filter By Selection, Filter By Form, or the Advanced Filter definition facility. Open the frmCollege form and click the Filter By Form button on the toolbar. Access adds features to the form to let you enter filter criteria, as shown in Figure 12-22.

In this example, we're looking for all verified colleges (colleges that returned my questionnaire) in Florida that have a Competitive rating. As you learned with datasheets, you can enter one set of criteria and then click on an "Or" tab to enter additional criteria. If you don't like some of the criteria you've entered, click the Clear Grid button on the toolbar to start over. Click the Apply Filter button on the toolbar to filter your records. Click the Cancel button to exit the Filter window without applying the new filter.

Clear Grid button

Apply Filter button

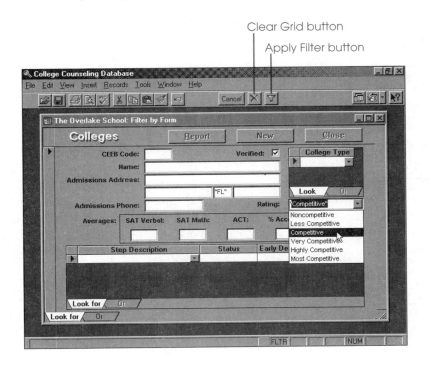

FIGURE 12-22
The Filter window for the frmCollege form.

To turn off the filter, click the Remove Filter button on the toolbar or choose the Remove Filter/Sort command from the Records menu. To see the filter definition, choose Filter from the Records menu and then choose Advanced Filter/Sort from the submenu. After you apply the filter shown in Figure 12-22 and do a descending quick sort on Zip, the Advanced Filter window should look something like that shown in Figure 12-23.

> **NOTE** If you used one of the Quick Sort buttons, you'll discover that quick sort uses the form's filter definition to create the sorting criteria. For example, if you did a quick sort to arrange zip codes in descending order, you'll find the zip code field in the form filter with the Sort row set to Descending when you click the Edit Filter/Sort button.

FIGURE 12-23

The Advanced Filter window for the frmCollege form with criteria previously entered using Filter By Form.

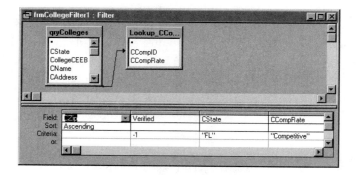

If you often use the same filter with your form, you can save the filter as a query and give it a name. Open the Advanced Filter/Sort window and create the filter. Choose the Save As Query command from the File menu and type in a name for the query when Access prompts you. You can also load an existing query definition to use as a filter. Open the Advanced Filter/Sort window, and choose the Load From Query command from the File menu. Access presents a list of valid select queries (those that are based on the same table or tables as the form you're using).

Printing Forms

You can use a form to print information from your table. When you design the form, you can specify different header and footer information for the printed version. You can also specify which controls are visible. For example, you might define some gridlines that are visible on the printed form but not on the screen.

An interesting form to print in the College Counseling database is the frmCollegeSummary form. Open the form, and then click the Print Preview button on the toolbar or choose the Print Preview command from the File menu. You probably won't be able to read any of the data unless you have a large screen. Click the Zoom button and scroll to the top of the first page. You should see a screen that looks like the one shown in Figure 12-24. Notice that the form headers and footers that you saw earlier in Figure 12-1 will not appear in the printed version.

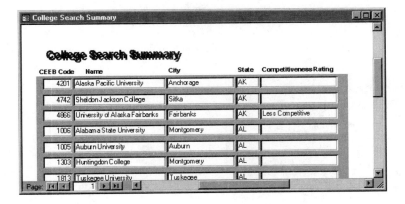

FIGURE 12-24

The window for the frmCollege-Summary form, zoomed in Print Preview.

You can use the scroll bars to move around on the page. Use the page number box in the lower left corner of the form in the same way that you use the record number box on a form or in a datasheet. Click the Zoom button again to see the entire page on the screen.

Choose Page Setup from the File menu to customize the way the form prints. Access displays the Page Setup dialog box. Click on the Margins tab to set top, bottom, left, and right margins. Click on the Page tab (shown in Figure 12-25 on the next page) to select Portrait or Landscape print mode, the paper size and source, and the printer. Access will store these specifications with your form definition.

FIGURE 12-25

FIGURE 12-25

The Page tab of the Page Setup dialog box for forms.

Click on the Layout tab of the Page Setup dialog box to see additional options, as shown in Figure 12-26. If the data in your form appears in a fairly narrow width, you can ask Access to stack the data from the form either horizontally or vertically across the page.

FIGURE 12-26

The Layout tab of the Page Setup dialog box for forms.

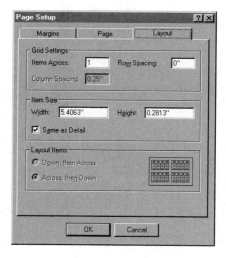

You should now have a good understanding of how forms work and of many design elements that you can include when you build forms. Now, on to the fun part—building your first form in the next chapter.

Chapter 13

Building Forms

433

F rom the perspective of daily use, forms are the most important objects you'll build in your Microsoft Access application. Forms are what users see and work with every time they run the application. This chapter shows you how to design and build forms in Access. You'll learn how to work with a Form window in Design view to build a basic form based on a single table, and you'll learn how to use a Form Wizard to simplify the form-creation process. The last section of this chapter shows you how to use some of the special form controls to simplify data entry on your forms.

Forms and Object-Oriented Programming

Microsoft Access was not designed to be a full object-oriented programming environment, yet it has many characteristics found in object-oriented application development systems. Before you dive into building forms, it's useful to examine how Access implements objects and actions, particularly if you come from the world of procedural application development.

In classic procedural application development, the data you need for the application is distinct from the programs you write to work with the data and from the results produced by your programs. Each program works with the data independently and generally has little structural connection with other programs in the system. For example, an order-entry program will accept input from a clerk and then write the order out to data files. Later, a billing program will process the orders and print invoices. Another characteristic of procedural systems is that events must occur in a specific order and cannot be executed out of sequence. A procedural system has difficulty looking up supplier or price information while in the middle of processing an order.

In an object-oriented system, however, all objects are defined in terms of a subject and an action performed on that subject. Objects can contain other objects as subjects. When an object defines a new action on another object, it inherits the attributes and properties of the other object and expands on the object's definition. In Access, queries define actions on tables, and the queries then become new logical tables known as *recordsets*. You can define a query based on another query with the same effect. Queries inherit the integrity and formatting rules defined for the tables. Forms further define actions on tables or queries, and the fields you include in forms initially inherit the underlying properties, such as formatting and validation rules, of the fields in the source tables or queries. You can define different formatting or more restrictive rules, but you cannot override the rules defined for the tables.

Within an Access database, you can interrelate application objects and data. For example, you can set startup properties or define an initial macro (called *Autoexec*) that prepares your application to run. As part of startup, you will usually open a switchboard form in your application. The switchboard form might act on some of the data in the database, or it might offer controls that open other forms, print reports, or close the application.

See Also For more information about startup properties and the *Autoexec* macro, see Chapter 23, "The Finishing Touches."

Figure 13-1 shows the conceptual architecture of an Access form. In addition to operating on tables or queries in a database, forms can contain other forms. These subforms can, in turn, define actions on other tables, queries, or forms, and can trigger additional macro actions or Microsoft Visual Basic for Applications (VBA) procedures. As you'll learn when you read about advanced form design, macro actions and VBA procedures can be triggered in many ways. The most obvious way to trigger an action is by clicking a command button on a form. But you can also define macros or VBA procedures that execute when an event occurs, such as clicking in a field, changing the data in a field, pressing a key, adding or deleting a row, or simply moving to a new row in the underlying table or query.

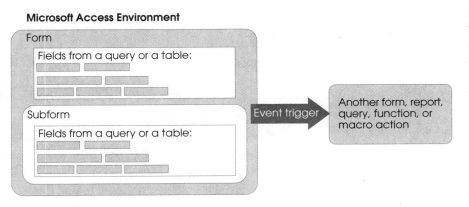

Microsoft Access Environment

FIGURE 13-1

The conceptual architecture of an Access form.

In Chapter 22, "Automating Your Application with VBA," you'll learn how several of the more complex forms in the College Counseling and Entertainment Schedule sample databases are automated with VBA. Figure 13-2 shows a few of the automated processes for the frmContracts form in the Entertainment Schedule database. For example, there's a command button to print the contract currently displayed in the form.

FIGURE 13-2
Some of the automated processes for the frmContracts form.

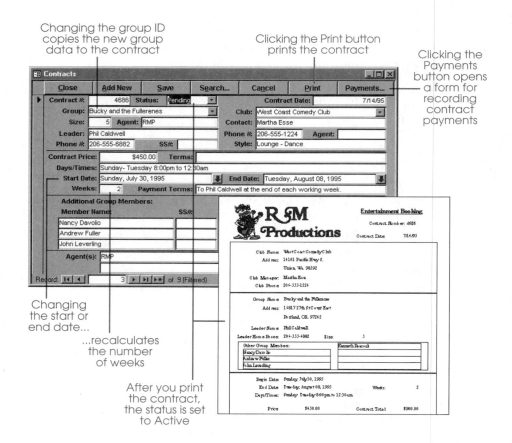

Changing the group ID copies the new group data to the contract

Clicking the Print button prints the contract

Clicking the Payments button opens a form for recording contract payments

Changing the start or end date...

...recalculates the number of weeks

After you print the contract, the status is set to Active

When you print the contract, another VBA procedure marks the contract "Active." If the contract is issued by RM Productions (the first agent code is RMP), a VBA procedure generates one payment record in the tblCommissions table for each week of the contract with the appropriate commission due. Clicking the Payments button opens a form to allow recording of payments for the current contract. If you change the group name in the contract, other procedures copy in the group member information. (This application copies the group member information because the group membership can change over time; each contract records the band members at the time the contract is issued.) When you change the start or end date of a contract, a VBA procedure automatically calculates the number of weeks.

Object-oriented systems are not restricted to a specific sequence of events. So a user entering a contract in Access can minimize the contract form and start a search in a groups table for musical style or start a search in a clubs table without first having to finalize the contract. You might provide a simpler way for the user to do this in your application by means of a command button on the contract form.

Starting from Scratch— A Simple Input Form

To start, you'll create a simple form that accepts and displays data in the tblClubs table in the Entertainment Schedule database. Later, you'll create a form for the College Counseling database using a Form Wizard.

Building a New Form with Design Tools

To begin building a new form, open your database. In the Database window, select the table or query that you want to use for the form. Select New Form from the New Object toolbar button's drop-down list, or choose Form from the Insert menu, and Microsoft Access opens the New Form dialog box, shown in Figure 13-3.

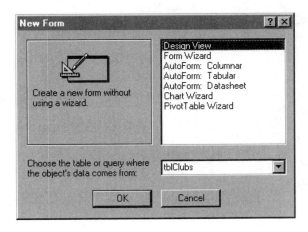

FIGURE 13-3
The New Form dialog box.

In the combo box in the lower part of the dialog box, Access displays the name of the table or query that you selected in the Database window. If you want to select a different table or query, you can open the combo box's drop-down list to see all the tables and queries in your database. You'll build this first form without the aid of a Form Wizard so that you'll understand all the components that go into form design.

Select Design View in the dialog box and then click the OK button. Access opens the Form window in Design view and with it a toolbox that contains several design tools, as shown in Figure 13-4. (You might not see all the windows shown in Figure 13-4.) In this figure, the Form window is in the background, the toolbox is in the lower left corner, the field list is in the upper center, and the property sheet for the form is in the lower right corner. If you've already experimented with forms in Design view and have moved some of the windows around, Access opens them where you last placed them on the screen.

FIGURE 13-4

A Form window in Design view with its design tools.

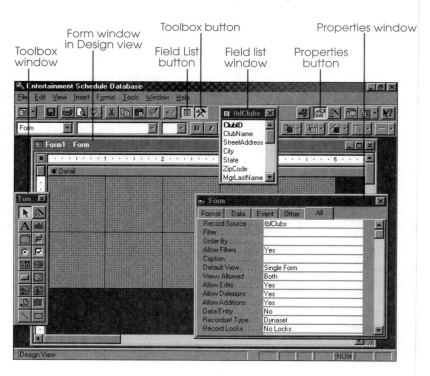

Access starts with a form that has only a Detail section (a gray grid). You can click on the edge of the Detail section with your mouse pointer and drag the edge to make the section larger or smaller. You can remove the grid dots from the Detail section by choosing the Grid command from the View menu. If you want to add headers or footers to the form, choose the Form Header/Footer command from the View menu.

The Detail section starts out at 5 inches (12.7 centimeters) wide by 2 inches (5.08 centimeters) high. The "inch" gradations on the rulers are relative to the size and resolution of your screen. On a standard 640×480 VGA screen, the full screen is approximately 6.5 "inches" wide by 5 "inches" high. By default, Access sets the grid at 24 dots per inch horizontally and 24 dots per inch vertically. You can change the density of the grid dots by altering the Grid X and Grid Y property settings on the form's property sheet.

The Grid X and Grid Y property settings determine the intervals per unit of measurement in the grid. You can enter a number from 1 (coarsest) through 64 (finest). You set the unit of measure (English or metric) by default when you select a country from the drop-down list on the Regional Settings tab of the Regional Settings Properties dialog box. (You access this dialog box by double-clicking on the Regional Settings icon in the Windows Control Panel.)

For example, if your unit of measurement is inches and you specify a Grid X setting of 10, Access divides the grid horizontally into .1-inch increments. When your measurement is in inches and you set the Grid X and Grid Y values to 24 or less, Access displays the grid dots on the grid. In centimeters, you can see the grid dots when you specify a setting of 9 or less. If you set a finer grid, Access won't display the grid dots but you can still use the grid to line up controls. Access always displays grid lines at 1-inch intervals (English) or 1-centimeter intervals (metric), even when you set fine Grid X or Grid Y values.

The following sections describe some of the tools you can use to design a form.

The Toolbox

The toolbox, shown in Figure 13-5 on the next page, is the "command center" of form design. You can move the toolbox around on your screen by dragging its title bar, and you can change the shape of the toolbox by dragging its sides or corners. You can even move the toolbox to the top of the workspace and "dock" it as a toolbar. You can close the toolbox by clicking the Close button in the upper right corner of the toolbox, by choosing the Toolbox command from the View menu, or by clicking the Toolbox button on the toolbar.

TIP   If you don't see the toolbox displayed with the Form window in Design view, choose the Toolbox command from the View menu or click the Toolbox button on the toolbar.

FIGURE 13-5
The toolbox.

The toolbox contains buttons for all the controls you can use on a form. To place a particular control on a form, you click the control's button in the toolbox. When you move the mouse pointer over the form, the mouse pointer turns into an icon that represents the tool you selected. Position the mouse pointer where you want to place the control, and press the left mouse button to place the control on the form. If you want to size the control as you place it, click and drag the mouse pointer to the size you want. (You can also size a control after it's placed by dragging its sides or corners.)

Left to right, top to bottom, the tools in the toolbox are as follows:

 Select Objects tool. This is the default tool. Use this tool to select, size, move, and edit controls.

 Control Wizards button. Click this toggle button to activate the Control Wizards. When this button appears pressed, a Control Wizard will help you enter control properties whenever you create a new option group, combo box, list box, or command button.

 Label tool. Use this tool to create label controls that contain fixed text. By default, most controls have a label control attached. You can use this tool to create stand-alone labels for headings and for instructions on your form.

Text Box tool. Use this tool to create text box controls for displaying text, numbers, dates, times, and memo fields in a form. You can bind a text box to one of the fields in the underlying table or query. If you allow a text box that is bound to a field to be updated, you can change the value in the field in the underlying table or query by entering a new value in the text box. You can also use a text box to calculate values using expressions.

 Option Group tool. Use this tool to create option group controls that contain one or more toggle buttons, option buttons, or check boxes. (See the description of these controls on this page and on the next page.) You can assign a separate numeric value to each button or check box that you include in the group. When you have more than one button or check box in a group, you can select only one button or check box at a time, and the value assigned to that button or check box becomes the value for the option group. You can select one of the buttons or check boxes in the group as the default value for the group. If you bind the option group to a field in the underlying query or table, you can set a new value in the field by selecting a button or a check box in the group.

 Toggle Button tool. Use this tool to create a toggle button control that holds an on/off, true/false, or yes/no value. When you click a toggle button, its value becomes −1 (to represent *on, true,* or *yes*) and the button appears pressed. Click the button again, and its value becomes 0 (to represent *off, false,* or *no*). You can include a toggle button in an option group and assign the button a unique numeric value. If you create a group with multiple controls, selecting a new toggle button will deselect any previously selected toggle button, option button, or check box in that group. If you bind the toggle button to a field in the underlying table or query, you can toggle the field's value by clicking the toggle button.

 Option Button tool. Use this tool to create an option button control (sometimes called a *radio button control*) that holds an on/off, true/false, or yes/no value. When you click an option button, its value becomes −1 (to represent *on, true,* or *yes*) and a filled circle appears in the center of the button. Click the button again, and its value becomes 0 (to represent *off, false,* or *no*). You can include an option button in an option group and assign the button a unique numeric value. If you create a group with multiple controls, selecting a new option button will deselect any previously selected toggle button, option button, or check box in that group. If you bind the option button to a field in the underlying table or query, you can toggle the field's value by clicking the option button.

Check Box tool. Use this tool to create a check box control that holds an on/off, true/false, or yes/no value. When you click a check box, its value becomes –1 (to represent *on, true,* or *yes*) and a check mark appears in the box. Click the check box again, and its value becomes 0 (to represent *off, false,* or *no*) and the check mark disappears from the box. You can include a check box in an option group and assign the check box a unique numeric value. If you create a group with multiple controls, selecting a new check box will deselect any previously selected toggle button, option button, or check box in that group. If you bind the check box to a field in the underlying table or query, you can toggle the field's value by clicking the check box.

 Combo Box tool. Use this tool to create a combo box control that contains a list of potential values for the control and an editable text box. To create the list, you can enter the values in the Row Source property of the combo box. You can also specify a table or a query as the source of the values in the list. Access displays the currently selected value in the text box. When you click the down arrow to the right of the combo box, Access displays the values in the list. Select a new value in the list to reset the value in the control. If the combo box is bound to a field in the underlying table or query, you can change the value in the field by selecting a new value in the list. You can bind multiple columns to the list, and you can hide one or more of the columns in the list by setting the column's list width to 0. You can bind the actual value in the control to a hidden column. In a multiple-column list, Access displays the value in the first column whose width is greater than 0 when the list is closed. Access displays all nonzero-width columns when you open the list.

 List Box tool. Use this tool to create a list box control that contains a list of potential values for the control. To create the list, you can enter the values in the Row Source property of the list box. You can also specify a table or a query as the source of the values in the list. List boxes are always open, and Access highlights the currently selected value in the list box. You select a new value in the list to reset the value in the control. If the list box is bound to a field in the underlying table or query, you can change the value in the field by selecting a new value in the list. You can bind multiple columns to the list, and you can hide one or more of the columns in the list by setting the column's list width to *0*. You can bind the actual value in the control to a hidden column. Access displays all nonzero-width columns that fit within the defined width of the control.

 Command Button tool. Use this tool to create a command button control that can activate a macro or a VBA procedure.

 Image tool. Use this tool to store a static picture on your form. You cannot edit the picture on the form, but Access stores it in a format that is very efficient in terms of application speed and size. If you want to store a picture as the entire background of your form, you can set the form's Picture property.

 Unbound Object Frame tool. Use this tool to add an object from another application that supports Object Linking and Embedding (OLE). The object becomes part of your form, not part of the data from the underlying table or query. You can add pictures, sounds, graphs, or slides to enhance your form.

 Bound Object Frame tool. Use this tool to make available on your form an OLE object from the underlying data. Access can display most pictures and graphs directly on a form. For other objects, Access displays the icon of the application in which the object was created. For example, if the object is a sound object created in Sound Recorder, you'll see a speaker icon on your form.

 Page Break tool. Use this tool to add a page break between multiple pages of a form.

 Subform/Subreport tool. Use this tool to embed another form in the current form. You can use the subform to show data from a table or a query that is related to the data in the main form. Access maintains the link between the two forms for you.

 Line tool. Use this tool to add lines to a form to enhance its appearance.

 Rectangle tool. Use this tool to add filled or empty rectangles to a form to enhance its appearance.

TIP   When you select a tool other than the Select Objects tool, it becomes deselected after you use it to place a control on your form. If you plan to create several controls using the same tool—for example, a series of check boxes in an option group—double-click the control button in the toolbox to "lock" it on. You can unlock it by clicking any other tool button (including the Select Objects tool).

See Also   For more information about using controls on forms, see Chapter 14, "Customizing Forms," and Chapter 15, "Advanced Form Design."

The Field List

Use the field list in conjunction with the toolbox to place bound controls (controls linked to fields in a table or a query) on your form. You can open the field list by clicking the Field List button on the toolbar or by choosing the Field List command from the View menu. Access displays the name of the underlying table or query in the field list title bar, as shown in Figure 13-6. You can drag the edges of the window to resize the field list so that you can see any long field names. You can drag the title bar to move the window out of the way. Use the scroll bar along the right side of the window to move through the list of available field names.

FIGURE 13-6
A field list showing the names of the fields in the underlying table or query.

To use the field list to place a control for a field on a form, first select the tool you want. (The default tool is for a text box control.) Then drag the field you want from the field list and drop it into position on the form. If you select a control that's inappropriate for the data type, Access selects the default control for the data type. For example, if you select anything but a Bound Object Frame control for an OLE object, Access creates a Bound Object Frame control for you anyway. If you try to drag and drop a field using the subform/subreport, unbound object frame, line, rectangle, or page break control, Access creates a text box control or bound object frame control instead.

The Property Sheet

The form, each section of the form (header, detail, footer), and each control on the form has a list of properties associated with it, and you set these properties using the property sheet. The kinds of properties you can specify vary depending on the object. To open the property sheet for an object, first select the object, and then click the Properties button on the toolbar or choose the Properties command from the View menu. Access opens a window similar to the one shown in Figure 13-7.

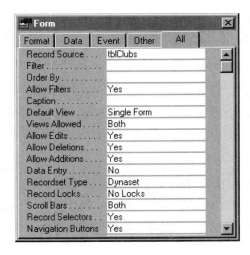

FIGURE 13-7
The property sheet for a form.

You can drag the title bar to move the property sheet window around on your screen. You can also drag the edges of the window to resize it so that you can see more of the longer property settings. Because a form has more than 70 properties that you can set and because many controls have more than 30 properties, Access provides tabs at the top of the property sheet so that you can choose to display all properties (the default) or to display only format properties, data properties, event properties, or other properties. A form property sheet displaying only the data properties is shown in Figure 13-8.

FIGURE 13-8
A form property
sheet displaying
only the data
properties.

When you click in a property box that provides a list of valid values, a down arrow button appears on the right side of the property box. Click this button to see a drop-down list of the values. For properties that can have a very long value setting, you can use Shift-F2 to open a Zoom box. The Zoom box provides an expanded text box for entering or viewing an entry.

Even better than the Zoom box are the builders that help you create property settings for properties that can accept a complex expression, a query definition, or code (a macro or a VBA procedure) to respond to an event. When a builder is available for a property setting, Access displays a small button with an ellipsis (...) next to the property box when you select the property; this is the Build button. If you click the Build button, Access responds with the appropriate builder dialog boxes. For example, display the property sheet for the form, click on the Data tab to display the form's data properties, select the Record Source property, and then click the Build button next to Record Source to start the Query Builder. Access asks whether you want to build a new query based on the table that currently is the source for this form.

If you click Yes, Access opens a new Query window in Design view with the tblClubs field list displayed in the upper part of the window, as shown in Figure 13-9.

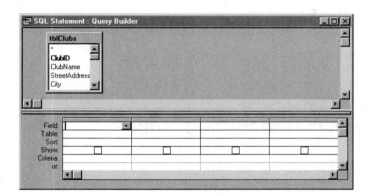

FIGURE 13-9
Using the Query Builder to create a query for the form's Record Source property.

Suppose that you want to base this form on a query that sorts the clubs in ascending order by club name. You'll need all the fields in the tblClubs table for this form, so select them and drag them to the design grid. For ClubName, specify Ascending as the sorting order. Your result should look like that shown in Figure 13-10.

TIP To easily select all the fields from a field list displayed in the upper part of the Query window, double-click on the title bar of the field list. Access highlights all the fields for you. Then simply click on any of them and drag them to the design grid.

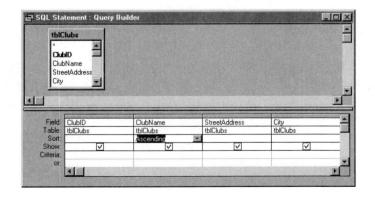

FIGURE 13-10
Building a query for the Record Source property of the form.

If you close the Query window at this point, Access asks whether you want to update the property. If you click Yes, Access stores the SQL text for the query in the Record Source property box. A better approach is to save the query and give it a name, such as *qryClubsSorted-ByName,* so do that now. When you close the query, Access asks whether you want to save the query and update the property. If you click Yes, Access places the query name (rather than the SQL text) in the property sheet.

Building a Simple Input Form for the tblClubs Table

Now let's create a simple input form for the tblClubs table in the Entertainment Schedule database. If you've followed along to this point, you should already have a blank form based on the qryClubsSortedByName query that you created using the Query Builder. If you haven't done so already, switch to the Database window, open the Tables list, select the tblClubs table, and select New Form from the New Object toolbar button's drop-down list (or choose Form from the Insert menu). Select the Design View option in the New Form dialog box. You'll see the Form window in Design view and a set of design tools, as shown earlier in Figure 13-4. If necessary, open the toolbox, field list, and property sheet by clicking the appropriate buttons on the toolbar. Select the Record Source property, and then click the Build button and follow the procedures discussed in the previous sections, whose results are shown in Figures 13-9 and 13-10 on the previous page; this will create the query you need and make it the source for the form.

In the blank form for the qryClubsSortedByName query, drag down the bottom of the Detail section to make some room to work. Because you'll be using default text boxes, you don't need to select a tool from the toolbox. If you'd like to practice, though, double-click on the Text Box tool in the toolbox before dragging fields from the field list. In this way, you can drag fields one at a time to the Detail section of the form. Follow this procedure to drag each of the fields between the ClubID field and the ClubFaxNumber field from the field list to the Detail section. Your result should look something like that shown in Figure 13-11.

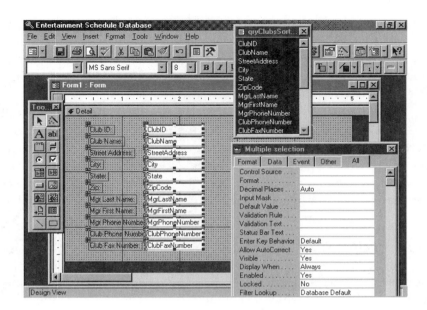

FIGURE 13-11

The text box controls that are created on a form when you drag and drop fields from the qryClubsSorted-ByName field list.

TIP A quick way to place several successive fields on a form is to click on the first field you want in the field list, scroll down until you see the last field you want, and then hold down the Shift key while you click on the last field. This procedure selects all the fields between the first and last fields you selected. You can also double-click on the title bar of the field list to select all the fields, and then click on any of the highlighted fields and drag the fields as a group to the Detail section of the form.

When you position the field icon that you're dragging from the field list, the upper left corner of the new text box will be at the position of the mouse pointer when you release the mouse button. For default text boxes, Access attaches a label that displays the field's Caption property (or field name, if you didn't specify a Caption property when you designed the field), 1 inch to the left of the text box. So you should drop each text box about 1.25 inches (3 centimeters) from the left edge of the Detail section to leave room to the left of the text box for Access

449

to place the control labels. If you don't leave room, the text boxes will overlap the labels. Even if you do leave room, notice that if a caption is too long to fit in the 1-inch space between the default label and the default text box (for example, *Club Phone Number* in Figure 13-11), the text box will overlap the label.

In the example in Figure 13-11, the property sheet indicates that you have selected multiple controls. (In this case, all the selected fields were dragged to the Detail section at one time.) Whenever you select multiple controls on a form in Design view, Access displays the properties that are common to all the controls you selected. If you change a property in the property sheet while multiple controls are selected, Access makes the change to all of the controls.

Moving and Sizing Controls

By default, Access creates text boxes that are 1 inch wide. For some of the fields, 1 inch is larger than necessary to display the field value—especially if you are using the default 8-point font size. For other fields, the text box isn't large enough. You probably also want to adjust the location of some of the controls.

To change a control's size or location, you usually have to select the control first. Be sure that the Select Objects tool is selected. Click the control you want to resize or move, and moving and sizing handles will appear around the control. The handles are small boxes that appear at each corner of the control—except at the upper left corner, where the larger handle indicates that it cannot be used for sizing. In Figure 13-11, handles appear around all the text boxes, indicating that they are all selected. To select just one control, click anywhere in the blank area of the form; this changes the selection to the Detail section. Then click the control you want. If the control is wide enough or high enough, Access provides additional handles at the midpoints of the sides of the control.

To change the size of a control, you can use the sizing handles on the sides, in either of the lower corners, or in the upper right corner of the control. When you place the mouse pointer over one of these sizing handles, the pointer turns into a double arrow, as shown in Figure 13-12. With the double-arrow pointer, drag the handle to resize the control. You can practice on the form by shortening the ClubID text box so that it's .5 inch long. The name and address fields need to be stretched until they are each about 1.75 inches long. You might also want to adjust the state, zip code, and phone number fields.

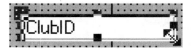

FIGURE 13-12
You can drag
a corner handle
of a selected
control to change
the control's width
or height or both.

To move a control that is not currently selected, click the control and drag it to a new location. After you select a control, you can move it by placing your mouse pointer anywhere along the edge of the control between the handles. When you do this, the mouse pointer turns into an open hand, as shown in Figure 13-13, and you can then drag the control to a new location. Access displays an outline of the control as you move the control to help you position it correctly. When a control has an attached label, moving either the control or the label moves both of them.

FIGURE 13-13
You can drag
the edge of a
selected control
to move the
control.

You can position a control and its attached label independently by dragging the larger handle in the upper left corner of the control or label. When you position the mouse pointer over this handle, the pointer turns into a hand with a pointing finger, as shown in Figure 13-14. Drag the control to a new location relative to its label. You can delete a label from a control by selecting the label and pressing the Del key. If you want to create a label that is independent of a control, you can use the Label tool. If you inadvertently delete a label from a control and you've made other changes so that you can no longer undo the deletion, you can attach a new label by doing the following:

1. Create a new unattached label.

2. Select the label, and then choose Cut from the Edit menu to move the label to the Clipboard.

3. Select the control to which you want to attach the label, and then choose Paste from the Edit menu.

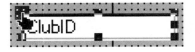

FIGURE 13-14
You can drag the
large handle of a
selected control
to move the con-
trol independent
of its label.

The Formatting Toolbar

The Formatting toolbar, shown in Figure 13-15, provides a quick and easy way to alter the appearance of a control by allowing you to click options rather than set properties.

FIGURE 13-15
The Formatting
toolbar.

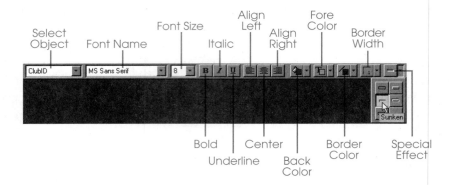

This toolbar is also handy for setting background colors for sections of the form. Left to right on the toolbar, the options are as follows:

Select Object	Use this list box to select a specific object on your form. This is particularly handy if you stack multiple controls on top of each other.
Font Name	Use to set the font for labels, text boxes, command buttons, toggle buttons, combo boxes, and list boxes.
Font Size	Use to set font size.
Bold	Click to set font style to bold.
Italic	Click to set font style to italic.
Underline	Click to underline text.
Align Left	Click to left-align text.
Center	Click to center text.
Align Right	Click to right-align text.
Back Color	Use to set the background color of the control or form area. You can also set the background color to transparent.
Fore Color	Use to set the foreground color of the control.
Border Color	Use to set the border color of the control. You can also set the border color to transparent.
Border Width	Use to set the border width from hairline to 6 points wide.
Special Effect	(Shown with options opened.) Use to set the look of the control to flat, raised, sunken, etched, shadowed, or chiseled.

NOTE You can select only one of the alignment buttons—
Align Left, Align Right, or Center—at a time. If you do not
click a button, alignment is set to General—text data aligns
left and numeric data aligns right.

Depending on the object you select, some of the Formatting
toolbar options might not be available. For example, you can't set text
color on a bound object frame control. Nor can you set fill or border
colors on a toggle button because these areas are always set to gray for
this button. If you have the property sheet open and you scroll through
it so that you can see the properties the Formatting toolbar sets, you
can watch the settings in the property sheet change as you click different options on the toolbar.

Setting Text Box Properties

The next thing you might want to do is to change some of the text box
properties. Figure 13-16 shows the first 45 properties for the ClubID
control. (The remaining properties are all Event properties—see Chapter 18, "Advanced Report Design," for details.) Because the ClubID
field in the Entertainment Schedule database is an AutoNumber field,
which the user cannot change, you should change this control to prevent it from being selected on the form. To prevent the selection of a
control, set the control's Enabled property to No. Because Access
shades a control if it isn't enabled and isn't locked, you should set the
Locked property to Yes to indicate that you won't be updating this control. The control will not be shaded, and you will not be able to tab to
it or select it on the form in Form view.

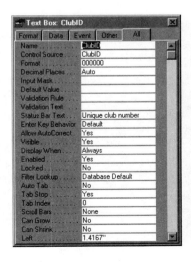
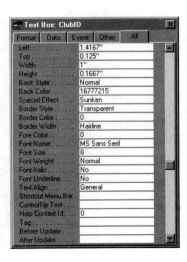

FIGURE 13-16

The first 45
properties for
the ClubID text
box control.

If you specify a Format, Decimal Places, or Input Mask property setting when you define a field in a table, Access copies these settings to any text box that is bound to the field. Any data you enter using the form must conform to the validation rule defined in the table; however, you can define a more restrictive rule for this form. New rows inherit default values from the table unless you provide a different default value in the property sheet. The Status Bar Text property derives its value from the Description property setting you entered for the field in the table.

At the end of the list in Figure 13-16, you can see properties labeled *Before Update* and *After Update*. If you scroll beyond this point or click on the Event tab, you'll see a host of additional properties with the word *On*. By entering macro names as values here, you can make certain events trigger certain actions. (See Chapter 19, "Adding Power with Macros.") You can also reference VBA procedures that are stored separately in modules or locally with this form. (See Chapter 21, "Visual Basic for Applications Fundamentals," and Chapter 22, "Automating Your Application with VBA.") Other properties in this property sheet can be set to customize a form. (See the next chapter.)

Setting Label Properties

You can also set separate properties for the labels attached to controls. Click on the label for ClubID to see the property sheet shown in Figure 13-17. Access copies the Caption property from the field in the underlying table to the Caption property in the associated control label. Notice that in Figure 13-17 the caption has been changed from *ClubID* (the field name) to *Club ID* (which includes a space for readability).

FIGURE 13-17

The property sheet for the ClubID label control.

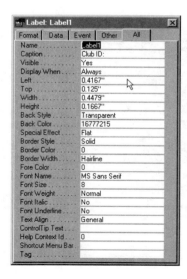

You also can correct the caption inside a label by selecting the label, moving the mouse pointer inside the label until the pointer changes into an I-beam, and then clicking to set the insertion point inside the label text. You can delete unwanted characters, and you can type in new information. When you finish correcting a label caption, you might find that the control is either too large or too small to adequately display the new name. You can change settings using the property sheet to adjust the size of a label, or you can select the control and drag the control's handles to adjust the size and alignment.

TIP To quickly adjust the size of a label, click on the label, choose the Size command from the Format menu, and then choose To Fit from the submenu.

Setting Form Properties

You can display the form's properties in the property sheet (as shown in Figure 13-18) by clicking anywhere outside the Detail section of the form or by choosing the Select Form command from the Edit menu. In Figure 13-18, the caption has been set to *Club Names and Addresses*. This value will appear on the Form window's title bar in Form view or in Datasheet view.

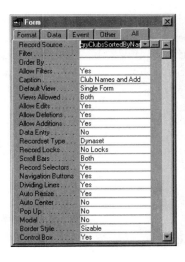
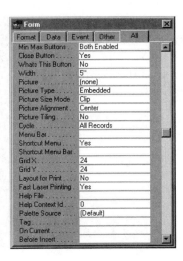

FIGURE 13-18
The first 46 properties for the tblClubs form.

455

The properties beginning with On Current in the property sheet can be set to run macros or VBA procedures. The events associated with these properties can trigger macro actions.

In the second part of the list of properties are the Grid X and Grid Y properties that control the density of dots on the grid. The defaults are 24 dots per inch across (Grid X) and 24 dots per inch down (Grid Y) if your measurements are in English units. For metric measurements, the defaults are 5 dots per centimeter in both directions. Access also draws a shaded line on the grid every inch or centimeter to help you line up controls. If you decide to use the Snap To Grid command from the Format menu to help you line up controls on your form, you might want to change the density of the grid dots to give you greater control over where you place objects on the form.

> NOTE You won't see the grid dots if you set either the Grid X or Grid Y property to more than 24 in English measurements or more than 9 in metric measurements.

Checking Your Design Results

When you finish working on this form in Design view, it might look something like the one shown in Figure 13-19. To make the fields on the form stand out, you can click in the Detail section and then set the background to dark gray using the Back Color button on the Formatting toolbar. To make the labels stand out against this dark background, drag the mouse around all the label controls or click on the horizontal ruler directly above all the label controls, and then set the Back Color to white. If you also want to make the Detail section fit snugly around the controls on your form, drag in the edges of the Detail section with the mouse pointer.

First click here to select all labels...

...and then choose white as the background color

FIGURE 13-19

Adding contrast to the Club Names and Addresses form.

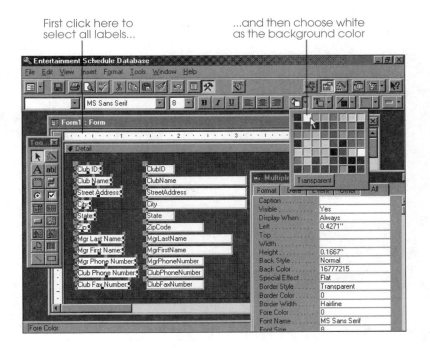

 TIP To select all controls in a vertical area, click on the horizontal ruler above the area containing the controls you want to select. Likewise, to select all controls in a horizontal area, click on the vertical ruler.

Click the Form View button on the toolbar to see your form. It will look similar to the form shown in Figure 13-20 on the next page. To size the Form window to exactly fit the boundaries of your form design, choose Size To Fit Form from the Window menu, as shown in the figure. Click the Save button on the toolbar or choose Save from the File menu to save your new form design.

FIGURE 13-20

The finished
Club Names
and Addresses
form in Form
view.

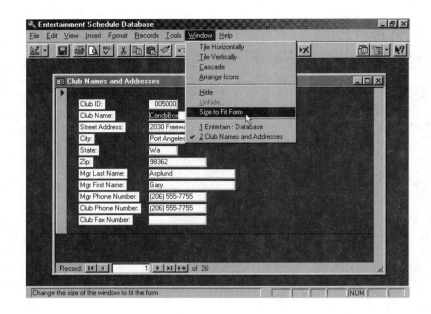

Working with Form Wizards

Now that you understand the basic mechanics of form design, you could continue to build all your forms "from scratch" in Design view. However, even the most experienced developers take advantage of the many wizards built into Microsoft Access to get a jump-start on design tasks. This section shows you how to use a Form Wizard to quickly build a custom form.

> **NOTE** The remaining examples in this chapter are based on the College Counseling sample database.

Creating the Colleges Form with a Form Wizard

Begin by opening the College Counseling database, and then switch to the Database window and select the Colleges table. Next, select New Form from the New Object toolbar button's drop-down list or choose Form from the Insert menu. Access opens the New Form dialog box, as shown in Figure 13-21.

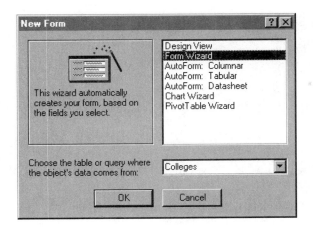

FIGURE 13-21
The New Form
dialog box, in
which you select
a Form Wizard.

As you can see, you have seven choices in this dialog box: Design View (which you used in the previous section), Form Wizard, AutoForm: Columnar, AutoForm: Tabular, AutoForm: Datasheet, Chart Wizard, and PivotTable Wizard. The AutoForm Wizards quickly build a form, selecting all the defaults along the way. The Chart Wizard builds a form containing a graph object and walks you through all the steps to define the data for the graph and customize the way the graph works. The PivotTable Wizard creates a form with an embedded Microsoft Excel object and then shows you how to use Excel's pivot table capabilities to create a data summary for display in your Access application. Note that in the New Form dialog box you can change the data source for your form by changing the table or query name displayed in the combo box.

For this example, select Form Wizard and click OK. Access opens the window shown in Figure 13-22 on the next page. You can select any field in the Available Fields list and click the single right arrow button to copy that field to the Selected Fields list. You can also click the double right arrow button to copy all available fields to the Selected Fields list. If you copy a field in error, you can select the field in the Selected Fields list and click the single left arrow button to remove the field from the list. You can remove all fields and start over by clicking the double left arrow button. For this example, click the double right arrow button to use all the Colleges table's fields in the new form.

FIGURE 13-22

The Form
Wizard window
for selecting
fields.

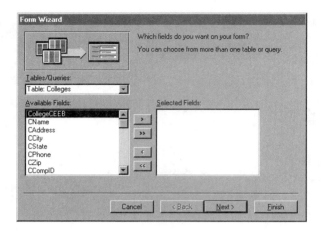

As you'll learn later in Chapter 15, "Advanced Form Design," you can select fields from one table or query and then change the data source name in the Tables/Queries combo box to select a different but related table or query. If you have defined the relationships between tables in your database, the Form Wizard can determine how the data from multiple sources is related and can offer to build either a simple form to display all the data or a more complex one that shows some of the data in the main part of the form with related data displayed in an embedded subform. You'll use this technique to build a more complex form in Chapter 15.

At any time, you can click the Finish button to go directly to the last step of the wizard. You can also click the Cancel button at any time to stop creating the form.

After you select all the fields you want from the Colleges table, click Next. In the following window, the wizard gives you choices for the layout of your form. You can choose to display the controls on your form in columns, arrange the controls across the form in a tabular format (this also creates a continuous form), or create a form in Datasheet view. For this example, select the Columnar format, and then click Next.

If you select the Columnar or Tabular format, the wizard displays a window in which you can select a "look" for your form, as shown in Figure 13-23. The nice thing about this window is that the wizard shows you a sample of each selection on the left side of the window. You can look at them all and decide which one you like best. In this example, the Stone built-in style is selected. In Chapter 14, "Customizing Forms," you'll learn how use the AutoFormat facility to create a look for your own custom form.

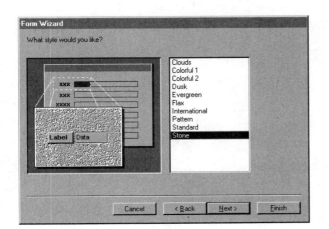

CAUTION When you select a style in the Form Wizard, the new style becomes the default for any new forms you create until you change the style setting again either in the Form Wizard or in the Auto-Format facility. See Chapter 14 for details.

In the final window, the Form Wizard asks for a title for your form. Type in an appropriate title, such as *Colleges*. The wizard places this title in the Caption property of the form and also saves the form with this name. Select the Open The Form To View Or Enter Information option, and then click the Finish button to go directly to Form view. Select the Modify The Form's Design option and then click Finish to open the new form in Design view. The finished form is shown in Figure 13-24 on the next page.

FIGURE 13-24

The Colleges form in a columnar format.

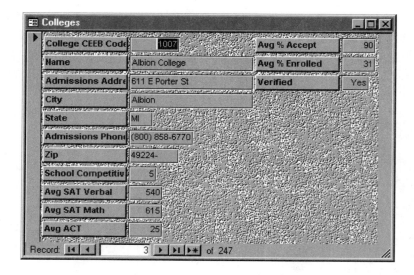

If you're curious to see the Tabular format, you can start a new form on the Colleges table and use the Form Wizard again. Select the CollegeCEEB, CName, CAddress, CCity, CState, and CZip fields. Select Tabular and set the style back to Standard. For a title, type *Colleges - Tabular*, and open the new form in Form view. It should look something like the form shown in Figure 13-25. Close this form when you finish looking at it.

FIGURE 13-25

The Colleges form in a tabular format.

ge CEEB Code	Name	Admissions Address	City	Stab	Zip
1005	Auburn University	105 Samford Hall	Auburn	AL	36849-3
1006	Alabama State University	P.O. Box 271	Montgomery	AL	36101-0
1007	Albion College	611 E Porter St	Albion	MI	49224-
1008	Alcorn State University		Lorman	MS	39096-
1017	Antioch College	795 Livermore St	Yellow Springs	OH	45387-
1051	Ball State University	2000 University Avenue	Muncie	IN	47306-
1056	Bellarmine College	Newburg Road	Louisville	KY	40205-
1058	Belmont University	1900 Belmont Blvd	Nashville	TN	37212-3
1059	Beloit College	700 College Street	Beloit	WI	53511-
1069	Bowling Green State Uni	110 McFall Center	Bowling Green	OH	43403-0
1135	Columbia College	600 South Michigan	Chicago	IL	60605-
1229	Franklin University	201 South Grant Ave	Columbus	OH	43215-5

Record: 1 of 247

Modifying the Colleges Form

The Form Wizard took care of some of the work, but there's still a lot you can do to improve the appearance and usability of this form. And even though the Form Wizard adjusted the display control widths, they're still not perfect; the display controls for CName and CAddress should be larger. Several other controls could be narrower. Also, you could make better use of the space on the form if you rearranged the field columns.

You can either start with the columnar format form you created in Figure 13-24 or start a new form with the Standard style. Open the form in Design view. To help align controls, click outside the Detail section so that the form is selected (or choose the Select Form command from the Edit menu), and make sure that Grid X and Grid Y on the form's property sheet are set to 24. (Leave the settings at Grid X = 5 and Grid Y = 5 if you're working in metric measurements.) Be sure the Grid command is checked on the View menu. Move controls around until the form looks similar to the one shown in Figure 13-26. Change the alignment of all the labels to left align; delete the labels from the city, state, and zip controls and place the controls in a row; and lengthen the name and address controls to approximately 2.5 inches (6.35 centimeters). Also, remove the redundant *Avg* from all the statistical field labels, position the labels on top of their respective display controls, and line up the controls along the bottom of the Detail section. Add the descriptive label *Averages:* in a bold font.

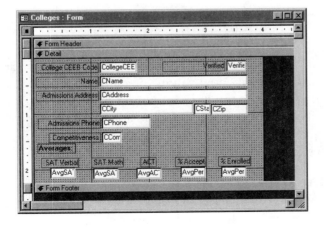

FIGURE 13-26

The modified Colleges form in Design view.

Now switch to Form view. Your form should look something like the one shown in Figure 13-27. The form now looks a bit more customized—and somewhat more like the frmCollege form in the College Counseling application.

FIGURE 13-27

The modified
Colleges form in
Form view.

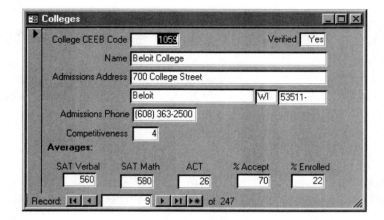

Simplifying Data Input with a Form

One drawback to working with a relational database is that often you have to deal with information stored in multiple tables. That's not a problem if you're using a query to link data, but multiple tables can be confusing if you're entering new data. Microsoft Access provides some great ways to show information from related tables, thus making data input much simpler.

Combo Boxes and List Boxes

In Chapter 12, "Form Basics," you saw that you can use a combo box or a list box to present a list of potential values for a control. To create the list, you can type the values in the Row Source property of the control. You can also specify a table or a query as the source of the values in the list. Access displays the currently selected value in the text box portion of the combo box or as a highlighted selection in the list.

Creating a Combo Box to Display the College Competitiveness Rating

Codes don't mean much to the people who read a form, but for efficiency's sake you need a code, not a description, to identify the competitiveness rating in the Colleges table. If you really plan ahead, you can use the Display Control property of the CCompID field in the table to define a combo box in advance for all your queries and forms. In this example, the Display Control property is set to Text Box so that you can learn how to create a combo box for the CCompID field. You can build a combo box that shows the user the related rating description fields but stores the code in the Colleges table when the user chooses a description.

To see how a combo box works, you can replace the CCompID text box control with a combo box on the Colleges form. In Design view, select the CCompID text box control and then press the Del key to remove the text box control from the form. Be sure the Control Wizards button is selected in the toolbox, and then click the Combo Box button in the toolbox and drag the CCompID field from the field list to the form. A new control appears on the form, and then Access starts the Combo Box Wizard, as shown in Figure 13-28, to help you out.

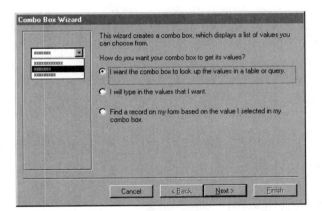

FIGURE 13-28
The first window of the Combo Box Wizard.

TIP To change a text box to a different type of control, select the text box, choose Change To from the Format menu, and then choose the new type of control from the submenu. To change a text box to a combo box, however, you have to set the properties to create the display list yourself.

Follow this procedure to build your combo box:

1. You want the combo box to display values from the zCompete-List table, so leave the first option selected and click the Next button to go to the next window.

2. In the second window, the wizard displays a list of tables and queries. Scroll down in the list until you see the zCompeteList table. Select it, and then click Next.

3. In the third window, the wizard displays a list of available fields from the table and a list of columns in your combo box. Click the double right arrow button between the two lists to move both fields from the zCompeteList table to the columns in your combo box, and then click Next.

4. In the fourth window, the wizard displays the fields you selected in the previous window. You use this window to set the width of any columns you want displayed when you open the combo box on the form. Also, you can use this window to change the order of the fields. This is important, because Access displays only the data in the first of these fields when the combo box is closed. Notice that the wizard has hidden the CCompID field. The wizard figured out that the CCompID field probably contains a code since its name and data type match the field you're trying to set in the Colleges table. You can deselect the Hide Key Column check box to see the code column. But since you really need to see only the rating description, you should leave this check box selected. You can adjust the size of the CCompRate column to make sure it displays all of the available descriptions properly. Your result should look like that shown in Figure 13-29. Click Next to go on.

FIGURE 13-29

The results of setting column widths in the fourth window of the Combo Box Wizard.

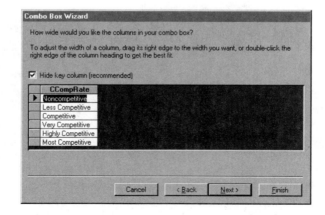

5. In the next window, the wizard asks whether you want to bind the control to a value in the table or query that you're updating with this form or simply save the value selected in an unbound control. You'll see in Part 6 of this book that unbound controls are useful for storing calculated values or for providing a way for the user to enter parameter data for use by your macros or VBA procedures. In this case, you want to update the CCompID field, so be sure to select the Store That Value In This Field option and select CCompID from the drop-down list. Click Next to go to the last window of the wizard.

6. In the final window, shown in Figure 13-30, notice that the wizard has chosen the caption from the bound field as the label for the combo box. Because you'll be showing descriptions and not codes in the combo box, change the caption as shown. Click Finish, and you're all done.

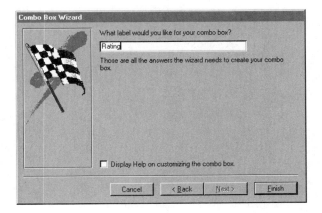

FIGURE 13-30
The final window of the Combo Box Wizard.

If you have the property sheet open, you can study the properties set by the Combo Box Wizard, as shown in Figure 13-31 on the next page. The Control Source property shows that the combo box is bound to the CCompID field. The Row Source Type property indicates that the data filling the combo box comes from a table or a query. You can also specify a list of values, or you can ask Access to create a list from the names of fields in the query or table specified in the Row Source property.

FIGURE 13-31

The properties
set by the
Combo Box
Wizard.

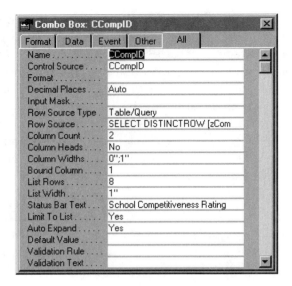

The Row Source property shows the SQL statement that the wizard created to retrieve the CCompID and CCompRate fields from the zCompeteList table. The wizard doesn't specify any sorting criteria or save the query. To add sorting criteria to the query and then save it, you can click in the Row Source property box and then click the Build button, as you learned earlier in this chapter. In the design grid, set the CCompRate field to be sorted in ascending order and save the query as *qryCompRatingsSorted.* When you exit the builder, ask it to update the Row Source property so that the property refers to the query that sorts the descriptions.

The Column Count property is set to 2 to indicate that two columns should be used from the query. You have the option of asking Access to display column headings when the combo box is open, but you don't need that for this example, so leave the Column Heads property set to No. Notice that the first entry in the Column Widths property is 0 inches. This is how you "hide" a column in a combo box. Remember, you don't want to show the competitiveness rating code, but you do want to save it in the table when you select a description from the combo box. The next property, Bound Column, indicates that the "hidden" first column (the CCompID field) is the one that sets the value of the combo box and, therefore, the bound field in the table.

When you open the form in Form view, it should look like the one shown in Figure 13-32. Notice that the Rating combo box now shows meaningful descriptions instead of numbers; the description you select will set the correct rating code in the record.

> **TIP** If you want Access to select the closest matching entry when you type a few leading characters in a combo box, set the Auto Expand property to Yes.

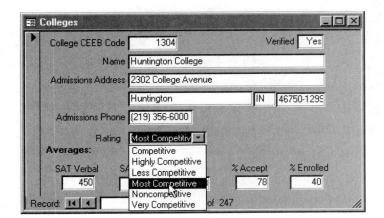

FIGURE 13-32
The finished
Rating combo
box in operation.

Toggle Buttons,
Check Boxes, and Option Buttons

If your table contains a field that has a yes/no, true/false, or on/off value, you can choose from three types of controls that graphically display and set the status of this type of field: toggle buttons, check boxes, and option buttons.

The Colleges table has a Verified field that indicates whether the particular college has responded to a questionnaire and whether the data in the table has been verified. As you can see in the original text box control created by the Form Wizard, the word *Yes* or *No* appears depending on the value in the underlying field. This field might be more graphically appealing and understandable if it is displayed in a check box control.

To change the Verified control on the Colleges form, first delete the Verified text box control. Next, select the Check Box tool and then drag the Verified field from the field list onto the form in the open space you left in the top right corner of the form. Your form in Design view should now look like the one shown in Figure 13-33.

FIGURE 13-33

The Colleges form with a check box control to display the Verified field.

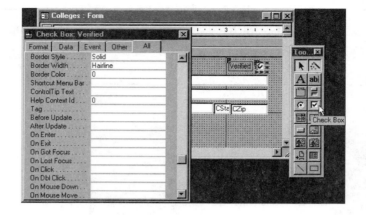

Click the Form View button to see the result. Your form should look like the one shown in Figure 13-34. One of the interesting side effects of using a special control to display data in a form is that the control properties carry over to Datasheet view. Switch to the Datasheet view of this form. The Rating field is displayed as a drop-down list on the datasheet and the Verified field still looks like a check box. You might decide to design some forms to be used in Datasheet view, but you can customize the look of the datasheet by using controls other than text boxes while in Design view. By the way, this design sample is saved as *frmXmplCollege1* in the College Counseling database.

FIGURE 13-34

The final Colleges form in Form view.

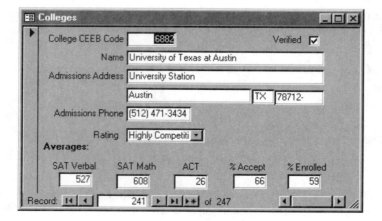

By now, you should be getting a feel for the process of designing and building forms. In the next chapter, you'll learn how to customize the appearance of your forms.

Chapter 14

Customizing Forms

n the previous chapter, you learned how to create a basic form by building it from scratch or by using a Form Wizard. In this chapter, you'll look at ways that you can refine your form's appearance.

Creating a Custom Toolbar

One of the nicest features of Microsoft Access is that it allows you to modify any of the built-in ("standard") toolbars or to define your own custom toolbars. You can build a custom application toolbar or a custom design toolbar. Much of this chapter explains how to enhance the appearance of your forms, so first you'll learn how to create a custom toolbar that gives you direct access to all the aligning and sizing commands.

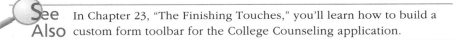

See Also In Chapter 23, "The Finishing Touches," you'll learn how to build a custom form toolbar for the College Counseling application.

Defining a New Toolbar

To begin, open your database and then open the Toolbars dialog box by choosing Toolbars from the View menu. You can also click with the right mouse button on any open toolbar to open the toolbar shortcut menu, and then choose Toolbars from that menu. The Toolbars dialog box is shown in Figure 14-1.

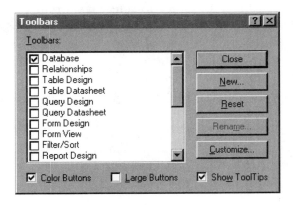

FIGURE 14-1
The Toolbars dialog box.

473

On the left side of the Toolbars dialog box you can see the names of all the built-in toolbars in Access. You can make any of the toolbars visible by selecting the check box next to the toolbar name. If you scroll to the bottom of the list, you'll see three special built-in toolbars that Access displays only if you select them in this dialog box: Microsoft, Utility 1, and Utility 2. The Microsoft toolbar contains buttons that launch seven Microsoft applications: Microsoft Excel, Word, PowerPoint, Mail, FoxPro, Project, and Schedule+. The two utility toolbars are empty, so you can customize these by adding buttons of your choice. If you have either the College Counseling or the Entertainment Schedule sample database open, you can see one of the custom toolbars already defined at the bottom of the list.

> **NOTE** If you open one of the built-in toolbars in a context in which the toolbar would not normally be open, the toolbar remains open until you close it. For example, if you open the Toolbars dialog box from the Database window and then open the Form Design toolbar, the toolbar remains open no matter where you are in Access. Likewise, if you close a toolbar in a context in which that toolbar is normally open (for example, if you close the Formatting toolbar in a Form window in Design view), that toolbar will remain closed until you specifically open it in the Toolbars dialog box.

Across the bottom of the Toolbars dialog box are check boxes you can use to select buttons with color icons, to select large buttons, and to display ToolTips. If you're working on a large monitor at a high resolution (1024×768 or 1280×1024), you might find the larger toolbar buttons easier to work with. The large buttons are approximately 50 percent wider and taller than the standard buttons.

If you have made changes to one of the built-in toolbars, you can select it in the dialog box and click the Reset button to return the toolbar to its installation default. Access prompts you to confirm this action so that you don't inadvertently erase any custom changes you've made.

You can click the New button to begin defining a new toolbar. Access will prompt you for a name for your new toolbar. You'll see the new name appear at the bottom of the Toolbars list, and an empty toolbar in the form of a tiny, gray window will open in the Access workspace.

Any new toolbar that you define is available only in the database that you had open at the time you created the toolbar. If you want to define a custom toolbar that is available in all databases, you must modify one of the built-in toolbars. You can use the two "blank" toolbars—Utility 1 and Utility 2—to create a custom set of toolbar buttons that is available in any database. The only drawback to these two toolbars is that you cannot give them custom names.

Because you'll probably want to use form alignment tools in every database that you design, it's a good idea to use one of the blank toolbars to define your custom buttons. Scroll down the Toolbars list until you see the Utility 1 toolbar name. Select it and then click its check box to open the toolbar. The empty Utility 1 toolbar appears in the Access workspace.

Next, click the Customize button in the Toolbars dialog box to open the Customize Toolbars dialog box, shown in Figure 14-2. This dialog box allows you to change the buttons on any open toolbar. On the left side of the dialog box is a list of all the button categories that Access provides. Because you want buttons to help with form sizing and alignment, select the Form & Report Design category. The buttons in that category appear on the right side of the dialog box. As you move your mouse pointer over the various buttons in the group, Access displays a description of the button in the box at the bottom of the dialog box. If you have ToolTips turned on, you'll also see a short description appear just below the mouse pointer.

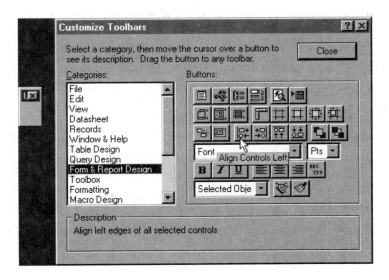

FIGURE 14-2

The Customize Toolbars dialog box and the Form & Report Design category buttons. The empty Utility 1 toolbar is open at the left.

Buttons that are useful for form design include the Tab Order button (the fourth button in the top row), all the buttons in the second group in the second row (Ruler, Show/Hide Grid, Snap To Grid, Size To Grid, Align To Grid), and all the buttons in the third row (Duplicate Control, Size To Fit, Align Controls Left, Align Controls Right, Align Controls Top, Align Controls Bottom, Bring To Front, Send To Back). Drag and drop these buttons one at a time onto your new toolbar. You might find it easiest to line up the buttons in the proper order if you add them to the toolbar from right to left. You'll notice that Access displays the name of the toolbar in the toolbar window's title bar as soon as you add enough buttons to make the toolbar wide enough to show the entire name. Your toolbar with all the added buttons should look something like the one shown in Figure 14-3.

FIGURE 14-3
The Utility 1 custom toolbar under construction.

Unless you're building the toolbar while a form is open in Design view, all buttons will appear gray (disabled). As soon as you open a form in Design view, the appropriate buttons will become available for use.

Customizing the Look of Your New Toolbar

After you build a toolbar, you can rearrange the buttons and add spacing between them. To make any changes, first open the toolbar. Choose Toolbars from the View menu to open the Toolbars dialog box, and select the check box next to the Utility 1 toolbar. Then click the Customize button to open the Customize Toolbars dialog box.

TIP   You can also open the Customize Toolbars dialog box by clicking on the toolbar with the right mouse button to open the toolbar shortcut menu and then choosing Customize from that menu.

When you open the Customize Toolbars dialog box, all toolbar buttons become editable. You can:

- Remove any button from any open toolbar (including any built-in one) by clicking the button and dragging it off its toolbar

- Move any button by clicking it and dragging it to a new location on its toolbar

- Add a button by dragging it from the Buttons display to any toolbar

To make buttons easier to use, it's often useful to "cluster" buttons that perform similar functions and to create a space between those clusters. To create a space to the left of any button, hold down the Shift key and then click the button and move it to the right. (You might need to resize the toolbar window to make the space visible.)

On the Utility 1 toolbar, the Tab Order button should probably stand on its own. The Ruler and Show/Hide Grid buttons should probably come next. The Snap To Grid, Size To Grid, Align To Grid, and Size To Fit buttons would make a good group. The Duplicate Control button should probably stand on its own. The four alignment buttons seem logical together, followed finally by the Bring To Front and Send To Back buttons. After you make these modifications, your toolbar should look like the one shown in Figure 14-4. Close the Customize Toolbars dialog box when you finish.

FIGURE 14-4
The Utility 1 custom toolbar with buttons arranged in clusters.

 TIP   You can drag the edges of a toolbar to change its shape. You can also "dock" the toolbar at the top, sides, or bottom of the workspace.

Adding a Custom Button to a Built-In Toolbar

It might be nice to add a button to the built-in Form Design toolbar that opens and closes your new Utility 1 toolbar. To do this, you need to create a simple macro and add a custom button to the Form Design toolbar.

Creating a Macro to Open Your Toolbar

As you'll see in a minute, you can create a custom toolbar button that can run any macro in your database. If you want a button that will open your custom Utility 1 toolbar, you need a macro that you can call from the custom toolbar button. Switch to the Database window and click on the Macros tab. Click New to open a new Macro window, as shown in Figure 14-5. In the first Action row, type *ShowToolbar*, or select ShowToolbar from the drop-down list. Press F6 to jump down to the Toolbar Name argument text box, and type *Utility 1*—the name of the built-in toolbar you just customized. Enter *Yes* in the Show argument text box. Choose Save from the File menu and name your macro *Form Tools*.

FIGURE 14-5

A macro to show the Utility 1 toolbar.

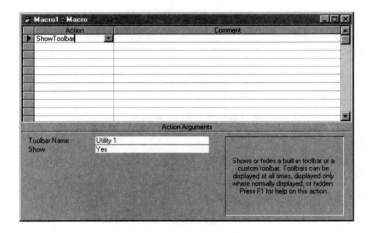

Now you're ready to add a custom button to the Form Design toolbar.

Defining a Button to Run Your Macro

In this section you'll spend some time working with the Colleges form that you built in the last chapter. (You can find a copy of this form saved as *frmXmplCollege1* in the College Counseling sample database.) Open this form in Design view. You should see the Form Design toolbar. If you can't see the toolbar, choose Toolbars from the View menu and be sure that the Form Design check box is selected in the Toolbars dialog box.

Move your mouse pointer over the toolbar and click with the right mouse button to open the shortcut menu, as shown in Figure 14-6. Choose Customize from this menu to open the Customize Toolbars dialog box again.

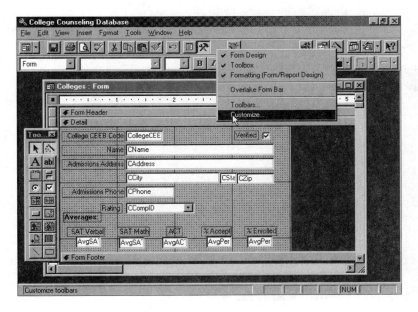

FIGURE 14-6

Using the shortcut menu to open the Customize Toolbars dialog box.

If you're working on a screen with a 640×480 resolution or if you've selected the large toolbar buttons, you might want to remove one of the standard buttons from the Form Design toolbar to make room for a new button. I don't know about you, but I rarely need to see a form in Print Preview. You can click the Print Preview button and drag it off the Form Design toolbar to remove it. If you're working with normal sized buttons, there's plenty of space on the Form Design toolbar between the AutoFormat and Code buttons.

Next, you need to find the macro you just created. Scroll down the Categories list in the Customize Toolbars dialog box and select All Macros. Access displays all the macros in your database in the Objects list, as shown in Figure 14-7. Select the *Form Tools* macro from the list, drag it to the Form Design toolbar, and drop it between the existing Auto-Format and Code buttons. Your toolbar should look like the one shown in Figure 14-8.

FIGURE 14-7

Selecting a macro to use for a custom toolbar button.

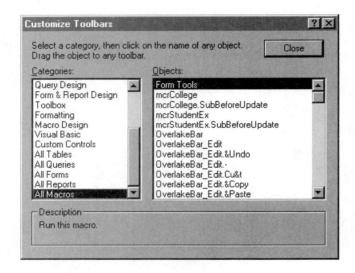

FIGURE 14-8

Placing a custom toolbar button on the Form Design toolbar.

The default picture that Access displays when you create a button to run a macro is the macro icon. As you can see, the ToolTip says *Run macro 'Form Tools'*. Fortunately, Access lets you change both the icon and the ToolTip. While you still have the Customize Toolbars dialog box open, right-click the new button to open a shortcut menu. Choose the Choose Button Image command to open the Choose Button Image dialog box, as shown in Figure 14-9. (The shortcut menu also includes a command to edit the existing button icon and a command to paste an icon you've copied to the Clipboard from another application.)

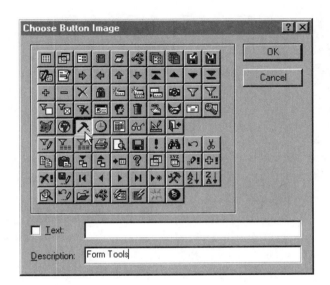

FIGURE 14-9
Selecting a custom button icon and description in the Choose Button Image dialog box.

There's a handy hammer-and-nail icon in the fifth row of available icons that will do quite nicely for this new button. You can also shorten the description to simply *Form Tools*—this description will show up as a ToolTip when you move the mouse pointer over the button. Click OK and then close the Customize Toolbars dialog box. You can now click your new toolbar button to open the Utility 1 toolbar that contains your custom set of form design buttons, as shown in Figure 14-10 on the next page.

FIGURE 14-10

The new custom toolbar button that opens the Utility 1 toolbar.

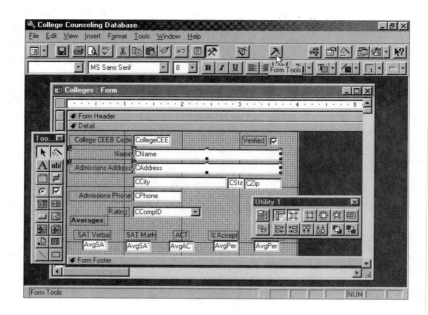

When the Utility 1 toolbar is open, you can "dock" it at the top, bottom, or sides of your workspace or leave it floating. If you want to continue to use this custom toolbar in other databases, be sure to copy the *Form Tools* macro to those databases.

Aligning and Sizing Controls

In the previous chapter, you built a form based on the Colleges table in the College Counseling sample database, as shown in Figure 14-10. This form looks pretty good, but the labels and fields are different sizes and are out of alignment. If you threw the form together quickly to help you enter some data (as you did to create a simple Clubs input form in the Entertainment Schedule database in the previous chapter), it probably doesn't matter if the form doesn't look perfect. But if you're designing the form to be used continuously in an application, it's worth the extra effort to fine-tune the design. Otherwise, your database will look less than professional, and users might suffer eyestrain and fatigue.

NOTE If you follow along precisely with the alignment steps described in this chapter, your results might vary slightly. All of the alignment commands are sensitive to your current screen resolution. When your screen driver is set to a high resolution (for example, 1024x768), the distance between grid points might be smaller than it is when the screen driver is set to a low resolution (such as 640x480). You should design your forms at the same resolution as the machines that will run your application.

To examine the alignment and relative size of controls on your form, you can open the property sheet in Design view and click various controls. For example, Figure 14-11 shows the property sheets for the CPhone and CCompID controls. You can see by looking at the values for the Left property (the distance from the left edge of the form) that the CPhone control is a bit closer to the left margin than is the CCompID control.

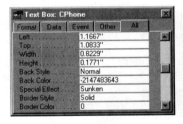 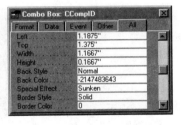

FIGURE 14-11
The properties that define the placement and size of the CPhone and CCompID controls.

You could move around the form and adjust controls so that they fit your data. You could painstakingly enter values for each control's Left property to get all controls in a column to line up exactly and then set the Top property (defining the distance from the top of the Detail section) for controls that you want to appear in a row. You could also adjust the values for the Width and Height properties so that controls and labels are the same width and height where appropriate. Fortunately, there are easier ways to make all of these adjustments.

Sizing Controls to Fit Content

One of the first things you can do with the Colleges form is to be sure that all the controls are the right size for displaying your data. Access has a command called Size/To Fit that sizes label controls to fit around the label text. This command also ensures that text boxes, combo boxes, and list boxes are tall enough to display your data using the font size you've selected.

Because you created all of the controls and labels on this form using the same font, it makes sense to resize them all at once. First, choose Select All from the Edit menu to highlight all the controls on your form. To select a specific group of labels or controls, click on the first one and then hold down the Shift key as you click on each control or label that you want to select. You can also drag the mouse pointer across the form (as long as you don't start dragging while you are over a control), and the mouse pointer will delineate a selection box. Any controls that are inside the selection box when you release the mouse button will be selected. After you select the controls you want, choose the Size/To Fit command from the Format menu. (If the custom Form Design toolbar that you created earlier in this chapter is open, you can click the Size To Fit button on that toolbar. The Detail section should look something like that shown in Figure 14-12.

FIGURE 14-12
The Colleges
form after you
select the
controls and
choose the
Size/To Fit
command.

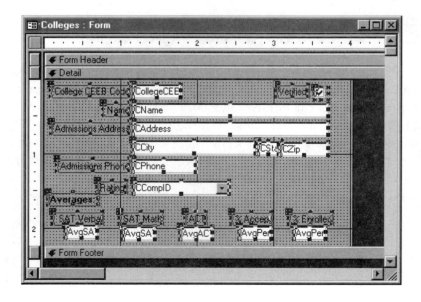

TIP   If you think you'll be selecting multiple controls often, you might want to experiment with an option setting that governs how you can select controls with your mouse pointer. From the Tools menu, choose Options, and then click on the Forms/Reports tab of the Options dialog box. When you select the Partially Enclosed option, the selection box you draw with your mouse needs only to touch any part of a control to select it. If you select the Fully Enclosed option, the selection box must contain the entire control in order for the control to be selected. Fully Enclosed is most useful for complex forms with many controls that are close to each other—that way you don't have to worry about inadvertently selecting controls that you touch with the selection box.

You can also select all controls in a vertical or a horizontal band by making the rulers visible and then dragging the mouse along the top or side ruler.

 TIP   You can "size to fit" any individual control or label by double-clicking on its lower left corner.

"Snapping" Controls to the Grid

It's a good idea to verify that all the controls are spaced evenly down the form. One way to do this is to take advantage of the grid. You can adjust the density of the grid by changing the Grid X and Grid Y properties of the form. Be sure that the property sheet is open, and then choose Select Form from the Edit menu. Also, be sure that the Grid command on the View menu has a check mark in front of it.

For this example, set the Grid X and Grid Y properties to 16 (.0625 inch between grid points). This works well for the default 8-point MS Sans Serif font because the "sized to fit" text boxes will be .17 inch high. You can place these text boxes every .25 inch (four grid points) down the form, which leaves adequate space between the controls.

You can "snap" the controls to the grid in one of two ways. If you want to handle each control individually, choose the Snap To Grid command from the Format menu. (You'll see a check mark in front of this command when it is active.) Now click on each control and drag it vertically every .25 inch (every fourth grid point) down the grid. When you release the mouse button, you'll see the upper left corner of the control "snap" to the nearest grid point. As you saw in the previous chapter, Access moves a control and its label as a unit. So if you previously moved the label up or down independent of the attached control, you might need to use the positioning handle in the upper left corner of the control or the label to align them horizontally.

A faster way to snap all controls to the grid is to choose Select All from the Edit menu, and then choose Align/To Grid from the Format menu. The result might look something like that shown in Figure 14-13—and it might look like you made it worse instead of better! Snapping to the grid helps spread the controls apart to make them easier to work with. You'll see in the next few steps that it's easy to line them all up.

FIGURE 14-13

The Colleges form after you "snap" the controls to the grid.

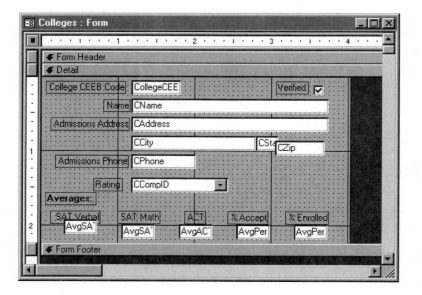

Lining Up Controls

You now have your controls spaced evenly down the form, but they probably aren't vertically aligned. That's easy to fix. Select all the labels in the far left column. You do this by clicking on the first label (not its associated control) and then holding down the Shift key as you click on all the remaining labels in the column. When you have selected them all, your grid should look something like the one shown in Figure 14-14. Notice that Access also shows the large handles in the upper left corner of all the related controls but no sizing handles on the controls.

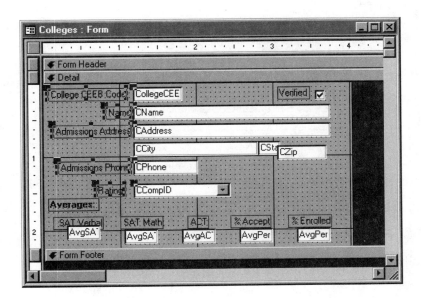

FIGURE 14-14
The Colleges form with a column of labels selected.

The labels will look best if their right edges align. You have two choices at this point. If you turn off the Snap To Grid command, you can have Access align all the labels with the label whose right edge is farthest to the right, even if that edge is between dots on the grid. If you leave on Snap To Grid, you can have Access align the labels with the label farthest to the right and then snap the entire group to the nearest grid point.

When you're ready to align the selected controls on your form, choose the Align command from the Format menu. Choose the Right command from the submenu, as shown in Figure 14-15 on the next page, and then click inside the grid. Your form should look similar to the one shown in Figure 14-16. (Again, if you're using the Utility 1 toolbar, you can simply click the Align Right button instead of using the menu commands.)

FIGURE 14-15
The Align
command and
its submenu.

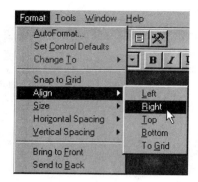

FIGURE 14-16
The labels from
Figure 14-14 are
right-aligned.

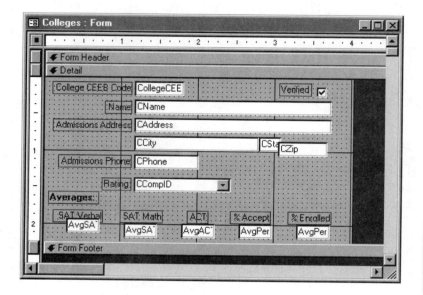

To further improve the alignment of the controls on the Colleges form, do the following:

1. To fix any overlap of the CCity, CState, and CZip controls, select all three controls and then choose Align/Left from the Format menu.

2. Select the CollegeCEEB, CName, CAddress, CCity, CPhone, and CCompID controls. Choose Align/Left from the Format menu.

3. Select the College CEEB Code and Verified labels and their corresponding controls. Choose Align/Top from the Format menu.

4. Select the Name label and control. Choose Align/Top.

5. Select the CCity, CState, and CZip controls. Choose Align/Top.

6. Select the Admissions Phone label and control. Choose Align/Top.

7. Select the Rating label and control. Choose Align/Top.

8. Select the CollegeCEEB, CName, CAddress, CCity, CPhone, and CCompID controls. Choose Vertical Spacing/Make Equal from the Format menu.

9. Realign the CState and CZip controls with the CCity control by selecting all three and choosing Align/Top or Align/Bottom as appropriate.

10. Select the five Averages text boxes. Choose Align/Bottom.

11. Select the five labels for the Averages text boxes (but not the text boxes themselves). Choose Align/Top.

12. Select the Averages label and move it down closer to the five Averages labels.

After you complete these steps, your form should look something like the one shown in Figure 14-17.

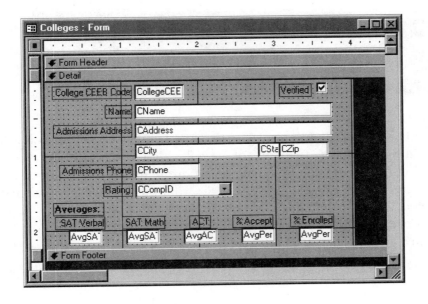

FIGURE 14-17
The controls and labels are aligned horizontally and vertically.

Adjusting Control Width

Two long controls—CName and CAddress—stretch most of the way across the Colleges form. You aligned their left edges, but it would be nice if their right edges also aligned with the CZip and AvgPercent-Enrolled controls. You can do this by adjusting the Width property of the CZip control and moving the AvgPercentEnrolled control.

To determine what adjustment you need (if any), first take a look at the Left and Width properties of the CAddress control's property sheet, as shown in Figure 14-18. In this example, the CAddress text box starts 1.1875 inches from the left edge of the form and is 2.5521 inches wide. This means that the right edge is 3.7396 inches from the left edge of the form. Next, take a look at the Left and Width properties of the CZip control. You don't want to move this control from its location 3.0625 inches from the left edge because it's left-aligned with the other controls in that row. The sum of the Left and Width properties of the CZip control should equal 3.7396 inches in order to align the right edge of the CZip control with the right edge of the CAddress control. So you need to change the CZip control's Width property to .6771 inch (3.7396 minus 3.0625) to achieve the desired result. (Access might adjust this length slightly to align with the nearest display pixel.)

FIGURE 14-18

The values for the Left and Width properties can be compared and adjusted to align the right edges of two controls.

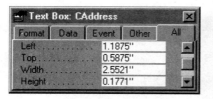

Next, click on the grid to deselect the CZip control. Click on the AvgPercentEnrolled control and drag it slightly to the left so that its right edge is clearly to the left of the right edge of the CAddress control. Select both the AvgPercentEnrolled control and the CZip or CAddress control and then choose Align/Right from the Format menu. Finally, select all five Averages controls along the bottom of the form and choose Horizontal Spacing/Make Equal from the Format menu to get equal spacing across the bottom.

TIP   If you want to move one or more controls only horizontally or only vertically, hold down the Shift key as you select the control (or the last control in a group) that you want to move, and then drag either horizontally or vertically. When Access detects movement either horizontally or vertically, it "locks" the movement and won't let the objects stray in the other plane. If you inadvertently start to drag horizontally when you mean to move vertically (or vice versa), click the Undo button and try again.

When you finish, switch to Form view and choose Size To Fit Form from the Window menu. Your form should look something like the one shown in Figure 14-19.

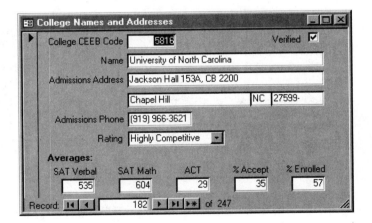

FIGURE 14-19
The Colleges form with controls aligned and sized.

TIP   Forms have an Auto Resize property. If you set this property to Yes, Access sizes the Form window to exactly fit the form. Note that Access won't automatically resize a form if you've switched from Design view to Form view.

You can also set the Auto Center property to Yes to center the Form window in the current Access workspace.

491

Enhancing the Look of a Form

When you first built the Colleges form using a Form Wizard and specified the Standard format, the wizard automatically added one enhance-
ment—a gray background color. In this section, you'll learn about
additional enhancements you can make to your form's design.

Lines and Rectangles

Microsoft Access comes with two drawing tools, Line and Rectangle,
that you can use to enhance the appearance of your forms. You can
add lines to visually separate parts of your form. Rectangles are useful
for surrounding and setting off a group of controls.

On the Colleges form, it might be helpful to add a line to separate
the primary information about the college from the statistical information in the five Averages controls. To make room for the line, you need
to move the Averages information down about two grid points. The
easiest way to do this is to switch to Design view, use the pointer tool
to highlight all the affected controls and labels, and then move them as
a group. Start by clicking on the left ruler (if you can't see the rulers, be
sure that Ruler is checked on the View menu) just above the Averages
label and then dragging in the ruler until the selection box surrounds
all the Averages text boxes. Release the mouse button, and all the controls inside the selection box will be selected. Grab a handle on any of
the controls and slide the entire selection box down two grid points.
(You might have to first drag the bottom margin of the Detail section
down to make room.)

Next, select the Line tool from the toolbox. To draw your line,
click on the left side of the form, about one grid row below the Rating
label, and drag across to the form's right edge. If the line isn't exactly
straight, you can drag the right end up or down to adjust it. You can
also set its height to 0 in the property sheet. Use the Border Width button on the toolbar to make the line a little thicker if you want. Your
form should now look similar to the one shown in Figure 14-20.

Border Width button

FIGURE 14-20
Use the Line tool
to draw a line on
a form, and use
the Border Width
button to adjust
the line width.

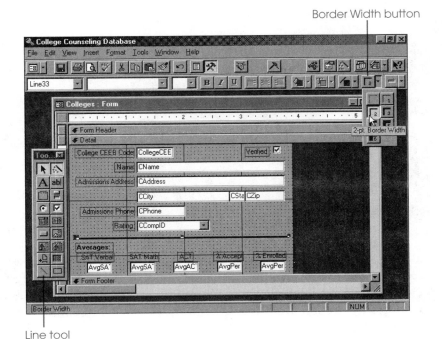

Line tool

You can add emphasis to the form by drawing a rectangle around all the controls. To do this, you might first need to move all the controls down and to the right a bit and make the Detail section slightly wider and taller. First, expand your form by about .5 inch across and down. Choose Select All from the Edit menu, and then click on any control and drag all the controls so that you have about .25 inch of space around all the edges. (This might seem like too much space, but we'll use the extra space to have some fun a bit later.) Select the Rectangle tool, click where you want to place one corner of the rectangle, and drag to the intended location of the opposite corner. When you draw a rectangle around all the controls, your form will look similar to the one shown in Figure 14-21 on the next page.

FIGURE 14-21

The Colleges
form after a
rectangle with a
default etched
look is added.

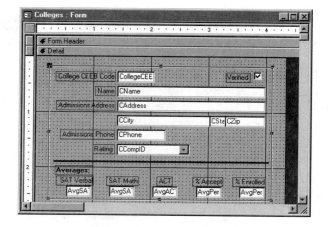

Note that the default rectangle is transparent with an etched special effect. If you ever want to create a solid rectangle, you can select the Rectangle tool and then use the Back Color button on the toolbar to select the color you want. When you add a solid control like this after you've created other controls, the solid control will cover the previous controls. You can choose Send To Back from the Format menu to unhide the covered controls and keep the solid control in the background.

Now switch to Form view and choose Size To Fit Form from the Window menu. Your Colleges form should now look similar to the one shown in Figure 14-22.

FIGURE 14-22

The Colleges
form in Form view
with a line and a
rectangle added.

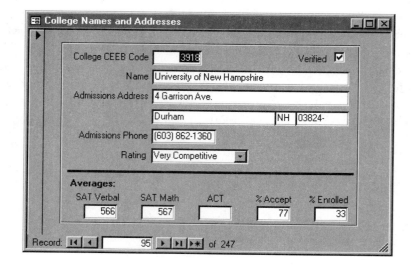

Colors and Special Effects

The Form Wizard added a light gray color to the background of the Colleges form when you first created it. You can also use color and special effects to highlight objects on your form. For example, you can make all the controls appear to "float" on a raised surface on the form. To do so, switch to Design view and select the rectangle you just created. Use the Back Color button on the toolbar to set the background color to light gray. Use the Special Effect button to change the rectangle from Etched to Raised. Choose Send To Back from the Format menu to make sure all the other controls appear on top of the colored background. Your form will look similar to the one shown in Figure 14-23.

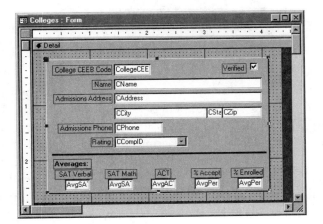

FIGURE 14-23

The rectangle behind the controls is now "raised" and light gray in color.

Next, select the Rectangle tool again, and set Back Color to dark gray and Special Effect to Sunken using the buttons on the toolbar. Draw a second rectangle so that it forms a border about halfway between the edge of the first rectangle and the edge of the grid. Choose Send To Back from the Format menu to send this latest rectangle to the background. Switch to Form view to see the result. The controls now appear to float on the light gray rectangle on the form, surrounded by a "moat" of dark gray, as shown in Figure 14-24 on the next page.

FIGURE 14-24

Controls
appear to float
on the form
using special
effects.

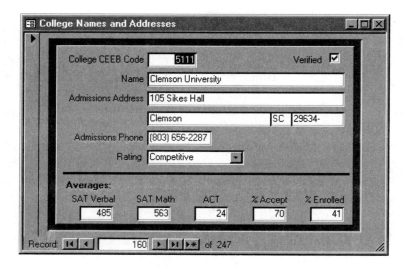

Fonts

Another way you can enhance the appearance of your forms is by varying the fonts and font sizes you use. When you select any control or label that can display text or data, Access makes font, font size, and font attribute controls available on the Formatting toolbar so that you can easily change how that control or label looks. Simply click the down arrow next to the Font Name combo box on the Formatting toolbar to open a list of all the available fonts, as shown in Figure 14-25. Select the font you want for the selected control or label.

FIGURE 14-25

The list of fonts in
the Font Name
combo box.

If you want to add some variety, you can use bold or italic type in a few key places. In this case, you might select all the labels on the form and select a serif font such as Times New Roman. You can add a label to the header of the form to display a title such as *Colleges*. (This is probably overkill since the form caption already tells us the subject of this form.) Set the label in the header to the Arial font (a sans serif font), bold, italic, and 14 points in size. You can see a portion of this work under way in Figure 14-26.

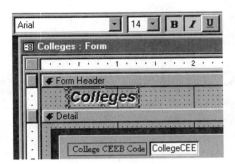

FIGURE 14-26
Using special font settings in a form header label.

You can create the special "shadowed" effect you see in this label by first creating the label with a black foreground color. Copy the label to the Clipboard and paste it in the header. Change its foreground color to white and then choose Send To Back from the Format menu. Drag the white label so that it is slightly lower and to the right of the first label. When you finish, the form should look similar to the one shown in Figure 14-27. (You can find this form saved in the College Counseling database as *frmXmplCollege2*.)

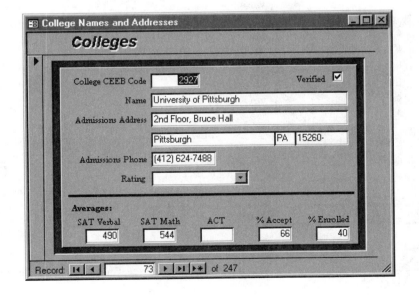

FIGURE 14-27
The Colleges form using some different fonts for variety.

You should note that a form with too many fonts or font sizes will look too busy and jumbled. In general, you should use only two or three fonts per form. Use one font and font size for most data in controls and labels. Make the label text bold or colored for emphasis. Select a second font for controls in the headers and perhaps a third (at most) for information in the footers.

Setting Control Properties

Microsoft Access gives you several additional properties for each control to allow you to customize the way your form works. These properties affect formatting, the presence or absence of scroll bars, and the enabling or locking of records.

Formatting Properties

In the property sheet for each text box, combo box, and list box are three properties that you can set to determine how Access displays the data in the form. These properties are Format, Decimal Places, and Input Mask, as shown in Figure 14-28.

FIGURE 14-28

The list of format settings for the AvgSATVerbal control, which uses the Number data type.

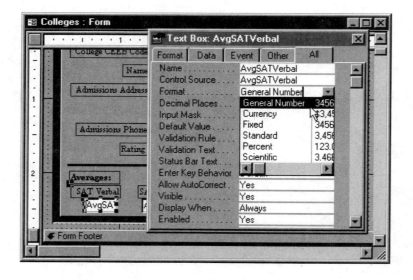

See Also   For details on the Input Mask property, see Chapter 5, "Building Your Database in Microsoft Access."

Access copies these properties from the definition of the fields in the underlying table. If you haven't specified a Format property in the field definition, Access sets a default Format property for the control, depending on the data type of the field bound to the control. In the control's property sheet, you can customize the appearance of your data by selecting a format setting from the Format property's drop-down list or by entering a custom set of formatting characters. The following sections present the format settings and formatting characters available for each data type.

Numbers and Currency

If you don't specify a Format property setting for a control that displays a number or a currency value, Access displays numbers in the General Number format and currency in the Currency format. You can choose from among six Format property settings, as shown in Figure 14-29.

Number/Currency Format	Description
General Number	Displays numbers as entered with up to 11 significant digits. If a number contains more than 11 significant digits, Access first rounds the number to 11 decimal places and then uses scientific (exponential) notation for very large or very small numbers (more than 10 digits to the right or to the left of the decimal point).
Currency	Displays numeric data according to the Currency setting in the Regional Settings section of the Windows Control Panel. In the U.S. layout, Access uses a leading dollar sign, maintains two decimal places (rounded), and encloses negative numbers in parentheses.
Fixed	Displays numbers without thousands separators and with two decimal places.
Standard	Displays numbers with thousands separators and with two decimal places.
Percent	Multiplies the value by 100, displays two decimal places, and adds a trailing percent sign.
Scientific	Displays numbers in scientific (exponential) notation.

FIGURE 14-29
The Format property settings for the Number and Currency data types.

You can also create a custom format. You can specify a different display format for Access to use (depending on whether the numeric value is positive, negative, 0, or Null) by providing up to four format specifications in the Format property. The specifications must be separated by semicolons. When you enter two specifications, Access uses the first for all nonnegative numbers and the second for negative numbers. When you provide three specifications, Access uses the third specification to display numbers with a value of 0. Provide the fourth specification to indicate how you want Null values handled.

To create a custom number format, use the formatting characters shown in Figure 14-30. Notice that you can include text strings in the format and specify a color to use to display the number on the screen.

FIGURE 14-30

The formatting characters for the Number and Currency data types.

Formatting Character(s)	Usage
Decimal separator	Use to indicate where you want Access to place the decimal point. Use the decimal separator defined in the Regional Settings section of the Windows Control Panel. In the English (United States) layout, the separator is a period (.).
Thousands separator	Use to indicate placement of the thousands separator character that is defined in the Regional Settings section of the Windows Control Panel. In the English (United States) layout, the separator is a comma (,).
0	Use to indicate digit display. If no digit exists in the number in this position, Access displays 0.
#	Use to indicate digit display. If no digit exists in the number in this position, Access displays a blank space.
- + $ ( ) or a blank space	Use these characters anywhere you want in your format string.
"*text*"	Use double quotation marks to embed any text you want displayed.

(continued)

FIGURE 14-30 *continued*

Formatting Character(s)	Usage
\	Use to always display the immediately following character (the same as including a single character in double quotes).
!	Use to force left alignment.
*	Use to generate the immediately following character as a fill character. Access normally displays formatted data right-aligned and filled with blank spaces to the left.
%	Use to multiply the value by 100 and include a trailing percent sign.
E- or e-	Use to generate scientific (exponential) notation and to display a minus sign preceding negative exponents. It must be used with other characters, as in *0.00E-00*.
E+ or e+	Use to generate scientific (exponential) notation and to display a minus sign preceding negative exponents and a plus sign preceding positive exponents. It must be used with other characters, as in *0.00E+00*.
[*color*]	Use brackets to display the text in the color specified. Valid color names are Black, Blue, Green, Cyan, Red, Magenta, Yellow, and White. A color name must be used with other characters, as in *0.00[Red]*.

For example, to display a number with two decimal places and comma separators when positive, enclosed in parentheses and shown in red when negative, *Zero* when *0*, and *Not Entered* when Null, you would specify the following:

    #,##0.00;(#,##0.00)[Red];"Zero";"Not Entered"

To format a U.S. phone number and area code from a numeric field, you would specify the following:

    (000) 000-0000

Text

If you don't specify a Format property setting for a control that displays a text value, Access displays the data in the control left-aligned. You can also specify a custom format with one to three entries separated by semicolons. If you include a second format specification, Access uses that specification to show Null and empty values. If you include a third format specification, Access uses the second specification to show empty values and the third specification to show Null values. Notice that when you specify formatting for text, Access displays the data in the control right-aligned.

If a text field contains more characters than the number of formatting characters you provide, Access uses up the formatting characters and then appends the extra characters at the end with the fill character (if any) in between. Figure 14-31 lists the formatting characters that are applicable to character strings.

Formatting Character(s)	Usage
@	Use to display any available character or a space in this position.
&	Use to display any available character in this position. If no characters are available to display, Access displays nothing.
<	Use to display all characters in lowercase.
>	Use to display all characters in uppercase.
- + $ ( ) or a blank space	Use these characters anywhere you want in your format string.
"*text*"	Use double quotation marks to embed any text you want displayed.
\	Use to always display the immediately following character (the same as including a single character in double quotes).
!	Use to force left alignment. This also forces placeholders to fill left to right instead of right to left.

(continued)

FIGURE 14-31 *continued*

Formatting Character(s)	Usage
*	Use to generate the immediately following character as a fill character. Access normally displays formatted data right-aligned and filled with blank spaces to the left. The asterisk must be used with other characters, as in >*@-@@@.
[*color*]	Use brackets to display the text in the color specified. Valid color names are Black, Blue, Green, Cyan, Red, Magenta, Yellow, and White. A color name must be used with other characters, as in >[*Red*].

For example, if you want to display a six-character part number with a hyphen between the second character and the third character, left-aligned, specify the following:

!@@-@@@@

To format a check amount string in the form of *Fourteen Dollars and 59 Cents* so that Access displays an asterisk (*) to fill any available space between the word *and* and the cents amount, specify the following:

**@@@@@@@@

Using the above format in a text box wide enough to display 62 characters, Access displays *Fourteen Dollars and 59 Cents* as

Fourteen Dollars and ********************************59 Cents

and *One Thousand Two Hundred Dollars and 00 Cents* as

One Thousand Two Hundred Dollars and *****************00 Cents

Date/Time

If you don't specify a Format property setting for a control that displays a Date/Time value, Access displays the date/time in the General Date format. You can also select one of the six other Format property settings shown in Figure 14-32 on the next page.

FIGURE 14-32

The Format
property
settings for
the Date/Time
data type.

Date/Time Format	Description
General Date	Displays the date as numbers separated by the date separator character. Displays the time as hours and minutes separated by the time separator character and followed by an AM/PM indicator. If the value has no time component, Access displays the date only. If the value has no date component, Access displays the time only. Example: 3/15/95 06:17 PM.
Long Date	Displays the date according to the Long Date setting in the Regional Settings section of the Windows Control Panel. Example: Wednesday, March 15, 1995.
Medium Date	Displays the date as dd-mmm-yy. Example: 15-Mar-95.
Short Date	Displays the date according to the Short Date setting in the Regional Settings section of the Windows Control Panel. Example: 3/15/95.
Long Time	Displays the time according to the Time setting in the Regional Settings section of the Windows Control Panel. Example: 6:17:12 PM.
Medium Time	Displays the time as hours and minutes separated by the time separator character and followed by an AM/PM indicator. Example: 06:17 PM.
Short Time	Displays the time as hours and minutes separated by the time separator character using a 24-hour clock. Example: 18:17.

You can also specify a custom format with one or two entries separated by semicolons. If you include a second format specification, Access uses that specification to show Null values. Figure 14-33 lists the formatting characters that are applicable to Date/Time data.

Formatting Character(s)	Usage
Time separator	Use to show Access where to separate hours, minutes, and seconds. Use the time separator defined in the Regional Settings section of the Windows Control Panel. In the English (United States) layout, the separator is a colon (:).
Date separator	Use to show Access where to separate days, months, and years. Use the date separator defined in the Regional Settings section of the Windows Control Panel. In the English (United States) layout, the separator is a forward slash (/).
c	Use to display the General Date format.
d	Use to display the day of the month as one or two digits, as needed.
dd	Use to display the day of the month as two digits.
ddd	Use to display the day of the week as a three-letter abbreviation. Example: Saturday = Sat.
dddd	Use to display the day of the week fully spelled out.
ddddd	Use to display the Short Date format.
dddddd	Use to display the Long Date format.
w	Use to display a number for the day of the week. Example: Sunday = 1.
ww	Use to display the week of the year (1–53).

FIGURE 14-33
The formatting characters for the Date/Time data type.

(continued)

FIGURE 14-33 *continued*

Formatting Character(s)	Usage
m	Use to display the month as a one-digit or two-digit number, as needed.
mm	Use to display the month as a two-digit number.
mmm	Use to display the name of the month as a three-letter abbreviation. Example: March = Mar.
mmmm	Use to display the name of the month fully spelled out.
q	Use to display the calendar quarter number (1–4).
y	Use to display the day of the year (1–366).
yy	Use to display the last two digits of the year.
yyyy	Use to display the full year value (within the range 0100–9999).
h	Use to display the hour as one or two digits, as needed.
hh	Use to display the hour as two digits.
n	Use to display the minutes as one or two digits, as needed.
nn	Use to display the minutes as two digits.
s	Use to display the seconds as one or two digits, as needed.
ss	Use to display the seconds as two digits.
ttttt	Use to display the Long Time format.
AM/PM	Use to display 12-hour clock values with trailing AM or PM, as appropriate.
A/P or a/p	Use to display 12-hour clock values with trailing A or P, as appropriate.

(continued)

FIGURE 14-33 *continued*

Formatting Character(s)	Usage
AMPM	Use to display 12-hour clock values using forenoon/afternoon indicators as specified in the Regional Settings section of the Windows Control Panel.
- + $ ( ) or a blank space	Use these characters anywhere you want in your format string.
"*text*"	Use quotation marks to embed any text you want displayed.
\	Use to always display the immediately following character (the same as including a single character in double quotes).
!	Use to force left alignment.
*	Use to generate the immediately following character as a fill character. Access normally displays formatted data right-aligned and filled with blank spaces to the left. The asterisk must be used with other characters, as in *A/P*#*.
[*color*]	Use brackets to display the text in the color specified. Valid color names are Black, Blue, Green, Cyan, Red, Magenta, Yellow, and White. A color name must be used with other characters, as in *ddddd[Red]*.

For example, to display a date as full month name, day, and year (say, *December 20, 1996*) with a color of cyan, you would specify the following:

mmmm dd, yyyy[Cyan]

Yes/No

You can choose from among three standard formats—Yes/No, True/False, or On/Off—to display Yes/No data type values, as shown in Figure 14-34 on the next page. The Yes/No format is the default. As you saw earlier, it's often more useful to display Yes/No values using a check box or an option button rather than a text box.

FIGURE 14-34

The Format
property settings
for the Yes/No
data type.

Yes/No Format	Description
Yes/No (the default)	Displays *0* as No and any nonzero value as Yes.
True/False	Displays *0* as False and any nonzero value as True.
On/Off	Displays *0* as Off and any nonzero value as On.

You can also specify your own custom word or phrase for Yes and No values. To do that, specify a format string containing three parts separated by semicolons. Leave the first part empty, specify a string enclosed in double quotation marks (and with an optional color modifier) in the second part for Yes values, and specify another string (also with an optional color modifier) in the third part for No values.

To display *Invoice Sent* in red for Yes and *Not Invoiced* in blue for No, you would specify the following:

;"Invoice Sent"[Red];"Not Invoiced"[Blue]

NOTE If you specify both an Input Mask setting (see Chapter 5, "Building Your Database in Microsoft Access") and a Format setting, Access uses the Input Mask setting to display data when you move the focus to the control and uses the Format setting at all other times. If you don't include a Format setting but do include an Input Mask setting, Access formats the data using the Input Mask setting. Be careful not to define a Format setting that conflicts with the Input Mask. For example, if you define an Input Mask setting for a phone number that looks like

!\(###") "000\-0000;0;_

(this stores the parentheses and hyphen with the data) and a Format setting that looks like

(&&&) @@@-@@@@

your data will display as

(206() 5) 55--1212

Adding a Scroll Bar

When you have a field that can contain a long data string (for example, the Comments field in the Students table), it's a good idea to provide a scroll bar in the control to make it easy to scan through all the data. This scroll bar appears whenever you select the control. If you don't add a scroll bar, you must use the arrow keys to move up and down through the data.

To add a scroll bar, first open the form in Design view. Select the control and open its property sheet. Then set the Scroll Bars property to Vertical. For example, if you open the frmStudent form in Form view and tab to (or click in) the Comments text box on the second page, the vertical scroll bar appears, as shown in Figure 14-35.

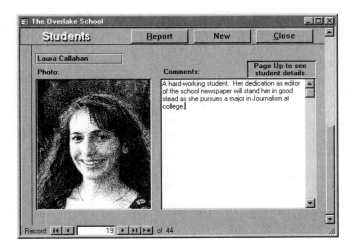

FIGURE 14-35
The Comments text box with a scroll bar added.

Enabling and Locking Controls

You might not want users of your form to select or update certain controls. You can set these conditions with the control's Enabled and Locked properties. For example, if you use a control to display an AutoNumber field, you can be certain that Access will provide the field's value. So it's a good idea to set the control's Enabled property to No (so that the user can't select it) and the control's Locked property to Yes (so that the user can't update it). Figure 14-36 on the next page shows the effects of the Enabled and Locked property settings.

FIGURE 14-36

The combinations
of settings for
the Enabled
and Locked
properties.

Enabled	Locked	Description
Yes	Yes	Control can have the focus. Data is displayed normally and can be copied but not changed.
No	No	Control can't have the focus. Control and data appear dimmed.
Yes	No	Control can have the focus. Data is displayed normally and can be copied and changed.
No	Yes	Control can't have the focus. Data is displayed normally but can't be copied or changed.

In some cases, you might want to allow a control to be selected with the mouse but to be skipped over as the user tabs through the controls on the form. You can set the control's Tab Stop property to No while leaving its Enabled property set to Yes. This might be useful for controls for which you also set the Locked property to Yes. Setting the Tab Stop property to No keeps the user from tabbing into the control, but the user can select the control with the mouse to use the Find command or to copy the data in the control to the Clipboard.

Setting Form Properties

The form itself has a number of properties that you can use to control its appearance and how it works.

The Default View and Views Allowed Properties

When the Form Wizard built the original Colleges form for you, it set the Default View property of the form to Single Form. This is the view you'll see first when you open the form. Note that with the Single Form setting, you can see only one record at a time. You have to use the record number box, the arrows to the left and right of the record number box, or the Go To command on the Records menu to move to another record. If you set the Default View property of the form to Continuous Forms, you can see multiple records on a short form, and you can use the scroll bar on the right side of the form to scroll through the records. Because one record's data in the Colleges table fills the form, the Single Form setting is probably the best choice.

Another property, Views Allowed, lets you control whether a user can change to the Datasheet view of the form. The default setting is Both, meaning that a user can use the toolbar or the View menu to switch between views. If you're designing a form to be used in an application, you will usually want to eliminate either Form or Datasheet view. For the Colleges form, set the Views Allowed property to Form; the Datasheet View option on the Form View toolbar button's drop-down list should become grayed out (disabled).

Setting the Tab Order

After the Form Wizard built the Colleges form, you moved several controls around and changed the CCompID control to a combo box and the Verified control to a check box. As you design a form, Access sets up the tab order for the controls in the order in which the controls are defined. When you delete a control and replace it with another, Access places the new control at the end of the tab order. You can set a different tab order, however. Choose the Tab Order command from the View menu to open the Tab Order dialog box, as shown in Figure 14-37.

FIGURE 14-37
The Tab Order dialog box.

As you can see, the CCompID and Verified controls don't appear where they should in the Custom Order list. Click the Auto Order button to reorder the controls so that the tab order corresponds to the arrangement of the controls on the form, from left to right and from top to bottom. You can make additional adjustments to the list by clicking the row selector for a control to highlight it and then clicking the row selector again and dragging the control to its new location in the list. Click OK to save your changes to the Custom Order list.

You can also change an individual control's place in the tab order by setting the control's Tab Index property. The Tab Index property of the first control on the form is *0*, the second is *1*, and so on. If you assign a new Tab Index setting to a control and some other control already has that Tab Index setting, Access reorders the Tab Index settings as if you had dragged the control to that relative position in the Tab Order dialog box.

The Record Selectors, Scroll Bars, and Navigation Buttons Properties

Because the Colleges form you've been designing displays one record at a time, it might not be useful to display the row selector on the left side of the form. You've also designed the form to show all the data in a single window, so a scroll bar along the right side of the window isn't necessary. You probably should keep the record number box at the bottom of the form, but you don't need the horizontal scroll bar. To make these changes, set the form's Record Selectors property on the property sheet to No, the Scroll Bars property to Neither, and the Navigation Buttons property to Yes. Your form should look something like the one shown in Figure 14-38.

FIGURE 14-38

The Colleges form without a row selector or scroll bars.

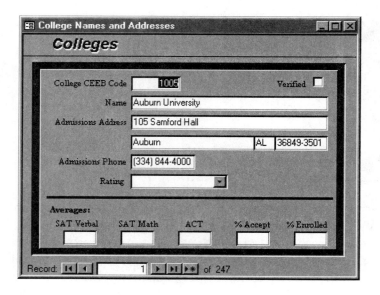

The Pop Up and Modal Properties

You might occasionally want to design a form that stays on top of all other forms even when it doesn't have the focus. Notice that the toolbox, property sheet, and field list in Design view all have this characteristic. These are called *pop-up forms.* You can make the Colleges form a pop-up form by setting the form's Pop Up property to Yes. Figure 14-39 shows the Colleges form as a pop-up form on top of the Database window that has the focus. (Note: If you play with the frmXmplCollege2 form to do this, be sure to set the form's Pop Up property back to No.)

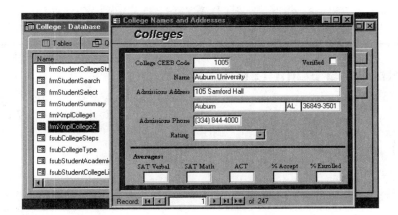

FIGURE 14-39
The Colleges form as a pop-up form on top of the Database window that has the focus.

As you'll learn in Part 6 of this book, it's sometimes useful to create forms that ask the user for information that's needed in order to perform the next task. Forms have a Modal property that you can set to Yes to "lock" the user into the form when it's open. The user must make a choice in the form or close the form in order to go on to other tasks. When a modal form is open, you can switch to another application, but you can't select any other form, menu, or toolbar button in Access until you dismiss the modal form. You've probably noticed that most dialog boxes are modal forms. Modal isn't a good choice for the Colleges form, but you'll use it later to help control application flow.

CAUTION   As you'll see later, you can set a form's Control Box property to No to remove all control features from the form's title bar. This means that both the Control-menu box (which contains the Close command) and the form's Close button (at the right end of the title bar) will not appear. If you also set the form's Modal property to Yes, the only way to close the form is to use the special Windows Ctrl-F4 key combination. You should always provide an alternative way to close a modal form, such as a Command button that runs a Close macro action. (See Chapter 18, "Advanced Report Design," for details.)

Controlling Editing and Filtering

You can set several properties on forms to control whether data in the form can be updated or whether data in the underlying tables can change. You can also prevent or allow user-applied filters on the form. These properties and their settings are as follows:

Allow Filters	Determines whether a user can see selected records by applying filtering and sorting criteria and whether the user can see all records by choosing the Show All Records command from the Records menu. If you set the Data Entry property to Yes and set the Allow Filters property to No, the user can enter only new data and cannot change the form to view other existing records. The valid settings for the Allow Filters property are Yes and No.
Allow Edits	Determines whether the user can change records in this form. The valid settings are Yes and No.
Allow Deletions	Determines whether a user can delete records in this form. The valid settings are Yes and No.
Allow Additions	Determines whether a user can add records using this form. The valid settings are Yes and No.
Data Entry	Determines whether the form opens a blank record in which you can insert new data. Access won't retrieve rows from the form's recordset. Allow Additions must be set to Yes to set Data Entry to Yes.

The Control Box and Min Max Buttons Properties

In some cases, you might want to prevent the user from opening the form's Control menu (the Control menu contains the Restore, Move, Size, Minimize, Maximize, Close, and Next commands) or to minimize or maximize the form. If you want to perform special processing before a form closes, you might want to provide a command button to do the processing and then close the form. You can set the form's Control Box property to No to remove the Control-menu box from the upper left corner of the form window and the Close button from the upper right corner. This also removes the Minimize and Maximize buttons.

You can set the form's Close Button property to No to remove the Close button but leave the Control-menu box (with Close disabled on the Control menu). You can set the form's Min Max Buttons property to Both Enabled, None, Min Enabled, or Max Enabled. If you disable a Minimize or Maximize button, the related command on the form's Control menu becomes grayed out. Finally, you can set the Whats This Button property to Yes to display the Help button, but you must set the Min Max Buttons property to No.

 CAUTION If you remove the form's Control-menu box, the only way you can close the form is to use the Ctrl-F4 key combination. If you create an *Autokeys* macro that intercepts the Ctrl-F4 key combination, you must provide an alternative way to close the form—most likely with a command button. See Chapter 18, "Advanced Report Design," for details on adding a command button to close a form.

Setting the Border Style

In most cases, you'll want to create forms with a normal border that allows you to size the window and move it around. Forms have a Border Style property that lets you define the look of the border and whether the window can be sized or moved. The Border Style property settings are shown on the next page.

None | The form has no borders, Control-menu box, title bar, or Minimize and Maximize buttons. You cannot resize or move the form when it is open. You can select the form and press Ctrl-F4 to close it unless the form's Pop Up property is set to Yes. You should provide an alternative way to close this type of form.

Thin | The form has a thin border, signifying that the form cannot be resized.

Sizable | This is the default setting. The form can be resized.

Dialog | If the Pop Up property is set to Yes, the form's border is a thick double line (like that of a true Windows dialog box), signifying that the form cannot be resized. If the Pop Up property is set to No, the Dialog setting is the same as the Thin setting.

Setting Form and Control Defaults

You can use the Set Control Defaults command on the Format menu to change the defaults for the various controls on your form. If you want to change the default property settings for all new controls of a particular type, select a control of that type, set the control's properties to the desired default values, and then choose the Set Control Defaults command from the Format menu. The settings of the currently selected control will become the default settings for any subsequent definitions of that type of control on your form.

For example, you might want all new labels to show blue text on a white background. To make this change, place a label on your form and set the label's Fore Color property to blue and its Back Color property to white using the Fore Color and Back Color toolbar buttons. Choose the Set Control Defaults command from the Format menu while this label is selected. Any new labels you place on the form will have the new default settings.

You can also create a special form to define new default properties for all your controls. To do this, open a new blank form, place controls on the form for which you want to define default properties, modify the properties of the controls to your liking, and save the form with the name *Normal*. The Normal form becomes your *form template*. Any new control that you place on a form (except forms for which you've already changed the default for one or more controls) will use the new default property settings you defined for that control type on the Normal form. To define a name other than *Normal* for your default form and report templates, choose Options from the Tools menu, and then click on the Forms/Reports tab.

Working with AutoFormat

After you define control defaults that give you the "look" you want for your application, you can also set these defaults as an AutoFormat that you can use in the Form Wizards. To create an AutoFormat definition, open the form that has the defaults set the way you want them, and then click the AutoFormat button on the toolbar or choose AutoFormat from the Format menu. Click the Customize button to open the dialog box shown in Figure 14-40. Select the "Create a new AutoFormat" option to save a format that matches the form you currently have open, and then click OK. In the next dialog box, type in a name for your new format, and then click OK. Your new format will now appear in the list of form AutoFormats. As you saw in Chapter 13, "Building Forms," you can select any of the defined form AutoFormats to dictate the look of a form created by the wizards.

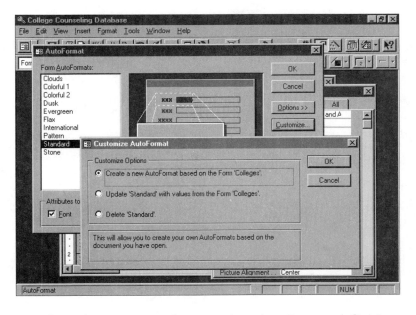

FIGURE 14-40

Creating a new AutoFormat definition.

If you have previously created an AutoFormat definition, you can update it or delete it using the AutoFormat dialog box. You cannot update or delete any of the built-in formats, however.

Now you should be comfortable with designing forms and adding special touches to make your forms more attractive and usable. In the next chapter, you'll learn advanced form design techniques: using multiple-table queries in forms, building forms within forms, and performing simple form linking using command buttons.

Chapter 15

Advanced
Form Design

n the two previous chapters, you learned how to design a form that works with data in a table and you saw how to display data from another table by using a combo box or a list box. In this chapter, you'll learn how to consolidate in a form the information from multiple tables. You'll find out how to:

- Create a form using a query that joins multiple tables
- Embed a subform in a main form so that you can work with related data from two tables or queries at the same time
- Create a form that spreads many data fields across multiple pages
- Link two related forms using a simple command button

Basing a Form on a Multiple-Table Query

In Chapter 8, "Adding Power with Select Queries," you learned how to bring together data from multiple tables using select queries. The result of a select query is called a *recordset*. A recordset contains all the information you need, but it's in the unadorned Datasheet view format. Forms enable you to present this data in a more attractive and meaningful way. And in the same way that you can update data in queries, you can also update data using a form that is based on a query.

A Many-to-One Form

As you discovered in the previous two chapters, it's easy to design a form that allows you to view and update the data from a single table. You also learned how to include selected single fields from related tables using a list box or a combo box. But what if you want to see more information from the related tables? The best way to do this is to design a query based on the two (or more) related tables and use that query as the basis of your form.

When you create a query with two or more tables, you're usually working with one-to-many relationships among the tables. As you learned earlier, Microsoft Access lets you update any data in the table that is on the "many" side of the relationship and any nonkey fields on the "one" side of the relationship. So when you base a form on a query, you can update all of the fields in the form that come from the "many" table and most of the fields from the "one" side. Because the primary purpose of the form is to search and update records on the "many" side of the relationship while reviewing information on the "one" side, this is called a *many-to-one form.*

In Chapter 8, you learned how to build a multiple-table query that displays both Club and Contract information in the Entertainment Schedule sample database. In Chapter 13, "Building Forms," you explored the fundamentals of form construction by creating a simple form to display club data. The key task in the Entertainment Schedule database is the creation of contracts that define which groups have agreed to play in which clubs on specific dates and for a specific fee. You clearly need a form to edit the tblContracts table to do this. While the tblContracts table does carry forward some of the details about the group (such as the names of the current group members), it has only the ClubID field to link you back to the club information. When you look at contract data in a form, you probably want to see more than just the club ID.

You learned near the end of Chapter 13 how to create a combo box control to display more meaningful data from the "one" side of a many-to-one relationship. You could use a combo box to display a club name instead of a number in the contract form. But what if you want to see the club address and manager name or phone number when you select a new club? And how can you make the current data from the tblGroups table available to procedures that you might create with the form to automatically copy over the current group information to a new contract? To perform these tasks, you need to base your contract form on a query that joins multiple tables.

Designing a Many-to-One Query

Open a new Query window in Design view and add the tblClubs, tblContracts, and tblGroups field lists using the Show Table dialog box that appears. You should see a relationship line from the ClubID field in the tblClubs field list to the ClubID field in the tblContracts field list. Similarly, you should see a relationship line linking the GroupID field in the tblGroups field list to the GroupID field in the tblContracts list. If you don't see these lines, you should close the Query window and switch back to the Database window, choose the Relationships command from the Tools menu, add the appropriate one-to-many relationships between the tblClubs and tblContracts tables and the tblGroups and tblContracts tables, and then open a new Query window and add the three field lists.

You want to be able to update all fields in the tblContracts table, so drag the special "all fields" indicator (*) from the tblContracts field list to the design grid. From the tblGroups table, you need most of the detail fields, such as group leader name (first and last name fields), address, phone numbers, and group size. Do not include the GroupID field from tblGroups; you want to be able to update the GroupID field, but only in the tblContracts table. If you include the GroupID field from the tblGroups table, it might confuse you later as you design the form. From the tblClubs table, you need fields such as manager name, address, phone numbers, days and times the club is open, and so forth.

You can find a query already built for this purpose in the Entertainment Schedule database named *qryXmplContracts*, as shown in Figure 15-1. If you explore the database and look up the row source for the frmContracts form, you'll discover that it uses the qryContracts query. In this query, many of the fields from the tblGroups table have been given aliases to make them easy to distinguish from fields of the same name in the tblContracts table. Also, the group leader name and the club manager name are each a single field in the tblContracts table but are separate first and last names in the original tables. This query uses expressions to concatenate these names into a single field. Finally, the query eliminates any contracts that have a deleted ("D") status code. There's no point in editing or cluttering up the display with contracts that have been deleted. For this example, the simpler query with only the names and addresses from the two tables related to contracts will do quite nicely.

FIGURE 15-1

The qryXmplContracts query in Design view.

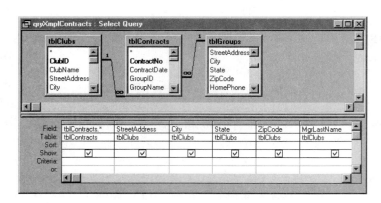

Designing a Many-to-One Form

Now that you have the query you need, find the query definition in the Database window and open a new form based on the query. You can use the Form Wizard if you like. From the tblContracts table, include the ContractNo, ContractDate, GroupID, ClubID, ContractPrice, Contract-Terms, BeginningDate, EndingDate, and NumberOfWeeks fields. From tblClubs, include the StreetAddress, City, State, ZipCode, MgrLastName, MgrFirstName, and DaysTimes fields. From tblGroups, select the Size, LeaderFirstName, LeaderLastName, StreetAddress, City, State, and Zip-Code fields. If you're using the Form Wizard, your field selections should be the same as those shown in Figure 15-2. Click Next to go to the second window of the wizard.

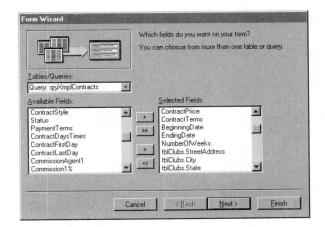

FIGURE 15-2

Selecting fields from a multiple-table query in the Form Wizard.

When you start with a query containing multiple tables or if you select fields from multiple tables in the first window of the Form Wizard, the wizard gives you some interesting choices if it can determine which tables are on the "one" side and which are on the "many." As you can see in Figure 15-3 on the next page, the wizard assumes that you want to see all the fields as a single view from the "many" (tblContracts) side of this relationship. If you select either "by tblClubs" or "by tblGroups" from the list on the left, the wizard changes the display on the right to offer either a main form and subform or linked forms. You'll learn about building subforms in the next section. If you select linked forms, the wizard creates two forms for you. The first form displays only the information from the "one" side (either tblGroups or tblClubs). A command button on the first form opens the second form, which displays the information from the "many" side (tblContracts).

FIGURE 15-3

Selecting a single form for fields from multiple tables.

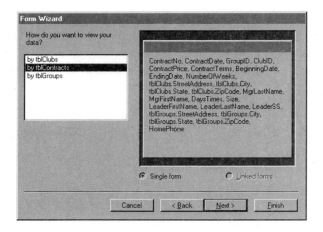

For now, select "by tblContracts" to see all the fields on one form. Select a columnar layout in the next window, and select the style you want in the window that follows. Give your form a title of *Contracts* in the last step. When the wizard finishes, you should see a form similar to that shown in Figure 15-4.

FIGURE 15-4

A "many-to-one" form to display data from multiple tables.

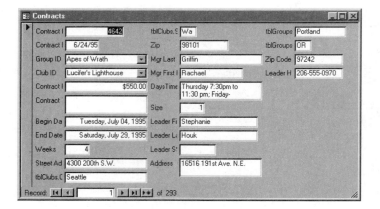

This form could use some polishing, but the wizard has very nicely placed everything on the form for us. Note the combo boxes for Group ID and Club ID. The wizard placed these on the form because the tblContracts table had Lookup properties set for both of these fields to display a more meaningful group or club name. Perhaps you can begin to appreciate how important it is to pay attention to these sorts of details when you design your table. Doing so will save you a lot of work as you build your application.

Try changing the club ID on the first contract to something else and watch what happens. You should see the corresponding manager name and club address information pop into view, as shown in Figure 15-5. Since you haven't done anything to set the Locked property for any of the fields, you can also update the address and city information for the displayed club. If you do this, the new club information appears for all contracts created for that club.

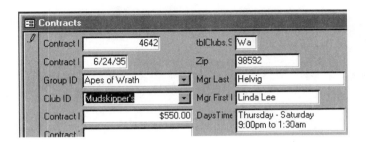

FIGURE 15-5
Changing the club ID automatically displays new related club information.

You'll discover later when you explore the actual frmContracts form that the query automatically pulls in the related "one" side information if you change the foreign key on the "many" side. In the contracts form in the application, Visual Basic for Applications (VBA) code behind the form runs whenever you change either the club ID or the group ID. This code copies the new data to the appropriate fields in the contracts table. Since this sample form isn't designed to do that yet, you shouldn't change the club ID or the group ID in too many contracts using this form.

Creating and Embedding Subforms

If you want to show data from several tables and be able to update the data in more than one of the tables, you probably need to use something more complex than a standard form. In the College Counseling database, the main college information is in the Colleges table. Colleges can be categorized in many different ways—Public or Private; College or University; Rural, Small Town, Urban, or Suburban; and so forth. The CollegeTypes table lists all the possible categories tracked by this database.

Because any one college might be classified in many different ways and any college type might apply to many colleges, the Colleges table is related to the CollegeTypes table in a many-to-many relationship. (See Chapter 5, "Building Your Database in Microsoft Access," for a review of relationship types.) The CollegeTypeLink table establishes the necessary link between the colleges and their classifications.

When you are viewing information about a particular college, you might also want to see and edit the classification information. You could create a single form that displays Colleges joined with CollegeTypeLink, similar to the frmContracts form you built in the previous section. However, the focus would be on the links, so you would see many records in the form for the same college—one for each different classification for each college.

Subforms can help solve this problem. You can create an outer form that displays the college information (you already did this in the two previous chapters) and embed in it a subform that displays all the related rows from the linking table. If you use a combo box on the subform, you can display the names of the classifications that match the codes in the CollegeTypeLink table.

Specifying the Subform Source

You can embed forms within forms up to three layers deep. It's often easier to start by designing the innermost form and working outward. Begin by deciding on the data source for the subform.

In the example described above, you want to create or update rows in the CollegeTypeLink table to create, modify, or destroy links between colleges in the Colleges table and college classifications in the CollegeTypes table. You also want to modify the display because the CollegeTypeLink table contains only the two linking fields—not very useful information to display on a form. You need to make sure that the Lookup properties for the CTypeID are set to display the classification names from the CollegeTypes table. (They are.) Since it makes sense to sort the data by the classification name, you need to include the CollegeTypes table in the subform data source so you can sort by the name, not by the code.

Start by opening a new query in Design view. In the Show Table dialog box, add the field lists for the CollegeTypeLink and CollegeTypes tables to the Query window. You want to be able to update all the fields in the CollegeTypeLink table, so copy them to the design grid. Add the CTypeName field from the CollegeTypes table so that you can sort on it (in ascending order). Deselect the Show check box because you don't need this field in your subform. Your query should look similar to the one shown in Figure 15-6.

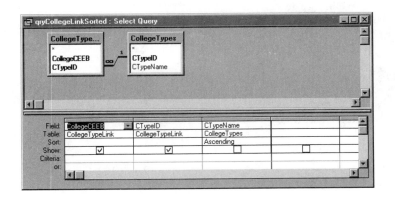

FIGURE 15-6
A query for updating the CollegeTypeLink table from a subform.

Notice that the CollegeTypes table has a one-to-many relationship with the CollegeTypeLink table. This means that you can update any field in the CollegeTypeLink table (including both primary key fields as long as you don't create a duplicate row) because the CollegeTypeLink table is on the "many" side of the relationship. Save the query and name it *qryCollegeLinkSorted* so that you can use it as you design the subform. (If you're working in the College Counseling database, you'll find this query already defined.)

Designing the Subform

You'll end up displaying the single CTypeID field bound to a combo box that shows the classification names. For this purpose, a form in Datasheet view will do quite nicely. Start by opening a new form based on the qryCollegeLinkSorted query you just created. Try creating the form without using the Form Wizard.

Figure 15-7 on the next page shows the design for the subform. Once you're in Design view for the subform, you need only drag and drop the CTypeID field onto the detail area of the subform. Again, because the Lookup properties are defined properly in the source table, you get the combo box that you want. All you have left to do is to set the subform's Default View property to Datasheet, set the Scroll Bars property to Vertical Only (it would be silly to have a horizontal scroll bar for one field), and set the Navigation Buttons property to No (you can use the vertical scrollbar to move through the multiple rows).

FIGURE 15-7

The new
subform in
Design view.

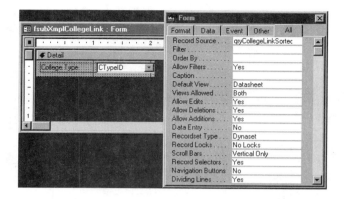

You need to switch to the subform's Datasheet view to make a few adjustments. You can see the datasheet in Figure 15-8. Since you'll be using the subform in Datasheet view when it's embedded in the frmCollege form, you have to adjust how the datasheet looks and save the subform from Datasheet view to preserve the look you want. Note that the single column has inherited its caption from the label attached to the combo box in Design view. The label must be attached to the combo box for this to work. If the label isn't attached, you'll see the field's name displayed—it won't even inherit the caption property from the field.

FIGURE 15-8

The new
subform in
Datasheet
view.

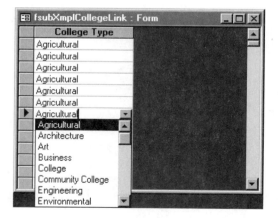

You can drop down one of the combo boxes to make sure it's wide enough to display the widest college type description. You can also choose Font from the Format menu to make sure the datasheet font matches what you'll be using on the main form. Note that the datasheet font is independent of the font you might have selected for the combo box in Design view; you must set the datasheet font in Datasheet view. Once the datasheet looks the way you want, choose Save As from the File menu. You can find this example saved as *fsubXmplCollegeLink* in the College Counseling database.

Specifying the Main Form Source

Now it's time to move on to the main form. You need a table or a query as the source of the form. You want to be able to view, update, add, and delete colleges, so you can use the Colleges table as the source. In this case, it might be a good idea to sort the college data by state and then by city. Start a new query on the Colleges table and include all the fields in the design grid. Drag the State field so that it comes before the City field in the design grid. (You'll recall from Chapter 8, "Adding Power with Select Queries," that the sequence of fields in the design grid is important for sorting.) Set both the State and City fields to Ascending sorting order. Your query should look something like that shown in Figure 15-9.

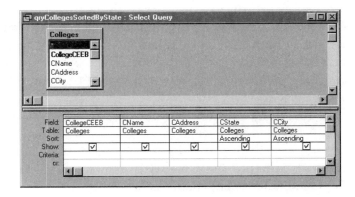

FIGURE 15-9

A query for updating the Colleges table from a main form.

Creating the Main Form

Building the form for the Colleges table is fairly straightforward. In fact, you can select the query you just created and use a Form Wizard to build the basic form in columnar format. I actually started with the frm-XmplCollege1 form we built in Chapter 13, "Building Forms"; changed the record source to point to the sorted query; and moved a few things around. The sample design shown in Figure 15-10 on the next page has a space just above the Rating control where you can place the subform to display classification data.

FIGURE 15-10

A main form
to display
college data,
with space
for a subform.

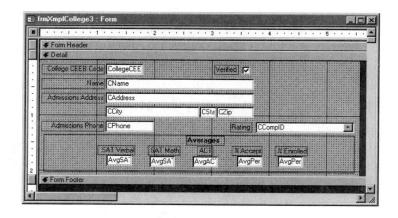

Embedding a Subform

You can use a couple of techniques to embed the subform in your main form. First, you can deselect the Control Wizards button in the toolbox, select the Subform/Subreport tool in the toolbox, and then click on the upper left corner of the main form's free area and drag the mouse pointer to create a subform control. If you leave the Control Wizards active, Access starts a wizard to help you build a subform from scratch when you create the subform control on your main form. Since you already built the subform, you don't need that bit of help. Once the control is in place, set its Source Object property to point to the subform you built.

Another way to embed the subform (if you have a big enough screen to do this) is to place the Form window and the Database window side by side, find the form you want to embed as a subform, and then drag and drop it from the Database window onto your form. In any case, your result should look something like Figure 15-11.

Access should be able to readily identify that the CollegeCEEB field on the main form matches the same field on the subform. If you create any other form or subform in this way, you should check the subform control's Link Child Fields and Link Master Fields properties to be sure that Access has linked the forms correctly. When the subform links to the main form with multiple fields, you must enter the field names in these properties in sequence and separate the names with semicolons.

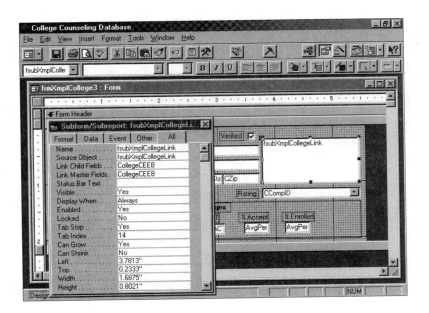

FIGURE 15-11

The new subform embedded in the frmCollege form.

NOTE If the source of the subform contains a table related to a table in the source of the main form, and if you've defined a relationship between the two tables, Access generates the link properties (Link Master Fields and Link Child Fields) for you using the related fields when you drag and drop the subform onto the main form. Access also links a subform to a main form when you embed a subform control in the main form and then set the Source Object to a form that contains a related table.

Sizing a subform that you display in Form view is quite simple. Choose the subform control, and then choose Size/To Fit from the Format menu. In this case, you're using a subform in Datasheet view, so unless the form's Design view is exactly the same size as the datasheet, using Size/To Fit won't work. You have to switch in and out of Form view and manually adjust the size of the subform control.

When you finish, click the Form View button on the toolbar to see the completed form, as shown in Figure 15-12 on the next page. If you see a partial row displayed on the subform, return to Design view and adjust the height of the subform control. You can find this sample form saved as *frmXmplCollege3* in the College Counseling database.

FIGURE 15-12
The frmCollege
form with a
subform.

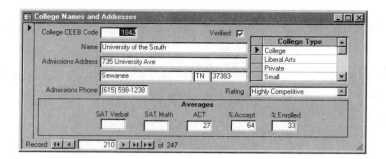

By the way, you can also use a Form Wizard to create a form or a subform. The wizard creates a single-column form for the main form and a Datasheet view of the subform.

Creating Multiple-Page Forms

As you've seen, Microsoft Access makes it easy to display a lot of related information about one subject in a single form either by using a query as the source of the form or by displaying the related information in a subform. But what do you do if you have too much information to fit in a single, screen-sized form? One possibility to consider is splitting the form into multiple "pages."

You can create a form that's up to 22 logical inches high. If you're working on a basic 640×480 pixel screen, you cannot see more than about 3 logical inches vertically at one time (if toolbars are displayed). If the information you need to make available in the form won't fit in that design height, you can split the form into multiple pages using a page break control. When you view the form, you can use the PgUp and PgDn keys to move smoothly through the pages.

Creating a smoothly working multiple-page form takes a bit of planning. First, you should plan to make all pages the same height. You should also design the form so that the page break control is in a horizontal area by itself. If the page break control overlaps other controls, your data might display across the page boundary. You also need to know that when you set the form's Auto Resize property to Yes, Access sizes the form to the largest page. If the pages aren't all the same size, you'll get choppy movement using the PgUp and PgDn keys.

The frmStudent form in the College Counseling database is a good example of a multiple-page form. If you open the form in Design view and select the Detail section of the form, you can see that the height of this area is 6.5 inches, as shown in Figure 15-13. If you click on the page break control shown at the left edge of the Detail section in Figure 15-13, you'll find that it's set at exactly 3.25 inches from the top of the page.

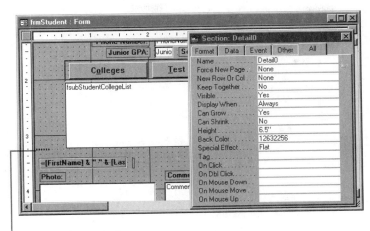

Page break control

FIGURE 15-13
The frmStudent form with a page break control added.

When you look at this form in Form view (as shown in Figures 15-14 and 15-15) and use the PgUp and PgDn keys, you'll see that the form moves smoothly from page to page. (You need to open this form from the Database window, not from Design view, to get it to size properly.) In fact, if you're on the second page of the form and you press PgDn again, you'll move smoothly to the second page of the next record. Note that certain key information (such as the student name) is duplicated on the second page so that it's always clear what record you're editing.

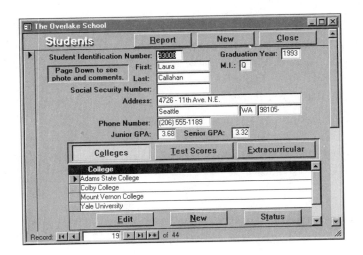

FIGURE 15-14
The first page of the frmStudent form.

533

FIGURE 15-15

The second
page of the
Students form.

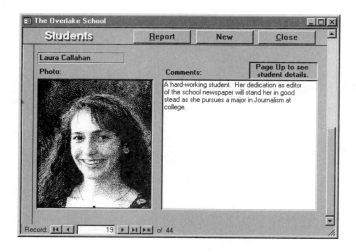

Linking Forms with a Command Button

One of the most useful features of Access is its ability to trigger macros or VBA procedures when events occur on forms. Let's go back to the Entertainment Schedule database for this example. Suppose you're browsing through the club records. Once you find a club that interests you, wouldn't it be nice to have an easy way to see all the contracts for the current club? Although later you'll learn how to do this with VBA, it's easy to create a macro and a command button to accomplish the same thing.

Creating a Macro

If you've looked at any of the form or control property sheets in any detail, you've probably noticed several properties with names such as *On Load, Before Update, On Close,* and the like. These properties refer to events for which you can define actions that Access will execute when the event happens. For example, selecting a control, clicking a button, and typing characters in a text box are events to which Access can respond.

You can use a macro to define most of the actions you'll ever need. Access also gives you the option of handling events with VBA—either as procedures attached to forms and reports or as procedures in separate modules. (You'll learn more about both macros and VBA in the last part of this book.)

Macros provide more than 40 different actions that you can use as responses to events. To define a simple macro, go to the Database window, click on the Macros tab, and then click the New button. Access opens the Macro window, as shown in Figure 15-16. The Macro window looks a lot like the Table window in Design view and works in much the same way. You enter action names and comments in the upper part of the window, and you use the F6 function key to jump down to the lower part of the window to set arguments for each action. When you select an action in the upper part of the window, Access asks for the appropriate arguments in the lower part the window. You don't even have to remember the names of all the actions. If you click in the Action column, Access displays a down arrow button that you can click to reveal a list of all macro actions.

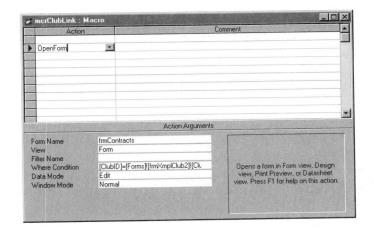

FIGURE 15-16

A macro that opens the frmContracts form.

It's time to try creating your own macro. Your macro will open the frmContracts form in the Entertainment Schedule database. Open a new Macro window and move the window to the side a bit so that you can see the Database window. Find the frmContracts form in the Database window, and drag and drop it onto the upper part of the Macro window. When you drop a form onto a Macro window, Access creates an OpenForm action for you with all the correct arguments filled in, as shown in Figure 15-16.

You might want to type an appropriate comment in the Comment field next to the OpenForm action. In this example, you want the frmContracts form to show only the contracts for the club displayed in the frmXmplClub2 form (which you created in Chapter 13, "Building

Forms"). To do this, you need to put a condition on the OpenForm action. Type the following in the Where Condition argument text box:

[ClubID]=[Forms]![frmXmplClub2]![ClubID]

You'll learn more about referencing open forms later. The argument you just typed in asks Access to open the requested form "where the ClubID in the records in the form you are opening matches the ClubID in the form called frmXmplClub2." Now all you have to do is save your macro. Choose the Save As command from the File menu, and give your macro a name. You can find this macro saved as *mcrClubLink* in the sample database.

Adding a Command Button

It's easy to create a command button for your newly created macro. Open the frmXmplClub2 form in Design view. Choose Header/Footer from the View menu and add a label, leaving some room on the right end of the header. Move the Form window to the side a bit so that you can see the Database window. Locate your new *mcrClubLink* macro in the Database window, and drag and drop it onto the Form Header section of your form. Access creates a command button that runs the macro you selected. Change the caption of the Command button to *Contracts*. Set the ControlTip Text property to *Show Contracts for this Club*. The result is shown in Figure 15-17.

FIGURE 15-17
A Contracts
command button
added to the
Clubs form.

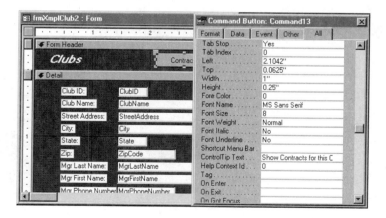

Choose Save As from the File menu and save the form as *frmXmplClub2* (or you can rename the *frmXmplClub2a* form that's already in the sample database). Open the form in Form view. Place the mouse pointer over the command button for a second (but don't click) to see the new ToolTip, as shown in Figure 15-18.

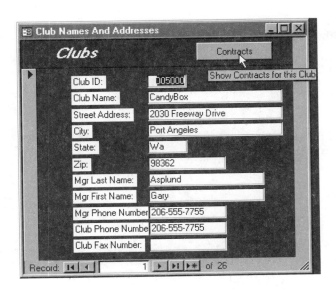

FIGURE 15-18
The Clubs form command button shows a ToolTip.

Click the command button and the frmContracts form opens, showing the contracts for the club you currently have displayed in the first form, as shown in Figure 15-19.

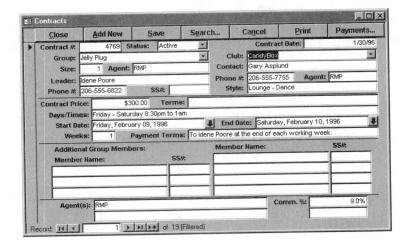

FIGURE 15-19
The frmContracts form opens when you click the new command button on the Clubs form.

This is the last chapter on forms. You'll learn a few more design tricks when you start to build an application using macros and VBA in Part 6 of this book. Now it's time to learn about reports in Part 5.

PART 5

Creating Reports

Chapter 16

Report Basics

In previous chapters you learned that you can format and print tables and queries in Datasheet view and that this technique is useful for producing printed copies of simple lists of information. You also learned that you can use forms not only to view and modify data, but also to print data—including data from several tables. However, because the primary function of forms is to allow you to view single records or small groups of related records displayed on screen in an attractive way, forms aren't the best way to print and summarize large sets of data in your database.

This chapter explains when you should use a report instead of another method of printing data, and it describes the features that reports offer. The examples in this chapter are based on the College Counseling and Entertainment Schedule sample databases. After you learn what you can do with reports, you'll look at the process of building reports in the following two chapters.

Uses of Reports

Reports are the best way to create a printed copy of information that is extracted or calculated from data in your database. Reports have two principal advantages over other methods of printing data:

- Reports can compare, summarize, and subtotal large sets of data.

- Reports can be created to produce attractive invoices, purchase orders, mailing labels, presentation materials, and other output you might need in order to efficiently conduct business.

Reports are designed to group data, to present each grouping separately, and to perform calculations. They work as follows:

- You can define up to 10 grouping criteria to separate the levels of detail.

- You can define separate headers and footers for each group.

- You can perform complex calculations not only within a group or a set of rows but also across groups.

- In addition to page headers and footers, you can define a header and a footer for the entire report.

As with forms, you can embed pictures or graphs in any section of a report. You can also embed subreports or subforms within report sections.

A Tour of Reports

You can explore reports by examining the features of the sample reports in the College Counseling and Entertainment Schedule databases. A good place to start is the rptContractStatusByGroupAll report in the Entertainment Schedule database. Open the database and go to the Database window. (If you let the application start, click the Exit button on the main switchboard form.) Click on the Reports tab and scroll down the list of reports until you see the rptContractStatusByGroupAll report, as shown in Figure 16-1. Double-click on the report name (or select it and click the Preview button) to see the report in Print Preview—a view of how the report will look when printed.

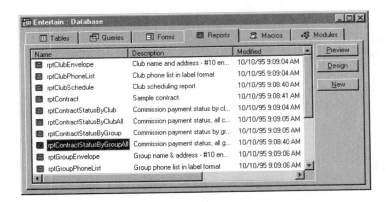

FIGURE 16-1
The Reports list in the Database window.

Print Preview—A First Look

The rptContractStatusByGroupAll report is based on the qryActivePaidContracts query, which brings together information from the tblClubs, tblContracts, and tblCommissions tables. When the report opens in Print Preview, you'll see a view of the report in the Contract Status By Group window, as shown in Figure 16-2 on the next page. When you open the report from the Database window, the report shows information for all active contracts. If you start the application (by opening frmCopyright), click the Reports button on the main switchboard form, and then click the Group Contract Status button on the Reports switchboard form, you'll see a dialog form that displays the status for only a selected group or a specific date range.

FIGURE 16-2

The rptContract-
StatusByGroupAll
report in Print
Preview.

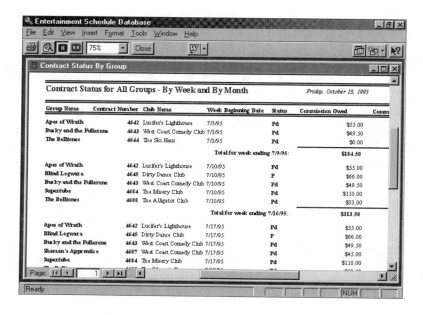

You can expand the window in Print Preview to see a large portion of the rptContractStatusByGroupAll report at one time. Use the vertical and horizontal scroll bars to position the report so that you can see most of the upper half of the first page, as shown in Figure 16-2. You can also use the arrow keys to move up, down, left, and right. If you are using a standard VGA screen (640×480 pixels), select 75% in the Zoom Control box on the toolbar (as shown) to see a bit more of the report.

To view other pages of the report, use the page number box at the bottom left of the window, as shown in Figure 16-3. To move forward one page at a time, click the arrow button immediately to the right of the page number box. You can also click on the page number (or press F5 to select the page number), change the number, and press Enter to skip to the page you want. As you might guess, the arrow button immediately to the left of the page number box moves you back one page, and the two outer arrows (each pointing to a vertical bar) on either end of the page number box move you to the first or last page of the report. You can also move to the top of the page by pressing Ctrl-up arrow, move to the bottom of the page by pressing Ctrl-down arrow, move to the left margin of the page by pressing Home or Ctrl-left arrow, and move to the right margin of the page by pressing End or Ctrl-right arrow. Pressing Ctrl-Home moves you to the upper left corner of the page, and pressing Ctrl-End moves you to the lower right corner of the page.

FIGURE 16-3
The page number box in a Report window in Print Preview.

Headers, Detail Sections, Footers, and Groups

Although the rptContractStatusByGroupAll report shown in Figure 16-2 looks simple at first glance, it actually contains a lot of information. On the first page you can see a report header that displays a title for the report and the date on which you open the report. Below that is a page header that appears at the top of every page. As you'll see later when you learn to design reports, you can choose whether to print this header on the page that also displays the report header.

The data in this report is grouped by week and then by month. You could, if you wanted, print a heading for each group in your report. This report could easily be designed, for example, to display the month name in a header line, the beginning date of the week in another header line, and then the related detail lines. (Since the dates are repeated in the detail line in this report, adding those headers seems redundant.)

Next, Access prints the detail information, one line for each row in the recordset formed by the query. In the Detail section of a report, you can add unbound controls to calculate a result using any of the columns in the record source. You can also calculate percentages over a group or over the entire report by including a control that provides a summary in the group or report footers and then referencing that control name in a percentage calculation in the Detail section. Access can do this because its report writer can look at the detail data twice—once to calculate any group or grand totals and a second time to calculate expressions that reference those totals.

On the first or second page of the report, you can see the group footer for one of the weeks and the group footer for the first month, as shown in Figure 16-4 on the next page. If you scroll down to the bottom of the page you'll see a page number, which is in the page footer.

FIGURE 16-4
The rptContract-
StatusByGroupAll
report has sub-
totals by week
and by month.

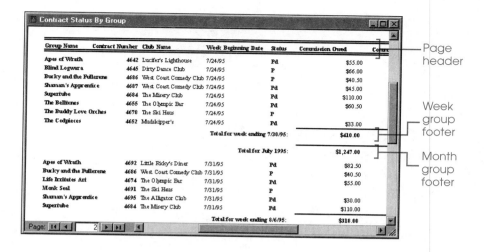

If you skip to the last page of the report (about page 40—note that the page number might vary slightly depending on the printer you're using), you can see the total calculations for the last weeks and the last month, plus the grand total commission for the report, as shown in Figure 16-5. The grand total is in the report footer.

NOTE If you're working in a report with many pages, it might take a long time to move to the first or last page or back one page. You can press Esc to cancel your movement request. Microsoft Access displays the most recent page it attempted to format.

FIGURE 16-5
The rptContract-
StatusByGroupAll
report's grand
total calculation
is in the report
footer.

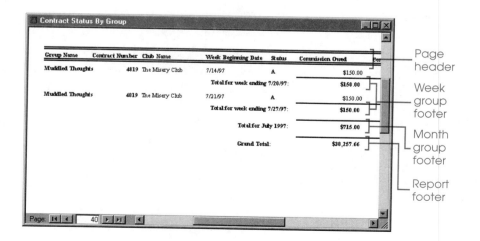

Subreports

Just as you can embed subforms within forms, you can also embed subreports (or subforms) within reports. Subreports are particularly useful for showing related details or totals for the records that make up the source rows of your report. For example, you can create a report to calculate grand totals by quarter and then embed that report as a subreport in one of the headers of your main report. In the College Counseling database, the student information includes related colleges, test scores, and extracurricular activities. The college information includes related application steps and classification data. You can place the detail data (application steps or classification types) in a subreport and then embed that subreport in the detail section of a report that displays college data—much as you did for the frmCollege form exercise in the previous chapter.

You can see an example of this use of a subreport in the rptCollege report and in the rsubCollegeSteps and rsubCollegeType subreports in the College Counseling database. Open the College Counseling database and switch to the Database window. (If you let the application start, click the Exit button on the main switchboard form to return to the Database window.) Open the rsubCollegeSteps subreport in Design view by selecting the subreport in the Database window and then clicking the Design button, as shown in Figure 16-6. The Report window in Design view is shown in Figure 16-7 on the next page.

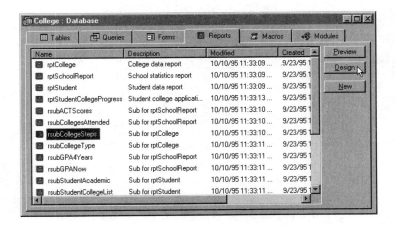

FIGURE 16-6

The rsubCollege-Steps subreport about to be opened in Design view.

FIGURE 16-7

The Report
window for the
rsubCollegeSteps
subreport in
Design view.

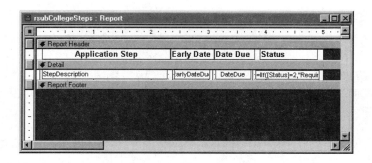

Notice that this subreport looks very much like a normal report
with Report Header and Detail sections. If you look at the Record
Source property for the subreport, you'll find that it uses the
CollegeSteps table, which has a CollegeCEEB code field but no other
meaningful information about which step belongs to which college. In
fact, this subreport doesn't display any college information at all. Open
the subreport in Print Preview. You'll see a simple list of various application steps, as shown in Figure 16-8.

FIGURE 16-8

The rsubCollege-
Steps subreport
in Print Preview.

Application Step	Early Date	Date Due	Status
SAT		12/15	Required
SAT II		12/15	Required
Application part 1		12/15	Required
Application part 2		12/15	Required
School report		12/15	Required
Interview		12/15	Required
Campus visit		12/15	Recommended
Counselor recommendation		12/15	Required
FAFSA		12/15	Recommended
SAT		01/01	Required
Application part 1		01/01	Required
Application part 2		01/01	Required
School report		01/01	Required
Campus visit		01/01	Recommended
Counselor recommendation		01/01	Required

Close the subreport and run the rptCollege report, shown in Figure 16-9. Notice as you move from page to page that the data displayed
in the two subreports changes to match the currently displayed college.
The data from the rsubCollegeSteps subreport now makes sense within
the context of a particular college. Access links the data from each subreport in this example using the Link Master Fields and Link Child

Fields properties of the subreport (which are set to the linking CollegeCEEB field)—just like the subform you created in the previous chapter.

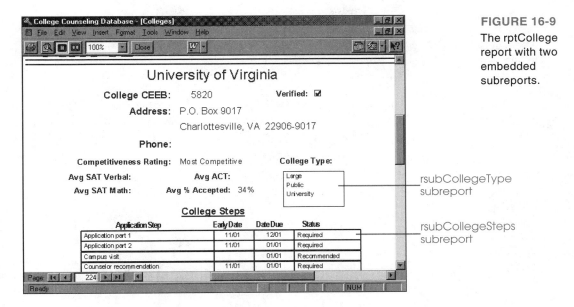

FIGURE 16-9
The rptCollege report with two embedded subreports.

As you'll see in the next section when we examine some features of the rptStudent report, that report also uses subreports to link information from three related tables to each displayed row from the Students table.

Objects in Reports

As with forms, you can embed OLE (Object Linking and Embedding) objects in reports. The objects embedded in or linked to reports are usually pictures or charts. You can embed a picture or a chart as an unbound object in the report itself, or you can link a picture or a chart as a bound object from data in your database.

The rptStudent report in the College Counseling database has both unbound and bound objects. When you open the rptStudent report in Print Preview, you can see the Overlake School logo (a stylized font graphic) embedded in the report title as an unbound bitmap image object, as shown in Figure 16-10 on the next page. This object is actually a part of the report design.

FIGURE 16-10

An unbound
bitmap image
object (the
Overlake
School logo)
embedded in
the rptStudent
report.

**College
Counseling**

Nancy Q. Davolio

If you scroll down the first page of the report, you can see a picture displayed on the form, as shown in Figure 16-11. This picture is a bound bitmap image object from the Students table (a picture of the student—in this case borrowed from the Northwind Traders sample database's employee data).

FIGURE 16-11

A bound bitmap
image object
displayed in the
rptStudent report.

Nancy Q. Davolio

Class of	1992
Student ID:	92001
Address:	507 - 20th Ave. E.
	Seattle, WA 98122
Phone:	(206) 555-9857
Junior GPA:	3.3
Senior GPA:	3.45

Colleges applied to

College Name	Applied	Accepted	Attended
Adams State College	Yes	Yes	No
Alcorn State University	Yes	Yes	Yes
Bethel College	Yes	No	No

Printing Reports

Earlier in this chapter you learned the basics of viewing a report in Print Preview. Here are a few more tips and details about setting up reports for printing.

Print Setup

Before you print a report, you might first want to check its appearance and then change the printer setup. Select the rptStudent report (which you looked at earlier) in the Database window, and click the Preview button to run the report. After Microsoft Access shows you the report, click the Zoom button and then enlarge the window to see the full-page view. Click the Two Pages button to see the first two pages side-by-side, as shown in Figure 16-12. This report is narrow enough to print two pages side-by-side in landscape mode on 14-inch-long paper. To print it that way, you need to modify some parameters in the Page Setup dialog box.

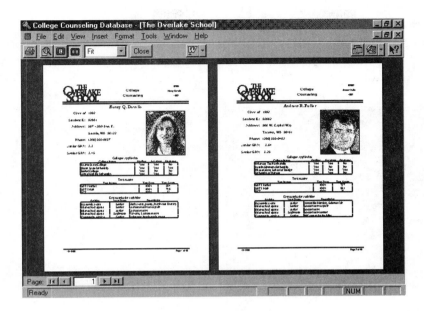

FIGURE 16-12

The two-page view of the rptStudent report in Print Preview.

Open the Page Setup dialog box by choosing Page Setup from the File menu. (You can also define the page setup for any report without opening the report: Select the report in the Database window and choose Page Setup from the File menu.) Access displays a dialog box similar to the one shown in Figure 16-13.

FIGURE 16-13

The Page Setup dialog box.

To print the rptStudent report with two logical pages per physical page, you first need to adjust the margins as shown in Figure 16-13. You haven't changed the page orientation yet, so the settings that are currently the "top" and "bottom" will become the "left" and "right" margins once you rotate the page. The pages need to print very close to the edge of the paper, so set the top and bottom margins to .25 inch and set the left and right margins to .5 inch. Click on the Page tab to display the next set of available properties, as shown in Figure 16-14.

FIGURE 16-14
The Page tab of the Page Setup dialog box.

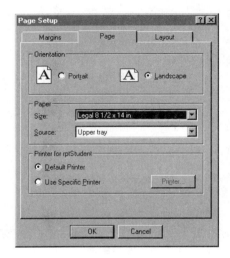

On the Page tab, you can select the orientation of the printed page—Portrait to print vertically down the length of the page or Landscape to print horizontally across the length of the page. Since we're trying to print two pages across a single sheet of paper, select the Landscape option. The report is also about 6½ inches wide, so you'll need wider paper to fit two logical pages to a printed page. Select 8½-by-14-inch paper.

In general, it's best to leave the printer set to the default printer that you specified in your Windows 95 settings. If you move your application to another computer that's attached to a different type of printer, you won't have to change the settings. You can print any report you design in Access to any printer supported by Windows 95 with good results. However, if you've designed your report to print on a specific printer, you can save those settings via the Page Setup dialog box. On the Page tab, select the Use Specific Printer option, and then click the Printer button to open an additional dialog box in which you can select any printer installed on your system. Click the Properties button in that dialog box to adjust settings for that printer in the Properties dialog box shown in Figure 16-15. Note that the Properties dialog box you see might look different depending on the capabilities of the printer you selected and how Windows 95 supports that printer.

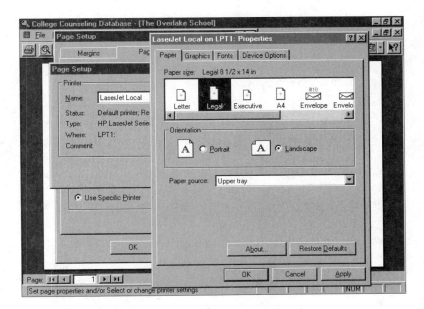

FIGURE 16-15
Setting properties for a specific printer.

After you set the page orientation to Landscape, click on the Layout tab as shown in Figure 16-16 on the next page to set up a multiple-column report. In this case, you want to print two "columns" of information. After you set the Items Across property to a value greater than 1 (in this case, 2), you can set spacing between rows and spacing between columns. You can also set a custom width and height that are larger or smaller than the underlying report design size. Note that if you specify a smaller size, Access crops the report. When you have detail data that fits in more than one column or row, you can also tell Access whether you want the detail produced down and then across the page or vice versa.

FIGURE 16-16
Setting report
layout properties.

After you enter the settings shown in Figures 16-13, 16-14, and 16-16, your report in Print Preview should look like the one shown in Figure 16-17.

FIGURE 16-17
The rptStudent
report in Print
Preview displayed
in landscape
orientation and in
two columns.

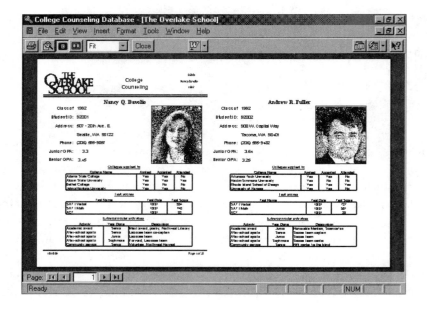

NOTE If you created the report or have modify design permission for the report, you can change the page layout settings and save them with the report. The next time you print
or view the report, Access will use the last page layout settings you specified. All of the reports in the sample databases were created using the default "Admin" user ID. If
you start Access without security or sign on with the default
ID, you will have full ownership of all objects in the sample
databases.

That covers the fundamentals of reports and how to view them
and set them up for printing. The next two chapters show you how to
design and build reports for your application.

Chapter 17

Constructing a Report

onstructing a report is very similar to building a form. In this chapter, you'll apply many of the techniques that you used in working with forms, and you'll learn about some of the unique features of reports. After a quick tour of the report design facilities, you'll build a simple report for the Entertainment Schedule database, and then you'll use a Report Wizard to create the same report.

Starting from Scratch— A Simple Report

You're most likely to use a report to look at the "big picture," so you'll usually design a query that brings together data from several related tables as the basis for the report. In this section, you'll build a relatively simple report as you tour the report design facilities. The report you'll build uses the tblClubs and tblContracts tables in the Entertainment Schedule sample database. The report groups contract data by club, prints a single summary line for each contract, and calculates the number of contracts, the total number of booked weeks, and the total contract amount for each club.

Building the Report Query

To construct the underlying query for the report, you need the ContractNo, GroupName, BeginningDate, and NumberOfWeeks fields from the tblContracts table. Create a new query based on the tblContracts table, and then add these fields to the design grid. You need to create one calculated field in your query that multiplies NumberOfWeeks times ContractPrice to determine the total value of the contract. Call that field ContractAmount and be sure to set its Format property to Currency. You also need the Status field from tblContracts to be able to select only Active ("A") and Paid ("Pd") contracts. Add the Status field to the design grid, and then type in the criterion *"A" Or "Pd"* in its Criteria row. You could include a list box on the report to extract the matching ClubName field from the tblClubs table, but it's more efficient to include that information in a query that provides the data for the report rather than to include the information in the report itself. So, add the tblClubs table to the query, and then add the ClubID and ClubName fields to the design grid. Figure 17-1 shows the query you need for this first report. (You can find this query saved as *qryXmplClubContractReport* in the Entertainment Schedule database.)

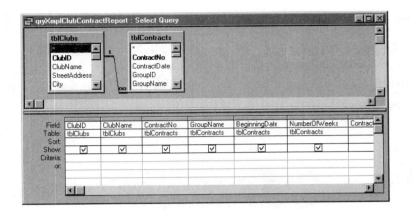

FIGURE 17-1

A query that
selects contract
data for a report.

Designing the Report

Now you're ready to start designing the report. In the Database window, select the query you just built, and then select New Report from
the New Object toolbar button's drop-down list (or choose Report
from the Insert menu). Microsoft Access displays the New Report dialog
box, as shown in Figure 17-2.

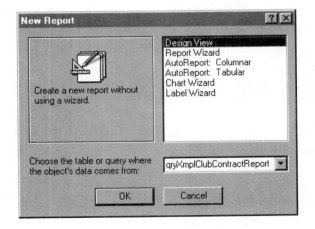

FIGURE 17-2

The New Report
dialog box.

The name of the query you just selected appears in the combo
box in the lower part of the dialog box. (If you want to select a different table or query, open the drop-down list to see a list of all the tables
and queries in your database and select another.) Later in this chapter,
you'll use a Report Wizard to create a report. But for now, select Design
View and click OK to open a new Report window in Design view, as
shown in Figure 17-3 on the next page. You can see both the Report

Design toolbar and the Formatting toolbar at the top of the Access window. The Report window is in the background (but on top of the Database window), and the field list, property sheet, and toolbox are open to assist you in building your report. (If necessary, you can use the Field List, Properties, and Toolbox commands on the View menu to open these windows.)

FIGURE 17-3

The Report window in Design view.

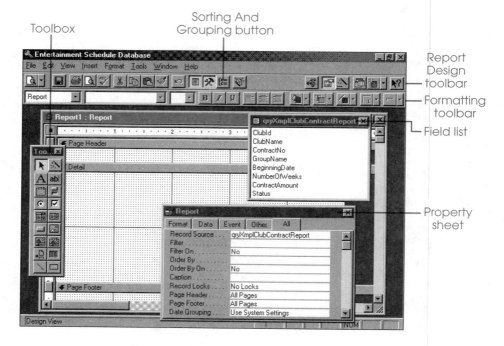

The blank report has Page Header and Page Footer sections and a Detail section between them that is 2 inches high and 5 inches wide. The rulers along the top and left edges of the Report window help you plan space on the printed page. If you want standard 1-inch side margins, the body of the report can be up to 6½ inches wide for an 8½-by-11-inch page. The available vertical space depends on how you design your headers and footers and how you define the top and bottom margins. As with forms, you can drag the edge of any report section to make the section larger or smaller. Note that the width of all sections must be the same, so if you change the width of one section, Access changes the width of all other sections to match.

Within each section you can see a grid that has 24 dots per inch horizontally and 24 dots per inch vertically, with a solid gray line displayed at 1-inch intervals. If you're working in centimeters, Access divides the grid into 5 dots per centimeter both vertically and horizontally. You can change these settings using the Grid X and Grid Y properties in the report's property sheet. (If the dots are not visible in your Report window, choose the Grid command from the View menu; if the Grid command is checked and you still can't see the dots, try resetting the Grid X and Grid Y properties in the property sheet.)

The page header and page footer will print in your report at the top and bottom of each page. You can choose the Page Header/Footer command from the View menu to add or remove the page header and page footer. You can also add a report header that prints once at the beginning of the report and a report footer that prints once at the end of the report. To add these sections to a report, choose the Report Header/Footer command from the View menu. You'll learn how to add group headers and group footers later in this chapter.

See Also   The field list, the property sheet, the toolbox, and the Formatting toolbar are similar to the features you used in building forms. See Chapter 13, "Building Forms," for detailed descriptions of their uses.

Sorting and Grouping Information

A key way in which reports differ from forms is that you can group information for display on reports using the Sorting And Grouping window. Click the Sorting And Grouping button on the toolbar (shown in Figure 17-3) to open the Sorting And Grouping window, as shown in Figure 17-4 on the next page. In this window you can define up to 10 fields or expressions that you will use to form groups in the report. The first item in the list determines the main group, and subsequent items define groups within groups. (You saw this nesting of groups in the previous chapter within the rptContractStatusByGroupAll report in this same database; each month had a main group and a subgroup within that main group for each week.)

FIGURE 17-4

The Sorting And
Grouping window.

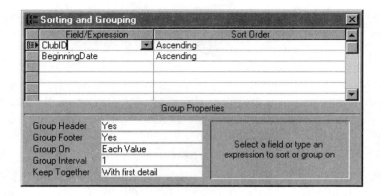

In the simple report you're creating for contracts, you need to group data by club ID so that you can total the number of contracts, the number of weeks, and the contract amounts for each club. If you click in the first row of the Field/Expression column, a down arrow button appears on the right side of the field. Click this arrow (or press Alt-down arrow) to open the list of fields from the underlying table or query. Select the ClubID field to place it in the Field/Expression column. You can also use the Field/Expression column to enter an expression based on any field in the underlying query or table. By default, Access sorts each grouping value in ascending order. You can change the sorting order by selecting Descending from the drop-down list that appears when you click in the Sort Order column. In this case, you're asking the report to sort the rows in ascending numeric order by club ID. If you want to see the clubs in alphabetic order by name, you can group/sort on the ClubName field.

You need a place to put a header for each group (at least for the ClubID field) and a footer for the calculated fields (the counted and summed values). To add these sections, change the settings for the Group Header and the Group Footer properties to Yes, as shown in Figure 17-4. When you do that, Access adds those sections to the Report window for you. You'll learn how to use the Group On, Group Interval, and Keep Together properties in the next chapter. For now, leave them set to their default values. It would also be nice to see the contracts in ascending date order for each club. Add the Beginning-Date field below ClubID, but don't set Group Header or Group Footer to Yes. Close the Sorting And Grouping window by clicking the Close button on its title bar or by clicking the Sorting And Grouping button on the toolbar.

NOTE You can specify sorting criteria in the query for a report, but once you set any criteria in the Sorting And Grouping window, the report ignores any sorting in the query. The best way to ensure that your report data sorts in the order you want is to always specify sorting criteria in the Sorting And Grouping window and not in the underlying query.

Completing the Report

Now you're ready to finish building a summary report based on the tblContracts table. Take the following steps to construct a report similar to the one shown in Figure 17-5. (You can find this report saved as *rptXmplClubContractSummary1* in the Entertainment Schedule database.)

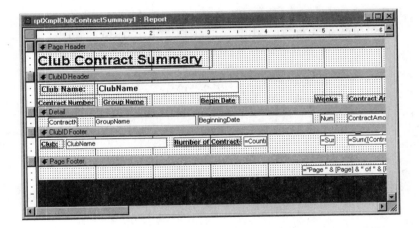

FIGURE 17-5

The Report window in Design view for the Club Contract Summary report.

1. Place a label control on the Page Header section and type *Club Contract Summary* as the label's caption. Select the label control and then, from the Formatting toolbar, select the Arial font in 18-point bold and underlined. Choose Size/To Fit from the Format menu to set the control size to accommodate the new font size.

2. Drag the ClubName field from the field list and drop it onto the ClubID Header section. Use Arial 10-point bold for the label and the control.

3. You'll need some column labels in the ClubID Header section. The easiest way to create them is to set up the text box control so that it has an attached label with no colon, set the defaults for the label control to the font you want, and then drag and

drop the fields you need onto the Detail section. First, make sure the Property window is open, and then click on the Text Box tool in the toolbox. Scroll down the Property window and make sure the Auto Label property is set to Yes and the Add Colon property is set to No. Click on the Label tool and set its font to Arial 8-point bold and underlined. Now lengthen the Detail section to give yourself some room, and then drag and drop the ContractNo, GroupName, BeginningDate, NumberOf-Weeks, and ContractAmount fields from the field list onto the Detail section. Select the label for ContractNo, and then choose the Cut command from the Edit menu (or press Ctrl-X) to separate the label from the control and place the label on the Clipboard. Click on the ClubID Header bar, and then choose the Paste command from the Edit menu (or press Ctrl-V) to paste the label into the upper left corner of the header section. You can now place the label independently in the ClubID Header section. (If you try to move the label before you separate it from the control to which it's attached, the control moves with it.) Separate the labels from the GroupName, BeginningDate, NumberOfWeeks, and ContractAmount controls one at a time, and move the labels to the ClubID Header section of the report.

4. Line up the column labels in the ClubID Header section, placing the Contract Number label near the left margin, the Group Name label about 1.1 inches from the left margin, the Begin Date label about 2.8 inches from the left margin, the Weeks label about 4.8 inches from the left margin, and the Contract-Amount label about 5.4 inches from the left margin. (You might also want to edit the ContractAmount label to add a space between the two words.) You can set these distances in the Left property of each label's property sheet. Line up the tops of the labels by dragging a selection box around all five labels using the Pointer tool and then choosing the Align command from the Format menu and choosing Top from the submenu.

5. You can enhance the appearance of the report by placing a line control across the top of the ClubID Header section. Click on the Line tool in the toolbox and place a line in the ClubID Header section. Select the line control, open its property sheet, and set the following properties: Left 0, Top 0, Width 6.5, and Height 0.

6. Align the controls for ContractNo, GroupName, BeginningDate, NumberOfWeeks, and ContractAmount under their respective headers. The controls for ContractNo and NumberOfWeeks can be made smaller. You'll need to make the GroupName control about 1.75 inches wide and the BeginningDate control about 2 inches wide. Set the Text Align property for Beginning-Date to Left.

7. The height of the Detail section determines the spacing between lines in the report. You don't need much space between report lines, so make the Detail section smaller until it's only slightly higher than the row of controls for displaying your data.

8. Now add two lines at the top edge of the ClubID Footer section, one about .3 inch wide aligned under NumberOfWeeks, and a second about .75 inch wide aligned under ContractAmount. (You can use a single line if you prefer.) Drag and drop the Club-Name field again onto the left end of the ClubID Footer section. It's a good idea to repeat the grouping information in the footer in case the detail lines span across a page boundary. Add three more unbound text boxes to the ClubID Footer section.

9. Change the caption label of the first unbound text box to read *Number of Contracts:* and size it to display the entire label. In the Control Source property of the text box, enter the formula *=Count([ClubID])*. This counts the number of rows in the group.

10. Delete the label of the second unbound text box. Enter the formula *=Sum([NumberOfWeeks])* in the Control Source property of the text box. This formula calculates the total booked weeks of all the contracts within the group. Align this control under the NumberOfWeeks control in the Detail section.

11. Delete the label of the third unbound text box. Enter the formula *=Sum([ContractAmount])* in the Control Source property of the text box. This formula calculates the total of all the contracts within the group. Align this control under the Contract-Amount column and set its Format property to Currency.

12. Finally, create an unbound text box in the lower right corner of the Page Footer section and delete its label. Enter the formula *="Page " & [Page] & " of " & [Pages]* in the Control Source property of the text box. *[Page]* is a report property that contains the current page number. *[Pages]* is another report property that contains the total number of pages in the report.

After you finish, click the Print Preview button on the toolbar to see the result, as shown in Figure 17-6. (I scrolled to page 3 of the report to show some smaller groups so you could see the effect of the page header, group header, and group footer in one example.) Notice that in this figure, the detail lines are sorted in ascending order by Begin Date. You'll recall from Figure 17-4 that the sorting and grouping specifications include a request to sort within group on BeginningDate.

FIGURE 17-6

The Club Contract Summary report in Print Preview.

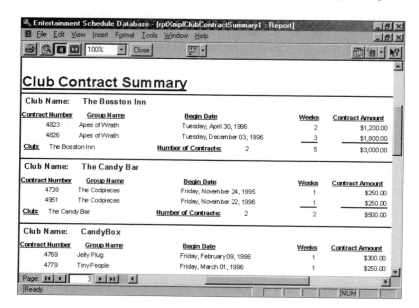

Using a Report Wizard

The Report Wizards that Microsoft Access provides to assist you in constructing reports are similar to the Form Wizards you used earlier to create forms. To practice using a Report Wizard, build the Club Contract Summary report again. Open the Database window, click on the Queries tab, and select the qryXmplClubContractReport query. Select New Report from the New Object toolbar button's drop-down list or choose Report from the Insert menu to open the New Report dialog box.

Selecting a Report Type

The New Report dialog box offers the following six options, as shown in Figure 17-7.

Design View	You selected this option in the first example in this chapter to create a report from scratch in Design view.
Report Wizard	This option opens the main Report Wizard, where you can select the fields you want to include and select formatting options, grouping options, and summary options. (You'll use this wizard in this exercise to create the Club Contract Summary report again.)
AutoReport: Columnar	Using this Report Wizard is the same as selecting AutoReport from the New Object toolbar button's drop-down list. This option creates a very simple columnar report that lists the fields from a table or a query in a single column down the page.
AutoReport: Tabular	This Report Wizard displays the data from fields in a query or a table in a single row across the report. If the wizard detects a one-to-many relationship in a query, it automatically creates a group for the data from the "one" side, but it does not generate any totals. It generates a report using the last style you selected in a wizard or via Auto-Format in a Report window in Design view.
Chart Wizard	This Report Wizard helps you create an un-bound OLE Object containing a Microsoft Graph application object to chart data from your database.
Label Wizard	This Report Wizard lets you select name and address fields and format them to print mailing labels. You can select from a number of popular label types. The Label Wizard will size the labels correctly.

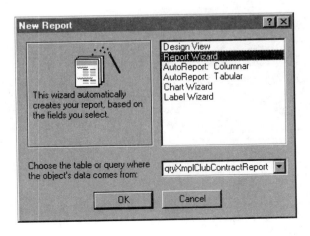

FIGURE 17-7
The Report Wizard options in the New Report dialog box.

Because you want to control all options, including setting a group and subtotals, select the Report Wizard option, and click OK.

Specifying Wizard Options

In the first window of the wizard, shown in Figure 17-8, you select the fields you want in your report. You can select all available fields in the order in which they appear in the underlying query or report by clicking the double right arrow (>>) button. If you want to select only some of the fields or if you want to specify the order in which the fields appear in the report, select one field at a time in the list box on the left, and click the single right arrow (>) button to move the field to the list box on the right. If you make a mistake, you can select the field in the list box on the right and then click the single left arrow (<) button to move the field to the list box on the left. Click the double left arrow (<<) button to remove all selected fields from the list box on the right and start over.

You can also select fields from one table or query, and then change the table or query selection in the Tables/Queries combo box. The Report Wizard uses the relationships you defined in your database to build a new query that correctly links the tables or queries you specify. If the wizard can't determine the links between the data you select, it warns you and won't let you proceed unless you include data only from related tables.

FIGURE 17-8

Selecting
fields in the
Report Wizard.

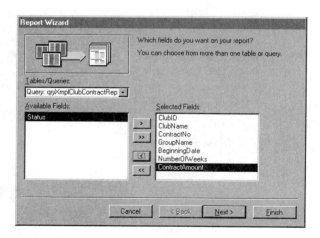

568

To create the Club Contract Summary report, you should select all of the fields except Status. When you finish selecting fields, click the Next button to go to the next window.

The wizard examines your data and tries to determine whether there are any "natural" groups in the data. Since this query includes information from tblClubs that is related one-to-many to information from tblContracts, the wizard assumes that you might want to group the information by clubs (ClubID and ClubName), as shown in Figure 17-9. If you don't want any groups or you want to set the grouping criteria yourself, select "by tblContracts." In this case, the wizard has guessed correctly, so click Next to go to the next step.

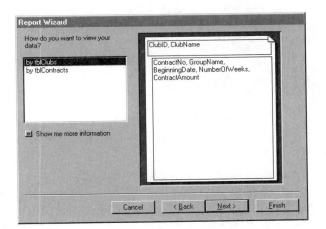

FIGURE 17-9

Verifying primary grouping criteria in the Report Wizard.

In the next window, the wizard asks which additional fields you want to use for grouping records, as shown in Figure 17-10 on the next page. If you chose to set the criteria yourself, you will see a similar window with no first group selected. You can select up to four grouping levels. The wizard doesn't allow you to enter an expression as a grouping value—something you can do when you build a report from scratch. If you want to use an expression as a grouping value in a Report Wizard, you have to include that expression in the underlying query. For this report, you could also group within each club by the group name. If you select an additional field, the wizard makes the Grouping Options button available. You can click this button to see the Grouping Intervals dialog box, also shown in Figure 17-10. For text fields, you can group by the entire field or by one to five of the leading characters in the fields. For date/time fields, you can group by individual values or by year, quarter, month, week, day, hour, or minute.

For numeric fields, you can group by individual values or in increments of 10, 50, 100, 500, 1000, and so on, up to 500,000. If you want to closely duplicate the report you built earlier, don't select any additional grouping fields, and click Next to go to the next step.

FIGURE 17-10
Setting the grouping interval on an additional grouping field in the Report Wizard.

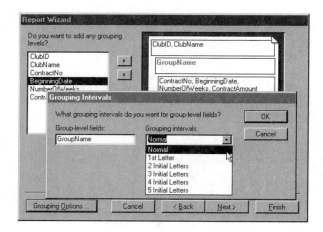

In the next window, shown in Figure 17-11, the wizard asks you to specify any additional sorting criteria for the rows in the detail section. You can select up to four fields from your table or query to sort the data. By default, the sorting order is ascending. Click the control button to the right of the field selection combo box to change the order to descending. Again, you can sort only on fields in your query. You can't enter expressions as you can in the Sorting And Grouping window. In this report, you need to sort in ascending order on the BeginningDate field, as shown in the figure.

FIGURE 17-11
Specifying sorting criteria in the Report Wizard.

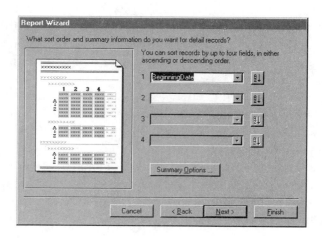

Click the Summary Options button to open the dialog box shown in Figure 17-12, in which you can ask the wizard to display summary values for certain fields in the group footers. The wizard shows you any numeric fields that would be appropriate for summary calculations. In this case, you want the Sum for both the NumberOfWeeks and ContractAmount fields. Note that you also have choices to calculate the average (Avg) of values over the group or to display the smallest (Min) or largest (Max) value. You can select multiple options. You can also indicate that you don't want to see any of the detail lines by selecting the Summary Only option. (Sometimes you're interested only in the totals for the groups in a report, not all of the detail.) If you select the Calculate Percent Of Total For Sums option, the wizard will also display, for any field for which you have selected the Sum option, an additional field that shows what percent of the grand total this sum represents. When you have the settings the way you want them, click OK to close the dialog box. Click Next in the Report Wizard window to go on.

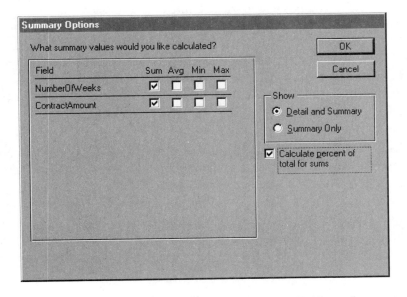

FIGURE 17-12

Selecting summary options in the Report Wizard.

In the next window, shown in Figure 17-13 on the next page, you can select a layout style and a page orientation for your report. When you select a layout option, the wizard displays a preview on the left side of the window. In this case, the Stepped layout option in Portrait orientation will come closest to the "hand-built" report you created earlier in this chapter. You should also select the check box for adjusting the field widths so that all of the fields fit on one page.

FIGURE 17-13

Selecting a layout style and page orientation in the Report Wizard.

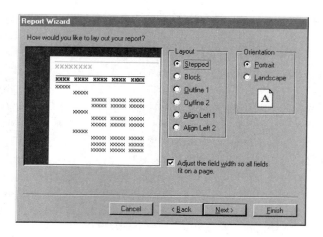

Click Next to go to the next-to-last window of the wizard (not shown). In this window you can select from several built-in report styles. If you defined your own custom report style using AutoFormat in a Report window in Design view (similar to the way you defined a format for a form in Chapter 14, "Customizing Forms"), you can also select your custom style. The built-in styles include Bold, Casual, Compact, Corporate, Formal, and Soft Gray. The Bold and Casual styles are probably best suited for informal reports in a personal database. The other formats look more professional. For this example, select the Corporate style. Click Next to go to the last window of the wizard.

In the final window, shown in Figure 17-14, you can type in a report title. Note that the wizard uses this title to create the report caption, the label in the report header, and the report name. It's probably best to type in a title that's appropriate for the caption and label and to not worry about the title being a suitable report name. If you're using a naming convention (such as prefixing all reports with *rpt* as I've done in the Entertainment Schedule sample database), it's easy to switch to the Database window after the wizard is done to rename your report.

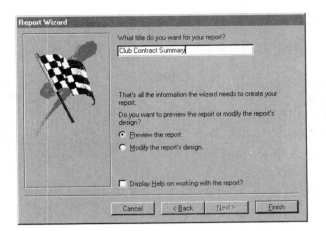

FIGURE 17-14
The Report
Wizard window
for specifying a
report title.

Viewing the Result

Select the Preview The Report option in the final window, and then click the Finish button to create the report and display the result in Print Preview, as shown in Figures 17-15 and 17-16.

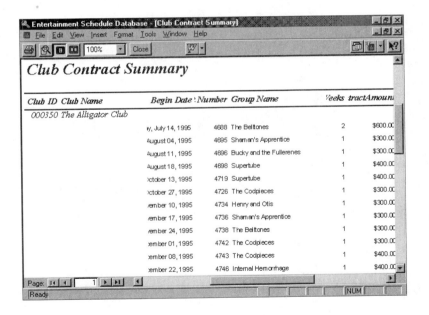

FIGURE 17-15
The first page of
the Club Contract
Summary report
created using a
wizard.

FIGURE 17-16

A later page in
the Club Contract
Summary report
showing club
summary data.

Club ID Club Name	Begin Date	Number	Group Name	Weeks	tractAmount
	vember 15, 1996	4949	Shaman's Apprentice	1	$300.00
	vember 22, 1996	4950	The Belltones	1	$300.00
	vember 29, 1996	4955	The Codpieces	1	$300.00
	vember 06, 1996	4956	The Codpieces	1	$400.00
	vember 20, 1996	4958	Internal Hemorrhage	1	$400.00

Summary for 'ClubId' = 350 (35 detail records)

Sum				36	$13,550.00
Percent				6.06%	3.54%

000400 The Baby Seal Club

You can press Esc at any time to return to Design view. It's easy
to use Design view to modify minor items (such as adjusting the width
and alignment of the BeginningDate field and resizing the labels) to
obtain a result nearly identical to the report you constructed earlier.
You can find this report saved as *rptXmplClubContractSummary2* in the
Entertainment Schedule database. As you might imagine, Report Wizards
can help you to get a head start on more complex report designs.

You should now feel comfortable with constructing reports. In the
next chapter, you'll learn how to build more complex reports that contain subreports and calculated values.

Chapter 18

Advanced
Report Design

n the previous chapter, you learned how to create a relatively simple report with a single subtotal level. You also saw how a Report Wizard can help you construct a new report. This chapter shows you how to:

- Design a report with multiple subtotal groups
- Add complex calculations to a report
- Embed a report within another report
- Create a complex "spreadsheet" report

To learn how to work with these features, you'll create a Group Contract Status report for the Entertainment Schedule database. In a second example, you'll learn how to use the results from two advanced queries in embedded subreports to produce an easy-to-use report that displays openings in club and group schedules. In the final example in this chapter, you'll learn a creative way to design a report around a total query to display multiple categories of totals across by month and down by group, similar to a spreadsheet.

Building the Group Contract Status Report Query

As noted in the previous chapter, because reports tend to bring together information from many tables, you are likely to begin constructing a report by designing a query to retrieve the data you need for the report. For this example, you need information from the tblClubs, tblContracts, and tblCommissions tables in the Entertainment Schedule database. Open a new Query window in Design view and add these tables to the query.

This report needs to include not only contracts marked Active and Paid but also those marked Pending (contracts that have been booked but not confirmed). As you'll learn in Chapter 22, "Automating Your Application with VBA," when you study the main frmContracts form, code behind the form creates appropriate matching tblCommissions rows (one row per contract week—a contract might span several weeks, but commission payments are due weekly from the group) whenever a contract is marked Active or Paid. However, contracts marked Pending don't have any matching tblCommissions rows. You'll recall from Chapter 8, "Adding Power with Select Queries," that you get only rows that match on both sides of a join unless you change the join criteria. Double-click on the join line between tblContracts and tblCommissions to open the Join Properties dialog box. Select the option to select all records from tblContracts and matching records from tblCommissions. The upper part of the Query window should look similar to the one shown in Figure 18-1. Add the fields listed in Figure 18-2 to the design grid. (You can find this query saved as *qryActivePaidContracts* in the sample database.)

FIGURE 18-1
The qryActive-
PaidContracts
query for the
Group Contract
Status report.

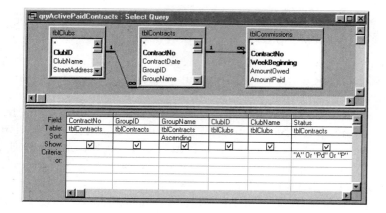

FIGURE 18-2
The fields in the
qryActivePaid-
Contracts query.

Field/Expression	Source Table	Criterion
ContractNo	tblContracts	
GroupID	tblContracts	
GroupName	tblContracts	Sort: Ascending
ClubID	tblClubs	
ClubName	tblClubs	
Status	tblContracts	"A" Or "Pd" Or "P"
BeginningDate	tblContracts	
EndingDate	tblContracts	
WeekBegin:→ IIf(IsNull([WeekBeginning]),→ [BeginningDate]-Weekday→ ([BeginningDate],2)+1,→ [WeekBeginning])		
WeekBeginning	tblCommissions	
AmountOwed	tblCommissions	
AmountPaid	tblCommissions	
CommissionAgent1	tblContracts	"RMP"

When there are matching rows in the tblCommissions table, this query generates one output row per week of the contract. Remember that some contracts won't have any weekly commissions rows yet. However, the report that uses this query is designed to subtotal by week and by month. The WeekBeginning date would work to produce the subtotal breaks if every row had commissions. The WeekBegin calculated field tests for rows that don't have commissions. (The WeekBeginning field will be Null.) When no WeekBeginning date is available, WeekBegin calculates the date of the Monday preceding the BeginningDate field in the tblContracts table by subtracting an offset using the *Weekday* built-in function. This results in a field in the query that you can use in the report to create the necessary subtotals. You should click on the WeekBegin field, open its property sheet, and set the Format property to Short Date and the Caption property to Week Beginning Date.

Either save your query and select it in the Database window or select the qryActivePaidContracts query in the Database window and then select New Report from the New Object toolbar button's drop-down list. Select Design View in the New Report dialog box to open the Report window in Design view. (Because there are so many fields in this report, it is easier to build the report without a Report Wizard.)

Defining Sorting and Grouping Criteria

The first thing you need to do is define the sorting and grouping criteria for the report. Click the Sorting And Grouping button on the toolbar to open the Sorting And Grouping window. This report should display the contract and commission data by group and then by month, with the detail showing the weekly contract and commission data from the query. Select the GroupName field in the first line of the Sorting And Grouping window and then set the Group Footer property to Yes. Notice that when you set the Group Header or Group Footer property to Yes for any field or expression in the Sorting And Grouping window, Microsoft Access shows you a grouping symbol on the row selector for that row. Access also adds an appropriate section to your report. You want to make sure that a group header doesn't get "orphaned" at the bottom of a page, so set the Keep Together property to With First Detail. Note that you can also ask Access to attempt to keep all the detail for this level of grouping on one page by setting the Keep Together property to Whole Group. When you do this, Access will move to a new page if all the detail for the next group won't fit on the current page. Because we know that many of the groups have too many contract rows to fit on a single page, you can set the Keep Together property to Whole Group. As you'll see a bit later, the report sections also have properties that you can set to force a new page with the start of each group.

The WeekBegin field from the query returns the date of Monday for each week over the life span of each contract. However, commission payments are due at the end of the week. We want this report to also provide subtotals by month, but the months should be grouped on dates when the payments are due. You can ensure the correct grouping by specifying an expression in the Sorting And Grouping window. If WeekBegin is always a Monday, then [WeekBegin]+6 must be the Sunday at the end of the week. Type this expression in the Field/Expression column, and set the Group Footer property to Yes and the Group On property to Month. (The following section discusses other grouping options that depend on data type.) Finally, you should sort the detail rows by the week ending date by typing in =[*WeekBegin*]+6 again in the Field/Expression column (but without changing any of the group properties). Even though the qryActivePaidContracts query has sorting criteria, you must also define the sorting criteria you want in the report definition. Reports ignore any sorting specification from the source query if you define any criteria in the Sorting And Grouping window. Your result should look something like that shown in Figure 18-3.

FIGURE 18-3
The sorting and grouping criteria for the Group Contract Status report.

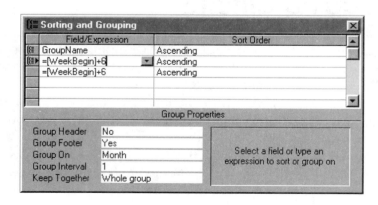

Setting Group
Ranges by Data Type

For each field or expression in the upper part of the Sorting And Grouping window, you can set Group On and Group Interval properties. Normally, you'll want to start a new grouping of data whenever the value of your field or expression changes. You can, however, specify that a new grouping start whenever a field or an expression changes from one range of values to another. The kind of range you can specify varies depending on the data type of the field or the expression.

For text grouping fields, you can ask Microsoft Access to start a new group based on a change in value of one or more leading characters in the string. For example, you can create a new group based on a change in the first letter of the field (rather than on a change anywhere in the field) to create one group per letter of the alphabet—a group of items beginning with *A,* a group of items beginning with *B,* and so on. To group on a prefix, set the Group On property to Prefix Characters, and set the Group Interval property to the number of leading characters that will differentiate each group.

For numbers, you can set the Group On property to Interval. When you specify this setting, you can enter a setting for the Group Interval property that will cluster multiple values within a range. Access calculates ranges from 0. For example, if you specify 10 as the interval value, you'll see groups for the values −20 through −11, −10 through −1, 0 through 9, 10 through 19, 20 through 29, and so on.

For date/time fields, you can set the Group On property to calendar or time subdivisions and multiples of those subdivisions, such as Year, Qtr, Month, Week, Day, Hour, or Minute. Include a setting for the Group Interval property if you want to group on a multiple of the subdivision—for example, set Group On to Year and Group Interval to 2 if you want groupings for every two years.

NOTE When you create groupings in which the Group Interval property is set to something other than Each Value, Access sorts only the grouping value, not the individual values within each group. If you want Access to sort the detail items within the group, you must include a separate sort specification for those items. For example, if you group on the first two letters of a Name field and also want the names within each group sorted, you must enter *Name* as the field in the Sorting And Grouping window with Group Header (and possibly Group Footer) set to Yes, Sort Order set to Ascending, Group On set to Prefix Characters, and Group Interval set to 2, and then you must enter *Name* as the field again with Sort Order set to Ascending and Group On set to Each Value.

Creating the Basic Group Contract Status Report

Now that you've defined the groups, you're ready to start building the report. Before you go any further, choose the Save As command from the File menu, and save the report as *rptMyGroupContractStatus*. (The completed report is saved as *rptContractStatusByGroup* in the Entertainment Schedule database.) You can create the basic report by taking the following steps. Figure 18-4 shows the results of the steps described.

FIGURE 18-4

The upper section of the Group Contract Status report in Design view.

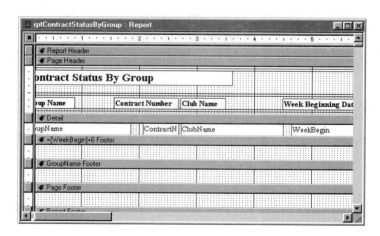

1. Choose Page Setup from the File menu to open the Page Setup dialog box. Click on the Page tab and set the page orientation to Landscape. Click on the Margins tab and set the top and bottom margins to 1 inch and the left and right margins to .5 inch. Drag the right border of the Detail section to widen the report to about 10 inches.

2. Place a label in the page header and type *Contract Status By Group*. Select the label, set the font to Times New Roman, and select a font size of 14 points from the toolbar. Click the Bold button to make the title stand out. Choose the Size To Fit command from the Format menu to expand the label to fit your text. Set the Top property to approximately .1 inch. Add a line control to the Page Header section. Set its Top property to .05 inch, Left property to 0 inch, Height property to 0 inch, and Width property to 10 inches. Choose Duplicate from the Edit menu five times to create six copies of the line that stretch all the way across the Page Header section. Drag the bottom edge of the Page Header section to make it just under 1 inch tall. Move the lines so that two of them are above the label you just created. Move the remaining four lines two at a time to create a band for your column heading labels. Leave approximately .25 inch between the two bands of lines for the labels.

3. Click on the Label tool in the toolbox and make sure that its default font is Times New Roman, Font Size 10, and Font Weight Bold. Click on the Text Box tool in the toolbox and make sure that its default font is Times New Roman, Font Size 10, Font Weight Normal, Auto Label Yes, and Add Colon No.

4. Open the field list and drag and drop the following fields onto the Detail section: GroupName, ContractNo, ClubName, WeekBegin, Status, AmountOwed, and AmountPaid.

5. Select all the labels on the controls you just added to the Detail section and cut them to the Clipboard. Click in the Page Header section and paste the labels there. Move the Group Name label to the left edge between the two rows of line controls. Place the Contract Number label approximately 1.5 inches from the left edge. Place Club Name at 2.7 inches, Week Beginning Date at 4.6 inches, Status at 5.8 inches, Amount Owed at 6.7 inches,

and Amount Paid at 8.5 inches. Select all of these column heading labels and choose the Align/Top command from the Format menu to align the tops of the controls. Adjust the entire group vertically so that the text box controls are evenly spaced between the two rows of line controls.

6. In the Detail section, move all of the text box controls so that they line up under their respective labels along the top edge of the section. Make the GroupName and ClubName controls about 1.85 inches wide. Set ContractNo and Status to .75 inch wide. Make WeekBegin about 1 inch wide, and set AmountOwed and AmountPaid to 1.5 inches wide. Make sure that your report is still 10 inches wide. Drag the bottom of the Detail section up so that it is the same height as the text box row.

7. Change the Amount Owed label's caption to *Commission Owed* and change the Amount Paid label's caption to *Commission Paid*.

Your report design should now look something like that shown in Figures 18-4 and 18-5.

FIGURE 18-5

The right side of the Group Contract Status report in Design view.

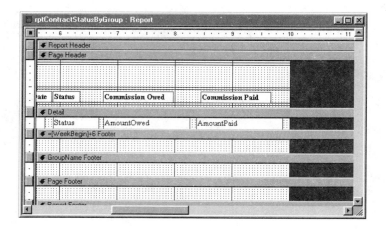

When you click the Print Preview button on the toolbar and maximize the Report window, the result should look something like that shown in Figure 18-6.

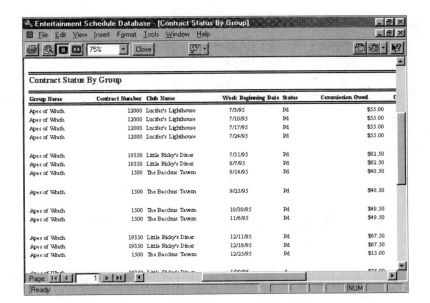

FIGURE 18-6
The Group
Contract Status
report in Print
Preview.

Setting Section and Report Properties

You've probably noticed that Microsoft Access has a property sheet for each section in the Report window in Design view. You can set section properties not only to control how the section looks but also to control whether Access should attempt to keep a group together or start a new page before or after the group. There's also a property sheet for the report as a whole. You don't need to change any more of these properties at this point, but the following sections explain the available property settings.

Section Properties

When you click in the blank area of any group section or detail section of a report and then click the Properties button, Access displays a property sheet, such as the one shown in Figure 18-7 on the next page.

585

FIGURE 18-7

A property
sheet for a
report section.

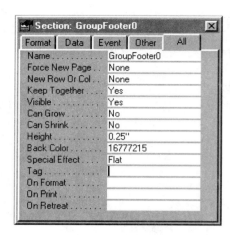

The available properties and their uses are described below:

Name	Access automatically generates a unique section name for you.
Force New Page	Set this property to Before Section to force the section to print at the top of a new page. Set this property to After Section to force the next section to print at the top of a new page.
New Row Or Col	When you use the Page Setup dialog box to format your report with more than one column (vertical) or more than one row (horizontal) of sections, you can set this property to Before Section, After Section, or Before & After to produce the section again at the top, bottom, or both top and bottom of a new column or row. This property is useful for forcing headers to print at the top of each column in a multiple-column report.
Keep Together	Set this property to No to allow a section to flow across page boundaries. The default Yes setting tells Access to attempt to keep all lines within a section together on a page. You can ask Access to attempt to keep lines with group headers and footers together by setting the Keep Together property to Yes for the grouping specification in the Sorting And Grouping window.
Visible	Set this property to Yes to make the section visible or to No to make the section invisible. This is a handy property to set from a macro or from a Visual Basic for Applications (VBA)

routine while Access formats and prints your report. You can make sections disappear, depending on data values in the report. (See Chapter 19, "Adding Power with Macros," for details.)

Can Grow

Access sets this value to Yes when you include any control in the section that also has its Can Grow property set to Yes. This allows the section to expand to accommodate controls that might expand because they display memo fields or long text strings. You can design a control to display one line of text, but you should allow the control to expand to display more lines of text as needed.

Can Shrink

This property is similar to Can Grow. You can set it to Yes to allow the section to become smaller if controls in the section become smaller to accommodate less text. You'll use Can Shrink later in this chapter to make a control disappear when the control contains no data.

Tag

Use this property to store additional identifying information about the section. You can use this property in macros and in VBA procedures to temporarily store information that you want to pass to another routine.

On Format

Enter the name of a macro or a VBA procedure that you want Access to execute when it begins formatting this section. (See Chapter 19, "Adding Power with Macros," and Chapter 21, "Visual Basic for Applications Fundamentals," for details.)

On Print

Enter the name of a macro or a VBA procedure that you want Access to execute when it begins printing this section or when it displays the section in Print Preview. (See Chapter 19 for details.)

On Retreat

Enter the name of a macro or a VBA procedure that you want Access to execute when it has to "back up" over a section after it finds that the section won't fit on the current page and you've set the Keep Together Property to Yes. This event happens after On Format but before On Print, so you can use it to undo settings you might have changed in your On Format routine. Access calls On Format again when it formats the section on a new page.

The remaining properties in the property sheet (Height, Back Color, and Special Effect) control how the section looks. Whenever you adjust the height of the section by dragging its lower border, Access resets the section's Height property. You can set the Back Color and Special Effect properties using the Formatting toolbar.

For page headers and footers, only the Name, Visible, Height, Back Color, Special Effect, Tag, On Format, and On Print properties are available.

Report Properties

If you choose the Select Report command from the Edit menu or click in the Report window beyond the right edge of the Detail section, and then click the Properties button, Access displays the report's properties in the property sheet, as shown in Figure 18-8.

FIGURE 18-8

The property sheet for a report.

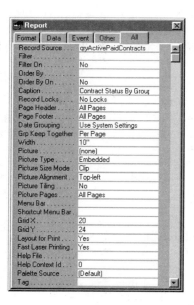

The available properties and their uses are described below:

Record Source	This property displays the name of the table or query that provides the data for your report.
Filter	This property shows any filter inherited from the Record Source property or applied by a macro or VBA procedure the last time the report was opened.

Filter On	Set this property to Yes if you want the filter defined for the report to be automatically applied each time the report opens. Note that you can set the Filter and Filter On properties from a macro or a VBA procedure.
Order By	This property shows any ordering criteria inherited from the Record Source property or applied by a macro or a VBA procedure the last time the report was opened.
Order By On	Set this property to Yes if you want the Order By property defined for the report to be automatically applied each time the report opens. Note that you can set the Order By and Order By On properties from a macro or a VBA procedure.
Caption	Use this property to enter the text that appears in the title bar when you open the report in Print Preview.
Record Locks	Set this property to All Records if the data for your report is on a server shared by others and you want to be sure that no one can update the records in the report until Access creates every page in the report. You should not set this property to All Records for a report that you plan to view in Print Preview because you'll lock out other users for the entire time that you're viewing the report on your screen.
Page Header	This property controls whether the page header appears on all pages. You can choose to not print the page header on the first and last pages if these pages contain a report header or a report footer.
Page Footer	This property controls whether the page footer appears on all pages. You can choose to not print the page footer on the first and last pages if these pages contain a report header or a report footer.
Date Grouping	Use this property to determine how Access groups date and time values that you've specified in the Sorting And Grouping window. You can set this property to US Defaults or Use System Settings. For US Defaults, the first day of the week is Sunday and the first week of the year starts on January 1. If you specify Use System Settings, the first day of the week and first week of the year are determined by the Regional Settings in the Windows Control Panel.

(continued)

Grp Keep Together	Set this property to Per Page if you want Access to honor the Sorting And Grouping Keep Together property by page. Set it to Per Column for a multiple-column report if you want Access to attempt to keep a group together within a column.
Width	Access sets this property when you increase the width of the report in the design grid.
Picture, Picture Type	For these properties, you enter the full path-name and filename of a bitmap that you want to use as the background of the report. If you set the Picture Type property to Embedded, Access copies the bitmap to the Report object and sets the Picture property to (bitmap). If you set the Picture Type property to Linked, Access uses the path name stored in the Picture property to load the bitmap each time you open the report. The Picture and Picture Type properties are also available on forms.
Picture Size Mode	When your background picture is not the same size as your page, you can set the Picture Size Mode property to adjust the size. The Clip setting displays the picture in its original size, and if the page is smaller than the picture, Access clips the right and bottom edges of the picture. The Zoom setting maintains the aspect ratio and shrinks or enlarges the picture to fit the page. If your picture doesn't have the same horizontal-to-vertical dimension ratio as your page, Access might show some blank space at the right or bottom edge of the page. The Stretch setting expands the picture to fit the page size and might distort the image if the aspect ratio of the picture does not match the aspect ratio of the page.
Picture Alignment	When you set the Picture Size Mode property to Clip, you can use Picture Alignment to place the picture in the center of the page or in one of the corners before the picture is clipped.
Picture Tiling	When you set the Picture Size Mode property to Clip and your picture is smaller than the page size, you can set the Picture Tiling property to Yes so that Access will place multiple copies of the picture across and down the page.
Picture Pages	You can set this property to show the picture on All Pages, First Page, or No Pages.

Menu Bar	Enter the name of the macro that defines a custom menu bar that Access displays when you open the report in Print Preview. (See Chapter 23, "The Finishing Touches," for details.) If you want to hide the menu bar when your report opens, set this property to True.
Shortcut Menu Bar	Enter the name of the macro that defines a custom shortcut menu that Access displays when you open the report in Print Preview and right-click in the Report window.
Grid X, Grid Y	Specify the number of horizontal (X) or vertical (Y) divisions per inch or per centimeter for the dots in the grid. When you use inches (when English [United States] is set in the Regional Settings section of the Windows Control Panel), you can see the dots whenever you specify a value of 24 or less for both X and Y. When you use centimeters (when Measurement is set to Metric), you can see the dots when you specify values of 9 or less.
Layout For Print	When this property is set to Yes, you can select from among several TrueType and printer fonts for your design. When this property is set to No, only screen fonts are available.
Fast Laser Printing	Some laser printers support the drawing of lines (such as the edges of rectangles, the line control, or the edges of text boxes) with rules. If you set the Fast Laser Printing property to Yes, Access sends rule commands instead of graphics to your printer to print rules. Rules print faster than graphics.
Help File, Help Context Id	You can create custom help text using the Microsoft Help Compiler provided in the Microsoft Win32 Software Development Kit or in the Microsoft Access Developer's Toolkit for Windows 95. (See the development kit documentation for details.)
Palette Source	With this property, if you have a color printer, you can specify a device-independent bitmap (dib) file, a Microsoft Windows Palette (pal) file, a Windows icon (ico) file, or a Windows bitmap (bmp) file to provide a palette of colors different from those in the Access default.
Tag	Use this property to store additional identifying information about the report. You can use this property in macros and in VBA procedures to temporarily store information that you want to pass to another routine.

The following additional Report properties are not shown in Figure 18-8 on page 588:

On Open	Enter the name of a macro or a VBA procedure that you want Access to execute when it begins printing your report or when it displays the report in Print Preview. (See Chapter 19, "Adding Power with Macros," for details.)
On Close	Enter the name of a macro or a VBA procedure that you want Access to execute when you close Print Preview or when Access has finished sending the report to your printer. (See Chapter 19 for details.)
On Activate	Enter the name of a macro or a VBA procedure that you want Access to execute when the Report window gains the focus in Print Preview. This property provides a convenient method of opening a custom toolbar.
On Deactivate	Enter the name of a macro or a VBA procedure that you want Access to execute when the Report window loses the focus in Print Preview. This property provides a convenient method of closing a custom toolbar.
On No Data	Enter the name of a macro or a VBA procedure that you want Access to execute when the report opens but the record source contains no data.
On Page	Enter the name of a macro or a VBA procedure that you want Access to execute when all the sections of a page have been formatted but have not yet been printed. In VBA, you can use special methods to draw custom graphics on the page.
On Error	Enter the name of a macro or a VBA procedure that you want Access to execute when any errors occur in the report.

Using Calculated Values

Much of the power of Microsoft Access reports comes from their ability to perform both simple and complex calculations on the data from your underlying tables or queries. Access also provides dozens of built-in functions that you can use to work with your data or to add information to your report. The following sections provide examples of the types of calculations you can perform.

Adding the Print Date and Page Numbers

One of the pieces of information you might frequently add to a report is the date on which you prepared the report. You'll probably also want to add page numbers. Access provides two built-in functions that you can use to add the current date and time to your report. The *Date* function returns the current system date as a Date/Time value with no time component. The *Now* function returns the current system date and time as a Date/Time value.

To add the current date to your report, create an unbound text box control on the Page Header section and set its Control Source property to =Now( ). Then, in the Format property box, specify a Date/Time setting. Go back to the report and type in a meaningful caption for the label, or delete the label if you don't want a caption. You can see an example of using the *Now* function in Figure 18-9. The result in Print Preview is shown in Figure 18-10.

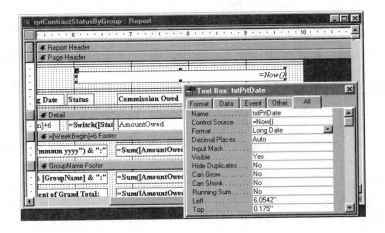

FIGURE 18-9

Using the *Now* function to add the date to a report.

FIGURE 18-10

The current date displayed in the report in Print Preview.

To add a page number, use the Page property for the report. You can't see this property in any of the property sheets because it is maintained by Access. Access also provides the Pages property, which contains a count of the total number of pages in the report. To add the current page number to a report (in this example, in the Page Footer section), create an unbound text box control and set its Control Source property to ="Page " & [Page] & " of " & [Pages], as shown in Figure 18-11.

TIP You can reset the value of the Page property in a macro or a VBA procedure that you activate from an appropriate report property. For example, if you're printing several multiple-page invoices for different customers in one pass, you might want to reset the page number to 1 when you start to format the page for a different customer. You can include a Group Header section for each customer and then use a macro or a VBA procedure to set the Page property to 1 each time Access formats that section (indicating that you're on the first page of a new customer invoice).

Performing Calculations

Another task you might perform frequently is calculating extended values from detail values in your tables. You'll recall from Chapter 4, "Designing Your Database Application," that it's usually redundant and wasteful of storage space to define in your tables the fields that you calculate from other fields. (The only situation in which this is acceptable is when saving the calculated value will greatly improve performance in parts of your application.)

Performing a Calculation on a Detail Line

You can use arithmetic operators to create complex calculations in the Control Source property of any control that can display data. You can also use any of the many built-in functions or any of the functions you define yourself in a module. If you want, you can use the Expression Builder that you learned about in Chapter 8, "Adding Power with Select Queries," to build the expression for any control. You let Access know that you are using an expression in a Control Source property by start-ing the expression with an equal sign (=).

In the Detail section of this report, you can make a couple of en-hancements to the way data is displayed. First, even though the con-tracts are listed in the query by week beginning date, the report summarizes by week ending date and by month. So the report might display a detail line with a week beginning date of Monday, April 29, 1996, but total that detail line in May because the payment isn't due until Sunday, May 5. This might be confusing, so it makes more sense to display a week ending date for each detail line. Change the label for Week Beginning Date to Week Ending Date. Set the Control Source property of the text box in the Detail section to =[WeekBegin]+6 and change the name of the text box to something other than WeekBegin. If you don't change the control name, you will create a circular reference in the control source because the reference to [WeekBegin] in the Con-trol Source property first looks for a control by that name. If no control has a matching name, Access looks for a field in the record source by that name—which is what you want to have happen in this case. If you've ever seen a report control display *#ERROR* in Print Preview, it's probably because of a circular reference—the control references itself.

The second calculation you can perform on the detail line re-places the status code with a word that matches the code. Before you built this report and its query, you could have gone to the tblContracts table and set the Lookup property of the Status field to a list box that displays a matching value from a list (as you learned to do in Chapter 6, "Modifying Your Database Design"). Since this query returns only three status codes, you can get the same effect by using a built-in function called *Switch* to replace the codes with names. The *Switch* function lets you enter up to seven pairs of expressions. If the first expression in a pair evaluates to True, *Switch* returns whatever is in the second expres-sion. Once it finds a true expression, it stops, so it's a good idea to put the most common test first.

Change the name of the Status text box to txtStatus, and then en-ter an expression using the *Switch* function in the Control Source prop-erty box, as shown in Figure 18-12 on the next page. As you can see, this expression asks *Switch* to first test Status for "A" and return "Ac-tive" if true, and then test for "Pd" and return "Paid", and finally test for "P" and return "Pending".

FIGURE 18-12

A calculated
expression using
the *Switch*
function.

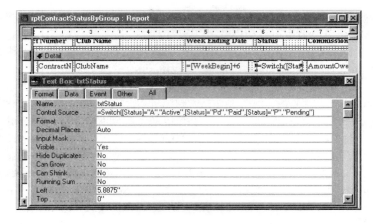

Figure 18-13 shows the result in Print Preview. (The figure also shows some additional total values that you'll add in the next section.) You can see that Access has performed the required calculations on each status value and displayed a more meaningful result for each.

FIGURE 18-13

The calculated
detail line values
and monthly
totals within a
group in Print
Preview.

umber	Club Name	Week Ending Date	Status	Commission Owed	Commission Paid
4642	Lucifer's Lighthouse	7/9/95	Paid	$55.00	$55.00
4642	Lucifer's Lighthouse	7/16/95	Paid	$55.00	$55.00
4642	Lucifer's Lighthouse	7/23/95	Paid	$55.00	$55.00
4642	Lucifer's Lighthouse	7/30/95	Paid	$55.00	$55.00
				$220.00	$220.00
4692	Little Ricky's Diner	8/6/95	Paid	$82.50	$82.50
4692	Little Ricky's Diner	8/13/95	Paid	$82.50	$82.50
4697	The Bacchus Tavern	8/20/95	Paid	$40.50	$40.50
				$205.50	$205.50
4727	The Bacchus Tavern	10/1/95	Paid	$40.50	$40.50
				$40.50	$40.50

Adding Values Across a Group

Another task commonly performed in reports is adding values across a group. You saw a simple example of this in the previous chapter that used the built-in *Sum* function. In this report, you have two levels of grouping: first by group and then by month within group. When you specified sorting and grouping criteria earlier in this chapter, you asked Access to provide group footers. This gives you sections in your report in which you can add unbound controls that use any of the aggregate functions (*Sum, Min, Max, Avg, Count, First, Last, StDev,* or *Var*) in expressions to display a calculated value for all the rows in that group. In this example, you can create unbound controls in the GroupName and =[WeekBegin]+6 footers to hold the totals, by group and by month, for commission owed and commission paid, as shown in Figure 18-14. You can also add a line control at the top of each footer section to provide a visual clue that the values that follow are totals.

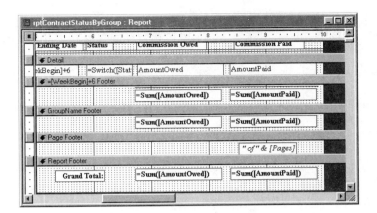

FIGURE 18-14
Adding
summaries
by group and
by month.

If you switch to Print Preview at this point, the result should look like that shown in Figure 18-13.

TIP   An important point to remember about using an aggregate expression in a group section is that the expression cannot refer to any controls in the Detail section. So, for example, you cannot create a calculated field in the Detail section that multiplies two numbers and then reference that control in the summary expression. You can, however, repeat the calculation expression in the summary. If a detail control named Total has an expression such as *=[Quantity] * [Price]*, you must use an expression such as *=Sum([Quantity] * [Price])* in your grouping section, not *=Sum([Total])*.

TIP   You can use a text box control's Running Sum property to calculate extended totals and to ask Access not to reset totals at the end of a group. If you set the Running Sum property to Over Group, Access accumulates the total over all groups at this level until it encounters a new group value at the next-highest level. If you set the property to Over All, Access accumulates one total and does not reset totals for new groups.

Creating a Grand Total

Use the Report Footer section to create grand totals for any values across the entire set of records in a report. You can use any of the aggregate functions in the report footer just as you did in the two grouping section footers. Figure 18-13 also shows you two *Sum* functions used in controls in the report footer. If you switch to Print Preview and go to the last page in the report, you should see a result similar to that shown in Figure 18-15.

> **NOTE** If you want to create percentage calculations for any of the groups over the grand total, you must create the control for the grand total in the report footer so that you can reference the total in percentage calculation expressions. (See the section titled "Calculating Percentages" later in this chapter.) If you don't want the total to print, set the control's Visible property to No.

FIGURE 18-15

The grand totals are displayed in the report in Print Preview.

4851	The Sourdough Cafe	6/1/97	Active	$80.00	$0.00
4851	The Sourdough Cafe	6/8/97	Active	$80.00	$0.00
4851	The Sourdough Cafe	6/15/97	Active	$80.00	$0.00
4851	The Sourdough Cafe	6/22/97	Active	$80.00	$0.00
4851	The Sourdough Cafe	6/29/97	Active	$80.00	$0.00
				$400.00	$0.00
4851	The Sourdough Cafe	7/6/97	Active	$80.00	$0.00
				$80.00	$0.00
				$3,379.00	$756.00
		Grand Total:		$36,901.66	$12,593.26

Concatenating Text Strings and Hiding Redundant Values

You probably noticed in several of the preceding examples that the GroupName, ContractNo, and ClubName fields print for every detail line. When a particular detail line has values that match the previous line, the report looks less readable and less professional. You can control this by using the Hide Duplicates text box property (which is available only in reports). You can switch to the Design view of this report and set the Hide Duplicates property to Yes for the GroupName text box in the Detail section to print the group name only once per group or page. When Access moves to a new grouping level or page, it prints the group name even if it matches the previous value displayed.

In this report, you could also set the Hide Duplicates property for both the ContractNo and ClubName fields. Note, however, that Hide Duplicates works on a field-by-field basis. In this database, a couple of the groups have more than one contract in a month for the same club. If you set the Hide Duplicates property to Yes for the two separate fields, you'll find instances in which the new contract number prints but the club name doesn't print because it's the same as the previous line. It would be less confusing to hide duplicates for the <u>combination</u> of contract number and club name. To do that, you have to use text string concatenation to display the data in a single control for which you can set Hide Duplicates.

Figure 18-16 shows a text string concatenation as a Control Source property setting. You need to remove both the ContractNo and ClubName text boxes and replace them with a single text box that spans the area covered by the two column heading labels. The special ampersand (&) character indicates a concatenation operation of three text strings. The first string derives from the *Format* function applied to the ContractNo field to return precisely six digits. The second string adds some spaces between the two data fields. The last string is the ClubName field from the record source. You can now set the Hide Duplicates property of this control to Yes to hide redundant data only when both the ContractNo <u>and</u> ClubName fields are the same.

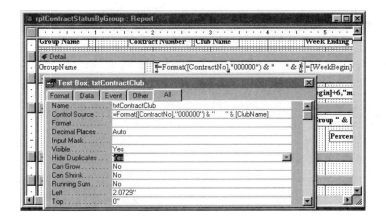

FIGURE 18-16

The control source expression that allows the Hide Duplicates property to eliminate duplicate ContractNo and ClubName values.

Another good use of string concatenation is to display data that looks like a label but that also includes information from the record source. Sometimes it's useful to combine descriptive text with a value from a text field in the underlying query or table or to combine multiple text fields in one control. In Figure 18-17, you can see a descriptive label (created by a single text box control) on one of the subtotal lines. (The figure shows the control source expression in the Zoom window [Shift-F2] to make it easy to read.) This "label" concatenates the words *Total for* with an expression that uses the *Format* function applied to the week ending date (*[WeekBegin]+6*) to get the name of the month and the year, and an ending string containing a colon, as shown in Figure 18-18. You could certainly define a label followed by a text box followed by another label to create the same display. The advantage of using a single control is that you don't have to worry about lining up three controls or setting the font characteristics. In fact, because the string in the middle containing the month and the year will vary in length, you cannot create three separate controls that correctly line up all possible values end-to-end. As you can imagine, you can use the same technique in the group footer to create a "label" that reads *Total for group* followed by the group name and a trailing colon. Set the Text Alignment property of these controls to Right so that they line up correctly next to the summary controls.

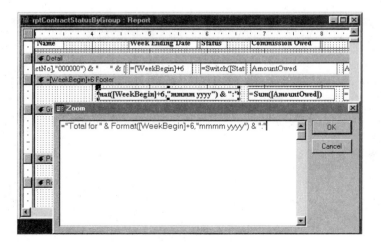

FIGURE 18-17

A text constant and string derived from a field in the record source are concatenated as a "label" in a text box.

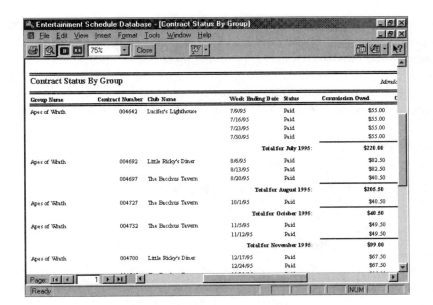

FIGURE 18-18
The total lines now have descriptive captions using data from the record source.

When you look at the report in Print Preview, you can see that the duplicate values for GroupName and for the combination of Contract-No and ClubName have been eliminated. You can also see the nice result from using a concatenated string in a text box to generate labels for the total lines.

Calculating Percentages

In any report that groups and summarizes data, you might want to determine what percentage of an outer group total or the grand total is represented in a particular sum. You can do this in a report because Access makes two passes of the data. On the first pass, it calculates simple expressions in detail lines, sums across groups, sums across the entire report, and calculates the length of the report. On the second pass, it resolves any expressions that reference totals calculated in the first pass. Consequently, you can create an expression in a detail or group summary section that divides by a sum in an outer group or the grand total to figure percentages.

Figure 18-19 shows an example of a percentage calculation in the GroupName Footer section. The expression divides the sum of the AmountOwed field for this group and then divides it by some value in a field called txtGrandOwed. If you look in the Report Footer section, you'll find that this is the name of the text box containing the grand total for the AmountOwed field.

FIGURE 18-19

Adding a calculation for a percentage of a grand total.

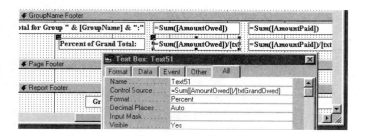

Set the Format property to Percent and switch to Print Preview. Scroll down to find a group total, and you'll also see the percent of the grand total, as shown in Figure 18-20.

FIGURE 18-20

A percentage calculation for one group in Print Preview.

Contract Status By Group

Group Name	Contract Number	Club Name	Week Ending Date	Status	Commission Owed
Apes of Wrath	004842	Little Ricky's Diner	11/3/96	Active	$82.50
			11/10/96	Active	$82.50
			11/17/96	Active	$82.50
			11/24/96	Active	$82.50
			Total for November 1996:		$330.00
Apes of Wrath	004826	The Bosston Inn	12/8/96	Active	$60.00
			12/15/96	Active	$60.00
			12/22/96	Active	$60.00
	004959	The Bacchus Tavern	12/29/96	Active	$15.00
			Total for December 1996:		$195.00
			Total for Group Apes of Wrath:		$1,971.00
			Percent of Grand Total:		5.34%

Creating and Embedding a Subreport

In many of your reports, you will probably design the detail section to display a single line of detail information from the underlying record source. As you learned in the previous sections, it's fairly easy to link several tables to get lots of detail across several one-to-many relationships in your database. You also saw how to use the Hide Duplicates property to visually create a hierarchy across several rows of detail.

However, just like the forms with subforms that you learned about in Chapter 15, "Advanced Form Design," you can embed subreports in the detail section of your report to display multiple detail lines from a table or query that has a "many" relationship to the one current line printed in the detail section. This technique is particularly useful when you want to display information from more than one "many" relationship on a single page. In the College Counseling database, for example, the rptCollege report prints the main college information as the detail, all of the classification categories in one subreport, and all of the application steps in another subreport. The rptStudent report combines the basic student information in the main report with the list of all colleges that interest the student in one subreport, test scores in a second subreport, and extracurricular activities in yet a third subreport. You could create a very complex query that joins all the information, but you'd get one row for each unique combination of college, test score, and activity per student—far more rows than you actually need to solve the problem.

Ray McCann, the owner of RM Productions, presented me with a particularly interesting and challenging problem that I solved with subreports, as you'll see in the following sections. Although an entertainment contract might span several weeks, all of the clubs and groups that Ray deals with like to schedule on a week-to-week basis. He needed a report that would show him for each of several upcoming weeks which clubs and groups for which he acts as an agent were not yet booked. Armed with this report, he could easily create a working list of unbooked groups that could be of interest to the open clubs. It would then be a simple matter of calling each club manager to suggest an available group and perhaps book it on the spot. Also, if a club or group for which he is not the usual agent were to call him to request a booking during a certain week, he could quickly generate this report to let the caller know what is available.

As you'll see in the following sections, queries can extract the open club or group information that Ray needs. A creative use of subreports puts all this information on one page per week to make it extremely easy to use.

Building the Subreport Queries

If you read to the end of Chapter 11, "Advanced Query Design—SQL," you already learned about some advanced techniques for wringing information out of the tables in the Entertainment Schedule database. The queries to solve the "open club or group" problem use some of the same techniques.

What makes this problem difficult is that the tblContracts table contains only one row per contract for a time period that might span several weeks. It doesn't make sense to store one row per week—that would mean a lot of redundant data. But as mentioned earlier, clubs and groups like to book (and take care of payments) on a week-to-week basis. (In Chapter 22, "Automating Your Application with VBA," you'll learn about some special procedures in the frmContracts form that set up the necessary weekly payment records in tblCommissions.) The queries to solve this problem use a "driver" query to separate each contract row into multiple weekly booking rows to perform the necessary analysis.

Since we're trying to find open weeks, we first need a query that generates one row per club or group for each available week on the calendar. You'll use a query that lists all clubs for all weeks in an outer join with a query that lists the booked weeks for each club to determine which weeks are open for the club. There's a companion set of queries that deal with groups.

In the sample database, you can find a table called tblDates that lists all dates from January 1, 1990, through the end of the year 2099. The query named *qryMondays* creates a row for Monday of each week (the start of the week for most group and club bookings). If you include this query in another query along with either the tblClubs table or the tblGroups table, you can generate one row per club or group for each week. You can see the query for clubs in Figure 18-21. (The query has been optimized by adding a parameter to reference the outer report that will include the subreport that uses this query.)

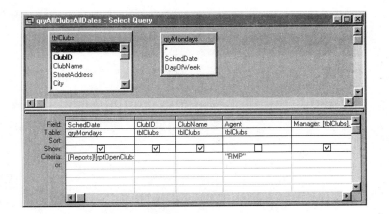

FIGURE 18-21
A query to return
one row for each
week for all clubs.

To build the new query, you'll need the ClubID, ClubName, MgrFirstName, MgrLastName, and ClubPhoneNumber fields from the tblClubs table. Because there is no join line between the table and the query, you get the *Cartesian product* of the rows in the two record sources. That is, you get each row in tblClubs matched up with each row in qryMondays. That's a lot of rows. In most cases, Ray will want to look at only a few weeks at a time. Rather than extract all rows every time this query runs, you can restrict the rows returned by the query to only the weeks of interest.

When I built this query, I knew that I was going to use it in a subreport embedded in a main report called rptOpenClubsAndGroups. Furthermore, I knew that the outer report would use the SchedDate field from qryMondays to print one week per page. You'll learn more about how to reference open forms and reports in Chapter 20, "Automating Your Application with Macros." For now, it's sufficient to know that *[Reports]![rptOpenClubsAndGroups]![SchedDate]* references the value in the SchedDate field on the current page of the report we're about to build. This limits the query to one week per page so that the report takes a few seconds per page to calculate instead of several minutes. You can find the qryAllClubsAllDates and qryAllGroupsAllDates queries in the sample database.

Now we need a query to produce one row per booked week for every contract. You can start with a query that joins tblClubs to tblContracts. You can output from this query one row per contract that includes the club name, manager name, club phone number, group name, group leader name, group phone number, contract status, and beginning and ending dates of the contract. To get one row per week, you can add our old friend qryMondays to the mix and use a special type of join to get the required result. Remember, if you didn't create a join between qryMondays and the other tables, you'll get one row for all weeks for all contracts. What you want is one row from the join across clubs and contracts linked with each row from qryMondays that represents a week within the span of the contract. As long as the Monday from qryMondays is not more than seven days earlier than the start of the contract and that same date is also less than or equal to the date of the end of the contract, at least part of the contract will fall during that week.

The only way to specify this sort of join is in SQL. You can see the query (which is saved as *qrySchedDates* in the sample database) in Figure 18-22. (This query is also optimized to reference the outer report.) If you studied Chapter 11, "Advanced Query Design—SQL," you know that the list following the SELECT DISTINCTROW includes all the fields to be output by the query. The FROM clause lists the source tables or queries and specifies how Access should link them. The "magic" part of the query is this phrase:

```
(qryMondays.SchedDate > tblContracts.BeginningDate - 7) AND
(qryMondays.SchedDate <= tblContracts.EndingDate)
```

This states in "SQL-ese" the link criteria necessary to get one row per week. In English, this says, "Link the rows from qryMondays with the rows from tblContracts where the week defined by the row in qryMondays spans any part of the contract in tblContracts." As with the qryAllClubsAllDates query, the WHERE clause restricts the output of this query to the date on the current page of the report to get the best performance.

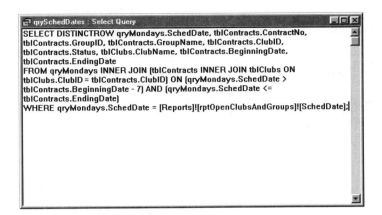

FIGURE 18-22

A complex query that returns one row per week for each contract (which might span multiple weeks) in the database.

The final queries link either qryAllClubsAllDates or qryAllGroups-AllDates with qrySchedDates using an outer join to find the unbooked dates. (Figure 18-23 shows the final query that returns one row per unbooked week for each club.) As you'll recall from Chapter 8, "Adding Power with Select Queries," you can set the join properties to include all rows from one table or query and any matching rows from the second table or query. When there is no match, Access returns the special Null value in the columns from the second table or query. If you test for Null, the query returns only the unmatched rows—in this case, the weeks for any club or group in which that club or group is not booked.

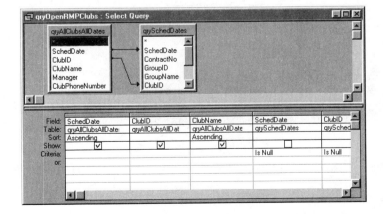

FIGURE 18-23

A complex query that returns one row per unbooked week for each club.

You can find the qryOpenRMPClubs and qryOpenRMPGroups queries in the sample database; they return the open weeks for clubs and groups, respectively. The next step is to use these queries as the row source for two subreports.

Designing the Subreport

Select either query in the Database window, and select New Report from the New Object toolbar button's drop-down list. Select Design View in the New Report dialog box and click OK to open the Report window in Design view.

Open the View menu and be sure the Page Header/Footer command is not checked. Access won't display page headers and footers in a subreport. In the final report, the list of open clubs should appear side-by-side with the list of open groups, so each subreport should be narrow enough to fit both of them across a standard-width page—about 3 inches will work. You don't need the SchedDate field from the underlying query on the report, but that field will form the link to the outer report, as you'll see in a moment. For clubs, you need the ClubName, Manager, and ClubPhoneNumber fields, as shown in Figure 18-24.

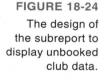

FIGURE 18-24

The design of the subreport to display unbooked club data.

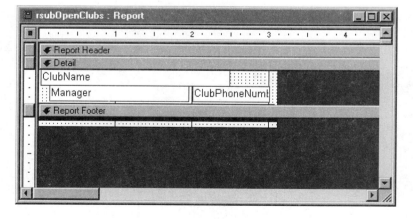

For Groups, you need the GroupName, Leader, and HomePhone fields, as shown in Figure 18-25. Choose Report Header/Footer from the View menu and shrink the header to a height of 0. Make the report footer about .125 inch tall and place a thick black line control across the top of the section. If the list is long enough to span more than one page, this line will provide a visual indicator of the end of the list. You can find the two subreports saved as *rsubOpenClubs* and *rsubOpenGroup* in the sample database.

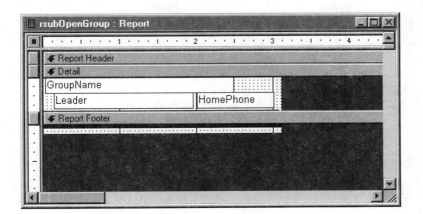

FIGURE 18-25
The design of the subreport to display unbooked group data.

Embedding the Subreport

Now comes the payoff. Start a new report on the qryMondays query. Make the report 6.5 inches wide. (This works well with the default 1-inch margins.) Create a title in the Page Header section using a label control, and add a text box to display today's date if you want. Drag and drop the SchedDate field from the field list onto the Page Header section. Change the text box's caption to Week Beginning. Add a label on the left side for clubs and another on the right side for groups. In the Detail section, add two subreport controls next to each other, and make them both about 3 inches wide and .5 inch high.

To embed the rsubOpenClubs subreport in the left control, enter *Report.rsubOpenClubs* in the Source Object property box of the subreport control, as shown in Figure 18-26 on the next page. Because you can also include a form in the report, the *Report* prefix tells Access to include a report, not a form. As you did with a subform, you need to define linking fields. In this case, the SchedDate field on the main report (which is set in the Link Master Fields property box) matches the SchedDate field on the subreport (which is set in the Link Child Fields property box). You need to set both the Can Shrink and Can Grow properties to Yes to allow the subreport to expand or shrink as necessary.

FIGURE 18-26

The subreport
is linked to the
main report.

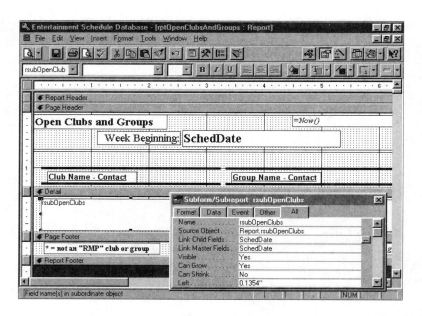

Follow the same procedure to embed the rsubOpenGroup report in the subreport control on the right. Finally, choose Size/To Fit from the Format menu for both subreport controls to make sure that they are sized correctly to display all the data in the subreports.

If you find that you need to make some adjustments to the subreport (or, for that matter, to any subreport or subform), you can edit it directly from the Design view of the main report or form. Be sure that the subreport control isn't selected, and then double-click on the subreport control to open the subreport in Design view. Save and close the subreport in its Report window after you finish making changes. To update the subreport control to reflect these changes in the main report's Report window, select the subreport control, click on it, and highlight the source object name in the upper left corner of the control. Press Enter to update the subreport definition in the main report.

Remember that three of the queries contain references to the outer report's SchedDate field to obtain optimum performance. If you want to save your own copy of this report, you must also go to each of the three queries and change the reference to point to your report. You can then open your own report to see how it works. Because your report isn't restricted in any way, you'll see open dates starting with January 1, 1990. If you want to see how this report works in the "live" application, go on to the next section.

Viewing the Embedded Result

To see how this report works in "real life," go to the Database window and open the frmMain form. Click the Reports button on that form to open the Reports switchboard form. On that form, click the Open Clubs And Groups button to open a dialog box in which you can specify a date range, as shown in Figure 18-27.

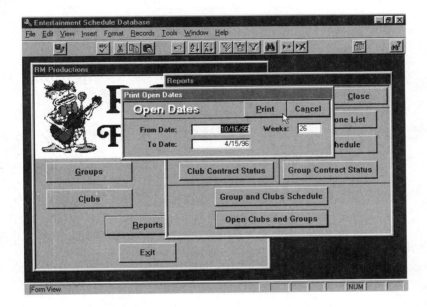

FIGURE 18-27

Specifying a date range for the Open Clubs And Groups report in the sample application.

The sample database contains contract data from June 1995 to December 1996. If you specify a date range beginning in mid-October 1995 and click the Print button in the Print Open Dates dialog box, you should see the result shown in Figure 18-28 on the next page. Do you suppose the No One Wants to Work Here club would be interested in booking Bucky and the Fullerenes? Better ask Ralph first! (You'll recall from Chapter 8 that this is the one club that has never had any bookings.)

FIGURE 18-28

The Open Clubs
And Groups
report showing a
result from two
subreports.

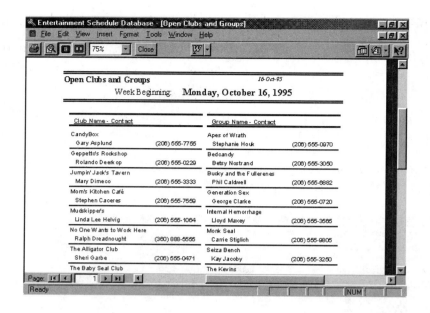

Creating a "Spreadsheet" Report

You can easily create sophisticated reports with grouped totals down the page, like the Group Contract Status report you built in the previous sections. But what if you want a monthly summary of number of contracts, total weeks booked, <u>and</u> total commissions all in one report? Crosstab queries work well for summarizing data by groups and dates, but they can display only a single summarized value.

You could export the data to a Microsoft Excel spreadsheet using the Office Links button on the toolbar. Once in Excel, you could use the PivotTable Wizard to create your report. You could also use the PivotTable Form Wizard in Microsoft Access to produce an Excel spreadsheet linked to an Access form. However, the form created by the PivotTable Form Wizard must be linked to static data—that is, you must summarize data in the source query either for a specific year or for all years. You can find an example of such a form in the sample database, frmGroupSummary1996, that was created using the PivotTable Form Wizard and a query based on 1996 data. If you want something more flexible that lets the user specify the reporting year, you can use the reporting facilities in Access to create what you want.

Building a Summary Query

First, you need a query to summarize contract data for the year by group and by month. This query will be very similar to the crosstab query you built in Chapter 8, "Adding Power with Select Queries," but it creates totals for the number of contracts, the number of contract weeks, and total commission on these contracts from the tblContracts table.

You can find the query you need saved as *qryGroupSpreadsheet* in the sample database. This query includes a parameter that prompts the user to enter the year of interest. The query outputs the parameter as a calculated column result and also uses the parameter to restrict which contracts are considered. You can see the query in Figure 18-29 and in Figure 18-30 on the next page.

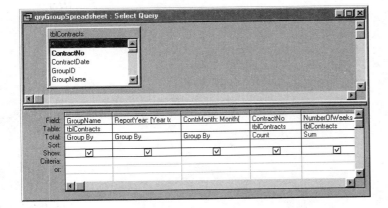

FIGURE 18-29

The first five fields in a query to summarize group contract data by month.

This query groups the data by GroupName, by Year (the parameter field), and by contract Month (using the *Month* built-in function on the BeginningDate field). In addition, the query counts the contracts, sums the NumberOfWeeks field, and sums an expression that calculates the commission on each contract. The query is restricted to contracts for which RM Productions is the commissioning agent and the contract is marked either Active or Paid.

FIGURE 18-30

The remaining
fields in a query
to summarize
group contract
data by month.

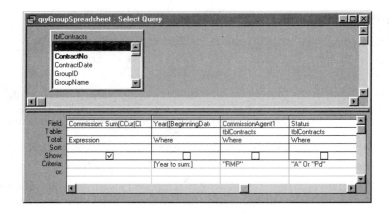

Designing a "Summaries Only" Report

The report you need in order to display the contract count, number of
weeks, and total commission dollars by month in a spreadsheet-like
format won't actually have any detail lines. Start by selecting the
qryGroupSpreadsheet query, and then select New Report from the New
Object toolbar button's drop-down list. Open the report in Design
view. Start by defining a group on the GroupName field, and set the
Group Footer property to Yes. Access will display a GroupName Footer
section for you. Your Sorting And Grouping window should look like
the one shown in Figure 18-31.

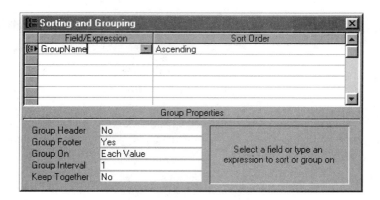

Open the Report Header and Report Footer sections by choosing
Report Header/Footer from the Format menu. Be sure you also have a
page header and a page footer. In the Report Header section, create a
label control as a title for the report.

In the Page Header section, insert a Group Name label at the left edge. Move about 1.5 inches to the right and start inserting labels for each of the month groups. Create a label containing the month name centered above the three labels for Contracts, Weeks, and Comm. Add a line control on either side of each month group to highlight the "columns" you'll be creating below. Each group of labels should be no more than 1.5 inches wide. Create groups for the months of January through June, extending the report to 10.5 inches wide. Drag the GroupName field from the field list onto the GroupName Footer section, remove its label, and set the control to display Arial 8-point text. Your result should look something like that shown in Figure 18-32.

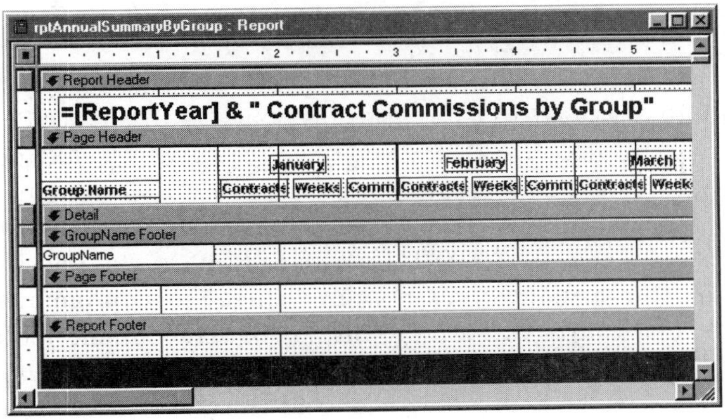

FIGURE 18-32

A spreadsheet report under construction.

To create the monthly totals you want, you need three unbound text boxes per month in the GroupName Footer section—one to display the sum of the contract count, one to display the sum of the number of weeks, and one to display the sum of the total commission amount. You want to use the *Sum* function to total the CountOfContractNo, SumOfNumberOfWeeks, and Commission fields from the query. However, for each month, you want the *Sum* function to add up only the values for the month in that column. Here's where the *IIF* function comes in handy. In the unbound text box control for the total contract count in January, test to see whether the month in the "current" row being processed by the *Sum* function has a month value of *1*. If the month is *1*, give the *Sum* function the CountOfContractNo value to work with, as shown in Figure 18-33 on the next page. If the month is not *1*, pass a *0* to the *Sum* function. The formula in the Control Source property box is as follows:

=Sum(IIf([ContrMonth]=1,[CountOfContractNo],0))

FIGURE 18-33

Creating a total
of selected
month values.

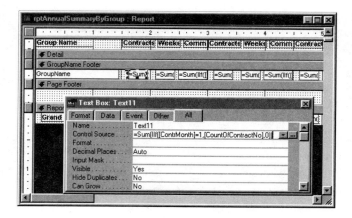

You'll enter a similar formula for the controls that total contract weeks. The formula for January looks like this:

=Sum(IIf([ContrMonth]=1,[SumOfNumberOfWeeks],0))

And, as you might expect, the formula for the commission text boxes looks like this:

=Sum(IIf([ContrMonth]=1,[Commission],0))

For the controls in the other months, change the month number to pick out the total values you want to display in that column. (February is 2, March is 3, and so on.) In the sample report in the Entertainment Schedule database, lines are drawn on either side of each group of monthly total controls so that they align with the lines in the page header.

You'll notice that the columns for the first six months will fit within a 10.5-inch-wide report, and that a standard 8.5-inch-wide page would be too narrow. To fix this, choose Page Setup from the File menu, select Landscape mode, and set the left and right margins to .25 inch. This gives you a 10.5-inch-wide print area on standard 8.5-by-11-inch paper.

To set up the second logical page for the last six months, stretch your report to 21 inches wide. Select all the controls in the first "half" of the report, section by section, and then choose Duplicate from the Edit menu. You can move these duplicated controls to the area between 10.5 and 21 inches. Change the month labels and change each of the formulas to test for the month in that column.

To create grand totals in the report, copy all the calculation controls from the GroupName Footer section to the Clipboard, click in the Report Footer section, and paste the controls there. You don't have to make any changes to any of the formulas, although you'll need to delete the GroupName controls and add labels for the grand totals. The totals in the GroupName Footer section will be for the rows matching that group. The totals in the Report Footer section will be for all rows returned by the query. Your report in Design view should now look something like that shown in Figure 18-34.

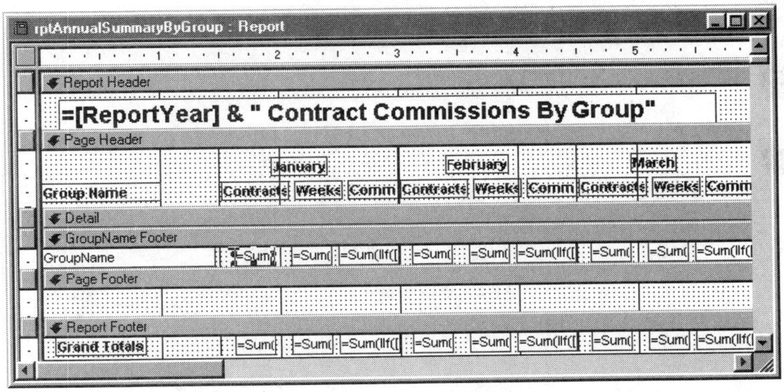

FIGURE 18-34 The completed spreadsheet report in Design view.

Switch to Print Preview, respond to the year prompt by entering *1996*, and your result should look similar to that shown in Figure 18-35.

1996 Contract Commissions By Group

	January			February			March			April	
Group Name	Contracts	Weeks	Comm.	Contracts	Weeks	Comm.	Contracts	Weeks	Comm.	Contracts	Weeks
Apes of Wrath	1	2	$150.00	0	0	$0.00	2	2	$50.50	2	5
Blind Logwara	1	1	$44.00	0	0	$0.00	2	4	$240.00	0	0
Bucky and the Fullerenes	2	5	$130.00	0	0	$0.00	0	0	$0.00	1	2
Cornish Game Hens	0	0	$0.00	0	0	$0.00	0	0	$0.00	0	0
Generation Sex	0	0	$0.00	1	20	$1,300.00	0	0	$0.00	0	0
Henry and Otis	1	1	$25.00	1	2	$121.00	1	1	$55.00	0	0
Internal Hemorrhage	1	1	$27.00	0	0	$0.00	1	1	$25.00	0	0
Jelly Plug	1	5	$0.00	1	1	$27.00	0	0	$0.00	1	4
King Tut and the Uncommon	0	0	$0.00	0	0	$0.00	0	0	$0.00	2	4
Life Imitates Art	0	0	$0.00	1	1	$30.00	0	0	$0.00	0	0
Monk Seal	0	0	$0.00	1	3	$225.00	0	0	$0.00	0	0
Muddled Thoughts	0	0	$0.00	0	0	$0.00	1	4	$500.00	1	5
Seltza Bench	0	0	$0.00	0	0	$0.00	0	0	$0.00	0	0
Shaman's Apprentice	1	1	$40.00	1	2	$130.00	1	2	$0.00	2	3
Supertube	1	1	$55.00	1	2	$72.00	3	3	$126.00	1	1
The Belltones	3	4	$166.00	1	1	$33.00	3	3	$100.00	1	2
The Buddy Love Orchestra	0	0	$0.00	0	0	$0.00	0	0	$0.00	1	2
The Codpieces	0	0	$0.00	3	3	$87.00	1	1	$22.00	0	0
The Keuhs	0	0	$0.00	0	0	$0.00	1	2	$99.00	0	0
The Yurts	0	0	$0.00	0	0	$0.00	0	0	$0.00	0	0
Tiny People	0	0	$0.00	0	0	$0.00	2	2	$58.00	1	1
Urban Runoff	0	0	$0.00	1	1	$70.00	2	2	$57.00	2	6
Grand Totals:	12	21	$537.00	12	36	$2,096.00	20	27	$1,442.50	15	35

FIGURE 18-35 The spreadsheet report in Print Preview.

You can find this report saved as *rptAnnualSummaryByGroup* in the Entertainment Schedule database.

At this point, you should thoroughly understand the mechanics of constructing reports and working with complex formulas. The final part of this book shows you how to bring together all that you've learned to build an application.

Part 6

SELECT EDITION

Creating an Application

619

Chapter 19

Adding Power
with Macros

n Microsoft Access, you can define a macro to execute just about any task you would otherwise initiate with the keyboard or the mouse. The unique power of macros in Access is in their ability to automate responses to many types of events. The event might be a change in the data, the opening or closing of a form or a report, or even a change of focus from one control to another. Within a macro, you can include multiple actions and define condition checking so that different actions are performed depending on the values in your forms or reports.

In this chapter, first you'll learn about the various types of actions you can define in macros. Next, you'll tour the macro design facility and learn how to build both a simple macro and a macro with multiple defined actions. You'll also learn how to manage the many macros you need for a form or a report by creating a macro group. Finally, you'll see how to add conditional statements to a macro to control the actions Access performs. At the end of the chapter, you'll find summaries of the macro actions and of the events that can trigger a macro. You might find these sections useful as a quick reference when you're designing macros for your applications.

Uses of Macros

Microsoft Access provides various types of macro actions that you can use to automate your application:

- You can use macros to open any table, query, form, or report in any available view. You can also use a macro to close any open table, query, form, or report.

- You can use macros to open a report in Print Preview or to send a report directly to the printer. You can also send the output data from a report to a Rich Text Format (rtf) file, a Microsoft Windows Notepad (txt) file, or a Microsoft Excel (xls) file and then open the file in Microsoft Word, Windows Notepad, or Microsoft Excel.

- You can use macros to execute a select query or an action query. You can base the parameters of a query on the values of controls in any open form.

- You can use macros to base the execution of an action on any condition that tests values in a database, a form, or a report.

You can use macros to execute other macros or to execute Visual Basic for Applications (VBA) functions. You can halt the current macro or all macros, cancel the event that triggered the macro, or quit the application.

■ You can use macros to set the value of any form or report control. You can also emulate keyboard actions and supply input to system dialog boxes, and you can refresh the values in any control based on a query.

■ You can use macros to apply a filter to, go to any record in, or search for data in a form's underlying table or query.

■ You can use macros with any form to define a custom menu bar to replace the standard menu bar in Access. You can enable or disable and check or uncheck items on custom menus, including shortcut menus and global menus. You can also open and close any of the standard Access toolbars or your own custom toolbars.

■ You can use macros to execute any of the commands on any of the Access menus.

■ You can use macros to move and size, minimize, maximize, or restore any window within the Access workspace. You can change the focus to a window or to any control within a window. You can select a page of a report to display in Print Preview.

■ You can use macros to display informative messages and to sound a beep to draw attention to your messages. You can also disable certain warning messages when executing action queries.

■ You can use macros to rename any object in your database. You can make another copy of a selected object in your database or copy an object to another Access database. You can delete objects in your database. You can use a macro to save an object. With macros you can also import, export, or attach other database tables or import or export spreadsheet or text files.

■ You can use macros to start an application and exchange data with the application using Dynamic Data Exchange (DDE) or the Clipboard. You can send data from a table, query, form, or report to an output file and then open that file in the appropriate application. You can also send keystrokes to the target application.

Consider some of the other possibilities for macros. For example, you can make it easy to move from one task to another using command buttons that open and position forms and set values. You can create very complex editing routines that validate data entered in forms, including checking data in other tables. You can even check something like the customer name entered in an order form and open another form so that the user can enter detailed data if no record exists for that customer.

NOTE Macros are particularly useful for building small, personal applications or for prototyping larger ones. As you'll learn in Chapter 21, "Visual Basic for Applications Fundamentals," you probably should use VBA for complex applications or for applications that will be shared by several users over a network. Even if you think you're ready to jump right into VBA, you should study all the macro actions first. You'll find that you'll use nearly all of the available macro actions in VBA, so learning macros is an excellent introduction to programming in Access in general.

Creating a Simple Macro

Near the end of Chapter 15, "Advanced Form Design," you learned how to create a macro that opens a form when a button is clicked on another form. This section explains the macro design facility in Access in more detail.

The Macro Window

Open the Wedding List sample database, and close the Wedding List data entry form to return to the Database window. As you'll discover a bit later in this chapter, a special macro called *Autoexec* runs each time you open the database. We'll look at that macro in some detail to see how it hides a few items and opens and maximizes the main data entry form to start the application.

Click on the Macros tab in the Database window, and click the New button to open a new Macro window similar to the one shown in Figure 19-1 on the next page. In the upper part of the Macro window you define your new macro, and in the lower part you enter settings, called *arguments,* for the actions you've selected for your macro. The upper part shows at least two columns, Action and Comment. You can view all four columns shown in Figure 19-1 by clicking the Macro Names and Conditions buttons on the toolbar.

FIGURE 19-1
A new Macro
window.

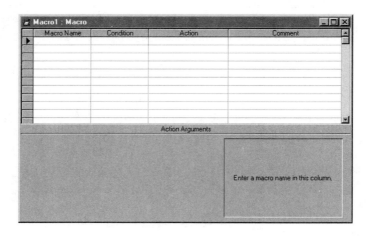

Notice that the area at the lower right displays a brief Help message. The message changes depending on where the cursor is located in the upper part of the window. (Remember: You can always press F1 to open a context-sensitive Help topic.)

In the Action column, you can specify any one of the 49 macro actions provided by Access. If you click in any box in the Action column, a down arrow button will appear at the right side of the box. Click this button to open a drop-down list of the macro actions, as shown in Figure 19-2.

FIGURE 19-2
The drop-
down list of
macro actions.

To see how the Macro window works, select the MsgBox action now. You can use the MsgBox action to open a pop-up modal dialog box with a message in it. It's a great way to display a warning or an informative message in your database without defining a separate form.

Now, assume that this message will be a greeting, and type *Greeting message* in the corresponding box in the Comment column. You'll find the Comment column especially useful for documenting large macros that contain many actions. In the Comment column, you can enter additional comments in any blank box (that is, any box without an action next to it).

After you select an action such as MsgBox, Access displays argument boxes in the lower part of the window (shown in Figure 19-3), in which you enter the arguments for the action.

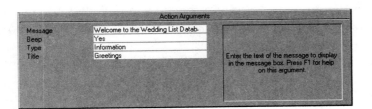

FIGURE 19-3
Arguments
for a MsgBox
action that
displays a
greeting
message.

TIP As you can in the Table and Query windows in Design view, you can use the F6 key to move between the upper and lower parts of the Macro window.

The setting in the Message argument box is the message that you want Access to display in the dialog box you're creating. The setting in the Beep argument box tells Access whether to sound a beep when the message is displayed. In the Type argument box, you can set a graphic indicator, such as a red critical icon, that will appear along with your message. In the Title argument box, you can type the contents of your dialog box's title bar. Use the settings shown in Figure 19-3 in your macro. (The message should read, "Welcome to the Wedding List Database.")

Saving Your Macro

You must save a macro before you can run it. Choose the Save (or Save As/Export) command from the File menu. When you choose Save, Access opens the dialog box shown in Figure 19-4 on the next page. Enter the name *TestGreeting* and click OK to save your macro.

FIGURE 19-4

The Save As
dialog box for
saving a macro.

Testing Your Macro

You can run some macros (such as the simple one you just created) directly from the Database window or from the Macro window because they don't depend on controls on an open form or report. If your macro does depend on a form or a report, you must link the macro to the appropriate event and run it that way. (You'll learn how to do this later in this chapter.) However you run your macro, Access provides a good way to test it by allowing you to single-step through the macro actions.

To activate single-stepping, first switch to the Database window, click on the Macros tab, select the macro you want to test, and click the Design button. These steps open the macro in the Macro window. Either click the Single Step button on the Macro toolbar or choose the Single Step command from the Run menu. Now when you run your macro, Access opens the Macro Single Step dialog box before executing each step. In this dialog box, you'll see the macro name, the action, and the action arguments.

Try this procedure with the *TestGreeting* macro you just created. Open the Macro window, click the Single Step button, and then click the Run button. The Macro Single Step dialog box opens, as shown in Figure 19-5. If you click the Step button in the dialog box, the action you see in the dialog box will run, and you'll see the modal dialog box with the message you created, as shown in Figure 19-6. Click the OK button in the modal dialog box to dismiss it. If your macro had more than one action defined, you would have returned to the Macro Single Step dialog box, which would have shown you the next action. In this case, your macro has only one action, so Access returns you to the Macro window.

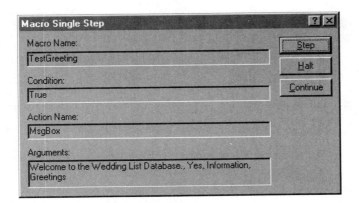

FIGURE 19-5
The Macro Single
Step dialog box.

FIGURE 19-6
The dialog box
you created with
the *TestGreeting*
macro.

If you encounter an error in any macro during normal execution of your application, Access first displays a dialog box explaining the error it found. You then see an Action Failed dialog box, which is similar to the Macro Single Step dialog box, containing information about the action that caused the problem. At this point, you can click only the Halt button. You can then edit your macro to fix the problem.

Before you read on in this chapter, you might want to return to the Macro window and click the Single Step button again so that it's no longer selected. Otherwise you'll continue to single-step through every macro you run until you exit and restart Access.

Defining Multiple Actions

In Microsoft Access, you can define more than one action within a macro, and you can define the sequence in which you want the actions performed. The Wedding List database contains several good examples of macros that have more than one action. Open the database, and close the Wedding List data entry form to return to the Database window. Click on the Macros tab, and select the macro named *Autoexec.* Click the Design button to open the Macro window. The macro is shown in Figure 19-7.

FIGURE 19-7

The *Autoexec* macro, which defines multiple actions that Access executes automatically when you open the Wedding List database.

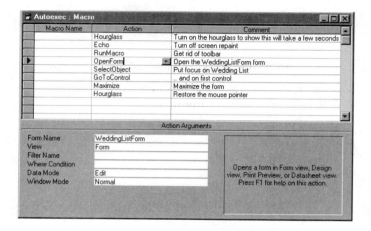

You can see eight actions defined in this macro that Access executes automatically whenever you open the database. First, the Hourglass action displays an hourglass mouse pointer to give the user a visual clue that the next several steps may take a second or two. It's always a good idea to turn on this visual cue, even if you think the next several actions won't take very long. Next, the Echo command executes (its Echo On argument is set to No) to ask Access not to repaint the screen after any of the succeeding actions. When you plan to execute several actions in a row that can each potentially cause changes to the screen display, you can turn repainting off to minimize annoying screen flashing. As you'll learn later in Chapter 21, "Visual Basic for Applications Fundamentals," a similar command is available in VBA (the Echo method of the Application object) to halt screen flashing.

TIP If you create a macro and name it *Autoexec,* Access runs the macro each time you open the database in which it is stored. You can keep Access from running this macro if you hold down the Shift key as you open the database. (For details, see Chapter 23, "The Finishing Touches.")

The next action, RunMacro, runs another macro that hides the standard Form View toolbar. You'll find this technique handy if you use any short series of actions again and again in macros. Create a macro with the repeated commands, and then call that macro wherever you need to execute those common actions. If you open the *Offbars* macro that's called from this RunMacro action, you can see that it contains a ShowToolbar action to hide the Form View toolbar.

The next action, OpenForm, opens the WeddingListForm form. As you can see in Figure 19-7, the macro action sets four arguments to define how it should work. The Form Name argument indicates the form you want to open. The View argument tells Access what view you want. (The four choices for the View argument are Form, Design, Print Preview, and Datasheet.) Edit is the default for the Data Mode argument, which allows the user to add, edit, or delete records while using this form. (The choices for this argument are Add, Edit, and Read Only.) The default setting for the Window Mode argument is Normal. This opens the form in the mode set by its design properties. You can override the design property settings to open the form in Hidden mode, as an Icon, or in the special Dialog mode. When you open a form in Dialog mode, Access does not run further actions or VBA statements until you close the form.

Access doesn't always wait for one action to complete before going on to the next one. For example, an OpenForm action merely starts a task to begin opening the form. Particularly if the form displays a lot of data, Access might take several seconds to load all the data and finish displaying the form. Since you're running Windows 95, your PC can handle many tasks at once. Access takes advantage of this by going to the next task without waiting for the form to completely open. However, since the *Autoexec* macro wants to maximize the WeddingListForm form, the form must be completely open in order for this to work.

You can force a form to finish opening by asking Access to put the focus on the form. The *Autoexec* macro does this by using the Select-Object action to identify the object to receive the focus (in this case, the WeddingListForm form) followed by the GoToControl action to put the focus on a specific control on the form. Once the GoToControl action puts the focus on the control, the Maximize action sizes the active window (the window containing the object that currently has the focus) to fit the entire screen. The final action in the *Autoexec* macro (the Hourglass action again) restores the mouse pointer to let the user know that the macro is done.

Learning to define multiple actions within a macro is very useful when you want to automate the tasks you perform on a day-to-day basis. Now that you've learned how to do this, the next step is to learn how to group actions by tasks.

Macro Groups

You'll find that most of the forms you design for an application require multiple macro actions—some to edit fields, some to open reports, and still others to respond to command buttons. You can design a macro for each of these actions, but you'll soon have hundreds of separate macros in your application. You can create a simpler design (with only a few macro files) by defining a macro group for each form or report. Another technique is to create a group for each type of action in your database. For example, you might create one macro group containing all the OpenForm actions you need to run. In a macro group, you can define a number of individual macros. You give each macro in the group a name in the Macro Name column of the Macro window. As you saw earlier in the *Autoexec* example, naming a macro object in a RunMacro action asks Access to run the actions it finds in that macro object. You ask Access to run a specific macro within a macro group by entering the name of the macro group, a period, and the name of the macro within the group. You can also define actions without a name at the beginning of a macro group. Access executes these actions when you ask it to run the macro group with no qualifying name.

Figure 19-8 shows the PrintOptions form of the Wedding List database in Form view. This form contains two command buttons, each of which triggers a different macro. The two macros are contained within a macro group called DoReport. To look at the macro group, switch to the Database window, click on the Macros tab, and then select DoReport from the list of macros in the Database window. Click the Design button to open this macro group in the Macro window. The macro group is shown in Figure 19-9.

The DoReport macro group has a Macro Name column. (If you don't see the Macro Name column, click the Macro Names button on the toolbar.) Each of the seven names in this column represents an individual macro within the group. (You have to scroll down to see the other names.) The first macro (triggered by the Print Report button on the WeddingListForm form) opens the PrintOptions form, and the second macro determines which report was selected. The next four macros display the appropriate report in Print Preview mode, based on the result of the second macro. The last macro merely closes the PrintOptions form if the user clicks the Cancel button. As you might have guessed, Access runs a macro starting with the first action of the macro name specified and executes each action in sequence until it encounters a StopMacro action, another macro name, or no further actions. As you'll see a bit later, you can control whether some actions execute by adding tests in the Condition column of the macro.

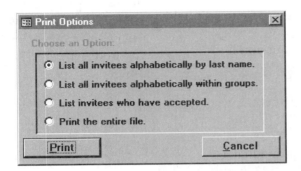

FIGURE 19-8
The Wedding List PrintOptions form.

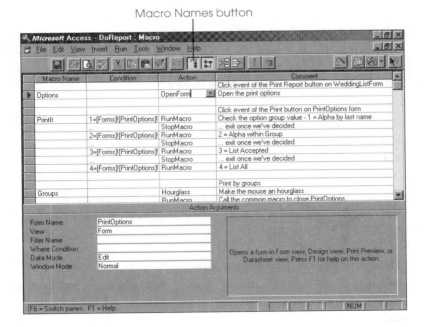

FIGURE 19-9
The DoReport macro group.

If you open the PrintOptions form in Design view (see Figure 19-10 on the next page) and look at the properties for each of the command buttons, you'll see that the On Click property contains the name of the macro that executes when the user clicks the command button.

If you open the drop-down list for any event property, you can see that Access lists all macros and macro groups for you to make it easy to select the one you want. Remember, the macro name is divided into two parts. The part before the period is the name of the macro group, and the part after the period is the name of a specific macro within the group. So, for the first command button control, the On Click property is set to *DoReport.PrintIt*. When the user clicks this button, Access runs the *PrintIt* macro in the DoReport group. When you have specified a macro name in an event property, you can click the Build button next to the property, and Access will open that macro in Design view.

FIGURE 19-10
The On Click
property of a
command button
set to execute a
macro.

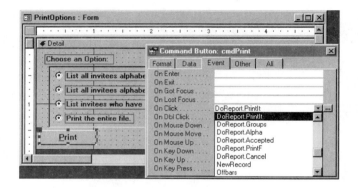

Conditional Expressions

In some macros, you might want to execute some actions only under certain conditions. For example, you might want to update a record, but only if new values in the controls on a form pass validation tests. Or you might want to display or hide certain controls based on the value of other controls.

The *PrintIt* macro in the DoReport macro group is a good example of a macro that uses conditions to test whether an action should proceed. Select DoReport from the list of macros in the Wedding List database, and click the Design button to see the Macro window. Click in the Condition column of the first line of the *PrintIt* macro and press Shift-F2 to open the Zoom edit window shown in Figure 19-11. If you can't see the Condition column, click the Conditions button on the toolbar.

Conditions button

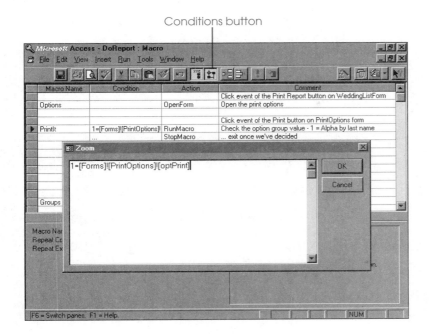

FIGURE 19-11

A condition in the Wedding List *DoReport* macro shown in the Zoom edit window.

As you saw earlier, this macro is triggered by the On Click property of the Print button on the PrintOptions form. This form allows the user to print a specific report by selecting an appropriate option button and then clicking the Print button. If you look at the form in Design view (see Figure 19-10), you'll see that the option buttons are actually located within an Option Group control on the form. Each option button sets a specific numeric value (in this case *1* for the first button, *2* for the second button, *3* for the third button, and *4* for the fourth button) in the option group, which you can test in the Condition column of a macro.

When you include a condition in a macro, Access won't run the action on that line unless the condition evaluates to True. If you want to run a group of actions based on the outcome of a test, you can enter the test in the Condition column on the first action line and enter ellipses (...) in the Condition column for the other actions in the group. This causes Access to evaluate the condition only once and execute additional lines with an ellipsis in the Condition column as long as the original test evaluated to True.

In this particular example, the condition tests the value of the option group control on the form. You can reference any control on an open form by using the syntax

FORMS!<*formname*>!<*controlname*>

where *formname* is the name of an open form and *controlname* is the name of a control on that form. In this case, the direct reference is *[FORMS]![PrintOptions]![optPrint]*. (*optPrint* is the name of the option group control. You can see this in the Name property on the Other tab of the Properties window for this control.)

> **TIP** In most cases, you don't need to surround the FORMS keyword or *formname* with square brackets when you use this syntax to reference a control on a form. Access will insert the brackets as needed.

Once you understand how to refer to the value of a control on a form, you can see that the *PrintIt* macro tests for each of the possible values of the option group control. When it finds a match, *PrintIt* runs the appropriate macro within the group that opens the report requested and then stops. If you look at the individual report macros, you'll see that they each run a common macro to close the PrintOptions form (you don't need it anymore once you figured out what choice was made) and then open the requested report in Print Preview and put the focus on the window that displays the report.

Using macro groups is a good way to consolidate your macros so that they are easy to find and maintain. You can group macros not only by task, but by "function." Suppose you have a form that contains several command buttons and each button is assigned a macro that performs a specific task. You can gather these macros together to form a macro group and then give the group a name that relates it to the form containing the command buttons. If you have a Customer form that includes several command buttons, you can create a macro group and name it *CustomerFormMacros*. This macro group will contain the macros that will be assigned to the command buttons on the form.

The rest of this chapter summarizes all the actions you can include in macros and the events that trigger macros. You'll find it useful to browse through these sections to become familiar with the available actions and events before going on to the next chapter, in which you'll see how other parts of the Wedding List database are automated. You'll find this action and event reference useful as you begin to study how to automate applications with VBA in later chapters.

Summary of Macro Actions

This section summarizes the actions available for you to use in macros. The summaries are organized in the following functional categories:

- Opening and closing tables, queries, forms, and reports
- Printing data
- Executing a query
- Testing conditions and controlling action flow
- Setting values
- Searching for data
- Building a custom menu and executing menu commands
- Controlling display and focus
- Informing the user of actions
- Renaming, copying, deleting, saving, importing, and exporting objects
- Running another application

Opening and Closing Tables, Queries, Forms, and Reports

Macro Action	Purpose
Close	Closes either the specified window or the active window for a table, query, form, or report. If the Database window has the focus when you run a Close action with no window specified, Access closes the database. You can also indicate whether to save the object when it's closed.
OpenForm	Opens a form in Form, Datasheet, or Design view or in Print Preview. You can also apply a filter or a Where condition in Datasheet or Form view or in Print Preview.

(continued)

continued

Macro Action	Purpose
OpenModule	Opens a module in Design view and displays the named procedure. To see an event procedure, specify the name of the module in which the procedure is located. This is necessary because event procedures are private and don't appear in the global name space. To open an event procedure of a form or report, the form or report itself must be open.
OpenQuery	Opens a query in Datasheet or Design view or in Print Preview. If you specify an action query, Access performs the updates specified by the query. (See RunSQL in the upcoming section titled "Executing a Query" to specify parameters for an action query.) You can indicate whether records can be added or modified or whether they should be "read only."
OpenReport	Opens a report in Print Preview (the default), prints the report, or opens the report in Design view. For Print and Print Preview, you can also specify a filter or a Where condition.
OpenTable	Opens a table in Datasheet or Design view or in Print Preview. You can designate whether the data should be "read only" or whether data can be added or modified.

Printing Data

Macro Action	Purpose
OpenForm	Optionally opens a form in Print Preview. You can specify a filter or a Where condition.
OpenQuery	Optionally opens a query in Print Preview.
OpenReport	Prints a report or opens a report in Print Preview. You can specify a filter or a Where condition.
OpenTable	Optionally opens a table in Print Preview.

(continued)

continued

Macro Action	Purpose
OutputTo	Outputs the named table, query, form, report, or module to a Microsoft Excel (xls), Microsoft Word (rtf), or Windows Notepad text (txt) file and optionally starts the application to edit the file. For forms, the data output is from the form's Datasheet view. For reports, Access outputs all controls containing data (including calculated controls) except OLE controls.
PrintOut	Prints the active datasheet, form, module, or report. You can specify a range of pages, the print quality, the number of copies, and collation. Use an "Open" action first if you want to apply a filter or a Where condition.

Executing a Query

Macro Action	Purpose
OpenQuery	Runs a select query and displays the recordset in Datasheet or Design view or in Print Preview. Executes an action query. To specify parameters for an action query, use the RunSQL action.
RunSQL	Executes the specified action query statement (INSERT INTO, DELETE, SELECT... INTO, UPDATE) or data definition query statement (CREATE TABLE, ALTER TABLE, DROP TABLE, CREATE INDEX, DROP INDEX). (Note: You can't enter more than 256 characters in the SQL Statement argument. If you need to run a more complex query, define a query object and use the OpenQuery action.)

Testing Conditions and Controlling Action Flow

Macro Action	Purpose
CancelEvent	Cancels the event that caused this macro to run. You can't use a CancelEvent action in a macro that defines menu commands or in the OnClose event for a report. CancelEvent can cancel the following events: ApplyFilter, BeforeDelConfirm, BeforeInsert, Before-Update, DblClick, Delete, Exit, Filter, Format, KeyPress, MouseDown, NoData, Open, Print, and Unload.
DoMenuItem	Executes a command on a standard Access menu. You can use a DoMenuItem action in a macro that defines a custom menu bar or a custom shortcut menu to make selected Access menu commands available on the custom menu.
Quit	Closes all Access windows and exits Access.
RunCode	Executes a VBA function procedure. Other actions following this action execute after the function completes. (Note: To execute a VBA sub procedure, call that procedure from a function procedure.)
RunMacro	Executes another macro. Actions following this action execute after the other macro completes.
StopAllMacros	Stops all macros, including any macros that called this macro.
StopMacro	Stops the current macro.

Setting Values

Macro Action	Purpose
Requery	Refreshes the data in a control that is bound to a query (such as a list box, a combo box, a subform, or a control based on an aggregate function such as *DSum*). When other actions (such as inserting or deleting a row in the underlying query) might affect the

(continued)

continued

Macro Action	Purpose
	contents of a control that is bound to a query, use the Requery action to update the control values. Use Requery without an argument to refresh the data in the active object (form or datasheet).
SendKeys	Stores keystrokes in the keyboard buffer. If you intend to send keystrokes to a modal form or a dialog box, you must execute the SendKeys action before opening the modal form or the dialog box.
SetValue	Changes the value of any control or property that you can update. For example, you can use the SetValue action to calculate a new total in an unbound control or to affect the Visible property of a control (which determines whether you can see that control).

Searching for Data

Macro Action	Purpose
ApplyFilter	Restricts the information displayed in a table, form, or report by applying a named filter, a query, or an SQL WHERE clause to the records of the table or to the records of the underlying table or query of the form or report.
FindNext	Finds the next record that meets the criteria previously set by a FindRecord macro action or in the Find In Field dialog box.
FindRecord	Finds a record that meets the search criteria. You can specify in the macro action all the parameters available in the Find In Field dialog box.
GoToRecord	Moves to a different record and makes it current in the specified table, query, or form. You can move to the first, last, next, or previous record. When you specify the next or the previous record, you can move by more than one record. You can also go to a specific record number or to the new-record placeholder at the end of the set.

Building a Custom Menu and Executing Menu Commands

Macro Action	Purpose
AddMenu	Adds a drop-down menu to a custom menu bar or a custom shortcut menu for a form or a report. This is the only action allowed in a macro referenced by a MenuBar property or ShortcutMenuBar property. The arguments to AddMenu specify the name of this menu bar and the name of another macro that contains all the named commands for the menu and the actions that correspond to those commands. An AddMenu action can also build submenus by referring to another macro that uses an AddMenu action.
SetMenuItem	Sets the state of a menu item on a custom menu bar or a custom shortcut menu. Menu items can be enabled or disabled, checked or unchecked.
DoMenuItem	Executes a command on one of the standard Access menus. Use this macro action within a custom menu bar or a custom shortcut menu to make selected Access menu commands available on the custom menu.

Controlling Display and Focus

Macro Action	Purpose
Echo	Controls the display of intermediate actions while a macro runs.
GoToControl	Sets the focus to the specified control.
GoToPage	Moves to the specified page in a form.
Hourglass	Changes the mouse pointer to an hourglass icon while a macro runs.
Maximize	Maximizes the active window.
Minimize	Minimizes the active window.
MoveSize	Moves and sizes the active window.

(continued)

continued

Macro Action	Purpose
RepaintObject	Forces the repainting of the window for the specified object. Forces recalculation of any formulas in controls on that object.
Requery	Refreshes the data in a control that is bound to a query (such as a list box, a combo box, a subform, or a control based on an aggregate function such as *DSum*). When actions (such as inserting or deleting a row in the underlying query) might affect the contents of a control that is bound to a query, use the Requery macro action to update the control values. Use Requery without an argument to refresh the data in the active object (form or datasheet).
Restore	Restores a maximized or minimized window to its previous size.
SelectObject	Selects the specified object. Restores the object's window if it was minimized. If the object is in the process of opening (for example, a form referenced in a previous OpenForm action), SelectObject forces the object to finish opening before going on to the next action. Use this action after OpenForm when you need to immediately reference the form, a property of a control on the form, or data in a control on the form.
SetWarnings	When enabled, causes an automatic Enter key response to all system warning or informational messages while a macro runs. For warning messages displayed in a dialog box, pressing the Enter key selects the default button (usually OK or Yes). Does not halt the display of error messages. Use this macro action with the Echo action set to No to avoid displaying the messages.
ShowAllRecords	Removes any filters previously applied to the active table, query, or form.
ShowToolbar	Shows or hides any of the standard toolbars or any custom toolbars.

Informing the User of Actions

Macro Action	Purpose
Beep	Produces a sound.
MsgBox	Displays a warning or an informational message and optionally produces a sound. You must click OK to dismiss the dialog box and proceed.
SetWarnings	When enabled, causes an automatic Enter key response to all system warning or informational messages while a macro runs. For warning messages displayed in a dialog box, pressing the Enter key selects the default button (usually OK or Yes). Does not halt the display of error messages. Use this macro action with the Echo action set to No to avoid displaying the messages.

Renaming, Copying, Deleting, Saving, Importing, and Exporting Objects

Macro Action	Purpose
CopyObject	Copies any database object to the current database using a new name or copies any database object to another Access database using any specified name.
DeleteObject	Deletes any table, query, form, report, macro, or module.
Save	Saves any table, query, form, report, macro, or module.
OutputTo	Outputs the named table, query, form, report, or module to an Excel (xls), Word (rtf), or Windows Notepad text (txt) file and optionally starts the application to edit the file. For forms, the data output is from the form's Datasheet view. For reports, Access outputs all controls containing data (including calculated controls) except OLE controls.

(continued)

continued

Macro Action	Purpose
Rename	Renames the specified object in the current database.
SendObject	Outputs a table datasheet, a query datasheet, a form datasheet, data in text boxes on a report, or a module listing to an Excel (xls), Word (rtf), or Windows Notepad text (txt) file and embeds the data in an electronic mail message. You can specify to whom the message is to be sent, the message subject, additional message text, and whether the message can be edited before it is sent. You must have e-mail software installed that conforms to the Mail Application Programming Interface (MAPI) standard.
TransferDatabase	Exports data to or imports data from another Access, dBASE, Paradox, Microsoft FoxPro, Btrieve, or SQL database. You can also use this action to attach tables or files from other Access, dBASE, Paradox, FoxPro, Btrieve, or SQL databases, or from text or spreadsheet files.
TransferSpreadsheet	Exports data to or imports data from Excel or Lotus 1-2-3 spreadsheet files.
TransferText	Exports data to or imports data from text files.

Running Another Application for MS-DOS or Microsoft Windows

Macro Action	Purpose
RunApp	Starts another application for MS-DOS or Windows.

Summary of Events That Trigger Macros

Microsoft Access provides more than 40 event properties on forms and reports that can trigger macros (or VBA procedures). This section summarizes those events and organizes them in the following functional categories:

- Opening and closing forms and reports
- Changing data
- Detecting focus changes
- Trapping keyboard and mouse events
- Printing
- Activating a custom form, report, or application menu
- Trapping errors
- Detecting timer expiration

Opening and Closing Forms and Reports

Event Property	Event Name	Description
OnClose	Close	Runs the specified macro or user-defined event procedure when you close a form or a report but before Access clears the screen. You can't use a CancelEvent macro action in the OnClose routine. The Close event occurs after the Unload event.
OnLoad	Load	Runs the specified macro or user-defined event procedure when Access loads a form and then displays its records. You can use the event procedure to set values in controls or to set form or control properties. The

(continued)

continued

Event Property	Event Name	Description
		Load event occurs after the Open event and before the Resize event. You cannot cancel a Load event.
OnOpen	Open	Runs the specified macro or user-defined event procedure when you open a form or a report but before Access displays the first record. To access a control on the form or report, the routine must specify a GoToControl action to set the focus on the control. The Open event occurs before Access retrieves the form or report recordset, so you can use the event procedure to prompt the user for parameters and to apply filters.
OnResize	Resize	Runs the specified macro or user-defined event procedure when a form changes size. This event also occurs when a form opens, after the Load event but before the Activate event. You can use this event to force immediate repainting of the resized form or to recalculate variables that are dependent on the size of the form.
OnUnload	Unload	Runs the specified macro or user-defined event procedure when you close a form but before Access removes the form from the screen. You can cancel an Unload event if you determine that a form should not be closed. (Caution: You must carefully test any routine that can cancel the unloading of a modal form.)

Changing Data

Event Property	Event Name	Description
AfterDelConfirm	AfterDelConfirm	Runs the specified macro or user-defined event procedure after a row has been deleted via a form and the user has confirmed the deletion. The AfterDelConfirm event also occurs if the event procedure for the BeforeDelConfirm event cancels the deletion. In a VBA procedure, you can test a status variable to determine whether the deletion was completed, was canceled by the event procedure for the BeforeDelConfirm event, or was canceled by the user. If the deletion was successful, you can use the Requery action within the event procedure for the AfterDelConfirm event to refresh the contents of the form or combo boxes. You can also provide automatic deletion of dependent rows in another table (for example, of all the orders for the customer just deleted) by executing a delete query. You cannot cancel this event.
AfterInsert	AfterInsert	Runs the specified macro or user-defined event procedure after a new row has been inserted. You can use this event to requery a recordset after Access has inserted a new row. You cannot cancel this event.

(continued)

continued

Event Property	Event Name	Description
AfterUpdate	AfterUpdate	Runs the specified macro or user-defined event procedure after the data in the specified form or control has been updated. You cannot cancel this event. In the AfterUpdate event of a control, you can, however, use a DoMenu-Item action to choose the Undo command from the Edit menu. This event applies to all forms and to combo boxes, list boxes, option groups, and text boxes as well as to check boxes, option buttons, and toggle buttons that are not part of an option group.
BeforeDelConfirm	BeforeDelConfirm	Runs the specified macro or user-defined event procedure after rows have been deleted via a form but before Access displays the standard confirmation dialog box. If you cancel this event, Access replaces the deleted rows and does not display the confirmation dialog box. In a VBA routine, you can display a custom confirmation dialog box and then set a return parameter to suppress the standard confirmation dialog box.
BeforeInsert	BeforeInsert	Runs the specified macro or user-defined event procedure when you type the first character in a new row. This event is useful for providing additional information to a user who

(continued)

continued

Event Property	Event Name	Description
		is about to add records. If you cancel this event, Access erases any new data on the form. This event occurs before the Before-Update event.
BeforeUpdate	BeforeUpdate	Runs the specified macro or user-defined event procedure before the changed data in the specified form or control has been saved to the database. You can cancel this event to stop the update and place the focus on the updated control or record. This event is most useful for performing complex validations of data on forms or in controls. This event applies to the same controls as the AfterUpdate event.
OnChange	Change	Runs the specified macro or user-defined event procedure whenever you change any portion of the contents of a combo box or a text box control. You cannot cancel this event. (Caution: You can cause an endless loop if you change the contents of this control within the event procedure for the Change event.)
OnDelete	Delete	Runs the specified macro or user-defined function just before one or more rows are deleted. You can use this event to provide a customized warning message. You can also provide automatic deletion of dependent rows in another table (for example,

(continued)

continued

Event Property	Event Name	Description
		of all the orders for the customer about to be deleted) by executing a delete query. You can cancel this event if you need to stop the rows from being deleted.
OnNotInList	NotInList	Runs the specified macro or user-defined event procedure when you type an entry in a combo box that does not exist in the RowSource property for the combo box. You cannot cancel this event. You can use this event to allow a user to create a new entry for the combo box (perhaps by adding a row to the table on which the RowSource property is based). In VBA, you can examine a parameter passed to the event procedure that contains the unmatched text. You can also set a return value to cause Access to display the standard error message, display no error message (after you've issued a custom message), or requery the list after you've added data to the RowSource property.
OnUpdated	Updated	Runs the specified macro or user-defined event procedure after the data in a form's object frame control changes. You cannot cancel this event. In a VBA procedure, you can examine a status parameter to determine how the change occurred.

Detecting Focus Changes

Event Property	Event Name	Description
OnActivate	Activate	Runs the specified macro or user-defined event procedure in a form or a report when the Form or Report window receives the focus and becomes the active window. You cannot cancel this event. This event is most useful for displaying custom toolbars when a form or a report receives the focus. This event does not occur for pop-up or modal forms. This event also does not occur when a normal Form or Report window regains the focus from a pop-up or modal form unless the focus moves to another form or report.
OnCurrent	Current	Runs the specified macro or user-defined event procedure in a bound form when the focus moves from one record to another but before Access displays the new record. Access also triggers the Current event when the focus moves to the first record as a form opens. This event is most useful for keeping two open and related forms synchronized. You cannot cancel this event. You can, however, use a GoTo-Record or other action to move to another record if you decide you do not want to move to the new record.

(continued)

continued

Event Property	Event Name	Description
OnDeactivate	Deactivate	Runs the specified macro or user-defined event procedure when a form or a report loses the focus to another window inside the Access application that is not a pop-up or modal window. This event is useful for closing custom toolbars. You cannot cancel this event.
OnEnter	Enter	Runs the specified macro or user-defined event procedure when the focus moves to a bound object frame, a combo box, a command button, a list box, an option group, or a text box, as well as when the focus moves to a check box, an option button, or a toggle button that is not part of an option group. You cannot cancel this event. This event occurs only when the focus moves from another control on the same form. If you change the focus to this control with the mouse, this event occurs before the GotFocus, MouseDown, MouseUp, and Click events in this control. If you change the focus to this control using the keyboard, this event occurs after the KeyDown event in the control you leave but before the KeyUp and the KeyPress events in this control.

(continued)

continued

Event Property	Event Name	Description
OnExit	Exit	Runs the specified macro or user-defined event procedure when the focus moves from a bound object frame, a combo box, a command button, a list box, an option group, or a text box, as well as when the focus moves from a check box, an option button, or a toggle button that is not part of an option group to another control on the same form. You cannot cancel this event. This event does not occur when the focus moves to another window. If you leave a control using the mouse, this event occurs before the MouseDown and MouseUp events in the new control. If you leave a control using the keyboard, the KeyDown event in this control occurs, and then the Exit, KeyUp, and Key-Press events occur in the new control.
OnGotFocus	GotFocus	Runs the specified macro or user-defined event pro-cedure when an enabled form control receives the focus. If a form receives the focus but has no enabled controls, the GotFocus event occurs for the form. You cannot cancel this event. The GotFocus event occurs after the Enter event. Unlike the Enter event, which occurs only when the focus moves from

(continued)

continued

Event Property	Event Name	Description
		another control on the same form, the GotFocus event occurs every time a control receives the focus, including from other windows.
OnLostFocus	LostFocus	Runs the specified macro or user-defined event procedure when an enabled form control loses the focus. The LostFocus event for the form occurs whenever a form that has no enabled controls loses the focus. You cannot cancel this event. This event occurs after the Exit event. Unlike the Exit event, which occurs only when the focus moves to another control on the same form, the LostFocus event occurs every time a control loses the focus, including to other windows.

Trapping Keyboard and Mouse Events

Event Property	Event Name	Description
OnClick	Click	Runs the specified macro or user-defined event procedure when you click a command button or click on an enabled form or control. You cannot cancel this event.
OnDblClick	DblClick	Runs the specified macro or user-defined event procedure when you double-click on a bound object frame, a combo box, a

(continued)

continued

Event Property	Event Name	Description
		command button, a list box, an option group, or a text box, as well as when you double-click a check box, an option button, or a toggle button that is not part of an option group. The Click event always occurs before DblClick. Access runs the macro before showing the normal result of the double-click. You can cancel the event to prevent the normal response to a double-click on a control, such as activating the application for an OLE object in a bound control or highlighting a word in a text box.
OnKeyDown	KeyDown	Runs the specified macro or user-defined event procedure when you press a key or a combination of keys. You cannot cancel this event. In a VBA procedure, you can examine parameters to determine the key code and whether the Shift, Ctrl, or Alt key was also pressed. You can also set the key code to *0* in VBA to prevent the control from receiving keystrokes. If the form has a command button whose Default property is set to Yes, KeyDown events do not occur when the Enter key is pressed. If the form has a command button whose Cancel property is set to Yes, KeyDown events do not occur when the Esc key is pressed.

(continued)

continued

Event Property	Event Name	Description
OnKeyPress	KeyPress	Runs the specified macro or user-defined event procedure when you press a key or a combination of keys. You cannot cancel this event. In a VBA procedure, you can examine the ANSI key value.
OnKeyUp	KeyUp	Runs the specified macro or user-defined event procedure when you release a key or a combination of keys. You cannot cancel this event. In a VBA procedure, you can examine parameters to determine the key code and whether the Shift, Ctrl, or Alt key was also pressed. If the form has a command button whose Default property is set to Yes, KeyUp events do not occur when the Enter key is released. If the form has a command button whose Cancel property is set to Yes, KeyUp events do not occur when the Esc key is released.
OnMouseDown	MouseDown	Runs the specified macro or user-defined event procedure when you press any mouse button. You cannot cancel this event. In a VBA procedure, you can determine which mouse button was pressed (left, right, or middle); whether the Shift, Ctrl, or Alt key was also pressed; and the X and Y coordinates of the mouse pointer (in twips) when the button was pressed. (Note: A *twip* is $\frac{1}{20}$ point or $\frac{1}{1440}$ inch.)

(continued)

continued

Event Property	Event Name	Description
OnMouseMove	MouseMove	Runs the specified macro or user-defined event procedure when you move the mouse over a form or a control. You cannot cancel this event. In a VBA procedure, you can determine whether a mouse button was pressed (left, right, or middle) and whether the Shift, Ctrl, or Alt key was also pressed. You can also determine the X and Y coordinates of the mouse pointer (in twips) when the button was released.
OnMouseUp	MouseUp	Runs the specified macro or user-defined event procedure when you release any mouse button. You cannot cancel this event. In a VBA procedure, you can determine which mouse button was released (left, right, or middle); whether the Shift, Ctrl, or Alt key was also pressed; and the X and Y coordinates of the mouse pointer (in twips) when the button was released.

Printing

Event Property	Event Name	Description
OnFormat	Format	Runs the specified macro or user-defined event procedure just before Access formats a report section to print. This event is useful for hiding or displaying controls in the report

(continued)

continued

Event Property	Event Name	Description
		section based on data values. If Access is formatting a group header, you have access to the data in the first row of the detail section. Similarly, if Access is formatting a group footer, you have access to the data in the last row of the detail section. You can test the value of the FormatCount property to determine whether the Format event has occurred more than once for a section (due to page overflow). You can use the CancelEvent action to keep a section from appearing on the report.
OnNoData	NoData	Runs the specified macro or user-defined event procedure after Access formats a report that has no data for printing and just before the reports prints. You can use this event to keep a blank report from printing.
OnPage	Page	Runs the specified macro or user-defined event procedure after Access formats a page for printing and just before the page prints. You can use this event to draw custom borders around a page or add other graphics to enhance the look of the report.
OnPrint	Print	Runs the specified macro or user-defined event procedure just before Access prints a formatted section of a report. If you use the CancelEvent action in a macro triggered by a

(continued)

continued

Event Property	Event Name	Description
		Print event, Access leaves a blank space on the report where the section would have printed.
OnRetreat	Retreat	Runs the specified macro or user-defined event procedure when Access has to retreat past already formatted sections when it discovers that it cannot fit a "keep together" section on a page. You cannot cancel this event.

Activating a Custom Form, Report, or Application Menu

Event Property	Event Name	Description
MenuBar	(N/A)	Defines the macro that creates the custom menu for a form or a report. The macro triggered by the MenuBar property must contain only named AddMenu actions. Each AddMenu action refers to another macro that defines the individual commands for that menu. You can define submenus by including additional Add-Menu actions in macros referenced by an AddMenu

(continued)

continued

Event Property	Event Name	Description
		action. From a VBA macro or procedure, you can set the Application.MenuBar property to define a custom menu bar for the database. Set the MenuBar property to =True to hide the menu bar when this form or report has the focus.
ShortcutMenuBar	(N/A)	Defines the macro that creates the custom menu or shortcut menu for a form or a report.

Trapping Errors

Event Property	Event Name	Description
OnError	Error	Runs the specified macro or user-defined event procedure whenever a run-time error occurs while the form or report is active. This event does not trap errors in VBA code; use On Error in the VBA procedure instead. You cannot cancel this event. If you use a VBA procedure to trap this event, you can examine the error code to determine an appropriate action.

Detecting Timer Expiration

Event Property	Event Name	Description
OnTimer	Timer	Runs the specified macro or user-defined event procedure when the timer interval defined for the form elapses. The form's TimerInterval property defines how frequently this event occurs in milliseconds. If the TimerInterval property is set to 0, no Timer events occur. You cannot cancel this event. However, you can set the TimerInterval property for the form to 0 to stop further Timer events from occurring.

You should now have a basic understanding of macros and how you might use them. In the next chapter, you'll see macros in action.

Chapter 20

Automating Your Application with Macros

Here you'll learn how to validate data that is being entered into a field and how to set the values of other fields based on the success of the validation. This technique goes beyond using the validation rule for a field in a table by giving you more control over how the data is checked and how Access responds if the validation fails.

Throughout this book, you've learned how to perform common tasks using menu commands and toolbar buttons. In working with your database, you've probably also noticed that you perform certain tasks repeatedly or on a regular basis. You can automate these tasks by using macros to execute the actions you perform and then associating the macros with various form or control events, such as the OnCurrent event of a form, the OnClick event of a command button, or the OnDblClick event of a text box control.

All of the examples in this chapter are based on the Wedding List sample database.

Referencing Form and Report Objects

As you create macros to automate the tasks that you commonly perform, you'll often need to refer to a report, a form, or a control on a form to set its properties or values. The syntax for referencing reports, forms, controls, and properties is described in the following sections.

Rules for Referencing Forms and Reports

You can refer to a form or a report by name, but you must first tell Microsoft Access which *collection* contains the named object. Open forms are in the Forms collection, and open reports are in the Reports collection. To reference a form or a report, you follow the collection name with an exclamation point to separate it from the name of the object to which you are referring. You <u>must</u> enclose an object name that contains blank spaces or special characters in brackets ([ ]). If the object name contains no blanks or special characters, you can simply enter the name. However, it's a good idea to always enclose an object name in brackets so that your name reference syntax is consistent.

To reference a form named WeddingList, enter the following:

Forms![WeddingList]

To reference a report named WeddingList, enter the following:

Reports![WeddingList]

Rules for Referencing
Form and Report Properties

To reference a property of a form or a report, follow the form or report name with a period and the property name. You can see a list of most property names for a form or a report by viewing the form or the report in Design view and opening the property sheet while you have the form or the report selected. You can change most form or report properties while the form is in Form view or from the Print and Format events of reports as Access prints or displays them.

To reference the ScrollBars property of a form named CityInformation, enter the following:

Forms![CityInformation].ScrollBars

To reference the MenuBar property of a report named CityInformation, enter the following:

Reports![CityInformation].MenuBar

NOTE The names of properties do not contain embedded blank spaces, even though the property sheet shows blanks within names. For example, BackColor is the name of the property listed as Back Color in the property sheet.

Rules for Referencing Form and
Report Controls and Their Properties

To reference a control on a form or a report, follow the form or report name with an exclamation point and then the control name enclosed in brackets. To reference a property of a control, follow the control name with a period and the name of the property. You can see a list of most property names for controls by opening a form or a report in Design view, selecting a control (note that different control types have different properties), and opening its property sheet. You can change most control properties while the form is in Design view.

To reference a control named State on the WeddingListForm form, enter the following:

Forms![WeddingListForm]![State]

To reference the Visible property of a control named Accepted on the report named WeddingListForm, enter the following:

Reports![WeddingListForm]![Accepted].Visible

Rules for Referencing Subforms and Subreports

When you embed a subform in a form or a report, the subform is contained in a *subform control*. A subreport embedded in a report is contained in a *subreport control*. You can reference a subform control or a subreport control exactly as you would any other control on a form or a report. For example, suppose you have a subform called RelativesSub embedded in the WeddingListForm form. To reference the subform control on the WeddingListForm form, enter the following:

    Forms![WeddingListForm]![RelativesSub]

Likewise, you can reference properties of a subform or a subreport by following the control name with a period and the name of the property. To reference the Visible property of the RelativesSub subform control, enter the following:

    Forms![WeddingListForm]![RelativesSub].Visible

Subform controls have a special Form property that lets you reference the form that's embedded in the subform control. Likewise, subreport controls have a special Report property that lets you reference the report embedded in the subreport control. You can follow this special property name with the name of a control on the subform or the subreport to access the control's contents or properties. For example, to reference the LastName control on the RelativesSub subform, enter the following:

    Forms![WeddingListForm]![RelativesSub].Form![LastName]

To reference the FontWeight property of the LastName control, enter the following:

    Forms![WeddingListForm]![RelativesSub].Form![LastName].FontWeight

Opening a Secondary Form

As you learned in Chapter 12, "Form Basics," it's easier to work with data by using a form. You also learned in Chapter 15, "Advanced Form Design," that you can create multiple-table forms by embedding subforms in a main form, thus allowing you to see related data in the same form. However, it's impractical to use subforms when

- You need two or more subforms to see related data

- The main form is too small to display the entire subform

- You need to see the related information only some of the time

The solution is to use a separate form to see the related data. You can open this form by responding to one of several events. For example, you can use a command button or the OnDblClick event of a control on the main form to give your users access to the related data. This technique helps reduce screen clutter, makes the main form easier to use, and helps to speed up the main form when moving from record to record.

You can make use of this technique in the WeddingListForm form. Currently, clicking the City Info button on the form opens the City-Information form, which displays all records from the CityNames table, including the best airline to take and the approximate flying time from each city to Seattle. However, if you're talking to Aunt Sara in Boston, it would be convenient for the CityInformation form to display only Boston-related data rather than the data for all cities. In the following section, you'll create a macro that opens the CityInformation form based on the city that's displayed for the current record shown in the WeddingListForm form.

Creating the *SeeCityInformation* Macro

In the Database window, click on the Macros tab, and then click the New button. When the Macro window opens, maximize it so that it fills the entire screen. Next, click the Macro Names button and the Conditions button on the toolbar to display the Macro Name and Condition columns in the Design window. Although you're not going to use these columns for this macro, it's a good idea to get in the habit of displaying them whenever you create new macros in case you need them.

 TIP   You can display the Macro Name and Condition columns by default by choosing Options from the Tools menu. In the Options dialog box, click on the View tab and select both options in the Show In Macro Design section. The next time you create a new macro, the columns will be displayed automatically.

The macro you need is shown in Figure 20-1. You can change the City Info command button to execute this macro. You can also use the

OnDblClick event of the City combo box on the WeddingListForm form. The macro contains only one action, OpenForm. The OpenForm action not only opens the CityInformation form but also applies a filter so that the city that will be displayed matches the city currently displayed in the WeddingListForm form. Use the Where Condition argument of the macro to enter

[CityName]=Forms![WeddingListForm]![City]

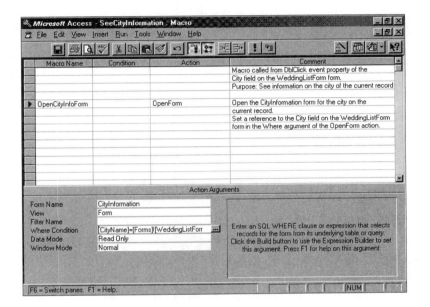

FIGURE 20-1
The actions for the *SeeCity-Information* macro.

The Where Condition argument causes the OpenForm action to open the requested form showing only the rows in the form's record source whose CityName equals the value currently shown in the City combo box on the open WeddingListForm form. A bit later, you'll learn how to create a macro to synchronize these two forms as you move to different rows in the WeddingListForm form.

Type the comments shown in the first three lines of the Comment column shown in Figure 20-1. It's a good idea to use the Comment column to document your macro. Documenting your macro in this manner makes it easy to debug, modify, or enhance in the future. It's also easier to read, in English, what each macro action does rather than have to view the arguments for each action line by line.

669

After you finish creating the action for the macro, choose Save from the File menu and save the macro as *SeeCityInformation*. (You can also find the completed macro saved as *XmplSeeCityInformation* in the Wedding List database.) The Save As dialog box is shown in Figure 20-2.

FIGURE 20-2

The Save As dialog box for macros.

Next, you can associate the macro with the City combo box control on the WeddingListForm form. Click on the Forms tab in the Database window. Select WeddingListForm and open the form in Design view. Click on the City combo box control and then click the Properties button on the toolbar. When the property sheet opens, click on the Event tab. You'll trigger the *SeeCityInformation* macro from the OnDblClick event. Select the macro from the OnDblClick event property's drop-down list. After you select the macro, the property sheet should look like the one shown in Figure 20-3.

FIGURE 20-3

The property sheet of the City combo box control.

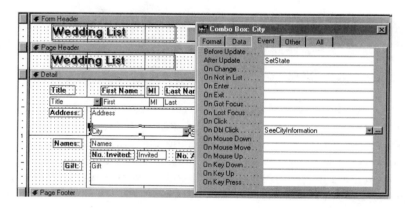

You can also choose the City Info button you created earlier and change its OnClick event to point to this new macro. Save and close the WeddingListForm form. When you return to the Database window, open the form in Form view and then maximize it. Scroll down two or three rows and double-click on the City combo box. The data displayed in the CityInformation form should be for the city in the current record in the WeddingListForm form. Your screen should look like the one shown in Figure 20-4.

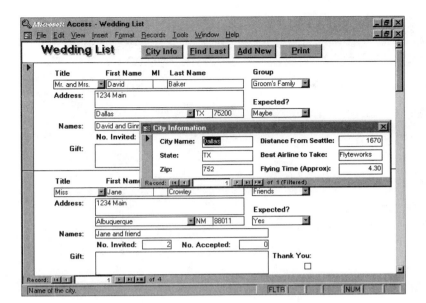

FIGURE 20-4
The CityInformation and Wedding-ListForm forms.

Opening a related form in this manner is very useful, but what happens to the data displayed in the CityInformation form when you move to a new record in the WeddingListForm form? Try it, and you'll find that the data in the CityInformation form doesn't change as you move through the records in the WeddingListForm form. The data doesn't change because the forms aren't synchronized. In the next section, you'll learn a technique for synchronizing the data in the two forms.

Synchronizing Two Related Forms

In the previous section, you learned how to open a secondary form from a main form based on matching values of two related fields in the two forms. You also learned that the data in the secondary form doesn't change as you move through the data in the main form. In this section, you'll create a macro that synchronizes the data in the two forms.

Creating the *SyncWeddingListAndCityInfoForms* Macro

In the Database window, click on the Macros tab, and then click the New button. When the Macro window opens, maximize it so that it fills the entire screen. The actions and comments you'll create for this macro are shown in Figure 20-5 on the next page.

671

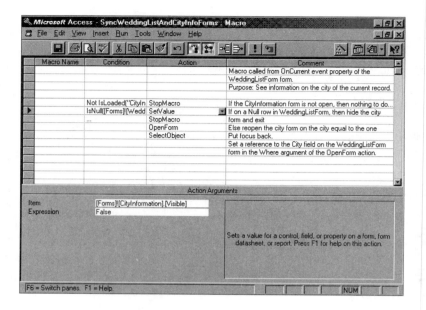

You'll create this macro in the same basic manner that you created the *SeeCityInformation* macro. Select the actions from the Action column and type the associated comments in the Comment column. The settings for the actions are shown in Figure 20-6.

FIGURE 20-6

The settings for the actions in the *SyncWedding-ListAndCity-InfoForms* macro.

Condition	Action	Argument Box	Setting
Not IsLoaded→ ("CityInformation")	StopMacro		
IsNull([Forms]!→ [WeddingListForm]!→ [City])	SetValue	Item	[Forms]!→ [CityInformation].→ [Visible]
		Expression	False
...	StopMacro		
	OpenForm	Form Name	CityInformation
		View	Form
		Where Condition	[CityName]=[Forms]!→ [WeddingListForm]!→ [City]
		Data Mode	Read Only
		Window Mode	Normal

This macro has a couple of conditions that determine what parts of the macro execute. The first condition, in plain English, states:

"If the CityInformation form is not currently loaded, execute the first action."

This condition uses the *IsLoaded* function, which is included in the modUtility module of the Wedding List database. This function checks to see whether a form (whose name you've provided to the function) is currently open. (The form can be hidden.) The syntax for the function is IsLoaded("*<formname>*"), where *formname* is the name of the form in question. You must enclose the name of the form in double quotation marks in order for the function to work. The *Not* before the function expression in Figure 20-6 asks Access to evaluate the converse of the True/False value returned from the function. So this condition will be true only if the form is *not* loaded. If the companion form isn't open, there's nothing to do, so the macro action on this line—StopMacro—executes and the macro ends.

You can use an ApplyFilter action to refilter the open CityInformation form, but ApplyFilter works only for the form that currently has the focus. A SelectObject action would solve that problem, but why use two macro actions when one would suffice? As it turns out, you can execute OpenForm again with the same Where condition to display the matching row you want. If the form is already open, OpenForm puts the focus on that form (and unhides it if it's hidden) and applies any Where condition that you've specified.

However, it's a bad idea to reference an "empty" value in a Where condition. In fact, in some cases you'll get an error message. When you move beyond the last row in the WeddingListForm form or choose Go To from the Edit menu and then choose New from the submenu, you'll be in a new blank row in which the City field has no value. In this case, OpenForm will show you a blank row in the CityInformation form. It probably makes more sense to test for an "empty" or Null value and hide the companion form if you're in a new row in the Wedding-ListForm form. The second line in this macro uses the *IsNull* built-in function to check for this condition. If City is Null, the macro hides the CityInformation form by setting its Visible property to False, and then the macro ends. Note that the form is <u>still open</u> even though you can't see it. If you move back to a row that contains data, this macro executes again and makes the form visible when the OpenForm action runs.

Finally, the OpenForm action in this macro is just like the one you saw earlier in the *SeeCityInformation* macro. In fact, you could just as well use a RunMacro action here to run that macro again to open the form (or to put the focus on it if it's already open) and apply the filter specified in the Where Condition argument.

Once you have the synchronization macro you need, the last step is to associate the macro with the OnCurrent event of the Wedding-ListForm form. Click on the Forms tab in the Database window and open the WeddingListForm form in Design view. Once you're in Design view, click the Properties toolbar button to open the property sheet for the form, and then click in the OnCurrent property box. Use the drop-down list to select the *SyncWeddingListAndCityInfoForms* macro. Your screen should look like the one shown in Figure 20-7.

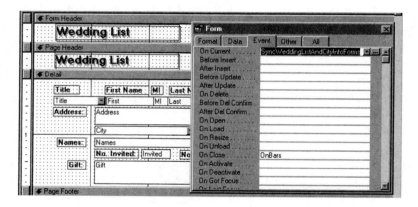

When you finish, save and close the form. Open the form in Form view and double-click in the City combo box control. Your screen should look like the one shown in Figure 20-4, assuming you're positioned on Mr. and Mrs. David Baker's record.

Test the macro by moving through the records in the Wedding-ListForm form. As you move from record to record, the data in the CityInformation form should change to reflect the city displayed in the current record of the WeddingListForm form. If you move to the blank record at the end of the recordset, the CityInformation form disappears. Move back to a row containing data, and it reappears!

In this section, you've learned how to synchronize two forms containing related data. This technique works well with almost any set of forms and can be used in a number of situations. In the next section, you'll learn how to create a more complex macro known as a *macro group*. Macro groups use the idea of grouping macros by task, which, as you'll soon see, is quite useful.

Validating Data and Presetting Values

Two tasks you'll commonly automate in your applications are validating data that a user enters in a field and automatically setting values for specific fields. In this section, you'll create a macro group containing macros that will perform these tasks. You'll associate these macros with both the WeddingListForm form and the CityInformation form.

Validating Data

A problem you'll often encounter when you create database applications is ensuring that the data the users enter is valid. The three types of invalid data are unknown entries, misspelled entries, and multiple versions of the same entry.

- *Unknown entries*—A good example of this is an entry such as *AX* in a state field. As we all know, no state name is abbreviated as *AX*, but a user who tries to enter *AZ* might accidentally hit the X key instead of the Z key.

- *Misspelled entries*—This is quite common among users with poor typing or spelling skills and among very fast typists. In this case, you might see *Settle*, *Seatle*, or *Saettle* for *Seattle*.

- *Multiple versions*—These are common in poorly designed databases and in databases that are shared by a number of users. You might see entries such as *ABC Company, Inc.; ABC Company, Incorporated; ABC Co., Inc.;* or *A B C Company Inc.*

In the next section, you'll create a macro for the WeddingListForm form that performs the following tasks:

1. Validates the city that the user enters in the City field. (The following steps will execute only if the city doesn't exist in the CityNames table.)

2. Displays a message indicating that the city is currently unlisted and asks if the user wants to enter a new city name.

675

3. If the user wants to create a new city record, another macro runs that opens the CityInformation form in data-entry mode and copies the city name the user just typed.

4. If the user successfully saves a new row, a macro in the After-Insert event of the CityInformation form sets a flag on the WeddingListForm form.

5. Back in the WeddingListForm form, the city name gets revalidated, and if the city entry is a new one, a macro triggered by AfterUpdate of the city name makes sure that the new name appears in the combo box. When the city name is validated, this macro also automatically enters the state name and the first three digits of the zip code.

Creating the ValidateCitySetStateAndZip Macro Group

In the Database window, click on the Macros tab and create a new macro. Be sure the Macro Name and Condition columns are displayed. The first macro and its associated actions are shown in Figure 20-8.

FIGURE 20-8
The Macro window for the first two macros in the ValidateCity-SetStateAndZip macro group.

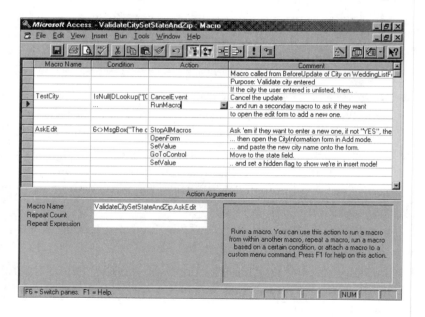

After you type the first three lines of comments, type *TestCity* in the Macro Name column. This will be the name of the first macro in the macro group. Next, select the actions listed in Figure 20-9 and set the arguments as indicated. When you finish, enter the appropriate comments for each action that you see in Figure 20-8. Don't worry about the conditions for now.

Action	Argument Box	Setting
CancelEvent		
RunMacro	Macro Name	ValidateCitySetStateAndZip.AskEdit

FIGURE 20-9
The actions and arguments in the *TestCity* macro.

Now let's take a look at the condition that validates the city name and executes these actions if the city name doesn't exist in the City-Names table. Click in the Condition box to the left of the CancelEvent action, and then open the Zoom box using the right mouse button's shortcut menu. Enter the expression shown in Figure 20-10.

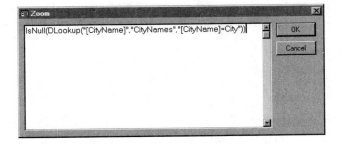

FIGURE 20-10
The conditional expression used in the *TestCity* macro.

This condition uses two built-in functions: *IsNull* and *DLookup*. The *DLookup* function looks up the city name in the CityNames table. The *IsNull* function checks the return value of the *DLookup* function. If the *DLookup* function doesn't find the city name, it returns a Null value. This, in turn, causes the *IsNull* function to return a True value because the return value of the *DLookup* function is indeed Null. So if no row in the CityNames table matches the current city name in the WeddingListForm form, Access executes the action associated with this condition because the condition evaluated to True. In this case, a CancelEvent macro action tells Access not to store the new value in the City field. By including an ellipsis (…) in the Condition column of the second action, you ask Access to run this action only if the previous condition is true. (When you use an ellipsis, you need enter the condition only once and Access performs the evaluation only once.) So if the city doesn't exist in the CityNames table, the RunMacro macro action on the second line calls the *AskEdit* macro, which we'll look at in a moment.

On the other hand, if the *DLookup* function does find the city name, it returns the city name to the *IsNull* function. The *IsNull* function then returns a value of False since the return value of the *DLookup* function is not Null. Access disregards the action associated with this condition. Because you included an ellipsis on the second condition line, the False evaluation applies there also, so ultimately the macro ends without taking any further action. When you don't cancel a Before-Update event on a control, Access accepts the changes and gives you a chance to look at the result in the AfterUpdate event. As you'll see a bit later, this application uses AfterUpdate on this control to fill in the correct state and part of the zip code.

So what happens if the user enters a city name that's not yet in the database? The *AskEdit* macro runs, and the first thing it does is evaluate another condition. As you'll learn in later chapters, this sort of IF...THEN...IF logic testing is much easier to do in VBA. With macros, you have to do the first test in one macro, and then if that's true you have to call another nested macro to perform a further test.

The condition on the first line of the *AskEdit* macro is as follows:

6<>MsgBox("The city you entered is not in the database. →
    Do you want to enter a new one?",36)

You've seen the MsgBox action before. This condition uses a built-in function called *MsgBox* that's a lot more powerful. The *MsgBox* function lets you not only display a message but also lets you specify what icon you want displayed, and it provides several options for buttons to display in the message box. You set these options by adding number selections and providing the result as the second argument to *MsgBox*. In this case, *36* is the sum of *32,* which asks for a question icon, and *4,* which requests Yes and No buttons. (Intuitive, isn't it?) You can find all the option settings by searching for *MsgBox* in Help. In addition, the function returns an integer value depending on the button the user clicks in the message box. If you look at the MsgBox Help topic, you'll find out that when the user clicks Yes, *MsgBox* returns a *6.* So if the user <u>doesn't</u> click Yes, the first line of this macro—a

StopAllMacros action—executes and the macro ends. If the user does click Yes, the rest of the macro executes. The actions and arguments are listed in Figure 20-11.

Action	Argument Box	Setting
StopAllMacros		
OpenForm	Form Name	CityInformation
	View	Form
	Data Mode	Add
	Window Mode	Normal
SetValue	Item	[Forms]![CityInformation]![CityName]
	Value	[Forms]![WeddingListForm]![City]
GoToControl	Control Name	State
SetValue	Item	[Forms]![CityInformation]![AddFlag]
	Value	True

FIGURE 20-11
The actions and arguments in the *AskEdit* macro.

This macro contains several actions that Access executes if the user enters the data for a new city name. First, Access opens the CityInformation form and copies the city name from the Wedding-ListForm form to the CityName field of the CityInformation form. It does this for two reasons: for user convenience and to ensure that the user starts with the name just entered. After the macro copies the city name to the CityName field, Access moves the cursor to the State field. Finally, the macro sets the value of a hidden text box on the CityInformation form to indicate that the user is in data entry mode. The macro attached to the AfterInsert event checks this flag to determine whether it should notify the AfterUpdate event of the City control on the WeddingListForm form to refresh its list.

Passing Status Information Between Linked Forms

As you just saw, the *AskEdit* macro sets a special hidden control on the CityInformation form to tell the form's AfterInsert event macro that the WeddingListForm form needs to know if a new row has been successfully added. Likewise, when a new row is added to the CityInformation form, the macro that runs in response to an AfterInsert event (the event that Access uses to let you know when a new row has been added via a form) needs to check the flag and pass an indicator back to the WeddingListForm form. You'll learn in later chapters that you can do this sort of "status indicator" passing much more easily using variables than you can by hiding controls on open forms.

Figure 20-12 shows the macro you need in order to respond to the AfterInsert event of the CityInformation form. The first line has a condition that tests to make sure that the user asked to add a new row. The condition is as follows:

Not [Forms]![CityInformation]![AddFlag]

FIGURE 20-12

The *Refresh-CityList* macro.

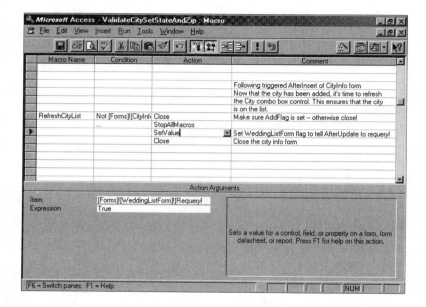

If the flag is not set, the first action closes the form, and the StopAllMacros action causes the macro to end. If the flag is set, the SetValue action sets the flag on the WeddingListForm form (to let it know that it must refresh the list in the City combo box at its earliest opportunity) and then closes the CityInformation form. Note that you could be in the AfterInsert event as a result of the user entering new data and then clicking the form's Close button. Access is kind enough not to generate any error from either of the Close actions in this macro if this is the case. If the user triggers the AfterInsert event by moving to another row, it makes sense to close the form after adding the one row you need. If the user closes the form without entering any new data, the AfterInsert event won't happen. The user will be back in the WeddingListForm form with the unmatched city data still typed in the City combo box.

Presetting Values

Validating data is just one of the many ways you can ensure data integrity in a database. Presetting values for certain fields is another way. Although you can set the Default property of a field, sometimes you'll need to set the value of a field based on the value of another field in a form. For example, you'll want to set the values of the State field and the Zip field in the WeddingListForm form based on the value of the City field. You can accomplish this with a macro.

In this section, you'll examine actions in the ValidateCitySetState-AndZip macro group that set the values of the State and Zip fields in the WeddingListForm form based on the city entered. If you scroll down in this macro, you can see the additional actions, as shown in Figure 20-13.

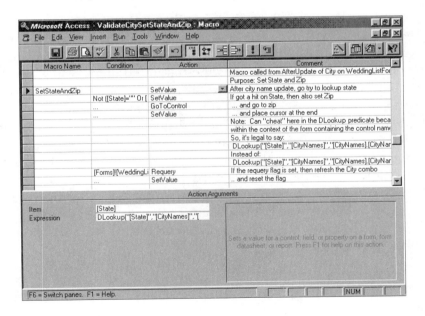

FIGURE 20-13

Data entry actions in the *SetStateAndZip* macro of the ValidateCitySet-StateAndZip macro group.

Figure 20-14 lists the actions and arguments in this macro.

FIGURE 20-14

The actions and arguments in the *SetState-AndZip* macro of the ValidateCity-SetStateAndZip macro group.

Action	Argument Box	Setting
SetValue	Item	[State]
	Expression	DLookup("[State]","[CityNames]", "[CityNames].[CityName]=City")
SetValue	Item	[Zip]
	Expression	DLookup("[Zip]","[CityNames]", "[CityNames].[CityName]=City")
GoToControl	Control Name	Zip
SetValue	Item	[Forms]![WeddingListForm]! [Zip].SelStart
	Expression	255
Requery	Control Name	City
SetValue	Item	[Forms]![WeddingListForm]! [RequeryFlag]
	Value	False

When the user enters a valid city name, the first SetValue action uses the *DLookup* built-in function to retrieve the matching State value from the CityNames table. If the value for State isn't blank or Null, the second SetValue action retrieves the first three digits of the zip code from the table, moves the focus to the Zip control with a GoToControl action, and sets the SelStart property of the Zip control to a high value (255) to place the cursor at the end of the data displayed in the control. Pressing the F2 key after you move into a control also places the cursor at the end of the data in the control, so you can use a SendKeys action here. However, setting the SelStart property is faster and more reliable. (See Access Help for more information on the SelStart property.) The user can now enter the last two digits of the zip code and move on to the Expected field. The Condition column for the second action is as follows:

Not ([State]="" Or [State] Is Null)

The macro group is now complete. You've implemented data integrity by validating data and presetting specific values. This decreases the likelihood that users can make errors. Now you'll see how to associate these macros with the appropriate events on the WeddingList-Form form and the CityInformation form.

Click on the Forms tab in the Database window and open the WeddingListForm form in Design view. Click on the City combo box control and then click the Properties toolbar button. After the property sheet opens, click on the Event tab. You should see the *ValidateCity-SetStateAndZip.TestCity* macro associated with the BeforeUpdate event of the City combo box. Remember, this is the macro you should run to verify whether the user has entered a valid city name. The AfterUpdate event property should be set to *ValidateCitySetStateAndZip.SetState-AndZip*. This macro automatically sets the matching State and Zip values whenever the user specifies a new City value. Figure 20-15 shows the result.

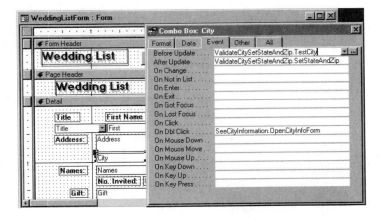

FIGURE 20-15

Setting the event properties for the City control on the WeddingListForm form.

Save and close the WeddingListForm form. Open the CityInformation form in Design view, and click the Properties toolbar button to open the property sheet. Click on the Event tab and then click in the AfterInsert property box. From the drop-down list, select the *Validate-CitySetStateAndZip.RefreshCityList* macro. You're associating the macro with this particular event so that it will run only after the user has entered new city data in the CityInformation form. Your property sheet should look like the one shown in Figure 20-16 on the next page.

FIGURE 20-16

Associating the
*ValidateCity-
SetStateAndZip.-
RefreshCityList*
macro with the
AfterInsert
event property
of the CityInfor-
mation form.

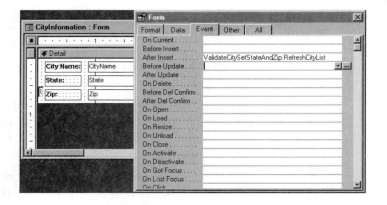

Save and close the CityInformation form. Now that you've defined
the macros and associated them with the appropriate objects and
events, you're ready to test your work. Begin by clicking on the Macros
tab in the Database window and running the *Autoexec* macro. Move to
a new record after the WeddingListForm form opens and enter a title, a
name, an address, and a group. When the cursor moves to the City
combo box, enter *Yakima* (a city in Washington state). After you
press Enter or Tab, Access runs the *ValidateCitySetStateAndZip.TestCity*
macro. Since this city doesn't currently exist in the CityNames table, the
AskEdit macro runs and Access displays the message box shown in
Figure 20-17.

FIGURE 20-17

The message box
displayed by the
AskEdit macro.

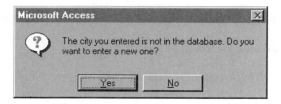

After the user clicks the Yes button, Access executes the remaining actions in the macro. Access opens the CityInformation form, copies the city name to the City field of the form, and moves the cursor to
the State field. The result of these actions is shown in Figure 20-18.

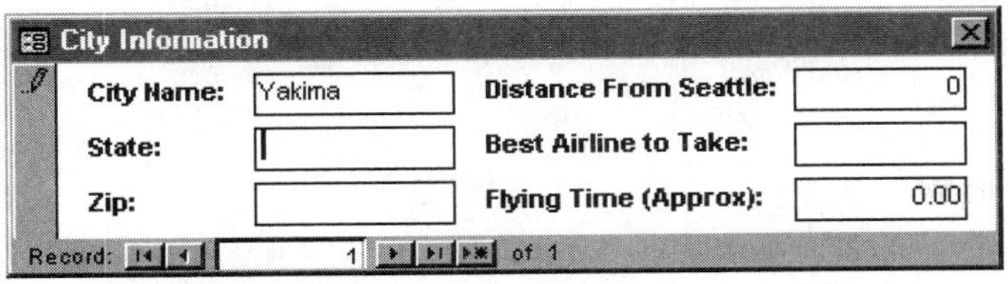

FIGURE 20-18
The result
of the remaining
actions in the
AskEdit macro.

After the user enters information in the remaining fields and closes the CityInformation form, the AfterInsert event of the form triggers the *ValidateCitySetStateAndZip.RefreshCityList* macro. After the form closes, Access moves the focus back to the WeddingListForm form. When the user finally leaves the now valid City control, the macro triggered by AfterUpdate requeries the City combo box control and automatically updates the State and Zip fields.

In this chapter, you've learned how to validate data and set the values of fields in a form. You've also learned a little more about data integrity in the process. In the next two chapters, you'll learn more about the power of VBA.

SELECT EDITION

Chapter 21

Visual Basic for Applications Fundamentals

W hether you've realized it or not, you've already been using Visual Basic for Applications (VBA) procedures. For example, the *IsLoaded* function you used with macros in the previous chapter is a custom VBA procedure. In this chapter and in the following one, you'll learn more about VBA and how to use it to automate your applications.

Using VBA Instead of Macros

As you saw in previous chapters, you can make lots of magic happen with macros. In fact, as you explore the Northwind Traders, Orders, and Solutions databases that come with Microsoft Access or the Wedding List database included with this book, you'll discover many additional ways that you can use macros to automate tasks in your database.

However, macros have certain limitations. For example, you learned from examining the list of available events in Chapter 19, "Adding Power with Macros," that many events require or return parameters that can't be passed to or read from a macro. Also, even though you can write a macro to handle general errors in forms and reports, you can't really analyze errors effectively within a macro or do much to recover from an error.

When to Use Macros

Use macros in your application in any of these circumstances:

- You don't need to trap errors.

- You don't need to evaluate or set parameters passed by certain events, such as AfterDelConfirm, BeforeDelConfirm, Error, KeyDown, KeyPress, KeyUp, MouseDown, MouseMove, Mouse-Up, NotInList, and Updated.

- Your application consists of only a few forms and reports.

- Your application might be used by nonprogrammers who will want to understand how your application is constructed and possibly modify or enhance it.

- You're developing an application prototype, and you want to rapidly automate a few features to demonstrate your design.

There are actually a few things that can be done only with macros:

- Creating custom menus and submenus for forms.

- Defining alternative actions for certain keystrokes.

- Running a routine from a toolbar button.

- Creating a startup routine that runs when your database opens. Most of the time, you'll run a startup routine by attaching it to a startup form; however, in some circumstances you might find it useful to create an *Autoexec* macro startup routine.

You'll learn about most of these specialized tasks for macros in Chapter 23, "The Finishing Touches."

When to Use VBA

Although macros are extremely powerful, a number of tasks cannot be carried out with macros or are better implemented using a VBA procedure. Use a module instead of a macro in any of the following circumstances:

- You need discrete error handling in your application.

- You want to define a new function.

- You need to handle events that pass parameters or accept return values (other than Cancel).

- You need to create new objects (tables, queries, forms, or reports) in your database from application code.

- Your application needs to interact with another Microsoft Windows–based application via OLE Automation or Dynamic Data Exchange (DDE).

- You want to be able to directly call Windows API functions.

- You want to place part of your application code in a library.

- You want to be able to manipulate data in a recordset on a record-by-record basis.

- You need to use some of the native facilities of the relational database management system that handles your attached tables (such as SQL Server procedures or data definition facilities).

- You want maximum performance in your application. Because modules are compiled, they execute slightly faster than macros. You'll probably notice a difference only on slower processors.

The VBA Development Environment

VBA replaces the Access Basic programming language included with previous versions of Microsoft Access. The two are very similar; in fact, both VBA and Access Basic evolved from a common early design component. So if you already know Access Basic, VBA will be familiar territory. In recent years, VBA has become the common programming language for Microsoft Office applications, including Access, Microsoft Excel, and Microsoft Project.

Having a common programming component across applications provides several advantages. You have to learn only one programming language, and you can easily integrate objects across applications by using VBA and OLE Automation. In addition to these obvious advantages, VBA improves on the programming environment of Access Basic by providing color-coded syntax, an Object Browser, and other improvements. It also provides better tools for testing and confirming the proper execution of the code you write.

Modules

You save all VBA code in your database in modules. Access provides two ways to create a module: as a module object or as part of a form or report object.

Module Objects

You can view the module objects in your database by clicking on the Modules tab in the Database window. Figure 21-1 on the next page shows the modules in the Entertainment Schedule database. You should use module objects to define procedures that can be used from queries or from several forms or reports in your application. A procedure defined in a module object can be called from anywhere in your application.

To create a new module, click the New button to the right of the Modules list. It's a good idea to name modules based on their purpose. For example, a module that contains procedures to perform custom calculations for queries might be named modQueryFunctions, and a module containing procedures to work directly with Windows functions might be named modWindowsAPIFunctions.

FIGURE 21-1

The module
objects in the
Entertainment
Schedule
database.

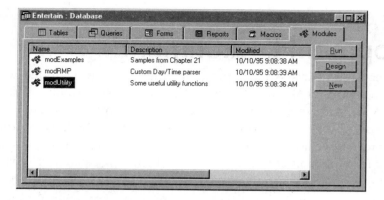

Form and Report Modules

To make it easy to create VBA procedures that respond to events on
forms or reports, Access provides a module associated with each form
or report that can contain procedures to respond directly to events.
You can also create special procedures within a form or report module
that will be used only by that form or report. You can edit the module
for a form or a report by opening the form or report in Design view and
then clicking the Code button on the toolbar or choosing Code from
the View menu.

Form and report modules offer two main advantages over module
objects:

- All the code you need to automate a form or a report resides
  with that form or report. You don't have to remember the name
  of a separate form-related or report-related module object.

- Access loads module objects into memory when you first reference any procedure or variable in the module and leaves it
  loaded as long as the database is open. It loads the code for a
  form or a report only when the form or the report is open.
  Therefore, form and report modules consume memory only when
  you're using the form or the report to which they are attached.

The Module Window

When you open a module in Design view, Access opens the Module
window for the module and displays the Declarations section, in which
you define any variables that are shared by all procedures in the module. Click on the Modules tab in the Database window, select the
modRMP module, and then click the Design button to see the Module
window for the modRMP module, as shown in Figure 21-2.

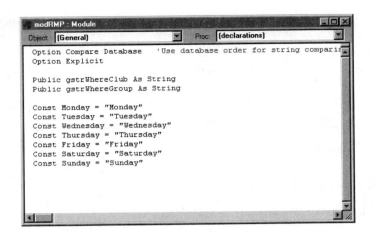

FIGURE 21-2
The modRMP
module in a
Module window.

At the top of the window, just below the title bar, are two drop-down list boxes:

- *Object list box.* When you're editing a form or report module, open this list to select the form or the report, a section on the form or the report, or any control on the form or the report that can generate an event. The Proc list box then shows the available event procedures for the selected object. Select (General) to select the Declarations section of the module. When you're editing a module object, this list displays only the (General) option.

- *Proc list box.* Open this list to select a procedure in the module and display that procedure in the Module window. When you're editing a form or report module, this list shows the available event procedures for the selected object and displays in bold type the event procedures that you have coded and attached to the form or the report. When you're editing a module object, the list displays in alphabetic order all the procedures you coded in the module.

In Figure 21-2, you can see the Declarations section of the module, in which public variables named *gstrWhereClub* and *gstrWhere-Group* are declared. These variables are shared by all procedures in the database (and are not reset each time a procedure runs). In a Module window, you can use the arrow keys to move horizontally and vertically. You'll find one blank line after the last line in this section, on which you can enter additional variable declarations. When you enter a new line of code and press Enter, Access verifies the syntax of the new line and warns you of any problems it finds.

From the Declarations section, you can press the PgDn key to move to the first procedure in this module. You can also select any procedure from the Proc list box. When you press PgDn while in the modRMP module, you see the *ValDaysTimes* function procedure, as shown in Figure 21-3.

FIGURE 21-3

The *ValDays-Times* function procedure as it appears in the modRMP module.

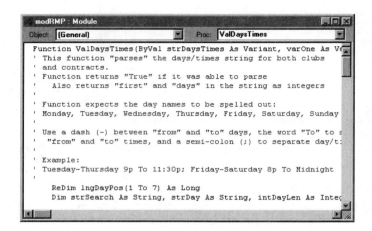

If you want to create a new procedure in a module, you can type in either a *Function* statement or a *Sub* statement on any line and then press Enter, click the Insert Procedure button on the toolbar, or choose Procedure from the Insert menu. Access starts a new procedure for you (it does not embed the new procedure in the procedure you were editing) and inserts an *End Function* or *End Sub* statement for you. If you're working in a form or report module, you can select an object in the Object list box and then open the Proc list box to see all the available events for that object. An event name displayed in bold type means you have created a procedure to handle that event. Select an event whose name isn't displayed in bold type to create a procedure to handle that event.

The Debug Window

One of the most useful tools for working with modules is the Debug window. While a Module window is open, click the Debug Window button on the toolbar or choose Debug Window from the View menu to open the Debug window, shown in Figure 21-4. (You can open the Debug window at any time by pressing Ctrl-G.)

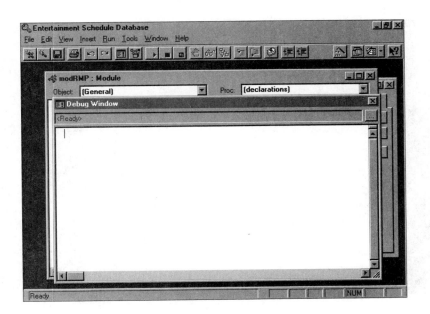

FIGURE 21-4
The Debug
window for the
modRMP module.

In the Debug window, you can type and immediately execute any legal VBA statement. For example, you can set the value of the gstrWhereClub variable to *"Winthrop"* by typing

```
gstrWhereClub = "Winthrop"
```

and pressing the Enter key.

The object used to debug VBA code is called *Debug*. The Debug object has a special method called *Print* that you can use to display the value of data in the Debug window. To display the current value of the gstrWhereClub variable in the Debug window, type

```
Debug.Print gstrWhereClub
```

and press Enter. You can try out these commands using the Debug window for the modRMP module. Set the value of gstrWhereClub to some string, and then use the *Debug.Print* method to display the value you just set, as shown in Figure 21-5 on the next page.

695

FIGURE 21-5

Setting and
displaying a
variable in the
Debug window.

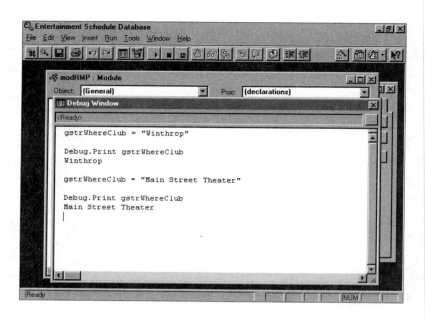

Debug.Print also has a shorthand syntax—a single question mark
(?). Therefore,

```
? gstrWhereClub
```

is the same as

```
Debug.Print gstrWhereClub
```

If you want to run a function procedure from the Debug window,
you can either assign the return value of the function procedure to a
variable or use *Debug.Print* to run the function and display the value
(if any) that it returns. If you want to try this out with the modRMP
module, enter the following:

```
? ValDaysTimes("Tuesday-Thursday 9p To 11:30p", 1, 1)
```

You should see the result shown in Figure 21-6—the function returns a value of −1, the numeric equivalent of True. This means that
the function was able to successfully evaluate the specified string,
"Tuesday-Thursday 9p To 11:30p".

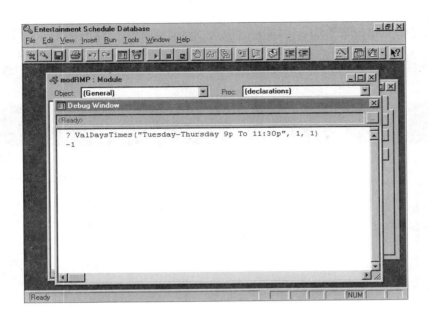

FIGURE 21-6

Using the Debug window to run the *ValDaysTimes* function procedure.

Variables and Constants

In addition to being able to use VBA code to work with the controls on any open forms or reports (as you can with macros), you can declare and use named variables in VBA code for storing values temporarily, calculating a result, or manipulating any of the objects in your database. So instead of defining "hidden" controls on forms to hold data that you want to pass from one routine to another, you can define a global variable (as you did in the modRMP module).

Another way to store data in VBA is with a constant. A *constant* is a data object with a fixed value that you cannot change. You've already encountered some of the "built-in" constants in Microsoft Access— Null, True, and False. VBA also has a large number of "intrinsic" constants that you can use to test for data types and other attributes or that you can use as fixed arguments in functions and expressions. You can view the list of intrinsic constants by searching for the Constants topic in Access Help. You can also declare your own constant values to use in code that you write.

In the following sections, you'll learn about using variables to store and calculate data and to work with database objects.

Data Types

VBA supports data types that are similar to the data types you use to define fields in tables. The data types are described in the following table.

Data Type	Size	Data-Typing Character	Can Contain
Byte	1 byte	(none)	Binary data ranging in value from 0 through 255
Integer	2 bytes	%	Integers from −32,768 through 32,767
Long	4 bytes	&	Integers from −2,147,483,648 through 2,147,483,647
Single	4 bytes	!	Floating-point numbers from approximately -3.4×10^{38} through 3.4×10^{38}
Double	8 bytes	#	Floating-point numbers from approximately -1.79×10^{308} through 1.79×10^{308}
Currency	8 bytes	@	A scaled integer with four decimal places from −922,337,203,685,477.5808 through 922,337,203,685,477.5807
String	1 byte per character	$	Any text or binary string up to approximately 2 billion bytes in length, including text, memo data, and "chunks" from an OLE object
Boolean	2 bytes	(none)	True or False
Date	8 bytes	(none)	Date/time values ranging from January 1, 100, to December 31, 9999
Object	4 bytes	(none)	Any Object reference

(continued)

continued

Data Type	Size	Data-Typing Character	Can Contain
Variant	1 byte through approximately 65,535 bytes	(none)	Any data, including Empty, Null, and date/time data (use the *VarType* function to determine the current data type of the data in the variable)
User-defined	Depends on elements defined	(none)	Any number of variables of any of the above data types

You can implicitly define the data type of a variable by appending a data-typing character, as noted in the above table, the first time you use the variable. For example, a variable named *MyInt%* is an integer variable. If you do not explicitly declare a data variable that you reference in your code and do not supply a data-typing character, Access assigns the Variant data type to the variable. Note that while the Variant data type is the most flexible (and, in fact, is the data type for all controls on forms and reports), it is also the least efficient because Access must do extra work to determine the current data type of the data in the variable before working with it in your code. The Variant data type is also the only data type that can contain the Null value.

 TIP   Access includes by default an *Option Explicit* statement in the Declarations section of every module. This helps you avoid errors that can occur when you use a variable in your code that you haven't properly declared in a *Dim, Public, ReDim, Static,* or *Type* statement or as part of the parameter list in a *Function* statement or a *Sub* statement. (See the next section.) Using an *Option Explicit* statement helps you find variables that you might have misspelled when you entered your code.

The Object data type listed in the table on the previous page lets you define variables that can contain object definitions. (See the section titled "Collections, Objects, Properties, and Methods" later in this chapter for details about objects that you can work with in VBA.) The object types are Application, Container, Control, Database, Document, Error, Field, Form, Group, Index, Parameter, Property, QueryDef, Recordset, Relation, Report, TableDef, User, and Workspace.

Variable and Constant Scope

The scope of a variable or a constant determines whether the variable or the constant is known to just one procedure, all procedures in a module, or all procedures in your database. You can create variables or constants that can be used by any procedure in your database (public scope). You can also create variables or constants that apply only to the procedures in a module or only to a single procedure (private scope). You can pass variables from one procedure to another using a parameter list, but the variables might be known by different names in the two procedures. (See the sections on the *Function*, *Sub*, and *Call* statements later in this chapter.)

To declare a public variable, use the *Public* statement in the Declarations section of a module. To declare a public constant, use the Public keyword with a *Const* statement in the Declarations section of a module. The *Public* statement and keyword replace the *Global* statement and keyword in previous versions.

To declare a variable or a constant that can be used by all procedures in a module, define that variable or constant in the Declarations section of the module object or the form or report module. To declare a variable or a constant used only in a particular procedure, define that variable or constant as part of the procedure.

Unlike previous versions of Access, Access for Windows 95 allows you to use the same name for variables or constants in different module objects or at different levels of scope. In addition, you can now declare public variables and constants in form and report modules as well as in module objects.

To use the same name for public variables and constants in different module objects or form or report modules, simply specify the name of the module to which it belongs when you refer to it. For example, you can declare a public variable named *intX* in a module object named *modMyModule* and then declare another public variable named *intX* in a second module object named *modMyOtherModule*. You can then refer to intX in modMyModule as follows:

```
modMyModule.intX
```

You can also declare variables or constants with the same name at different levels of scoping within a module object or a form or report module. For example, you can declare a public variable named *intX* and then declare another "local" variable named *intX* within a procedure. (You can't declare a public variable within a procedure.) References to intX within the procedure refer to the local variable, while references to intX outside the procedure refer to the public variable. To refer to the public variable within the procedure, simply qualify it with the name of the module, just as you would refer to a public variable in a different module.

Declaring a public variable or a constant in a form or report module can be useful for declaring variables and constants that are logically associated with a particular form or report but that you might also want to use elsewhere. Like the looser naming restrictions, however, this feature can sometimes create confusion. In general, it's still a good idea to keep common public variables and constants in module objects and to try to give public variables and constants unique names.

Syntax Conventions

The following conventions describe the VBA syntax for statements you'll encounter in this chapter.

Convention	Meaning
Boldface	Boldface type indicates keywords and reserved words that you must enter exactly as shown. Note that Microsoft Access understands keywords entered in uppercase, lowercase, and mixed case type.
Italic	Italicized words represent variables that you supply.

(continued)

continued

Convention	Meaning
Angle brackets < >	Angle brackets enclose syntactic elements that you must supply. The words inside the angle brackets describe the element but do not show the actual syntax of the element. Do not enter the angle brackets.
Brackets [ ]	Brackets enclose optional items. If more than one item is listed, the items are separated by a pipe character (|). Choose one or none of the elements. Do not enter the brackets or the pipe; they're not part of the element. Note that Access in many cases requires that you enclose names in brackets. When brackets are required as part of the syntax of variables that you must supply in these examples, the brackets are italicized, as in *[MyTable].[MyField]*.
Braces { }	Braces enclose one or more options. If more than one option is listed, the items are separated by a pipe character (|). Choose one item from the list. Do not enter the braces or the pipe.
Ellipsis ...	Ellipses indicate that you can repeat an item one or more times. When a comma is shown with an ellipsis (,...), enter a comma between items.
Underscore _	You can use a blank space followed by an underscore to continue a line of VBA code to the next line for readability. You cannot place an underscore in the middle of a string.

You must enter all other symbols, such as parentheses and colons, exactly as they appear in the syntax line.

The following sections show the syntax of the statements you can use to define constants and variables in your modules and procedures.

Const Statement

Use a *Const* statement to define a constant.

Syntax:

```
[Public | Private] Const {constantname [As type]=⏎
    <const expression>},...
```

Notes:

Include the Public keyword in the Declarations section of a module object or a form or report module to define a constant that is available to all procedures in all modules in your database. Include the Private keyword to declare constants that are available only within the module where the declaration is made. Constants are private by default.

The type entry is the data type of the constant; it can be Byte, Boolean, Integer, Long, Currency, Single, Double, Date, String, or Variant. Use a separate As type clause for each constant being declared. If you don't declare a type, the constant is given the data type that is most appropriate for the expression provided.

The *<const expression>* cannot include variables, user-defined functions, or VBA built-in functions (such as *Chr*). You can include simple literals and other previously defined constants.

Example:

To define the constant PI to be available to all procedures in all modules, enter the following in the Declarations section of any module object:

```
Public Const PI = 3.14159
```

Dim Statement

Use a *Dim* statement in the Declarations section of a module to declare a variable or a variable array that can be used in all procedures in the module. Use a *Dim* statement within a procedure to declare a variable used only in that procedure.

Syntax:

```
Dim {variablename [([<array dimension>],... )]
    [As [New] data type]},...
```

where *<array dimension>* is

```
[lowerbound To ] upperbound
```

Notes:

You cannot declare an array using an object data type. You can declare arrays using a *Dim* statement only in the Declarations section of a module. To declare an array in a procedure, use a *ReDim* or *Static* statement. If you do not include an *<array dimension>* specification, you must include a *ReDim* statement in each procedure that uses the array to dynamically allocate the array at run time. You can define an array with up to 60 dimensions. If you do not include a *lowerbound* value in an *<array dimension>* specification, the default lower bound is 0. You can reset the default lower bound to *1* by including an *Option Base 1* statement in the module Declarations section. You must specify a *lowerbound* value of at least −32,768 and an *upperbound* value that does not exceed 32,767.

Valid data type entries are Byte, Boolean, Integer, Long, Currency, Single, Double, Date, String (for variable-length strings), String * *length* (for fixed-length strings), Object, Variant, or one of the object types described in the section titled "Data Types" earlier in this chapter. You can also declare a user-defined variable structure using the *Type* statement and then use the user type name as a data type. Use the New keyword to indicate that a declared object variable is a new instance of an object.

Access initializes declared variables at compile time. Numeric variables are initialized to zero (0); variant variables are initialized to empty; variable-length string variables are initialized as zero-length strings; and fixed-length string variables are filled with ANSI zeros (Chr(0)). If you use a *Dim* statement within a procedure to declare variables, Access reinitializes the variables each time you run the procedure.

Examples:

To declare a variable named *intMyInteger* as an integer, enter the following:

```
Dim intMyInteger As Integer
```

To declare a variable named *dbMyDatabase* as a database object, enter the following:

```
Dim dbMyDatabase As Database
```

To declare an array named *strMyString* that contains fixed-length strings that are 20 characters long and contains 50 entries from 51 through 100, enter the following:

```
Dim strMyString (51 To 100) As String * 20
```

TIP It's a good idea to prefix all variable names you create with a notation that indicates the data type of the variable, particularly if you create complex procedures. This helps ensure that you aren't attempting to assign or calculate incompatible data types. (For example, the names will make it obvious that you're creating a potential error if you try to assign the contents of a long integer variable to an integer variable.) It also helps ensure that you pass variables of the correct data type to procedures. Finally, including a prefix helps ensure that you do not create a variable name that is the same as an Access reserved word. The following table suggests data type prefixes that you can use for many of the most common data types:

Data Type	Prefix		Data Type	Prefix
Integer	int		Control	ctl
Long	lng		Form	frm
Single	sgl		Report	rpt
Double	dbl		Database	db
Currency	cur		Field	fld
String	str		Index	idx
Variant	var		QueryDef	qry
User-defined (using the *Type* statement)	usr		Recordset	rcd
			TableDef	tbl

Public Statement

Use a *Public* statement in the Declarations section of a module object or a form or report module to declare variables that you can use in any procedure anywhere in your database.

Syntax:

```
Public {variablename [([<array dimension>],... )]⤳
    [As [New] data type]},....
```

where *<array dimension>* is

```
[lowerbound To ] upperbound
```

Notes:

You cannot declare an array using an object data type. If you do not include an *<array dimension>* specification, you must include a *ReDim* statement in each procedure that uses the array to dynamically allocate the array at run time. You can define an array with up to 60 dimensions. If you do not include a *lowerbound* value in an *<array dimension>* specification, the default lower bound is *0*. You can reset the default lower bound to *1* by including an *Option Base 1* statement in the module Declarations section. You must specify a *lowerbound* value of at least −32,768 and an *upperbound* value that does not exceed 32,767.

Valid data type entries are Byte, Boolean, Integer, Long, Currency, Single, Double, Date, String (for variable-length strings), String * *length* (for fixed-length strings), Object, Variant, or one of the object types described in the section titled "Data Types" earlier in this chapter. You can also declare a user-defined variable structure using the *Type* statement and then use the user type name as a data type. Use the New keyword to indicate that a declared object variable is a new instance of an object.

Access initializes declared variables at compile time. Numeric variables are initialized to zero (0); variant variables are initialized to empty; variable-length string variables are initialized as zero-length strings; and fixed-length string variables are filled with ANSI zeros (Chr(0)).

Example:

To declare a long variable named *lngMyNumber* that can be used in any procedure in the database, enter the following:

```
Public lngMyNumber As Long
```

ReDim Statement

Use a *ReDim* statement to dynamically declare an array within a procedure or to redimension a declared array within a procedure at run time.

Syntax:

```
ReDim [Preserve] {variablename (<array dimension>,....)⤶
    [As type]},....
```

where *<array dimension>* is

```
[lowerbound To ] upperbound
```

Notes:

If you're dynamically allocating an array that you previously defined with no *<array dimension>* in a *Dim* or *Global* statement, your array can have no more than 8 dimensions. If you declare the array only within a procedure, your array can have up to 60 dimensions. If you do not include a *lowerbound* value in an *<array dimension>* specification, the default lower bound is *0*. You can reset the default lower bound to *1* by including an *Option Base 1* statement in the module Declarations section. You must specify a *lowerbound* value of at least −32,768 and an *upperbound* value that does not exceed 32,767. If you previously specified dimensions in a *Global* or *Dim* statement or in another *ReDim* statement within the same procedure, you cannot change the number of dimensions.

Include the Preserve keyword to ask Access not to reinitialize existing values in the array. When you use Preserve, you can change the bounds of only the last dimension in the array.

Valid data type entries are Byte, Boolean, Integer, Long, Currency, Single, Double, Date, String (for variable-length strings), String * *length* (for fixed-length strings), Object, Variant, or one of the object types described in the section titled "Data Types" earlier in this chapter. You can also declare a user-defined variable structure using the *Type* statement and then use the user type name as a data type. You cannot change the data type of an array that you previously declared with a *Dim* or *Global* statement. After you establish the number of dimensions for an array that has module or global scope, you cannot change the number of its dimensions using a *ReDim* statement.

Access initializes declared variables at compile time. Numeric variables are initialized to zero (0); variant variables are initialized to empty; variable-length string variables are initialized as zero-length strings; and fixed-length string variables are filled with ANSI zeros (Chr(0)). If you use a *ReDim* statement within a procedure to both declare and allocate an array (and you have not previously defined the array with a *Dim* or *Global* statement), Access reinitializes the array each time you run the procedure.

Example:

To dynamically allocate an array named *strProductNames* that contains 20 strings, each with a fixed length of 25, enter the following:

```
ReDim strProductNames (20) As String * 25
```

Static Statement

Use a *Static* statement within a procedure to declare a variable used only in that procedure that Access does not reinitialize while the module containing the procedure is open. Access opens all module objects when you open the database containing those objects. Access keeps form or report modules open only while the form or the report is open.

Syntax:

```
Static {variablename [({<array dimension>},...)]↴
  [As [New] data type]},...
```

where *<array dimension>* is

```
[lowerbound To ] upperbound
```

Notes:

You cannot declare an array using an object data type. You can define an array with up to 60 dimensions. If you do not include a *lowerbound* value in an *<array dimension>* specification, the default lower bound is *0*. You can reset the default lower bound to *1* by including an *Option Base 1* statement in the module Declarations section. You must specify a *lowerbound* value of at least −32,768 and an *upperbound* value that does not exceed 32,767.

Valid data type entries are Byte, Boolean, Integer, Long, Currency, Single, Double, Date, String (for variable-length strings), String * *length* (for fixed-length strings), Object, Variant, or one of the object types described in the section titled "Data Types" earlier in this chapter. You can also declare a user-defined variable structure using the *Type* statement and then use the user type name as a data type. Use the New keyword to indicate that a declared object variable is a new instance of an object.

Access initializes declared variables at compile time. Numeric variables are initialized to zero (0); variant variables are initialized to empty; variable-length string variables are initialized as zero-length strings; and fixed-length string variables are filled with ANSI zeros (Chr(0)).

Examples:

To declare a static variable named *intMyInteger* as an integer, enter the following:

```
Static intMyInteger As Integer
```

To declare a static array named *strMyString* that contains fixed-length strings that are 20 characters long and contains 50 entries from 51 through 100, enter the following:

```
Static strMyString (51 To 100) As String * 20
```

Type Statement

Use a *Type* statement in a Declarations section to create a user-defined data structure containing one or more variables.

Syntax:

```
[Public | Private] Type typename
    {variablename As data type}
      . . .
End Type
```

Notes:

A *Type* statement is most useful for declaring sets of variables that can be passed to procedures (including Windows API functions) as a single variable. You can also use the *Type* statement to declare a record structure. After you declare a user-defined data structure, you can use the *typename* in any subsequent *Dim*, *Global*, or *Static* statement to create a variable of that type. You can reference variables in a user-defined data structure variable by entering the variable name, a period, and the name of the variable within the structure. (See the second part of the example that follows.)

Include the Public keyword to declare a user-defined type that is available to all procedures in all modules in your database. Include the Private keyword to declare a user-defined type that is available only within the module in which the declaration is made.

You must enter each *variablename* entry on a new line. You must indicate the end of your user-defined data structure using an *End Type* statement. Valid data type entries are Byte, Boolean, Integer, Long, Currency, Single, Double, Date, String (for variable-length strings), String * *length* (for fixed-length strings), Object, Variant, another user-defined type, or one of the object types described in the section titled "Data Types" earlier in this chapter.

Example:

To define a user type structure named *MyRecord* containing a long integer and three string fields, declare a variable named *usrContacts* using that user type, and then set the first string to Jones, enter the following:

```
Type MyRecord
    lngID As Long
    strLast As String
    strFirst As String
    strMid As String
End Type
```

Within a procedure, enter the following:

```
Dim usrContacts As MyRecord
usrContacts.strLast = "Jones"
```

Collections, Objects, Properties, and Methods

You've already dealt with two of the main collections supported by Microsoft Access—Forms and Reports. The Forms collection contains all the forms that are open in your application, and the Reports collection contains all the open reports.

You don't need a thorough understanding of collections, objects, properties, and methods to perform most application tasks. It's useful, however, for you to know how Access organizes these items so that you can better understand how Access works. If you want to study advanced code examples available in the Microsoft Access Solutions Pack or in the many sample databases that you can download from public forums, you'll need to understand collections, objects, properties, and methods and how to correctly reference them.

The Access Application Architecture

Access has two major components—the application engine, which controls the programming and the end-user interface, and the JET DBEngine, which controls the storage of data and the definition of all the objects in your database. Figure 21-7 shows the architecture of Access. When you open a database, the application engine uses the database engine to determine the names of all the tables, queries, forms, reports, macros, and modules to display in the Database window. The application engine establishes the top-level Application object, which contains a Forms collection (all the open forms) and a Reports collection (all the open reports). Each form and report, in turn, contains a Controls collection (all of the controls on the form or the report).

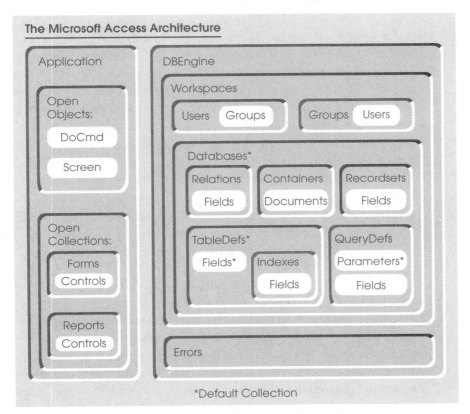

FIGURE 21-7
The Access application architecture.

The Application object also contains two special objects, the Screen object and the DoCmd object. The Screen object has four very useful properties: ActiveControl, ActiveForm, ActiveReport, and Previous-Control. Without knowing the actual names, you can reference the control (if any) that currently has the focus, the form (if any) that has the focus, the report (if any) that has the focus, or the name of the control that previously had the focus. (Additional details about referencing properties of objects appear later in this chapter.) The DoCmd object lets you execute most macro actions within VBA. (See the section titled "Running Macro Actions" later in this chapter.)

The Application object has a single property, DBEngine, that serves as a bridge between the application engine and the JET DBEngine. The DBEngine property represents the DBEngine object, the top-level object in the database engine object hierarchy. The DBEngine object controls all the database objects in your database through a hierarchy of collections, objects, and properties. When you open an Access database, the DBEngine first establishes a *Workspaces* collection and a default Workspace object. If your workgroup is secured, Access prompts you for a password and a user ID so that the DBEngine can create a User object and a Group object within the default workspace. If your workgroup is not secured, the DBEngine creates a default user called Admin in a default group called Admins.

Finally, the DBEngine creates a Database object within the default Workspace object. The DBEngine uses the current User and/or Group object information to determine whether you're authorized to access any of the objects within the database.

After the DBEngine creates a Database object, the application engine checks the database's startup options to find out whether to display a startup form, menu bar, and title or use one or more of the other startup options. You can set these options by choosing the Startup command from the Tools menu. After checking the startup options, the application engine checks to see whether a macro group named Autoexec exists in the database. If it finds Autoexec, the application engine runs this macro group. In previous versions of Access, you'd often use the Autoexec macro group to open a startup form and run startup routines. In Access for Windows 95, however, you should use the startup options to specify a startup form, and then use the event procedures of the startup form to run your startup routines.

See Also   See Chapter 23, "The Finishing Touches," for details on creating an Autoexec macro group.

You can code VBA procedures that can create additional Database objects in the Databases collection by opening additional mdb files. Each open Database object has a Containers collection that the DBEngine uses to store the definition (using the Documents collection) of all your tables, queries, forms, reports, macros, and modules.

You can use the TableDefs collection to examine and modify existing tables. You can also create new TableDef objects within this collection. Likewise, the Relations collection contains Relation objects that define how tables are related and what integrity rules apply between tables. The QueryDefs collection contains QueryDef objects that define all the queries in your database. You can modify existing queries or create new ones. Finally, the Recordsets collection contains a Recordset object for each open recordset in your database.

> **NOTE** In the example at the end of this chapter, you'll learn how to create a new TableDef object and then open a Recordset object on the new table to insert rows.

Referencing Collections, Objects, and Properties

In the previous chapter, you learned the most common way to reference objects in the Forms and Reports collections and controls on those objects and their properties. There are two alternative ways to reference an object within a collection. The three ways to reference an object within a collection are as follows:

- *CollectionName![Object Name]*. This is the method you used in the previous chapter. For example: *Forms![My Form]*.

- *CollectionName("Object Name")*. This method is similar to the first method but uses a string constant to supply the object name, as in *Forms("My Form")*.

- *CollectionName(RelativeObjectNumber)*. Access numbers objects within a collection from zero (0) to *CollectionName.Count* minus *1*. For example, you can determine the number of open forms by referring to the Count property of the Forms collection: *Forms.Count*. You can refer to the second open form in the Forms collection as *Forms(1)*.

Forms and Reports are relatively simple because they are top-level collections within the application engine. As you can see in Figure 21-7, shown earlier in this chapter, when you reference a collection or an object maintained by the DBEngine, the hierarchy of collections and objects is quite complex. If you want to find out how many Workspace objects exist in the Workspaces collection, you need to reference the Count property of the Workspaces collection. For example, you reference the Count property like this:

```
DBEngine.Workspaces.Count
```

(You can create additional workspaces from VBA code.)

Using the third method described on the previous page to reference an object, you can reference the default Workspace object by entering the following:

```
DBEngine.Workspaces(0)
```

Likewise, you can refer to the currently open database by entering the following:

```
DBEngine.Workspaces(0).Databases(0)
```

When you want to refer to an object that exists in an object's default (or only) collection (see Figure 21-7), you do not need to include the collection name. Therefore, because the Databases collection is the default collection for the Workspaces collection, you can also refer to the currently open database by entering the following:

```
DBEngine.Workspaces(0)(0)
```

NOTE When you use *DBEngine.Workspaces(0).Databases(0)* to set a database object, Access establishes a pointer to the current database. You can have only one object variable set to the actual copy of the current database, and you must never close this copy. A safer method is to set your database variable using the *CurrentDb* function. Using this method opens a new database object that is based on the same database as the current one. You can have as many copies of the current database as you like, and you can close them when you finish using them.

As you can see, even with this shorthand method, object names can become quite cumbersome if you want to refer, for example, to a particular field within an index definition for a table within the current database in the default Workspace object. (Whew!) If for no other reason, object variables are quite handy to help minimize name complexity.

In particular, you can reduce name complexity by using an object variable to represent the current database. When you set the variable to the current database, you can call the *CurrentDb* function rather than using the database's full qualifier. For example, you can declare a Database object variable, set it to the current database by using the *CurrentDb* function, and then use the Database object variable name as a starting point to reference the TableDefs, QueryDefs, and Recordsets that it contains. (See page 716 for the syntax of the *Set* statement.)

When to Use "!" and "."

You've probably noticed that a complex, fully qualified name of an object or a property in Access contains exclamation points (!) and periods (.) that separate the parts of the name. Use an exclamation point preceding a name when the name refers to an object that is in the preceding object or collection of objects. A name following an exclamation point is generally the name of an object you created (such as a form or a table). Names following an exclamation point must be enclosed in brackets ([ ]) if they contain embedded blank spaces or a special character, such as an underscore (_). To make this distinction clear, you might want to get into the habit of always enclosing in brackets names that follow an exclamation point, even though brackets are not required for names that don't use blank spaces or special characters. Access automatically inserts brackets around names in property sheets, design grids, and action arguments.

Use a period preceding a name that refers to a collection name, a property name, or the name of a method that you can perform against the preceding object. (Names following a period should never contain blank spaces.) In other words, use a period when the following name is of the preceding name (as in the TableDefs collection of the Databases(0) object, the Count property of the TableDefs collection, or the *MoveLast* method of the Recordset object). This distinction is particularly important when referencing something that has the same name as the name of a property. For example, the reference

```
DBEngine.Workspaces(0).Databases(0).TableDefs(10).Name
```

refers to the name of a TableDef object in the current database. In the Entertainment Schedule database, if you use *Debug.Print* to display this reference, Access returns the value *tblClubs*. However, the reference

```
DBEngine.Workspaces(0).Databases(0).TableDefs(10)![Name]
```

refers to the contents of a field called Name (if one exists) in the 11th TableDef object in the current database. In the Entertainment Schedule database, this reference returns an error because there is no Name field in the tblClubs table.

Assigning an Object Variable— the *Set* Statement

As noted earlier, you can use object variables to simplify name references. Also, using an object variable is less time-consuming than using a fully qualified name. At run time, Access must always parse a qualified name to first determine the type of object and then determine which object or property you want. If you use an object variable, you have already defined the type of object and established a direct pointer to it, so Access can quickly go to that object. This is especially important if you plan to reference, for example, many controls on a form. If you create a form variable first and then assign the variable to point to the form, referencing controls on the form via the form variable is much simpler and faster than using a fully qualified name for each control.

Syntax:

> **Set** *variablename* = *objectreference*

Notes:

You must first declare *variablename* using a *Dim*, *Public*, or *Static* statement as an Application, Container, Control, Database, Document, Error, Field, Form, Group, Index, Parameter, Property, QueryDef, Recordset, Relation, Report, TableDef, User, or Workspace object. The object type must be compatible with the object type of *objectreference*. You can use another object variable in an *objectreference* to qualify an object at a lower level. (See the examples below.) You can also use an object *method* to create a new object in a collection and assign that object to an object variable. For example, it's common to use the *OpenRecordset* method of a QueryDef or TableDef object to create a new Recordset object. (See the example in the next section, "Object Methods.")

An object variable is a reference to an object, not a copy of the object. So you can assign more than one object variable to point to the same object and change a property of the object, and all variables referencing the object will reflect the change as well. The one exception is that several Recordset variables can refer to the same recordset, but each can have its own Bookmark property pointing to different rows in the recordset.

Examples:

To create a variable reference to the current database, enter the following:

```
Dim dbMyDB As Database
Set dbMyDB = CurrentDb()
```

To create a variable reference to the tblClubs table in the current database using the *dbMyDB* variable defined above, enter the following:

```
Dim tblMyTable As TableDef
Set tblMyTable = dbMyDB![tblClubs]
```

Notice that you do not need to explicitly reference the Table-Defs collection of the database, as in *dbMyDB.TableDefs![tblClubs]* or *dbMyDB.TableDefs("tblClubs")*, because TableDefs is the default collection of the database. Access assumes that *[tblClubs]* refers to the name of an object in the default collection of the database.

To create a variable reference to the Notes field in the tblClubs table using the *tblMyTable* variable defined above, enter the following:

```
Dim fldMyField As Field
Set fldMyField = tblMyTable![Notes]
```

Object Methods

When you want to apply an action to an object in your database (such as open a query as a recordset or go to the next row in a recordset), you apply a *method* of either the object or an object variable that you have assigned to point to the object. In some cases, you'll use a method to create a new object. Many methods accept parameters that you can use to further refine how the method acts on the object. For example, you can tell the *OpenRecordset* method whether you're creating a recordset against a local table, a dynaset (an updatable recordset), or a read-only snapshot.

Access supports many different object methods—far more than there's room to properly document in this book. Perhaps one of the most useful groups of methods is the group you can use to create a recordset and then read, update, insert, and delete rows in the recordset.

To create a recordset, you must first declare a Recordset object variable. Then open the recordset using the *OpenRecordset* method against the current database (specifying a table name, a query name, or an SQL string to create the recordset) or against a QueryDef, TableDef, or other Recordset object. You can specify options to indicate whether you're opening the recordset as a local table (which means you can use the *Seek* method to quickly locate rows based on a match with an available index), as a dynaset, or as a read-only snapshot. For updatable recordsets, you can also specify that you want to deny other updates, deny other reads, open a read-only recordset, open the recordset for append only, or open a read-only forward scroll recordset (which allows you to move only forward through the records).

717

For example, to declare a recordset for the tblClubs table in the Entertainment Schedule database and open the recordset as a table so that you can use its indexes, enter the following:

```
Dim dbEntSched As Database
Dim rcdClubs As RecordSet
Set dbEntSched = CurrentDb()
Set rcdClubs = dbEntSched.OpenRecordSet("tblClubs", _
  dbOpenTable)
```

To open the qryActivePaidContracts query as a dynaset, enter the following:

```
Dim dbEntSched As Database
Dim rcdAPContracts As RecordSet
Set dbEntSched = CurrentDb()
Set rcdAPContracts = _
  dbEntSched.OpenRecordSet("qryActivePaidContracts")
```

(Note that opening a recordset as a dynaset is the default when the source is a query.)

After you open a recordset, you can use one of the *Move* methods to move to a specific record. Use *recordset.MoveFirst* to move to the first row in the recordset. Other *Move* methods include *MoveLast, MoveNext,* and *MovePrevious.* If you want to move to a specific row in the recordset, use one of the *Find* methods. You must supply a string variable containing the criteria for finding the records you want. The criteria string looks exactly like an SQL WHERE clause (see Chapter 11, "Advanced Query Design—SQL") but without the WHERE keyword. For example, to find the first item in the qryActivePaidContracts query's recordset whose AmountOwed entry is greater than $100, enter the following:

```
rcdAPContracts.FindFirst "AmountOwed > 100"
```

To delete a row in an updatable recordset, simply move to the row you want to delete and then use the *Delete* method. For example, to delete the first row in the qryActivePaidContracts query's recordset whose AmountOwed entry equals *0,* enter the following:

```
Dim dbEntSched As Database
Dim rcdAPContracts As RecordSet
Set dbEntSched = CurrentDb()
Set rcdAPContracts = _
  dbEntSched.OpenRecordSet("qryActivePaidContracts")
rcdAPContracts.FindFirst "AmountOwed = 0"
' Test the recordset NoMatch property for "not found"
```

```
If Not rcdAPContracts.NoMatch Then
    rcdAPContracts.Delete
End If
```

If you want to update rows in a recordset, move to the first row you want to update and then use the *Edit* method to lock the row and make it updatable. You can then refer to any of the fields in the row by name to change their values. Use the *Update* method on the recordset to save your changes before moving to another row. For example, to increase by 10 percent the AmountOwed entry of the first row in the qryActivePaidContracts query's recordset whose AmountOwed value is greater than $100, enter the following:

```
Dim dbEntSched As Database
Dim rcdAPContracts As RecordSet
Set dbEntSched = CurrentDb()
Set rcdAPContracts = _
    dbEntSched.OpenRecordSet("qryActivePaidContracts")
rcdAPContracts.FindFirst "AmountOwed > 100"
' Test the recordset NoMatch property for "not found"
If Not rcdAPContracts.NoMatch Then
    rcdAPContracts.Edit
    rcdAPContracts![AmountOwed] = _
        rcdAPContracts![AmountOwed] * 1.1
    rcdAPContracts.Update
End If
```

Finally, to insert a new row in a recordset, use the *AddNew* method to start a new row. Set the values of all required fields in the row, and then use the *Update* method to save the new row. For example, to insert a new club in the Entertainment Schedule tblClubs table, enter the following:

```
Dim dbEntSched As Database
Dim rcdClubs As RecordSet
Set dbEntSched = CurrentDb()
Set rcdClubs = dbEntSched.OpenRecordSet("tblClubs")
rcdClubs.AddNew
rcdClubs![ClubName] = "Winthrop Brewing Co."
rcdClubs![StreetAddress] = "155 Riverside Ave."
rcdClubs![City] = "Winthrop"
rcdClubs![State] = "WA"
rcdClubs![ZipCode] = "98862"
rcdClubs![ClubPhoneNumber] = "(509) 996-3183"
rcdClubs.Update
```

For more information about object methods, search on "Methods" in Access Help.

Functions and Subroutines

You can create two types of procedures in VBA—functions and subroutines (also known as function procedures and sub procedures). Both types of procedure can accept *parameters*—data variables that you pass to the procedure that can determine how the procedure operates. Functions can return a single data value, but subroutines cannot. In addition, you can execute a function from anywhere in Microsoft Access, including from expressions in queries and from macros. You can execute a subroutine only from a function, from another subroutine, or as an event procedure in a form or a report.

Function Statement

Use a *Function* statement to declare a new function, the parameters it accepts, the variable type it returns, and the code that performs the function procedure.

Syntax:

```
[Public | Private] [Static] Function functionname→
  ([<arguments>]) [As data type]
    [<function statements>]
    [functionname = <expression>]
    [Exit Function]
    [<function statements>]
    [functionname = <expression>]
  End Function
```

where *<arguments>* is

```
{[Optional][ByVal | ByRef][ParamArray] argumentname→
  [As data type]},...
```

Notes:

Use the Public keyword to make this function available to all other procedures in all modules. Use the Private keyword to make this function available only to other procedures in the same module. When you declare a function as private in a module object, you cannot call that function from a query or a macro or from a function in another module.

Include the Static keyword to preserve the value of all variables declared within the procedure, whether explicitly or implicitly, as long as the module containing the procedure is open. This is the same as using the *Static* statement (discussed earlier in this chapter) to explicitly declare all variables created in this function.

You can use a type declaration character at the end of the *functionname* entry or use the *As* clause to declare the data type returned by this function. If you do not declare a data type, VBA assumes that the function returns a variant result. You set the return value in code by assigning an expression of a compatible data type to the function name.

You should declare the data type of any arguments in the function's parameter list. Note that the names of the variables passed by the calling procedure can be different from the names of the variables known by this procedure. If you use the ByVal keyword to declare an argument, VBA passes a <u>copy</u> of the argument to your function. Any change you make to a ByVal argument does not change the original variable in the calling procedure. If the argument passed by the calling procedure is an expression, VBA treats it as if you had declared it a ByVal. If you use the ByRef keyword, VBA passes the actual memory address of the variable, allowing the procedure to change the variable's actual value. VBA always passes arrays by reference (ByRef).

Use the Optional keyword to declare an argument of the Variant data type that isn't required. If you declare an optional argument, all arguments that follow in the argument list must also be declared optional. Use the *IsMissing* built-in function to test for the absence of optional parameters. You can also use the ParamArray argument to declare an array of optional elements of the Variant data type. When you call the function, you can then pass it an arbitrary number of arguments. The ParamArray argument must be the last argument in the argument list.

Use the *Exit Function* statement anywhere in your function to clear any error conditions and exit your function normally, returning to the calling procedure. If VBA runs your code until it encounters the *End Function* statement, control is passed to the calling procedure but any errors are not cleared. If this function causes an error and terminates with the *End Function* statement, VBA passes the error to the calling procedure. (See the section titled "Trapping Errors" later in this chapter for details.)

Example:

To create a function named *MyFunction* that accepts an integer argument and a string argument and returns a double value, enter the following:

```
Function MyFunction (intArg1 As Integer, strArg2 As _
   String) As Double
      <function statements>
End Function
```

Sub Statement

Use a *Sub* statement to declare a new subroutine, the parameters it accepts, and the code in the subroutine.

Syntax:

```
[Public | Private] [Static] Sub subroutinename ⤷
   ([<arguments>])
   [As data type]
     [ <subroutine statements> ]
     [Exit Sub]
     [ <subroutine statements> ]
   End Sub
```

where *<arguments>* is

```
{[Optional][ByVal | ByRef][ParamArray] argumentname⤷
   [As data type]},...
```

Notes:

Use the Public keyword to make this subroutine available to all other procedures in all modules. Use the Private keyword to make this procedure available only to other procedures in the same module.

Include the Static keyword to preserve the value of all variables declared within the procedure, whether explicitly or implicitly, as long as the module containing the procedure is open. This is the same as using the *Static* statement (discussed earlier in this chapter) to explicitly declare all variables created in this subroutine.

You should declare the data type of all arguments that the subroutine accepts in its argument list. Note that the names of the variables that are passed by the calling procedure can be different from the names of the variables as known by this procedure. If you use the ByVal keyword to declare an argument, VBA passes a <u>copy</u> of the argument to your subroutine. Any change you make to a ByVal argument does not change the original variable in the calling procedure. If the argument passed by the calling procedure is an expression, VBA treats it as if you had declared it a ByVal. If you use the ByRef keyword, VBA passes the actual memory address of the variable, allowing the procedure to change the variable's actual value. VBA always passes arrays by reference (ByRef).

Use the Optional keyword to declare an argument of the Variant data type that isn't required. If you declare an optional argument, all arguments that follow in the argument list must also be declared as optional. Use the *IsMissing* built-in function to test for the absence of optional parameters. You can also use the ParamArray argument to declare an array of optional elements of the Variant data type. When you call the subroutine, you can then pass it an arbitrary number of arguments. The ParamArray argument must be the last argument in the argument list.

Use the *Exit Sub* statement anywhere in your subroutine to clear any error conditions and exit your subroutine normally, returning to the calling procedure. If VBA runs your code until it encounters the *Exit Sub* statement, control is passed to the calling procedure but any errors are not cleared. If this subroutine causes an error and terminates with the *End Sub* statement, VBA passes the error to the calling procedure. (See the section titled "Trapping Errors" later in this chapter.)

Example:

To create a subroutine named *MySub* that accepts two string arguments but can modify only the second argument, enter the following:

```
Function MySub (ByVal strArg1 As String, ByRef strArg2 _
  As String)
    <subroutine statements>
End Sub
```

Controlling the Flow of Statements

VBA provides many ways for you to control the flow of statements in procedures. You can call other procedures, loop through a set of statements either a calculated number of times or based on a condition, or test values and conditionally execute sets of statements based on the result of the condition test. You can also go directly to a set of statements or exit a procedure at any time. The following sections demonstrate some (but not all) of the ways you can control flow in your procedures.

Call Statement

Use a *Call* statement to transfer control to a subroutine.

Syntax:

> **Call** *subroutinename* [(*<arguments>*)]

or

> *subroutinename* [*<arguments>*]

where *<arguments>* is

> {[**ByVal** | **ByRef**] *<expression>* },...

Notes:

If the subroutine accepts arguments, the names of the variables passed by the calling procedure can be different from the names of the variables as known by the subroutine. The ByVal and ByRef keywords can be used in a Call statement only in certain circumstances, such as when you are making a call to a dynamic-link library (DLL) procedure. If you use the ByVal keyword to declare an argument, VBA passes a <u>copy</u> of the argument to the subroutine. The subroutine cannot change the original variable in the calling procedure. If the argument passed by the calling procedure is an expression, VBA treats it as if you had declared it a ByVal. If you use the ByRef keyword, VBA passes the actual memory address of the variable, allowing the procedure to change the variable's actual value.

Examples:

To call a subroutine named *MySub* and pass it an integer variable and an expression, enter the following:

```
Call MySub (intMyInteger, curPrice * intQty)
```

An alternative syntax is

```
MySub intMyInteger, curPrice * intQty
```

Do...Loop Statement

Use a *Do...Loop* statement to define a block of statements that you want executed multiple times. You can also define a condition that terminates the loop when the condition is false.

Syntax:

```
Do [{While | Until} <condition>]
    [<procedure statements>]
    [Exit Do]
    [<procedure statements>]
Loop
```

or

```
Do
    [<procedure statements>]
    [Exit Do]
    [<procedure statements>]
Loop [{While | Until} <condition>]
```

Notes:

The <condition> is a comparison predicate or expression that VBA can evaluate to True (nonzero) or False (zero or Null). The *While* clause is the opposite of the *Until* clause. If you specify a *While* clause, execution continues as long as the <condition> is true. If you specify an *Until* clause, execution of the loop stops when <condition> is true. If you place a *While* or an *Until* clause in the *Do* clause, the condition must be met for the statements in the loop to execute at all. If you place a *While* or an *Until* clause in the *Loop* clause, VBA executes the statements within the loop before testing the condition.

You can place one or more *Exit Do* statements anywhere within the loop to exit the loop before reaching the *Loop* statement. Generally you'll use the *Exit Do* statement as part of some other evaluation statement structure, such as an *If...Then...Else* statement.

Example:

To read all the rows in the tlbClubs table until you reach the end of the recordset, enter the following:

```
Dim dbEntSched As Database
Dim rcdClubs As RecordSet
Set dbEntSched = CurrentDb()
Set rcdClubs = dbEndSched.OpenRecordSet("tblClubs")
Do Until rcdClubs.EOF
    <procedure statements>
    rcdClubs.MoveNext
Loop
```

For...Next Statement

Use a *For...Next* statement to execute a series of statements a specific number of times.

Syntax:

```
For counter = first To last [Step stepamount]
    [<procedure statements>]
    [Exit For]
    [<procedure statements>]
Next [counter]
```

Notes:

The *counter* must be a numeric variable that is not an array or a record element. VBA initially sets the value of *counter* to *first*. If you do not specify a *stepamount*, the default *stepamount* value is *+1*. If the *stepamount* value is positive or *0*, VBA executes the loop as long as *counter* is less than or equal to *last*. If the *stepamount* value is negative, VBA executes the loop as long as *counter* is greater than or equal to *last*. VBA adds *stepamount* to *counter* when it encounters the corresponding *Next* statement. You can change the value of *counter* within the *For* loop, but this might make your procedure more difficult to test and debug. Changing the value of *last* within the loop does not affect execution of the loop.

You can nest one *For* loop inside another. When you do this, you must choose a different name for each *counter*.

Example:

To list the names of all the first five queries in the Entertainment Schedule database, enter the following:

```
Dim dbEntSched As Database
Dim intI As Integer
Set dbEntSched = CurrentDb()
For intI = 0 To 4
    Debug.Print dbEntSched.QueryDefs(intI).Name
Next intI
```

For Each...Next Statement

Use a *For Each...Next* statement to execute a series of statements for each item in a collection or an array.

Syntax:

```
For Each item In group
  [<procedure statements>]
  [Exit For]
    [<procedure statements>]
Next [item]
```

Notes:

The *item* must be a variable that represents an object in a collection or an element of an array. The *group* must be the name of a collection or an array. VBA executes the loop as long as at least one item remains in the collection or the array. All the statements in the loop are executed for each item in the collection or the array.

You can nest one *For Each* loop inside another. When you do this, you must choose a different *item* name for each loop.

Example:

To list the names of all the queries in the Entertainment Schedule database, enter the following:

```
Dim dbEntSched As Database
Dim qdf As QueryDef
Set dbEntSched = CurrentDb()
For Each qdf In dbEntSched.QueryDefs
    Debug.Print qdf.Name
Next qdf
```

GoTo Statement

Use a *GoTo* statement to jump unconditionally to another statement in your procedure.

Syntax:

```
GoTo {label | linenumber}
```

Notes:

You can label a statement line by starting the line with a string no more than 40 characters long that starts with an alphabetic character and ends with a colon (:). A line label cannot be a VBA or Access reserved word. You can also optionally number the statement lines in your procedure. Each line number must contain only numbers, must be different from all other line numbers in the procedure, must be the first nonblank characters in a line, and must contain 40 characters or less. To jump to a line number or a labeled line, use the *GoTo* statement and the appropriate *label* or *linenumber*.

Example:

To jump to the statement line labeled *SkipOver:*, enter the following:

```
GoTo SkipOver
```

If...Then...Else Statement

Use an *If...Then...Else* statement to conditionally execute statements based on the evaluation of a condition.

Syntax:

```
If <condition1> Then
    [<procedure statements 1>]
[ElseIf <condition2> Then
    [<procedure statements 2>]]...
[Else
    [<procedure statements n>]]
End If
```

or

```
If <condition> Then <thenstmt> [Else <elsestmt>]
```

Notes:

The *<condition>* is a numeric or string expression that Access can evaluate to True (nonzero) or False (0 or Null). The *<condition>* can also be the special *TypeOf...Is* test to evaluate a control variable. The syntax for this test is

```
TypeOf <ControlObject> Is <ControlType>
```

where *<ControlObject>* is the name of a control variable and *<ControlType>* is one of the following: BoundObjectFrame, CheckBox, ComboBox, CommandButton, Chart, CustomControl, Image, Label, Line, ListBox, OptionButton, OptionGroup, PageBreak, Rectangle, Subform, Subreport, TextBox, ToggleButton, or UnboundObjectFrame.

If the *<condition>* is true, Access executes the statement or statements immediately following the Then keyword. If the *<condition>* is false, Access evaluates the next *ElseIf <condition>* or executes the statements following the Else keyword, whichever occurs next.

The alternative syntax does not need an *End If* statement, but you must enter the entire *If...Then* statement on a single line. Both

<thenstmt> and *<elsestmt>* can be either a single VBA statement or multiple statements separated by colons (:).

Example:

To set an integer value depending on whether a string begins with a letter from *A* through *F*, from *G* through *N*, or from *O* through *Z*, enter the following:

```
Dim strMyString As String, strFirst As String, _
  intVal As Integer
strFirst = UCase$(Mid$(strMyString, 1, 1))
If strFirst >= "A" And strFirst <= "F" Then
    intVal = 1
ElseIf strFirst >= "G" And strFirst <= "N" Then
    intVal = 2
ElseIf strFirst >= "O" And strFirst <= "Z" Then
    intVal = 3
Else
    intVal = 0
End If
```

Select Case Statement

Use a *Select Case* statement to execute statements conditionally based on the evaluation of an expression compared to a list or range of values.

Syntax:

```
Select Case <test expression>
    [Case <comparison list 1>
        [<procedure statements 1>]]

    ...
    [Case Else
        [<procedure statements n>]]
    End Select
```

where *<test expression>* is any numeric or string expression; where *<comparison list>* is

```
{<comparison element>,...}
```

where *<comparison element>* is

```
{expression | expression To expression |⤶
   Is <comparison operator> expression}
```

and where *<comparison operator>* is

```
{= | <> | < | > | <= | >=}
```

Notes:

If the <*test expression*> matches a <*comparison element*> in a *Case* clause, VBA executes the statements that follow that clause. If the <*comparison element*> is a single expression, the <*test expression*> must equal the <*comparison element*> for the statements following that clause to execute. If the <*comparison element*> contains a To keyword, the first expression must be less than the second expression (either in numeric value if the expressions are numbers or in collating sequence if the expressions are strings) and the <*test expression*> must be between the first expression and the second expression. If the <*comparison element*> contains the Is keyword, the evaluation of <*comparison operator*> expression must be true.

If more than one *Case* clause matches the <*test expression*>, VBA executes only the set of statements following the first *Case* clause that matches. You can include a block of statements following a *Case Else* clause that VBA executes if none of the previous *Case* clauses matches the <*test expression*>. You can nest another *Select Case* statement within the statements following a *Case* clause.

Example:

To assign an integer value to a variable, depending on whether a string begins with a letter from *A* through *F*, from *G* through *N*, or from *O* through *Z*, enter the following:

```
Dim strMyString As String, intVal As Integer
Select Case UCase$(Mid$(strMyString, 1, 1))
    Case "A" To "F"
        intVal = 1
    Case "G" To "N"
        intVal = 2
    Case "O" To "Z"
        intVal = 3
    Case Else
        intVal = 0
End Select
```

Stop Statement

Use a *Stop* statement to suspend execution of your procedure.

Syntax:

```
Stop
```

Notes:

A *Stop* statement has the same effect as setting a breakpoint on a statement. You can use the VBA debugging tools, such as the Step Into and the Step Over buttons and the Debug window, to evaluate the status of your procedure after VBA halts on a *Stop* statement.

While...Wend Statement

Use a *While...Wend* statement to continuously execute a block of statements as long as a condition is true.

Syntax:

```
While <condition>
    [<procedure statements>]
Wend
```

Notes:

A *While...Wend* statement is similar to a *Do...Loop* statement with a *While* clause, except that you can use an *Exit Do* statement to exit from a *Do* loop. VBA provides no similar *Exit* clause for a *While* loop. The *<condition>* is an expression that VBA can evaluate to True (nonzero) or False (0 or Null). Execution continues as long as the *<condition>* is true.

Example:

To read all the rows in the tblClubs table until you reach the end of the recordset, enter the following:

```
Dim dbEntSched As Database
Dim rcdClubs As RecordSet
Set dbEntSched = CurrentDb()
Set rcdClubs = dbEntSched.OpenRecordSet("tblClubs")
While Not rcdClubs.EOF
    <procedure statements>
    rcdClubs.MoveNext
Wend
```

With Statement

Use a *With* statement to simplify references to complex objects in code. You can establish a "base" object using a *With* statement and then use a shorthand notation to refer to objects, collections, properties, or methods on that object until you terminate the *With* statement.

Syntax:

```
With <object reference>
    [<procedure statements>]
End With
```

Example:

To use shorthand notation on a recordset object to add a new row to a table, enter the following:

```
Dim rst As Recordset, db As Database
Set db = CurrentDb()
Set rst = db.OpenRecordset("MyTable", dbOpenDynaset, _
    dbAppendOnly)
With rst
    ' Start a new record
    .Addnew
    ' Set the field values
    ![FieldOne] = "1"
    ![FieldTwo] = "John"
    ![FieldThree] = "Viescas"
    .Update
    .Close
End With
```

Running Macro Actions

Within VBA, you can also execute most of the macro actions. Only a few of the macro actions have direct VBA equivalents. To execute a macro action, use the methods of the DoCmd object, described below.

DoCmd Object

Use the methods of the DoCmd object to execute a macro action within a VBA procedure.

Syntax:

```
DoCmd.actionmethod [actionargument],...
```

Notes:

Some of the macro actions you'll commonly execute from VBA include ApplyFilter, Close, DoMenuItem, FindNext and FindRecord (for searching the recordset of the current form and immediately displaying the result), Hourglass, Maximize, Minimize, MoveSize, Open-Form, OpenQuery (to run a query that you don't need to modify),

OpenReport, and ShowToolBar. Although you can run the Echo, GoTo-Control, GoToPage, RepaintObject, and Requery actions from VBA using a method of the DoCmd object, it's more efficient to use the *Echo, SetFocus, GoToPage, Repaint,* and *Requery* methods of the object to which the method applies.

NOTE Microsoft Access provides built-in constants for many of the macro action parameters. For more information, search on "Macro Action Constants" in Access Help.

Examples:

To open a form named Customer in Form view for data entry, enter the following:

```
DoCmd.OpenForm "Customer", acNormal, , , acAdd
```

To close a form named Supplier, enter the following:

```
DoCmd.Close acForm, "Supplier"
```

Actions with VBA Equivalents

A few macro actions cannot be executed from a VBA procedure. All but one of these actions, however, have equivalent statements in VBA, as shown in the following table:

Macro Action	VBA Equivalent
AddMenu	No equivalent
MsgBox	*MsgBox* statement or function
RunApp	*Shell* function
RunCode	*Call* subroutine
SendKeys	*SendKeys* statement
SetValue	Variable assignment (=)
StopAllMacros	*Stop* or *End* statement
StopMacro	*Exit Sub* or *Exit Function* statement

Trapping Errors

One of the most powerful features of VBA is the ability to trap all errors, analyze them, and take corrective action. To enable error trapping, use an *On Error* statement, as described on the next page.

On Error Statement

Use an *On Error* statement to enable error trapping, establish the routine to handle error trapping, skip past any errors, or turn off error trapping.

Syntax:

```
On Error {GoTo lineID | Resume [Next] | GoTo 0}
```

Notes:

Use a *GoTo lineID* statement to establish a code block in your procedure that handles any error. The *lineID* can be a line number or a label. In your error handling statements, you can examine the built-in *Err* variable to determine the exact nature of the error. You can use the *Error* function to examine the text of the error message associated with the error. If you use line numbers with your statements, you can use the built-in *Erl* function to determine the line number of the statement that caused the error. Use a *Resume* statement, after taking corrective action, to retry execution of the statement that caused the error. Use a *Resume Next* statement to continue execution at the statement immediately following the statement that caused the error. You can also use an *Exit Function* or *Exit Sub* statement to reset the error condition and return to the calling procedure.

Use a *Resume Next* statement to trap errors but skip over any statement that causes an error. You can call the *Err* function in a statement immediately following the statement that you suspect might have caused an error to see whether an error occurred. *Err* returns *0* if no error has occurred.

Use a *GoTo 0* statement to turn off error trapping for the current procedure. If an error occurs, VBA passes the error to the error routine in the calling procedure or opens an error dialog box if there is no previous error routine.

Examples:

To trap errors but continue execution with the next statement, enter the following:

```
On Error Resume Next
```

To trap errors and execute the statements that follow the *MyError:* label when an error occurs, enter the following:

```
On Error GoTo MyError:
```

To turn off error trapping in the current procedure, enter the following:

```
On Error GoTo 0
```

A Complex VBA Example

A good way to learn VBA techniques is to study complex code that has been developed and tested by someone else. In the Entertainment Schedule database, I created a function that dynamically creates a new table and then inserts into the table a complete list of all the error codes used by Microsoft Access and the text of the error message associated with each error code. You can find a partial list of the error codes in Access Help, but the table provides the best way to see a list of all the error codes. You might find this table useful as you begin to create your own VBA routines and set error trapping in them.

The name of the function is *CreateErrTable*, and you can find it in the modExamples module. The function statements are listed below. You can execute this function by entering the following in the Debug window:

```
? CreateErrTable
```

NOTE I've added line numbers to some of the lines in this code listing so that you can follow along with the line-by-line explanations in the table that follows the code listing.

```
01 Function CreateErrTable ()
02     ' Declare variables used in this function
03     Dim dbMyDatabase As Database, tblErrTable As _
          TableDef, fldMyField As Field
04     Dim rcdErrRecSet As Recordset, lngErrCode As _
          Long, intMsgRtn As Integer
05     Dim varReturnVal As Variant, varErrString As _
          Variant, ws As Workspace

       ' Create Errors table with Error Code and Error
       ' String fields
       ' Initialize the MyDatabase database variable to
       ' the current database
06     Set dbMyDatabase = CurrentDb()
07     Set ws = DBEngine.Workspaces(0)
       ' Trap error if table doesn't exist
       ' Skip to next statement if an error occurs
08     On Error Resume Next
09     Set rcdErrRecSet = _
          dbMyDatabase.OpenRecordset("ErrTable")
10     Select Case Err    ' See whether an error was raised
```

(continued)

```
11        Case 0        ' No error--table must already exist
12          On Error GoTo 0   ' Turn off error trapping
13          intMsgRtn = MsgBox("ErrTable already " & _
              "exists. Do you want to delete and " & _
              "rebuild all rows?", 52)
14        If intMsgRtn = 6 Then
              ' Reply was YES--delete rows and rebuild
              ' Turn off SQL warning
15            DoCmd.SetWarnings False
              ' Run quick SQL to delete rows
16            DoCmd.RunSQL "Delete * From ErrTable;"
              ' Turn warnings back on
17            DoCmd.SetWarnings True
18        Else                    ' Reply was NO--done
19            rcdErrRecSet.Close   ' Close the table
20            Exit Function        ' And exit
21        End If

22        Case 3011, 3078        ' Couldn't find table,
                                  ' so build it
23          On Error GoTo 0   ' Turn off error trapping
            ' Create a new table to contain the error rows
24          Set tblErrTable = _
              dbMyDatabase.CreateTableDef("ErrTable")
            ' Create a field in ErrTable to contain the
            ' error code
25          Set fldMyField = _
              tblErrTable.CreateField("ErrorCode", dbLong)
            ' Append the "ErrorCode" field to the fields
            ' collection in the new table definition
26          tblErrTable.Fields.Append fldMyField
            ' Create a field in ErrTable for the error
            ' description
27          Set fldMyField = _
              tblErrTable.CreateField("ErrorString", _
              dbText)
            ' Append the "ErrorString" field to the fields
            ' collection in the new table definition
28          tblErrTable.Fields.Append fldMyField
            ' Append the new table to the TableDefs
            ' collection in the current database
29          dbMyDatabase.TableDefs.Append tblErrTable
            ' Set text field width to 5" (7200 twips)
            ' (calls sub procedure)
```

```
30        SetFieldProperty tblErrTable![ErrorString], _
            "ColumnWidth", dbInteger, 7200
          ' Set recordset to Errors Table recordset
31        Set rcdErrRecSet = _
            dbMyDatabase.OpenRecordset("ErrTable")

32      Case Else
          ' Can't identify the error--write message and
          ' bail
33        MsgBox "Unknown error in CreateErrTable " & _
            Err & ", " & Error$(Err), 16
34        Exit Function

35    End Select

      ' Initialize the progress meter on the status bar
36    varReturnVal = SysCmd(acSysCmdInitMeter, _
        "Building Error Table", 32767)
      ' Turn on hourglass to show this might take a while
37    DoCmd.Hourglass True

      ' Start a transaction to make it go fast
38    ws.BeginTrans

      ' Loop through Microsoft Access error codes,
      ' skipping codes that generate
      ' "Application-defined or object-defined error"
      ' message
39    For lngErrCode = 1 To 32767
40        varErrString = AccessError(lngErrCode)
41        If Not IsNothing(varErrString) Then
42            If varErrString <> "Application-" & _
                "defined or object-defined error" Then
                ' Add each error code and string to
                ' Errors table
43                rcdErrRecSet.AddNew
44                rcdErrRecSet("ErrorCode") = lngErrCode
                ' Some error messages are longer
                ' than 255--truncate
45                rcdErrRecSet("ErrorString") = _
                    Left(varErrString, 255)
46                rcdErrRecSet.Update
47            End If
48        End If
```

(continued)

```
                        ' Update the status meter
49              varReturnVal = SysCmd(acSysCmdUpdateMeter, _
                    lngErrCode)
                        ' Process next error code
50      Next lngErrCode

51      ws.CommitTrans

        ' Close recordset
52      rcdErrRecSet.Close
        ' Turn off the hourglass--we're done
53      DoCmd.Hourglass False
        ' And reset the status bar
54      varReturnVal = SysCmd(acSysCmdClearStatus)
        ' Select new table in the Database window
        ' to refresh the list
55      DoCmd.SelectObject acTable, "ErrTable", True
        ' Open a confirmation dialog box
56      MsgBox "Errors table created."
57 End Function
```

The following table lists the statement line numbers and explains the code on each line in the preceding VBA code example.

Line Number	Explanation
01	Declares the beginning of the function. The function has no arguments.
02	Notice that you can begin a comment anywhere on a statement line by preceding the comment with a single quotation mark. You can also create a comment statement using the *Rem* statement.
03	Declares local variables for a Database object, a TableDef object, and a Field object.
04	Declares local variables for a Recordset object, a long integer, and an integer.
05	Declares local variables for a Variant that is used to accept the return value from the *SysCmd* function, a Variant that is used to accept the error string returned by the AccessError function, and a Workspace object.
06	Initializes the Database object variable by setting it to the current database.

(continued)

continued

Line Number	Explanation
07	Initializes the Workspace object by setting it to the current workspace.
08	Enables error trapping, but executes the next statement if an error occurs.
09	Initializes the Recordset object variable by attempting to open the ErrTable table. If the table does not exist, this generates an error.
10	Calls the *Err* function to see whether an error occurred. The following *Case* statements check the particular error values that interest us.
11	The first *Case* statement that tests for an *Err* value of *0*, indicating no error occurred. If no error occurred, the table has opened successfully.
12	Turns off error trapping because we don't expect any more errors.
13	Uses the *MsgBox* function to ask whether you want to clear and rebuild all rows in the existing table. The value *52* asks for an exclamation-point Warning icon (*48*) and Yes/No buttons (*4*). The statement assigns the value returned by *MsgBox* so that we can test it on the next line.
14	If you click Yes, *MsgBox* returns the value *6*.
15	Turns off the standard system warnings because we're going to run an SQL statement to delete all the rows in the error table.
16	Runs a simple SQL statement to delete all the rows in the error table.
17	Turns warnings back on.
18	The *Else* clause that goes with the *If* statement on line 14.
19	Closes the table if the table exists and you clicked the No button on line 13.
20	Exits the function.
21	The *End If* statement that goes with the *If* statement on line 14.
22	The second *Case* statement. Error code 3011 is "object not found."
23	Turns off error trapping because we don't expect any more errors.

(continued)

continued

Line Number	Explanation
24	Uses the *CreateTableDef* method on the database to start a new table definition. This is the same as clicking on the Tables tab in the Database window and then clicking the New button.
25	Uses the *CreateField* method on the new table to create the first field object—a long integer named ErrorCode.
26	Appends the first new field to the Fields collection of the new Table object.
27	Uses the *CreateField* method to create the second field—a text field named ErrorString.
28	Appends the second new field to the Fields collection of the new Table object.
29	Saves the new table definition by appending it to the TableDefs collection of the Database object. If you were to halt the code at this point and repaint the Database window, you would find the new ErrTable listed.
30	Calls the *SetFieldProperty* subroutine in this module to set the column width of the ErrorString field to 7200 twips (5 inches). This ensures that you can see most of the error text when you open the table in Datasheet view.
31	Opens a recordset by using the *OpenRecordset* method on the table.
32	This *Case* statement traps all other errors.
33	Shows a message box with the error number and the error message.
34	Exits the function after an unknown error.
35	This *End Select* statement completes the *Select Case* statement on line 10.
36	Calls the *SysCmd* function to place a "building table" message on the status bar and initializes a progress meter. The *CreateErrTable* function will look at 32,767 different error codes.
37	Turns the mouse pointer into an hourglass to indicate that this routine will take a few seconds.

(continued)

continued

Line Number	Explanation
38	Uses the *BeginTrans* method of the Workspace object to start a transaction. Statements within a transaction are treated as a single unit. Changes to data are saved only if the transaction completes successfully with a *CommitTrans* method. Using transactions when you're updating records can speed performance by reducing disk access.
39	Starts a *For* loop to check each error code from 1 through 32,767.
40	Assigns the error text returned by the *AccessError* function to the variable varErrString.
41	Calls the *IsNothing* function in the modUtility module of the sample database to test whether the text returned is blank. We don't want blank rows, so don't add a row if the *AccessError* function for the current error code returns a blank string.
42	Lots of error codes are defined as "Application-defined or object-defined error." We don't want any of these, so adds a row only if the *AccessError* function for the current error code doesn't return this string.
43	Uses the *AddNew* method to start a new row in the table.
44	Sets the ErrorCode field equal to the current error code.
45	Some error messages are very long. We want to save only the first 255 characters, so sets the ErrorString field equal to the first 255 characters of error text. The text is stored in the varErrString variable.
46	Uses the *Update* method to save the new row.
47	This *End If* statement completes the *If* statement on line 42.
48	This *End If* statement completes the *If* statement on line 41.
49	After handling each error code, updates the progress meter on the status bar to show how far we've gotten.

(continued)

continued

Line Number	Explanation
50	This *Next* statement completes the *For* loop begun on line 39. Access increments *lngErrCode* by 1 and executes the *For* loop again until *lngErrCode* is greater than 32,767.
51	The *CommitTrans* method completes the transaction begun on line 38.
52	After looping through all possible error codes, closes the table.
53	Changes the mouse pointer back to normal.
54	Clears the status bar.
55	Puts the focus on the ErrTable table in the Database window.
56	Displays a message box confirming that the function has completed.
57	End of the function.

You should now have a basic understanding of how to create functions and subroutines using VBA. In the final two chapters of this book, you'll use what you've learned to complete major parts of the Entertainment Schedule application.

SELECT EDITION

Chapter 22

Automating Your Application with VBA

ow that you've learned the fundamentals of using Microsoft Visual Basic for Applications (VBA), it's time to put this knowledge into practice. In this chapter, you'll learn how to perform many of the automation tasks you saw in Chapter 20, "Automating Your Application with Macros," but this time you'll use VBA in form modules.

You can find dozens of examples of automation in the College Counseling and Entertainment Schedule sample databases included with this book. As you explore the databases, whenever you see something interesting, you can open the form or report in Design view and take a look at the VBA code behind the form or report. This chapter walks you through a few of the more interesting examples in the two databases.

Automating Data Selection

One of the most common tasks to automate in a database application is filtering data. Particularly when a database contains thousands of records, users will rarely need to work with more than a few records at a time. If your edit forms always display all of the records, performance can suffer greatly. So it's a good idea to enable the user to easily specify a subset of records. This section examines three ways to do this.

Working with a Multiple-Selection List Box

You work with list boxes all the time in Microsoft Windows 95 and in Microsoft Access. For example, the file list in Windows Explorer is a list box, and the List view in the Access Database window is a list box. In the Database window, you can select only one object from the list at a time. If you click on a different object, the previous object is deselected. This is a simple list box. In Windows Explorer, you can select one file, select multiple noncontiguous files by holding down the Ctrl key and clicking, or select a range of files by holding down the Shift key and clicking.

Suppose the school counselors using the College Counseling database are interested in looking at the details for several colleges at one time but will rarely want to look at the entire list. If you open the application and click the Colleges button on the main switchboard form, the application opens the frmCollegeSelect form, which contains a multiple-selection list box, as shown in Figure 22-1.

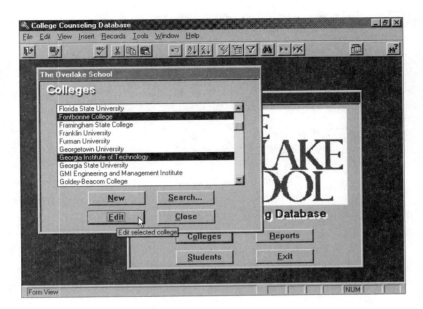

FIGURE 22-1
Selecting multiple college records to edit.

In this list box, the colleges are shown in alphabetic order. You can type the first letter of a college name to jump to the first college that begins with that letter. You can move the highlight up or down using the arrow keys. You can hold down the Shift key and use the arrow keys to extend the selection to multiple names. Finally, you can hold down either the Shift key or the Ctrl key and use the mouse to select multiple names. Figure 22-1 shows two college names selected using the Ctrl key and the mouse. When you click the Edit button, the application opens the frmCollege form with only the records you selected, as shown in Figure 22-2 on the next page. Note that the caption to the right of the record number box indicates two available records and that the recordset is filtered.

FIGURE 22-2
Editing a selected
college record.

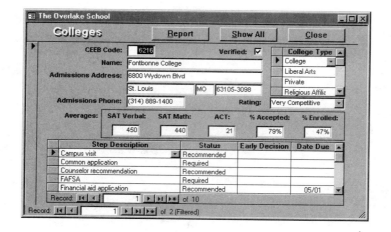

To see how this works, you need to go behind the scenes of the frmCollegeSelect form. Click Exit on the main switchboard form to return to the Database window. Select frmCollegeSelect and open the form in Design view, as shown in Figure 22-3. Click on the list box control and open its property sheet to see how the list box is defined. The list box uses two columns from the qryAllColleges query, displaying the CName field in the first column but hiding the CollegeCEEB field (the primary key that will provide a fast lookup) in the second column. The key to this list box is that its Multi Select property is set to Extended. The default for this property is None, which lets you select only one value at a time. You can set it to Simple if you want to select multiple noncontiguous values using the mouse. Using the Extended setting gives you the full Ctrl-click or Shift-click features that you see in most list boxes in Windows.

FIGURE 22-3
The multiple-
selection list
box on the
frmCollegeSelect
form and its
property sheet.

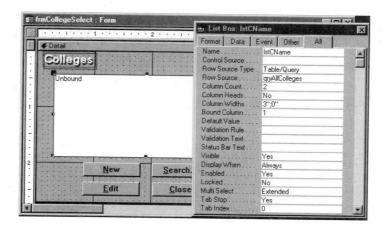

746

If you scroll down to the Event properties, you'll find an event procedure defined for On Dbl-Click. The code for this event procedure runs only the *Edit_Click* procedure. Right-click on the Edit command button and choose Build Event from the shortcut menu to jump to the *Edit_Click* procedure that does all the work, as shown in Figure 22-4.

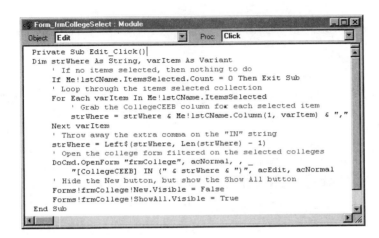

FIGURE 22-4

The VBA procedure that responds to a college edit request.

When you set the Multi Select property of a list box to something other than None, you can examine the control's ItemsSelected collection to determine what (if anything) is selected. In the *Edit_Click* procedure, the VBA code first checks the Count property of the control's ItemsSelected collection to determine whether anything is selected. If the Count is *0*, there's nothing to do, so the procedure exits.

The ItemsSelected collection is composed of variant values, each of which provides an index to a highlighted item in the list box. The For Each loop asks VBA to loop through all the available variant values in the collection, one at a time. Within the loop, the code uses the value of the variant to retrieve the CollegeCEEB code from the list. List boxes also have a Column property, and you can reference all the values in the list using

```
Me!ListBoxName.Column(ColumnNum, RowNum)
```

where *ListBoxName* is the name of your list box control, *ColumnNum* is the relative column number (the first column is 0, the second is 1, and so on), and *RowNum* is the relative row number (also starting at 0). The variant values in the ItemsSelected collection return the relative row number. This VBA code uses column 1 and the value from ItemsSelected to return each CollegeCEEB code and append it to a string variable, separated by commas. You'll recall from studying the IN predicate in Chapter 8, "Adding Power with Select Queries," and Chapter 11, "Advanced Query Design—SQL," that a list of values separated by commas is ideal for an IN clause.

After retrieving all of the CollegeCEEB codes, the next statement removes the trailing comma from the string. The DoCmd.OpenForm command uses the resulting string of comma-separated values to create a filter clause as it opens the form. The last two statements set up the New and Show All buttons on the frmCollege form. Since you're looking at a filtered list, it doesn't necessarily make sense to add new rows. (You can do that directly from the New button on the frmCollegeSelect form anyway.) However, you might be interested in looking at all rows, so this code hides the New button and reveals the Show All button. If you look at the Form Header section of the frmCollege form in Design view, you'll find the Show All button stacked on top of the New button.

Providing a Custom Query By Form

Suppose you want to do a more complex search on the frmCollege form—based on criteria such as location, competitiveness rating, or college type rather than simply by college name. You could teach your users how to use the Filter By Form features to build the search, or you could use Filter By Form to easily construct multiple OR criteria on simple tests. But if you want to find, for example, all colleges that are both Private and Liberal Arts (or some other AND combination), there's no way to construct this request using standard filtering features. In fact, when you define a filter for a subform using Filter By Form, you're filtering only the subform rows. You're not finding colleges that have only a matching subform row.

The only solution, then, is to build a custom Query By Form that provides options to search on all the important fields and build the complex query to solve the multiple AND criteria problem using VBA code. This particular example builds a very complex query using subqueries to satisfy the test for a college that meets multiple classification criteria. Without the complex query, it's fairly simple to build the filter criteria you need to implement a custom Query By Form.

To see how this works, open the College Counseling application (if you have exited to the Database window, you can reopen the application by opening afrmMain), click the Colleges button on the main switchboard form, and then click the Search button on the frmCollegeSelect form. You should see the frmCollegeSearch form, as shown in Figure 22-5.

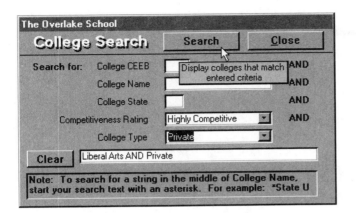

FIGURE 22-5
Using a custom
Query By Form
to perform a
complex search.

Try selecting Highly Competitive from the Competitiveness Rating drop-down list, and specify Liberal Arts AND Private for College Type by selecting Liberal Arts and then Private from the College Type drop-down list. When you click the Search button, you should see the frmCollege form open, displaying five schools.

To see how this works, you need to explore the design of the frmCollegeSearch form. Switch to the Database window and open the form in Design view. You should see a window like that shown in Figure 22-6. Notice that the form is not bound to any record source. The unbound controls exist to accept any criteria values that the user might enter.

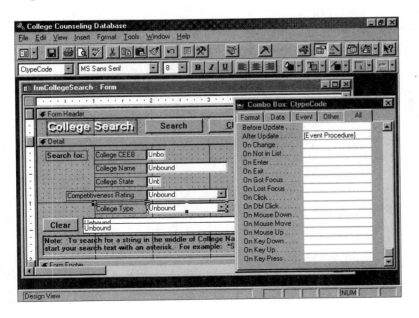

FIGURE 22-6
The frmCollege-
Search form in
Design view.

Part of the secret of this form is the CtypeCode combo box and its After Update event. Whenever you select a new type classification in the combo box, the following event procedure executes:

```
Private Sub CtypeCode_AfterUpdate()
    If IsNothing(Me!CTypeCodes) Then
        Me!CTypeCodes = Me!CtypeCode
        Me!CTypeList = Me!CtypeCode.Column(0)
    Else
        Me!CTypeCodes = Me!CTypeCodes & ", " & Me!CtypeCode
        Me!CTypeList = Me!CTypeList & " AND " & _
          Me!CtypeCode.Column(0)
    End If
    intInCount = intInCount + 1
End Sub
```

This code creates an IN clause that contains the matching type codes and keeps a count in a variable called intInCount of the number of classifications selected. Note that this code does not check to see whether you selected the same classification twice; you could add this feature to enhance the way the code works. This code stores the IN string in a hidden text box control on the form. (Its Visible property is set to No.) To see how this works, select the CTypeCodes control, set its Visible property to Yes, and switch to Form view. When you select a new classification, you can see the contents of both controls get updated.

All the work happens when you click the Search button. The code for the event procedure for the click event of the Search button is shown below.

```
Private Sub Search_Click()
    Dim db As DATABASE, rst As Recordset
    Dim strWhere As String, lngCount As Long
    Dim intRtn As Integer
    ' Call the routine to build a Where clause
    strWhere = Parse()
    ' If nothing to do, tell them and exit
    If IsNothing(strWhere) Then
        MsgBox "No criteria specified.", 32
        Exit Sub
    End If
    ' Hide myself and turn on Hourglass
    Me.Visible = False
    DoCmd.Hourglass True
    ' Find out if any colleges satisfy the Where clause
    Set db = CurrentDb
    Set rst = db.OpenRecordset("SELECT DISTINCTROW " & _
```

```
        "Colleges.CollegeCEEB " & _
        "FROM zCompeteList RIGHT JOIN Colleges ON " & _
        "zCompeteList.CCompID = Colleges.CCompID " & _
        " WHERE " & strWhere & ";")
    ' If none found, tell them and make me visible to
    ' try again
    If rst.RecordCount = 0 Then
        DoCmd.Hourglass False
        MsgBox "No Colleges meet your criteria", _
          vbInformation
        Me.Visible = True
        rst.Close
        Exit Sub
    End If
    ' Move to last row to get an accurate record count
    rst.MoveLast
    lngCount = rst.RecordCount
    DoCmd.Hourglass False
    ' If more than 20, ask if they want to see only a
    ' summary
    If lngCount > 20 Then
        intRtn = MsgBox( _
          "More than 20 colleges meet your criteria. " & _
          "Click Yes to see a summary list for all " & _
          "lngCount & colleges found, " & _
          "No to see complete data on all that match, " & _
          "or Cancel to try again.", _
          vbInformation + vbYesNoCancel)
        Select Case intRtn
            Case vbCancel    ' Cancel - Try again
                Me.Visible = True
                Exit Sub
            Case vbYes       ' Yes - show summary form
                DoCmd.OpenForm "frmCollegeSummary", _
                  acNormal, , strWhere
                DoCmd.Close acForm, Me.Name
                Forms!frmCollegeSummary.SetFocus
                Exit Sub
        End Select
    End If
    ' Replied NO or not more than 20, show full details
    DoCmd.OpenForm "frmCollege", acNormal, , strWhere
    Forms!frmCollege!New.Visible = False
    Forms!frmCollege!ShowAll.Visible = True
    ' Close me, and we're done
    DoCmd.Close acForm, Me.Name
End Sub
```

This code first calls another procedure in the form module (*Parse*) that examines all the unbound controls on the form and builds a valid SQL Where clause. We'll take a look at the *Parse* function in a moment. If *Parse* completes successfully, it returns the Where clause as a string. If it finds no criteria, the Where string will be empty and this procedure will exit.

The next part of the procedure builds a simple recordset on the tables used in both the frmCollege and frmCollegeSummary forms, applying the Where clause returned by the *Parse* function. If it finds no records, it uses the *MsgBox* function to inform the user and then gives the user a chance to try again. When you first open a recordset object in code, its RecordCount property is 0 if the recordset is empty and it is some value greater than 0 if the recordset contains some qualifying records. The RecordCount property of a recordset object contains only a count of the number of rows visited and not the number of rows in the recordset. So if it finds some rows, the procedure moves to the last row in the temporary recordset to get an accurate count. When the record count is greater than 20, the procedure lets the user view a summary of the records found in the frmCollegeSummary form, view all data in the full frmCollege form, or try again. This is a good example of using the *MsgBox* function to not only display some variable data but also to respond to a user choice. We'll examine how the frmCollege-Summary form works a bit later.

The key to making this Query By Form work is the *Parse* function, which examines the contents of the unbound controls and builds a valid Where clause. The *Parse* function is listed below:

```
Private Function Parse() As String
    Dim strWhere As String
    ' Set up an error trap
    On Error GoTo Parse_Exit
    ' Check for a CEEB specified
    If Not IsNothing(Me!CollegeCEEB) Then
        strWhere = "[CollegeCEEB]= " & Me!CollegeCEEB
    End If
    ' Check for a College Name string - use LIKE
    If Not IsNothing(Me!CName) Then
        If IsNothing(strWhere) Then
            strWhere = "[CName] Like " & Chr$(34) & Me!CName
        Else
            strWhere = strWhere & " AND [CName] Like " & _
```

```
                    Chr$(34) & Me!CName
        End If
        If Right$(Me![CName], 1) = "*" Then
            strWhere = strWhere & Chr$(34)
        Else
            strWhere = strWhere & "*" & Chr$(34)
        End If
    End If
End If
' Check for a State string - use LIKE
If Not IsNothing(Me!CState) Then
    If IsNothing(strWhere) Then
        strWhere = "[CState] Like " & Chr$(34) & _
            Me!CState
    Else
        strWhere = strWhere & " AND [CState] Like " & _
            Chr$(34) & Me!CState
    End If
    If Right$(Me!CState, 1) = "*" Then
        strWhere = strWhere & Chr$(34)
    Else
        strWhere = strWhere & "*" & Chr$(34)
    End If
End If
' Check for a competitiveness rating - use LIKE
If Not IsNothing(Me!CCompRate) Then
    If IsNothing(strWhere) Then
        strWhere = "[CCompRate] LIKE " & _
            Chr$(34) & Me!CCompRate
    Else
        strWhere = strWhere & _
            " AND [CCompRate] LIKE " & _
            Chr$(34) & Me!CCompRate
    End If
    If Right$(Me!CCompRate, 1) = "*" Then
        strWhere = strWhere & Chr$(34)
    Else
        strWhere = strWhere & "*" & Chr$(34)
    End If
End If
' Check for any classification codes - build a subquery
If Not IsNothing(Me!CTypeCodes) Then
    If Not IsNothing(strWhere) Then
        strWhere = strWhere & " AND "
```

(continued)

753

```
                         End If
                         strWhere = strWhere & "[CollegeCEEB] IN " & _
                           "(SELECT DISTINCTROW " & _
                           "CollegeTypeLink.CollegeCEEB " & _
                           "FROM CollegeTypeLink " & _
                           "WHERE CollegeTypeLink.CTypeID " & _
                           "In (" & Me!CTypeCodes & _
                           ") GROUP BY CollegeTypeLink.CollegeCEEB " & _
                           "HAVING Count(CollegeTypeLink.CTypeID)=" & _
                           intInCount & ")"
                 End If
         Parse_Exit:
             Parse = strWhere
         End Function
```

This function "builds up" a WHERE string by looking at the unbound controls one at a time. When the field is a number, the function builds a simple *[FieldName] = ControlValue* clause. If the field is a
string, it builds a test using the LIKE predicate so that whatever the user
enters can match any part of the field in the underlying table. When the
function adds a clause, it inserts the AND keyword between clauses if
other clauses already exist.

The only really tricky part to the function is the SQL subquery
it builds to solve the problem of selecting only colleges for which all
the classification criteria match. The subquery is actually a total query
that counts all the rows for any college for which the code in
CollegeTypeLink matches any of the entered codes. It then selects only
those rows for which the count of codes found matches the count of
codes requested. If, for example, a college matches only two of three
selection criteria, it won't be selected. This particular subquery works
because we know that the CTypeID is part of the primary key of the
CollegeTypeLink table—which means that each code exists only once
for each college.

You can use a similar technique any time you want to determine
which rows match some set of criteria on the "many" side of a relationship. If the rows on the many side aren't unique, you can make them
unique by basing the total query on a DISTINCT query. For example,
this technique works to determine which customers have ordered both
"Chocolade" and "Vegie-spread" in the Northwind Traders sample database that comes with Access.

Selecting from a Summary List

As you saw in the *Search_Click* procedure in the previous section, the user gets to make a choice if more than 20 rows meet the entered criteria. To see how this works, specify both Private and Liberal Arts for the College Type criteria in the frmCollegeSearch form. The result should look like that shown in Figure 22-7, in which 38 colleges match both criteria.

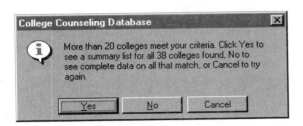

FIGURE 22-7

The message box that appears when the *Search_Click* procedure returns more than 20 rows.

When you click Yes, the *Search_Click* procedure opens the frm-CollegeSummary form, as shown in Figure 22-8. You can scroll down to any row, put the focus on that row (be sure the row selector indicator is pointing to that row), and then click the View Details button to open the frmCollege form and view the details for the one college you selected. You can see that this is a very efficient way to help the user narrow a search to one particular row.

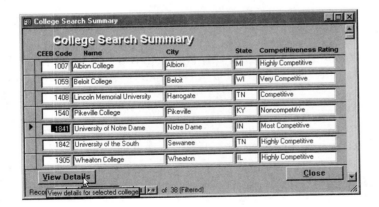

FIGURE 22-8

Selecting a specific college from a search summary.

Behind the View Details button is a simple VBA procedure, shown below, that uses the current value of the CollegeCEEB field on the form to build a filter for the OpenForm method.

```
Private Sub Details_Click()
    DoCmd.OpenForm "frmCollege", acNormal, , _
      "[CollegeCEEB] = " & Me!CollegeCEEB
    DoCmd.Close acForm, Me.Name
    Forms!frmCollege.SetFocus
    Forms!frmCollege!New.Visible = False
    Forms!frmCollege!ShowAll.Visible = True
End Sub
```

Handling Complex Data Display

So far, you've learned three very useful techniques to enable users to select the exact rows they want to work with. However, even after filtering down to specific rows, you might find that a record contains more information than will fit in a single form. The following sections suggest a couple of ways to deal with this problem.

Using Multiple Subforms

After you filter out all the data related to a single student in the College Counseling database, you might still have more detail than will fit in a reasonably sized single form. One way to deal with this is to create a multiple-page form that shows the most important data on the first page and the less frequently used data on subsequent pages. The frmStudents form uses this multiple-pages technique to display most of the student-specific data of interest to the school counselors. However, the counselors also want to be able to instantly see related college interest data, test scores, and extracurricular activities all in the same form. Since this data is located in several tables that have a "many" relationship to each student row, it makes sense to work with the data in a subform. However, to place all three categories of information in separate subforms would take up a lot of space in the form and would be cumbersome to work with.

One solution is to design the form so that all the information is available but only one subclass of information appears at a time. If you open the frmStudent form, as shown in Figure 22-9, you'll see three toggle buttons across the center of the form (Colleges, Test Scores, and Extracurricular), which indicate that additional information is available.

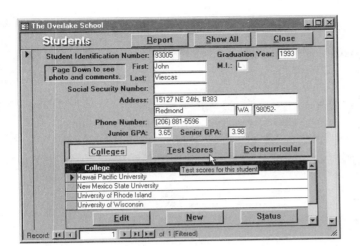

FIGURE 22-9
Providing a
simple way to
view multiple
complex
relationships.

The form opens with the Colleges button selected and showing
the list of colleges in which the student has expressed interest. If you
click one of the other buttons, the related test scores or extracurricular
activities appear in the subform window, as shown in Figure 22-10.

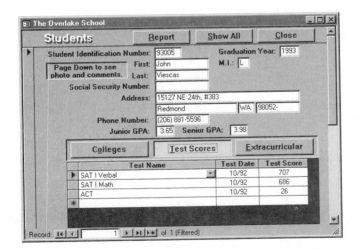

FIGURE 22-10
Viewing a second
set of related data
in a single form.

The key to this form is that three subforms are embedded in the
form and the three toggle buttons that control which subform is displayed are contained in an option group control. Open the frmStudent
form in Design view, click on the fsubStudentCollegeList subform, and
move it slightly to one side and down. You can see another subform
behind it that's in exactly the same location and is sized the same.
Figure 22-11 on the next page shows all three subforms moved slightly

apart. If you open the Property window and click on each subform, you can see that they have the same Height and Width property settings. They were originally stacked by selecting all three subforms and then manually setting the Top and Left properties identically. Note also that the Visible property for fsubStudentCollegeList is Yes, but the Visible property for the other two forms is No.

FIGURE 22-11

The three embedded subforms in the frmStudent form (moved apart to show the detail).

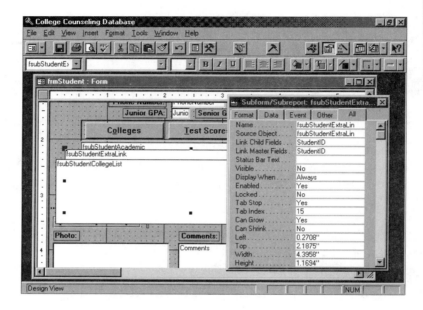

When the three subforms are stacked on top of each other, you can get to each one individually in Design view by selecting it in the Select Object drop-down list on the Formatting toolbar. (By the way, if you moved the subforms as instructed above, don't save your changes when you close the form!)

When you place toggle buttons within an option group, each has an Option Value property that you can set to an integer. (In this case, Colleges is 1, Test Scores is 2, and Extracurricular is 3.) One unique property of an option group is that only one of the controls within it can be "on" at one time. If you click on another control in the option group, the previously selected one turns off. Clicking on a different control also sets the underlying value of the option group to the Option Value of that control. In addition to toggle buttons, you can use check boxes or option buttons within an option group.

As shown in Figure 22-12, the Default Value property of the option group is set to 1 to match the subform that has its Visible property set to Yes. When you're in Form view, clicking a different button resets the value of the option group. It's a simple matter to create a VBA procedure that responds to the After Update event of the option group to reset the Visible properties of the subforms based on the button you clicked. The event procedure code is as follows:

```
Private Sub optOption_AfterUpdate()
    Select Case Me!optOption
        Case 1
            Me![fsubStudentExtraLink].Visible = False
            Me!fsubStudentCollegeList.Visible = True
            Me![fsubStudentAcademic].Visible = False
        Case 2
            Me![fsubStudentExtraLink].Visible = False
            Me!fsubStudentCollegeList.Visible = False
            Me![fsubStudentAcademic].Visible = True
        Case 3
            Me![fsubStudentExtraLink].Visible = True
            Me!fsubStudentCollegeList.Visible = False
            Me![fsubStudentAcademic].Visible = False
    End Select
End Sub
```

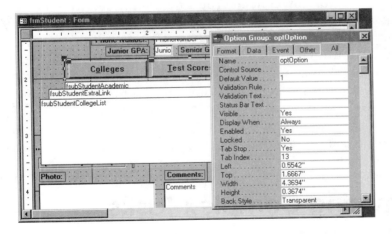

FIGURE 22-12

The option group on the frmStudent form that controls which subform is displayed.

Linking to Related Data in Another Form

Another way to handle additional related data is to display the details of that data in another form. In the fsubStudentCollegeList subform, the form footer has three additional command buttons to link the user to

759

other actions. The Edit button opens the college application step detail form for the current college displayed in the subform, as shown in Figure 22-13.

FIGURE 22-13

Using a
second form
to edit data
related to one
of the Student
subforms.

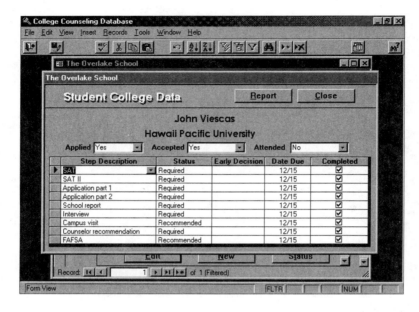

This provides an easy way to view and edit the student's application progress for any college. The New button lets you add a new college to the student's list. When you click this button, the VBA procedure opens a form that has a list box showing all the colleges that aren't currently on the student's list. There's also a button on that form to let you add a new college. When you select a college, VBA code not only adds it to the StudentCollegeLink table for the current student but also copies over the current application steps from the CollegeSteps table. You can explore all of these VBA procedures on your own in the frmStudent, fsubStudentCollegeList, frmCollegeList, and frmStudentCollegeSteps forms.

Automating Complex Tasks

Let's switch to the Entertainment Schedule database and take a look at the frmContracts form that is the "action central" of this application. RM Productions's business centers around booking groups into clubs, issuing contracts, and tracking commission payments. This section explores a few of the tasks that are automated in the frmContracts form.

Linking to a Related Task

You just learned one technique for linking to a related task using a command button. One of the key tasks in the main frmContracts form, shown in Figure 22-14, is tracking commission payments for active contracts. As you move from contract to contract in this form, the Payments button will either be disabled or available depending on the status of the particular contract. The form's On Current event procedure (*Form_Current*) examines the contract status field and sets the Enabled property of the button accordingly.

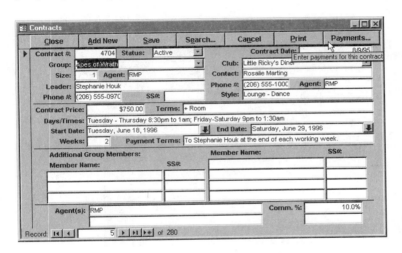

FIGURE 22-14

The frmContracts form in the Entertainment Schedule database.

Move to an active contract and click the Payments button to see what happens. You should see the frmPayments form open, as shown in Figure 22-15. This form, in which you enter payments for the current contract, opens as a modal form so that the user must enter all payments before moving to another contract.

FIGURE 22-15

Posting a payment for a specific contract.

If you open the frmPayments form in Design view, as shown in Figure 22-16, you'll discover that it has no record source! So how does this form work? Since we know that this form will always be used for editing data for exactly one contract, there's no point in incurring the overhead to open another recordset on the tblContracts table, especially since you don't need to edit the contract data in the Payments form. The subform <u>is</u> bound to the tblCommissions table, and its subform control's Link Master Fields property references the unbound ContractNo control on the outer form. The other controls on the form are there merely to confirm the contract data and are in locked (not updatable) controls.

FIGURE 22-16

The property settings for the frmPayments form. Note that the form has no record source.

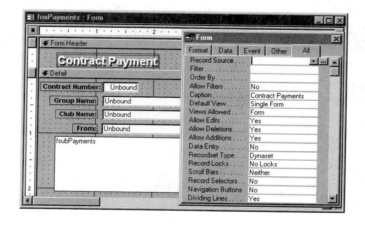

This form is opened and filled in by the OnClick event procedure for the Payment button on the main frmContracts form. The code is as follows:

```
Private Sub cmdPayment_Click()
    Dim frm As Form
    ' Check for unsaved data on this form
    If Me.Dirty Then
        ' If so, then must have a valid GroupID and ClubID
        If IsNothing(Me!GroupID) Or IsNothing(Me!ClubID) Then
            MsgBox "You can't save a contract without a " & _
                "Group Name and Club Name.", vbCritical, _
                "Payments"
            Me!GroupName.SetFocus
            Exit Sub
        End If
        ' Save the "dirty" data
        DoCmd.DoMenuItem acFormBar, acRecordsMenu, _
            acSaveRecord, , acMenuVer70
```

```
      End If
      ' Open the related payments form, hidden
      DoCmd.OpenForm "frmPayments", acNormal, , , acHidden
      ' Set a form variable for efficiency
      Set frm = Forms!frmPayments
      ' Plug in the unbound data on payments
      ' ... the ContractNo is what makes the subform work
      frm!ContractNo = Me!ContractNo
      frm!GroupName = Me!GroupID.Column(0)
      frm!ClubName = Me!ClubID.Column(0)
      frm!BeginningDate = Me!BeginningDate
      frm!EndingDate = Me!EndingDate
      ' Move the focus to the subform
      frm!fsubPayments.SetFocus
      ' and make the form visible
      frm.Visible = True
End Sub
```

After making sure that any changes are saved, the code opens frmPayments as a hidden form (so you won't see it pasting in the contract data), copies the display data to the form, and then makes the form visible. Note that there are no forms to enter new commission rows in the database. The commission rows are created automatically by another VBA procedure that runs each time an update completes on the frmContracts form (in the AfterUpdate event). The code is as follows:

```
Private Sub Form_AfterUpdate()
    Dim db As DATABASE, rst As Recordset, qd As QueryDef
    Dim varMonday As Variant, curOwed As Currency
    Dim intWeeks As Integer, intI As Integer
    On Error GoTo LoadComBail
    Set db = CurrentDb()
    ' If not an active or pending RMP contract,
    ' then make sure Commissions file is clean
    If IsNothing(Me!Status) Or Me!Status = "D" _
      Or Me!Status = "SB" Or Me!CommissionAgent1 <> "RMP" _
      Or IsNull(Me!CommissionAgent1) Then
        ' Create a temporary querydef to delete commission
        ' rows
        Set qd = db.CreateQueryDef("", _
          "Delete * From qryCommissions;")
        ' Fill in the parameter required by qryCommissions
        qd![Forms!frmContracts!ContractNo] = Me!ContractNo
        qd.Execute
        qd.Close
        Exit Sub
```

(continued)

763

```
                              End If
                              ' Active, Pending or Paid RMP contract --
                              ' make sure commissions are correct
                              ' Open a recordset on tblCommissions
                              Set qd = db.QueryDefs("qryCommissions")
                              ' Point to contract on this form
                              qd![Forms!frmContracts!ContractNo] = Me!ContractNo
                              Set rst = qd.OpenRecordset(dbOpenDynaset)
                              ' Calculate the weekly commission amount
                              curOwed = CCur(CLng(Me!ContractPrice * _
                                Me![Commission1%] * 100) / 100)
                              ' Figure out the Monday previous to Beginning Date
                              varMonday = Me![BeginningDate] - _
                                WeekDay(Me![BeginningDate], 2) + 1
                              ' If contract terms span a Monday,
                              ' then adjust first billing week day
                              If Me![ContractLastDay] > 7 Then _
                                varMonday = varMonday + 7
                              ' Calculate number of weeks
                              intWeeks = CInt(Me!EndingDate - varMonday + 7) \ 7
                              ' Set up an array containing all the valid weeks for this
                              ' contract
                              ReDim varWeekBeginning(1 To intWeeks + 1) As Variant
                              ReDim intHit(1 To intWeeks + 1) As Integer
                              For intI = 1 To intWeeks
                                  varWeekBeginning(intI) = varMonday
                                  varMonday = varMonday + 7
                              Next intI
                              ' Insert a dummy "high" date
                              varWeekBeginning(intWeeks + 1) = #1/1/2099#
                              intI = 1
                              ' Find the matching commission records
                              ' and make sure they're updated
                              Do Until rst.EOF
                                  Do Until varWeekBeginning(intI) >= rst!WeekBeginning
                                      intI = intI + 1
                                  Loop
                                  If varWeekBeginning(intI) = rst!WeekBeginning Then
                                      rst.Edit
                                      rst!AmountOwed = curOwed
                                      If Me!Status = "Pd" Then rst!AmountPaid = curOwed
                                      ' Mark this week "found" in the weekly array
                                      intHit(intI) = True
                                      rst.UPDATE
```

```
            Else
                ' If it's not a week in the array, delete it
                rst.Delete
            End If
            rst.MoveNext
    Loop
    ' Now add in any missing ones
    For intI = 1 To intWeeks
        If Not intHit(intI) Then
            rst.AddNew
            rst!ContractNo = Me!ContractNo
            rst!WeekBeginning = varWeekBeginning(intI)
            rst!AmountOwed = curOwed
            If Me!Status = "Pd" Then rst!AmountPaid = curOwed
            rst.UPDATE
        End If
    Next intI
    rst.Close
    Exit Sub
LoadComBail:
    MsgBox "Unexpected Error. " & Err & " " & Error, 16
    Exit Sub
End Sub
```

In a nutshell, this procedure does the following:

1. It verifies that this is an active contract for which RM Productions is the main commissioning agent. If the contract is not active, the routine makes sure that no rows exist for this contract in the tblCommissions table and exits.

2. Based on the contract BeginningDate and EndingDate values, the procedure builds an internal array containing the date of Monday in a contract week and another array containing a flag to indicate if that week already exists in the tblCommissions table. The procedure also calculates the weekly commission amount.

3. The procedure loops through any existing rows for this contract, looking for matching weeks. If it finds a week that doesn't match, it deletes the row. If it finds a matching week, it sets the "found" flag and makes sure the commission amount is correct.

4. For any weeks in the calculated array that it doesn't find in the tblCommissions table, the procedure builds a new row.

Validating Complex Data

VBA is a powerful language that includes many built-in functions that you can use to test and validate data. Although most of the time you will handle data validation using simple validation rule expressions in tables and forms, you can, when needed, create a validation procedure to parse and validate complex data.

An example in the Entertainment Schedule database is the Days/Times text string that exists in both the tblClubs and tblContracts tables. In a club record, the string defines the "default" days and times for which the club normally books entertainment. When you select a new club in the frmContracts form, a procedure in the AfterUpdate event of the ClubID combo box copies this information to the contract. However, for any particular contract, the days and times that the booked group is to perform might change from the club default. Since this is a field that ends up in the club and group booking contract, it needs to be validated for correct days of the week. Also, the beginning and ending dates of the contract need to match the Days/Times text. You can open a contract and try to enter an invalid day name in the Days/Times string. When you enter an invalid string, you should see an error message like the one shown in Figure 22-17.

FIGURE 22-17
The error message that appears when you try to enter an invalid day name in the frmContracts form.

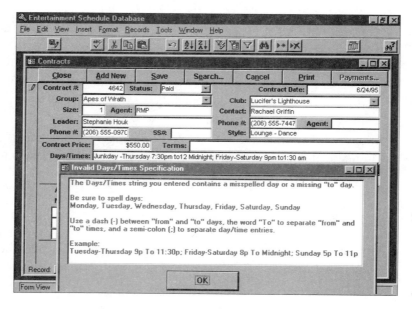

As discussed in the previous chapter, the *ValDaysTimes* function in the module named modRMP provides this validation. It not only checks for valid spellings of days of the week but also makes sure the string has the following form:

> dayname [- dayname] [booking times] [; dayname [- dayname]
> [booking times]…]

That is, the string must begin with a valid day name. A range of days for the same booking times can be specified by including a hyphen and a second day name. Any subsequent set of booking days must be delimited with a semicolon. Also, the *ValDaysTimes* function calculates the day of the week of the first day it finds in the booking string and the last day and returns the values based on Monday as the first day of the week. If the "last" day falls earlier in the week than the "first" day, the function assumes that the booking dates span a weekend and adds 7 to the ending date to indicate this. Here's the VBA code in the BeforeUpdate event procedure of the Days/Times string:

```
Private Sub ContractDaysTimes_BeforeUpdate(Cancel As Integer)
    Dim intReturn As Integer, intFirst As Integer
    Dim intLast As Integer
    intReturn = ValDaysTimes(Me!ContractDaysTimes, _
      intFirst, intLast)
    If Not intReturn Then
        DoCmd.OpenForm "frmDaysTimesError"
        Cancel = True
    End If
    Me!ContractFirstDay = intFirst
    Me!ContractLastDay = intLast
End Sub
```

Note that this procedure passes local variables called intFirst and intLast to the function rather than passing the fields from the contract. VBA passes form control variables by value, so they can't be updated directly by the called function. If the parse is successful, the procedure updates the first and last contract days in the underlying contract recordset. As you'll see in the final section of this chapter, these beginning and ending day of week values are used by other VBA procedures to validate the beginning and ending days of the contract.

Using the Calendar Custom Control

If you open the frmContracts form in Form view, you'll see down arrow buttons next to both the Start Date and End Date fields on the form. If you click one of these buttons, you'll see a graphical calendar display, as shown in Figure 22-18 on the next page.

767

FIGURE 22-18

Using one of
the calendar
custom con-
trols on the
frmContracts
form.

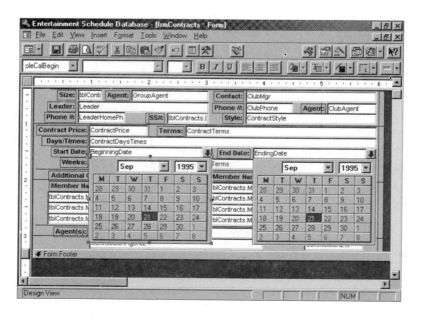

This display is part of the calendar custom control that comes with
Access. If you open the frmContracts form in Design view, as shown in
Figure 22-19, you'll see the two calendar controls overlaid on the form
just below the Start Date and End Date fields. The Visible property of
each control is set to No. As you might expect, the code behind the
toggle button that has the down arrow icon is responsible for displaying the calendar control.

FIGURE 22-19

The embedded
calendar con-
trols on the
frmContracts
form.

To place a calendar control on a form, you can open the form in Design view and then choose Custom Control from the Insert menu. (You won't find custom controls in the toolbox.) Because custom controls use OLE technology, you can purchase additional controls from various software vendors. In fact, the Microsoft Access Developer's Toolkit for Windows 95 contains additional custom controls that you can use in your applications.

You can bind the calendar control to data in the record source of your form. When you select a new date on the calendar, the control updates the field. However, if you need to validate the value before the control stores it in the field, you should leave the calendar control unbound. The calendar control does have an Updated event that informs you whenever data changes. However, the Updated event fires when you make any change to the control, so selecting a new month (but not selecting a new day) updates the control. Moving to a new record also updates the control and triggers the Updated event. If you leave the control unbound, you can decide when to respond to the Updated event and provide data validation only when necessary.

The Current event procedure for the form makes sure that both calendar controls are in sync with the data in the current record. Because the Current event "updates" the controls, it sets a form variable called intCurrent to tell the Updated event procedure of each control to ignore the event. Other procedures that update the calendar controls also use intCurrent to bypass the calendar control Updated event procedure. For example, the Click event procedure of the tglBegin button (the one next to Start Date) does the following:

```
Private Sub tglBegin_Click()
    ' Signal the calendar updated event to not do anything!
    intCurrent = True
    ' Reset the visibility of the calendar
    Me!oleCalBegin.Visible = Me!tglBegin
    If Me!tglBegin Then
        If IsNothing(Me!BeginningDate) Then
            Me!oleCalBegin.Year = Year(Date)
            Me!oleCalBegin.Month = Month(Date)
            Me!oleCalBegin.Value = Date
        Else
            Me!oleCalBegin.Year = Year(Me!BeginningDate)
            Me!oleCalBegin.Month = Month(Me!BeginningDate)
            Me!oleCalBegin.Value = Me!BeginningDate
        End If
```

(continued)

```
        End If
        DoEvents
        intCurrent = False
End Sub
```

If the toggle button is "pressed" (its value is True), this procedure makes sure that the respective calendar control shows a date that matches. If no date is set in BeginningDate, the procedure changes the calendar to today's date. When you open the calendar control by clicking the down arrow button, you can use the two combo boxes at the top of the control to select a different month or year. When you select a different date by clicking one of the date buttons, the Updated event procedure executes as follows:

```
Private Sub oleCalBegin_Updated(Code As Integer)
    ' Don't do anything if update is a result of Current
    ' event
    If intCurrent Then Exit Sub
    ' Also don't do anything if calendar value
    ' still equals BeginningDate
    If Me!oleCalBegin.Value = Me!BeginningDate Then Exit Sub
    If Not ValBegin(Me!oleCalBegin.Value) Then Exit Sub
    Me!BeginningDate = Me!oleCalBegin.Value
    Me!BeginningDate.SetFocus
    BeginningDate_AfterUpdate
    Me!tglBegin = False
    tglBegin_Click
End Sub
```

Note that this routine ignores the event if intCurrent is set. It also ignores the event if the current value of the control equals the value in the related bound date control. (Remember, the Updated event also fires when you move to a different month.) If, in fact, you have selected a new value, this procedure validates the new value (using the same procedure called by the BeforeUpdate property of the date control), copies the value to the companion control, calls the date control's AfterUpdate event procedure, resets the toggle button, and hides the calendar control by calling the toggle button's Click event procedure.

As you've seen in this chapter, VBA is an incredibly powerful language, and the tasks you can accomplish with it are limited only by your imagination. In the final chapter of this book, you'll learn how to set startup properties, create custom menus, and build a main switchboard form for your application.

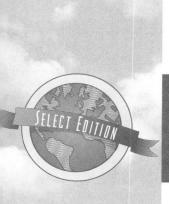

SELECT EDITION

Chapter 23

The Finishing Touches

Y

ou're in the home stretch. You have just about all the forms and reports you need for the tasks you want to implement in your application, but you need some additional forms to make it easier to "navigate" and to provide a jumping-off place to all your tasks. Your application could also use a custom menu bar and a custom toolbar to add a professional touch. Finally, you need to set the startup properties of your database to let Microsoft Access know how to get your application rolling, and you need to perform a final compile of your VBA code to get maximum performance.

Creating a Custom Form Toolbar

When your application is running, you probably won't want or need some of the Access design features. And you might want some additional toolbar buttons that provide direct access to commands, such as Save Record and Find Next, on your form toolbar. You can address these needs by creating a custom toolbar that opens for all forms in the application.

Click in the Database window, choose Toolbars from the View menu, and click the New button in the Toolbars dialog box to create and open a new custom toolbar. Access allows you to give the toolbar a meaningful name. You can click the Customize button in the Toolbars dialog box to add buttons to the toolbar and adjust the spacing between buttons. As you learned in Chapter 14, "Customizing Forms," you can also change the button faces.

Figure 23-1 shows the Overlake Form Bar custom toolbar from the College Counseling database. As you can see, buttons the user won't need, such as Form View, Save, Print and Print Preview (none of the forms in the College Counseling database are designed to be printed), Format Painter, and New Object, aren't available. A Save Record button has been added, and the Help button has been changed to open Access Help at the Contents screen. A bit later, you'll see the Visual Basic for Applications (VBA) procedure in the main menu form that makes this toolbar available for all forms in the application.

FIGURE 23-1

The Overlake Form Bar custom toolbar in the College Counseling database.

772

In the College Counseling application, this custom form toolbar is open whenever a form is open, as shown in Figure 23-2. You'll also see later that all the reports have VBA procedures that hide or reveal this toolbar when you move to or from a report in Print Preview.

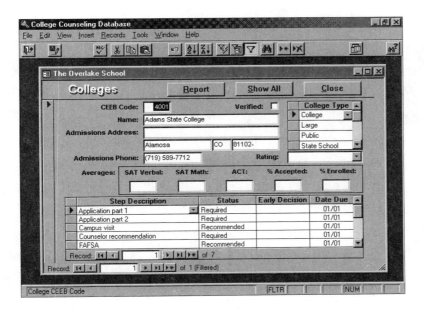

FIGURE 23-2

The Overlake Form Bar is open for all forms in the College Counseling application.

Creating a Custom Form Menu Bar

After you build a custom form toolbar, it would be helpful (and consistent) to replace the built-in form menu bar with a custom menu bar. You can then set the Menu Bar property of your forms to point to this menu bar's macro.

To define a custom menu bar, you must first create a menu bar macro that defines the menus that will appear on the menu bar itself. For each menu, you must add a line in the macro that executes an AddMenu macro action and set the Menu Name argument to identify the name of the menu. Use the Menu Macro Name argument to identify macros that define the commands on each menu.

Figure 23-3 on the next page shows the macro that creates the custom form menu bar in the College Counseling application. If you click in the first row's Action box and examine the action arguments, you can see that the first line defines another macro for the File menu that adds commands to the menu. Notice the use of the ampersand (&) to denote the access key for this menu.

FIGURE 23-3

The macro for
the custom form
menu bar in the
College Counsel-
ing application.

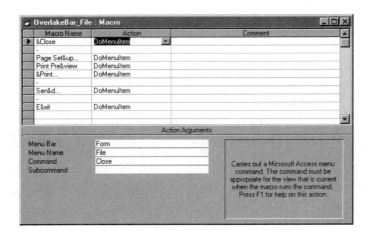

Figure 23-4 shows the macro that adds commands to the File menu on this custom menu bar. You list each command in the Macro Name column. Remember that you can designate an access key by preceding it with the & character. You can insert a line between sections of the menu by entering a minus sign (-) in the Macro Name column. Each macro that adds a menu command can execute either another AddMenu macro action to add a submenu or a series of macro actions to define the actions that you want Access to execute when you choose this command. In many cases, you'll use the DoMenuItem macro action to make a built-in menu command available through your custom menu bar. But you can also execute any other macro actions, including those that run another macro or a VBA function.

FIGURE 23-4

The macro that
defines the
commands on
the File menu
on the custom
form menu bar.

You can see that defining an entire set of menu macros can be quite laborious. It is especially tedious if you need to define different custom menu bars for different forms. Fortunately, Access includes a wizard called the Menu Builder to help you build menu macros. Click in the Database window, choose Add-ins from the Tools menu, and then choose Menu Builder from the submenu. Access starts the Menu Builder and displays the first dialog box, shown in Figure 23-5.

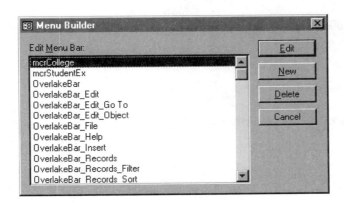

FIGURE 23-5
The first dialog box of the Menu Builder.

The dialog box lists all of the available macros in your database. You can select a macro that you know is a menu bar macro and click Edit to review and change the menu bar definition. You can also select a macro and click Delete to delete that macro. If the macro you delete is a menu bar macro, the Menu Builder also deletes any menu macros that add commands to the menu. Click the New button to start a new set of menu bar macros. The Menu Builder displays the dialog box shown in Figure 23-6.

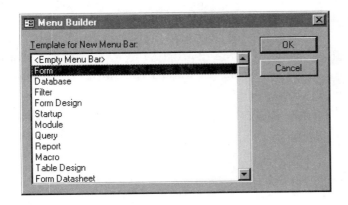

FIGURE 23-6
Selecting a template for a new set of menu bar macros.

You can either start a new menu bar or select one of the templates that duplicate the built-in menu bars in Access. Because you want a slightly modified menu for all the forms in this application, the Form menu bar template is a good place to start. Select Form and click OK, and the Menu Builder shows the Form menu bar's template in the Menu Builder edit dialog box, as shown in Figure 23-7.

FIGURE 23-7

The Menu Builder edit dialog box.

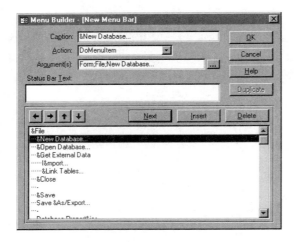

Within this dialog box, you can select each element of the menu definition in the lower list box and view the detailed definition in the controls above. If the element executes a macro action, you'll see the macro action and its arguments in the appropriate controls in the upper part of the dialog box. The Menu Builder supports the AddMenu, DoMenuItem, RunMacro, and RunCode macro actions. If you need to build a menu command that does something more complex, you can build a skeleton macro with the Menu Builder and then edit the resulting macro.

After you select an element in the lower list box, you can use the up and down arrow buttons in the dialog box to move the element up or down in the list. You can use the left arrow button to promote an element to a higher level or the right arrow button to demote an element to a lower level. Click the Next button to move the highlight down one element at a time. You can move the highlight past the last element to define a new element at the end of the list. If you need to create an element in the middle of the list, select the element below where you want to insert a new element and then click the Insert button. If you need to remove an element, select the element and then click the Delete button.

In many end-user applications, you don't want the user opening objects in Design view or creating new objects, so you might want to remove all of the New commands from the File menu. You probably don't need the Save and Save As/Export commands either. On the View menu, you might want to remove the Form Design and Toolbars commands. You might not need the Hide, Unhide, and Size To Fit Form commands on the Window menu. The custom form menu bar for the College Counseling application includes a custom command that displays an information dialog box from the Help menu. In Figure 23-8, you can see a line element inserted below the About Microsoft Access element and a new element for the About College Counseling command.

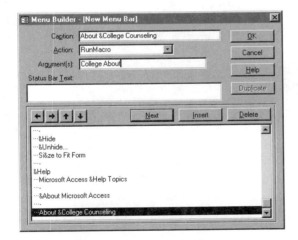

FIGURE 23-8

Additions to the Help menu on the custom form menu bar.

After building the basic custom menu bar using the Menu Builder, I modified the macro created in this step to open the frmAbout custom form, as shown in Figure 23-9 on the next page.

FIGURE 23-9

Modifying the
work of the
Menu Builder.

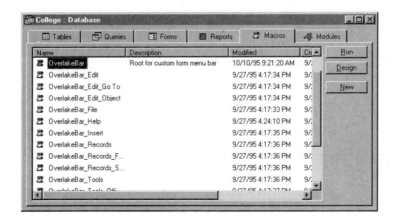

When you finish defining your menu bar, click OK to save it. If it's a new menu bar, the Menu Builder asks you to name the menu bar macro. The Menu Builder created 16 new macros, as shown in Figure 23-10: one for the main menu bar, one for each menu, and one for each submenu. If you set the Menu Bar property of your forms to point to the menu bar macro (*OverlakeBar*), you can see the new menu when you open the form, as shown in Figure 23-11.

FIGURE 23-10

The list of menu
macros built
by the Menu
Builder.

FIGURE 23-11
The custom form
menu bar's new
Help menu.

Fine-Tuning with the Performance Analyzer Wizard

Even the most experienced database designers (including me) don't always take advantage of all the available techniques to improve performance in an Access application. Fortunately, Access provides a Performance Analyzer Wizard to help you do a final analysis after you build most of your application. To start the wizard, switch to the Database window and choose Analyze from the Tools menu, and then choose Performance from the submenu. Access opens the window shown in Figure 23-12.

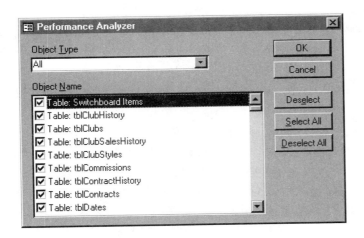

FIGURE 23-12
The main
selection window
of the Perfor-
mance Analyzer
Wizard.

You can select a specific category of objects to analyze—Current Database (which lets you analyze the table relationships), Table, Query, Form, Report, Macro, Module, or All objects. Within a category, you can click the check box next to an object name to select it for analysis. You can also click the Select All button to ask the wizard to examine all objects, or click Deselect All if you made a mistake and want to start over. Click OK to run the wizard. The wizard will open a window that shows you its progress through all the objects you selected. When it is finished, it will display the results of its analysis, similar to that shown in Figure 23-13.

FIGURE 23-13

An analysis from the Performance Analyzer Wizard.

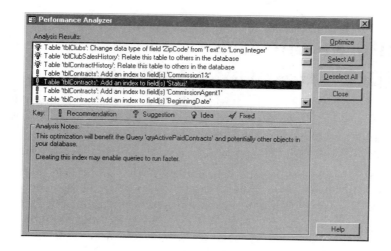

You can scan the list of recommendations, suggestions, and ideas displayed by the wizard. Click on any recommendation or suggestion that you like and then click the Optimize button to have the wizard implement the change on the spot. After the wizard implements a change, you'll see a check mark next to the item. If you like, you can click the Select All button to highlight all the recommendations and suggestions, and then click Optimize to implement all the fixes.

You can't implement ideas directly from the wizard. Most ideas are changes that could potentially cause a lot of additional work. For example, changing a data type of a field in a table might improve performance slightly, but it might also cause problems in dozens of queries, forms, and reports that you've already built using that table field. Other ideas are fixes that the wizard isn't certain will help, depending on how you designed your application.

Defining the Main Switchboard Form

Usually the last form that you need to build is a main switchboard form that gives the user direct access to the major tasks in the application.

Designing a Switchboard Form

Your main switchboard form should be a simple form with a logo, a title, and perhaps up to eight command buttons. The command buttons open the forms that you defined in the application. Figure 23-14 shows the main switchboard form for the Entertainment Schedule database in Design view.

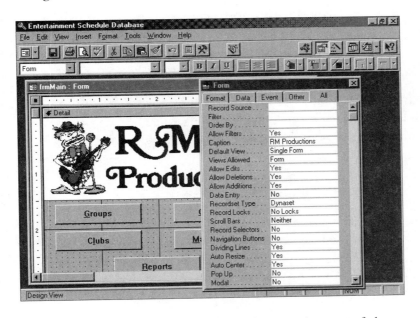

FIGURE 23-14
The main switchboard form for the Entertainment Schedule database in Design view.

One feature worth mentioning here is the use of the ampersand (&) character in the setting for each control's Caption property to define an access key for the control. In the Caption property for the Groups command button, for example, the ampersand precedes the letter *G*. The letter *G* becomes the access key, which means that you can "push" the Groups button by pressing Alt-G as well as by using the more traditional methods of clicking with the mouse or tabbing to the control and pressing the Spacebar or the Enter key. You must be careful, however, not to duplicate another access key letter.

781

NOTE The access key for the Clubs command button in this example is *L* to avoid conflict with the *C* access key for the Contracts command button.

You can use an access key to make it easier to select any control that has a caption. For command buttons, the caption is part of the control itself. For most other controls, you can find the caption in the attached label. For example, you can define access keys to select option buttons or toggle buttons in an option group.

For each command button, you need a simple event procedure to handle the Click event and to open the appropriate form. Here is the procedure for the Groups button:

```
Private Sub cmdGroups_Click()
    DoCmd.OpenForm "frmGroups"
End Sub
```

If you have a custom form menu macro, you should set the Menu Bar property of your switchboard form to point to the "root" macro of the custom menu. If you also have a custom form toolbar, you must add a procedure in your main form's Load or Open event to handle the toolbar. Here's the procedure from the frmMain Load event in the Entertainment Schedule database:

```
Private Sub Form_Load()
    ' Halt screen flashing
    Application.Echo False
    ' Select an object in the Database window
    DoCmd.SelectObject acForm, "frmMain", True
    ' And hide the window
    DoCmd.DoMenuItem acFormBar, 7, 4, , acMenuVer70
    ' Hide the form toolbar
    DoCmd.ShowToolbar "Form View", acToolbarNo
    ' and show the RMP custom toolbar
    DoCmd.ShowToolbar "McCann Form Bar", acToolbarYes
    ' Show 'em what we've done
    Application.Echo True
End Sub
```

Note that the procedure hides the Database window (although you'll see later that you can also set startup properties to hide this window), closes the standard Form View toolbar, and reveals the custom toolbar. This particular application is designed to "close" when this main form closes, so there's also a procedure to handle the Close event:

```
Private Sub Form_Close()
    DoCmd.ShowToolbar "Form View", acToolbarWhereApprop
    DoCmd.ShowToolbar "McCann Form Bar", acToolbarNo
    DoCmd.SelectObject acForm, "frmMain", True
End Sub
```

Note that this code opens the Form View toolbar again, but only where appropriate. If you opened it with acToolbarYes, the Form View toolbar would be visible all the time, even when you don't have a form open. Of course, there's no "where appropriate" for custom toolbars, so in some parts of your application you must hide the custom form toolbar when you don't need it. In both the College Counseling and Entertainment Schedule applications, a single custom form toolbar is used for all forms. But what about reports? Surely you don't want to see the custom form toolbar when you're in Print Preview. Here's where the Activate and Deactivate events in a report come in handy. For the Activate event (triggered when the report gets the focus in Print Preview) for all reports in the Entertainment Schedule database, the code is as follows:

```
Private Sub Report_Activate()
    DoCmd.ShowToolbar "McCann Form Bar", acToolbarNo
End Sub
```

Since we didn't hide the standard Print Preview toolbar, it will be open by default. If you were to design a custom Print Preview toolbar, you would use this same event to show the custom Print Preview toolbar after hiding your custom form toolbar. Likewise, you would need a bit of code in the Deactivate event to display the custom form toolbar when the application is running. The following code tests to see whether the main switchboard form is open (an indication that the application is running) before it shows the custom form toolbar again:

```
Private Sub Report_Deactivate()
    If Isloaded("frmMain") Then
        DoCmd.ShowToolbar "McCann Form Bar", acToolbarYes
    End If
End Sub
```

The *IsLoaded* function is a custom VBA procedure that you can find in the modUtility module of all the sample databases.

Using the Switchboard Manager

If your application is reasonably complex, it could take you a while to build all the individual switchboard forms you need to provide navigation through your application. Access has a Switchboard Manager utility that helps you get a jump-start on building your switchboard forms. This utility uses a creative technique to handle all switchboard forms using a single form. It uses a driver table called Switchboard Items to allow you to define any number of switchboard forms with up to eight command buttons each.

To start the Switchboard Manager, choose Add-ins from the Tools menu and then choose Switchboard Manager from the submenu. The utility will check to see whether you already have a switchboard form and a Switchboard Items table in your database. If you don't have these, the Switchboard Manager displays the message box shown in Figure 23-15, which asks you if you want to build them.

FIGURE 23-15

The message box that appears if the Switchboard Manager does not find a valid switchboard form and table in your database.

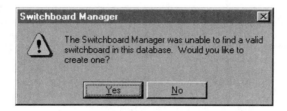

After the Switchboard Manager builds a skeleton switchboard form and a Switchboard Items table (or after it establishes that you already have these objects in your database), it displays the main Switchboard Manager window, as shown in Figure 23-16. To build an additional switchboard form (page), click the New button and enter a name for the new switchboard form in the resulting dialog box. Click OK to create it.

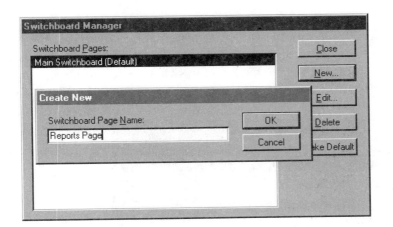

FIGURE 23-16
Adding an
additional
switchboard
form to the
main switch-
board form.

After you create the additional switchboard forms that you need, you can select one in the main Switchboard Manager window and click the Edit button to begin defining actions on the form. You'll see a window similar to the one shown in Figure 23-17, in which you can create a new action, edit an existing action, or change the order of actions. Figure 23-17 shows a new action being created. The Switchboard Manager can create actions to go to another switchboard form, open a form in add or edit mode, open a report, switch to Design view, exit the application, or run a macro or a VBA procedure. When you create a new action, the Switchboard Manager places on the switchboard form a command button that executes that action.

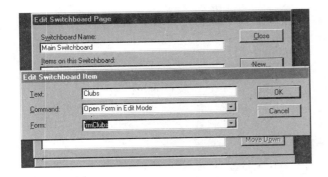

FIGURE 23-17
Creating a
new action
on a switch-
board form.

On the main switchboard form, you should create actions to go to other forms. You should also consider creating an action to exit the application. On each subsequent form, you should always provide at least one action to navigate back up the switchboard form tree or at least to go back to the main switchboard form, as shown in Figure 23-18.

FIGURE 23-18
Creating an action to return to the main switchboard form from another switchboard form.

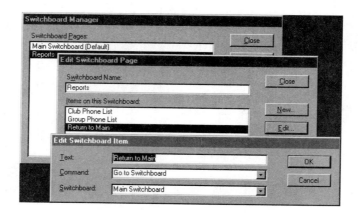

After you finish, the Switchboard Manager saves the main switchboard form with the name *Switchboard*. You can rename this form. If you want to rename the Switchboard Items table, be sure to edit the VBA procedures stored with the switchboard form to change all references to that table. You'll also need to change the record source of the form.

Figure 23-19 shows an example Switchboard form for the Entertainment Schedule database. I edited the form design to add the RM Productions logo.

FIGURE 23-19
The resulting main switchboard form.

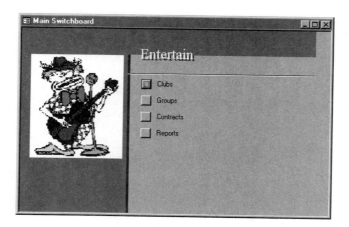

Setting Startup Properties for Your Database

At this point, you know how to build all the pieces you need to fully implement your database application. But what if you want your application to start automatically when you open your database? If you create a macro named *Autoexec*, Microsoft Access will always run it when you open the database (unless you hold down the Shift key when you open the database). However, a better way to start your application is to specify an opening form in the startup properties for the database. You can set these properties by switching to the Database window and then choosing Startup from the Tools menu. Access opens the Startup dialog box. Click the Advanced button to see the entire dialog box, as shown in Figure 23-20.

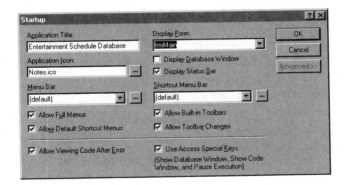

FIGURE 23-20
Setting startup properties for your database.

You can specify which form opens your database by selecting a form from the Display Form drop-down list. You can also specify a custom title for the application, an icon for the application, and default menu and shortcut menu root macros to override the standard menus for all forms. If you deselect the Display Database Window check box, Access hides the Database window when your application starts. You can also hide the status bar if you like by deselecting the Display Status Bar check box. Access has a set of condensed built-in menus that don't provide, for example, access to design commands. If you deselect the Allow Full Menus check box, Access provides these shortened menus as the default. You can hide all the built-in toolbars (you should provide your own custom toolbars in this case), and you can disallow toolbar changes.

In the lower part of the Startup dialog box, you can disallow view-ing of your code if there's an untrapped error. (You <u>do</u> trap all errors, don't you?) If you deselect this option, the application will exit on an error. Finally, you can disable some of the special keys—such as F11 to reveal the Database window, Ctrl-G to open the Debug window, or Ctrl-Break to halt code execution. As you can see, you have a host of powerful options for customizing how your application starts and how it operates.

Performing a Final VBA Compile

The very last task you should perform before placing your application "in production" is to compile and save all of your VBA procedures. When you do this, Access stores a compiled version of all the code in your database that it can use when it needs to execute a procedure you have written. If you don't do this, Access has to load and interpret your procedures the first time you reference them. For example, if you have several procedures in a form module, the form will open more slowly the first time because Access has to also load and compile the VBA procedures.

To compile and save all your VBA procedures, open any module—either a module object or a module behind a form or report. Choose Compile All Modules from the Run menu, as shown in Figure 23-21. After the module compiles, choose Save All Modules from the File menu. Close your database and compact it as described in Chapter 6, "Modifying Your Database Design." Do not change the database name when you compact the database. Renaming your database "decompiles" your code. If you need to rename the database, be sure to compile all the modules again to get the best performance when running the database.

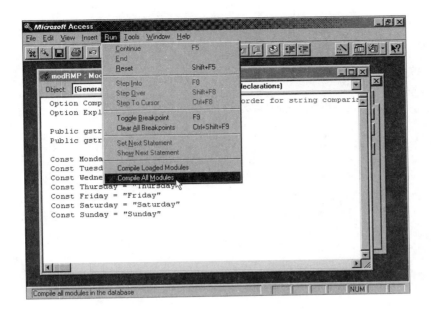

FIGURE 23-21
Choosing the Compile All Modules command from the Run menu to compile all the VBA procedures in your database.

I hope you're as impressed as I am by the power and simplicity of Microsoft Access as an application development tool. As you've seen in this book, you can quickly learn to build complex applications for the Windows 95 or Windows NT version 3.51 (or later) operating systems. You can use the relational database management system in Access to store and manage your data locally or on a network, and you can access information in other popular database formats or in any server-hosted or mainframe-hosted database that supports the Open Database Connectivity (ODBC) standard. You can get started with macros to become familiar with event-oriented programming and to prototype your application. With a little practice, you'll soon find yourself writing VBA event procedures like a pro.

Whether you use Access to build your own personal applications or to create applications for others to use, I'm confident you'll find it one of the most powerful and easy-to-use products you've ever worked with.

Appendix

Installing
Microsoft Access

To install Microsoft Access for a single user, you need a Microsoft Windows–compatible computer with the following configuration:

- An 80486 or higher microprocessor (80486/25 recommended as a minimum)

- At least 12 MB of RAM (16 MB or more recommended; 32 MB or more if you plan to run multiple applications at one time)

- A hard drive with at least 33 MB of free space for a typical installation

- A high-density floppy-disk drive (either a 3.5-inch 1.44 MB drive or a 5.25-inch 1.2 MB drive)

- A mouse or another pointing device

- A VGA or higher display

- Windows 95 or Microsoft Windows NT version 3.51 or later

  To run Access as a server on a network, you need:

- Network software that supports named pipes, such as Microsoft LAN Manager, Novell NetWare, or Banyan VINES

- A Windows-compatible computer with at least 11 MB of free disk space for the Access software plus additional space for user databases

- User workstations configured as specified above for a single user

Before you run the Access Setup program, be sure that no other applications are running on your computer, and then start Windows. If you're installing Access from floppy disks, place the first installation disk in your floppy-disk drive, and choose the Run command from the Windows 95 Start menu. In the Run dialog box, type *a:\ setup.exe* (where *a* is the drive letter for your floppy-disk drive), and then press Enter. If you're installing from the Microsoft Office Professional CD-ROM, type *x:\ setup.exe* (where *x* is the drive letter of your CD-ROM drive). To install from a network drive, use Windows Explorer to find the directory to which your system manager has copied the Access Setup files. Run Setup.exe in that directory. If you're installing Access from a Master License Pack, include an /L switch in the command line when you run Setup, as in *a:setup.exe/L*. If you're installing from a network (without a Master License Pack), include an /N switch in the command line when you run Setup, as in *a:setup.exe/N*.

The Access Setup program asks for your name and your company name and then lets you select the directory in which you want to install the Access files. It then asks whether you want a Typical, Compact, or Custom setup. A Typical setup installs the most frequently used Access components. A Compact setup installs only the Access program files. A Custom setup lets you select which Access components to install, including program files, Help files, database drivers, Microsoft Graph, and the sample databases. A Typical setup requires approximately 33 MB of hard-disk space; a Compact setup requires approximately 14.8 MB; a Custom setup requires a maximum of 42 MB.

Managing ODBC Connections

If you want to use Microsoft Access to connect to SQL databases that support the Open Database Connectivity (ODBC) standard, you must install both the ODBC driver for that database and the Microsoft ODBC administrator. The ODBC driver for Microsoft SQL Server is included with Access.

To install or modify your ODBC setup, double-click on the 32bit ODBC icon in the Windows Control Panel. The Data Sources dialog box opens, as shown in Figure A-1. To add new data sources, you must first define a logical name for each available ODBC server type. Select an available ODBC driver from the list, and then click the Add button to see the Setup dialog box for the driver. Click the Options button to expand the dialog box, as shown in Figure A-2 on the next page.

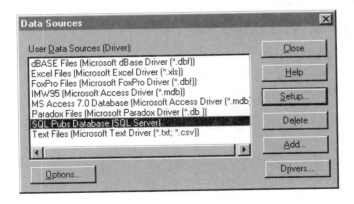

FIGURE A-1
The Data Sources dialog box.

FIGURE A-2

The ODBC SQL
Server Setup
dialog box, which
configures the
SQL driver.

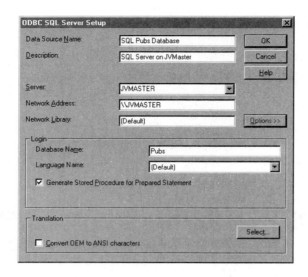

Specify the appropriate information, and then click the OK button to return to the Data Sources dialog box. (See your network administrator to determine the appropriate information.) After you finish setting up your ODBC drivers, click the Close button in the Data Sources dialog box.

Within Access, you'll use the data source name to attach to each SQL ODBC server. (For details, see Chapter 10, "Importing, Linking, and Exporting Data.")

Converting from a Previous Release

Although version 7 of Access can work with the data and tables in a database file created by version 1.*x* or version 2, you cannot use version 7 to modify the forms, reports, queries, macros, or modules in an earlier version database. You might be able to run your version 1.*x* or version 2 database application using version 7, but your application will fail if it attempts to modify queries, forms, or reports as part of its normal execution.

You can easily convert a version 1.*x* or version 2 database file to version 7. Start the Access version 7 program, and cancel the opening choices dialog box. Choose Database Utilities from the Tools menu and then choose Convert Database from the submenu. In the Database To

Convert From dialog box, select the version 1.*x* or version 2 file that you want to convert. Access opens the Convert Database Into dialog box. You must specify a different file for your version 7 database because Access won't let you replace your previous version file directly.

Conversion Issues

Access version 7 will report any objects or properties that it is unable to convert by creating a table in your converted database called Convert Errors. The most common problems you're likely to encounter are field validation rules that reference another field, an Access built-in function, or your own user-defined function. Because field and table validation rules are enforced by the JET DBEngine, you cannot use functions to validate data as you can in version 1.*x*. (See Chapter 21, "Visual Basic for Applications Fundamentals," for a discussion of the Access version 7 architecture.) However, this means that the validation rules you define are always enforced, regardless of whether your data is being accessed from the Access application environment or from another application environment, such as Visual Basic.

Other changes that might affect your application code or how your application runs include the following:

- Access version 1.*x* allows you to perform a Save Record menu command on a form even if the data in the form has not changed. Versions 2 and 7 generate an error. Be sure to check the Dirty property of the form before using Save Record.

- Version 1.*x* supports a CancelEvent action in the OnClose event handler of a form. Beginning with version 2, you must use CancelEvent in the OnUnload event handler. OnClose no longer supports a cancel. The conversion utility correctly changes OnClose to OnUnload in most cases.

- Version 1.*x* allows you to specify the default value of a text field without including double quotation marks. Beginning with version 2, you must enclose all text default values in double quotation marks. The conversion utility adds double quotation marks in most cases.

- Many more query fields are updatable in versions 2 and 7. For example, if you do not want to allow certain fields on the "one" side of a query to be updatable in a form, you must set the Locked property of the form controls to Yes in version 2 or later.

- You should use the *CurrentDb* function to open a new copy of the current database in Visual Basic for Applications (VBA) code when you set a database object variable. You can still reference DBEngine(0)(0), but you must never close an object based on a direct reference to the current database.

- Many objects and collections support a Name property. You must be careful to distinguish between references to a Name property and references to a Name object or field by using the correct syntax in code.

- If your Access Basic code makes calls to external library functions, you must convert these calls to the 32-bit equivalent functions. Version 7 does not support calls to 16-bit library functions.

- Properties related to the Windows interface are now Long or Variant variables rather than Integer variables. For example, the hWnd property of a Form object is now a 32-bit integer (Long) rather than a 16-bit value. The channel ID returned from a *DDEInitiate* function is now a Long rather than an Integer.

- VBA executes macro actions as methods of the new DoCmd object. VBA does not support a *DoCmd* statement. The conversion routines handle this change for you.

- The Parent property of a control in an option group and any attached label no longer return a Form or Report object. For attached labels, the Parent property returns the control to which the label is attached. For controls in an option group, the Parent property returns the option group control.

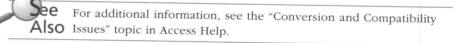

See Also   For additional information, see the "Conversion and Compatibility Issues" topic in Access Help.

PSS Q&A

Troubleshooting Tips from Microsoft Product Support Services

The following are some common questions that people ask Microsoft Product Support Services (PSS) about Microsoft Access, along with the answers.

> **NOTE** Microsoft provides recorded and faxed answers to common technical problems via its Microsoft FastTips service. FastTips operates 24 hours a day, 7 days a week, and it requires only a touch-tone telephone to use. The toll-free number is (800) 936-4100; recorded menus will guide you to the solution to your technical problem. (You can also get standard PSS telephone support for Access by calling (206) 635-7050 on weekdays between 6 a.m. and 6 p.m. Pacific time.)

Setup and Conversion

Can I Run Access Version 7 in Other Versions of Windows?

You can run Access version 7 (Access for Windows 95) only in Microsoft Windows 95 or in Microsoft Windows NT version 3.51 or later. You cannot run it in earlier versions of Windows.

What Components Do I Get with the Typical Installation of Access?

The Typical installation of Access includes the following components:

- Access application
- Access Help
- Access wizards
- Microsoft Excel ISAM
- Text ISAM
- xBASE ISAM
- Microsoft Graph version 5
- Northwind.mdb sample database
- MSINFO
- Uninstall application
- Briefcase replication
- Calendar custom control

The Typical installation of Access does not include the following components:

- Language reference
- Developer tools
- Paradox ISAM
- Lotus ISAM
- SQL ODBC driver
- Desktop ODBC drivers
- Solutions.mdb sample database
- Orders.mdb sample database

For more information about the components installed by each type of Setup—Typical, Compact, and Complete—you can order item number Q136132 by selecting the FastTips Technical Library option from the FastTips main menu.

How Do I Add or Remove Access Components?

To add or remove Access components in Windows 95, take these steps:

1. Choose Settings from the Microsoft Windows 95 Start menu and then choose Control Panel from the submenu.

2. Double-click on the Add/Remove Programs icon, and then follow the instructions on the Install/Uninstall tab.

In Microsoft Windows NT version 3.51 or later, double-click on the Microsoft Access Setup icon in the Microsoft Office group (or in the group that contains your Access icons).

Should I Keep My Earlier Version of Access?

If you plan to create or modify databases that are compatible with an earlier version of Access, you should keep the earlier version until you have converted all your databases and are comfortable working in Access version 7.

For example, if you maintain a database that is shared by people who have not yet upgraded to version 7, you must use the previous version of Access to make modifications to that database. You can use Access version 7 to open databases created by previous versions and work with data in those databases, but you cannot use version 7 to modify or create objects in a database created by a previous version unless you first convert that database to the version 7 format.

When I Opened, Instead of Converted, a Database That Was Created in a Previous Version of Access, the File Size Increased. Why?

Access version 7 supports Visual Basic for Applications (VBA), which is common to Microsoft Office applications. To use a version 1.*x* or version 2 database without changing its format, Access version 7 creates a new system table to hold the VBA translation of the database's Access Basic procedures. This new system table enables you to run your application in version 7 without converting your database and accounts for the increase in the size of your database file.

For more information about using version 1.*x* and version 2 databases in Access version 7, you can order item number Q136131 by selecting the FastTips Technical Library option from the FastTips main menu.

Why Didn't My Access Basic
DoCmd Statements Convert Correctly?

During the conversion of your Access version 2 database, you might see a message that says, "There were compilation errors during the conversion or enabling of this database," the result being that some of your old DoCmd statements do not get converted to new DoCmd objects.

This error is usually caused by uncompiled modules in the version 2 database. To solve the problem, open the database in version 2, open all of your form and report modules that contain Access Basic code, and choose Compile Loaded Modules from the Run menu. Then convert your database to Access version 7.

For more information about conversion issues, you can order item number Q136133 by selecting the FastTips Technical Library option from the FastTips main menu. You can also find information in the *Building Applications with Microsoft Access for Windows 95* manual that comes with Access, and in the appendix to this book.

Why Doesn't Setup Work After I Have
Installed Access on Four Different Machines?

Setup compliance checking is strict now. You cannot install Access on more than four different machines.

Why Doesn't My Custom Control Work After I Convert
My Access Version 2 Database to Access Version 7?

Access version 2 supports 16-bit custom controls, while Access version 7 supports 32-bit custom controls. When you convert a version 2 database that uses a 16-bit custom control, Access version 7 automatically updates the control to its 32-bit version if a 32-bit version exists and is registered on your computer. If you do not have a 32-bit version of a 16-bit control, Access version 7 generates an error message during the conversion process.

You can update a 16-bit custom control by installing its 32-bit version and registering it. Then you can open the converted database, save any forms or reports containing the control, and then close and reopen the database.

You can contact the manufacturer of a 16-bit custom control to find out whether a 32-bit version is available. The Microsoft Access

Developer's Toolkit version 2 includes three 16-bit custom controls: Calendar, Data Outline, and Scroll Bar. A 32-bit version of the Calendar control ships with Access version 7. A 32-bit version of the Data Outline control is included with the Microsoft Access Developer's Toolkit for Windows 95. The Scroll Bar control has no 32-bit version. However, you can replace the 16-bit Scroll Bar control with the 32-bit Slider control (which ships with Windows 95) to provide similar functionality.

Tables and Queries

How Can I Optimize My Queries?

Access uses Rushmore, a data-access technology that permits sets of records to be queried very efficiently.

Here are some useful query performance tips:

- Run the Performance Analyzer and see what it suggests.
- Index the fields used in sorts and criteria.
- Index the fields used in joins in both tables.
- Use multiple-field indexes on fields with multiple-column joins between the tables.
- If a table has a single-field primary key, do not add a separate index to the primary key field. If a table has a multiple-field primary key, the performance of queries on that table might improve if you have a separate index on each field.
- Use outer joins only when necessary—they limit the options for Rushmore's query optimizer.

For more information about query performance, use the Answer Wizard from the Access Help menu to search on the phrase "How do I optimize my query," and then view "Tell Me About: Optimizing query performance." Or you can order item number Q112112 by selecting the FastTips Technical Library option from the FastTips main menu.

How Can I Print the Relationships Window?

Access does not have a built-in option for printing the Relationships window. However, you can press Alt+Print Scrn to copy the image to the Clipboard, and then paste the image into another application, such as Paint in Windows 95 or PaintBrush in Windows NT, for printing.

Suddenly I See Tables in My Database with Names That Start with *MSys.* How Did They Get There, and Can I Delete Them?

You definitely do not want to delete these tables. They are part of every mdb file, and they keep track of the objects in your database. To hide these tables from view, choose Options from the Tools menu. On the View tab of the Options dialog box, deselect the System Objects check box.

Access Automatically Joins My Tables When I Add Them to a Query. Can I Turn Off This Feature?

Yes. There is a new option for this in Access version 7. To disable the AutoJoin feature, choose Options from the Tools menu. On the Tables/Queries tab of the Options dialog box, deselect the Enable AutoJoin check box.

I Like the New Lookup Properties for Fields in a Table, but How Can I Remove These Properties for Fields in My Query?

To change the control type back to a text box in a query:

1. Open the query in Design view.

2. Right-click on the field in the design grid, and then choose Properties from the shortcut menu.

3. Click on the Lookup tab, and set the Display Control property to Text Box.

You probably noticed that the Display Control setting was blank. This property was inherited from the field's Display Control property in the table. Changing the property in the query has no effect on the property in the table.

For more information about lookup fields, use the Answer Wizard from the Access Help menu to search on the phrase "What is a lookup field," and then view "How Do I: Create a field that looks up or lists values in tables."

On the Lookup Tab, What's the Difference Between Setting Display Control to Combo Box and Setting It to List Box? They Look the Same When I View My Table.

In Datasheet view, the field or the control will appear as a combo box. However, when you create a form using a wizard or when you drag fields to the form in Design view using the field list, you will get the control type that was specified in the field's Display Control property.

How Do I Create a One-to-One Relationship?

There is no longer an option for this in the Relationships window because Access version 7 is smart enough to know whether a relationship is one-to-one or one-to-many. It recognizes a one-to-one relationship when the join field or fields are the primary keys or have unique indexes in the respective tables.

What Are These Strange Fields in My Table, Such as s_GUID? I Didn't Make Them!

Access adds these system fields when you replicate a database. To hide these fields, choose Options from the Tools menu. On the View tab of the Options dialog box, deselect the System Objects check box.

Forms and Reports

I Get *#Error?* in a Control When I Run My Form or Report. What Does This Mean?

This value means that Access cannot evaluate the expression. The most common cause of this error is a circular reference. For example, a control with the following Name and Control Source properties will produce the error:

Name: FirstName

Control Source: =[FirstName] & " " & [LastName]

When Access evaluates [FirstName] in the Control Source property, it looks for a control with that name on the form. Since the control references itself, we call this a circular reference.

To solve the problem, you can change the Name property to FullName because FullName is not part of the Control Source expression. Since there is no longer a control called FirstName, Access will look for a field called FirstName when evaluating the expression in the Control Source property.

For more information about *#Error?* and other error values, you can order item number Q112103 by selecting the FastTips Technical Library option from the FastTips main menu.

When I Print My Report, Every Other Page Is Blank. How Can I Correct This?

This problem occurs when the total width of your report exceeds the width of the paper specified in the Page Setup dialog box. For example, blank pages print if your report form is 8 inches wide and your left and right margins are 1 inch wide (for a total width of 10 inches), and the paper size specified in the Print Setup dialog box is only 8.5 inches wide.

In this example, if any controls (such as text boxes) extend beyond the 8.5 inches, the controls print on a second page. If none of the controls extends beyond the 8.5 inches, you see a warning message stating that some pages might be blank. Blank pages generated after the warning are not counted in the total pages of your report.

For more information about preventing blank pages, you can order item number Q95920 by selecting the FastTips Technical Library option from the FastTips main menu.

How Do I Cancel a Report That Does Not Contain Any Records?

Access has a report event property called OnNoData. As its name implies, the macro or event procedure attached to this property is triggered when you preview or print a report without data. For example, you can set the OnNoData event property to a macro containing both a MsgBox action that tells the user there is no data and a Cancel-Event action.

For more information about canceling reports without data, use the Answer Wizard from the Access Help menu to search on the phrase "How do I cancel a report without records," and then view "How Do I: Cancel the printing of a report when it doesn't contain any records."

How Can I Get My Combo Box or List Box to Default to the First Item in the List?

When you move to a new record on a form that has a combo box or a list box, the combo box will be blank or the list box will not have any value selected. The combo box or list box might have a table or a query defined in its Row Source property that provides the list of items to display in the box. Since the data in the underlying Row Source property will vary with the addition or deletion of records, it is difficult to know which item will appear at the top of the list when the form is used.

In Access version 2 or later, you can use the ItemData method to cause a list box or a combo box to default to any row. To have the first row selected automatically, set the box's Default Value property to

    =[MyCombo].[ItemData](0)

where MyCombo is the name of your combo box.

How Do I Print a Report for Only the Current Record in the Form?

You can use the Where Condition argument of the OpenReport action to print a report for the current record in a form. For example, if you have a form called MyForm and a primary key field in both the form and the report called ID, you can use the following expression in the Where Condition argument:

    [ID]=Forms![MyForm]![ID]

For more information about printing a report for the current record in a form, use the Answer Wizard from the Access Help menu to search on the phrase "How do I print a report for the current record in a form," and then view "How Do I: Create a command button that prints the current record."

How Can I Check for Duplicate Records Right After I Enter a Value in a Primary Key Field?

Normally, Access does not check the values in primary key fields for duplicates until you move to the next record. If you want to check for duplicate values immediately after entering a value in a primary key field, use a macro in the control's BeforeUpdate event property. The macro should use the *DLookup* function to check for duplicates and then display an appropriate message.

For example, open the Customers form in the Northwind Traders sample database (Northwind.mdb) in Design view. The Before-Update event property of the CustomerID control is set to the *Customer.ValidateID* macro. To see the contents of the macro, click the builder button next to the BeforeUpdate event property.

For more information about using the *DLookup* function, you can order item number Q136122 by selecting the FastTips Technical Library option from the FastTips main menu.

How Do I Turn Off the Control Wizards That Start When I Add Certain Types of Controls to My Form?

Control Wizards help you create list boxes, combo boxes, option groups, and command buttons. Once you are comfortable working with these controls, you can turn off the Control Wizards so you don't have to cancel them each time you add one of these controls. To turn off the Control Wizards, click on the Control Wizards tool in the Toolbox.

How Do I Bypass the Switchboard Form When I Open a Database?

You can bypass a database's startup properties (which control the display of the main switchboard form) and its *Autoexec* macro by holding down the Shift key when you open the database.

For more information about startup properties, use the Answer Wizard from the Access Help menu to search on the phrase "What startup options are available," and then view "How Do I: Control how a Microsoft Access database or application starts."

How Can I Add My Own Styles to the Form Wizards and Report Wizards?

First, open the form or report that has the styles you want to copy. Then choose AutoFormat from the Format menu. In the AutoFormat window, click the Customize button to display the Customize Auto-Format window. Select the "Create A New AutoFormat Based On" option and click OK. Access creates a new AutoFormat based on the styles in your form or report.

Macros and Modules

What New Macro Actions Are Available in Access Version 7?

Access version 7 has two new macro actions: Save and SetMenuItem. The Save action saves a specified Access object or the active object if none is specified. The SetMenuItem action enables you to dim (gray out) or select (check) menu items on your custom menus.

You might notice another new macro action called PrintOut. This action is simply the Print action from previous versions of Access with a new name.

For more information about new macro actions, use the Answer Wizard from the Access Help menu to search on the phrase "What's new with macros," and then view "Tell Me About: What's new with macros, modules, and developing applications?"

How Do I Turn Off Warning Messages, Such as the One That Tells Me My Query Is About to Update Records?

Use the SetWarnings macro action, and set its Warnings On argument to No. After you use this action in a macro, you don't have to turn warning messages back on. Warning messages will automatically turn back on when the macro ends. However, if you use this macro action in a VBA procedure, warning messages will stay off until you explicitly set the Warning On argument back to Yes.

How Can I Convert My Macro to VBA Code?

You can easily convert your macros to VBA procedures by taking the following steps:

1. In the Database window, click on the Macros tab, and then select the macro object.

2. Choose Save As/Export from the File menu.

3. In the Save As dialog box, choose Save As Visual Basic Module, and then click OK.

4. In the Convert Macro window, click Convert to create a VBA module that duplicates the macro object's functionality.

If you chose a Typical or Compact installation when you ran Windows 95 Setup, the Developer Tools were not installed, and you will see an error message after step 3 above. To install the Developer Tools in Windows 95, do the following:

1. Choose Settings from the Microsoft Windows 95 Start menu, and then choose Control Panel from the submenu.

2. Double-click on the Add/Remove Programs icon, and then follow the instructions on the Install/Uninstall tab.

To install the Developer Tools in Windows NT version 3.51 or later, double-click on the Microsoft Access Setup icon in the Microsoft Office group (or in the group that contains your Access icons).

For more information about converting macros, use the Answer Wizard from the Access Help menu to search on the phrase "How do I convert a macro to code," and then view "How Do I: Convert macros to Visual Basic for applications."

Why Can I No Longer Run Macro Actions from My Module Using the DoCmd Statement?

The DoCmd statement has been replaced by a DoCmd object in Access version 7. When you use the DoCmd object to run a macro action, you specify the DoCmd object followed by a method of the object. Access provides methods with the same name as macro actions, so typically the syntax will look the same as in previous versions of Access, except with a period between DoCmd and the method name. For example,

```
DoCmd OpenForm "MyForm"
```

changes to the following in Access version 7:

```
DoCmd.OpenForm "MyForm"
```

What Happened to the Immediate Window?

The Immediate window is now part of the Debug window in Access version 7. The Debug window consists of two panes—an Immediate pane that functions much like the Immediate window in previous versions of Access, and a Watch pane. The Watch pane makes debugging VBA code easier because it enables you to watch the values of variables and expressions as your code runs. You can open the Debug window by pressing Ctrl+G from anywhere in Access.

For more information about the Debug window, use the Access Help Topics Index to search on the phrase "Debug window," and then view "Using the Debug Window."

I Am Using On Error to Trap Errors in My VBA Code, but Access Still Displays Error Dialog Boxes. What Gives?

You might have the Break On All Errors check box selected in the Options dialog box. To turn off this option, choose Options from the Tools menu. On the Module tab of the Options dialog box, be sure that the Break On All Errors check box is not selected.

The Break On All Errors option forces Access to display an error dialog box for every error that it encounters in your VBA code, including errors trapped using On Error.

The VBA Code That Was Created When I Converted My Macro Contains References to "CodeContextObject." What Does This Mean?

CodeContextObject is a new property that gives you a generic reference to the object in which the VBA code is executing. For example, if the code is executing in a form, CodeContextObject refers to that particular form, and if the code is executing in a report, it refers to that particular report.

When I Type in Long VBA Statements, Can I Continue Them on the Following Line or Lines?

Yes. This is a nice new feature in Access version 7. The underscore (_) character tells Access that the statement is continued on the next line. Here is an example:

```
X = MsgBox("This is the first part of my string, " _
    & "and this is the second part of my string.")
```

As a rule, it is best to leave a space before the underscore character and place operators, such as the ampersand (&), on the continuation line.

> **NOTE** You can't use the underscore character to break a line of code in the middle of a string constant. Use the string concatenation operator as shown in the example to assemble a string constant that must span multiple lines.

Can I Change the Font in the Module Window?

Yes. Choose Options from the Tools menu, click on the Modules tab, and then select a font from the Font drop-down list box. You can also change the size and color of the font and many other display attributes in this dialog box.

How Do I Search for Text in a Library Database?

Access allows you to search for text in one database at a time. To search in a library database, you must open a module in that database and begin the search from there. Press F2 to open the Object Browser, select a library from the Libraries/Databases list, double-click on a module in the Modules/Classes list, and then search in that module for text in the library database.

Interoperability

What Types of Files Can Access Import or Link?
Access can import and link the following file types:

- Btrieve
- Microsoft FoxPro versions 2, 2.5, 2.6, and 3
- dBASE III, III+, IV, and 5
- Paradox versions 3.*x*, 4.*x*, and 5
- Data SQL tables
- Data from programs and databases that support the ODBC protocol
- Microsoft Excel versions 2.*x*, 3, 4, 5, and 7
- Lotus 1-2-3, wks, wk1, and wk3 formats (import only)
- Delimited text files
- Fixed-width text files

For more information about importing and linking data, use the Answer Wizard from the Access Help menu to search on the phrase "What files can I import," and then view "How Do I: Import or link data from other programs and file formats."

I Don't See the File Type I Want to Import in the List. Does That Mean I Can't Import It?
You usually can import your file by first saving it as one of the file types supported by Access. For example, most applications have a "save as" or "export" option for delimited text files or for dBASE III+. You can save your file as one of those file types by using the other application and then importing the file to Access.

Why Can't I See My Text File in the List When I Try to Import It?
By default, Access filters out all but the common text file extensions, such as txt and csv. To see files with other extensions in the Import window, type *.* in the File Name text box and press the Enter key.

What Kinds of Graphics Files Does Access Support?

The answer depends on whether you are storing a graphic as an OLE object or in the new image control. When you use a bound object frame or an unbound object frame, you can link or embed any file type that has an OLE Server application registered on your computer. For example, if you have a Windows-based application that supports bmp files, such as Paint in Windows 95 or PaintBrush in Windows NT version 3.51 or later, and that application is an OLE Server application, you can embed or link that file in a bound or unbound object frame on a form or a report.

If you are using the image control that is new in Access version 7, you can use bitmaps (bmp or dib extension) or metafiles (wmf or emf extension).

For more information about object frames and the image control, use the Answer Wizard from the Access Help menu to search on the phrase "When should I use an object frame vs. an image control," and then view "Tell Me About: Which type of object frame should I use and should I embed or link my object?"

What ODBC Drivers Are Included with Access?

Access contains ODBC drivers for:

- Microsoft SQL Server
- Desktop Drivers (Access, FoxPro, dBASE, Excel, Paradox, text files)

The Desktop Drivers are not for use by Access. Access installs them so that other applications, such as Excel, can connect to Access databases and other data files through ODBC. Access uses built-in drivers called ISAMs to connect to these file types instead.

Can I Add an Access Database to a Microsoft Office Binder?

No. You can add only Microsoft Word documents, Microsoft Excel worksheets and charts, and Microsoft PowerPoint presentations to a binder. Although you can't add an Access database to a binder, you can embed a binder in an OLE field in an Access table.

My ODBC Tables Aren't
Updating Correctly. What's Wrong?

You'll get unpredictable results if you attempt to update a table via ODBC and the unique index you specified doesn't contain unique data values. To fix this problem, you must delete the table, relink it, and then specify an index with unique data values.

Advanced Topics

How Can I Create an Expression
to Extract a Portion of a Text Field?

To extract a portion of a text field, you can use expressions containing the *Left*, *Right*, *InStr*, and *Mid* functions. These expressions are commonly used in the Update To line of an update query to place a portion of a larger field into a new field.

For example, to extract "John" from a field containing "John Doe," you can use the following expression:

    Left([FullName],InStr(1,[FullName]," ")-1)

To extract "Doe" from "John Doe," you can use the following expression:

    Right(Trim([FullName]),Len(Trim([FullName]))-InStr(1,[FullName]," "))

For more information about parsing character strings, you can order item number Q115915 by selecting the FastTips Technical Library option from the FastTips main menu.

How Can I Create an Expression to Return a Value
from a Table or a Query Using the *DLookup* Function?

The *DLookup* function enables you to return (look up) a value from a specified set of records such as a table or a query. The syntax of the *DLookup* function is as follows:

    DLookup(Expression, Domain [, Criteria])

The function has three arguments:

- Expression: Identifies the field that contains the data in the domain that you want returned.

- Domain: Identifies the table or query that contains the data you want returned.

■ Criteria: An optional string expression, similar to a WHERE clause in an SQL statement, that restricts the range of data used in the function.

The *DLookup* function returns one value from a single field even if more than one record satisfies the criteria. If no record satisfies the criteria or if the domain contains no records, *DLookup* returns Null.

For more information about using the *DLookup* function, you can order item number Q136122 by selecting the FastTips Technical Library option from the FastTips main menu.

How Can I Calculate Date/Time Data to Display Specific Dates or Elapsed Time?

Access stores the Date/Time data type as a double-precision, floating-point number (up to 15 decimal places). Use the integer portion of the double-precision number to calculate dates; use the decimal portion to calculate time. Because a date/time value is stored as a double-precision number, you can receive incorrect formatting results when you try to display specific dates or calculate elapsed time of more than 24 hours.

For more information about calculating date/time data, you can order item number Q88657 by selecting the FastTips Technical Library option from the FastTips main menu.

How Do I Create Synchronized Combo Boxes?

Synchronized combo boxes enable you to restrict the selections in a combo box based on a filter that is selected in a second combo box. For a detailed example of creating synchronized combo boxes, you can order item number Q98660 by selecting the FastTips Technical Library option from the FastTips main menu.

Can I Open Multiple Copies of the Same Form?

Yes. Access allows you to open multiple instances of the same form. Opening multiple instances of a form gives you the flexibility to work on more than one record at once. For example, in an Order Entry application you can start taking an order, pause and take a second order, and then return to the first order—without losing any data.

For more information about opening multiple instances of a form, you can order item number Q135369 by selecting the FastTips Technical Library option from the FastTips main menu.

Index

Note: *Italicized* page references indicate figures or tables.

N

O

P

Q

The manuscript for this book was prepared and submitted to Microsoft Press in electronic form. Text files were prepared using Microsoft Word 6 for Windows. Pages were composed by Microsoft Press using Aldus PageMaker 5.0a for Windows, with text in Garamond and display type in Avant Garde Bold. Composed pages were delivered to the printer as electronic postscript files.

Cover Designer
Rebecca Geisler

Cover Illustrator
designlab

Interior Graphic Designers
Kim Eggleston
Amy Peppler Adams (designlab)

Interior Graphic Artist
David Holter with Michael Victor

Principal Compositor
Barbara Remmele

Principal Proofreader/Copy Editor
Lisa Theobald

Indexer
Foxon-Maddocks Associates

MICROSOFT® ACCESS FOR WINDOWS® 95 STEP BY STEP helps you quickly and efficiently learn how to organize and manage database information with Microsoft Access for Windows 95. The easy-to-follow lessons include clear objectives and real-world business examples so you can learn exactly what you need to know, at your own speed.

With MICROSOFT ACCESS FOR WINDOWS 95 STEP BY STEP, you'll learn how to:

- Use Microsoft Access to input, organize, manipulate, and store all kinds and quantities of information, and have it readily available

- Save time by creating forms that make it simple to complete calculations and find information, and that warn you of incorrect data input

- Create separate tables and queries for extraordinary flexibility in the ways you can bring related data together

- Use wizards to develop all aspects of your database quickly and easily

- Work with information from other database formats by importing it into Microsoft Access or by linking it directly to a particular database

- Customize your forms and reports by changing text styles and colors, and by adding pictures, controls, and OLE objects

- Quickly create detail and grouped reports that display your data in easy-to-read, professional-looking formats

Like the other books in the *Step by Step* series, MICROSOFT ACCESS FOR WINDOWS 95 STEP BY STEP takes a procedural, hands-on approach to get you up and using the product as quickly as possible.

097-000-680

Register Today!

Return this
Running Microsoft® Access for Windows® 95
registration card for a Microsoft Press® catalog

U.S. and Canada addresses only. Fill in information below and mail postage-free. Please mail only the bottom half of this page.

1-55615-886-6A   *Running Microsoft Access for Windows 95*   *Owner Registration Card*

_____
NAME

_____
INSTITUTION OR COMPANY NAME

_____
ADDRESS

_____

_____   STATE   ZIP
CITY

Microsoft® *Press*
Quality Computer Books

**For a free catalog of
Microsoft Press® products, call
1-800-MSPRESS**

BUSINESS REPLY MAIL
FIRST-CLASS MAIL   PERMIT NO. 53   BOTHELL, WA

POSTAGE WILL BE PAID BY ADDRESSEE

MICROSOFT PRESS REGISTRATION
RUNNING MICROSOFT ACCESS
FOR WINDOWS 95
PO BOX 3019
BOTHELL WA   98041-9946

Running Microsoft Access quick reference card

Wizards, Builders, and Add-Ins

Name	What it does	How to start it
Database Wizard	Creates a database for you	Choose New Database from the File menu, and then double-click on the icon for the type of database you want to create
Table Analyzer Wizard	Helps make your database more efficient by normalizing the data	Click on the table you want to analyze, choose Analyze from the Tools menu, and then click Table
Simple Query Wizard	Creates a single-table or multiple-table query for you and helps you group and summarize your data	Click on the Queries tab in the Database window, click the New button, and then double-click Simple Query Wizard
Form Wizard	Creates a single-table or multiple-table form and allows you to select fields from any table in your database; helps you create subforms	Click on the Forms tab in the Database window, click the New button, and then double-click Form Wizard
Report Wizard	Creates a single-table or multiple-table report and allows you to select fields from any table in your database; helps you create subreports	Click on the Reports tab in the Database window, click the New button, and then double-click Report Wizard
Subform/Subreport Field Linker	Helps you link forms or reports if you created your form and subform or report and subreport without using a wizard	In Design view, click on the subform or subreport control, display the property sheet, click in the Link Child Fields property box, and then click the Build button
Import Wizard	Allows you to view your data while importing or linking spreadsheet or text data so that you can select the correct field headings, data types, and so on	Runs automatically when you choose Get External Data from the File menu and then import or link a spreadsheet or text file
Text Export Wizard	Allows you to view your data while exporting Access data as text so that you can select the correct field delimiters, data types, and so on	Runs automatically when you choose Save As/Export from the File menu, select To An External File Or Database in the Save As dialog box, and select Text Files from the Save As Type drop-down list in the Save In dialog box
Lookup Wizard	Helps you create a list in a form or a datasheet that looks up values from another table	In the table's Design view, select Lookup Wizard as the data type for a field; in the table's Datasheet view, choose Lookup Column from the Insert menu
Label Wizard	Creates different types of labels in reports, including mailing labels	Click on the Reports tab in the Database window, click the New button, select the table or query you want to use as the source for the report, and then double-click Label Wizard
Control Wizards	Help you build an option group, combo box, list box, command button, chart, or subform/subreport control on your form or report	In Design view, be sure that the Control Wizards button appears pressed in the toolbox. Click the Option Group, Combo Box, List Box, Command Button, or Subform/Subreport tool in the toolbox and place the control on your form or report to start the respective wizard. For charts, choose Chart from the Insert menu.

Wizards, Builders, and Add-Ins

Name	What it does	How to start it
Input Mask Wizard	Helps you customize the list of input masks directly from the wizard	Click the Build button next to the Input Mask property box in the property sheet
PivotTable Wizard	Creates a control on a form that allows you to summarize data in your database using a Microsoft Excel pivot table	Click on the Forms tab in the Database window, click the New button, and then double-click PivotTable Wizard
Chart Wizard	Creates charts for your forms and reports	Open the form or report that will display the data, switch to Design view, choose Chart from the Insert menu, and then click on the form or report in which you want to place the chart
Database Splitter Wizard	Allows you to maintain a single source of data on the network by splitting a database into two files: one that contains the tables and one that contains the queries, forms, reports, macros, and modules	Choose Add-ins from the Tools menu, and then click Database Splitter
Menu Builder	Creates custom shortcut menu bars	In Design view, display the property sheet for the form, report, or subform control; click the Shortcut Menu Bar property; and then click the Build button
Macro to Visual Basic for Applications Converter	Converts your macros to Visual Basic for Applications (VBA)	Select the macro that you want to convert in the Database window, choose Save As/Export from the File menu, click Save As Visual Basic Module, and then click OK
Linked Table Manager	Allows you to view or refresh links when the structure or location of one or more linked tables has changed; allows you to easily switch between back-end databases	Choose Add-ins from the Tools menu, and then click Linked Table Manager
Conflict Resolver	Helps you manage conflicts that occur when you merge changes to a replicated copy of a database back into a master database	Choose Replication from the Tools menu, and then click Resolve Conflicts
Performance Analyzer	Analyzes any or all of the objects in your database and makes suggestions to improve database performance	Choose Analyze from the Tools menu, and then click Performance
User-Level Security Wizard	Helps you establish user-level security for a database	For more information, choose the "Secure a database using the Security Wizard" topic in Microsoft Access Help
Microsoft Word Mail Merge Wizard	Helps you create a Microsoft Word document that uses data merged from tables or queries in your database	Select Merge It from the OfficeLinks toolbar button's drop-down list